RAVEN ROCK

The Story of the U.S. Government's Secret Plan
to Save Itself—While the Rest of Us Die

GARRETT M. GRAFF

SIMON & SCHUSTER

New York   London   Toronto   Sydney   New Delhi

Simon & Schuster
1230 Avenue of the Americas
New York, NY 10020

First Simon & Schuster hardcover edition May 2017

SIMON & SCHUSTER and colophon are registered trademarks of Simon & Schuster, Inc.

For information about special discounts for bulk purchases, please contact Simon & Schuster
Special Sales at 1-866-506-1949 or business@simonandschuster.com.

The Simon & Schuster Speakers Bureau can bring authors to your live event. For
more information or to book an event, contact the Simon & Schuster Speakers
Bureau at 1-866-248-3049 or visit our website at www.simonspeakers.com.

Interior design by Ruth Lee-Mui

Manufactured in the United States of America

5   7   9   10   8   6

Library of Congress Cataloging-in-Publication Data is available.

ISBN 978-1-4767-3540-5
ISBN 978-1-4767-3545-0 (ebook)

PHOTO CREDITS

All photos are courtesy of the U.S. government unless otherwise indicated.

Insert 1:
Page 9: Courtesy of the Greenbrier; page 16, bottom: Courtesy of the author

Insert 2:
Page 4, top and bottom: Courtesy of the Greenbrier; page 5, all: Courtesy of the Greenbrier;
page 8, bottom: Courtesy of the author; page 13, top: Photo by Genesisman26;
page 13, middle: Photo by the Canadian Armed Forces; page 13, bottom:
Photo by Dan Brown; page 16, top: Photo by Lutz Lehmann

To KFB, who encourages my curiosity

CONTENTS

Doomsday is near. Die all, die merrily.

—*Henry IV, Part 1*, Shakespeare

INTRODUCTION

For Richard Nixon, August 9, 1974, may have marked the end of his presidency, but for Dexter McIntyre, it was just another workday—a Friday like any other in a workplace unlike almost any other. He arrived early in the morning at the secret AT&T facility in Stanfield, North Carolina, entered the access code at the outer fence, parked his car in the small aboveground lot, and walked through a small door built into the hillside.

The complex had existed since 1965, when AT&T began to dig a big hole about two miles from McIntyre's childhood home in Locust, North Carolina, about thirty miles east of Charlotte. He had been nineteen when construction started, and recalls, "There was a lot of curiosity about what was going on there." No one really knew what the hole was for—or even really who was digging. Some locals swore it was a secret facility for communicating with aliens; others believed it was a secret submarine base—despite the fact that it was about 150 miles from the ocean. The truth, as it turned out, was almost as strange as the fiction.

In 1967, McIntyre found himself reporting to work at the newly completed facility as a technician. The big hole that had so fascinated the community now contained a nuclear-hardened, department-store-sized concrete bunker, protected by twin 20,000-pound blast doors, that helped run an AT&T "long line" cable from Miami to Boston, skirting major metropolitan areas that might be nuclear targets. It was one of dozens of specially built facilities that ran air-to-ground communications for VIP military aircraft like Air Force One and various airborne alert command posts—programs with code names like NIGHTWATCH and LOOKING GLASS—that ensured that in the event of a nuclear strike someone in America would be able to launch from the ashes a devastating retaliatory blow against the Soviet Union.

For a quarter century, one eight-hour shift at a time, McIntyre and his colleagues—all technically AT&T staff—tended this hidden mountaintop redoubt, maintaining the telecommunications gear that kept the government ready, a key link in the massive "Continuity of Government" machine.* In the event of an attack, food and rations inside could keep the staff functioning for at least thirty days. The whole facility was mounted on massive metal springs to cushion the impact of a nuclear blast. Communications gear and lights hung from springs—even the toilets were mounted on springs and linked with rubber plumbing. The staff worked closely with other "AT&T" technicians at another North Carolina bunker in Chatham, similarly about thirty miles west of Raleigh, which served as the southern-most link in the government's massive "relocation arc," a network of nearly 100 bunkers built into the mountains of Pennsylvania, Maryland, Virginia, West Virginia, and North Carolina. The Chatham facility had a special nuclear-hardened troposcatter microwave relay for post-Apocalypse communications and its own special Continuity of Government functions that not even the fellow Stanfield employees understood. Even though they all had special security clearances, the Chatham programs were, as the military said, "need to know." None of the technicians even told their families what they really did. "You just didn't talk about it," McIntyre recalls. "What do you do? 'I work on telephone circuits.'" It wasn't an answer that encouraged follow-up questions.

As McIntyre's shift began on the morning of August 9, the Stanfield Klaxon sounded, signifying that an Air Force One flight was being readied at Andrews Air Force Base in Washington. McIntyre often served as the facility's air-to-ground communications technician, and so he closeted himself in the radio room to listen as the plane took off. His first step was to open the office safe and look up his station's daily call sign; each month, a

* McIntyre would work there until it closed in 1991, a victim of advancing technologies and the end of the Cold War.

courier delivered to Stanfield a sealed envelope with different call signs for each day of the month to make it impossible for any radio eavesdroppers to determine Air Force One's flight path. He looked over the plane's route, saw it was heading west, and knew that that day, he'd play only a minor role. With a westward flight path, he'd quickly hand over communications to the facility in Williamstown, Kentucky. As Air Force Colonel Ralph Albertazzie and his copilot readied for takeoff and as Air Force One passed through 10,000 feet, McIntyre in the Stanfield facility began to pick up a signal. He called in to the Waldorf, Maryland, ground communications station, "I've got acquisition of signal. I can take the flight." He tuned in to listen.

As Air Force One began to bank west, each of its thirty-four passengers watched the advancing time. Richard Nixon, in his private compartment, interrogated Sergeant Lee Simmons: "Is that clock right?" He gestured to the three digital clocks lining the cabin wall, a legacy that remained from Lyndon Johnson's presidency. LBJ had loved to summon staff to his cabin to tell him the time: *What time was it in Washington? At their destination? Where we are right now?* Finally, Air Force stewards installed a trio of clocks to provide constant answers. Now all three ticked down the final minutes of his successor's presidency.

"I think I'd like a martini," Nixon said.

Chief Steward Chuck Palmer knew exactly how the president liked it—a chilled glass filled with ice, just a hint of dry vermouth, a lemon peel twist lightly rubbed around the edge. Gin. Stirred quickly and served. Palmer had honed the technique during hundreds of hours of flight with the thirty-seventh commander-in-chief, who had visited twenty-eight countries, including the closed empire of China, traveling 137,500 miles internationally in his six years in office, more than any predecessor.

In the cockpit, copilot Les McClelland listened through headphones as a thousand miles away the chief justice and the vice president recited thirty-five words, phrase by phrase, concluding: ". . . preserve, protect, and defend the Constitution of the United States." The clock read three minutes and twenty-five seconds past noon. The Boeing 707, its blue-and-white paint job instantly recognizable around the world, was 39,000 feet above the Missouri plains, heading west at 600 miles an hour, still nearly three hours from its California destination.

Albertazzie keyed the radio: "Kansas City, this was Air Force One. Will you change our call sign to SAM 27000?"

"Roger, SAM 27000. Good luck to the president," a controller at the Kansas City Air Route Traffic Control Center replied.

On the ground in Stanfield, McIntyre was puzzled by Albertazzie's request. *Why was the plane changing call signs in midair?* It wasn't until that night when he watched the evening news at home that he realized he had heard history being made. He had been present, without realizing it, for the last moments of the Nixon administration.

Even as he prepared to hand over the office, becoming the first person to resign the presidency, Richard Nixon had promised he'd be commander-in-chief until the very end. Governing in the midst of the Cold War, he believed it critical for the nation to understand who possessed nuclear launch authority. With Soviet missiles never more than fifteen minutes away, the president led the National Command Authorities, the command and control structure that governed the use of nuclear weapons in case of an attack.

"As I am winging my way back to California tomorrow, I will still have the black box aboard," Nixon had said the day before at the White House. That black box was colloquially known as the Football—the briefcase, carried just a few steps from the president by a military aide, that contained the country's nuclear attack plans. The Football was the key to this vast and ever-growing arsenal, the Nuclear Triad of bombers, ICBMs, and submarines that kept the Soviet Union at bay, and it was always at the president's fingertips.

But not today. No one had told the president that, by one of the only measures that truly mattered, his presidency had already ended. The military aide never boarded the plane with the Football; the briefcase wasn't in its normal place on Air Force One, secured in the communications center just behind the cockpit. Even before Gerald Ford took the oath, the White House military apparatus had already taken from Richard Nixon the very power that defined his office.

In fact, days before the administration's dramatic denouement, Defense Secretary James Schlesinger had issued an unprecedented set of orders: If the president issued any nuclear launch order, military commanders should check with either him or Secretary of State Henry Kissinger before executing them. Schlesinger feared that the president, who seemed depressed and was drinking heavily, might order Armageddon. And on that August morning, the military and White House aides had left the nuclear codes with the incoming president.

In a country with no bejeweled crowns or royal thrones, the black Football briefcase is perhaps the only physical manifestation of our nation's sovereign, the outward sign of presidential power. And on that day it had already abandoned Richard Nixon.

On its surface, presidential succession seems such a simple idea, but it's what political scientist Ernst Kantorowicz called "a peculiar kind of scientific mysticism," whereby as mortal as any single officeholder may be, the office itself never dies. The president may be replaceable, but the presidency is not—it represents the very idea of the democratic traditions of the United States. "For me personally, no one ever elected to the office of the presidency was worth dying for, yet the office of the presidency was," recalled one Secret Service agent.

The King is dead, long live the King.

Nixon was gone, Ford was in.

The presidency always continues.

Gerald Ford's accession to the presidency in August 1974 heralded one of the most dramatic chapters of U.S. history, but it was all the more remarkable for just how unremarkable the actual event was—power transferred via a short letter delivered to the secretary of state. It was the third time in just three decades that a vice president had taken over, each time amid exigent circumstances: the natural death of the commander-in-chief in the midst of global war in 1945, the violent assassination of the leader of the free world as his vice president watched in 1963, and now the passing of the torch one step ahead of a forced removal by Congress. In each instance, though, there was no question but that the vice president would step forward.

Ford took office—and received the world-ending nuclear Football— without ever being elected to the vice presidency or the presidency. He had stepped into the vice presidency, nominated by Nixon and confirmed by

Congress, after Spiro Agnew's resignation amid scandal. Ford's ascension was a transition that literally couldn't have occurred a decade before; until just a few years earlier, when the Twenty-fifth Amendment was ratified, the nation had had no system for filling a vacancy in the vice presidency. It was a solution created out of necessity by the Cold War as the country came to grips with the fragility of its leadership, just one of the ways nuclear weapons had—and would—reshape the presidency for years to come.

For much of its existence, the American presidency had been a rather slow-moving enterprise. Presidents might take weeks or months to travel outside the capital, barely in contact with the mechanics of government. In September 1935, Franklin Roosevelt's car had become hopelessly lost in the canyons around the Hoover Dam, en route back to the train station in Las Vegas from the dam's dedication, and been completely out of touch for nearly two hours. No one knew where the president was, nor when he might reappear. Even as late as 1945, Vice President Harry Truman didn't receive Secret Service protection. Yet within a few short years, as Soviet missiles reduced monumental decisions to only fifteen-minute windows, such prolonged periods with the president incommunicado or the vice president's whereabouts unknown would be an artifact of history.

In the months after World War II ended and the arrival of the atomic bomb, Washington columnists Joseph and Stewart Alsop mused how the new weapons would complicate world relations and push America's government in new directions. In an era where an entire city could disappear in an instant, they argued that it wasn't going to be enough to just have a vice president on standby. "We shall have to organize a complete, specially trained emergency government as a sort of spare, and to keep it in a cavern until needed," they wrote. Oddly enough, that was almost exactly what the government would end up doing.

The need to command such powerful weapons on a hair-trigger alert pushed the office of the president into a new era of technology and new procedures; the commander-in-chief required instant, reliable communications, powerful new transportation, and detailed instructions to ensure that there was never a leadership vacuum. The White House Communications Agency would know where both would be every minute of every day, arranging in advance sophisticated communication tools to ensure that those in the newly designated National Command Authorities were always reachable. The need to keep the president and executive branch leaders secure, alive, and in communication gave rise to a massive infrastructure: gleaming Marine helicopters, the majestic Air Force One, hulking armored limousines, and screaming motorcades.

The nuclear age also transformed the presidency from a single person working in the White House to a much broader idea. While most Americans thought of a "president" as the person they elected every four years on the first Tuesday after the first Monday in November, the "presidency" by the 1970s represented a long line of men and women, stretching through both houses of Congress and through every cabinet agency—each ready to step into the void left by the deaths or incapacity ahead of them in the line of succession. While the person was replaceable, the position was not. The presidency literally had an A team, a B Team, and even a C team. In the event of an emergency, each team—and its designated "president"—had a different role and a different evacuation destination. The Alpha team, which in most cases included the elected president, would remain in Washington and, by design, be sacrificed almost immediately in an attack. The Bravo team would head to Mount Weather, a sprawling secret bunker in the hills of Virginia built to withstand a nuclear attack; the Charlie team would head to any of the nearly 100 hidden facilities available within an hour of Washington that the government would activate in an emergency. All this was meant to preserve the National Command Authorities, which began with the president and the secretary of defense, and continued with, as the wonderfully ambiguous phrase stated: "or persons acting lawfully in their stead."

Each of the nearly twenty offices in the presidential line of succession has its own unique hierarchy; dozens of civilian and military officials populate the succession line, for instance, for the defense secretary, which created possible paths to the presidency with potentially chaotic consequences. Under a truly horrific surprise attack that destroys the nation's leaders, the U.S. attorney for Chicago and northern Illinois might claim to be the president. Under no circumstances, though, would the presidency itself ever be vacant.

Beginning during the Cold War and continuing up to the present day, the Central Locator System, a special office of the Federal Emergency Management Agency (FEMA), tracks these officials and their whereabouts twenty-four hours a day, ready to whisk them away from their regular lives at a moment's notice. While many people are familiar with the military's DEFCON alerts—a system that tracks the U.S. military's state of readiness (Defense Condition) from DEFCON 5, representing peacetime, to DEFCON 1, representing complete global war—the analogous COGCON alert matrix, which tracks the government's "continuity condition readiness," is more obscure. COGCON 4 represents normal peacetime operations, while COGCON 1 calls for all the government's relocation bunkers and facilities to be fully staffed. Beginning at COGCON 3, personnel "warm up" the relocation facilities, and people like the head of the Department of Energy's Savannah River operations office in South Carolina, who stands eighteenth in line for succession to be energy secretary, must begin notifying the Watch Office every day by 8 a.m. ET his or her entire day's itinerary.

This nuclear world is filled with seemingly harmless gobbledygook, acronyms piled upon acronyms, that explains how the world would end in thermonuclear war. Under the MAD theory, if, for instance, BMEWS and NORAD confirmed a USSR BOOB attack on CONUS, the NCA—either POTUS, SECDEF, or the AEAO aboard the ABNCP—would see a PINNACLE/OP-REP3/NUCFLASH alert and turn to the NMCC, FEMA's HPSF, the ANMCC, or NEACP to issue EAMs activating SIOP, move the nation to DEFCON 1, mobilize COG and COOP plans, and notify DOD and SAC to attack and launch ICBMs, ALCMs, and SLBMs, raining MIRVs down upon USSR DGZs preselected by NSTAP and JSTPS.

The result of the president launching the nation's bombers, submarines, and missiles against Russia would almost surely destroy not only both countries but all human life on the entire planet. There were some 30,000 nuclear weapons in the U.S. arsenal, the rough equivalent, one CIA director calculated, of 55 billion traditional 500-pound TNT bombs from World War II. Enough, as he said, to carpet each state in the union with a billion bombs— and still have five billion bombs left over.

From start to finish, the entire process would take under an hour.

Even as the nation lay in ruins at the end of that hour, the government would have already carefully considered how the United States itself—how the idea of the United States—would continue forward. During the Cold War, the government secretly invested billions of dollars in a complicated set of plans known as "Continuity of Government" (COG), "Continuity of Operations" (COOP), and its most secretive level, "Enduring Constitutional Government" (ECG). Through these programs, planners gave deep thought to what activities and processes would be needed following a nuclear attack—and even what totems of American culture should be saved. The World War II command bunkers in London eventually inspired a breath-takingly audacious and complex network of dozens of bunkers, ships at sea, scores of helicopters and planes overhead, even secret rail trains, and convoys of tractor-trailers in the United States.

Prewritten presidential executive orders sat in office safes across Washington, as did secret draft legislation known as the Defense Resources Act, ready to be filled in Mad Libs–style with dates and emergencies, that laid out an entirely new structure and entirely new roles for how the government would function during a national emergency—effectively suspending the Constitution and Bill of Rights. The presidential Football is well known, but less well known is how the attorney general was accompanied through the darkest days of the Cold War by an "Emergency Briefcase" outlining FBI plans to sweep up thousands of Americans deemed a security threat. Long before Barack Obama made the Washington title "czar" popular, Dwight Eisenhower had imagined an expansive set of secret powers, preselecting nine men—mostly private citizens—who would be real czars, stepping in during an emergency to remake the private sector, seize assets coast to coast, and create new bureaucracies that would control nearly every aspect of American life until peace could be restored.

The Post Office would be in charge of registering the nation's dead; the National Park Service would run the refugee camps; the Department of Agriculture would distribute rationed food. Congress would retreat to a special bunker at a West Virginia resort; the Supreme Court would relocate to another resort in the North Carolina mountains; the Department of the Interior would move to the grounds of a former college in Harpers Ferry. The Federal Reserve kept an underground bunker stocked with a billion dollars cash inside Mount Pony, seventy miles south of Washington. FEMA would help the nation rebuild from regional bunkers in places like Denton, Texas, and Maynard, Massachusetts.

It was also carefully decided that at the National Archives, the Declaration of Independence would be saved before the Constitution, and at the National Gallery of Art, Leonardo da Vinci's Florentine masterpiece *Ginevra de' Benci* took priority over Rogier van der Weyden's Renaissance masterpiece *Saint George and the Dragon*. The Library of Congress knew it would save the Gettysburg Address ahead of George Washington's military commission, and in Philadelphia, a specially trained team of park rangers stood ready to evacuate the Liberty Bell into the mountains of Appalachia.

At every level, the COG system offered redundancy piled atop redundancy. It was a system that touched every state in the union—and nearly every state hosted a hidden COG facility. The scope of power involved was unlike anything our nation has ever experienced.

This book is a different type of Cold War history—it's not a traditional account focused on the "who," the great hawks and doves who shaped this momentous half century, nor is it really a story of the "why," the ideological and political struggles that played out from Washington to Moscow to Berlin to London. It's also not meant to be a comprehensive timeline; there are major events that merit barely a mention—Korea, McCarthyism, the Space Race, Vietnam—and major world figures, like Joseph Stalin, whose existence is only mentioned glancingly. Epochal domestic political issues—like civil rights and the 1960s—are discussed not at all. Instead, this book is meant to be the first definitive tour of the hidden architecture of the Cold War's shadow government. It is a history of "how." How nuclear war would have actually worked—the nuts and bolts of war plans, communication networks, weapons, and bunkers—and how imagining and planning for the impact of nuclear war actually changed the "why," as leaders realized the horrors ahead and altered the course of the Cold War at several key points in response.

In writing this account, I have been granted access to many new sources, sites, and facilities known only since the end of the Cold War, people newly willing to speak for the first time about their roles in this secret state, and hundreds of pages of newly declassified documents never before available to researchers. Yet it remains a hard world to re-create after the fact. For one thing, it's difficult to convey today just how dark the Cold War looked at key points. Though two generations of American leaders, from Harry Truman to Ronald Reagan, genuinely saw the Soviet Union as an existential threat—one that would destroy Europe, the United States, and free people everywhere at the first chance it had—we know now that the U.S. and the free world triumphed over Communism, quite peacefully, in fact.

Moreover, this story is a challenge to tell because much of the COG machinery remains shrouded in secrecy. Many of my requests to declassify even fifty-year-old reports and memos were denied. The National Archives refused my request to release, for instance, four Kennedy-era memos from 1962 and 1963 dealing with civilian emergency planning—arguing that all four still remain so vital to national security that not a single word of them could be declassified. It's hard—and troubling—to imagine what plans from an era where black-and-white television represented cutting-edge technology could still be relevant to our lives today.

For nearly fifty years, the inner workings of the nation's COG protocols were some of the government's best-kept secrets. These facilities and plans were huge surprises when they were unveiled in the 1990s by reporters like Ted Gup and William Arkin, as well as scholars and researchers like Bruce Blair and Tim Tyler. Even colleagues in the same office didn't know the scope of COG plans. When Aaron Sorkin was researching what would become *The American President* and *The West Wing*, Clinton aide George Stephanopoulos pulled out of his wallet what the Hollywood director first thought was a bus pass—it actually was the little card explaining how Stephanopoulos would be evacuated in the event of a nuclear attack. Sorkin incorporated that card into a later *West Wing* episode, where character Josh Lyman received such a card from the National Security Council and felt guilt because his co-workers wouldn't also be saved. While shooting the scene, set consultant Dee Dee Myers, the former press secretary to Bill Clinton, pulled Sorkin aside to tell him that the scene was unrealistic because those cards didn't actually exist. Sorkin was shocked: Even as a top aide, she'd never realized that her co-workers had exactly those cards—and she never did.

• • •

The story of COG is also the story of an unfolding technology revolution—both in terms of military firepower and communications infrastructure—that fundamentally reshaped both the presidency and much of today's world. The COG world developed the most elaborate communications apparatus ever designed. Nearly every person on the planet has seen their life altered by one of the most basic parts of this planning: It was, after all, the Defense Department's investment in creating a decentralized network that could ensure communication after a nuclear attack that helped drive development of the modern internet. The world's first online chat program—the forerunner of AOL Instant Messenger, Skype, Facebook Chat—was developed to help the main command bunker at Mount Weather respond to critical national shortages in an emergency. And the airline reservation system that every internet user accesses each time they use Orbitz, Expedia, or another travel site grew out of the air defense radar system built in the 1950s to prevent a surprise Soviet attack. As technology writer Frank Rose concluded, "The computerization of society, then, has essentially been a side effect of the computerization of war."

Beyond the information superhighway, America's concrete highways themselves grew out of the fear of attack—the 41,000 miles of interstates built under an Eisenhower program partly served to help the nation speed war matériel around the nation in case of a nuclear attack. The original name for the limited-access paved road network was the National System of Interstate and Defense Highways, and children of the era may recall the signs that sprouted up along the major roads that warned "In case of enemy attack, this road will be closed to all but military vehicles."

More broadly, though, the Cold War reshaped our nation's thinking about defense—it's where our national security state was created, where today's obsessive secrecy culture began, and where our government first set the precedent for the disproportionate response that has guided so much of our response to the modern threat of terrorism. The vast secrecy that surrounded the government's atomic weapons program—a culture of secret keeping that led to the development of the government's first formal security clearances and the now familiar classification system of "Confidential," "Secret," and "Top Secret"—grew not out of strength, but out of weakness. The original secret of the atomic age was just how few nuclear weapons the United States actually had. That secret begat a culture of rampant government classification, a problem that increasingly affects even basic and mundane information—and today sees more than five million Americans with security clearances, a group larger than the entire population of Norway, and more than 1.5 million with "Top Secret" clearances, a group larger than the entire population of either Maine, Hawaii, Idaho, or any of ten other states.

The stories and experiences told in this book are where men like Dick Cheney and Donald Rumsfeld, who practiced COG scenarios in bunkers in the 1970s and 1980s, first learned the instincts that would govern how they responded to the terrorist attacks of September 11, 2001—and where many of today's leading warriors started their careers. The Cold War was also where the president began asserting executive authority to lead the nation unilaterally into war, bypassing the traditional congressional declarations that had always guided such decision making, and laid the groundwork for presidential prerogatives used in Vietnam, Iraq, Syria, and so many other modern conflicts. Modern warfare necessitated quick action; in fact, as Dwight Eisenhower told a group of congressmen in 1954, nuclear war "will be a very quick thing," and he wouldn't have time to ask Congress's opinion before launching a retaliatory strike. Presidents began to invoke spurious ties to "national emergencies" that allowed them to take extraordinary action. In 1962, President John F. Kennedy turned to Truman's 1950 emergency declaration involving the invasion of South Korea as legal justification for his actions during the Cuban Missile Crisis. Half a century later, President Obama used a similar declaration from 9/11 to justify attacks in places like Yemen, Somalia, and Syria. In many ways, the Cold War mentality is alive and well today—especially as the world faces an emboldened Russia led by Vladimir Putin.

A generation before Ashton Carter took over the Pentagon as President Obama's fourth defense secretary, he had helped design the E-4B "Doomsday plane" meant to help the commander-in-chief run a nuclear war from the sky—the same plane is still in use today to ferry defense secretaries around the world. It sits every day on a runway in Omaha, Nebraska, fully staffed, with its engines turning, ready to launch in just minutes and run a nuclear war from the sky.

The history of our government's Doomsday planning is, as one historian wrote, "not a happy one." Even as the government's official outward appearance was optimistic—war would be (a) not that bad and (b) survivable—inside the corridors of power, leaders recognized that the public had virtually no hope of surviving. As Eisenhower said in one meeting, if war happened, the nation didn't have "enough bulldozers to scrape the bodies off the street." What began in the 1950s as an all-encompassing, nationwide push for civil defense, to ready every household and workplace, every village and city, for a Soviet attack, shrank decade by decade, until by 9/11, there was just one aspect of the grand plans left in operation: the evacuation of the nation's leaders to bunkers hidden under mountains. That September day, when Vice President Cheney and other officials retreated to "undisclosed locations," many went to Raven Rock, the bunker built near Camp David to house the military during the Cold War, and others flooded to Mount Weather, the government's other primary mountaintop bunker in Virginia. The terrorist attacks of September 11, 2001, and the subsequent anthrax attack on the U.S. Congress restarted a focus on COG and COOP planning that continues to this day. Today, this secret world still exists, just beneath the surface of our country. In many ways, it's actually more expansive, powerful, and capable today than it ever was during the twentieth century.

Today, a third generation of Doomsday planners are settling into life inside these bunkers, which are still staffed 24 hours a day, 365 days a year. While some new facilities have been built in the last two decades, the majority of the government's plans to preserve itself and our nation during an attack in the twenty-first century still rely upon bunkers built with slide rules.

Today, those same blue-and-gold Air Force helicopters still practice evacuating officials from Washington each day in the skies over the capital.

Today, each time a major event like a presidential inauguration or State of the Union speech occurs, there's still a "designated survivor" from the established line of succession, who skips the event and stays in a secure facility under guard until the event ends without incident. At the 2017 presidential inaugural, Senate President Pro Tem Orrin Hatch and outgoing Homeland Security Secretary Jeh Johnson waited outside Washington until President Trump safely assumed power.

Today, the Postal Service does not prepare to register the dead from a nuclear strike, nor do its mail trucks stand ready to be converted into "emergency casualty carriers," but it is the designated distributor of vaccines should a biological attack or health pandemic like smallpox or Ebola occur.

And, today, every day, there are still military aides who walk just steps behind the president and vice president toting a heavy black briefcase filled with all the instructions necessary to end the world as we know it.

Until that happens, of course, we'll never know if any of the plans outlined on the following pages would have ever worked—but, as readers will see, it seems unlikely.

RAVEN ROCK

Chapter 1

PROJECT S-1

Harry S. Truman, just hours after assuming the most awesome position in the world, knew exactly what his war secretary's obtuse note must mean. "I think it is very important that I should have a talk with you as soon as possible on a highly secret matter," Henry Stimson wrote. It must be, Truman knew, the new secret superweapon—the exact details of which were so classified that even as vice president he hadn't been privy to them. Until then, Truman had known only that it was a weapon that would create a "terrific explosion."

During his twelve years in office, FDR achieved many things as president, transforming a nation broken by the Great Depression into the most powerful economy and war-fighting machine the world had ever seen. Now it fell to his successor, a farmer-turned-haberdasher-turned-politician, to usher it all forward. At first glance, that was a tough order. Truman appeared a shadow of the elite, highly educated scion of a political dynasty who had led the country to the edge of victory in a two-theater world war.

Truman seemed about as ordinary a man as had ever occupied the White House. Had World War I not intervened, he likely would have remained content on his Missouri farm, an unremarked product of a simpler century, born in 1884, when the nation's hottest defense debate was whether to retain a wooden navy. By the time Woodrow Wilson rallied the U.S. into the "Great War" in 1917, Truman was thirty-three, two years older than the Selective Service's age limit. His eyes failed every branch's medical fitness requirements. And yet he volunteered anyway, setting off with the locally organized 129th Field Artillery, where his popularity and prior National Guard service led to a captainship. His unit, Battery D, performed admirably—even bravely at times—in battle on the stalemated Western Front. Nearly half the unit was killed or wounded. When Truman sailed back to the United States after the Allied victory, he did so full of newfound confidence, ambition, and a worldliness unsatisfied by crops and fieldwork. Back in Kansas City, he ran for county office backed by the local political machine and established a reputation as an honest, hardworking administrator. In 1934, he was elected to the U.S. Senate.

Though his first years in Washington were unmemorable, the outbreak of the war in 1941 established Truman as Congress's defense watchdog, leading the Senate Select Committee to Investigate the National Defense Program. Within months it came to be simply known as the Truman Committee. Traveling the country, he tirelessly led skilled investigators into every corner of the rapidly expanding military budget—except one. Then, in mid-1943, Truman's committee uncovered a massive, secret spending operation that funneled millions of dollars into industrial efforts in Tennessee and the American Southwest, none of which seemed to be producing anything. When Senator Truman called Stimson to investigate, the secretary of war demurred. "That's a matter which I know all about personally, and I am the only one of the group of two or three men in the whole world who know about it," Stimson said. "It's part of a very important secret development."

Now that Truman had unexpectedly become president, he was on the inside. He would finally find out the answer to his earlier questions. The answer to the mystery would forever transform the office for all of his successors.

The wartime vice presidency that Truman assumed in 1945 was an office in transition, as the nation realized the potential importance of its second in command. To Truman, the primary perk was the official car that picked him up in the morning at his $120-a-month apartment on Connecticut Avenue to take him up to the Capitol, where he spent much of his time in the Senate's small vice presidential office. He became the first vice president to be given a military aide, choosing his longtime friend from Battery D, Harry

Vaughan. A few days into Truman's new role, he noticed a young man sitting outside his office. For hours, the man sat patiently as the staff went about their day. Finally, Truman asked Vaughan, "Who is that young fellow who's been out here? Does he want to see me?"

Vaughan explained that the man was Secret Service—and so, it turned out, was the other nice young man who rode in the official car's front passenger seat with Truman in the morning. Truman was shocked. He had assumed the passenger was one of the driver's friends hitching a lift to work.

Apparently, Vaughan and the treasury secretary had discussed the incongruity of having a hundred Secret Service agents protect President Roosevelt even as Vice President Truman walked freely and unguarded through the capital. So, just a few days later, a detail of three agents—including the man outside his office and the one in the limo—began escorting the vice president around Washington as well.

Truman didn't take well to the new level of supervision. One day in April, he'd left his Secret Service detail behind and snuck away to Sam Rayburn's private hideaway office, where powerful lawmakers gathered for drinks and camaraderie. There, a message awaited him: *Tell no one, but get to the White House as soon as possible.* His driver raced him up Pennsylvania Avenue, still without any protection. Truman thought the president urgently needed to see him—an odd conclusion, given that the two had only met twice in the three months he'd been serving as vice president. Upon his arrival at the White House, Truman was ushered into the private quarters and found First Lady Eleanor Roosevelt. She explained that FDR had suffered a stroke in Warm Springs, Georgia: "Harry, the President is dead." It was just eighty-nine days into the new term.

"Is there anything I can do for you?" he said, after some time, as he struggled to wrap his mind around the announcement.

Eleanor countered quickly: "Is there anything we can do for you? For you are the one in trouble now."

The leadership began to assemble in the Cabinet Room in the West Wing. Nine members of the cabinet and assorted congressional leaders like Speaker Rayburn, as well as Chief Justice Harlan Fiske Stone, and Truman's wife, Bess, and daughter, Margaret. All stood waiting. As the transfer of power unfolded, one realization stood out to Truman. "We were in the final days of the greatest war in history," he later wrote. "In that war, the United States had created military forces so enormous as to defy description, yet now, when the nation's greatest leader in that war lay dead, and a simple ceremony was about to acknowledge the presence of his successor in the nation's greatest office, only two uniforms were present."

No one else noticed the military's absence, but Truman thought it a remarkable testament to American democracy that no one asked the country's powerful military leaders whom they supported as their next leader. "The very fact that no thought was given to it demonstrates convincingly how firmly the concept of supremacy of the civil authority is accepted in our land," Truman observed. The peaceful transition of civilian power represented a grand tradition in U.S. politics—the Continuity of Government from one leader to another, the continuity of an idea larger than any single officeholder.

Le roi est mort, vive le roi!

The president was dead, long live the president.

Truman raised his right hand and began the oath. Everyone around him was silent, except his wife. She'd been crying almost from the moment she heard the news.

The following days were a whirlwind. There was a war to win, first and foremost, but also a thousand administrative details as the presidency changed hands. The White House staff faced a huge adjustment to the new commander-in-chief, too. It had been more than a dozen years since a president who could move freely himself had occupied the White House. Soon after taking office, Truman needed to go to his bank, and without warning walked out the door toward the Hamilton National Bank two blocks away. The Secret Service and D.C. police raced to catch up, and a massive lunchtime traffic jam paralyzed downtown. The incident taught Truman that the president of the United States didn't go anywhere without warning and that the presidency, particularly under wartime security policies, erected huge literal and figurative walls between him and his fellow citizens.

Until the outbreak of World War II, the White House was just like any other D.C. government building: Tourists and passersby could walk right through the gates and inside. As late as the early 1910s, White House visitors could sit at the president's desk if he was absent. That quickly changed on December 7, 1941. Within hours of the attack on Pearl Harbor, Mike Reilly, the agent in charge of FDR's Secret Service detail, began hunting for an armored limousine for the president. The only suitable vehicle he could find was a 1928 Cadillac 341A Town Sedan that had belonged to Al Capone, sitting in a government impound lot years after the Treasury Department had seized it. Reilly had agents wash and prep the car in time for Roosevelt to ride in it to Congress to deliver his "Day of Infamy" speech. The president used Capone's car until the Secret Service fitted steel armor to his regular limo, equipping a 9,000-pound Lincoln behemoth with flashing lights, running boards, and grab handles for Secret Service agents.*

A new automobile was only part of the new protective bubble around the president. The treasury secretary, Henry Morgenthau—who supervised the Secret Service—spent much of December 7 peering out the White House windows for German bombers. Though his suggestions for the placement of sandbags and machine gun emplacements at the building's entrances were denied, all staff members were issued gas masks—Roosevelt's was attached to his wheelchair—and the White House architect, Lorenzo Winslow, began creating the building's first bomb shelter.

Two bunkers, in fact, were readied for the president. Workers added thick concrete walls to a forty-foot-by-forty-foot area of the basement under the East Wing, creating a two-room safe area that, theoretically, could protect up to 100 staffers. Accessible from two entrances—one in the East Wing and the other in the garden outside—it had food rations, water, medical supplies, and was built to withstand a hit by a 500-pound bomb. Workers also dug a sloped tunnel to the neighboring Treasury Building, so FDR could speed down the ramp in his wheelchair to the Treasury's basement, where a thick granite foundation and series of vaults provided even more protection and a spacious ten-room shelter, complete with carpeting and a kitchen.

The Secret Service eventually had the Army place antiaircraft guns atop nearby government buildings, although those weapons were initially in such short supply that some were merely realistic wooden replicas. A detachment from the Chemical Warfare Service was permanently stationed at the White

---

* Roosevelt, though, still preferred to keep the convertible roof down during public appearances, negating much of the car's protective ability.

House to defend against gas attacks. Weekly drills began practicing repelling an air raid on the White House; the D.C. police would close off four blocks around the building, an infantry battalion from Fort Myer would deploy to defend against parachutists, an engineer battalion would muster near the grounds with bulldozers to rescue anyone caught in a demolished building, and the D.C. Fire Department dispatched four fire engines. The president, depending on his location, would evacuate to the White House shelter, the neighboring Treasury Building, or to one of ten secret buildings in D.C. and Maryland.

Though Washington escaped an enemy attack during the war and the antiaircraft guns and gas masks eventually disappeared, the presidency never returned to its prewar levels of openness. In part, that was because by the time Truman tried to go to the bank, a new weapon was being readied in the U.S. arsenal—a weapon that would reshape the presidency forever.[*]

Twelve days after Truman became president, he met with Stimson on April 25. An elderly seventy-two, the secretary still preferred to be called "Colonel," his designated rank from the Great War. He explained to Truman that he was responsible for almost every detail of what was known as S-1, aka the Manhattan Project, and presented Truman with a short memo, the first sentence of which left little doubt of its seriousness: "Within four months we shall in all probability have completed the most terrible weapon ever known in human history, one bomb of which could destroy a whole city."

Stimson then introduced General Leslie Groves, head of the Manhattan Project, to provide further background and context. "This is a big project," Groves said. It was perhaps the day's only understatement. The secret effort was the biggest the government had ever undertaken, totaling nearly $2 billion in spending and involving 200,000 workers—many of whom lived in secret government cities in places like Oak Ridge, Tennessee, and Los Alamos,

---

[*] The only building damaged by the war was the Lincoln Memorial, which was hit by a burst of machine gun fire on the morning of September 3, 1942, when a soldier stationed at the antiaircraft gun emplacement on the roof of the Interior Department near the Mall accidentally fired a four-shot burst. Three of the bullets struck the north side of the Memorial's frieze, damaging the word "Wisconsin."

New Mexico. As the project advanced, a thicker and thicker cloak of secrecy surrounded the Manhattan research to secure it from leaks and spies. Mail from workers was censored, scientists were trailed by friendly surveillance teams, and staff traveled between facilities under pseudonyms—Groves himself was known simply as "99." As he and Stimson reported this to Truman, they saved the biggest news for last: It had all worked. The secrecy, the science, the engineering all led, by April 1945, to within a hairsbreadth of a workable device.

Stimson also added a warning, the import of which none of the men fully understood at the time. The United States and Great Britain had collaborated on the superweapon, but their monopoly on the technology would inevitably end. Only one nation could likely break it in the near term: Joseph Stalin's Soviet Union. Outside the Oval Office, World War II was quickly coming to an end. That very same day, Soviets advancing from the east and Americans advancing from the west united at the Elbe River in Germany. Five days later, Adolf Hitler committed suicide in his Berlin Führerbunker.

The only dilemma Truman faced, it seemed, was a moral one. He began to contemplate the destruction this kind of modern war could cause. When the Allied powers, led by Winston Churchill, Stalin, and Truman, gathered in Potsdam, Germany, to plot the war's final moves and shape the world that came after, Truman looked out the window of the presidential plane, the *Sacred Cow*, as it flew toward Berlin, passing over cities leveled by the Allied bombing. Sitting in his special observation seat, Truman became the first— and only—president to view firsthand the effects of aerial bombing on civilian targets. The destruction left him shaken. "Those two cities, viewed from the air, appeared to be completely destroyed," he later wrote. "I could not see a single house that was left standing." Churchill, who spent part of his time in Potsdam touring Hitler's headquarters and the bunker where he died, thought darkly: "This is what would have happened to us if they had won the war. We would have been in that bunker."

That same day—Monday, July 16—in the New Mexico desert the most fearsome weapon of all time became a reality. At 5:29 a.m. local time, 5,500 miles from Berlin, the first atomic bomb exploded at Alamogordo Air Force Base. George Kistiakowsky, who had helped lead development of the bomb and would go on to play a key role as a presidential science advisor in the Eisenhower administration, initially hugged lead scientist J. Robert Oppenheimer and then, more soberly, said, "I'm sure that at the end of the world—in the last millisecond of the earth's existence—the last human will see what we saw." That evening, Stimson carried a coded telegram to Truman in Berlin: OPERATED ON THIS MORNING. DIAGNOSIS NOT YET COMPLETE, BUT RESULTS SEEM SATISFACTORY AND ALREADY EXCEED EXPECTATIONS.

Truman had already made the decision to use the bomb. His goal was to forestall a land invasion of Japan, extending the war, and likely costing millions of lives. In part, Truman's resolve stemmed from how the world's views of targeting civilian populations had shifted radically over the course of the war. The 1937 Japanese bombardment of Shanghai caused outrage across much of the world, but by 1945 civilian targets were considered fair game for the Allies—massive bombardments and firebombings of Hamburg, Dresden, and later, Tokyo, Nagoya, Yokohama, Osaka, and Kobe caused little outcry from the public. General Curtis LeMay, the head of the Army Air Forces in the Pacific, had so embraced the mass bombardments, in fact, that war planners in Washington had been genuinely concerned by the spring of 1945 that there might not be a Japanese city left intact on which to demonstrate the new atomic bomb.

Truman, at the end of a day's negotiations in Potsdam, privately told Stalin that the U.S. had a new weapon of "unusual destructive force" to use against Japan. "All [Stalin] said was that he was glad to hear it and hoped we would make good use of it," Truman recalled later. The Soviet leader knew far more than he let on. Spies had been feeding the Soviets project secrets to accelerate Stalin's own atomic efforts. That night, he cabled Lavrenti Beria, the feared head of the secret police and head of the atomic initiative, to tell him to hurry. The Russians had to catch up with the Americans.

When the two leaders shook hands on the final day at Potsdam, neither Stalin nor Truman knew what the years ahead would bring. Though they would spend much of the next decade watching each other's moves warily, they would never again meet in person. They left in their wake a divided Europe, a partitioned Germany, a Soviet-occupied Poland, and a map that would haunt the world for nearly half a century.

As Truman sailed back to the United States aboard the USS *Augusta*, he was interrupted during lunch on August 6 by a message: HIROSHIMA BOMBED VISUALLY ... RESULTS CLEAR CUT SUCCESSFUL IN ALL RESPECTS. VISIBLE EFFECTS GREATER THAN IN ANY TEST. CONDITIONS NORMAL IN AIR-PLANE FOLLOWING DELIVERY. An aide from the White House Map Room helpfully circled Hiroshima on a map of Japan, showing the president the city he'd just wiped off the face of the planet. Truman shared the news with those around him in the mess hall, explaining that the U.S. had just dropped the world's most powerful weapon. "He was not actually laughing," journal-ist Merriman Smith recalled, "but there was a broad smile on his face. In the small dispatch which he waved at the men of the ship, he saw the quick end of the war written between the lines." Radios began to report the news, and the American public soon learned about the amazing new weapon and its stunning new power. On NBC radio, Don Goddard announced "the story of a new bomb, so powerful that only the imagination of a trained scientist could dream of its existence."

Four days later, another bomb—nicknamed Fat Man—dropped on Nagasaki. Amazingly, there was no separate presidential order for its de-ployment; Truman's initial orders in July had said to just continue dropping additional bombs as they became available. Nagasaki hadn't even been the primary target when the bomber *Bockscar* took off that morning—it had intended to bomb the city of Kokura, but there were too many clouds over the target city, so after an hour and three failed bombing runs, the plane diverted its lethal payload to Nagasaki. The citizens of Kokura continued on with their day, not realizing how close they'd come to death. Such were the vicissitudes of the new atomic age.

Twenty-four hours after the Nagasaki bombing, which killed an es-timated 70,000 people, the Japanese emperor decided to surrender. On Tuesday, August 14, the Swiss chargé d'affaires in Washington delivered the official surrender to President Truman. Jubilation broke out across the nation; in front of the White House in Lafayette Square, a conga line started.

Chapter 2

MR. RANCE

As the United States emerged from World War II, it wasn't looking to get into another war. Most Americans wanted just to "go to the movies and drink Coke," Averell Harriman said. In the weeks following the war's end, Truman announced a redesign of the presidential flag—the first since the Wilson years. Chief among the changes was the shifting of the eagle's head away from the arrows of war instead toward the olive branch of peace, reflecting the nation's desire for a universal peace. It was a hopeful gesture, but Truman understood reality as well. Buried in the midst of his post-Potsdam radio report, he gave an ominous warning: "No one can foresee what another war would mean to our own cities and our own people. What we are doing to Japan now—even with the new atomic bomb—is only a small fraction of what would happen to the world in a third World War."

For nearly its entire history, America's foreign policy had been unique in the Western world. Its physical isolation meant it possessed little need for a standing military or consistent security strategy, but new technologies and new weapons had opened the United States up to threats from abroad—one in particular. Assistant War Secretary John J. McCloy returned to Washington following a tour through ravaged Europe, Egypt, India, Burma, China, and Japan. He reported that he clearly heard the global fear of Soviet intentions. "Everywhere you go, the topic is up—the concern over Russia's ambitions, how far she is going to go, how to deal with her—it is in every aspect and every corner of the world," he said. He also saw the potential cost of a misstep ahead, as one of the few senior officials to tour Hiroshima. "All the pictures that you have seen of it cannot give you the complete picture of destruction which actually exists on the ground," he said. "One bomb did it."

While officials faced growing concerns, the nation initially experienced unbridled excitement over the newly discovered power of the atom.* General Mills offered an "atomic bomb ring" in exchange for a Kix cereal box top and 15 cents (the ring was "guaranteed not to blow everything sky high"), and some 750,000 children clamored for the prize. Books like *Almighty Atom: The Real Story of Atomic Energy* celebrated the possibility of using atomic weapons to melt the polar icecaps, gifting "the entire world a moister, warmer climate." It was an idea many people embraced, from World War I ace Eddie Rickenbacker to the head of UNESCO, who said he loved the idea of "atomic dynamite" for "landscaping the earth."

But the mood inside Washington turned grim as the long-term consequences of the bomb's invention sank in. The true horror of nuclear weapons became clear only after *The New Yorker* devoted its entire issue of August 31, 1946, to a 30,000-word article by war correspondent John Hersey, who explored the Hiroshima bombing by following six survivors in the subsequent hours, days, and months. Hersey's words, vivid details ("Heat stenciled dress figures onto the bodies of women"), and haunting statistics (62,000 of the city's 90,000 buildings had been destroyed) shocked and horrified readers. The magazine's entire print run sold out in hours; the ABC radio network ran special reports simply reading the article aloud. Turned quickly into a book, Hersey's work became a national bestseller. For many, it was the first-ever glimpse of the horrors of this new style of war. It's hard to contemplate today their shock, but many people had not yet seen photos or film from Hiroshima and Nagasaki, nor had they been bombarded on the nightly news with video and graphic images from combat zones. Suddenly, wartime Japan had made it to the living rooms of peacetime America.†

---

* The concept was so new that many people, reading the word for the first time, mispronounced it as "a-tome" instead of "ad-em."

† Not everyone yet saw atomic weapons, though, as a bad thing. "I read Hersey's report," one *New Yorker* subscriber wrote. "It was marvelous. Now let us drop a handful on Moscow."

Hersey's article came out just months after the top secret U.S. Strategic Bombing Survey delivered its own unvarnished and scientifically rigorous study of the Hiroshima and Nagasaki bombs. Together, they made hard
reading for government officials thinking about protecting the U.S. population from a similar attack. Paul Nitze, a thirty-nine-year-old strategist who
had worked on the survey and understood the effect of the massive Allied
bombardments, argued that while the atomic bomb was unique, that didn't
mean it was incalculably powerful. Citizens in Nagaski had been saved by
bomb shelters; buildings constructed of reinforced concrete had remained
standing even close to the center of the blast; parks had stopped spread-
ing fires. American cities could emulate these things—cities and industry
could be dispersed, firebreaks built into newly expanding urban and suburban areas.

A specific new fear—that a whole city could just disappear in an
instant—permeated the American consciousness in the wake of Hiroshima
and Nagasaki. Writer E. B. White captured that new fear in New York: "The
city, for the first time in its long history, is destructible. A single flight of a
plane no bigger than a wedge of geese can quickly end this island fantasy," he
wrote. "All dwellers in cities must live with the stubborn fact of annihilation."

Politically, the nation's reaction to the atomic bomb unfolded in distinct
phases. Leaders like Republican Harold Stassen—the GOP's 1940 convention keynoter—and scientists like Oppenheimer, the father of the atomic
bomb, first proposed grand ideas, arguing the world could ill afford national-
ism in the atomic age. In their view, the entire world must come under one
ruling body that possessed a monopoly on weaponry. The idea was endorsed
by such leading lights as Carl Spaatz, the head of the U.S. Army Air Forces,
and even Albert Einstein, who argued, "A World Government is preferable
to the far greater evil of wars, particularly with their intensified destructive-
ness." According to social historian Paul Boyer's estimates, a united world
government "won at least passive support from a third to half of the American people."

After discarding as impractical that initial idealism for peaceful world
government, the next phase of public debate argued for the comparatively
more modest goal of simply remaking American civilization. Military expert

Louis Bruchiss explained that large cities like New York were "all done." Atomic war—and atomic damage—was a "certainty" in the years ahead, and the only way to avoid it was to dig. The country needed a mass effort to bury urban populations inside mountains, linked by subterranean railroads. Meanwhile, Henry Luce's editors at *Life* magazine tried to put an optimistic spin on the idea that the atomic bomb would make life aboveground obsolete. "Consider the ant, whose social problems much resemble man," the magazine explained. "Constructing beautiful urban palaces and galleries, many ants have long lived underground in entire satisfaction." The military also touted the benefits of American society moving underground. "After all, sunlight isn't so wonderful. You have to be near a window to benefit by it. With fluorescent fixtures, you get an even light all over the place," one Pentagon official said, explaining that when Sweden buried factories underground during World War II, the plants were cheaper to run: "No paint bills, no roof-fixing, no window washing."

If cities weren't buried entirely, they at least had to be broken apart and dispersed. Urban architecture would be reimagined around atomic survival to ensure a single bomb couldn't do too much damage. They would be built in new design styles like "coiled rope," "ribbon," or "cellular" cities that were low-density, narrow, and composed of small "productive cells" connected by express highways. MIT professors proposed encircling urban centers with "life belts," large paved beltways that intersected radial highways to speed evacuations. The land around the "life belt" roads would be "reserved as parks and made ready for large tent cities which could quickly be erected to shelter the refugees."

Sociologist William Ogburn argued in 1946 that society must be broken up if there was any chance of surviving nuclear war—it could be done, he said, at a reasonable cost. "The Pueblo Indians once moved their cities from the plains, where they were the prey of their warlike enemies, and set them in caves scooped out of canyon walls high above the river," he wrote. Breaking the nation's 200 major cities into a thousand small ones would, he estimated, still cost less than the Second World War and "perhaps less than the cost of a third world war."

As the world rejected the "easy" road—international control and disarmament—the United States began a third phase of nuclear reality: an arms buildup and a new militaristic approach that expanded into civilian society. If atomic bombs represented the new normal, then the home front would become a war zone—each house its own ground zero. Cities like Allentown, Pennsylvania, distributed dogtags to every resident, and New York City gave the military-style IDs to every schoolchild. "See, it's bead chain, just like yours," a kid told a soldier in an ad promoting the program. Bert the Turtle taught a generation of schoolchildren to "duck and cover" when nuclear alarms sounded.

But in the years ahead enthusiasm for such plans waned. Efforts to protect civilian life fell by the wayside and a fourth and final grim phase of nuclear reality settled over the United States. Soon grandiose plans gradually shrank to just a single, all-consuming governmental goal: protect the idea of a democratic leadership and preserve the National Command Authorities—that virtually never-ending succession line of officials authorized to launch the nation's nuclear weapons. Rather than remake the entire society, the government would protect itself and let the rest of us die. That way, there was a chance that democracy could one day again blossom across the land of the free and the home of the brave.

Some people figured out this reality before others. Writing in *The Saturday Evening Post* in 1946, the well-connected Alsop brothers, Joseph and Stewart, sketched out emerging answers for the new atomic world. The nation's defense system would be "based upon the principle that 'the power to retaliate is the best deterrent of an attack,'" and would consist of "an immense, invulnerable mechanism of retaliation, which will be instantaneously set off by the first warning of enemy attack." They outlined, with remarkable and grim accuracy, the military's future, predicting a "great chain" of deep "concrete caverns" staffed by rocket squads "always at full readiness." "Deeper still, in some aseptic, scientifically ventilated, scientifically lighted, scientifically guarded hole somewhere in the United States, will be the master control center," they wrote. "If the system works as planned, in the very moment that death and ruin rain down upon this nation, an equal storm of death and ruin will be hurled outward."

That, though, was just the start. "The whole pattern of our life has been designed without a passing thought of future security," they continued. "We must initiate radical changes in the character of our national life." The U.S.

would have to invest deeply in the "most-effective secret intelligence . . . in a way and on a scale which are difficult to imagine." Key industrial plants would have to be buried and citizens made ready for when "our great cities will be reduced to radioactive shards." They whispered also about changes to the Constitution in the atomic age—after-the-fact investigations and prosecutions of saboteurs would not be enough. The U.S. would have to "reinterpret" the Constitution to provide for preemptive searches and seizures when atomic terrorism was involved. Remarkably, over the decades ahead, in almost every respect, the path the Alsops laid out in 1946 was almost precisely the one United States would take.

Military planners found themselves in largely uncharted territory as they explored what war with the Soviet Union would mean for the United States. The nation, unlike the other major players, had escaped damage to its mainland during World War II.* Thus, to prepare for a war against the Soviet Union, the U.S. military turned to Great Britain, where they found the first generation of what would come to be known as "Continuity of Government" facilities, meant to protect the national leadership from enemy attacks.

The British had learned their wartime lessons the hard way. During the Great War, imposing German Zeppelin airships bombed British cities regularly from 1915 onward. Raids often were carried out by just two or three airships at a time, dropping small bombs and grenades. Actual casualties and physical damage were mostly light—although one 1917 raid killed 162 Londoners—but the psychological impact was huge. The impregnable English Channel, which had left Britain beyond the reach of attackers for centuries, no longer offered protection.

With those horrible nights seared into their minds and new geopolitical storm clouds gathering, the British understood what larger air strikes with modern weaponry might mean; air raid planning began for the next war as early as 1924 and by 1937 officials were planning for the "Central War

* Luckily so—since Washington, D.C., had been badly unprepared for an enemy attack: Its first air raid drill, on December 21, 1941, had been a fiasco—the city's sole warning siren was left over from the First World War and after days of dramatic media warnings instructing residents to take cover when the alarm sounded, the siren emitted barely more than a rooster's squawk when a D.C. official activated it.

Room." The simplest idea was to build such a facility outside London, perhaps in the northwest countryside near Wales, but publicly evacuating the capital seemed bad for morale. Instead, the British Home Office developed its first Continuity of Government plans, secret procedures based around multiple scenarios. There was a "Yellow" move, which would disperse resources like the BBC's transmitting capabilities into the countryside as a precaution, and a "Black" move, which would come only if London had to be abandoned. The Home Office divided Britain and appointed thirteen regional commissioners who would oversee their respective portions of the country if London fell to air raids or invasion; their appointment and their identities were considered state secrets. As war neared, two teams of government officials—Group A and Group B—were readied for evacuation. Group A consisted of those deemed "essential" to war efforts and who would evacuate first to the suburbs; Group B were those not involved in military operations who could safely evacuate further outside London to the Midlands. The government provided resources for the public to protect itself, too, giving every civilian a gas mask and helping construct nearly two million backyard "Anderson Shelters," named after the head of the civil defense agency, Sir John Anderson, and able to shelter six adults.

The nation's valuables were dispersed, too. The National Gallery moved much of its collection to a slate quarry in North Wales; the Tate moved pieces to country estates outside London and into underground subway tunnels; the British Museum and the Victoria and Albert Museum evacuated key items to a stone quarry in Wiltshire; the Public Records Office decamped to a Surrey country estate; and essential state documents and the crown jewels were moved from the Tower of London. By June 1939 the Bank of England had completed a "shadow factory" for printing currency in Overton, sixty miles west of London, and designed special £1 notes in case coinage fell short during the war. The Bank moved thousands of tons of gold to Canada in secret to ensure the monarchy could continue to finance war operations in the face of a German invasion.

In secret, the military and cabinet moved ahead with building a protected central facility in the heart of London and a network of suburban bunker headquarters. George Rance, a veteran of the army's rifle brigades, had spent the years before the war in a mostly anonymous government post, helping procure furniture and office supplies; as war loomed, he became its key supplier. As the Cabinet War Rooms began construction, "Mr. Rance," as he was known to staff, doubled every legitimate supply request that passed through his office and delivered the surplus to the hidden warren of rooms growing under Whitehall. Deliveries "c/o Mr. Rance, Office of Public Works, Whitehall" filled the empty suites one by one.

By September 1939—within just a week of the declaration of war— the barebones Cabinet War Rooms opened for business, just steps from 10 Downing Street and Buckingham Palace. Winston Churchill toured the facility shortly after he became prime minister and declared, "This is the room from which I will direct the war."

From September 1939 onward, the operational hub of the War Rooms— the so-called Map Room—was staffed around the clock for six years, until August 1945. Over that time, Rance would become the War Rooms' clerk and custodian, carefully tending the facilities and setting the clocks each day. Life for the War Rooms staff proved damp, noisy, and stuffy. There was, one secretary recalled, always a "dense haze" in the air, and the high heels of female typists and secretaries echoed on the concrete floors. The bunker's air, marred by poor circulation, hardly seemed to move, and everyone from Churchill down smoked prodigiously. Residual cooking smells and fumes from the Elsan chemical toilets used throughout the facility didn't help the air's breathability. Staff came and went throughout the day, descending the guarded staircase from the buildings above, returning upstairs to shop or buy lunch, and departing at the end of their shifts for their own beds elsewhere.

The living quarters inside the sub-basement bunker, down the narrow stairs from the War Rooms, were tight and spartan, with ceilings just four feet high, and lit around the clock. "I propose to lead a troglodyte existence with several 'trogs,'" Churchill wrote in September 1940 as the bombing of London grew more intense, using the phrase that he coined to refer to the underground staff. They had mandatory sunlamp treatments to make up for their subterranean existence. Notice boards in the War Rooms announced the weather aboveground; as a joke, when a heavy air raid was occurring overhead, George Rance would list the weather as "windy." The Supreme Allied Commander, Dwight Eisenhower, kept his own bunker nearby, built adjacent to the Goodge Street underground station, with a direct pneumatic tube link to the Cabinet War Rooms to allow easy communications.

As unpleasant as the wartime experience had been, the British response proved critical to the early stages of the American postwar security planning. There was a lot still to learn—it had, after all, been more than a century since the U.S. had cared about homeland defense. The last time a continental American city had been attacked, Dolley Madison had fled Washington, D.C., with Gilbert Stuart's painting of George Washington. As she left the capital, the White House doorkeeper—known to everyone as "French John"—picked up the Madisons' pet macaw, locked the doors of the White House, and left the key to the presidential mansion with the friendliest member of the diplomatic corps: the Russian minister, André Daschkoff.

This coming era couldn't rely on the friendliness of the Russians.

Joseph Stalin took the stage at Moscow's Bolshoi Theatre on Saturday, February 9, 1946, to explain his view of East versus West and the grand historic battle he saw between Communism and capitalism. The two worldviews were simply incompatible, and Stalin made clear he foresaw war looming. As his foreign minister explained later, Stalin believed "the First World War pulled one country out of capitalist slavery. The Second World War created a socialist system, the third will put an end to imperialism once and for all."

Events around the world over the coming two weeks brought together the ingredients necessary for the new era—coincidences visible today only in retrospect. The day after Stalin's speech, the U.S. government told the 167 residents on the Bikini Atoll that they had to relocate. Their home island was being requisitioned for atomic testing, a task necessary, the islanders were told, for "the good of mankind and to end all world wars." Later that week, the U.S. Army unveiled its latest invention—the first electronic computer, known as ENIAC, the Electronic Numerical Integrator and Computer. The eight-ton room-sized device, its military inventors bragged, could complete "in ten days a job which would have required three months of concentrated effort." One of its first tasks would be calculating rocket trajectories to help speed war planning. Then, thirteen days after Stalin's speech, George Kennan, the deputy chief of mission at the Moscow embassy, sent a report to Washington on the state of Russian relations. Aptly known as the "Long

Telegram," his 8,000-word missive to the State Department laid out how the Soviet Union's leadership was fundamentally opposed to the American way of life. The United States must, Kennan argued, acknowledge Soviet ambitions and move to counter them. "The main element of any United States policy toward the Soviet Union must be that of a long-term, patient but firm and vigilant containment of Russian expansive tendencies," he wrote. Washington strategists and leaders desperate for a guiding principle in a threatening new world quickly seized upon Kennan's phrase "containment." Together, these three tools—nuclear weapons, computers, and Kennan's idea of containment—would define the next half century of the Cold War, and in the process reshape the world, the United States, and the American presidency.

On March 5, less than a month after Stalin's Bolshoi speech, Truman and a visiting Winston Churchill rode in the president's armored train car, called Ferdinand Magellan, to Westminster College in Missouri. There, Truman sat next to the eloquent British leader onstage as Churchill warned, "From Stettin in the Baltic to Trieste in the Adriatic an iron curtain has descended across the [European] Continent."

The Cold War was under way.

Few government bodies played as key a role in the Cold War's beginnings as the Atomic Energy Commission, the five-member panel created to balance the delicate relationship between civilian scientists, the military, and the presidency. Its first chair was David Lilienthal, a New Deal progressive of the first rank who had led the Tennessee Valley Authority (TVA), FDR's experiment to bring energy and economic growth to an underdeveloped region. In January 1946, Dean Acheson, then undersecretary of state, summoned Lilienthal to Washington to enlist his efforts in understanding the new nuclear world. Until then, the atom had been primarily a military project. Based on secrecy and necessity, General Leslie Groves's near-carte-blanche authority had stretched the Manhattan Project's scope far beyond normal democratic controls—he'd even entered into international uranium mining contracts with Belgium and the Congo without informing the State Department. Now, in the fresh sunlight of peace, Acheson and Truman wanted to establish a better model for the future. Lilienthal would lead the small commission to study the atomic project, the possibility for international control, and the extent necessary for ongoing secrecy.

Lilienthal immediately understood the central challenge: "What is there that is secret?" His hunch, he confided in his journal, was that "In the real sense there are no secrets (that is, nothing that is not known or knowable)" about the atomic project. The science was understood; the concept proved decisively; other countries could and would master the technology and design given time. Now, Lilienthal believed, "Military secrecy, as imposed by Army standards, may actually imperil security of the nation, in the short and the long run." Nearly everywhere Lilienthal now went, he was accompanied by AEC security officers, one of the first proliferations of the security culture that would dominate Washington in the decades ahead. His mind was now too valuable to leave unsecured. "There will surely never be a dull moment—not for quite a while," he wrote in his journal after accepting the AEC chairmanship.

In December 1946, when he was finally told "the numbers" by the military, Lilienthal was stunned to discover that his educated guess of the nation's nuclear arsenal had been nearly exactly correct, as had been his guess of the rough ratio between the number of bombs built versus the total amount of fissionable material the U.S. had created. One of the other commissioners laughingly teased Lilienthal: "You must have been peeking." But actually it was almost as he'd suspected earlier: There were no real secrets in the atomic program—except the big one about just how weak America's arsenal truly was.

When the AEC met with President Truman to present its report, Lilienthal and his team left a space blank. While reading the papers together with the president, Lilienthal delivered the atomic stockpile number verbally.

It was just thirteen.

Truman was shocked. That hardly seemed a firm redoubt to stop the Soviet advance.

Behind closed doors, Truman fretted as the Soviet Union consolidated its power in Eastern Europe. "Things look black," he wrote his daughter, Margaret, in March 1947. That month, in response to crises in Greece and Turkey, Truman addressed a joint session of Congress, arguing that the United

States had a duty to help democratic nations resist the spread of authoritarianism and, specifically, Soviet Communism. Secretary of State George C. Marshall expanded this Truman Doctrine that spring, proposing generous and large-scale economic aid to the devastated people of Europe, and Congress approved what came to be known as the Marshall Plan nearly a year later. Such visions marked a new development in U.S. policymaking, the rise of "national security." Policymakers in the past had always used terms like "national interest" or "national defense," but the idea of "national security" presaged something bigger and grander: It wasn't enough to be confident that an enemy could be stopped at the border—the United States needed to engage with the world beyond and stop threats long before they reached our shores. "Our national security can only be assured on a very broad and comprehensive front. I am using the word 'security' here consistently and continuously rather than 'defense,'" Navy Secretary James Forrestal explained in one 1945 congressional hearing.

"I like your words 'national security,'" Senator Edwin Johnson responded.

Forrestal tasked his friend Ferdinand Eberstadt, a powerful and respected Wall Street financier who dabbled in policymaking, to make recommendations for how the U.S. should align its military for peacetime after World War II. The resulting Eberstadt Report argued, "The changing content and scope of the phrase 'national security' is apparent from a contrast of our international commitments and responsibilities after World War I and World War II." The Eberstadt Committee suggested establishing a formal National Security Council, a Joint Chiefs of Staff, a National Security Resources Board for industrial preparedness, as well as a central intelligence agency. It served as the foundation for the seminal reshuffling of the 1947 National Security Act, modernizing and updating the military and intelligence community for the Cold War.

On June 24, as the Grand Old Party chose New York governor Thomas E. Dewey as Truman's opponent for the 1948 election, Russian forces closed the ground routes to the German capital of Berlin, leading Truman to order a massive airlift to resupply the city. In his first act of nuclear diplomacy, he dispatched B-29 bombers, the same type of planes that had dropped the bombs on Hiroshima and Nagasaki, to West Germany, the U.K., and Newfoundland. Although he didn't send nuclear weapons with them, as a

German newspaper reported, the Soviet foreign minister was "not likely to forget that the 90 Superfortresses stationed in Germany, when loaded with atom bombs, represent a destructive force which is four times as great as the entire Air Force of the United States in the Second World War." Never mind that there weren't ninety atomic bombs in the world at that point. That was a big secret. As Truman's secretary of state said, the atomic bomb was America's "gun behind the door." The United States, Truman argued, should never be in a position where Stalin could ignore its strength, and he often reminded visitors how Stalin brusquely dismissed the Vatican, mocking, "How many divisions did you say the Pope has?" Nuclear war wasn't necessarily the best option for defending the free world—it happened, though, to be the cheapest, far cheaper than trying to match Russian armies man-for-man on the fields of Europe.

In this new world, the Air Force—and specifically its nuclear weapons— would be the country's main strategic advantage. Air Force General Curtis LeMay—a tough, cigar-chomping power with a reputation for showy non-stop endurance flights—envisioned a new military doctrine, influenced by how World War II for the United States had started and ended—the surprise attack on Pearl Harbor and the bombing of Hiroshima and Nagasaki—and driven by the startlingly clear power of airborne attacks: Throughout the war, no nation had ever successfully defeated or turned back any attacker's bombing mission—in every bombing mission at least some bombers had gotten through to their target. In LeMay's mind, these three ingredients were the recipe for future wartime success: The devastating surprise of Pearl Harbor mixed with the devastating power of Hiroshima meant airpower could strike a decisive blow at the opening of the next war. As LeMay said, "There must be no ceiling, no boundaries, no limits to our airpower."*

Outside Omaha, at Nebraska's Offutt Air Force Base, LeMay started building a new military force fit for the age of nuclear weapons. On November 9, 1948—one week after Truman won the presidential election—Offutt,

---

* The general waxed almost poetically about nuclear weapons: "That beautiful devilish pod underneath, clinging as a fierce child against its mother's belly carries all the conventional bomb explosive force of World War II and everything which came before," he wrote. "One [bomber] can load that concentrated firepower and convey it to any place on the globe, and let it sink down, and let it go off, and bruise the stars and planets."

an old cavalry post from the 1800s, became the headquarters of the Strategic Air Command, chosen in part since its central location kept it well protected from a surprise Soviet attack. When LeMay arrived, SAC numbered about 45,000 personnel, spread across fourteen bomber wings, and he was disgusted by the undisciplined, shoddy organization he inherited. Over the months ahead, LeMay worked wing by wing, perfecting each unit before moving on to the next one.

Pentagon planners meanwhile settled on a list of forty-nine Soviet cities that, if destroyed, would effectively paralyze that country; hitting those cities would require, the Air Force estimated, 100 bombers and bombs, which meant the nation needed 200 nuclear-capable bombers and 200 nuclear weapons to successfully destroy the entire nation. The plan represented the Cold War's first atomic weapons tasking—the first in what would be a seemingly endless push for more weapons, bigger weapons, and more delivery vehicles.

In 1949, in an unprecedented move, the Navy's top leadership voiced public concern about the nascent atomic plans, saying they amounted to "mass slaughter of men, women, and children." "For a 'civilized society' like the United States, the broad purpose of a war cannot be simply destruction and annihilation of the enemy," wrote Admiral Daniel Gallery. As Rear Admiral Ralph Ofstie argued, current war plans aimed at "wholesale extermination of civilians" were "contrary to fundamental American ideals." While the broad-based objections of the admirals certainly had roots in the difficult inter-service rivalries of the postwar period—budget cuts and demobilization were hollowing out the once-strong naval fighting forces and the Air Force was gaining new technology and planes—the objections also stemmed from legitimate moral concerns about the new nuclear strategies. The Navy's argument, publicized during remarkable congressional hearings, came to be known as the "Admirals' Revolt," horrified other military leaders, and the "revolt" didn't last long. At the conclusion of the hearings, the Truman administration "retired" Admiral Louis Denfeld, who had led the objections on Capitol Hill, and two other admirals were reassigned before resigning their posts. Partly, the harsh reaction against the admirals was an unfortunate matter of timing; that same fall, the Soviet Union got the bomb and the government had little appetite for the appearance of weakness.

Truman, though, shared some of the admirals' concerns. The only man in history who had ever borne responsibility for a nuclear weapon's use, he stopped one Oval Office debate over civilian versus military control of the bombs cold, saying, "You have got to understand that this isn't a military weapon. It is used to wipe out women and children and unarmed people, and not for military uses. So we have got to treat this differently from rifles and cannons and ordinary things like that."

Chapter 3

CAMPBELL

During his time chairing the Atomic Energy Commission, David Lilienthal's escape was Martha's Vineyard, where he and his wife vacationed at the end of each summer. As the Lilienthals drove home from a friends' dinner party through a thick night fog on September 19, 1949, the car's headlights picked up a hatless figure at the end of their driveway, his thumb out like he was hitchhiking. "It's Jim McCormack," David said, startled. McCormack's face looked bemused, Lilienthal recalled, "as if I frequently found him on a windswept moor, in the dead of night, on an island, outside a goat field."

Army Brigadier General James McCormack, the highest-ranking military officer at the AEC, had traveled to the island with bad news. By the light of an oil lamp inside Lilienthal's cottage, he explained that a reconnaissance plane off Alaska had detected a radioactive cloud. Lavrenti Beria, the merciless KGB chief who had headed the Soviet nuclear effort, had achieved results years faster than anyone expected—testing a 22-kiloton bomb equivalent to the Fat Man that had exploded over Nagasaki. Lilienthal retrieved two beers from the icebox and the two leaders of the atomic age sat in quiet contemplation, absorbing what this meant for themselves, their work, and the world.

The test of "Joe-1," as the Soviet weapon became known, launched an immediate Washington debate over whether the U.S. should proceed with building a thermonuclear or hydrogen bomb, what was known in military circles as the "super." A thermonuclear bomb existed only theoretically, a nuclear-fusion-based weapon that would be ten times—or more—powerful than the fission-based bombs used on Japan. The military argued that if the Russians had mastered the atomic weapon, they would certainly push forward with a thermonuclear one. The United States couldn't be left behind. "The Russian bomb has changed the situation drastically," recorded Lilienthal, who for security purposes referred in his writings to the proposed weapon as "Campbell," as in the soup company, "soup" as short for "super." Lilienthal's commission argued against building the bomb, but a special study group at the National Security Council, known as the Z Committee, made a simple counterpoint: Delaying work on the bomb wouldn't delay the Soviets—and the American public wouldn't tolerate falling behind. In the final meeting, President Truman took just seven minutes to approve the weapon, asking only one question: "Can the Russians do it?"

Everyone nodded. Admiral Sidney Souers, from the National Security Council, made the only verbal reply: "We don't have much time."

"In that case, we have no choice," the commander-in-chief decided. "We'll go ahead."

The crash program for building the "super" dwarfed even the Manhattan Project. The AEC nearly tripled in size, growing from a handful of sites and 55,000 employees to 142,000 employees spread across more than a score of sites. It would devour nearly 7 percent of the nation's entire electrical output, and, according to historian Richard Rhodes, exceed in capital investment the combined market capitalization of Bethlehem Steel, U.S. Steel, Alcoa, DuPont, Goodyear, and General Motors. Albert Einstein, though, summed up the AEC's new project more succinctly than any statistics from the sidelines. As Lilienthal's AEC embarked on building Campbell, Einstein told a television interviewer: "General annihilation beckons."

Elsewhere inside the government, State Department policy planning chief Paul Nitze, working with both Secretary of State Dean Acheson and the Defense Department, prepared a fifty-eight-page document, dryly titled "United States Objectives and Programs for National Security," that would profoundly reshape U.S. policy for decades to come. The document, known as NSC-68, argued that the United States must commence a rapid and sustained buildup of the political, economic, and military strength of the free world. America must wrest the initiative from the Soviet Union, which at the time, between its nuclear weapons program and the rise of Communist China, seemed to have the global momentum. The document wasn't meant to harbor nuance; NSC-68, Acheson would later explain, was meant to "bludgeon the mass mind of 'top government.'"

The Pentagon continued to develop its own strategies for the day peace would end. Under the 1950 war plan OFF TACKLE, SAC would effectively expend all of its bombers, crews, and weapons within three months, believing that in an atomic war it would either be over within ninety days or there'd be no world left to fight over. There was also a subtle but important distinction in the plan's verbiage: Earlier plans had called for SAC to "direct" bombs against targets, whereas OFF TACKLE now called for SAC to "destroy" them.

Then, in June 1950, Communist North Korea invaded its American-backed neighbor to the south using Soviet-supplied tanks and weaponry, starting a new conflict. "My father made clear, from the moment he heard the news," Margaret Truman recalled later, "that he feared this was the opening round in World War III."

Two weeks later, Truman transferred eighty-nine atomic bombs to the U.S. Air Force bases in Great Britain, though he ordered the nuclear cores to remain stateside under the control of the Atomic Energy Commission. The military still badly wanted full custody of the weapons—and they knew, too, that in an emergency, they'd get them—presidential order or not. As General LeMay explained years later, "I felt that under certain conditions—say we woke up some morning and there wasn't any Washington or something—I was going to take the bombs." He dispatched an aide out to ABLE, the Atomic Energy Commission's facility in the Manzano Mountains outside Albuquerque where the nuclear cores were stored, to meet with its director and explain the military's perspective. "If we got into a position where the president was out of action or something else turned up, I was going to at least get the bombs and get them to my outfits and get them loaded and ready to go—at least do that much," LeMay recalled. "If I were on my own and half the country was destroyed and I could get no orders and so forth, I wasn't going to sit there fat, dumb, and happy and do nothing."

Between the Korean War and the search for an H-bomb, Truman asked Congress for $16.8 billion in additional defense spending and an extra billion dollars specifically for superbomb research—more than the entire original defense budget Truman had originally wanted. The new budgets and technological improvements combined to end the "doctrine of scarcity" that had long limited nuclear war planning. The regular stockpile briefings Lilienthal gave Truman now contained much larger numbers. "Boy, we could blow a hole clean through the earth," Truman said after one such meeting.

Meanwhile, the White House was falling down around the Trumans. Shoddy and delayed maintenance had taken a toll on the executive mansion even before Eleanor Roosevelt eschewed the building's $50,000 upkeep budget during the war to avoid public criticism. By the end of his first term, Truman had been forced to relocate his bedroom on the second-floor residence because engineers expressed concern that the entire floor might cave in. Then, one night, while daughter Margaret played the piano upstairs, the floor indeed gave way and the piano crashed through, sending plaster and rotted wood onto the executive mansion's first floor below.

The subsequent extensive and high-profile restoration provided the perfect cover to install a secret bomb shelter. On August 1, 1950, Truman's naval aide, Robert Dennison, wrote a memo to the renovation team, explaining, "The President has authorized certain protective measures which include alterations at basement level in and adjacent to the wings of the White House." The renovation had originally called for two basement levels of various utility and storage rooms. Instead, Dennison, aide David Stowe, and the project architect sketched out a large, heavily fortified facility on the northeast corner of the White House that would occupy much of the bottom basement level with an atomic shelter.

The new shelter's main door was four inches thick, with a retractable eye slit, that opened into a shower room, to allow occupants to rinse off radioactive fallout and discard their clothes before entering a room where they could don special, emergency-issue clothing. A larger, interior room was stocked with as many as seventy standard-issue Army cots, according to a diary by Roger Tubby, Truman's assistant press secretary. A communications room, powered by its own generator, allowed the president to remain (in theory, at least) in contact with the outside world, and direct lines connected the shelter to the Pentagon's own bomb shelter across the Potomac. A pantry held plentiful canned and packaged supplies for an extended stay. The president's private suite—an eight-foot-by-ten-foot room—included four bunk beds, a bookcase filled with reading material, and the president's own bathroom, dominated by a chemical toilet that would have been remarkably unpleasant within just a few days of use. Reinforced concrete walls and ceilings would protect an area potentially as large as 45,000 square feet, mostly extending out onto the North Lawn from under the White House's East Terrace. An elevator shaft off the mansion's northeast corner could provide quick access to those outside. As aide David Stowe explained, "As long as the White House facilities could be used we would operate from there with the situation determining the employment of our other plans."

As the renovation came to a close, rumors spread across Washington that the commander-in-chief had new protections in place. The front page of *The Washington Post* on April 18, 1951, blared: "Truman Digs into Special Fund for $881,000 A-Bomb Shelter." Congressmen who had approved and overseen the project fund expressed displeasure that they hadn't been told of the shelter construction—nor about the extra monies spent. But Truman and his advisors saw it as a necessary step—and not the last one that would be taken. That $881,000 was just a tiny down payment on the billions to come.

Despite the huge investment of time and money, Truman had no intention of ever seeking safety in the shelter he'd built. Even as construction progressed on the shelter and the early Continuity of Government plans were developed, he told Dennison, "Of course, you've got to go ahead with all of this planning and all of these arrangements, but I want to tell you one thing. If a situation ever develops where execution [of the evacuation plans] seems to be indicated, I don't intend to leave the White House. I am going to be right here." To the president, it was a matter of staying and fighting—and reassuring the nation. He added, "I would like to be as sure as I can that there's some way that I can get on the air to talk to the people of the United States, to assure them that I am here, that I'm not up in the hills some place, and to tell them what I can of the situation."

The tension of the Cold War was felt all around the presidency. Danger wouldn't just come from the sky, and the curtain of security around the president drew ever tighter as Truman's term unfolded. In the wake of the bombings of Hiroshima and Nagasaki, the Secret Service had ordered the roads adjoining the White House closed to traffic. "We are living in the atomic age," said Secret Service chief Frank Wilson. "We can't take a chance."*

Then, on the afternoon of November 1, 1950, Truman was napping upstairs at Blair House—the presidential guest residence across Pennsylvania Avenue where the Trumans had moved while the White House was under renovation—when two Puerto Rican nationalists tried to storm it and kill the president. A gunfight of less than a minute ensued, leaving one would-be assassin dead and a White House policeman mortally wounded. The assassination attempt ended Truman's days walking back and forth to the White House; now his armored limo carried him across the street with a police escort. Two days after the assassination attempt, the *Chicago Sun-Times* reported a new normal: The "President's guard [was now] on a war footing."

Bomb shelters and armored limos may have been the most visible changes the Cold War brought, but in offices across Washington planners were also reconsidering the very idea of a capital city. As they looked around D.C., officials saw Target #1 for the Soviet Union. "It gives me the willies every time I think of how concentrated we are in this town," one Pentagon leader said. "The country's got to disperse." The fears of a single, direct attack drove the government to expand its own plans, then referred to as "the continuity of the operation of the government." The National Security Act of 1947 had tasked the National Security Resources Board with planning for the strategic relocation of critical industries and government functions to ensure continuous operation. The Defense Department also began its first serious COG planning in 1949, calling into question even its new headquarters: "If we'd known there'd be an A-Bomb, the Pentagon would probably never have been built," General George Marshall said later. Indeed, when the AEC studied the effects of a nuclear attack on Washington, it found that just three Hiroshima-style bombs—targeted at the Capitol, the Pentagon, and the area around the White House—would "tear the guts out of Washington." Underground shelters would help some, but the AEC concluded that even those who made it to a shelter would suffer a sorry fate. "When

---

* As much as he disliked being watched and guarded, Truman liked the company of the agents: They were mostly from small towns like him, and in many ways shared more of his background than the Eastern elites around whom he spent much of his days as president.

the survivors emerged from hiding, they would wander helplessly through a useless city."

Congressman Chet Holifield proposed publicly creating an alternate seat of government to ensure that the "nerve center of our nation" couldn't be "paralyzed" by a Soviet atomic bomb. As Holifield explained, "The Continuity of Government functions in a national emergency created by atomic or hydrogen bomb disaster must be guaranteed. Such guaranty does not exist at the present time." *The New York Times* covered Holifield's proposal on its front page—the first time that the phrase "Continuity of Government" appeared in the newspaper. Other congressmen piled onto the debate; Mississippi congressman John Rankin called for setting up an alternate capital near Paducah, Kentucky, where Mammoth Cave, the longest cave system in the world, would provide the government safety in "the greatest storm cellar the world ever saw."* Truman asked Congress for $140 million to begin dispersal efforts, a request quickly backed by many in that body. The Senate Public Works Committee passed a bill to fund moving 20,000 federal jobs outside the downtown core and another 25,000 jobs even further away to reduce the capital's "target attractiveness."

Fears of attack permeated the rest of the country, too. Dispersal in the hills became a selling point for real estate agents: A *Wall Street Journal* ad for a fifteen-acre estate in upstate New York promoted the "large well furnished and equipped main house, large garage, accessory buildings, woods, garden, boats, fishing, swimming. Good bomb immunity." A D.C. newspaper carried ads touting the benefits of country living, "out of the radiation zone." One agent advertised "Small Farms—Out Beyond Range of Atomic Bombs."

The military buildup of the Korean War jump-started the debate over protecting the civilian population. Truman used Executive Order 10186 to create the Federal Civil Defense Administration on December 1, 1950. "So long as there is any chance at all that atomic bombs may fall on our cities, we cannot gamble on being caught unprepared," he explained in a speech a few months later. "Civil defense" did not have an auspicious history in

* Less serious was an Iowa congressman's suggestion that an alternate capital could be hidden in his home state's "tall corn."

the United States. Serious "civil defense" initiatives lasted for only a brief window during World War II; FDR had tapped New York mayor Fiorello La Guardia to lead the Office of Civilian Defense, but most plans, particularly La Guardia's most ambitious ones, like equipping a uniformed civilian defense corps, sputtered quickly. Eleanor Roosevelt stepped in to provide a softer approach, but anything more than token efforts quickly faded.

To head FCDA, Truman picked a former Florida governor, Millard Caldwell. His leadership quickly established what historian Dee Garrison has called four key precedents for the government's Cold War civil defense efforts: First, efforts were to be civilian-led, rather than military; second, civil defense would be a state and local effort rather than federal; third, the efforts would be more focused on propaganda because of persistent funding shortages to embark on real preparatory work; and, fourth, the effort would especially target women, enlisting them as wives and mothers, in ensuring that the home front was protected. One newspaper columnist at the time had a more succinct summation of the FCDA's shortcomings: "The Federal Civil Defense Administration has had no authority to do anything specific, or to make anyone else do it."

Such a conclusion was certainly true in peacetime, but buried in the legislation that created FCDA was a separate section, Title III, that granted the administrator sweeping authority in an emergency, including the power to "procure by condemnation or otherwise, construct, lease, transport, store, maintain, renovate, or distribute materials and facilities for civil defense, with the right to take immediate possession thereof without regard to the limitation of any existing law." The administrator could also "sell, lease, lend, transfer, or deliver materials or perform services for civil defense purposes on such terms and conditions as the Administrator shall prescribe and without regard to the limitations of existing law," and "employ temporarily additional personnel without regard to the civil service laws," among other various powers. The section represented just the tip of the iceberg of the hidden and sweeping powers that would accrue in the decades ahead to those tasked with wartime response and COG efforts.*

---

* Congress, in fact, was so concerned about the Title III powers granted FCDA that it set a specific sunset clause of June 30, 1954, after which the powers would expire unless

Caldwell's greatest legacy to the nation's defense plan came in the form of a 1,000-page, ten-volume report known as Project East River, commissioned in 1951. His "Bible of civil defense" represented the collected work of nine of the nation's best universities over eighteen months of study led by retired Army Major General Otto Nelson. All told, it made more than 300 recommendations to improve the nation's capability to defend, withstand, and rebuild following a Soviet attack.

Anyone who read through the entire report quickly understood that a sufficient civil defense plan would never exist—at least absent an expensive and complete rethinking of American society. Even the checklist of specific recommendations was misleadingly simple: Recommendation #92, for instance, proposed that the government research how to create a market for war insurance—an exceedingly difficult task that would require understanding first the rippling business effects of the cascading economic breakdown sure to follow a widespread nuclear attack. How would companies access capital markets if the New York Stock Exchange was destroyed? How would banks, whose own operations and record systems would be disrupted by an attack, ensure the liquidity necessary to fund private sector reconstruction? Beyond the financial sector, how would other industries even begin to restart operations given the destruction of facilities and interruption of supply chains, let alone the loss of a market for nearly all consumer goods? Britain and Germany had weathered the steadily escalating air attacks of World War II, adjusting economic processes as damage mounted, but no nation had ever contemplated the widespread and near-total destruction of potentially all its major commercial centers in a matter of hours. All of these complicated existential questions—and many others—were wrapped up in just one of the hundreds of recommendations Project East River addressed.

In the spring of 1951, David Stowe and Governor Caldwell traveled to Britain to study its civil defense operations, touring the country meeting with the officials who had overseen the domestic efforts during the war. The two men came back even more worried. Whereas Britain closely aligned its military and civilian planning, creating effectively a "fourth and vital arm

---

specifically renewed by Congress. (The authorities would be renewed every four years until 1974.)

of military defense," the U.S., they noted upon their return, effectively had
no joint planning, creating duplication, wasted effort, and lost utility. In
response, the government immediately began constructing a civil defense
college in Olney, Maryland, twenty-one miles outside Washington, headquartered in farm country inside a white-columned Georgian-style house.
The facility, whose construction was overseen by a British team, included
a full-sized "Rescue Street," a mock set based on the English civil defense
training during World War II that mimicked a bombed-out urban street
of residences and offices, filled with "rubble" and simulated broken gas and
water mains.

The public also got a taste of the experience: To raise awareness, the
FCDA sent out three "Alert America" convoys of tractor-trailers across
the country in 1952, stopping in seventy cities and attracting a million
visitors. The convoy exhibits showed civil defense tips and a "before" and
"after" depiction of the average American city, "City X," to help demonstrate the effects of a nuclear attack. Costumed staffers dressed as Bert
the Turtle handed out pamphlets and literature. Local officials held mock
air raid drills and "Miss Alert America" contests. As a recruitment tool
for civil defense volunteers, residents in Baltimore were treated to a mock
atomic bomb explosion on July 4, 1951—mushroom cloud included—that
knocked down two fake houses. Civil defense volunteers rushed in to treat
the "wounded."

The FCDA created dozens of films like *Survival Under Atomic Attack*,
Fire-fighting for House-holders, and *What You Should Know About Biological
Warfare*, and printed more than 20 million copies of the *Survival Under
Atomic Attack* pamphlet. Other brochures covered every possibility: being
stuck at the office, inside a vehicle, at the movies, school, or even walking
outside. The information appeared oddly pedestrian, with advice like draw
curtains to protect against flying glass; unplug appliances and turn off gas
lines; unlock doors to ensure rescuers can reach those inside easily. Lie flat
on your stomach, preferably under a table and covered by a blanket, again to
protect against glass and debris.

Signs posted in every New York taxicab explained that in the event of
an enemy attack, the cab would immediately pull to the curb and disgorge
its passengers. By the end of 1950, 10,000 of the city's 35,000 drivers had

enlisted in the "Emergency Taxi Corps," which would provide transportation for police and the military after an attack and transport supplies from fifty mobilization points located around New York City. "No time can be lost," the police commissioner, Thomas F. Murphy, said. "It's much later than most people think." New York City also distributed two million military-style dogtags to schoolchildren, to help officials both identify bodies and reunite separated families after an attack. Chicago's approach to "helping" kids was even more graphic: It recommended parents tattoo children's blood type under their armpit—but not on the arm itself in case it was blown off—which would help speed blood transfusions to avoid radiation poisoning.

Robert Landry, Truman's Air Force aide, met with representatives of Kansas City who proposed that the government locate its new underground installations in old quarry caves outside their city. The Kansas City boosters were more right than they knew: In the spring of 1947, the Army and the Navy began to study caves that might house future industrial factories, warehouses, residential homes, and government command centers. The military experimented with creating subterranean airplane factories, following the example of Germany's wartime facilities that had seen the V-1 and V-2 rockets assembled largely underground.

To map and identify the nation's most promising caves, the Munitions Board's Underground Sites Committee (USC) enlisted the help of the National Speleological Society, which estimated the nation possessed enough caves to protect all 145 million Americans. The head of the society, who was not an entirely disinterested party in the cave renaissance, proclaimed, "The cave is our main hope in an atomic war." The Army Map Service surveyed countless caves along West Virginia's Highway 220, which ran down the spine of the Blue Ridge Mountains.* In 1947, a *New Yorker* writer accompanied soldiers, amateur explorers, and a nuclear physicist on an expedition into Pendleton County's Trout Cave. A half mile deep into the cave, after

---

* Local entrepreneurs vied to turn their caverns into safe houses: Lester Dill, who owned Missouri's Meramec Caverns, applied for a million-dollar government loan to convert it into a five-story "modern Noah's Ark." The famous Explorers Club of New York got permission to convert the Endless Caverns outside New Market, Virginia, into an exclusive fallout shelter for its Washington chapter members and their families.

passing through several large chambers that could house industrial facilities
or government offices, they stumbled into a smaller chamber: "This might
even make a good office for the President," one man exclaimed. "He won't be
able to stay in the White House. He'll have to be in a safe place." *Boys' Life*,
the magazine for the Boy Scouts, promoted the cave exploration program in
its January 1948 issue, explaining, "Your country is in the throes of a gigantic
underground movement. . . . Even you may become part of this great Operation Underground."

Over the course of 1951 and 1952, commercial radio and television
broadcasting stations teamed up with civil defense authorities to launch
CONELRAD (CONtrol of ELectromagnetic RADiation), which would
warn the public an attack was under way while simultaneously confusing
Soviet bombers. Under CONELRAD, as an attack unfolded the radio
stations would shut down their normal broadcasting and more than 1,000
AM stations nationwide (each of which had voluntarily invested their
own money in such capabilities) would switch over to two designated frequencies, 640 kHz or 1240 kHz, and take turns broadcasting warnings
on those emergency channels. The special stations were marked with a
civil defense symbol on all radios built between 1953 and the program's
end in 1963. By taking turns broadcasting on the same frequencies, the
radio stations would confuse any Soviet bombers attempting to home in
on specific frequencies. Even as the Truman administration highlighted
the broadcasters' voluntary CONELRAD participation, the FCC didn't
leave them much choice: A 1951 executive order provided the commission
with the authority to seize and shut down all the nation's broadcasters in
time of war or national emergency anyway. That executive order, oddly,
cited the presidential proclamation on the Korean invasion to justify just
such a national emergency a year later. It wouldn't be the only time that
the government would use a crisis overseas to increase its emergency powers at home.

Harry Truman announced in mid-March 1952 that he would not seek reelection, and at the end of that month he finally moved back into the White
House, walking past the columns of Vermont marble for the first time in
nearly four years as a resident of the house. He was immensely proud of the

renovation and its careful attention to preserving history. As Truman wrote, "Only an earthquake or an atomic bomb—one of our latest, not the phony [ones] Russia talks about—could wreck the old building now."

Yet as confident as Truman might have been about the White House itself, the nation at large was still woefully unprepared for sudden attacks, as a freak event just weeks before the 1952 presidential election underscored. On Labor Day weekend, while most of the base's aircrews were off for the holiday, a hot Texas summer afternoon spawned a thunderstorm that devastated Carswell Air Force Base outside Fort Worth, a sprawling facility that had long been home to the nation's heavy bomber force and included an adjacent defense contractor's manufacturing plant for B-36s and their engines. The B-36 itself was a massive bomber—its wingspan covered most of a football field and its tail stood some five stories tall—but to the tornado that tore through just after 6 p.m., with winds of over 125 miles per hour, it may as well have been a child's toy. "Every aircraft on the base suffered some damage," a unit history reported. "The giant planes were lifted like toys and hurled into each other." One B-36 bomber was entirely destroyed and 106 others were knocked out of commission. All told, two thirds of the nation's entire strategic bomber force was grounded.

SAC scrambled to repair the damage, putting crews on eighty-four-hour workweeks and flying in more than 400 technicians and crew from other facilities. The tornado made front-page news in the nation's capital, partly because the number of damaged planes was actually larger than the total number of B-36 bombers that the government had previously admitted building—demonstrating to Americans, allies, and Russians that the bomber force was even more formidable than believed. The irony was that the secrecy that had long surrounded the nation's atomic forces, a secrecy originally conceived to conceal its fundamental weakness, now was unnecessary—serving only to cloak an increasingly large and growing nuclear superiority, a superiority that might have calmed hawkish views if anyone had been willing to acknowledge it.

Ten days after the Carswell tornado, on September 10, the National Security Resources Board sent a bulletin asking executive branch officials to design evacuation plans that specifically thought through the problems of relocation: How would power and legal authorities be delegated in the event of a surprise attack? How much space would an agency need? What communications capability would be required? NSRB outlined specific post-attack duties for agencies like the General Services Administration, which would assign available office space, and the Civil Service Commission, which would line up "standby" federal employees for emergency situations and set up registration points where they would report after an attack for their assignments. The government also distributed special "emergency passes" to allow critical federal employees freedom of movement. Such simple plans merely represented a stopgap, the NSRB explained: "A long-term emergency plan is currently in preparation, which is designed to provide for the operation of essential government functions at full wartime strength and for an indefinite period by utilizing space in existing college buildings, resort hotels, and other suitable quarters."

In December, as the government still grappled with repairing the planes damaged by the surprise tornado, Truman authorized construction of the nation's first air raid early warning system, which would provide three to six hours of warning in advance of approaching Soviet bombers. To supplement the electronic systems, the government expanded Operation SKYWATCH, a mass recruiting effort spread across twenty-seven states whereby more than 150,000 Ground Observer Corps civilian volunteers kept watch for enemy planes at some 6,000 stations across the nation. As Truman said, "If an enemy should try to attack us, we will need every minute and every second of warning that our skywatchers can give us." That same month, on December 12, he ran a government-wide air raid drill and command post exercise. "Exercises of this sort are essential for the proper indoctrination and training of the Federal employees in their civil defense duties," Truman explained to department and agency heads.

The earliest COG plans were relatively straightforward. While Truman was briefed on each successive set of plans, personally approving each, most officials had no sense of the emergency plans, which were kept secure in a guarded room at the Old Executive Office Building behind what David Stowe called "the biggest, fattest, secure door I've ever seen." Only two people had the clearances necessary to enter, including the FBI agent, on loan from J. Edgar Hoover, who oversaw the operational security for

COG. Only three government officials were then considered key to COG operations—Stowe, who had overseen the development of all the plans, Air Force aide General Robert Landry, who would coordinate the nation's military response, and naval aide Admiral Robert Dennison, who would become the chief operating officer of the nation's response and recovery.

While most White House, military, and government personnel had standing orders to report after an attack to designated Civil Service muster points and await further instructions, the three chosen men were to race to the president's side, wherever he was. "All three of us had those powerful little phones next to our bed," Stowe recalled later. "If the damn thing would have ever gone off I'm afraid I'd have had a heart attack before I could answer." The secret phones were checked each Wednesday at noon; the technician who installed them didn't even know what they were for. "When the telephone man put it in my house my wife said, 'You know, he wanted to know what kind of a phone this was, he said he couldn't find out where it went to or where it came from.'"

Early COG plans consisted of a few temporary locations that could hold a cabinet official and a small number of aides. "We had places all over the countryside for various parts of our Government to go. Greenbrier [the West Virginia luxury resort], for example, tied into where Congress would go—not the executive branch, obviously—and we had a very sophisticated, for that time, microwave communications link all over the place," Admiral Dennison explained years later.

"We had as sophisticated a plan as we could conceive, and I worked quite closely with Stowe, of course, and on paper our plans looked pretty good," Dennison said later. But the team knew that the temporary ad hoc nature couldn't last, as figuring out what (and where) to stock resources proved difficult. "There was also the problem of what files, what orders, what executive orders, many of which were pre-prepared, had to be available at each of these places; many of these had to be kept updated as we went along with sufficient copies so that wherever the President went they would be at hand," Stowe said. "Then there were other matters that were of such a sensitive nature that orders couldn't be prepared in advance or if they were there was only one copy which had to be with the President." The solution was clear:

The government would need to build permanent, hardened facilities like the British Cabinet War Rooms.

In the final year of his presidency, Truman hosted Winston Churchill, who at age seventy-seven had recently returned to the post of prime minister. The first night, the president brought his transatlantic friend on board the presidential yacht, USS *Williamsburg*, where they stayed up late talking world affairs. The two men didn't have to look any further than their vessel that night to see the world's anxiety. The *Williamsburg* was at once a key perk of the presidency and also now a key link in the government's expanding secret plans to save itself. A 244-foot private vessel purchased by the Navy in 1941, the *Williamsburg* had been converted in 1945 into the presidential yacht to replace FDR's beloved *Potomac*, a former Coast Guard cutter. The *Williamsburg* may not have been the most comfortable ride—hundreds of tons of iron had been placed in the bilge to ease the ship's time at sea and counter the heavy communications equipment added to keep Truman in touch with the military and White House—but the president loved the ship. He used it regularly on the Potomac, as well as down in Key West, where he liked to escape for vacations and where he became known for his love of tropical Hawaiian shirts. Entertaining guests like Churchill, he'd play poker on board late into the night while guests sipped Old Granddad whiskey, smuggled on board against Navy regulations.

The ship's recreational appearance masked its key purpose. "The *Williamsburg* was really a floating command post," Dennison recalled. In an emergency, it would be one of the best escape routes for the commander-in-chief, who could sail down the Potomac to safety in the Chesapeake Bay and the Atlantic Ocean. Despite the new expanded bunker at the White House, the goal was still to get the president out of town as quickly as possible. The *Williamsburg* represented one of three major presidential evacuation plans—by land, air, or water—that had been put in place since Truman took office. The White House also maintained special rail trains on both sides of the Potomac, north and south of the city, as well as plenty of pre-mapped road evacuation routes. Both the presidential rail car, known as U.S. Car No. 1 and nicknamed the Ferdinand Magellan, and a second special communications train car were always kept within an hour of Washington so that the president could be evacuated in an emergency. Other plans called for the president to be evacuated by helicopter or by plane—although both technologies were still far from sure bets at the time.

The main problem with evacuation was that while there were seven identified hiding spots for the president around Washington, and plenty of ways to get him out of town, few plans offered the chance to connect with the country. "The problem in any of these temporary command posts was to have facilities for the President to communicate on some kind of a broadcasting system—television if you could do it—and radio certainly," Dennison recalled. "The laying of cables and all of these matters was a very, very complicated problem, and also the interconnection between the President, the Vice President, and the Cabinet." In fact, the *Williamsburg* and the presidential camp at Shangri-La (later Camp David) were the only two facilities around Washington that possessed the communication links necessary to command the military if the White House and Pentagon had to be evacuated.

It wasn't entirely clear Truman would actually avail himself of any of the escape routes. "All these plans of moving by train or by car, or by ship, or whatever, really didn't appeal to the President. He wanted everybody else the hell out of there obviously . . . [and] he wanted to be sure that somewhere, somehow, the Government was going to continue," Dennison recalled. "But as far as he was concerned, he looked on himself as being expendable, provided the machinery for operating the Government still existed somewhere."

Indeed, the single time during his second term that an attack appeared imminent, Truman didn't blink. A radar operator, part of the nation's growing early warning system, alerted the White House that a squadron of unidentified aircraft were heading for Washington. Perhaps this was the surprise Russian attack that the Pentagon feared. The Secret Service warned Truman, and top aides evacuated the West Wing, heading for the new shelter underground. But Truman simply stayed at his desk, working. The public never learned of the false alarm. Without knowing it, Truman had answered the evacuation question the same way nearly all of his successors would— asked to choose in the years ahead between evacuating to safety and trying to provide an example of leadership, future presidents would all make the same decision Truman did.

Truman's farewell address on January 15, 1953, delivered five days before he left the renovated White House, is to this day one of the best speeches of the Cold War, containing insightful analysis and a prediction of how, decades later, it would end. "I suppose that history will remember my term in office as the years when the 'Cold War' began to overshadow our lives," he told the American people, speaking late at night from the Oval Office. Winning the Cold War wouldn't be easy—or fast—but the United States, he firmly believed, would win simply by holding the line. "Starting an atomic war is totally unthinkable for rational men," Truman explained. The Soviet Union would fail on its own, given time. Until then, the American people needed patience and needed to support other free people to help them remain as such.

Truman's message was even more critical than his audience knew at the time. Just days earlier, a thermonuclear test at Enewetak Atoll in the distant Pacific island chain of the Marshall Islands had succeeded. The world that Truman was leaving behind seemed, in many ways, more fragile than the one he inherited. Truman had taken office in 1945 when armaments were measured in tons of explosives, then served through an era when bombs leapt to "kilotons" of destructive power. Now his legacy was a world where bombs were spoken about with "megatons." Now it was his turn to share the secrets of the presidency with Dwight Eisenhower. And so, a few days after the election, Roy Snapp had boarded a plane to Georgia.

Chapter 4

THE BEARD LOT PROJECT

Roy Snapp realized moments before the president-elect arrived that he'd forgotten to turn in his pistol. The civilian secretary of the Atomic Energy Commission had flown down from Washington early that morning to the rainy and fog-shrouded Augusta Country Club, allowed briefly to interrupt Eisenhower's post-election golf vacation with news of great import. Snapp had carried a sidearm aboard the commercial flight to protect his satchel of secret documents; now, the president-elect was coming down the hall and the gun was still under Snapp's jacket. He alerted the Secret Service standing nearby, and the agent nonchalantly replied, "We're all carrying guns." And so the meeting began, with Dwight Eisenhower, unknowingly, the only man in the room unarmed. But he was about to have the deadliest weapon of all.

The men met in the golf course manager's office, an oddly incongruous setting for such a serious conversation. Snapp handed Eisenhower the memo from AEC chair Gordon Dean. "We have detonated the first full-scale thermonuclear device," Dean had written. The U.S. officials had exploded the first "super," a massive bomb that weighed more than 50 tons, code-named MIKE, that more resembled a small building than a weapon. While it would likely take another year to develop one properly sized for delivery by a bomber, the conclusion was clear: Hydrogen weapons could work—and they were awe-inspiring. It wasn't merely a larger atomic bomb; the first thermonuclear device, the first to harness the same fusion power that lit the sun, was clearly of a different variety entirely. The bomb was nearly 500 times more powerful than the atomic bomb that had destroyed Hiroshima. It exploded, in fact, with twice the power of all the explosive power of all the bombs used in World War II—a scale that Dwight Eisenhower, five-star General of the Armies, the Supreme Allied Commander, understood theoretically but could hardly process mentally. As Dean wrote in his memo, "The island of the Atoll which was used for the shot—Elugelab—is missing, and where it was there is now an underwater crater of some 1,500 meters in diameter."

For now, the existence of such a weapon was a secret kept by a few thousand personnel in the South Pacific, a few hundred people in Washington, and—now, with this memo—Dwight Eisenhower at the Augusta Country Club. Snapp and Eisenhower talked about nuclear weapons for quite some time; the old soldier began to realize how nuclear weapons—so scarce and so valuable just years before—were now becoming plentiful and affordable. He had a lot to learn and a lot to think about. For now, he wanted as little information as possible released about the new nuclear tests. An avid bridge player, he understood the value of long-term strategy. He valued time to think and consider his options. "Let's not make our mistakes in a hurry," he liked to say.

After Eisenhower left the club manager's office, Snapp stayed for a few minutes longer—he needed time to burn Dean's memo.

The horror of nuclear war never seemed far away as the Eisenhowers explored their new life in the White House. One night they took visiting friends on a tour of the bomb shelter as Mamie complained about the paltry budget to replace the White House towels; on another day, Eisenhower himself opened a locked drawer in the Oval Office to discover a secret report to Truman from J. Robert Oppenheimer, predicting an expensive and horrific arms race. The U.S. might, it said, face as many as 2,500 Soviet nuclear bombs in the years ahead, and while the nation might survive, survival would have "a rather specialized meaning," since the country would be blanketed by radioactive fallout.

Considering that he stood as one of the nation's greatest war heroes—ranking in a pantheon with perhaps only Ulysses S. Grant and George Washington himself, two other victorious generals who went on to the presidency with popular acclaim—Dwight D. Eisenhower's own experience with war was an odd one: He never personally faced combat as a soldier, though he became intimately acquainted with Europe's battlefields, the carnage left behind after both great wars, the mass graves, the broken souls. He loved soldiering, but hated war. On Memorial Day 1951, with the nation involved in a brutal war in Korea, he had written in his diary, "Another Decoration Day finds us adding to the number of graves that will be decorated in future years. Men are stupid." Now Eisenhower had inherited that stupid war, as well as the much larger Cold War, at a critical moment.

Eisenhower had campaigned on a "New Look" for the nation's foreign policy, one that promised greater focus, clarity, and strength than what his secretary of state, John Foster Dulles, had called Truman's "erratic" and "militaristic" foreign policy. The United States, Eisenhower said, needed "security with solvency." During one discussion, he dismissed the proposed expensive defense spending, saying, "We could lick the world if we were willing to adopt the system of Adolf Hitler." To Eisenhower, the point instead was to build the most secure free nation he could, consistent with a society and a tradition that put civilian leadership first and a high premium on the civilian quality of life. The U.S. would win the Cold War, not by outspending the Soviets, but by outliving them. As he wrote in early 1953, "If, on the other side of the Iron Curtain, a backward civilization with a second-rate production plant can develop the power to frighten us all out of our wits, then we, with our potential power can, through work, intelligence, and courage, build any countering force that may be necessary."

On March 4, 1953, word reached Washington that Joseph Stalin had died, alone, on the floor of his bedroom. It was as good an opportunity as any to reevaluate the Cold War. Ten days later, Eisenhower was in the Oval Office with his speechwriter, Emmett Hughes, expressing his desire to set a new tone during an upcoming speech to the national association of newspaper editors. As the president looked out over the South Lawn, toward the Washington Monument and the newly built Jefferson Memorial, an F-86 Sabre jet crossed into view, high above the capital. Eisenhower watched for a moment and then turned to his speechwriter—his mind focused and intense: "Here is what I would like to say. The jet plane that roars over your head costs three quarter of a million dollars. That is more money than a man earning ten thousand dollars every year is going to make in his lifetime. What world can afford this sort of thing for long? We are in an armaments race. Where will it lead us? At worst to atomic warfare. At best, to robbing every people and nation on earth of the fruits of their own toil." The resulting speech—delivered under duress as Eisenhower sweated profusely from a bout of food poisoning and the words swam before his eyes—became one of the best known of the Cold War. That day in April 1953, looking out at a room filled with newspaper executives, he explained, "Every gun that is made, every warship launched, every rocket fired signifies, in the final sense, a theft from those who hunger and are not fed, those who are cold and are not clothed."

To execute his "New Look," President Eisenhower launched Project Solarium, asking three teams of advisors to argue three different strategies: traditional containment, a foreign policy based on nuclear weapons, and increased covert efforts to turn back Communist aggression around the world. As he listened to the reports from the three groups, Eisenhower doodled, as he liked to do, on a yellow legal pad. The plans were each beautifully presented; each group seemed to believe wholeheartedly in its approach. But the presentation left him with one haunting thought that he carved into the pad of paper before him: "GLOBAL WAR AS DEFENSE OF FREEDOM/ ALMOST CONTRADICTION IN TERMS." At the conclusion of three hours of presentations, Eisenhower spoke for nearly forty-five minutes, summarizing and adding his own interpretations, and uniting the room around a blended policy. That strategy, eventually codified in NSC-162/2, called for containment in Europe, more aggressive efforts against Communist forces in the Third World, and a military posture built primarily around nuclear forces. Finally, within the United States, Eisenhower's strategy called for the defense of "our striking force, our mobilization base, and our people," an initiative that would launch some of the first widespread efforts to protect the nation from nuclear war.

As the U.S. government began to tie together the new Eisenhower strategy, the Russians exploded their first thermonuclear-like weapon on August 8, 1953, known as RDS-6 or by its U.S. moniker, Joe-4. While not quite a workable military device, the bomb's yield of 400 kilotons proved that the Soviets were close to possessing massive destructive power.

President Eisenhower tried to talk more openly about the dangers thermonuclear war presented to an ill-prepared nation, an effort his administration called Operation CANDOR, but fully explaining the new reality to the American public involved presenting a dark world vision. As C. D. Jackson, a White House staffer working on the draft speech, recalled, "[Operation CANDOR] had the basic defect that all it really contained was mortal Soviet attack followed by mortal U.S. counterattack—in other words, bang-bang, no hope, no way out at the end." Rather than focusing on the cost of war, the project instead evolved over the course of the fall to highlight the benefits of peace. On December 8, 1953, Eisenhower addressed the General Assembly of the United Nations, presenting what would become the most important atomic initiative of his presidency. He outlined the "fearful material damage and toll of human lives" that war would bring, and argued that the world should readjust its priorities, "mov[ing] out of this dark chamber of horrors into the light." Meant as a contrast to the superpower race for "atoms for war," his "Atoms for Peace" plan intended to foster international cooperation to pursue scientific efforts that could harness nuclear power for medicine, agriculture, energy, and other nonaggressive uses. The United States, he promised, would pledge "its entire heart and mind to find the way by which the miraculous inventiveness of man shall not be dedicated to his death, but consecrated to his life."

At the same time, Eisenhower's annual budget message to Congress in January 1954 suggested the nation embark on vast increases in spending on continental defense. The following month, a new planning document, known as NSC-5408, prioritized planning for a Soviet attack. "Emergency plans and preparations to insure the continuity of essential wartime functions of the Executive Branch should be completed with the utmost urgency," the document read in part, adding that "within the next two years, an emergency plan should be completed for the relocation of the Legislative and Judicial Branches of the Government."

Just days after the document was completed, Eisenhower convened the National Security Council to debate the first stages of a COG effort. More than thirty officials—including a half dozen cabinet officers and leaders from the Pentagon, the Atomic Energy Commission, the CIA, the Bureau of the Budget, and the Office of Defense Mobilization (ODM)—crammed into the room on February 17, 1954, to discuss the government's new relocation planning. Over the course of a nearly two-and-a-half-hour meeting, the men talked through how and where the government should begin planning to relocate during and after a Soviet attack. Retired Army General Willard Paul, a veteran of the Battle of the Bulge who worked for ODM, laid out a large map of Washington (which he inadvertently referred to as a "blow-up" of the capital), as well as two other large maps showing the proposed relocation arc and, more broadly, the backbone of the nation's communications networks. Circles were drawn around Washington at a radius of 30, 100, and 300 miles, and various agencies had been assigned suggested relocation areas around the city. Eisenhower wondered aloud whether relocation facilities even had to be that close to the capital, as long as adequate communications existed elsewhere. "With the use of telephonic communications it should be perfectly possible to relocate many of these agencies a thousand miles away from Washington," he said. Treasury Secretary George Humphrey chimed in that if the government reused existing facilities, he would bet the government wouldn't "have to spend a nickel for any new construction." As it turned out, Humphrey's estimate was way off—in the years ahead, the government would spend tens of billions of dollars constructing scores of new bunkers and facilities around the country.

Facilities to protect the nation were just one piece of the puzzle, though. That spring, Ike summoned a team of advisors to the White House on a Saturday morning and posed a question: What would a surprise attack mean for the United States? As MIT president James Killian, the group's leader, later recounted, "Modern weapons, [Eisenhower] warned, had made it easier for a hostile nation with a closed society to plan an attack in secrecy and thus gain an advantage denied to the nation with an open society." Ike's group, technically known as the Technological Capabilities Panel and nicknamed simply the Killian Committee, examined the nation's defense, offense, and intelligence capabilities—and found all of them lacking. "The United States is at present unacceptably vulnerable to surprise attack," it concluded. "Our cities could suffer millions of casualties and crippling damage, and enough SAC bombers and bases could be destroyed to reduce drastically our ability to retaliate."

The Killian Report scared officials in Washington, with its specific recommendations to boost U.S. defensive measures and invest in new technologies—like the U-2 spy plane and the Polaris submarine. The report, widely endorsed in the administration's top circles by those worried about the state of the nation's readiness, accelerated development of ballistic missile technology, and its harsh assessment encouraged further investment in the shadowy world of "Continuity of Government" and encouraged the first wide-scale readiness exercises in 1954, which would come to be known as Operation ALERT.

Then, on March 1, 1954, the nuclear world faced its scariest moment yet. The United States had returned to the Marshall Islands for a third series of nuclear tests—including the first use of a hydrogen bomb—and things went quickly awry. Thermonuclear bombs were still not well understood and the weapon, code-named CASTLE BRAVO, turned out to be three times more powerful than expected, a total of some 15 megatons. A four-mile-wide fireball engulfed everything around ground zero in under a second. Birds spontaneously combusted in the sky, and small animals as far away as 345 miles were found to have suffered retinal burns from the nuclear flash. Poisonous radioactivity ultimately covered an area nearly the size of New Jersey, including the unlucky twenty-six-man crew of the Japanese fishing vessel *Lucky Dragon* that turned out to be downwind of the test. One fisherman ultimately died and 400,000 outraged Japanese attended his funeral; Aikichi Kuboyama's dying words were "Please make sure that I am the last victim of the bomb."

North of Washington, none of the locals in Adams County initially understood why the government was buying up their surrounding land, just over the Pennsylvania line from Maryland. Or, more accurately, why the government was seizing so much land around what locals knew only as the Beard Lot, an old property dating back to the area's first white settlers. All told, the government appeared to be cobbling together about 1,100 acres from dozens of landowners. Some sold quickly; those that didn't faced court-ordered seizures. Government lawyers said the land was needed "to adequately provide for the establishment of facilities for the use of the Department of the Army and for other military uses incident thereto."

The most confusing thing was that the government agents said they wanted "access" to the properties, but weren't seeking to displace anyone. People could stay in their homes, and farmers could still farm the land. It seemed, some observed, like the government just wanted whatever was beneath the ground. The government took eight acres from Glenn and Ethel Martin, 280 acres from Alfred and Georgia Holt, forty-five acres from Eleanor Linebaugh, and so forth. Harold Carson and his wife, who owned some of the affected property and ran the local filling station, heard only that the government wanted their property "for an entrance."

An entrance to what?

The need for an "alternate Pentagon" came just six years after the Pentagon itself opened. A May 1948 memo from the Joint Chiefs to the defense secretary suggested that the military establish a command center outside the capital. Over the next two years, the military considered a variety of sites before settling on a mountain about six miles north of the president's vacation house at Shangri-La/Camp David, sixty-five miles north of Washington. Building a cavern under hundreds of feet of greenstone provided extensive natural protection—Pennsylvania's greenstone granite, the builders would brag, was one of the hardest rocks in the world.

Until the government arrived, the anonymous 1,500-foot-high granite ridge had been largely untouched since July 4, 1865, when Union and Confederate soldiers and cavalry battled around it during the retreat from nearby Gettysburg. Forests of chestnut oaks, poplars, and black oaks populated its slopes. The surrounding area had never seen permanent Indian settlements, and barely a thousand people, mostly descendants of the first German immigrant settlers, lived in the nearby valleys, many of whom worked for the Catoctin Iron Furnace.

Engineering firm Parsons Brinckerhoff took a lead role in the Beard Lot project, drawing on its expertise from projects like the New York City subway, the Detroit–Windsor Tunnel, and other massive construction efforts. In fact, the Cold War building boom begun by Truman had turned Parsons into "almost an adjunct of the Corps," in the words of Benson Bobrick, who wrote a history of the firm. "We started design [for Raven Rock] in 1948, under which time the project was under very tight security clearance," recalled engineer John O. Bickel. "We did not even tell our families what we were doing." The design project alone was massive; the engineering team spent weeks traveling through Europe, visiting underground facilities in Sweden and Germany and studying the Maginot Line defenses France had built between the world wars.* In Sweden, the engineers learned how to use rock roof bolts to hold back the mountain walls and seal them against water. "It involved unprecedented concepts," recalled engineer Walter J. Douglas. "We pioneered in the installation of blast valves, blast doors, and underground utilities."

Work began in earnest on January 22, 1951, with bulldozers, earth movers, and other equipment arriving at the site with a forty-person work crew. Local No. 1167 of the General Laborers' union set up a small headquarters and employment office across the road from the site, and a 300-person workforce arrived the next week, working around the clock with three shifts, earning $1.35 an hour. Many of the mining team came from New York's P. J. Healy Co., which had dug the Lincoln Tunnel just years earlier. Once the $17 million project was running full-steam, trucks rumbled out of the expanding site all day long, dumping the "spoil" into a nearby ravine, as workers carved a 3,100-foot tunnel out of the granite.†

In the project's initial days, locals camped out across Highway 16 from the tunnel's entrance to watch—some even brought lunches—but then new "No Parking" signs sprang up one night. "The cover that it was a mining operation could not be maintained for much longer. It did not take much time before *Life* magazine had a quite comprehensive description of the entire project," Bickel recalled. When a reporter cornered an Army officer at the local gas station, he harumphed a "no comment," saying, "Why don't you ask the people who live here? They seem to know more about it than we do."

On February 2, just weeks after the project broke ground, the local newspaper joked that Adams County's prognosticating groundhog emerged from the tunnel complaining about the new tenants and seeking new quarters. Locals called the mysterious project on the Beard Lot a number of names: the Little Pentagon, the Alternate Pentagon, and the Republicans in town called it derogatorily "Harry's Hole," after President Truman. By summer, the Army provided an official label—naming the mountain after a rock

---

* The Parsons Brinckerhoff team was notable at the time for including in its leadership a female architect, Priscilla Dalmas, during an era when the profession included few women.
† The ravine owners actually profited the most from the project: They sold the tunnel's detritus to a roofing manufacturer to make shingles.

pillar nearby: Raven Rock. Most government officials, though, knew it by its code name: SITE R. It became operational on June 30, 1953, five months after Eisenhower became president, with just over 100,000 square feet of office space, not counting the corridors, bathrooms, dining facility, infirmary, or the communications and utilities areas, and could hold about 1,400 personnel comfortably.

The following year, down in Virginia, the government began a similar construction project, building a bunker that would house the civilian arm of the government—it, too, would be known by a rotating set of names, most famously the one derived from the mountain site's former role as a weather forecasting facility: Mount Weather. The two facilities would serve together as the core of the government's Doomsday planning for the next seven decades.

Raven Rock's presence in the valley drew new people and new infrastructure into the region. Dozens of families moved into the area as the bunker staff arrived, boosting local school enrollments. Housing developments were upgraded at nearby Fort Ritchie, which would serve to support the bunker. Both Maryland and Pennsylvania widened and improved the highways leading toward the facility. The telephone company began to string new wires north and south. Government officials scouted surrounding airfields to ease quick evacuations.

At Eisenhower's urging, NSC aide Robert Cutler inspected Raven Rock one afternoon, reporting back to the president in person that night, and then repeating the presentation the next morning for the assembled National Security Council. The night before, Cutler had told Ike that Raven Rock cost $37 million, but in the morning, Cutler said $47 million. "That's not what you told me last night," Ike interrupted, looking up from his doodling.

"I know sir," Cutler replied. "This banker's face is red. I added the figures again last night and found I was ten million dollars off." Everyone laughed. The difference would prove irrelevant, merely drops in the bucket of the billions the government would secretly pour into the Pennsylvania mountain.

Multiple layers of security surrounded the facility, from fences and barbed wire around the outside exterior to gates guarded by military police and roaming K-9 units who patrolled the complex's interior with fierce German Shepherds. Four ground-level portals—two at each end—opened into 1,000-foot-long curved tunnels leading into the heart of the mountain. (The curved tunnels would dissipate the blast of a nuclear bomb nearby.) Two sets of massive thirty-four-ton blast doors protected the tunnels themselves. A pedestrian walkway ran along the vehicle road through the long tunnel of rough-hewn granite. According to security regulations, every person, vehicle, or package was inspected between the first blast door and the second.

At the center of the mountain was the core of the facility—protected by nearly a quarter mile of granite—five parallel caverns that each held large three-story buildings, carefully positioned on coiled springs to ease swaying during a nearby attack. While a communications team—comprised of a surprisingly large contingent of women for the era—kept the place running twenty-four hours a day, most of the facility sat deserted and unstaffed. Two independent power plants ran massive diesel-powered generators, with exhaust vents running to the surface far above. While air filters ran continuously, occupants often complained about the dirty tunnel air. Inside the mountain, guards patrolled the rooftops of the buildings inside the cave to ensure saboteurs didn't sneak in through air vents.*

Raven Rock was designed to be the centerpiece of a large military emergency hub. The Pentagon established contingency plans for Condition Able (the total loss of the entire DOD organization at the "Seat of Government") and Condition Baker (the partial destruction of the Pentagon and associated facilities). The secretary of defense would go to either Raven Rock or Mount Weather, while key military officials and the National Security Council would head directly to the former. The secretary of defense established his own line of succession for his service chiefs, ensuring that the secretaries of the Army, Air Force, and Navy—none of whom were covered by the constitutional presidential succession planning—would be rapidly replaced if needed during an emergency, as would the various vice chiefs of staff, who would take over if the service's Joint Chiefs were lost. A NATO team of allied

---

* Longtime staff pranked new arrivals by announcing "Submarine Drills" at Raven Rock's underground reservoirs: Experienced MPs would station new arrivals on the edge of the reservoir, to keep an eye out for the fictional submarine that supposedly carried VIPs and the president underwater from Camp David six miles away.

military commanders would set up operations at Mount St. Mary's College, further up Highway 15 in the Catoctin Mountains. Altogether, some 6,000 military leaders, aides, and support personnel would make their base in and around Raven Rock—half at the underground facility itself and half at the other surrounding facilities. More Army and Pentagon staff would be sent to other forts and installations surrounding Washington. Within ninety days of an attack, all Pentagon operations were supposed to be reconstituted at alternate locations.

If a surprise attack wiped out Washington's military leadership, the Army was prepared for that as well. It readied what it called the Department of the Army Alternate Command Element (DACE), a plan whereby the branch's leadership would be reconstituted by the faculty and staff at the Army War College in Carlisle, Pennsylvania, just outside Harrisburg. DACE, known on campus under its cover name, the Operations Group, and overseen by the school's commandant, hosted a permanent staff of about twenty soldiers and officers in several on-campus buildings, though it didn't have hardened facilities. The Air Force had a similar program set up at the Air University at Maxwell Air Force Base in Alabama.

As the Pentagon built its mountainside bunker, the country's diplomatic corps chose a more scenic option, outfitting a relocation site on the grounds of the U.S. Agriculture Department's Beef Cattle Research Station, a pastoral 6,000-acre facility about seventy-five miles outside Washington in Front Royal, Virginia.

In the summer of 1952, the State Department dispatched Earl G. Millison, part of its special services branch, to Front Royal to begin building out the facility, code-named RABBIT. The facility had first opened in 1914 as an Army cavalry station, and during World War II had been used as a prisoner of war camp and K-9 training post. By the time Millison arrived, it was mostly abandoned and housed a mishmash of government projects, including the USDA's experimental cattle breeding program, a long-running Bureau of Standards experiment about the effects of sunspots on radio transmissions, and the National Archives' collection of flammable acetate films. Miles of split-rail fences crisscrossed the research station, demarking pastures filled with Angus, Hereford, and Shorthorn cattle, and alfalfa fields that once fed Army mounts.* As Millison recalled, "The vines nearly covered the buildings, broken through the windows and filled some of the rooms." Until he could transform the research station, the State Department established a temporary relocation site at the nearby Randolph-Macon Academy for Boys.

Working with a seven-person maintenance team, Millison spent the first year just clearing roads and rehabilitating buildings, replacing plumbing and overhauling furnaces. Later, his team grew to nearly forty full-time staff to maintain the facility indefinitely. Since no one knew how many State Department staff would be needed to keep the agency's business going after an attack, planners "sort of picked out of the air" the figure of 1,200—a number that became gospel for Millison's planning. Under the State Department's emergency plans, known internally at the agency as the "Black Book," those 1,200 would relocate to the odd collection of fifty-eight buildings spread across nearly sixty acres.† The series of barns, converted stables, coal storage bunkers, veterinary clinics, administration buildings, and an old theater, plus a handful of purpose-built office facilities, were ready for occupancy with just a few hours' notice, fully stocked with supplies. A two-story, ten-room stucco house on the property would house the secretary of state and his wife. Most employees would stay at nearby motels and apartments requisitioned during an emergency, but for those lucky enough to bunk at the farm, each bed was equipped with a cot pad, a pillow, pillowcase, two sheets, a blanket, and a single towel.

Cryptologic facilities utilized radio and microwave relays built on top of the nearby hills, and in an emergency the radio transmitter was powerful enough to reach some U.S. diplomatic missions overseas. A diesel generator, stocked with a three-month supply of fuel, could power the entire campus, and Millison's team located three surplus dump trucks that they could use to haul coal over from West Virginia in a long-term emergency. Year-round a two-engine fire department protected the research station and the relocation

* Today, the facility houses the National Zoo's Conservation Biology Institute, where herds of cheetahs run free in the Virginia hills.
† For those not lucky enough—or quick enough—to be included in the evacuation, the State Department also maintained its own fallout shelter in the basement of its Foggy Bottom headquarters, stocked with food, water, and survival gear for 10,000 people.

site, a twenty-three-bed hospital on the grounds could be activated as necessary, and the seventy-five-person cafeteria would keep the evacuated workers
fed. At the site, a complement of 50 telephone lines, 203 manual typewriters,
9 adding machines, and 7 calculators, as well as a copier machine, 10,000
sheets of paper, and a microfilm reader, would have kept the secretaries busy
and paperwork flowing. Each afternoon at 3 p.m., a security officer patrolled
the surrounding mountains to check the facility's spring houses and natural
water sources, and each day through the end of the decade, couriers transported a selection of telegrams from the Foggy Bottom headquarters to the
relocation facilities to enable the emergency staff to pick up the country's
foreign affairs if needed.

Paper shuffling, in fact, was becoming a key part of the government's
planning. The National Security Resources Board had begun a Herculean
effort to back up the vast paper trail created by the federal bureaucracy and
ensure an attack wouldn't paralyze the government. As Senator Henry Cabot
Lodge said in one interview, "The multitude of records in Washington—
social security, tax records, Army and Navy files—would be gone in an atom
bomb attack." Even beyond the messages stored at Front Royal, the State
Department moved hard copies and microfilm of some 5,000 files, ranging from intelligence studies to phone books to operations handbooks, to
its new Records Evacuation Depository in Richmond, Virginia. The Treasury Department and the comptroller general maintained off-site storage
for the government's payroll files. The NSRB worked to preserve citizen-
ship records, which in wartime would be necessary for determining military
eligibility, and property ownership records, which would be needed to help
government acquisitions and industrial plant development. Another NSRB
effort enlisted people like the records custodian of Westinghouse Electric
and the archivist of the Firestone Tire Company to study what church or
business records might be necessary to protect. In an era where detailed
maps and especially aerial surveillance were scarce, the government carefully
maintained redundant map sources far from the capital: The Army built
a map depository in Omaha, Nebraska, the Navy maintained a hydrologic
chart depository in Louisville, Kentucky, and the Air Force maintained an
aeronautical chart library in St. Louis, Missouri.

Such in-depth planning efforts fit with the ethos of the period. It was a moment when the country as a whole embraced bureaucracies and large organizations, when plans, org charts, and long-term strategies became the coin of the realm, and throughout the COG and civil defense planning were echoes of the phenomenon that during the same decade gave rise to William Whyte's runaway bestselling 1956 management book, *The Organization Man*. The same logic and organization that made General Electric or General Motors factories so efficient seemed like it could be applied to something as chaotic—and unpredictable—as the aftermath of nuclear war. It seemed that we were only ever one more chart or one more report away from a perfectly planned nuclear holocaust.

Eisenhower, however, never harbored such illusions. During one NSC meeting, he candidly laid out his assessment of how nuclear war would unfold, openly scoffing at the section of a draft document dealing with the postwar planning, which he saw almost as an oxymoron. None of the world's nations would exist as we knew them, he argued, let alone be able to rise to the occasion of building a postwar peace. "The President said that, of course, his imagination as to the horrors of a third world war might be overdeveloped, but he believed that every single nation, including the United States, which entered into this war as a free nation would come out of it as a dictatorship," wrote Deputy Executive Secretary Everett Gleason in the meeting minutes. "This would be the price of survival."

In 1954, the 450 headquarters staff of the Federal Civil Defense Administration were moved out of the capital to a retired fifteen-story Italian Renaissance–style hospital in Battle Creek, Michigan, to help keep the nation's homeland defense secure from marauding Soviet bombers.* There, at the headquarters—code-named LOW POINT, as opposed to Mount Weather's code name, HIGH POINT—planners considered three different possibilities for civilian defense: dispersal, evacuation, or shelters. As Peterson explained,

---

* Nebraska Governor Val Peterson's deputy, Katherine Graham Howard, an heiress to the R. J. Reynolds tobacco fortune, was the first woman in any government agency or department to become its second in command. A committed civil defense leader, she was famous for carrying through the logic that nuclear bombs were "just another weapon" to an absurd degree, noting that hydrogen bombs were "neither particularly new nor particularly astonishing" and merely a "bigger A-Bomb."

"The alternatives are to dig, die, or get out—and certainly we don't want to die." The truth was the civilian population didn't have any good options if a war came. Cities would be leveled and excavated by a hydrogen bomb, destroying any benefit from a basement shelter—and no one seriously proposed digging civilian shelters hundreds or thousands of feet underground.

Nevertheless, the ornately decorated hallways of the new FCDA Michigan headquarters, a onetime Seventh Day Adventist sanitarium, were filled with optimistic plans, displays, and exhibits, like an improvised 200-bed hospital that could fit inside a single tractor-trailer and be erected in a temporary location like a school or church within just four hours of an attack. The $22,500 hospital prototype represented the first of thousands of such mobile facilities the FCDA hoped to pre-position outside target areas to aid in emergency response. Other exhibits traveled the country to trade conventions, state fairs, and local exhibit halls. More than 136,000 curious people tromped through the shelter exhibits at the 1955 Eastern States Exposition in Springfield, Massachusetts. One of its major campaigns was "Grandma's Pantry," urging families to stockpile a seven-day supply of food and water for an attack under the slogan "Grandma was always ready for an emergency." Sears, Roebuck & Co. erected FCDA-produced "Grandma's Pantry" exhibits in 500 of its stores, and women's magazines carried articles like "Take these steps now to save your family."* Yet even as the executive branch churned out the propaganda, it poured ever-rising billions into defense readiness, nuclear weapons, and its own COG planning and bunker building. The public got few glimpses of these weapons, bunkers, and tools other than the much-hyped annual exercises called Operation ALERT, or OPAL for short.

Operation ALERT 1954 became the government's first dress rehearsal for nuclear war—a drill that unfolded across the nation's capital in response to a 50-kiloton bomb "exploding" over the crowded heart of Washington.

---

* Despite all the activity and purported high-level interest, the FCDA remained perennially starved for funding, so many of its propaganda films ended up being sponsored by self-interested industries—the American Trucking Association paid for *Rehearsal for Disaster*, about the role truckers and tractor-trailers would have in an emergency, Chrysler's marine division paid for *Big Men in Small Boats*, about the vital role of personal watercraft in evacuations, and the National Automobile Dealers Association sponsored a film called *Escape Route* about how a family car would be life-saving in an evacuation.

The Eisenhowers were rushed to the White House bunker, police and civil defense wardens ushered civilians into fallout shelters, and, after the "attack," Civil Air Patrol volunteers practiced delivering medical supplies to a vacant parking lot near the D.C. Armory converted into an emergency landing strip.

A team of officials gathered at Mount Weather, which was still in the process of being constructed. "Water was dripping from the ceiling and oozing from the walls," recalled Innis Harris, one ODM official. The hours in the cave, while brief, were deeply informative—mainly about how far the government had to go to be ready for responding to an attack. "The participants needed information on the attack situation to determine what policies were actually necessary. They didn't have it. They needed assistance in the preparation of documents to reflect policy decisions. They didn't have it. They needed to communicate policy directives to the departments and agencies concerned. They couldn't do it. They needed to know that the agencies had a capability to carry out the policy directives if they could issue them. They had no way of knowing," Harris recalled. "So a new push was given to the development of physical features for carrying on government—relocation sites, an interagency communication system, and the further development of plans."

Chapter 5

APPLE JACK ALERT

At precisely 6:52 a.m. on Wednesday morning, June 15, 1955, Soviet foreign minister Vyacheslav Molotov, rested and relaxed, disembarked from the *Queen Elizabeth* in New York Harbor. It was a beautiful warm and sunny spring day, and like any tourist in the Big Apple, he had an ambitious sightseeing agenda. Four hours later, he walked, unexpected, into the Metropolitan Museum of Art. A Secret Service agent waved down a guide at the information desk, "This is Mr. Molotov, and he would like to have someone show him the pictures." The small delegation wandered the galleries for more than an hour, with the Soviet leader pondering the new abstract paintings of the unfamiliar Modern Art movement. "What does it mean?" he asked of one painting. Before another canvas by surrealist Bradley Walker Tomlin, he inquired, "Why do they have an unfinished painting in the museum?"

"Who knows?" Molotov's companion replied.

It was, altogether, an odd day for the Soviet minister in New York—in part because the city was practicing what would happen if his nation attacked it. As he continued his visit, the first nationwide Operation ALERT emptied streets and offices across the country. Just as Molotov left the Met, the FCDA's Civil Air Defense Warning System announced "Condition LEMON JUICE." From LEMON JUICE, the yellow warning that an enemy attack was considered probable, the Air Force then moved to its red alert: Condition APPLE JACK, an enemy attack was under way. Air raid sirens sounded in New York. City buses stopped and disembarked their passengers so they could seek shelter. As they exited, they were handed "raid checks" to allow them to reboard after the drill without paying. The stock market stopped, schoolchildren sought shelter, and 22,000 civil defense volunteers sprang into action as a "bomb" exploded over Brooklyn's Williamsburg neighborhood, at the corner of Kent Avenue and North Seventh Street.*

When the APPLE JACK alert sounded in Washington, 14,000 government workers stored and locked classified materials, closed their office windows and blinds, turned off electrical appliances, and then walked calmly out to the employee parking lots. There, the "evacuees" touched their car door handles, stood in place for a minute, and then returned to their offices, avoiding the certain traffic gridlock that would accompany a real emergency. About a thousand key personnel did, however, travel to relocation sites—a smiling Defense Secretary Charles Wilson evacuated on one of fourteen helicopters that shuttled Pentagon leaders to the mountain bunkers. The treasury secretary, George Humphrey, traveled incognito in an unmarked car. As air raid sirens sounded over Washington at 12:05 p.m., Eisenhower—clad in a summer tan suit and brown hat—hurried out of the Oval Office, checked his watch to time the evacuation, and climbed into the presidential limousine. As his Cadillac raced for HIGH POINT at 70 miles per hour on the narrow country roads, passing other evacuees who drove at a more stately pace, the president signed mock executive orders, which were then radioed ahead to the campsite to speed their implementation.

For the drill, most of the press corps was sent to Richmond, Virginia, where the FCDA set up a briefing room, code-named NEWPOINT. The exact location of Mount Weather was kept secret, with the press referring to the relocation headquarters as just a "mountainous wooded area within 300 miles of Washington."

When Eisenhower's limo arrived at that "mountainous wooded area," he found hundreds of other officials waiting, spread across Mount Weather's interior and rows of aboveground tents. The exercise at first had a lighthearted

---

* Not everyone embraced the mock evacuations; over the course of the twenty-six-hour drill, thirty-one New Yorkers were arrested for "non-compliance" with civil defense orders, a misdemeanor.

air. Secretary of Health, Education, and Welfare Oveta Culp Hobby showed up late at her assigned relocation point, confessing that she'd stopped for lunch. Atop Mount Weather, the mustachioed CIA director Allen Dulles sat relaxed on a camp chair in a suit and bow tie, smoking his ever-present pipe, chatting with other government leaders. Yet as the hours progressed, the scale of the issues the nation would face in an attack became clear to nearly everyone.

At the campsite atop Mount Weather, Ike ate lunch in the mess tent, and then, sitting in a metal folding chair and working from a wooden table covered in brown butcher paper, he confronted the various challenges the drill revealed. Later, he drove through the mountains to Raven Rock for a special four-hour National Security Council meeting, where the normal attendees were joined by J. Edgar Hoover, whose FBI would play a key role in any national emergency. For Eisenhower, a man for whom logistics and planning had formed the backbone of his successful military career, the sheer complexity of a nuclear attack deeply worried him.

He hoped that by injecting a level of uncertainty into the exercise, he could underscore the challenge of responding to a nuclear attack. He insisted that he not be tied down to a tight schedule. "The president desires no one know where he will be," his naval aide, Edward Beach, wrote in the days before the exercise. "His movements will be unpredicted and spontaneous." As part of that effort, Eisenhower declared "mock" martial law during the alert, explaining that he felt it "would be essential to the national interest under the circumstances until the Congress could come into session and normal channels of governmental control and action be established." The mock declaration came out of the blue for the exercise planners and participants. "No one was prepared," recalled Innis Harris, the ODM deputy assistant director for plans and readiness. "The decision caused no end of consternation to both civilian and military agencies. Everyone was speculating as to what it meant. Would the civilian agencies or the military make the allocations of resources, do the rationing and so forth and so on? The lawyers were running for the books to draft an appropriate proclamation, looking back to see what Abraham Lincoln did."

The mock order would have put most of the country under the control of the nation's six Army areas—based in New York, Maryland, Atlanta,

Houston, Chicago, and San Francisco. Governors, the administration explained, "would retain normal functions" but would report to their respective regional Army field commander. The goal behind the order wasn't so much control of the civilian population as it was control over the states themselves: The FCDA believed one of the "major problems" it would face was convincing undamaged cities and states "that the national interest demands they provide support to attacked areas." It was clear the FCDA's stockpiles were deeply inadequate for a large-scale emergency—its $411 million medical reserve, split among thirty-one warehouses and storage sites nationwide, could only treat the injured Operation ALERT "victims" for three days—and to aid recovery, the FCDA would need to extract state resources from unscathed areas, by military force if necessary.

Confusion continued to swirl throughout the exercise: A draft order from the U.S. Department of Agriculture lifting crop quotas was misinterpreted as a real order, leading to outraged farmers nationwide. In stories datelined from "Emergency Press Headquarters," the media reported how Agriculture Secretary Ezra Taft Benson worked "at fever pitch" to undo the damage, but it was a brief window into just how radical the government's changes would be in the event of an enemy attack.

Then there were unexpected obstacles: The biggest enemy the Justice Department discovered in the course of Operation ALERT '55 wasn't Communist saboteurs—it was West Virginia's local Jim Crow laws, which posed considerable difficulty for the attorney general, who struggled to find overnight accommodations for his black chauffeur. The State Department, too, had serious concerns about running operations in its Front Royal headquarters for an extended period of time since so much of its workforce was African American and the area had a serious "racial problem."

Another unexpected problem in emergency planning became apparent during the exercise: The wives of the cabinet leaders rebelled—the first in what would be a long line of spouses who realized that the government had planned for their partners' survival but not their own. As syndicated columnist Doris Fleeson wrote in a column entitled "Men First; Women, Children Last," "Apparently it had not dawned on those ladies until they actually saw their husbands pack a suitcase for a three-day stay that no such plans had been made for them or their children. Their wives' farewell embraces

were described by some of the men as rather lacking in warmth." Adding
to the domestic chill was the realization that 200 of the cabinet leaders'
secretaries—"Government Girls," as the newspapers referred to them—had
been afforded space in the relocation planning.* Spouses, meanwhile, were
left in Washington, where the four wives of the defense secretary, the Joint
Chiefs chairman, the secretary of the Navy, and the assistant defense secretary gathered during the exercise for a night of rummy.

Across the country, the government remade the landscape for war. Eisenhower had long been fascinated by transportation—it was hard to spend
any real time in the military without becoming a student of logistics. Years
earlier, he'd participated in the U.S. military's first cross-country convoy in
1919, a coast-to-coast study of the nation's poor road network. After invading Germany, Eisenhower had become fascinated with that country's advanced Autobahn, which helped Hitler rapidly move war matériel. Now,
as president, Ike wanted a similar robust road system for the United States,
especially since nuclear war would require speedy evacuations from urban
areas. By the middle of the 1950s, drivers had become familiar with highway
signs warning, "In case of enemy attack, this road will be closed to all but
military vehicles."

Eisenhower turned the interstates into a priority, selling them both as an
economic engine for a growing country and as a national security imperative.
As he argued to Congress in 1955, "In case of an atomic attack on our key
cities, the road net must permit quick evacuation of target areas, mobilization of defense forces and maintenance of every essential economic function.
But the present system in critical areas would be the breeder of a deadly
congestion within hours of an attack." His effort, known formally as the National System of Interstate and Defense Highways, became one of the most
ambitious public works projects the nation had ever undertaken, building
40,000 miles of interstate in just a decade. As the network of limited-access
highways grew, the Pentagon carefully negotiated the minimum vertical

---

* In Washington, where whispers had long existed about Ike's wartime friendship with his
driver, Kay Summersby, the protection for female aides but not for spouses led Fleeson to
write privately to Bess Truman, "Just like the war."

clearances over the interstates to ensure that its largest vehicles could maneuver across the country—forcing the Transportation Department to raise its minimum standard from fourteen feet to sixteen feet to accommodate the new generation of ICBM movers that would enter the nation's arsenal in the years ahead.

Across the government, agencies and departments were lending their efforts to war preparations. The same month as the 1955 Operation ALERT exercise, the Commerce Department's U.S. Weather Bureau began calculating twice-daily "fallout forecasts," tracking how winds and atmospheric conditions would direct radioactive fallout from seventy-two critical target areas across the country and transmitting the encoded forecasts to military bases and local civil defense centers. As part of the program, fifty-two weather stations daily sent balloons skyward to obtain atmospheric readings, and the Weather Bureau assigned a permanent staff of twenty meteorologists to FCDA headquarters in Battle Creek, as well as to each of the seven regional headquarters. Civil defense planners collected the forecasts for critical target areas within 500 miles of their own borders—1,000 miles in winter when fallout would spread further due to colder temperatures—and would be able to plot the impact of an attack on their home areas within just five minutes.

The forecasts would prove helpful as well to local cities and towns, many of which found themselves inspired by the OPAL drills and implemented their own drills. South Bend, Indiana, ran Operation EXIT, evacuating its own downtown, and on a much smaller level, the town of Bellows Falls, Vermont, hosted Operation BELLWIND, where 2,000 of the town's 3,000 residents participated in a civil defense drill. Mobile, Alabama, home to a major Air Force base, ran Operation KIDS, practicing evacuating all 37,000 of its schoolchildren to sites twelve miles outside the city—a process it got down to just forty minutes. On September 27, three months after OPAL '55, the city of Portland, Oregon, launched the most ambitious civil defense exercise of the Cold War: Operation GREENLIGHT, a full-scale evacuation of the city. More than 1,000 square blocks of the city were evacuated, including all 200,000 residents within a twenty-mile radius of "ground zero," with workers and residents streaming out to twelve different "reception areas" set up across the state to receive evacuees. Red Cross kitchens served the evacuees food. Actor Glenn Ford narrated a CBS TV

movie titled *A Day Called X* that traced Portland's experience and illus-
trated how Portland residents would react to an unfolding attack. The final
scene of the movie showed a police motorcycle patrolling the deserted city,
his only companion a stray dog.

Still, many ordinary Americans remained stubbornly disinterested in
nuclear war preparation, despite the abundant public awareness campaigns
surrounding them—efforts that included making civil defense knowledge
part of the judging for the Miss America beauty pageant in 1956. People
didn't like to be reminded regularly of just how precious and tenuous their
daily existence truly was in the age of nuclear weapons. It was simply difficult to keep up the fear, hard to keep up the psychological pressure that the
world might end at any moment.

After an initial fervor, the Air Force struggled to maintain Operation
SKYWATCH, its civilian ground observer corps. By the program's peak in
1956, 380,000 volunteers—many of them women—manned 17,000 posts
across every state in the nation, urged on to their patriotic duty by celebrity
spokesman Jack Webb, of *Dragnet* fame. Recruiting posters showed a child
holding his dog, saying "Wake up, sign up, look up!" More than 1,300 of the
stations—perched in places like church towers and racetrack grandstands—
were staffed twenty-four hours a day. "The awful truth is that, for the first
time in our history, a potential enemy has the power to make sudden, devastating attacks on any part of Canada or the United States," the observers'
manual began. More than a hundred pages of aircraft photos, drawings, and
technical specifications helped identify any civilian or military aircraft that
might pass through an observer's sector, from the Soviet IL-28 "Beagle"
bomber to the red, white, and blue livery of Japan Airlines. Still, the long
hours staring at a blank sky proved mind-numbing, and retaining unpaid
volunteers through years of peacetime proved challenging. Even the merit
awards, badges, and certificates the ground observers corps handed out to its
most dedicated volunteers helped only so much.

Luckily, as interest in skywatching patriotism waned, computer use
was on the rise. By the mid-1950s, the military began to deploy the Semi-
Automatic Ground Environment (SAGE) network, linking together
twenty-two regional radar centers into the first national airspace control
center. Costing about $10 billion (about $67 billion today), the SAGE

system was a marvel of computer engineering—the 250-ton CPUs, housed in massive four-story concrete blockhouses scattered across the country, used the first generation of modems, the first magnetic-core RAM, and the first generation of computer monitors—and became one of the first wide-area computer networks, inspiring much of the knowledge used a decade later to create ARPANet, the forerunner of the modern information superhighway. The computers could track hundreds of incoming radar targets and would form the backbone of the nation's air defense networks well into the Reagan administration.*

Through the 1960s, the government helped justify numerous civilian projects by explaining how useful they'd be in an enemy attack. The same day newspapers reported the first components of SAGE were rolling off the assembly line, the media also trumpeted the defense-related transformation of more terrestrial highways.

Thermonuclear war thoroughly frightened Eisenhower. As a staff officer in Panama in the 1920s, Eisenhower had read Carl von Clausewitz's classic *On War*, which drilled into him the belief that military commanders use "every weapon at hand." Wars and military endeavors were unpredictable, irrational, and difficult to control once started; they escalated in unintended ways, and military commanders would never admit defeat if they still had weapons to deploy. Eisenhower was certain any war with the Soviet Union would become a nuclear war, and any nuclear war would escalate into a full, all-out general nuclear exchange. That end, catastrophic for the planet, was just too awful to contemplate. As he told his advisors in one meeting, "You might as well go out and shoot everyone you see and then shoot yourself."

During a January 1956 meeting, he aggressively confronted members of the cabinet who wanted to trim back the nation's five-year strategic stockpile based upon the premise that a war with Russia might last just thirty to sixty days. None of his advisors, Eisenhower complained, had withdrawn into a

---

* IBM used the SAGE technology as the foundation of another airline-related project, SABRE, the Semi-Automatic Business-Related Environment, which grew into the modern computerized airline reservation system that the world still uses today.

quiet room and contemplated for a period of time the real nature of a future thermonuclear war. None of us, he said, could imagine "the chaos and destruction which such a war would entail." There would be no winner.

The best way, Eisenhower felt, to stop a small international incident from escalating into a nuclear war was to ensure that everyone understood that all wars would be nuclear war. Historian Campbell Craig argues that beginning in 1955, Eisenhower specifically pursued a defense strategy "to remove limited, non-nuclear military planning from American general war policy, so as to ensure that any war directly between the United States and the Soviet Union would escalate automatically into an all-out thermonuclear war."

Ike had seen studies that regardless of whether the U.S. detected an attack in advance, America would experience "practically total economic collapse, which could not be restored to any kind of operative conditions under six months to a year." He knew the only real way to mitigate losses would be to strike first in a surprise attack ordered on the sole authority of the president himself—an idea Eisenhower thought so "against our traditions" that it would be "impossible."

As Eisenhower told one group of congressmen, nuclear war "will be a very quick thing," and he wouldn't have time to ask Congress for a war declaration before launching a retaliatory strike: "If you were away and I waited on you, you'd start impeachment proceedings against me." He was even more blunt in a 1954 news conference. As reporters pressed him on whether he would launch a war on his own, he said—effectively—yes: "The element of surprise, always important in war, has been multiplied by the possibility of creating such widespread destruction quickly. Therefore, any President should be worse than impeached, he should be hanged, I should say, if he didn't do what all America would demand that he do to protect them in an emergency." Eisenhower's conclusion, while logical, represented a major departure from the Constitution's checks and balances—establishing for himself the right to launch a preemptive war before Congress even knew it was in the offing.

Yet Congress had done little to inspire Eisenhower's confidence that it was equipped to deal with the pressures of nuclear war. He'd tried repeatedly in 1954 and 1955, as the executive branch's relocation efforts expanded, to encourage Congress to do its own relocation planning—efforts that had all come to naught.

Similarly, the Supreme Court of the United States seemed to recognize that there was little future for the judiciary in a nuclear confrontation. The Court had made some minor efforts in the early 1950s to prepare itself for war—installing an air raid alarm system in the Court headquarters at One First Street and designating a shelter in the basement. The Court marshal also drew up a list of air raid tasks for staff like filling pre-positioned 30-gallon water drums. In 1955, as the Eisenhower administration proceeded with its relocation arc building projects, it tried to encourage the Court's efforts to do so as well. Chief Justice Earl Warren, who had taken over the Court in the fall of 1953, had once been an enthusiastic participant in civil defense planning. As attorney general of California during World War II, he'd strung blackout curtains after Pearl Harbor to help protect against submarine or air attacks, organized police chiefs, and generally done all he could to boost the war efforts. As governor of California at the dawn of the Cold War, he'd urged all Californians to build family fallout shelters.

As the leader of a branch of government in Washington, Warren had initially remained committed to civil defense. His staff met in mid-1955 with the Office of Defense Mobilization to discuss a judicial relocation facility, and Assistant ODM Director Willard Paul had pointed the Court toward the North Carolina mountains. Court Clerk Harold Willey was dispatched by Warren to spend a fall weekend scouting Asheville for a possible relocation facility. "Because all large cities are considered to be prospective enemy targets, a hotel in a secluded small city, wherein approximately one-hundred people could both live and work, with spaces available for a court room and clerical offices, seems a most appropriate facility for the Court," Willey wrote in his report to the chief justice.

Willey visited Asheville's three big local hotels and swung by some of the smaller transient hotels, and quickly settled on the palatial Grove Park Inn, set two miles from the center of town on the side of Sunset Mountain, a storied resort that had housed Axis diplomats during World War II and hosted a number of visiting U.S. presidents, ensuring it was familiar with government interlopers. Plus the Grove Park had a nice golf course and, Willey reported, the new owners were planning to build a swimming pool, too.

Willey also visited the local courthouse and examined the law library of the nearby District Court for Western North Carolina, housed in the Asheville Post Office, and found it adequate for ordinary needs, although it lacked the specialized materials on issues like taxation and interstate commerce that the Supreme Court would require. The available courtrooms, he thought, were not "sufficiently commodious for our use," although the expectation was that only in the most dire circumstances would they have to use the existing facilities. Instead, Willey's plan was for the Supreme Court to assemble its own law library and construct its own courtroom at the Grove Park Inn inside one of the inn's three banquet halls.

With Warren's approval, the court worked out an agreement with the inn that barely filled two pages of text. "In the event of an enemy attack or the imminence thereof . . . it is understood and agreed that you will permit The Supreme Court of the United States immediately to take possessions of the facilities described in Exhibit 'A,'" the letter from the Court read. That attached "Exhibit A" indicated the Court would take over the entire property, all thirty-four acres, 141 rooms, four cottages, two dining rooms, the forty-room staff dormitory, and twenty-three-car garage.

That brief agreement was about as far as the Supreme Court ever got, though. The Court's marshal sent the Grove Park Inn each year a roll of microfilm with the Court's payroll records, and the Court also sent microfilmed copies of its papers to a government storage facility in Denver, but no other documents or books were ever moved to North Carolina. And Warren, now that he had a front-row seat to Washington, soured quickly on the civil defense apparatus. The federal civil defense office, Warren felt, was "a shelter for worn-out political figures, and they were only heard from when some cold war exigency arose." The Supreme Court, which was in recess during the summer, didn't even bother participating in the annual summer Operation ALERT drills during the Eisenhower years. The justices were frequently out of town, and didn't see a point in bothering to return just to practice evacuating again.

The annual Operation ALERT exercises each raised new questions and problems for the government to address in its post-attack planning. For one thing, the OPAL '56 exercise badly underscored the limits of an evacuation by land. While the cabinet was evacuated by helicopter, Eisenhower was again driven in his limousine, which got stuck behind a slow farm truck on the narrow Catoctin Mountains roads on the way to Camp David. In a nuclear alert, speed mattered, and a faster, more reliable evacuation procedure was clearly needed. It was, the White House decided, finally time to send the president up in the air.

The Secret Service had grave concerns about allowing the president to fly in a helicopter. They insisted that the president not travel in single-engine aircraft, but the president's airplane pilot, Colonel William Draper, rejected using the military's large Sikorsky transport helicopters because of their noise and unreliability. Instead, he settled on trying a H-13J Bell Ranger helicopter, primarily used in the private sector by corporate executives. The regular H-13, with its distinctive Plexiglas bubble and open-framed tail, was one of the military's primary helicopters, serving as the workhorse of the Korean War and made famous by the opening sequence of *M*A*S*H*.

In February 1957, the White House announced the Air Force had purchased two new $60,000 helicopters for presidential transport. They were specially modified, with foot and arm rests in the presidential seat, a rotor brake, and all-metal rotor blades, which allowed it to lift a heavier load, but they otherwise had no special security or military equipment. In the months ahead, Draper conducted an extensive search process and hand-selected the first presidential helicopter pilot, tapping Major Joseph E. Barrett, an experienced helicopter aviator who had spent nineteen months as a German prisoner of war after being shot down and was later awarded a Silver Star for a long-range helicopter rescue mission in the Korean War. Barrett spent weeks practicing his landing on the White House lawn to prepare for July 12, 1957, when Ike and his Secret Service head, James Rowley, boarded the blue-and-white U.S. Air Force Bell Ranger helicopter for the flight to Camp David as part of Operation ALERT '57. The second Bell helicopter carried a Secret Service agent and the White House physician.

While Barrett's flying skills proved impeccable, his flight would become merely a historical footnote. With a top speed of about 100 miles an hour and a cruise speed of between 60 and 70, Eisenhower's trip to Camp David took fifty-seven minutes, about half the usual two-hour motorcade ride. The ride inside the small helicopter was particularly unpleasant, though, as Eisenhower baked in the July sun's glare, despite a special tinted blue Plexiglas nose bubble technicians had installed to deflect the sun's heat.

His aides, meanwhile, had a more pleasant ride: After Eisenhower departed, twenty staff and various reporters tromped down to the Ellipse and boarded six larger transport helicopters, including Army twin-rotor H-21s and a Marine Seahorse copter. With their greater speed, the transport helicopters arrived well before Eisenhower did. As Virgil Olson, who piloted the Marine transport helicopter that day, recalled years later, "When the president arrived, he was sweating from an uncomfortable ride and annoyed to find us on the ground, with the engines of our helicopter already off and cooled down." Although he completed the exercise, flying on to the Mount Weather relocation site for a meeting with the civil defense and national security teams, Ike made clear he would never board the Bell Ranger helicopter again.

Two months later, while the president was vacationing in Newport, Rhode Island, tensions during the integration of Little Rock Central High School threatened to boil over on September 7, 1957. Ike decided to return to the White House to meet with Justice Department officials—and he wanted to get there as soon as possible. The president called upon the Marine emergency evacuation helicopter that the White House Military Office had stationed nearby in the event of a surprise Soviet nuclear attack. The flight across Narragansett Bay lasted just six minutes, as opposed to the hour Eisenhower would have spent on the ferry—and the helicopter, piloted by Virgil Olson, was nearly triple the size of the Bell Ranger passenger-wise. This, Eisenhower decided, was a much better option.

Since the Air Force didn't possess the large transport helicopters Eisenhower desired, the Marine Corps took over the presidential helicopter fleet. Within two months—lightning speed in government time—the Marines established an executive flight squadron in Quantico, Virginia. Colonel Olson, an Iowan who had flown Marine dive-bombers in the Pacific during World War II and later volunteered to train on helicopters and fly in the Korean War, became the first commander of the presidential helicopter squadron known as HMX-1, a unit originally established to test out new helicopters (the "Experimental" mission is where the unit gets the X in its moniker).

No one wanted a repeat of the sweaty and irritated Eisenhower who had disembarked during the Operation ALERT drill, so the Sikorsky UH-34 Seahorse helicopters were painted white on top, to help reflect heat and lower the cabin temperature, and each was fitted with an automobile air conditioner to help keep the passengers cool. Their distinctive paint scheme came to be known as "white tops," and would designate helicopters used for VIP transport. Until the Ford presidency, the Army and the Marines alternated flying the same eight helicopters, designating them "Army One" when an Army officer piloted and "Marine One" when a Marine officer did.

By 1957, the idea of World War III was shifting dramatically. Jets—faster and more powerful—were on their way to replacing propeller-driven planes; ballistic missiles were coming online, reducing the warning time for a nuclear attack from several hours to just minutes. A major upgrade in May 1957 to the National Attack Warning System (NAWAS) reduced the time required to broadcast an alert from seven minutes to just four, and consolidated the system to three locations manned twenty-four hours a day by FCDA and military officials: the North American Air Defense headquarters, known as NORAD, in Colorado; the eastern air defense headquarters in Newburgh, New York, at Stewart Air Force Base; and the western air defense headquarters at Hamilton Air Force Base in California.

Post-attack planning expanded, too: In 1955, the Interior Department had been tasked with both ensuring adequate fuel supplies for attacked areas and for restoring electrical service to damaged cities. It divided the United States into sixteen electrical regions, each of them to be overseen post-attack by specially designated officials or their successors. Two years later, the Public Health Service launched a "Special Weapons Protection Branch" to work with hospitals in developing protective construction features that could help them withstand nuclear blasts. The Labor Department created handbooks of occupational titles and codes for post-attack planning, dividing the U.S. workforce into helpful skill sets, and developed plans for post-attack "income maintenance," under a program it called the "Federal Emergency Unemployment Payments Plan." DELNET, a dedicated teletype system for communication between relocation facilities, came online in time for Operation ALERT '57, part of the National Communications System No. 1

(NACOM 1), which included nearly 20,000 miles of telephone wires connecting Mount Weather, Battle Creek, the FCDA regional offices, and state and local civil defense headquarters. The cutting-edge technology could transmit up to seventy-five words a minute and even handle encoded classified messages. In the years ahead, the FCDA would also deploy NACOM 2, a radio backup system to link the various facilities.

The new speed of war caused the administration to reconsider some of its hard-and-fast rules about using nuclear weapons—it was no longer clear that the president or the National Command Authorities would necessarily have the time to issue their own official launch orders. On May 22, 1957, President Eisenhower signed a new policy, the "Authorization for the Expenditure of Nuclear Weapons," which provided instructions for circumstances under which military commanders could decide on their own accord to launch an atomic attack. Considered so secret that only eight copies of the order were created and its very existence was never made public, Eisenhower intended for the "pre-delegation" to apply when "time and circumstances do not permit a decision by the President" or "when immediate communications have become impossible between the President and responsible officials of the Department of Defense." Giving the military such control over the nuclear weapons marked the final step away from the careful civilian control that Truman had insisted upon. Eisenhower would probably have been horrified had he understood what his orders really meant on the ground—at many locations security was lax and there were few controls on the soldiers in charge of the nuclear weapons. In the field, Eisenhower's "pre-delegation" rules meant something like this: At Incirlik Air Force Base in Turkey, an American pilot would sit in the cockpit of an F-105 bomber, with nuclear weapons slung under its wings, watched over only by a Turkish soldier with a sidearm. The guard's sidearm was unloaded.

The new nuclear "pre-delegation" rules were just one step in the growing assortment of post-attack planning the government was developing. In March 1958, Strategic Air Command implemented a new system called "Fail-Safe," meant to prevent its force being caught on the ground by a surprise attack. In the event of what RAND strategist Albert Wohlstetter called a "serious yet not unambiguous warning," SAC could launch its bombers on its own, which would then advance toward their targets while SAC gathered further information and awaited an official launch order from the National Command Authorities. The bombers would wait at designated points in the air unless they received a second authenticated "Go Code" ordering them to proceed toward their targets. If they didn't receive such a confirmation order, they turned around. By the following year, one third of the SAC bomber force stood on "alert" status, ready to launch with just minutes' notice.*

FCDA also launched a major effort to boost COG planning by state and local officials, meeting with governors and working with Columbia University to draft sample legislation and constitutional amendments to help states adapt to the needs of nuclear succession planning. Veterans groups adopted the measures as a patriotic pet cause, pushing hard for them in state houses, and by 1959 such legislation was under consideration in forty-six states and thirty-four had established clear COG plans and new lines of succession.† During the 1960 election, voters in fourteen states decided whether to ratify new nuclear age COG and succession plans.

The FCDA also released "Battleground USA," a 120-page report on how local cities should manage their civil defense operations in an attack. It didn't skimp on gruesome details, explaining how after an attack a city should be divided into mortuary zones, with different mortuary zone chiefs overseeing "collection teams" who would be in charge of identification of bodies and interment, and how some 7,000 Post Office mail trucks were to be converted into casualty carriers after an attack. FCDA's stockpiles had soared by the late 1950s to more than 3.2 million square feet nationwide— up from just 400,000 square feet of warehouses in 1953. It included more than nine million burn dressings, 1.5 million paper blankets, 307,000 litters, and 1,400 gas masks. A dozen FCDA maintenance facilities managed more than sixty stockpiles of supplies and engineering equipment that dotted the

---

* While the "Fail-Safe" mechanisms became a favorite trope of novels during the 1950s and movies like *Dr. Strangelove*, it actually worked as proposed when tested in the real world. During scares in 1979 and 1980, when nuclear-armed bombers were scrambled, they were all recalled under "Fail-Safe" protocols.

† The state-by-state process created some oddities: Kansas's line of succession, for instance, included the chancellor of the University of Kansas, just ahead of the president of Kansas State. Texas includes the chief judges of its appeals courts; New Jersey includes its state highway commissioner.

country, including major depots in places like Stockton, California; Sidney, Nebraska; Lake Charles, Louisiana; Anniston, Alabama; Zanesville, Ohio; Crab Orchard, Illinois; and many others—all located between ten and fifty miles outside a major target.

More than 900 of the improvised emergency hospitals sat pre-positioned near major attack sites, waiting in storage in places like the federal prison in Danbury, Connecticut; the town hall in Adams, Massachusetts; the First Presbyterian Church in Warren, Pennsylvania; Beaver Dam's high school in Wisconsin; the VFW hall in Centralia, Illinois; and the Benedictine monastery in Mount Angel, Oregon. The FCDA trained hundreds of police officers across the country on "Emergency Traffic Control," to aid urban evacuations, and built special civil defense rescue trucks, dispatching hundreds of them to fire departments nationwide. The FCDA even planned in 1958 to distribute radiology monitoring kits to all 15,000 American high schools, so that science classes could begin to teach students how to monitor fallout levels after an attack.

In Kansas, officials calculated they could probably assemble two million pounds of food after an attack and that if survivors reduced consumption to an "austerity diet" of 2,000 calories, the state's food stocks could last nearly two months. Besides the official stocks, Kansas's wildlife could help, too: Its forests, plains, and waters contained, officials believed, 11 million "man-days" of food in rabbit meat, 10 million "man-days" of wild birds, five million "man-days" of edible fish, and—perhaps most macabre of all—nearly 20 million "man-days" of meat in residential pets. After an attack, officials also planned to confiscate household vitamins for the good of the general population and ration carefully the state's twenty-eight-day supply of coffee. But those calculations—and the countless others that made up the nation's post-attack planning—left some officials worried. "I don't think we are ever very realistic in our approaches," complained the Commerce Department's emergency planning coordinator, retired Army Brigadier General Ernest V. Holmes. "When we came up against a problem for which we had no answer, usually because 'we could never get the public to accept such a premise,' we tried to assume ourselves out of the predicament. Assumptions are great little solvers of problems."

Indeed, despite all the civilian planning of the first decade of civil defense efforts, it seemed clear that any plans involving the general public would fall far short. Even as the military's readiness surged and the nuclear arsenals expanded, homeland defense efforts seemed neglected.

In 1958 Eisenhower merged the civilian FCDA and the military's Office of Defense Mobilization into a single agency, the Office of Defense and Civilian Mobilization, located within the Executive Office of the President and headed by Leo Hoegh, who had taken over as the head of FCDA the year before. Within two months of its reorganization, Hoegh's new agency was renamed again as the Office of Civil and Defense Mobilization (OCDM) to emphasize the primacy of civilian protection. That pattern would repeat itself regularly. Despite well-meaning efforts beginning with Truman's new FCDA, bureaucratic indifference would mark nearly every aspect of the nation's homeland defense operations in the decades ahead, as the function migrated regularly between different departments and underwent nearly a dozen name changes and agency affiliations before eventually becoming the Federal Emergency Management Agency (FEMA) in the 1970s and, after yet another organizational reshuffling, would finally end up part of the Department of Homeland Security in 2003. No other seemingly key governmental duty has been so thoroughly reimagined so many times. That constant shuffling, perhaps, was indicative of what Eisenhower knew in his gut: Protecting the civilian population in a nuclear war was a mostly futile effort. It would be devastating beyond any imagination. "The destruction," Eisenhower told his cabinet at one point, "might be such that we might have ultimately to go back to bows and arrows."

Chapter 6

THE SPIRIT OF
CAMP DAVID

As the threat of nuclear war loomed, "protective structures" became its own construction specialty. The Defense Department created a Protective Structures Development Center at Fort Belvoir in Washington that included a demonstration area for manufacturers, and a special facility that simulated nuclear fallout to test structures for radiation protection. Officials from across the government journeyed to Fort Belvoir to view the demos, study shelter design, investigate pricing, and compare the layouts of two full-sized model shelters built on site—one that could hold 200 people and another that could hold 1,000 people. In theory, they were impressive, but the question remained: Were they effective?

To prove shelters made a difference, the government decided it needed to test the bunkers with actual atomic weapons. The nation's early atomic experiments had been in the South Pacific, but as such testing grew more regular and complicated, the logistical challenges of moving naval flotillas and scientific personnel halfway around the world made such far-flung tests cost-prohibitive. Plus, there were the security concerns: Soviet, Japanese, and Korean fishing trawlers became regular observers of the tests and there was little the Navy could do about them in international waters.

So in 1950, President Truman authorized a secret operation, code-named Project NUTMEG, to identify an unpopulated space inside the continental United States for weapons testing. The military and the AEC finally settled on a bombing and gunnery range in Nevada, located about sixty miles up a narrow two-lane highway from the small desert city of Las Vegas. Outside of Las Vegas and Reno, nearly 90 percent of Nevada is federal land, and during the 1950s, a huge swath of that was given over to secret Cold War experiments of one sort or another. Near Groom Lake at Nellis Air Force Base, at what came to be known as Area 51, the CIA ran tests for a secret program known as OXCART—developing the U-2 surveillance plane—among others. Adjacent to Area 51, the government found the perfect place for its nuclear tests.

The Nevada Test Site eventually grew to some 1,300 square miles, a secure area the size of Rhode Island, buried within an even larger block of restricted land that would be home to Nellis Air Force Base, Indian Springs Air Force Base (now Creech Air Force Base), the Tonopah Test Range, and other government reservations. The test site had been barely touched by human hands—its population consisted of little more than tortoises, antelope, kit foxes, and bighorn sheep.* Soon, it became home to a small secret government town named Mercury—complete with a bowling alley, a post office, rec facilities, and hotels—for the military and Atomic Energy Commission personnel brought out to the Mojave Desert to watch nuclear weapons explode.

The first of the domestic nuclear tests came on January 27, 1951, when a B-50 bomber dropped a bomb onto Frenchman Flat shortly before dawn. In a valley surrounded by forests of Joshua trees, past signs that read "If You Wouldn't Tell Stalin, Don't Tell Anyone," military and AEC personnel lined up on mountainsides and the desert flat itself to test the various effects of nuclear explosions. In the years ahead, it became the most scarred Cold War battlefield in the world, subjected to nearly a thousand nuclear explosion tests over forty years. The distant booms became a major source of entertainment for Las Vegas, where locals became skilled at spotting the increased level of activity that preceded a test; tourists would wake up early to see the bright flash and mushroom clouds rising from over the Nevada Test Site.†

In 1953 and 1955, the FCDA conducted two major tests focusing on

---

* The landscape is so barren and isolated that in the 1960s Apollo astronauts like Neil Armstrong and Buzz Aldrin trained at the Nevada Test Site because it resembled the moon.
† Not all of the local effects of the testing were entertaining: Local farmers, known as "down-winders," suffered unmistakable damage as scientists at the test site came to understand how radioactive fallout worked. In one 1953 series of tests, fallout killed thousands of grazing sheep downwind.

the nuclear effects on domestic Americana. They built a mock town named "Survival City," outfitted with specially constructed utility stations, gas stations, and full-sized Colonial-style houses, each containing furniture, appliances, and a total of fifteen tons of fresh food, spread among the tables, cupboards, shelves, and storage areas. Clothed mannequins were located in various rooms to test the effects of the blast and subsequent shockwaves on "Mr. and Mrs. America." Rows of mannequins were propped up in the desert, each wearing different colors and types of clothing to test their varying protective abilities. Donated automobiles, trailer homes, and three postal trucks were brought up from Las Vegas and parked around the intended blast zone. "We actually built a small city and we obliterated most of the city," recalled Ernest Williams, one of the project team members.

The results, captured on camera from reinforced positions, became famous. During the ANNIE test, a house just 3,000 feet from ground zero was obliterated in under three seconds. During the APPLE-2 test, other houses at 6,600 and 8,000 feet from ground zero fared better, although many of their occupants didn't. Mannequins in the homes aboveground "died" violent deaths, while those in the basement shelters all fared fine. The mannequins whose "lives" had been saved by the basement shelters were taken back to Las Vegas and displayed in the windows of the J.C. Penney store on Fremont Street. A sign nearby read, "These mannequins could have been real people, in fact, they could have been you."

At the Nevada site, engineers also studied differing window and glass configurations, built airplane hangars, railroad bridges, industrial facilities, and filled acres with various military matériel like tanks and armored personnel carriers to test their survivability. For one test, the government imported 145 mature ponderosa pines, most towering fifty or more feet into the air, and cemented them into the desert, to test the effects of a nuclear blast on a forest.

The atomic testing reached its peak in the summer of 1957, when Operation PLUMBBOB saw the Nevada Test Site explode twenty-four nuclear weapons between April and October. As part of the June 1957 test codenamed PRISCILLA, the government devoted months to building a variety of protective structures and bunkers across the desert of Frenchman Flat—and then blew it all up on June 24, 1957, with a 37-kiloton device exploded about 700 feet above the desert. The device, about double the magnitude of the

Hiroshima bomb, awed those present as the mushroom cloud roared eight miles up into the air.

Early observers found the awe-inspiring wonder of the nuclear blasts hard to capture. The experience of a blast was not easily described. As physicist I. I. Rabi tried to explain, "Suddenly, there was an enormous flash of light, the brightest light I have ever seen or that I think anyone has ever seen. It blasted; it pounced; it bored its way into you. It was a vision which was seen with more than the eye. It was seen to last forever. You would wish it would stop; altogether it lasted about two seconds." Early observers expressed wonder that a nuclear blast turned out to be a full-sensory experience—you could, as it turned out, even taste a nuclear explosion, as the passing shockwaves changed the atmospheric ozone as it blew by.

For the PRISCILLA test—which focused on fortifications and military equipment—engineers constructed machine gun emplacements, foxholes, and troop shelters just a few hundred meters from the detonation and then loaded a pig into the door of each machine gun emplacement. (The pigs fared poorly.) Dozens of other experiments tested various underground shelter designs. For those, the military built ten domed bunkers of varying designs and strengths, placed in arcs out from the detonation point that would test their survival at various predetermined distances from the blast. There were also fourteen international shelter designs from French, Swiss, and German engineers, and a "dual-use" massive underground parking garage that could hold several hundred cars—or as many as 900 people as a bomb shelter—and was protected by a four-foot-thick, 100-ton concrete blast door. Across the various bunkers and shelters, engineers varied the concrete aggregate and reinforcing rebar; some bunkers were entirely rounded, while others had hard 90-degree side edges. Lastly, for the PRISCILLA test, the Mosler Safe Company built a $500,000 bank vault in the middle of the desert and filled it with fake stocks, bonds, and other valuables to test its ability to withstand a nuclear blast. The company, based in Hamilton, Ohio, was already well known; its vault doors protected the gold at Fort Knox and four Mosler vaults had survived the Hiroshima bombing virtually unscathed inside that city's Teikku Bank. "It was our great luck to find that though the surface of the vault doors was heavily damaged, its contents were not affected at all and the cash and important documents were perfectly saved," the Japanese bank manager wrote Mosler. "Your products were admired for being stronger than the Atomic Bomb." Mosler advertised that success in magazines and newspapers across the United States, and banks began to brag about installing the same vaults that survived "the blast and heat of the atomic bomb." Now, they sought to prove it again.

The PRISCILLA blast scoured the sides, as a 70-psi overpressure wave twisted away the concrete rebar on the walls (.5 psi will shatter windows and 5 to 7 psi will destroy most nonconcrete buildings), but the vault itself was just fine. "The damage to the door was only ornamental trim, etc., the door being reopened without any difficulty," the company's after-action report concluded. "The interior of the above-ground vault was entirely protected by the door."

Over the course of the Cold War, the company became the gold standard for nuclear security, working on nearly every major nuclear bunker project. It established a special division to work on "protective construction" and helped build the vault that the National Archives used to hold the Declaration of Independence and the Constitution. Even as Mosler tested its doors in the Mojave Desert, the company was working on huge new challenging orders like building massive blast doors for facilities like the Greenbrier congressional bunker and the five-foot-thick shielding doors for the Oak Ridge National Laboratory, which the company bragged were the "largest and heaviest" hinged doors in the world, but still able to be closed by a single worker. Mosler also came to design and build blast doors for missile silos, as well as the safes that held the nuclear launch orders aboard the Navy's nuclear submarines. Its reputation took it beyond government work, though, to include nearly anything people hoped would survive the Apocalypse: Even the Mormon Church turned to Mosler blast doors to secure its genealogical records inside Utah's Granite Mountain.*

As Eisenhower's second term began, domestic concerns overtook much of his foreign policy agenda. The school desegregation came to a head in Little

---

* The security offered inside a bank safe even became fodder for a 1959 episode of *The Twilight Zone*, in which mild-mannered, bookish bank clerk Henry Bemis, who locked himself inside the bank's safe each day to read during his lunch break, emerged from the vault one day to find the world devastated by nuclear bombs.

Rock, even as Congress prepared to pass the first civil rights act since Reconstruction, and the country's economy, robust since World War II, faltered. Hoping to distract criticism of his defense agenda, Eisenhower gathered yet another study group to evaluate the nation's readiness in mid-1957. Led by H. Rowan Gaither, who headed the Ford Foundation and helped found the government-sponsored defense think tank RAND, it was at least the fourth blue-ribbon panel to study the nation's readiness in the 1950s—all of which continued to find the United States ill-equipped for war. The Gaither Committee's work was already under way when the Soviets launched the world's first ICBM that August. The success of the rocket alone struck a psychological blow—the first U.S. ICBM had blown up during a test in July—but the Soviets then surprised the world in October by launching a basketball-sized beeping orb named Sputnik into the heavens. The Air Force had diverted attention from its space program to speed completion of the B-52 bomber—and the cost of that trade-off was instantly clear, as every American household could tune their radio at night to hear the steady, ominous *beep-beep-beep-beep* of Sputnik passing high overhead. Texas senator Lyndon B. Johnson declared that the nation faced "another Pearl Harbor."

The Gaither Committee's final report, entitled "Deterrence and Survival in the Nuclear Age," was delivered on November 7, 1957, just four days after the Soviets underscored their space success by launching a dog, Laika, into orbit. The report didn't conclude what Eisenhower had hoped it would, instead echoing the alarmist Truman-era NSC-68 and calling for a massive shelter-building program and extensive modifications to the nation's defense structure, as well as a strategic shift offensively toward "counterforce" attacks. The concerns seemed valid: During a visit to SAC headquarters, the committee had viewed a surprise alert—only to find that not a single bomber was readied and in the air within six hours. (LeMay had brushed off the failure, saying his intelligence was too good to ever be met by a true surprise attack.)

In *The Washington Post*, journalist Chalmers Roberts explained, "the still top-secret Gaither Report portrays a United States in the gravest danger in its history. It pictures the nation moving in frightening course to the status of a second-class power." An irritated Eisenhower didn't agree. "We must get people to understand that we confront a tough problem, but one we can lick," Eisenhower said. He ended the meeting with the committee at the White House by emphasizing his conclusion that nuclear war was never a real option. The Gaither Report was wrong, he argued, because widespread, serious planning for a nuclear exchange was a waste of finite resources. As he told the departing committee after they presented the report to the National Security Council, it wasn't just a matter of building better weapons or deeper shelters if nuclear war came: "We don't have enough bulldozers to scrape the bodies off the street."

The morning after the Gaither Report arrived, on a gray and rainy fall day, Ike helicoptered out to Germantown, Maryland, to dedicate the new headquarters of the Atomic Energy Commission—an excursion that highlighted the odd mix of urgent concern and lackadaisical attitude that characterized much of the COG planning. Already that morning, he'd sworn in the new attorney general, William Rogers, making the former Wall Street lawyer the newest member of the presidential line of succession. The FBI had accordingly revised its war plans—passing the attorney general's emergency briefcase to Rogers, assigning two new details of agents, a primary team and a backup, to evacuate him in the event of an attack that came outside normal office hours, and giving each agent a top secret folder of maps and driving directions to Mount Weather and Raven Rock, as well as to the Justice Department relocation facilities in Shepherdstown and Quantico.

After Rogers's swearing-in, Eisenhower boarded his new Marine helicopter for the twenty-three-mile flight north to Germantown—a trip almost a decade in the making. Eight years before, in November 1949, AEC chair David Lilienthal had called for the dispersal of key government facilities like the AEC, which was headquartered across the street from the White House. As pressing as the Soviet threat seemed, Congress only moved so quickly. Left without a good relocation plan as time passed, the AEC—the civilian agency more responsible than anyone for the nation's nuclear stockpiles—instead planned for its own doom and decreed that once Washington was destroyed, the AEC's management would devolve to the head of its New Mexico operations at the Sandia National Laboratory.

Finally in 1955, Congress allowed the Atomic Energy Commission to move forward with a new headquarters, beginning a two-year project to construct a modern building for its 1,600-person staff on a 109-acre farm in

Maryland. Reinforced with concrete and covered in brick, the headquarters was specially shielded to absorb a blast radiating north from the capital. Two years later, it was complete.

Throughout the rainy dedication day speakers stressed both the glories and the horrors of the atom. Buried in the building's cornerstone was a time capsule of atomic age mementos, including a linen from the Dead Sea Scrolls that radiocarbon dating had identified as having been created in AD 38, a representative of the wondrous benefits nuclear technology would bring to civilian life. In his remarks, the president repeated the themes of his earlier "Atoms for Peace" initiative. This time, however, Eisenhower's dramatic conclusion inadvertently brought the crowd back to the scary reality of the modern world: He had to press a button to drop the curtain covering the building's dedication plaque, not exactly the best symbology for a nation anxious facing nuclear war. As he leaned over to the button, he said, "I certainly hope it [works]." It was the same question the whole nation was asking that fall about the nuclear "button," too.

Eisenhower's stubborn resistance to new defense spending crumbled in his final years as president. Publicly, the so-called Bomber Gap had become a major point of political concern, with calls to speed up production of the new B-52. But secretly the first photographs taken by the new U-2 high-altitude surveillance plane confirmed that the United States was far ahead militarily. The Soviet Union possessed no real strategic air force, possessing just 85 bombers to the United States' 1,750. Yet the administration couldn't really publicly refute the "Bomber Gap" without giving away its new secret intelligence and so the myth lingered with fear of the Soviet Union's creeping ambitions continuing to permeate American politics.

The junior Massachusetts senator, John F. Kennedy, warned that under the Eisenhower administration the United States was "behind, possibly as much as several years" in developing ICBM and rocket technology. He and others like columnist Joseph Alsop used the primal fear of that "Missile Gap" to bludgeon the former Supreme Allied Commander as weak and soft on defense. Eventually, Eisenhower approved plans to build the nation's first nine Polaris submarines, whose solid-liquid-fueled ballistic missiles would give the United States a nearly invulnerable second-strike capability—the submarines would become the third leg of the Nuclear Triad of bombers, subs, and ICBMs. But Ike—and his vice president, Richard Nixon—continued to resist an expansion of the national shelter program, with Nixon arguing in an NSC meeting, "If 40 million were killed, the United States would be finished." He did not believe the country would survive such a disaster. Eisenhower seemed to agree, later writing, "so far as I am personally concerned, I am not sure whether I would really want to be living if this country of ours should ever be subjected to a nuclear bath."

Behind the scenes, though, government Doomsday planners kept working to convince their colleagues that they should make plans to live through that "nuclear bath." In June 1959, the OCDM's liaison officer, Jack Hurley, took two CIA officers out to HIGH POINT to give them a tour. He drove them around the installation, pointing out the two-story cinder-block barracks where the chosen few would live atop Mount Weather. By September, he explained, the underground caverns would be ready for occupancy. By that point, sixteen agencies had full-time staff at HIGH POINT, rotating their watch staff through the facility every two weeks. Six other agencies would relocate to the site in an emergency, for a total of twenty-two. The air-conditioned underground bunker, 300 feet under the mountaintop, would be able to hold around 3,000 workers once finished, Hurley said. He took the CIA officers through the communications unit and showed them the above-ground war room, which shortly would be relocated inside what the team was calling "the Hole"; they wondered in awe at the large-scale wall map where planners would chart the nation's damage assessment and the spread of radioactive fallout. Finally, Hurley introduced them to J. Leo Bourassa, an ex-OSS officer from World War II who was then the deputy commander of HIGH POINT. While the CIA's headquarters and relocation sites already had communication links to Mount Weather, Bourassa argued that the CIA should consider stationing a team at the facility full-time. As the officers reported back to Langley, "He felt this would provide a person familiar with our operations who could intelligently answer questions that may arise."

Dwight Eisenhower's life as commander-in-chief was lonely, as all presidents inevitably found in the isolation of the White House, but the pressures of World War II and the fame it delivered him had pushed on him years earlier a particularly cocooned life. As a habit, he rose early, around 6 a.m., and during breakfast carefully pored over the morning newspapers. Nearly all of his mundane life tasks were outsourced; he didn't even put on his own underwear. His valet, John Moaney, dressed him each morning head to toe. He hadn't driven a car in years, eaten casually in a restaurant in more than a decade, learned to dial a telephone, shopped in a grocery store, written his own checks, or managed his own money. His rare escape from the pressures of the White House involved golf, short vacations, and he especially loved escapes to the presidential retreat in the Catoctin Mountains in Maryland on the Pennsylvania border.

That retreat, Camp David—now such a central part of the U.S. president's world—almost didn't survive until Eisenhower's presidency, coming close to the same fate as the first presidential retreat, Herbert Hoover's Camp Rapidan in the Shenandoah, which was abandoned soon after the end of Hoover's presidency. Franklin Roosevelt had preferred other activities, primarily sailing on the presidential yacht, *Potomac*, visiting his home in Hyde Park, New York, and his favorite vacation spot in Warm Springs, Georgia. Yet rationing and security concerns at the onset of World War II made each untenable in its own way: He needed to find a weekend escape closer to home.

The National Park Service found the most workable solution was Hi-Catoctin, Camp #3, sixty miles north of D.C., in the Catoctin Mountains, the easternmost ridge of the Blue Ridge Mountains that extend from the Great Smoky Mountains near Tennessee up to the Berkshires of New England. Catoctin is technically considered a single fifty-mile-long mountain that runs from the Pennsylvania border down across Frederick County, Maryland, and into Virginia, but nearly everyone refers to it as plural—the Catoctin Mountains. Lifted a billion years ago and made of especially hard granite, the Blue Ridge mountains in general—and Catoctin specifically— would in the years ahead become the favored home of the U.S. government during a nuclear attack.

Initially, the camp the Park Service proposed to FDR had been part of a New Deal program to build summer recreation sites for poor children. He was driven up the 1,800-foot mountainside to the rustic facility for the first time in April 1942 and loved it from first sight, proclaiming, "This is Shangri-La!" The mythical Asian paradise in James Hilton's 1933 novel,

Lost Horizon, had been at the forefront of his mind that week at the White House, where a day earlier he had celebrated with reporters one of the country's first "victories" in World War II, the surprise bombing of Tokyo and mainland Japan by carrier-launched bombers led by James Doolittle. When pressed for details of the raid, he joked, "I think the time has now come to tell you. They came from our new secret base at Shangri-La!" But the reference also carried real significance for him—he liked Hilton's book and Shangri-La represented a place unravaged by war or aging, both of which he was struggling with by 1942. This tranquil mountaintop, filled with pines, oaks, ferns, and wildflowers, and camouflaged from public eyes, the media, and German bombers, would be where he could escape the White House, host friends, and work on his stamp collection.

When he first saw Hi-Catoctin Camp #3, it had only small four-cot cabins, a pool, recreation hall, and communal showers. FDR outlined basic additions—a screened porch here, a new wheelchair ramp there—and the site was readied for presidential use on a budget of about $20,000. When he was in attendance, nearly 100 staff, from secretaries to security to a movie projectionist stayed nearby in primitive conditions—living in unheated cabins without running water. The Secret Service stayed in nearby Thurmont, Maryland, at the Cozy Motel until an old Civilian Conservation Corps barracks was readied for them and nicknamed by FDR "221B Baker Street."

Truman had inherited the camp as a matter of course, but shown little interest in it—or more accurately, the Truman women hated it: His daughter, Margaret, labeled it "terrible," "damp and cold," and First Lady Bess called it "dull." The president, a man from the Plains, considered the whole place overgrown. "I look out the window and there's nothing but trees," he complained. During his tenure, he seldom used it, eschewing it entirely for the final two and a half years of his presidency. Eisenhower expected to feel the same way—he first visited the camp as part of his plan to mothball it, amid a promised tightening of presidential perks that included also setting aside Truman's presidential yacht, the *Williamsburg*. But Eisenhower, who owned a farm nearby in Gettysburg, found that he absolutely loved Roosevelt's "Shangri-La."

Almost immediately, Mamie set about updating and redecorating the cabins. The presidential cabin, called "The Bear's Den" by FDR, became

Aspen Lodge, after the official tree of Mamie's home state, Colorado. The other cabins were named after trees as well: Laurel, Hickory, Birch, Dogwood, Red Oak, and so on. A famed New York golf course designer laid out a tiny putting area for the president, and the Navy expanded the support facilities nearby, building a new barracks and even a family housing complex. Eisenhower thought Roosevelt's name was "just a little fancy for a Kansas farm boy" and had the camp's sole sign changed, rechristening it "Camp David," after his grandson. (The Navy calls the camp "Naval Support Facility Thurmont," while the Secret Service and the White House Communications Agency code name for the facility is CACTUS.)

In the latter years of Eisenhower's administration, his preference for the Catoctin retreat was so well known that "an invitation to Camp David had come to confer a special distinction upon a guest." British prime minister Harold Macmillan visited Camp David on March 20, 1959, staying the night in Aspen Lodge. Mixing business and pleasure, Ike gave a tour of the recently enlarged bomb shelter to underscore the Cold War tensions both nations faced. Macmillan recalled in his diary later being shown the "underground fortress," "a sort of Presidential Command Post in the event of atomic war. It holds fifty of the President's staff in one place and one hundred and fifty Defence staff in another. The fortress is underneath the innocent looking huts in which we lived, hewn out of the rock. It cost 10 million dollars!" The Aspen bomb shelter, Ike explained, would have served as one of the main evacuation points for a president in an emergency and was carefully secured at all times. While the Marines primarily provided perimeter security—the Secret Service covered the camp's interior—a Marine with a loaded M-1 rifle always guarded the entrance to the bunker under the Aspen Lodge. Security was tight; during Op ALERT '57, the normal sentry outside the bunker was away and his substitute—a large, gruff Marine— even refused entry to the director of the Secret Service, James Rowley, who didn't have his appropriate badge. "No badge, no entry," the Marine explained, forcing the director to have one of the camp agents vouch for him.

In July 1959, Eisenhower invited Nikita Khrushchev to Camp David. Khrushchev, a peasant by birth who had risen to head the Soviet Union despite being only semiliterate, was dubious of the invitation because he had never heard of the facility. "What's that?" Suspicious of a possible slight, he asked his aides, "What sort of camp is it?" When the report came back that Camp David was the president's vacation home—his, so to speak, *dacha*—Khrushchev happily accepted, using the visit as a chance to embark on a long, roving, and bizarre cross-country tour in the fall of 1959, including stops in New York, California, Iowa, Pennsylvania, and Washington, D.C.

Finally, the two leaders arrived at Camp David, where they watched a Western and video of the USS *Nautilus* under the North Pole. The normally quiet escape had been transformed for the summit—dozens of U.S. and Soviet staff descended on the camps, filling all the available bedrooms and forcing some staff to sleep in the lounge areas.

Khrushchev had assumed the Soviet premiership in September 1953, inheriting the same awesome power that Dwight Eisenhower now possessed. His first briefing on the nation's nuclear stockpile had left him shaken, too. "I couldn't sleep for several days," he recounted later. "Then I became convinced that we could never possibly use these weapons, and when I realized that I was able to sleep again." He had, despite maintaining his boisterous rhetoric, subtly changed the Soviet Union's trajectory, nudging it toward peace. During the Soviet Union's 1956 Party Congress, just months after the successful test of the Joe-4 hydrogen bomb, Khrushchev had repudiated Joseph Stalin's tenet that a new world war was inevitable and instead endorsed "peaceful coexistence." "Either peaceful coexistence or the most destructive war in history," he declared, "there is no third way."

Still, a divide existed between the men. As Khrushchev and Ike posed for pictures on Camp David's wooden deck, the Soviet leader had no idea he was standing directly over the bomb shelter from which the U.S. president might someday lead a war against his nation. The talks, overall, were neither a step forward nor a step backward—all in all, a diplomatic win.

Eisenhower's final Operation ALERT exercise, scheduled for spring, was set to be the most realistic yet. On the third day of OPAL '60, Thursday, May 5, Eisenhower left the White House at 7:33 a.m. and helicoptered to Mount Weather, but other evacuations had a less smooth start. Given just an hour's warning, Defense Secretary Thomas Gates had been driven by his wife, still in her nightgown, to his designated helicopter site, only to discover he'd forgotten his pass and was initially blocked from entering by the guards at the

Anacostia Naval Station. Meanwhile, science advisor George Kistiakowsky had come out of his Georgetown home to find Allen Dulles's broken-down Cadillac blocking the street. The CIA director sputtered angrily at his car as Kistiakowsky helped him push it off to the side. The chairman of the Joint Chiefs, Air Force General Nathan Twining, meanwhile, missed his helicopter entirely and never made it to the evacuation site.

As helicopters across Washington ferried officials to HIGH POINT, the UPI wire carried a news bulletin just three minutes after Eisenhower left the White House: REUTERS SAYING KHRUSHCHEV SED IN SPEECH TDAY TT U.S. PLANE SHOT DOWN SUNDAY FOR VIOLATING SOVIET AIR SPACE. At Mount Weather, the facility's director, J. Leo Bourassa, interrupted the exercise to give the president the news. The irony was that the U-2 flight, piloted by Francis Gary Powers, was set to be one of the U-2's last: New spy satellites were arriving that would make the flights redundant and Eisenhower had been increasingly antsy about an incident. Despite the news, the Op ALERT continued at Mount Weather. Eisenhower toured the relocation site, and hosted a National Security Council meeting—but everyone's minds were on the downed U-2. Even as a CIA analyst and a Pentagon briefer provided a rundown of the Soviet missile threat inside the bunker's command center, other aides popped in with teletype updates on the U-2 situation. When the briefing wrapped up, Eisenhower asked senior officials to adjourn with him to another room, where they plotted a reaction to the shoot-down. After deciding to issue a statement through the State Department, Ike then turned back to the Op ALERT, giving a quick and inspiring closed-circuit TV speech to those at the classified location before helicoptering back to the White House. The day was wrecked; both superpowers were embarrassed and hopes for a productive summit scheduled in Paris later that month had been dashed. The event, though, had also raised questions about Mount Weather itself. Kistiakowsky recorded in his diary that the day's experience showed the bunker turned out not to be such a great place to manage an unfolding crisis. Even as large as the bunker was, it was quickly overwhelmed by the staff involved in a real emergency. Mount Weather, Kistiakowsky wrote, "is a really mammoth underground structure and is most impressive, but notwithstanding the air conditioning, the briefing room in which we had the NSC meeting was stuffy."

The 1960 readiness exercise did achieve one major secret milestone, bringing together for the first—and only—time the nine men selected to oversee the nation's private sector in an emergency. The secret program had been years in the making, drawing in a close circle of the men Eisenhower most trusted to stay calm in the midst of great chaos. The need for clear thinking and steady leadership in the face of a nuclear attack had long dogged Eisenhower's thoughts. COG plans, Eisenhower argued, must be as straightforward as possible. During a cabinet meeting, he'd reminded his department heads that nothing would go smoothly after an enemy attack, stressing that the job of government is to preserve some common sense in a situation where everyone is going crazy. "These will not be normal people— they will be scared, will be hysterical, will be absolutely nuts," he said. "This characterization will apply to department heads—to the president himself. We will be bewildered people. The plans for work at relocation centers should be drawn up on the simplest possible terms, in order to enable a man who will be beside himself with grief and apprehension about his family and his country to carry on and do something which will be of use."

Eisenhower used a series of secret draft executive orders to create an all-new structure for wartime government, rebuilt around nine departments and agencies—some had prewar analogues, but most would be entirely new. In two cases, those agencies would be headed by existing cabinet officials, but in the others the government would rely upon secret agreements with private sector leaders, the best minds Eisenhower felt he knew outside government, who would be deputized in a national emergency to become de facto industry czars. Andrew Goodpaster, the president's national security aide, recalled decades later, "He wanted to bring in the wisdom and competence to reinforce whatever elements of the government survived and provide some assurance that our government could not be decapitated."

The president's requests to join this secret shadow government had surprised those involved. CBS Television president Frank Stanton, who had become personal friends with the president, thought as he walked into the White House in the fall of 1957 that he'd been invited to commiserate over the Soviet success with Sputnik. But Eisenhower had something much bigger in mind. Instead, Eisenhower explained that he wanted Stanton to become the administrator of the Emergency National Communications

Agency, overseeing all the nation's radio, television, and other outlets, ensuring "the flow of essential national telecommunications." Stanton was stunned, but agreed. "I was surprised and startled by the breadth of the assignment," the CBS executive recalled decades later.

Over the course of the fall, Eisenhower had lined up half a dozen other private sector leaders—many of whom were also good friends—to lead his emergency government. His fishing buddy and father-in-law's financial advisor, Aksel Nielsen, was the administration's pick to lead the wartime National Housing Agency. Nielsen, a mortgage banker by trade, headed the Title Guaranty Company and would in a war coordinate "rent, housing prices, and real estate credit stabilization prices." Harold Boeschenstein, the Ohio head of Owens-Corning Fiberglass Corporation whom *Forbes* had named that year as one of the nation's top fifty business leaders, would lead a National Production Agency and administer "national policies and programs required to program, schedule, and control ... the production, manufacture, and use of raw materials." Boeschenstein, who had crossed paths with Eisenhower several times and shared a membership at New York's elite social hub for golfers, the Links Club on East 62nd Street, was well familiar with the powers of the wartime czar: He had left Owens-Corning during World War II to join the War Production Board, where he headed the Forest Products Bureau—a job that, among many other things, had put him in charge of newsprint rationing. J. Ed Warren, a longtime oil industry executive, would become the administrator of the National Energies and Minerals Agency and oversee the national policies and systems for producing and distributing all "solid fuels, petroleum, and gas."*

Frank Stanton's colleague, CBS News's Theodore Koop—the network's head of news and public affairs in Washington—was set to lead the new Office of Censorship. It was an odd position for Koop. He had served as part of the World War II government censorship agency, but by the 1950s he was a leading figure at *Face the Nation*, had just wrapped up a term as the president

---

* Warren might have been especially interested in czarlike powers: In the 1960s, when he was CEO of Cities Service—the forerunner to Citgo—he'd get in trouble for calling one person, one vote, "the single most portentous and harmful change in the course of government to occur in the past century."

of the National Press Club, and was at CBS extensively involved in delicate interviews with Soviet leaders. Yet he knew that in a national emergency he would be swept into government to work alongside the officials he covered on a daily basis—and would, with the stroke of the president's pen, become the wartime boss of all his journalism peers.

While many of Eisenhower's picks for secret shadow czars were friends, some were not politically advantageous: He appointed onetime Truman administration budget director and then president of the defense contractor General Dynamics Frank Pace Jr. to lead the National Transport Agency. Pace would exercise "control over the operation of domestic, overseas, and international" private shipping, personnel transport, the railroad system, and all nonmilitary airports. He would later resign from the theoretical position in 1959 and be replaced by the dean of the Harvard Business School, Dr. George Pierce Baker.

Eisenhower also asked his agriculture secretary, Ezra Taft Benson, to lead the National Food Agency; the chair of the Federal Reserve, a financial whiz named William McChesney Martin Jr., would head the National Stabilization Agency; and his labor secretary, James Mitchell, would lead the National Manpower Agency.

All nine men received similar secret form letters in early March 1958. As Eisenhower wrote in the letter to Pace, "In the event of an emergency, as soon as you have assured yourself, by any means at your disposal, that [your agency] has been activated, you shall immediately assume active direction of that agency and its function. This letter will constitute your authority. I have requested the Director of the Office of Defense Mobilization to communicate with you regarding any planning activities in connection with the creation of and activation of an Emergency Transport Agency." He added, "Until such time as an Emergency Transport Agency may be created, I am certain that you will treat your designation as Administrator as classified information and that you will impress upon any staff you select to assist you that their designations are to be treated similarly as classified information." Indeed, the appointments stayed secret until the end of the Cold War.

During OPAL '60, Leo Hoegh met with the secret appointees at Mount Weather and briefed them on their postwar responsibilities. Hoegh's expansive list of wartime preparations seemingly covered every aspect of post-attack government function—he'd even requested the Defense Department assign three clergy—a Protestant minister, a Jewish rabbi, and a Catholic priest—to Mount Weather to help provide spiritual care to those who would be locked inside the mountain during a nuclear war.

Now Hoegh outlined a plan for the nine men to name deputies and key staff in advance. In order to let them make arrangements and discuss possible postwar staffing, the Eisenhower administration established cover identities for their work—activating Executive Order 10660, a 1956 initiative that created a National Defense Executive Reserve, and provided training for more than 1,800 private sector leaders and corporate executives who would step into government roles during national emergencies helping to manage and run the nation's reaction to an enemy attack.

The scale of operations contemplated by this shadow government would be vast—more powerful than any government body since the establishment of the Constitution in 1789. The president, the plans said, "will take whatever actions are essential for national security and survival," even though many of the proposals seemed to exceed anything the Constitution had imagined. As just one example, Aksel Nielsen's Emergency Housing Agency would be in charge of "lodging post-attack through the allocation of control of existing housing (including billeting)," a minor parenthetical that would, in practice, likely violate the Third Amendment, which prohibited private military housing placement. Meanwhile, William Martin's Stabilization Agency would sweep up employees from the Departments of Agriculture, Commerce, Interior, and Labor, as well as the Housing and Home Finance Agency and parts of the Office of Defense Mobilization, and have broad-ranging power to control prices, rents, wages, and salaries. The Emergency Food Agency would have vast powers to dictate the production and distribution of foodstuffs, and the Emergency Transport Agency would effectively seize control of all the nation's merchant vessel fleet and all of the nation's highways—dictating who could drive on what roads when. It would also impound all airplanes of potential enemies that were at U.S. airports. Many plans were shockingly broad. "Commercial stocks in the hands of retailers will automatically be available to local governments to supplement local stockpiles," one section read.

Altogether, the government's outline for the "post-attack environment," known as "Plan D-Minus"—a reference to the plans created before an attack, which were known as D-Day in military parlance—stretched to hundreds of printed pages. It was so long that the document's forty-first annex was merely a fifteen-page index listing the major components of the previous forty annexes. Going into an emergency, the president could draw from at least forty-three prewritten directives and executive orders to reorganize the government along the proposed emergency lines, designating certain duties to each. "The National Plan is a statement of principles, responsibilities, re-quirements and broad courses of action," its introduction read. "While other documents concerning civil defense and defense mobilization will be issued as necessary, each will be subordinate to and compatible with this Plan." While primarily focused on a "general war" scenario, Plan D-Minus also included lesser mobilizations and policies for implementation both during increased international tensions and limited nonnuclear war. The govern-ment readied more than a dozen "Emergency Preparedness Orders" that de-lineated various departments' and agencies' responsibilities for a post-attack environment. In wartime, the Department of Labor would be primarily con-verted to a Stabilization Agency, focused on implementing a salary and wage stabilization system for wartime and the post-attack environment. The plans also called for at least two years of government "economic stabilization" pro-grams to ensure plenty of time for the private sector to rebuild following an attack. Nearly every industry would be pressed into service: The government identified 1,200 private aircraft that it designated the "National Emergency Air Fleet" to help meet the military's wartime transport needs. The trucking industry deputized three representatives who would be sworn into service as the nation's chief of operations, chief of administration, and chief of special staff of the emergency "Highway Transport Division" to help coordinate the nation's 10 million commercial vehicles in an attack. Meanwhile, the Emer-gency Housing Agency would, according to the plans of the Eisenhower era, be run through eight regional offices and forty-five branch offices set up around the country.

Yet just how legal any of these actions would have been was entirely unclear. Harry Truman had tried in 1952 to nationalize the steel industry when the United Steelworkers went out on strike over wages. During the standoff, Truman issued Executive Order 10340 and announced during a national address that he had ordered Commerce Secretary Charles Sawyer to seize the steel mills and continue running them with the existing workers and management, citing the national emergency of the Korean War. The industry immediately fought back, sending lawyers to the house of a federal judge in the middle of the night to ask for a restraining order. The case, known as *Youngstown Sheet & Tube Co. v. Sawyer*, quickly worked its way through the legal system to the Supreme Court, which ruled against the president in a 6–3 decision, stating that he lacked the power to seize private property during a national emergency unless Congress or the Constitution specifically authorized it. The Court, though, was badly divided—all six of the majority justices authored their own opinions, each laying out their own theories of what emergency powers the president did or did not possess. They all agreed it was hardly a clear-cut case. And it was hard to ignore the fact that the seizure stemmed from a national emergency invoked because of an unpopular war far from America's shores. Would the Supreme Court feel the same way about the presidential response to a devastating nuclear attack on the homeland? Would anyone even be able to find the Supreme Court in the North Carolina mountains to ask?

As Eisenhower's presidency came to a close, he received from the nation's defense leaders in November 1960 the nation's first Single Integrated Operational Plan (SIOP), uniting the targeting of the Navy and the Air Force. Fifteen years earlier, in late 1946, Eisenhower had told colleagues that the half dozen nuclear weapons in the U.S. stockpile represented "enough to win a war," and as late as 1956, Eisenhower hadn't believed the U.S. would ever need more than 150 "well-targeted" missiles. SAC's list of intended targets swelled to more than 20,000 sites and facilities, as aerial reconnaissance improved knowledge of the Soviet interior. In just the final two years of his presidency, Eisenhower watched the nuclear stockpile triple from 6,000 weapons to 18,000. That first SIOP, which enshrined in U.S. war planning the principle of "massive retaliation," called for bombing 1,050 "Designated Ground Zeros" at some 2,600 separate installations. Even a "Bolt Out of the Blue" (BOOB) Soviet attack would still allow all of the nation's alert aircraft and missiles to launch a devastating 1,400 weapons. The presentation, Eisenhower later told an aide, "frighten[ed] the devil out of me."

When Eisenhower's science advisor reviewed SIOP, his team was shocked by the overkill: One Soviet city roughly analogous to Hiroshima in size and military value was due to be hit by four separate nuclear attacks—a total of seven million tons of TNT. Hiroshima had been almost entirely annihilated by Little Boy's comparatively tiny 13,000.

With the clock running out on his presidency, Eisenhower handed the unedited plan, known as SIOP-60, over to the new administration. In his farewell address, Eisenhower argued against the emerging "military-industrial complex," saying that the nation's defense industry had too much power. The nation could ill afford to invest its precious resources in more war. His speech was forlorn, but proud. "As one who has witnessed the horror and the lingering sadness of war—as one who knows that another war could utterly destroy this civilization which has been so slowly and painfully built over thousands of years—I wish I could say tonight that a lasting peace is in sight. Happily, I can say that war has been avoided," he said.

By then, nuclear weapons had already affected every human on the planet. A 1959 Consumers Union study, *The Milk We Drink*, found that levels of strontium-90, fallout from atmospheric testing, were rising in America's milk. While the radioactive element was below "danger" levels, the magazine concluded, "This report cannot be ended with a clear recommendation. None exists. No doubt the Best Buy is milk without strontium-90, air without fallout, and adequate medical care without diagnostic x-rays. But none of these solutions are to be had."

This—and so many other aspects of the Cold War—would all be John F. Kennedy's problem now. He would inherit a world far more dangerous than the one that Truman had handed off to Ike. And to make Kennedy's new responsibility clear, Eisenhower arranged for a special little demonstration.

Chapter 7

THE NEW FRONTIER

The two men met at the White House on January 19, 1961, just hours before the transfer of power. As the president-elect, Kennedy, later recalled, "The President was at his desk looking very fit, pink-cheeked and unharrassed." That innocent appearance belied Eisenhower's purpose for the meeting; over the forty-five minutes that followed, he stressed the life-and-death power Kennedy was poised to inherit. They discussed at length the Emergency Action Plans, the loose-leaf notebooks and laminated cards that were never more than a few steps from the president inside a briefcase carried by a military aide. He was "an unobtrusive man," Eisenhower explained, "who would shadow the President for all of his days in office." The next morning, Eisenhower went on, then-president Kennedy would become part of the National Command Authorities and be given a wallet-sized laminated card containing secret codes to identify him to people in the military chain of command. Those codes, once successfully authenticated, would allow Kennedy to access and order different nuclear strikes.

Eisenhower handed Kennedy "Federal Emergency Plan D-Minus," walking through the post-attack options for the government, laying out who was authorized to live and who would be left to die, which governmental functions should continue to exist and which would be thrown by the wayside. Like every document in the emergency briefcase, Eisenhower had carefully read over and initialed it for the record. The copy Eisenhower presented to Kennedy, though, had a blank signature line where the new president would have to sign it the next day, agreeing to the government's Doomsday plans.

An unfolding nuclear emergency, Eisenhower cautioned, would require "immediate, split-second decisions." SIOP-60 consisted of sixteen graduated "options," depending on how much time the military had to prepare for a strike. Attacking only with the alert force, ready at a moment's notice with 1,447 weapons, was Option #1; it would take twenty-eight hours to "generate" the entire strategic force, totaling 3,423 weapons, which represented Option #16. The full-scale attacks, the Pentagon estimated, would kill 54 percent of the Soviet population and destroy four out of every five buildings in the nation. Those higher-numbered options, though, would include visible readiness steps that would tip off the Soviets of a looming attack. The president's main choice would be how to balance a more devastating attack against the potential of receiving an equally devastating attack on the United States.

Soon, Ike arrived at the grand finale—a demonstration for the soon-to-be commander-in-chief. He picked up the Oval Office phone and commanded, "OPAL Drill Three." Within minutes, a Marine helicopter thundered onto the White House lawn, ready to evacuate the president. After one of Eisenhower's naval aides boarded the helicopter, it immediately took off. In the event of a real emergency, the helicopter would have continued on to one of the Presidential Emergency Sites that Kennedy was learning about for the first time that day. Kennedy never forgot the impression the drill made, later calling it "chilling." This was a nation prepped for its own destruction.

As they wrapped up, Eisenhower offered a final warning to his succesor, "Only the tough problems get to you."*

In the early 1960s, the combination of Soviet bluster (Khrushchev had bragged his factories were turning out 250 ICBMs a year) and the Pentagon's

---

* Eisenhower, purposely or not, didn't share all the government's secrets that day: A year after Op ALERT '60 and four months after taking office, the Kennedy administration was surprised to discover the existence of the czar system Eisenhower had created. Kennedy was eager to shut it down, but wanted to wait until he had something ready to replace it with. In the end, it seems, Kennedy terminated the program without any analogous efforts of his own.

tendency to use worst-case scenarios had given the public appearance that the U.S. was far behind in the missile race. However, Kennedy, who had campaigned strongly on the "Missile Gap" issue, soon discovered as president that the Soviet Union didn't have the 500 missiles feared—it didn't even have one percent of that total. It had exactly four intercontinental missiles.

For the new defense secretary, Robert McNamara, the lack of a "Missile Gap" was just one of all too many eye-popping things he learned in his first months at the Pentagon. At just forty-four, he was a year older than President Kennedy and the youngest man to lead the Defense Department. An unexpected choice for the job, McNamara—a businessman known for his shrewd thinking and drive for efficiency—was barely a month into his new job as the head of Ford Motor Company when Kennedy summoned him to Georgetown after the election. McNamara's Lincoln Continental had idled at the curb outside Kennedy's house, its high-tech radio car phone keeping an open line to the Ford offices in Washington, which, in turn, had a long-distance line open to McNamara's wife in Ann Arbor to relay the news of the job offer. When McNamara took office in 1961, his official Pentagon limousine had an even more advanced car phone: He was one of fifty-six top government officials who had a special line connected directly to Mount Weather and Raven Rock. Beyond that technological flourish, though, McNamara didn't think much of the bureaucratic systems and mostly antiquated processes he inherited. "It didn't take me long, once we got in here, to find out the deficiency or bankruptcy in both strategic policy and in the force structure," he recalled later.

During his first week on the job, McNamara sat down with the Pentagon's Weapons Systems Evaluation Group (WSEG), which had just completed an intensive study, known as WSEG Report #50, that found that a Soviet surprise attack on only five locations—the White House, the Pentagon, Camp David, Raven Rock, and Mount Weather—would likely destroy all of the nation's command structure. Even simply hitting the first two would likely wipe out the military command structure, since Raven Rock and Mount Weather weren't normally manned with senior personnel. "Both the Presidential and the SecDef-JCS levels of command are presently subject to operational incapacitation by the same events," the report explained.

Hitting all the nation's major military commands and leadership sites would involve attacking just fourteen installations—a devastating blow that would require just thirty-five Soviet ICBMs, while providing a 90 percent probability of "destroying the entire higher political-military command of strategic nuclear forces." Such an attack would leave almost the entire nation, nearly all of its major cities, and the entire military apparatus intact—but without anyone left to guide it, no one to give orders, and no one left to negotiate with the Soviets.

WSEG found the broader COG system severely lacking—most members of the presidential line of succession had only a telephone number at the Pentagon that they were supposed to call in an emergency. Setting aside the chaos that would ensue if the Pentagon was destroyed and that sole telephone line was inoperable, there were no comprehensive or organized ways to tell who had survived an attack and who hadn't. The system left the Navy captain, Air Force major, or whoever happened to be on duty answering the phone in the Pentagon's Joint War Room to choose the presidential successor. "A judgment [would] be made by the senior officer on duty in the JWR as to when he has in fact received a communication from the senior non-incapacitated member of the list," the report explained. "The possibility exists that the man to wield Presidential authority in dire emergency might in fact be selected by a single field grade military officer."

Moreover, COG and COOP procedures that had made sense for the bomber age, when the nation would likely have three to seven hours of warning before an attack unfolded, needed to be updated for an era when the nation might have as little as two minutes (fifteen at maximum) before missiles began to strike the continental United States. To solve this problem, the WSEG report recommended expanding mobile command outposts like ships or trains, rather than simply relying on fixed underground bunkers.

McNamara was terrified by what he heard. "The chain of command from the President down to our strategic and defensive weapon systems is highly vulnerable in almost every link," he reported to Kennedy. Under their command, the military moved quickly to rectify the most obvious shortcomings. McNamara met with the WSEG on a Friday afternoon; within a week, SAC launched its first twenty-four-hour airborne command post, code-named LOOKING GLASS, ensuring that there would always be one senior military leader in the National Command Authorities who could order a retaliatory strike. He and Kennedy pushed quickly to boost SAC's readiness, increase the number of Minuteman missiles, and grow the Polaris submarine fleet, which brought a new capability to the nuclear arsenal—the stealthy subs couldn't be easily tracked by the weak Soviet navy. Submarines, which could hide beneath nearly 70 percent of the earth's surface, could strike at any time since, unlike land-based bombers and ICBMs, they didn't need to be deployed in an opening salvo or potentially lost forever. They were the perfect weapons for a more nuanced, flexible nuclear strategy.

As the spring unfolded, the Kennedy administration struggled with a Cold War that seemed to only grow darker, a struggle in which the U.S. seemed constantly off-balance. On April 12, 1961, cosmonaut Yuri Gagarin became the first human to journey into outer space and orbit the earth. Not even a week later, a CIA-trained and -backed force of Cuban émigrés invaded their native Caribbean island at the Bay of Pigs in an operation marred by poor planning, poor execution, and poor intelligence. With few reinforcements and without U.S. air cover for their invasion, the émigrés were quickly trapped by Cuban dictator Fidel Castro's forces and hunted down. Over the next two weeks, two U.S. rockets—part of the next major test of the Mercury project meant to catch up to the Soviet lead in space— blew up just seconds after takeoff. While it appeared the U.S. couldn't do anything right, the irony was that militarily, by the spring of 1961, the nation had never been stronger. Its successes were secret, the failures all too public.

The rise of Soviet ICBMs and escalating world tensions brought new life to Raven Rock in the Catoctin Mountains, too. In March, the facility switched to running the watch staff twenty-four hours, seven days a week, to help guard against the chance of a sneak missile attack on Washington. The round-the-clock operations would continue for thirty years. Of course, even the fifteen-minute ICBM warning time was academic at best, as it implied a Soviet attack would come from missiles. As the Kennedy administration quickly learned, the U.S. war planning suggested that they were much more likely to try sabotage or a sneak attack, for which the nation was ill-prepared.

Ever since the Truman administration, official U.S. war plans assumed that the Soviets would begin a nuclear exchange by exploding smuggled nuclear weapons inside their Washington, D.C., embassy and their U.N. mission in New York—thus ensuring that the opening salvo came without any warning whatsoever. In the early 1950s, the FBI had searched frantically for a nuclear weapon that a Brazilian informant told them had already been smuggled into one of the Soviet-bloc U.N. consulates in New York. They never found it—but that didn't mean it didn't exist.

Several months into his presidency, John F. Kennedy invited journalist Hugh Sidey to dinner in Palm Beach. After they enjoyed daiquiris on the patio while listening to Frank Sinatra records, Kennedy vented during dinner about his early dealings with Khrushchev and the Soviet leader's anger over West Berlin. Sidey tried to leaven the evening by comparing free Berlin to the Soviet embassy on 16th Street NW, saying, "We have a bustling communist enclave just four blocks from the White House."

Kennedy paused, fork between plate and mouth, and told Sidey, "You know, they have an atom bomb on the third floor of the embassy."

Sidey brushed off the remark, "Sure, why not?"

No, really, Kennedy replied. The president told Sidey that U.S. intelligence believed the Soviets had smuggled atomic bomb components into Washington using diplomatic pouches and assembled it in the embassy's attic. "If things get too bad and war is inevitable," he said, "they will set it off and that's the end of the White House and the rest of the city."

Sidey laughed, still not believing such a fantastic rumor. Kennedy replied, "That's what I'm told. Do you know something that I don't?"

The first time John F. Kennedy visited Camp David, it was out of political necessity, not for recreation. In fact, the Kennedys never thought they'd grow to like Camp David, as they already had plenty of vacation homes of their own, in Hyannis, Palm Beach, and the Virginia countryside. As Hugh Sidey wrote, the first family were "a branch of the jet set, people of means and inclination who roamed the world's resorts by plane more easily than the financial lords of the East Coast used to go to Newport around the turn of the century." Even before the inauguration, the wealthy clan had rented Glen Ora, a Virginia horse country estate near Middleburg, where the White House Communications Agency also installed massive communications equipment. It wasn't until the failed Bay of Pigs invasion that Kennedy traveled north to the traditional presidential retreat to confer with his predecessor, who helicoptered over from the Gettysburg Farm where he was enjoying his retirement.

The two presidents talked over lunch at the Aspen Lodge, where Kennedy outlined how badly off-course the invasion had gone, and then they walked the camp's grounds. "No one knows how tough this job is until after he has been in it a few months," Kennedy said, hoping for sympathy. He got none from Eisenhower—neither the president who had held the Cold War at peace for eight years, nor the general who had led successfully the largest amphibious invasion in world history would commiserate with the young leader.

Kennedy had gotten bad advice through the Bay of Pigs crisis and understood little about how to get thoughtful assessments from advisors. Eisenhower schooled him, cutting him off repeatedly during their long conversations, and chastising his terrible decision making. It was, Kennedy biographer Richard Reeves later wrote, "the tongue-lashing of his life." Over the course of their afternoon together, Eisenhower thought the new president—whom he'd never much respected—seemed "very subdued and more than a little bewildered." Yet the stern lecture was much appreciated by Kennedy, who needed tough advice from one of the few other people who understood the burdens of the presidency.

After Eisenhower left, Kennedy toured the bomb shelter under Aspen Lodge. Looking around the small space for the first time, it was hard to contemplate that if the Cold War continued to heat up or if in the next crisis Kennedy again miscalculated or received more bad advice, this would be one of the options for where he and a small group of aides could sit out the nuclear exchange.

Kennedy's gratitude for Eisenhower's advice that day shaped an important decision press secretary Pierre Salinger announced two days later. Ike had always assumed that, like the presidential yacht and airplane, the Catoctin retreat would be renamed by each successive president. At Naval Support Facility Thurmont, the "Camp David" sign had been taken down as Ike left office, and it was again referred to in government documents as Camp #3. In the early months of the Kennedy administration, the White House yacht had been renamed from Eisenhower's *Barbara Ann*, after his granddaughter, to Kennedy's *Honey Fitz*, the nickname for Kennedy's grandfather. Would

Catoctin be rechristened "Camp Caroline"? But the Kennedys realized that the presidential camp's name had become something of a public brand, and Kennedy was inclined to show his predecessor some respect.

And so, Salinger announced on April 24 that the retreat would have a permanent name: Camp David.

McNamara tasked retired Air Force General Earle Partridge with studying the country's command and control systems, a job made all the more urgent that summer as tensions mounted in Berlin. The general recommended tying together the existing bunkers and command facilities into a more unified structure, reporting clearly through to the president under a new process called the National Military Command System, headquartered at a new National Military Command Center at the Pentagon, which would replace the existing antiquated Joint War Room. Partridge also recommended that SITE R, the Raven Rock bunker, be officially designated the Alternate National Military Command Center (ANMCC), and that Project 425L, a new military bunker then under construction in the Colorado mountains for the military's North American Aerospace Defense Command (NORAD), be designated as the center of the continental defense efforts. As one Air Force historian would write, "If NORAD and its sensors were the body's eyes and ears, if SAC were its muscles and fists, the new command system would constitute its brain and central nervous system."

The White House Army Signal Corps maintained permanent detachments at Raven Rock, Mount Weather, and Camp David to ensure communications were always ready if the president had to evacuate. At the time, the nearby NATO relocation facility employed 47 people full-time, Raven Rock and Fort Ritchie had a staff of 527, and Mount Weather a staff of 329; altogether, the government was spending nearly $2 million a month just to keep the two facilities staffed and ready.

All told, the national military system possessed at the time something akin to bunker fever. According to a partially declassified memo buried in the National Archives, there were fifty-eight federal relocation sites scattered around the "arc" for civilian agencies by the end of the Eisenhower administration, not counting those like Raven Rock that were purposely built for the military.

While most of the government's hardened facilities were within the "relocation arc," bunkers sprouted almost anywhere there was part of the vast military web. The Pentagon maintained dozens of other specific relocation facilities for various agencies and units, including a backup facility for the Navy at Patuxent River, Maryland, a relocation site for the Air Force's Office of Special Investigations at Maxwell Air Force Base in Alabama, and another for the Office of Naval Intelligence in Princeton, New Jersey.

Strategic Air Command maintained its own series of locations, like "the Notch" in Hadley, Massachusetts. Built in 1958 into the side of Bare Mountain in the Holyoke range, SAC's two-story, 40,000-square-foot bunker would have served as the alternate command post for the Eighth Air Force, based five miles away at Westover Air Force Base. A key link in what the military called the Post-Attack Command and Control System (PACCS), the Notch could have supported, if needed, 135 personnel for a month, with seventy-five pre-positioned cots, some surplus World War II rations, and five water wells.

OCDM had also begun burying its regional command centers—the first project being in Denton, Texas. Each region had competed for that first bunker, but then director Leo Hoegh had been impressed by the efforts of local Denton businessmen to raise $25,000 to purchase and donate the necessary land near Loop 288. In 1959, Hoegh had guaranteed Welcome Wilson, the regional director, that his would be the first project built if Wilson could get Senate Majority Leader Lyndon Johnson, Speaker of the House Sam Rayburn, and House appropriations chair Albert Thomas to all call Hoegh within an hour. Wilson scrambled to contact all three of the powerful Texas legislators. "[Hoegh] was convinced Congress would not appropriate the money," Wilson said years later. "He felt like if he got them to call him and say they supported it, he could get the money to build it. So I got on the phone." All three men indeed called Hoegh—and the Denton facility moved forward.

When it finally opened, behind schedule and over budget, the twenty-acre, $2.7 million Federal Regional Center—which could have overseen emergency operations in Arkansas, Louisiana, New Mexico, Oklahoma, and Texas—included a 50,000-square-foot, two-level underground bunker that could support several hundred officials for thirty days, with its own

1,250-foot-deep well, laundry facilities, diesel generators, and thirteen-ton blast doors. The facility kitchen could serve 1,500 meals a day and its walk-in freezers would double as the facility's morgue; on ground level, three white cones marked special, shielded antennas meant to be raised post-attack if the facility's main communications links were destroyed. Altogether, it was a big step up from the previous relocation facility, inside Breckenridge Hall at the nearby Texas Women's University.

Similar Federal Regional Center facilities would follow in Maynard, Massachusetts; Thomasville, Georgia; Bothell, Washington; and Denver, Colorado. The centers also included duplicate copies of vital records, to help affected agencies maintain Continuity of Operations. Any of the facilities could be used by the president or other high-ranking government leaders if they happened to be caught nearby during an attack, and they had broad-cast booths ready to connect to the nation's Emergency Broadcast System. The bunkers, as advanced as they were at the time, were still austere and cramped—those who participated in drills didn't think much of the idea of being locked inside with 300 others for a month. "We'd be killing each other in a few days," said Millard Ireland, who helped run the Bothell Federal Regional Center. "That's my personal opinion."

Five states had by then also established protected command centers, and nineteen states had plans to do so by 1962. Even local governments began setting up protected emergency operations centers, so many that it maxed out a federal matching fund program meant to encourage such facilities. Portland, Oregon, built a $670,000 bunker on top of Kelly Butte, about six and a half miles east of downtown. The nearly 20,000-square-foot facil-ity, its main operations center framed by both the U.S. and Oregon State flags, could house 250 people for two weeks and was staffed full-time by seven workers. Buried under as much as thirty feet of dirt and protected by a twenty-six-inch reinforced-concrete roof, it held more than three million city documents backed up on microfilm and had a small cafeteria, radio transmission tower, living quarters, and generators.

Private corporations got into the mountain bunker craze, too. AT&T, whose communication networks were so key to the U.S. government, built an underground facility in Netcong, New Jersey, complete with steel gray desks carefully arranged in descending size by an executive's rank—the nameplates on each desk were always kept up-to-date. In 1951, businessman Herman Knaust started the Iron Mountain Atomic Storage Company—a series of underground vaults created inside an old iron mine outside Hudson, New York. For years, Knaust had been running the mine as an underground mushroom farm, but shifted focus when he recognized the business opportunities of the Cold War. "If an atom bomb burst right on top of us, it wouldn't even make a Geiger counter flicker here in the vaults," Knaust said. Under heavy security, the retrofitted mine became hugely successful, a repository for valuable artworks, corporate archives, and even, in wartime, the executives themselves. Companies like General Electric and IBM turned to it for records storage, while others, like Standard Oil and Shell Oil, actually built full-on emergency dormitories for their staff to shelter in during a war. The magazine *The Nation* called it a "20th Century Noah's Ark" for thousands of specially selected Wall Street employees. Part of the motivation was self-interest. During early readiness exercises, conducted in conjunction with government officials, Standard Oil management balked at the idea of their company being nationalized during a disaster, and the executives believed they would have a better chance at preserving private ownership of their company if they could demonstrate the seriousness of their war preparations.

"They had motels there, really," recalled Mary Howell, who lived nearby. "Some had food stored there for months, if not years. One company had their setup on seven different levels so people would get exercise going up and down" while trapped there during a nuclear holocaust. One wealthy woman moved her art collection into the Iron Mountain mine and hosted wine and cheese parties inside her vault for visitors to admire the priceless collection.

A similar facility was constructed 225 miles outside Kansas City, in an old salt mine near Hutchinson, Kansas, that included emergency space for the Kansas City Federal Reserve Bank and was stocked daily with microfilm backups of key records. Other companies struck out on their own: Westinghouse Electric, based in Pittsburgh, kept its own relocation facility in an old limestone mine. Standard Oil of New Jersey, the forerunner of Exxon, updated its corporate bylaws to include special rules to govern how the board of directors could respond to "an attack on the United States or any nuclear or atomic disaster."

There were so many underground projects going on nationwide that it was sometimes hard to keep track. On a Sunday morning in March 1961, amateur cave explorers from the Huntsville, Alabama, "Grotto" of the National Speleological Society hiked out to the historic Sauta Cave, a vast underground cavern known to house hundreds of thousands of bats. At the end of their hike, they were surprised to find not tranquil solitude but a detachment of soldiers, bulldozers, and earth-moving equipment: A National Guard battalion was converting the cave into a government shelter—digging roads, erecting lighting, and stringing water lines.

In an emergency, the Washington sky would be filled with evacuation helicopters swooping down into predesignated evacuation landing zones—the grounds of the Naval Observatory, the American University track and soccer field, the round ellipse of grass at the end of the Memorial Bridge in Virginia, the Pentagon's helipads, the South Lawn of the White House, the parking lot of D.C. Stadium, the CIA's landing pad in Langley, and other locations. For Vice President Johnson alone, the military had designated nineteen possible evacuation points across the city—any one of which the Secret Service could order a helicopter into at a moment's notice. Each seat on each helicopter had been carefully allocated. The Justice Department's war plans called for the attorney general, escorted by FBI agents, and his deputy to be evacuated to Mount Weather aboard two three-seat helicopters, which would land at 7th Street and Madison Avenue NW, on the edge of the National Mall near the department headquarters. Alternatively, if helicopters were unable to fly, officials could take an Immigration and Naturalization Service boat across the Potomac to Virginia to pick up ground transportation on that side. At Mount Weather, the Justice Department officials would be joined by FBI director J. Edgar Hoover, who didn't want to fly on the helicopters. Instead, his limousines had been furnished with roadmaps to Mount Weather, Raven Rock, and the department's relocation facility in Martinsburg, West Virginia.

Beyond the people at the top of the department hierarchy, though, departments had carefully thought through a much broader list of who would be evacuated. FBI agents were also responsible for evacuating the attorney general's family to a "safe place," although the cabinet member's family wasn't to be afforded space in an official relocation site. The families of Justice Department leaders would be evacuated to the Shenandoah Hotel in Martinsburg, while "non-essential" staffers and their families would take over the George Washington Hotel in nearby Winchester, Virginia. The ownership and staff of each of the hotels selected had been discreetly investigated by the FBI and found to be both patriotic and clean of criminal records and foreign ties.

Meanwhile "essential" operations staff would report to the Justice Department's own relocation site, set up in the federal courthouse and post office in Martinsburg, West Virginia. The Martinsburg location had been the department's third choice—it had initially preferred a site near Charlottesville, where it could access a good law library at the University of Virginia—but after much bureaucratic wrangling, it was assigned the top floors of a turreted red-brick Roman Revival building, a very Norman Rockwell–esque place in which to sit out a nuclear war. The White House Army Signal Corps, which was responsible for communications between relocation facilities, pre-positioned two Army tractor-trailers full of radio equipment at the Veterans Administration hospital in Martinsburg to support the DOJ and FBI facilities.*

Through the 1950s, the FBI had maintained its own relocation site on the grounds of Shepherd University, close to the Justice Department one in Martinsburg, but by the Kennedy era the FBI's executive team was supposed to report to the bureau's relocation site near the Marine Corps base at Quantico, about forty miles south of the capital. It'd be just one of a number of agencies swarming that base, which had become a critical component of the government's relocation arc. Quantico also served as an "Emergency Evacuation Transfer Point" for high-level officials and a "Joint Regrouping Point" for Defense Department personnel; a Marine Battalion Landing Team, too, stood ready there for emergency deployment. The FBI had held on to the Shepherdstown facility, though, as a relocation site for the Washington Field Office—each FBI field office across the nation also had its own designated relocation facilities.

---

* The hospital itself had been DOJ's second choice for a relocation facility, after Charlottesville, but department lawyers rejected it because using a hospital for wartime functions would violate the Geneva Conventions.

Relocation planning was logistics-intensive. In an era long before computerized records, the bureau also had to arrange to move thousands of files on FBI informants as well as those on suspected subversives and spies to the relocation sites, as well as to stockpile the necessary stationery and office supplies for emergency operations. Unsurprisingly, the plans weren't free of bureaucratic turf battles: At the relocation site, the INS commissioner would not be allowed to use the FBI radio system and would have to figure out his own communications plan.*

The State Department, meanwhile, fretted that whereas the Pentagon could evacuate senior leaders by helicopter from its own helipads, the secretary of state and selected undersecretaries were supposed to cross more than a mile of downtown Washington to be evacuated by helicopter from near the White House. "This may well prove to be the weakest part of the whole scheme," the department's emergency planner wrote.† The State Department's relocation planning was particularly shaky; its only major domestic staff outside the capital were in New York at the United Nations—and the international body was uniquely and purposely unprepared, lacking any fallout shelters or relocation sites. "The U.N. being a peace organization has absolutely no plans for an emergency resulting from a nuclear attack or even traditional hostilities," the State Department reported. The United Nations even denied local New York civil defense planners the chance to survey the complex for fallout shelters.

The CIA, meanwhile, settled on the Warrenton Training Center as a relocation site, a natural choice as the surrounding area had grown into a key military and intelligence hub. During World War II, the Army's Signals Intelligence Service built a 700-acre facility named Vint Hill Farms Station and brought thousands of intelligence officers to the area to man one of the country's most important secret listening posts. The Department of the Interior constructed a bomb shelter on the grounds of Storer College

---

* Who exactly could order a relocation was also a point of contention. The bureau's plans relied upon a declaration by the president, whereas DOJ's relied upon a declaration of a "yellow alert" by the military.

† The State Department's solution involved reinforcing the roof at Foggy Bottom to allow a helicopter to land directly on top, though its desire to have a helicopter permanently stationed on the roof never got off the ground.

in Harpers Ferry, West Virginia, a historically black college that, after the college went out of business, was later turned into a training center for the National Park Service. The Agriculture Department also went through several cycles of relocation planning—basing its emergency operations at the Beef Cattle Research Station in Front Royal, Virginia, where the State Department had located its emergency facility, before switching to Beltsville, Maryland. Later, that suburb proved too close to D.C. to escape damage, so it was finally assigned six counties in Pennsylvania near Penn State University, where Milton Eisenhower—Ike's brother—was president and the USDA had strong relationships at nearby universities like Shippensburg State Teachers College and Dickinson College.

Across the government, the scale of relocation planning varied widely. For the Bureau of Labor Statistics, set to relocate to the Hampden-Sydney College in southern Virginia, about 180 miles from the capital, the prep work involved outfitting each classroom with telephone jacks, and pre-positioning large metal desks, filing cabinets, and boxes of letterhead in the basement of the newly constructed Johns Auditorium. For the U.S. Information Agency, created by Eisenhower in 1953 to help spread the nation's message of freedom to other parts of the world through the Voice of America network, it was a much more extensive project.

USIA initially set up its relocation facility in Greenville, North Carolina, at East Carolina Teachers College (now East Carolina University), a location that avoided the northern auroral zone that interfered with radio waves but was close enough to Washington to minimize transmission costs. It built two radio studios, a command post, and a stockpile on the top floor of one of the school's buildings, Austin Hall, paying the campus $5,000 a year in rent for what school officials obliquely referred to as its "summer maneuvers," and retrofitted the campus radio station with its own transmitters, sharing the facility during peacetime with the student-run WWWS, 91.3 FM.

During Operation ALERT drills, USIA practiced broadcasting from Austin Hall. In 1956, a year after the site was first set up, Voice of America ran its Polish and Czech broadcasts from the heart of North Carolina's Tidewater region, listeners overseas none the wiser that they were part of a Continuity of Government experiment. Over the following years, USIA gradually expanded its facilities—eventually proposing to the college trustees that it build at government expense a 12,510-square-foot building on campus, which would be used by the college ten months of the year and be given over to USIA for the two summer months when Operation ALERT drills occurred.*

Greenville became the hub where USIA built its major East Coast broadcasting facility, an incredible 6,000-acre half-billion-wattage site that was the world's largest radio broadcasting facility. Split between two different locations outside the city, the transmitters could reach as far north as Greenland, as east as Sweden, Poland, Italy, Libya, and Mali, and south toward nearly all of Central and South America. The site had nearly thirty miles of private roads and its own fire department. Staffed with a small contingent under normal circumstances, the facility would see nearly 400 personnel flood down from Washington beginning at DEFCON 3, including a large contingent of English, Russian, and Chinese language experts. USIA also established a local executive and operational reserve of ninety-eight people—including East Carolina president John Messick, Columbia Journalism School dean Ed Barrett, and former ABC News anchor Leo Cherne—who could step in to run the agency if Washington and its leadership was destroyed.

The wide network of relocation sites and bunkers continued north of the border as well, where Canada, a NATO ally and NORAD partner, integrated its own defenses with the U.S. The secret Canadian Central Emergency Government Headquarters, known colloquially as the "Diefenbunker," after Prime Minister John Diefenbaker, had been built beginning in 1959, buried seventy-five feet underground about thirty-five minutes west of Ottawa. Known as CFS (Canadian Forces Station) Carp, the $22 million facility operated under the cover of an innocuous communications base. Next to a small parking lot in Carp, behind barbed wire fences, a small tin shed and a series of antennas were all that appeared aboveground. One of the only hints of its special function was the unit's crest, dominated by the three-headed dog Cerberus, who according to legend guarded the entrance to the underworld. The shed led down a long pedestrian tunnel into

---

*To hide the true purpose of the new building, known as Project 4PR, the Office of Defense Mobilization had the Housing and Home Finance Agency loan the college the money, then pay it back over a ten-year "lease" to the government.

a 100,000-square-foot facility that could hold 535 people, including the prime minister, the governor general, and other cabinet ministers, the Royal Canadian Mounted Police, and other agencies.* An attached vault for the Bank of Canada would store the nation's gold reserves, and a medical unit included an operating room. A fully equipped CBC radio station held the capability to broadcast to a nervous nation, as well as radio turntables and a stocked library of vinyl records to ensure that even after Armageddon the nation could hear broadcasts of jazz favorites like Duke Ellington's "In a Sentimental Mood" and the Wayne King Orchestra's "Melody of Love." The facility, staffed twenty-four hours a day for the following three decades, had a peacetime workforce of around 100 personnel, many of whom lived in the bunker full-time.

The Diefenbunker represented merely one link in Canada's own COG machinery, which included nearly fifty bunkers nationwide and six Regional Emergency Government Headquarters facilities in British Columbia, Alberta, Manitoba, Ontario, Quebec, and Nova Scotia. While the Diefenbunker was critical for the national government, Canada's most important link for continental defense efforts was still under construction in Ontario, 200 miles northeast. That site, Canadian Forces Station North Bay, opened on October 1, 1963, a $50 million project largely paid for by the U.S. government. The three-story military command center—which would serve as the backup to the NORAD complex in Cheyenne Mountain, Colorado, and would be staffed by 400 personnel in an emergency—was buried nearly 600 feet underground, nestled inside the two-billion-year-old granite of the Canadian Shield, and accessible only through mile-long tunnels at both ends of the facility.

As prepared as North America might have seemed, Europe was another matter. As Kennedy weathered a tense and difficult summer and Berliners saw the arrival of a wall dividing their city, the continent's security forces appeared an easy target. In 1954, NATO had built its own underground command center, Air Defense Operations Center—Kindsbach, inside an old Nazi mountain bunker outside Ramstein Air Force Base in southwestern Germany. The "Kindsbach Cave" had once served as Germany's western front command headquarters before it eventually became an integral link in

* As in the U.S., spouses and families weren't included in Canada's evacuation plans.

NATO's command system. Yet the relatively tiny 37,000-square-foot, sixty-seven-room bunker buried in the side of a well-known hill—and all the rest of NATO's command system—could have been destroyed by basic conventional weapons with less than ten minutes of warning, leaving Europe isolated from political and military leaders back in the United States. Britain, for its part, seemed better prepared with its emergency relocation site, code-named BURLINGTON and built in 1961 within a sprawling network of old limestone quarry tunnels just outside Corsham, 100 miles due west of London. Known also as Site 3, the massive thirty-five-acre site could have housed as many as 4,000 government workers and had a special suite for the prime minister with whitewashed walls, a BBC studio, and boxes of tea sets, ready to ensure the country's afternoon traditions continued after Armageddon.

As the Berlin Wall rose, the Pentagon and Kennedy aide Carl Kaysen put together a serious and straightforward plan to launch a first strike against the Soviet Union: A fifteen-minute-long surprise attack with just fifty-five long-range bombers targeting eighty-eight "Designated Ground Zeros," including seventy-two bomber bases and sixteen ICBM facilities that would deliver a blow that, Kaysen believed, "eliminated or paralyzed the nuclear threat to the United States sufficiently." The attack would likely kill under a million Russians, a manageable number that wouldn't blind the Soviet leadership with an "irrational urge for revenge," especially if it was coupled with a strong message to Khrushchev that the U.S. would limit follow-up attacks and avoid hitting civilian populations if the Soviets did the same. Kaysen acknowledged that the worst-case scenario for his plan included a full thermonuclear war that would kill seven out of every ten Americans, but that the risk might still be worth it given the escalating Berlin crisis. As he wrote, "The choice may not be between 'go' and 'no-go'; it may be between 'go' and SIOP-62." Kennedy received the plan in September and responded with a detailed list of questions, including one in particular: If he called the Joint War Room, who would answer the phone?

Kennedy's war preparations called for a "new start on civil defense," and he split the Office of Civil and Defense Mobilization between the Pentagon, which created a new Office of Civil Defense (OCD), and a new policy-focused Office of Emergency Planning (OEP) inside the White

House. He nominated Steuart L. Pittman, a forty-two-year-old Washington lawyer, as the new assistant secretary of defense for civil defense.* The veteran-turned-attorney didn't think the U.S. even possessed the "illusion of a defense against the rising threat from the new Soviet nuclear missiles," and began to shift the government's strategy away from urban evacuations to focusing on shelters only. From Pittman's time forward, evacuation would be a reasonable option only for senior government leaders.

That same August, the Army Corps of Engineers and the Navy's Bureau of Yard and Docks began an intensive shelter assessment training program for 1,200 civilian architecture and engineering students, at nine sites like the Army's Fort Belvoir and Worcester Polytechnic Institute (WPI). The men, working in teams of two, assembled a national list of possible fallout shelters, surveying nearly every school, church, hospital, civic building, and commercial building that could protect more than fifty people in a nuclear attack. They dutifully recorded building entrances and exits, interior passageways, windows, and floor space on Department of Defense Form 1356. The forms were then mailed to the Census Bureau's processing center in Jeffersonville, Indiana, where they were put onto microfilm and converted to magnetic tape before being sent on to the Bureau of Standards in Washington, where computers calculated how many civilians could fit in each of the half million surveyed buildings. Buildings that met the standards were then adorned with black-and-yellow "Fallout Shelter" signs on the exterior and interior of the building, and the government would deliver sufficient stockpile supplies.†

Pittman's "community shelter" effort clashed philosophically with the

---

* Pittman received a Silver Star for what was likely the last naval engagement of World War II: Leading a team of Chinese guerrillas in the South China Sea, his two junks were attacked by a Japanese junk six days after Japan's surrender. He'd taken the helm himself after the guerrilla helmsman was killed, maneuvering his junk in close to the Japanese craft to rake it with gunfire, killing forty-three Japanese and forcing the surrender of the remaining thirty-nine.
† The now iconic "Fallout Shelter" signs, designed by the Army Corps of Engineers, were often confused with the international radiation symbol, but the six points of the logo's bright yellow triangles were actually meant to represent the six benefits of a government-stocked shelter: (1) shielding from radiation; (2) food and water; (3) trained leadership; (4) medical supplies and aid; (5) communications with the outside world; and (6) radiological monitoring to determine safe areas and time to return home.

suggestions of other leading figures, like Republican Nelson Rockefeller, who as chair of the Governors' Civil Defense Committee advocated private home shelters. Rockefeller bordered on the obsessive about civil defense—he'd led a study panel in 1958 that pushed for shelters and had since adopted his own rhetoric. He had shelters built at the New York governor's mansion and his own Fifth Avenue residence and spearheaded construction of the nation's largest civilian fallout shelter in Albany—a $4 million project meant to protect some 700 preselected state employees, businessmen, lobbyists, and professionals. He proselytized every chance he could. Indian prime minister Jawaharlal Nehru, after meeting the governor during a visit to New York, remarked: "Governor Rockefeller is a very strange man. All he wants to talk about is bomb shelters. Why does he think I am interested in bomb shelters?"

The result of these two conflicting philosophies was a jumbled message delivered in October 1961, in which Kennedy endorsed both public and private shelters and a national goal of "fall-out protection for every American as rapidly as possible."* For a brief moment, Americans became fascinated by shelter living. The head of IBM, Thomas Watson Jr., promised all 60,000 employees loans to build fallout shelters—and arranged to sell any employees construction materials at cost. In the preceding years, the government had conducted several large-scale shelter experiments, including one with California inmates who received a day off their sentences for each day they lived in an underground shelter; nationally, 7,000 volunteers had participated in over 22,000 "man-days" of shelter living experiments. While some were highly scientific, others were simply for publicity: In one stunt sponsored by Bomb Shelters Inc., Melvin Mininson and his new bride, Maria, spent their honeymoon twelve feet underground in a Miami fallout shelter and emerged hot and dusty after fourteen days—and then promptly left on a real two-week honeymoon to Mexico, paid for by the builder.†

---

* In fact, there were legitimate reasons to avoid relying upon backyard shelters. For one thing, home shelters raised immediate and real inequities. Sure, middle-class white families in suburbs had basements or backyards in which to construct shelters, but what about the rest of the country? Many low-income homes, particularly in the South, had no basements at all, and many inner-city minorities lived in apartment buildings.

† Not everyone bought into the hype: Betty Friedan, in her classic *The Feminine Mystique*, mocked an article submitted to a women's magazine about how to give birth inside a shelter.

The proliferation of home shelters launched a national moral debate about how those with shelters should respond to their unprotected neighbors. In Austin, Texas, resident Charles Davis told *Time* magazine he was prepared both to defend his shelter from the inside and to recapture it if others got there first. Pointing to his cache of five guns and a four-inch-thick door, he said, "This isn't to keep radiation out, it's to keep people out." What came to be known as the "Gun Thy Neighbor" debate consumed social commentary, religious leaders, and even popular culture shows like *The Twilight Zone*, which featured an episode about just such an event. Jesuit L. C. McHugh wrote in an essay titled "Ethics at the Shelter Door" about how "a Christian has the obligation to ensure the safety of those who depend on him," while other spiritual thinkers argued the exact opposite.

Potential conflicts weren't limited to just neighbor-to-neighbor and street-to-street. In 1961, Las Vegas's civil defense leader, J. Carlton Adair, suggested forming a 5,000-man local militia who could help repel by force California refugees who would likely pour across the border after a nuclear attack "like a swarm of locusts." Similar concerns in Beaumont, California, which sat on the road from Los Angeles to Phoenix, led the county civil defense coordinator to encourage households to pack pistols in their nuclear survival kits in order to fend off the 150,000 Los Angelean refugees expected to pass through Riverside County as they fled the devastated coast.

Meanwhile, Edward Teller, the scientist known as the father of the H-bomb, tried to convince the Kennedy White House that much of American life should be moved underground to create vast shelter networks—public buildings like schools, libraries, and museums should be buried, he argued, since they could simultaneously help save lives and preserve "some of the chief reasons for living." Besides, underground schools, while windowless, would ensure students had "a really adequate playground" on the school's roof. Teller's confident and enthusiastic presentation to Kennedy in November 1961 left Kennedy and National Security Advisor McGeorge Bundy troubled. "I must say I am horrified by the thought of digging deeper as the megatonnage gets bigger," Bundy told the president.

The White House also heard from two RAND strategists: Herman Kahn, whose 1960 book *On Thermonuclear War* laid out in 500 grim pages the impact of nuclear war and strategized about how best to consider deterrence, and Thomas Schelling, whose book that same year, *The Strategy of Conflict*, explored the bargaining, negotiation, and game theory that world powers could deploy. Kahn sought to parse the "degrees of awfulness," complete with charts, tables, and graphs, and his book became an unlikely bestseller in policy circles. He talked starkly about the differences between a war that killed 100 million and one that "only" killed 50 million. "A properly prepared country is not 'killed' by even the destruction of a major fraction of its wealth," he wrote. "While recuperation times may range all the way from one to a hundred years, even the latter is far different from the 'end of history.'"*

Ultimately, Robert McNamara and the strategists—backed by retired General Maxwell Taylor's idea of a "flexible response" and a young scholar named Henry Kissinger—led the Kennedy administration away from Eisenhower's plan and into a new era of strategic thinking. McNamara settled on five escalating SIOP sub-plans that focused primarily on "counterforce" scenarios. The new plan, SIOP-62, would target in ascending order: (1) Soviet nuclear forces; (2) air defenses away from urban areas, like rural radar units; (3) air defenses near urban areas; (4) governmental and military command and control facilities; (5) the all-out "spasm" attack. Publicly, the U.S. trumpeted in the media its new, "friendlier," "humane" nuclear war plan.

The Cold War appeared in full force for Kennedy's first Christmas as president. The family spent the holiday in Florida, where they had owned a seven-bedroom estate since 1933 on Palm Beach's Ocean Boulevard, just a few blocks from the luxurious Palm Beach Country Club. As the Kennedy family relaxed—and the president's father recovered from a December stroke—a special team of contractors were busy constructing a corrugated metal Quonset hut that would serve as the Palm Beach Winter White House's fallout shelter. Securing the president's three main vacation

---

* The enthusiasm of Teller and Kahn would lead to both men being parodied in *Dr. Strangelove*. Kahn, when asked what life in a shelter would be like, dismissed any concerns: "Well, you're sipping a drink, munching on something tasteless, and it's dark and crowded—a Greenwich Village nightclub."

homes—in Virginia's horse country, in Palm Beach, and in Hyannis—had kept the security and communications teams busy that year.

On December 26, a special team of Navy Seabees arrived to finish the Florida bunker. Known as "Detachment Hotel," the unit had made something of a name for themselves building previous presidential shelters like the one for Eisenhower at Camp David. Earlier that summer, they had built another nearly identical shelter, hidden at a Nantucket submarine surveillance base and disguised as a fuel storage area, near Kennedy's family compound in Hyannisport.

To protect the president in Florida, military planners settled on a site on nearby Peanut Island, a seventy-nine-acre artificial island created from the dredging of Lake Worth Inlet in Palm Beach harbor. The island, named for a failed peanut oil shipping business that had once been based there, had been closed to the public since the arrival of a new Coast Guard base on the eve of World War II. The location was just minutes away from the Kennedy house, a quick boat ride or helicopter away to relative safety. To cover the purpose of the new facility, the government told local planning officials that the military needed a new ammunition depot on the island.

Since the high Florida water table made digging bunkers difficult, the Seabees built a Quonset hut, set amid the sand dunes, with its base just a few feet below the surface. While the government often complained that commercially available home fallout shelter plans were too flimsy to offer families real security, the military had ensured its own bunkers were robust through the testing in the Nevada desert. The bunker built for Kennedy in Palm Beach was a modified version of a design engineers had tested on Frenchman Flat during Operation Plumbbob in 1957. On Peanut Island, workers layered nearly twelve feet of sand, lead, and concrete on top of the buried Quonset hut, disguising it to look like any other high dune. During a one-week Christmas sprint, the ten-person Navy Seabee team painted, prepped, assembled furniture, and set up radio equipment to provide spartan living accommodations for the presidential party in the event of an emergency evacuation. The surface-level entrance to the shelter led visitors down a long corrugated metal tube before a sharp 90-degree turn, meant to protect against a nearby atomic blast. They then would pass through decontamination showers before entering the main room of the command post. All told the shelter was only about 1,500 square feet, though it was equipped to hold up to thirty people for a month, and outfitted with double bunks, its own diesel generator, and powerful air scrubbers to limit fallout, as well as an escape hatch that led up to a makeshift helicopter landing pad on the dunes. Unlike the more serious COG facilities at Raven Rock or Mount Weather, Peanut Island wasn't intended for long-term occupancy; instead, it would provide a safe haven for a few hours or a few days until the president could be evacuated to more secure and more robust facilities—either an underground bunker, a floating naval command post, or an airborne command post overhead. As the Seabees worked, they caught an occasional glimpse of Kennedy, his family, and aides sailing by aboard the presidential yacht, *Honey Fitz*.

On Valentine's Day 1962, McGeorge Bundy charged the Office of Emergency Planning with conducting a fresh top-to-bottom review of COG—the only major reevaluation of COG during the brief Kennedy administration. The lengthy report that came back in June 1962 was, like the WSEG #50 Report, not encouraging. The three-member committee, headed by Ed McDermott, the corporate lawyer Kennedy had appointed that same month to head the OEP, concluded that the government should plan for the near-total loss of its Washington leadership and create a shadow government-in-waiting outside target areas. "Prelocation appears more suitable," the report explained, recommending that staff should work day-to-day doing essential peacetime duties in hardened, protected facilities. Their emergency duties should be predelegated to them. One successor, the committee concluded, "on a rotational basis, shall be at all times outside the Washington target area at one of the pre location sites or a mobile command post."

McDermott's recommendation jibed with what other agencies were concluding around the same time: Washington was simply too vulnerable. The State Department, which had planned to send over a thousand personnel to its sprawling Front Royal farm, worried that Washington would be destroyed even before any headquarters staff could evacuate, and it explored building a standby executive service of retired Foreign Service officers who lived in northern Virginia close to Front Royal and who could step in to run the nation's diplomacy in the wake of a decapitation attack.

Those fears of Washington's vulnerabilities encouraged planners to move away from agency-specific relocation sites that would have supported hundreds of staff, replacing them with centralized relocation plans at hardened facilities. The General Services Administration initially hoped to build four satellite centers, fifteen to twenty miles outside D.C., that could house multiple agencies beyond the main blast zone, but that plan had been vetoed by a budget-conscious Congress. Instead, many agencies would end up at Raven Rock, which would be primarily focused on military and overseas missions with the State Department, and Mount Weather, which would be primarily concerned with restoring domestic operations.

The change in plans drastically reduced the number of personnel who would be evacuated to safety—the State Department, for instance, which suspended its operations at Front Royal in 1963, would see only 300 of its personnel housed at Mount Weather and another 100 at Raven Rock. All told, as many as 3,000 would be housed inside Raven Rock, only about a thousand of which would be active-duty military. In the mid-1960s, the Alternate National Military Command Center would have supported 348 Air Force personnel, 295 Army, 270 Navy, and 46 Marine Corps. These space reallocations set off tense and delicate behind-the-scenes negotiations of which agency got to take how many people to which facility—and not all of the allocations made sense. The Bureau of the Budget initially tried to lay claim to 400 of the 1,900 available spots at Mount Weather.

The new austere staffing plans also shrank the operations each agency could conceivably continue in an emergency. Those plans needed trimming anyway. It was important to focus on only the most critical government functions, Bundy's study group wrote: "Determinations as to which Federal functions are essential in the immediate postattack period have not been sufficiently austere." To do so, Bundy's study group stressed, officials should resist the easy route of relying upon military martial law to respond to an emergency. "Some segment of representative civil government must remain in control of government operations," the committee said.

The initiative to focus resources on Mount Weather and Raven Rock necessitated upgrading the hardened sites. A 1960 estimate showed Raven Rock would only provide "buttoned-up" capability for two to three days, and so the military embarked on a multimillion-dollar project to boost the air filtration system, expand the water reservoirs, and upgrade the facility such that it could remain "buttoned-up" for up to fifteen days. Congress autho-rized new construction and upgraded communications for the relocation arc's crown jewel at Raven Rock and in 1962 two more buildings—named D and E, to round out the existing buildings A, B, and C—were carved out of the mountain.

The newly expanded facility at Raven Rock hosted a large permanent staff; personnel who were permanently stationed at the facility were known as the "Landlords of the Rock." When bunker personnel transferred to their next post, they received a stuffed animal mole from their colleagues—meant to represent time served in what Raven Rock veterans called the "Fraternal Order of the Moles." The commander of the 1108th Signal Bri-gade unit, which ran much of the facility, was known colloquially as the "Mayor of Raven Rock" or the "The Grand High Mole." It was a strange working environment for the moles posted to the Pennsylvania mountain: The hollowed-out cavern was generally very dusty and layers of dirt cov-ered most interior surfaces; music was piped into the building hallways to help dampen any classified conversations, and job postings warned, "Daily ingress and egress from office requires walking through industrial and stor-age areas via concrete roadways and hallways up to a mile in length." The "Granite Cove" dining facility fed the regular staff, while crates of rations sat ready for an emergency. Over time the military added exercise facilities, racquetball courts, a barber shop, and a drugstore. Away from the main of-fice buildings inside the mountain, two large underground reservoirs—one for drinking, one for mechanical uses—extended off into the dark gloom of the cavern.

As communications infrastructure improved, the military worked closely with AT&T to build a series of facilities around the region that supported Raven Rock. There was Site A, a radio facility in Greencastle, Pennsylvania; Site B, another radio facility near Sharpsburg, Maryland; Site C, a com-munications site near Fort Ritchie on top of Mount Quirauk, which served as the primary Raven Rock link to the outside world. (Mount Quirauk was hundreds of feet taller than Raven Rock and one of the tallest in the re-gion.) Sites D, E, and F delineated microwave relay facilities in Damascus, Maryland, Tyson's Corner, Virginia, and Fort Meade in Maryland. Raven Rock's own communications site, on top of the mountain, was known as

Site RT—an antenna array so large and prominent that it's visible from the Gettysburg battlefield.*

A nearby buried communications tower, code-named CREED, had a ground-level entrance into a hollowed-out tower that led up through nine stories of rock to the top of the hill. Just one floor and a reinforced concrete microwave antenna station peeked out the top of the hill. Lower floors were dedicated to living quarters, a kitchen, administrative offices, maintenance, and communications. Over the next decade, similar hardened communication towers were built aboveground across the Washington area, though their purposes were never publicly disclosed: The CARTWHEEL tower near Fort Reno in upper northwest D.C.; the CORKSCREW tower near Lamb's Knoll, outside Frederick, Maryland, in 1962; CANNONBALL near Cross Mountain in Mercersburg, Maryland; and COWPUNCHER, a tower near Martinsburg, West Virginia. All had similar layouts and had to be line-of-sight to at least one other facility to ensure unobstructed microwave transmissions, which meant they were spaced generally about fifty miles apart. The two top levels were encased in Plexiglas to protect the radio equipment from weather without interfering with transmission. They operated, masquerading as water towers, well into the 1970s and most are still standing today. The government even hired water tankers to drive up the access roads from time to time to help the cover story.

Raven Rock maintained a fully operational black-and-white television facility that could broadcast nationwide, as needed, as well as to more than forty different locations within the complex itself for closed-circuit messages. The facility also housed mobile communications vans that could exit Raven Rock after an attack and help it reestablish contact with the rest of the government.

As more buildings were completed inside, Raven Rock could host as many as 5,400 people under tight emergency conditions, but it wouldn't have been comfortable living for any long period of time.† Unlike at Mount

---

* The Army unit primarily responsible for the communications at Site R would go through several different reorganizations in the years ahead, eventually becoming the 1111th U.S. Army Signal Battalion, part of the 1108th U.S. Army Signal Brigade based at Fort Ritchie. The unit bills itself as the "Signal Masters of the Rock."

† Today, Raven Rock is believed to have as much as 900,000 square feet of office space.

Weather, which had bunks for 1,000, Raven Rock offered no dormitories. Instead, it stocked 1,600 air mattresses; everyone—including cabinet officials and generals—would be sleeping on the mountain floor. The president—whoever that would end up being, whether the elected leader or a successor—had a special suite set aside, but little effort was ever put into upgrading those facilities. In later years, the presidential suite came to be known as the "Lucy and Desi Suite," after Lucille Ball and Desi Arnaz, because its decorating scheme seemed permanently frozen in the 1960s.

Planners divided the government's post-attack functions into three tiers: A ("must-continue, essential, non interruptible function"), B ("can be resumed later"), and C ("can be deferred"). For the most part, staffers didn't know who was included in evacuation plans, since circulating such lists would present a security risk. As one report explained, "Such a list would tell an enemy, 'These are the ones they must have, and these they can do without.' To disclose such a list would make an enemy's job much easier. As much doubt as possible is what is necessary." Few government workers understood, in fact, that in many cases private sector workers would be saved ahead of them. As one official sheepishly admitted, "Yes, there are certain nonfederal people, especially communications like the telephone company, who have priority." As the Raven Rock communications towers demonstrated, telecommunications giant AT&T was tightly integrated into the nation's security. When the company adopted a new slogan in the 1950s, "Communications is the foundation of democracy," the words were more true than the public ever knew. The nation's growing network of secret sites needed extensive private help—and many vital bunkers were doubly hidden, buried underground and buried behind a corporate cover. Few companies made more sense to hide behind than AT&T, whose national telephone network gave it every reason to build facilities in random locations around the country. In fact, this made them as critical in the mission as the government itself.

Unbeknownst to most Americans, AT&T ran two special telecommunications networks solely for the use of the government—networks that required scores of secret installations spread across nearly every state in the country. First, it ran in conjunction with the White House Communications Agency what was known as the Echo-Fox nationwide network, which provided air-to-ground telephone and radio capability for planes like Air Force One, LOOKING GLASS, and other VIP aircraft. Echo-Fox relied on a network of more than forty ground-entry-point stations around the country to ensure that the aircraft could call into the ground telephone system from anywhere in the sky.*

The second network, called Autovon, was built in the early 1960s.† The Automatic Voice Network, designed for the U.S. military and built apart from the civilian telephone system using approximately sixty reinforced bunkers, would become the military's primary telephone network until the early 1990s. The network featured special telephone keypads with four different levels of call importance: Routine, Priority, Immediate, and Flash. (A fifth emergency level, "Flash Override," was available only to the National Command Authorities.) Callers selected their precedence level before dialing, and the system would route each call accordingly; for instance, if all the circuits were busy and a "Priority" call came through, the system would automatically bump a "Routine" call. An "Immediate" call could bump either a "Routine" call or a "Priority" one, and so on. A major advance in telecommunications at the time, Autovon's multiple access tiers and routing links from facility to facility ensured that the most important calls could always get through—even if some relay facilities were destroyed. It would be one of the first distributed communications networks in the world—an early forerunner of the technology that would later power the internet.

Working closely with the military, AT&T built dozens of large underground Autovon relay stations around the country, mostly on mountaintops at the end of long gated roads, away from major metropolitan areas. The sites crisscrossed the nation, from Anaheim, California, and Ellisville, Florida, to Pittsfield, Massachusetts, and Fairview, Kansas; Boone, Iowa, and Delta, Utah, to Yakima, Washington, and Mounds, Oklahoma. Nuclear blast detectors ringed many of the Autovon sites to help COG officials in Appalachian bunkers or NORAD officials at Cheyenne Mountain determine

---

* More locally, AT&T ran a special maritime network that covered the Potomac River to allow ship-to-shore communications for the presidential yacht and a yacht used by the chief of naval operations.
† The system was expanded into Canada in the mid-1960s through another nine switching centers.

where the U.S. had been struck. "Close cooperation between AT&T and government agencies during the planning of these blast-resistant transmission facilities has produced a highly reliable communications system," the telephone company bragged in an internal document.

While some Autovon facilities shared real estate with AT&T's civilian long-distance services, five specially designated "Project Offices" were solely national security facilities, run by AT&T's "Potomac District," which wasn't a geographic unit but the unit that ran classified facilities. Those five Autovon bunkers constructed in the 1960s—in Hagerstown, Maryland; in Leesburg, Virginia, atop Short Hill Mountain; in Buckingham, Virginia, atop Spears Mountain; outside Charlottesville, atop Peters Mountain; and in Pittsboro, North Carolina—received special attention and could be used as COG facilities in an emergency, showed extra security, helipads, and sixty-car parking lots—larger than seemingly required for a simple transmission station. The only aboveground buildings at the sites were security huts and two-story concrete cubes that housed troposcatter microwave relay stations, to allow over-the-horizon radio communications.* Thirty feet under the ground, though, the Project Offices featured huge bunkers, shielded by a copper shell against a nuclear blast's electromagnetic pulse.

Normally staffed by thirty employees, the Project Offices could hold as many as ninety staff during an emergency. Local workers were sworn to secrecy, and often didn't know who or what might end up using the facilities in an emergency. A local North Carolina construction company received $7 million in 1962 to build the Pittsboro facility, digging a hole large enough to house a multistory bunker the size of a large department store, around 100,000 square feet—much larger than other similar AT&T Autovon stations, which ran "only" about 60,000 square feet. The whole facility was built atop gravel and spring coils meant to sway in a nearby attack. "The buildings themselves can shift six inches without cracking," AT&T reported. "The whole installation could roll with an atomic punch." The sites had their own power and water supplies, including a 300,000-gallon fuel tank and

---

* A small hardened aboveground garage at the sites also housed a bulldozer that could be used to clear debris from the site post-attack.

a 100,000-gallon tank for drinking water, as well as quarters for dozens of people to live for weeks. Just inside the massive double-blast doors—built by the Mosler Safe Company's Nuclear Division, the same company that provided doors for the government's bunkers and whose bank safe had survived the bombing of Hiroshima—decontamination showers and racks of fresh clothing ensured safe passage for employees after an attack.*

At almost every level, AT&T served as the backbone of the nation's wartime communications system. Among its many projects, it ran circuitry for the Ballistic Missile Early Warning System (BMEWS), the massive radar systems spread across the Arctic north that aimed to spot a Soviet missile launch the second a missile passed above the horizon—a moment that would give the United States about thirty minutes of warning. "Each one of those minutes is probably worth a plane for every runway that SAC has," AT&T executive Charles Duncan explained to a group of military leaders in 1960. "An interruption of fifteen minutes in one of these things might mean a difference between survival of the country or not. To put it more bluntly, it might mean the difference between the survival of Russia and us, if they attacked us." AT&T was so tightly integrated into the Pentagon that the Defense Department intervened to stop a Justice Department effort to break apart the powerful company on antitrust grounds, arguing that doing so would create a "hazard to national security."

Soon after its 1962 publication, Fletcher Knebel's riveting novel *Seven Days in May*, foretelling a military coup against the president, became a bestseller and generated curious speculation around Washington. Among other questions it raised, the book led President Kennedy to try to understand better the emergency briefcase that followed him around. The president asked his staff, "The book says one of those men sits outside my bedroom door all night. Is that true?" General Ted Clifton replied that the military aide actually waited downstairs through the night, but that, "We've timed it many times; he can make it even if he has to run up the stairs and not use the

---

* Visitors decades later to the defunct facilities would find boxes of shaving cream, military rations, sanitation supplies, and racks of 1968 Converse sneakers for facility staff to change into.

elevator—in a minute and a half," he said. "If he knocks at your door some night and comes in and opens the valise, pay attention."

The novel also featured a central scene that revolved around an emergency exercise at a fictional location called Mount Thunder—a bunker where the nation's leaders were supposed to retreat and "run the nation in the event of a nuclear attack on Washington." As Washington officials read the book by Knebel and his coauthor, Charles W. Bailey II, something surprising stood out: If you followed the book as it unfurled toward Mount Thunder, the driving directions to the bunker sounded eerily familiar. The character's Chrysler wheeled onto Route 50, then through the "jungle of neon lights and access roads at Seven Corners" onto Route 7, then right at the fork to Route 9. As the car climbed into the Blue Ridge Mountains, the character made a left on scenic Virginia 120.

With only two minor changes (skip Route 9 and look for Route 601, not 120, which didn't run anywhere close by), the route described would run right by the very real government facility known officially for over a decade as HIGH POINT or the "Special Facility." Different agencies over the years referred to it by other names as well, like the Western Virginia Office of Controlled Conflict Operations, but fifty miles west of Washington and 1,725 feet up into the Blue Ridge Mountains, it had never really shaken its original colloquial name: Mount Weather. Along with Raven Rock and the Greenbrier bunker, the site, overlooking the Piedmont and Shenandoah Valley, represented one of COG's cornerstones.

Mount Weather's name came from its first government service as an observatory for the Weather Bureau, which had purchased the property for just $2,513.15 in the 1890s. Using motor-operated rotating steel drums lined with as much as 40,000 feet of piano wire, the half dozen staff on Mount Weather's kite team did groundbreaking work, but as better technologies arrived, the Weather Bureau handed off the majority of the 100-acre facility to the Army to use as a World War I artillery range. The government had spent the better part of the 1920s trying to get rid of the property, finding little interest.*

---

* The Mount Weather Observatory shattered its own world altitude record in 1910, flying one kite 23,826 feet up into the air to record the lowest temperature (29 degrees Fahrenheit below zero) ever using such an instrument.

Finally, Calvin Coolidge proposed the idea of establishing a presidential vacation residence atop Mount Weather to Congress, which appropriated $48,000 to convert it to a summer White House. When Coolidge's successor came to office in 1929, though, Herbert Hoover promptly declared the fishing at Mount Weather inadequate and announced he'd find a different campsite.*

In 1936, Mount Weather became a Bureau of Mines testing facility, since the rock on the mountain was "exceptionally dense," and it excavated a narrow but lengthy tunnel to test blasting and drilling methods. In World War II, the government housed as many as 100 conscientious objectors there, pressing them into service as weather researchers to help develop better forecasts for the Northern Hemisphere. After the war, the facility went back to the Bureau of Mines, which redoubled its efforts at developing new drilling techniques. As a 1953 Interior Department publication bragged in a lengthy report on the "widely acclaimed" problems solved by the mountain's engineers, "From Mount Weather in the last few years has come a mass of technical data on drilling, steels to use in drills and rods, diamond drilling, and related subjects."

That publication, though, was one of the last mentions of the site for a generation; even as the Interior report went to press, the government began to erase the public existence of Mount Weather so it could adopt a new purpose. Given the distance from Washington, the exceptionally hard rock, the existing tunnel, and the pre-located drilling machines, it appeared the perfect site to outfit an executive branch bunker. The Bureau of Mines announced that it was closing Mount Weather in 1954—true to a certain extent, but the real tunneling at the site was just beginning. Just a year after Raven Rock became operational to the north, workers launched a four-year expansion project that would transform Mount Weather into a massive bunker complex. According to a perhaps apocryphal story, the first director of Mount Weather was given a simple commission directly from President Eisenhower: "I expect your people to save our government."

Gilbert Fowler, whose uncle Ernest had lived near the site since its

---

* He eventually paid for his own summer residence, Camp Rapidan, in the Shenandoah Valley.

earliest days, became one of the forty-person work crews in the around-the-clock excavation. Fowler, like many of the crew, had worked for years on the experimental mines, so it wasn't too different of a project. "That was some rough, tough, dirty work," he recalled in 2001. The Army Corps of Engineers project, code-named Operation HIGH POINT, enlarged the original tunnels, excavating hundreds of thousands of tons of greenstone and hollowing out a cavern large enough for a medium-sized city under the mountain. More than 21,000 iron bolts reinforced the roof. While the facility wasn't fully completed until 1958, it began serving as the executive branch's main relocation site almost immediately.

By the Kennedy years, Mount Weather included all the regular amenities and life-support systems familiar to other U.S. COG bunkers. Helicopter landing pads and a sewage treatment plant sat atop the mountain, and the underground facility held reservoirs for both drinking water and cooling needs, diesel generators, a hospital, radio and television broadcast facilities, cafeterias, its own fire department and police force. Some 800 blue-mesh hammocks sat ready for evacuated personnel, who would sleep in shifts throughout the day. Plastic flowers dotted the tables in the cafeteria. Mount Weather also hosted the National Damage Assessment Center, the NADAC, a team of analysts who would track enemy attacks and issue damage reports. In peacetime, the unit concerned itself with compiling exhaustive lists of local emergency resources and facilities that could aid evacuation, rescue, and reconstruction efforts.

The list of who would be admitted to the facility during a real emergency was comparatively small and carefully tracked. Security procedures held that each driver's-license-style ID card was duplicated and stored at the front gate—ensuring an extra level of protection against forgeries or unauthorized alterations. No matter how real an emergency pass looked, no one would be admitted to the facility unless that duplicate was on file with security. It was a procedure, in part, meant to forestall the very type of coup that played out in the pages of *Seven Days in May*.

The first atomic explosion in the New Mexico desert, codenamed TRINITY, on July 16, 1945, heralded a new era.

J. Robert Oppenheimer and General Leslie Groves, the two leaders of the Manhattan Project, inspect the site of the TRINITY explosion.

Fears of the Soviet Union drove the invention and test of a thermonuclear bomb, codenamed IVY MIKE, in the South Pacific on November 1, 1952.

General Groves and David Lilienthal helped shape how the government thought about the atomic age.

Truman would have used this presidential yacht, the USS *Williamsburg,* to escape Washington in an attack.

Harry Truman's
renovations to
the White House
served as perfect
cover to bury
a new bomb
shelter under
the north lawn.

Dwight Eisenhower, seated between George Kistiakowsky and James Killian Jr., listened to their warnings about how unprepared the nation was for nuclear war.

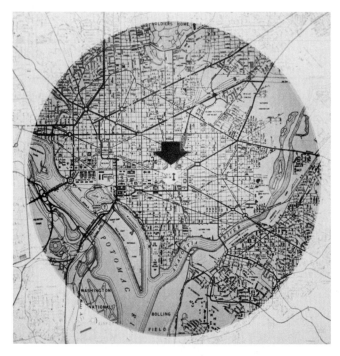

Cautionary maps like this, showing the effect of the IVY MIKE bomb on Washington, D.C., led the government to accelerate its Doomsday planning.

The national tour of the "Alert America" convoy aimed
to galvanize interest in civil defense.

Comics and "Bert the Turtle" tried to educate
(and calm) America's children.

Government demonstrations made fallout shelter living
look as normal, wholesome, and relaxing as possible.

Ike's annual Operation ALERTS saw officials decamp for relocation
sites around D.C., like Virginia's Mount Weather.

Government officials would practice restoring the nation to "normal"
after an attack, even though Ike doubted it would ever be possible.

Ike's first helicopter flight was one of the only times the president would ever fly aboard an Air Force helicopter. He found it too hot and miserable in the July sun.

By the time Kennedy took office, the White House had settled on larger Marine transport helicopters to fly (and evacuate) the president.

ARCHITECT OF THE CAPITOL
WASHINGTON, D. C.

March 28, 1956

Mr. Walter J. Tuohy, President
Chesapeake and Ohio Railway Company
Terminal Tower
Cleveland 1, Ohio

Dear Mr. Tuohy:

This is to introduce Mr. J. George Stewart, Architect of
the Capitol, who is calling upon you on matters of vital importance
to the Congress of the United States.

We, the undersigned, representing the leadership of the
United States Congress, will appreciate any cooperation you may
give us.

Sincerely yours,

Speaker of the House of
Representatives

Majority Leader of the Senate

Minority Leader of the House
of Representatives

Minority Leader of the Senate

Congressional leaders secretly began discussions about building
a bunker at the Greenbrier resort in West Virginia.

SAC spent the 1950s and 1960s finely tuning a war
machine of unprecedented destructive capability.

Upper right: General Curtis LeMay's exacting standards drove SAC,
even as his hawkishness led to his mockery in *Dr. Strangelove*.

SAC built itself a massive bunker outside Omaha, which is still in use today.

SAC's underground command post at Offutt Air Force Base in Nebraska was dominated by its massive "Big Board," manually updated by men on cherry-pickers.

The groundbreaking of the new NORAD bunker
under Cheyenne Mountain on June 16, 1961.

NORAD's tunnels extended thousands of feet into Cheyenne Mountain.

Inside the massive hollowed-out caverns,
engineers built free-standing three-story buildings
that would be the heart of NORAD.

For years in the Nevada desert, the military tested the effects of atomic weapons.

Mosler built a bank safe in the Nevada desert to ensure it could survive an atomic blast. It still stands there today.

Engineers erected houses and stocked them with mannequins to test buildings' sturdiness to nuclear blasts. The mannequins often fared poorly.

During the 1960s, the military built a half-dozen communications towers, like this one atop Fort Reno, in D.C., to keep the president in touch during a nuclear war.

Regional command posts, like this one in Denton, Texas, would have coordinated post-attack responsibilities for the government.

The Federal Regional Center in Maynard, Massachusetts, would have run New England after an attack.

The first White House command post, set up during the
Spanish-American War, was an elaborate affair.

JFK's new White House
"Situation Room" was built
after the Bay of Pigs fiasco.

Navy Seabees built this
presidential escape bunker
on Peanut Island, close to
JFK's vacation home in
Palm Beach, Florida.

Chapter 8

CUBAN MISSILE CRISIS

On October 30, 1961, the Soviet Union had resumed its nuclear testing, ending a 1958 test moratorium in spectacular fashion by exploding a weapon that came to be known as "Tsar Bomba" near the Arctic Circle. At 50 megatons, it was the largest man-made explosion in history—about 3,000 times more powerful than the Hiroshima bomb. Too large and too heavy to be militarily useful, the weapon still terrified, destroying every building in a village 34 miles away from ground zero and breaking windows as far as 500 miles away.

The United States had resumed testing weapons the following spring as well, and the two nations pounded away with experimental nuclear blasts one, two, even three times a week through the rest of the year. On a rainy Washington afternoon soon after, Kennedy had been briefed about the progress and resulting fallout by his science advisor, Jerome Wiesner. Midway through the briefing, he asked the MIT professor how contamination in the upper atmosphere reached the earth's surface. "The clouds are washed out by rain," Wiesner said.

Kennedy looked quickly out the Oval Office windows at the Rose Garden. "You mean it's in the rain out there?"

"Possibly," Wiesner replied.

Kennedy remained silent for several beats, thinking, and after the meeting finished, the president sat silently staring out at the rain. "I never saw him more depressed," aide Kenny O'Donnell said later.

The tests weren't just for geopolitical show—scientists and military planners were still learning about the myriad behaviors and effects of atomic weapons. In one July 1962 test, STARFISH PRIME, the United States exploded a 1.4-megaton warhead some 250 miles above Johnson Island, creating colorful auroras across much of the Pacific. Hotels in Hawaii, about 800 miles away, hosted "rainbow parties" for guests to watch the "spectacular pyrotechnic aftermath," and unexpectedly became the first civilians to experience a little-understood nuclear phenomenon: the electromagnetic pulse. The high-altitude blast's EMP wreaked havoc on electrical circuits and knocked out a chunk of Oahu streetlights. Enrico Fermi had theorized before the first nuclear tests in 1945 that the weapons' blasts would give off an electrical pulse similar to lightning's charge and could cause damage to electronics, but during surface tests, the EMP seemed minimal. Only as tests like STARFISH PRIME were conducted in the higher atmosphere did scientists understand how much more potent the EMP effect was in the earth's magnetic field. The EMP, it turned out, could be a dangerous weapon on its own and needed to be factored into the creation of protective structures. The new knowledge was applied almost immediately to NORAD's underground bunker in Cheyenne Mountain, Colorado, which was then still under construction in 1962 and would become the military's first EMP-shielded facility.

By that fall of 1962, Dwight Eisenhower had lost patience with President Kennedy's foreign policy. The Bay of Pigs appeared now a harbinger of what was to come; his successor had been rolled again and again by the more cunning Khrushchev—in Vienna at a disastrous summit, in Berlin by the crisis over the Wall, and by the Soviet resumption of nuclear testing. As midterm elections loomed in early November, Eisenhower felt comfortable publicly declaring Kennedy's foreign policy a failure. "It is too sad to talk about," he told Republican Party faithful at a Boston campaign dinner on October 15, 1962, drawing a sharp contrast between his own tough leadership and the wishy-washy junior Massachusetts senator who had let the Soviets walk all over him. The stunning remarks from the former commander-in-chief, a remarkable departure from the unspoken tradition of not criticizing one's successors as president, deeply irritated President Kennedy when he read them in bed the following morning at the White House; Eisenhower's speech was the lead story in *The New York Times*. The next item on Kennedy's schedule that Tuesday morning, however, would instantly overshadow Eisenhower's comments—and plunge the administration into the tensest period of the Cold War.

National Security Advisor McGeorge Bundy knocked on the president's bedroom door shortly after 8 a.m. with the daily intelligence briefing—which included a worrying report from Cuba: A U-2 surveillance flight showed what appeared to be Soviet missile bases under construction on the Caribbean island. Kennedy phoned his brother Robert: "We have the big trouble." By late morning, President Kennedy had gathered military leaders and senior White House aides for a briefing by the CIA's chief photo interpreter, who used a long pointer to highlight the missile trailers, erector launchers, and personnel tents on the nascent missile fields. Over the coming hours and days, the administration struggled to figure out an appropriate course of action; the missiles couldn't go unanswered, yet as the week unfolded, all options looked bad. Should the U.S. invade Cuba? Or could surprise air strikes level the missile sites? Would a naval blockade be seen as too weak a response? If they didn't attack the missiles, would it give Khrushchev confidence to move on Berlin?

On Saturday afternoon, Kennedy learned at least two of the missiles were already operational—and more would be shortly—meaning that nuclear missiles with "yields in the low megaton range" could blanket the southern United States with almost no warning. The advisors sat in the sitting room of the second-floor White House residence, debating their options. Bundy wanted air strikes—some 800 sorties over Cuba to level broad swaths of the island's offensive and defensive installations. McNamara and Dean Rusk, Kennedy's secretary of state, wanted a blockade. The president was leaning toward a blockade, but was still bullish on air strikes. Afterward he walked out on the Truman Balcony with his brother Bobby and speechwriter Ted Sorensen. It was a beautiful, crisp fall day in Washington, 74 degrees. There wasn't a cloud in the sky as they looked down the Ellipse towards the Washington Monument. "We are very, very close to war," Kennedy said gravely. Then he cracked a smile: "I hope you realize that there's not enough room for everybody in the White House bomb shelter."

The president planned a national address for Monday evening, and over the weekend the military began tracking down far-flung congressional leaders who were out on the pre-election recess. House whip Hale Boggs was fishing in the Gulf of Mexico when a Navy helicopter clattered out of the horizon, came to a low hover overhead, and dropped down a bottle with a note inside: CALL OPERATOR 18, WASHINGTON. URGENT MESSAGE FROM THE PRESIDENT. The helicopter's PA system directed the Louisiana congressman toward a nearby oil rig, where he was whisked away from the drilling platform to the closest Air Force base, put in the backseat of a fighter jet, and raced to Washington.

Kennedy didn't mince words in his speech from the Oval Office. Speaking to nearly two thirds of the nation's 145 million people, the largest U.S. audience ever assembled for a presidential address, he announced a naval "quarantine" of Cuba—a word carefully chosen, rather than blockade, to minimize comparisons of what the Soviets had done to Berlin. He condemned the new missile bases, asked for support from the international community, and drew a firm line against both the Soviet Union and Cuba. On NBC, anchor Chet Huntley called Kennedy's address "the toughest and most grim speech by a president since December 1941." The speech captivated the nation, instantly plunging the world into the midst of the crisis that Kennedy's White House had shouldered alone for nearly a week.

NORAD raised the nation's readiness level to DEFCON 3—an alert that would continue for the next thirty-six days, six hours, and ten minutes, the longest period of the Cold War. Troop trains packed with soldiers and matériel converged on the Southeast as the Army and Marines assembled a 140,000-strong invasion force. At sea, Navy ships steamed toward the Caribbean to enforce the quarantine line. As part of SAC's normal alert procedures, hundreds of planes were loaded with nuclear weapons and sent to dispersal airfields, many of which were unprepared to host nuclear bombers. B-47 bombers from the 509th Bombardment Wing, which had dropped the atomic weapons on Hiroshima and Nagasaki, headed for Boston's Logan Airport and parked in a little-used corner to find that few logistical details had been arranged. One pilot bought fuel for his bomber with his personal credit card, and the flight crews rented vehicles from Hertz and Avis to shuttle them to their aircraft if an alert sounded.

Across the country the military's communications infrastructure was equally unprepared. In forty-eight hours, AT&T raced to build communication lines at thirty-two airfields to ensure the nuclear forces were tied into the SIOP. Message traffic was so clogged that even "emergency" communications were delayed four hours; the second most urgent category, "operational-immediate," was delayed up to seven hours. SAC controllers worked feverishly to update the SIOP war plans, since they'd never factored in an airborne alert posture, rewriting war plans with bombers literally already in the air. Officials realized midway through the crisis that the EC-135 LOOK-ING GLASS planes had never developed a system to authenticate emergency launch orders from the ground and scrambled to outline how messages would be transmitted and authenticated. Those who received the proposal didn't think much of it: "This is a joke," the chief of naval operations wrote on his copy. He pointed out the "4 to 8 hr delay" in operational messages. What made the military think, given the backlog, that even an emergency launch order would make it through the circuits before Washington and SAC's bases were fried?

SAC's leader, General Thomas Power, addressed his worldwide command on Wednesday morning, October 24. As CINCSAC in Omaha, Power oversaw a vast empire, a quarter million personnel that represented the world's most destructive fighting force. Only a century before, a unit of blue-uniformed Union cavalry had occupied the same land at Fort Crook near the Missouri River, charged with protecting settlers from marauding Indians at the edge of the American frontier. Now, the reign of the fifty-seven-year-old Power reached every corner of the globe. He might have been less of a hawk than Curtis LeMay, but only marginally. When the Kennedy administration had pushed Power to modify the existing "overkill" strategy to focus solely on military targets, Power had objected: "Why are you so concerned with saving their lives? The whole idea is to kill the bastards." His next conclusion had abruptly ended the discussion: "Look—at the end of the war, if there are two Americans and one Russian, we win!"

Since taking over SAC from LeMay in June 1957, he'd pushed the organization toward greater levels of readiness, working to perfect an alert system that kept the nation's nuclear fleet "cocked." SAC perfected a ground alert system that could launch scores of planes in under fifteen minutes. Ground alert only went so far, and between 1959 and 1961, Power experimented with an airborne alert, keeping a handful of B-52s in the air at all times. He had wanted to greatly expand the program, known as KEEN AXE, but cost considerations kept it from being permanent. As part of Project LIFE INSURANCE, Kennedy had boosted the ground alert to half of all the nation's bombers and tankers. Over the course of 1962, the nation began to bring its nascent missile forces online, too—the Titan had arrived in April, the Atlas F in August. Now, with the Cuban Missile Crisis, Power finally had his chance to expand airborne alert, keeping two-plane B-52 teams, code-named CHROME DOME, flying regularly near the Arctic Circle and in the Mediterranean, within quick striking distance of the Soviet Union.

SAC's headquarters at Offutt Air Force Base, built in 1957 by contractor Leo A. Daly, and known officially as Building 501, was nicknamed the "molehole." It had replaced SAC's overburdened original building with an aboveground facility sixteen times larger than the original, as well as a huge new underground command post. The hulking aboveground facility, where most of the SAC staff worked, might have appeared intimidating, but it was what military engineers of the age called "Hollywood Hard," "fortress-like for the public, but often vulnerable." To get to the real center of SAC's operations, you walked down a sloped, eight-foot-wide ramp with thick concrete walls that led into the huge command bunker, buried nearly four stories under the earth. It contained space enough for 800 staff to work "buttoned-up" for two weeks with the necessary rations and an artesian well for drinking water. The three-foot-thick concrete walls wouldn't have withstood a direct hit from the nuclear bomb, but it would have survived a near-miss— and, besides, SAC's goal was to have the bombers and missiles launched and on their way long before anything could strike Omaha.

From his glass-walled office, Power could see SAC's "big board," a 264-foot-long series of maps, charts, and postings that summarized the global threat condition, the status and location of SAC's various forces, weather conditions, and so on. While state-of-the-art television cameras could broadcast briefings around the world and an advanced IBM 704 computer helped run the command center—one of the first machines to incorporate what came to be known as random access memory (RAM)—most data inside the command center was displayed through more pedestrian means: Personnel used cherry-picker lifts to update the big board on SAC's status throughout the day.

Power's daily life revolved around the two colored phones in his command post. As he liked to say, "Without communications, all I command is my desk, and that is not a very lethal weapon." Contrary to popular belief, it wasn't actually a red phone that connected him to the Pentagon and the president—it was gold. His movements were carefully planned and his schedule carefully coordinated so that wherever he went, any time of day or night, he could answer that gold phone within six rings. After receiving an order from the president or the National Command Authorities, Power would then use his own red phone, which linked him to the rest of the command.

Now, in that underground bunker, overlooking the big board, SAC's commander picked up that same red phone from which he'd order a nuclear war, and prepared to address the nation's nuclear forces. With the touch of the red ALARM button, he activated the Primary Alerting System, the dedicated telephone lines that linked SAC's 200 global bases and units.* A "warble" sounded in the other SAC command posts, alerting everyone to the announcement.

"This is General Power speaking," he began. "We are in an advanced state of readiness to meet any emergencies, and I feel we are well-prepared. I expect each of you to maintain strict security and use calm judgment during this tense period." Power's message was purposely broadcast in the clear—not encoded—to ensure that Soviets could eavesdrop and understand the stakes. His message was hardly the rousing battle speech one might expect; in fact, it underscored how nervous everyone was up and down the chain of command. On this day, his concluding final line, rather than some Shakespearean battle cry, was, instead, a much more tepid, "If you are not sure of what you should do in any situation, and if time permits, get in touch with us here."

As one SAC officer listening at a base in Puerto Rico recalled later, "You could hear a pin drop. It was highly unusual, like virtually never, to hear the voice of the Commander in Chief of SAC pipe in on the Primary Alerting

---

* Actually, the Primary Alerting System was two dedicated lines at each base—a primary and a backup. Each line was tested electronically every three seconds, to ensure that any outages were noticed immediately.

System. We were on the verge of world crisis and we all felt it." Power himself expected war; he "buttoned up" the SAC command post and permitted
the battle staff to each place one telephone call to family members to say a
final good-bye.

In the days after Kennedy's Oval Office address, Americans nationwide confronted the real possibility of war. Some reactions made sense—Caribbean
cruises were canceled and all the vacationing guests quickly checked out of
the Key Wester Motel in Florida—but even cities far removed from the immediate threat of Cuban missiles saw panic buying in supermarkets. Grocers
saw runs on sugar, salt, canned meats, and powdered milk. In just two days,
one Washington, D.C., store sold 900 cans of pemmican—a high-calorie
meat-and-berry concentrate—at 27 cents each. Not everyone, though, was
going to scrimp on Armageddon: "One woman walked out of here with an
entire case of our most expensive canned tuna," a market employee in the
San Fernando Valley told a reporter. In cities like Dallas and St. Peters-
burg, Florida, sporting goods stores saw big jumps in gun purchases. New
York City ordered hundreds of schools to run repeated air raid drills. An-
ecdotally, hundreds of thousands—and perhaps as many as several million
Americans—decamped from likely target cities for the countryside, visiting
rural family members, reopening summer homes, or checking into motels, in
hopes of escaping a nuclear holocaust.

For the first time, the general population began to pay attention to civil
defense. "The nation's flagging interest in civil defense began to undergo a
sharp rise yesterday in the wake of President Kennedy's speech," *The Washington Post* reported just after the televised address. The District's civil defense office stayed open late until 1 a.m. answering queries, even as the city
raced to man its relocation center in Lorton, Virginia, at the D.C. prison.
The dean of the Washington National Cathedral ordered its basement
flooded to secure drinking water for an emergency.

Across the country, schoolchildren were sent home with stockpile lists
and shelter tips. Newspapers published descriptions of air raid signals: A
steady-tone, five-minute blast meant a general "alert," indicating an attack
was at least an hour away; a rising-and-falling five-minute blast on the sirens
meant an imminent attack. Jacksonville, Florida, officials distributed the best

escape routes for those seeking to flee into Georgia. Residents of Memphis were told to drive fifteen miles outside the city limits, the so-called Safety Line, after which they were told ambiguously "arrangements will be made to feed, clothe, and shelter the thousands who need help." Chicago school officials mapped which students lived close to school to determine who could conceivably make it home during an alert and who should be held at school to experience nuclear war with their teachers.

In truth, the few existing community shelters wouldn't have made for a pleasant two weeks of living, the length of time recommended to minimize radiation exposure. Each shelter was stocked with twenty-one-inch-tall fiberboard drums, lined with plastic, that would start out as water storage and then, once empty, be converted into toilets. Sanitary kits (one for every twenty-five people) would include a portable toilet seat, chemicals to minimize septic problems, toilet paper, and a small privacy screen. The Office of Civil and Defense Mobilization's plans called for shelters to stock just 10,000 calories of food per person and 3.5 gallons of drinking water per person, meant to stretch across two weeks.

Most of that 1.5 quarts of daily water ration presumably would have been used to swallow the shelter's *menu du jour*: lots and lots and lots of bulgur wheat crackers, some mixed with "carbohydrate supplement," aka hard candy. This "survival cracker" recipe grew out of an extensive 1958 study with the Department of Agriculture and the Department of Health, Education, and Welfare, and then—after the government purchased some three million bushels of surplus wheat to manufacture them—was mass-produced, as much as 150 million pounds of crackers, by companies like Kroger, Nabisco, and the United Biscuit Company (now Keebler), and sealed in seven-pound tins that held precisely 434 crackers. "This is one of the oldest and most proven forms of food known to man," explained Deputy Assistant Secretary of Defense Paul Visher. "It has been the subsistence ration for many portions of the earth for thousands of years. Its shelf life has been established by being edible after 3,000 years in an Egyptian pyramid." The specially made bulgur crackers were indeed nearly unchanging: A fifty-page USDA report on the crackers and their chemistry found merely a "discernible but inconsequential decrease" in flavor after fifty-two months of storage. Perhaps, though, that "inconsequential" decrease was due to the fact that the wafers tasted terrible to begin with. About the highest compliment ever paid to the survival crackers was that they tasted like "cardboard." Nevertheless, since there was little else to do in a shelter, OCDM literature encouraged serving six small "meals" per day of precisely 125 calories. As one official explained, "Although this may seem somewhat austere, nutrition experts consider it adequate and in accord with minimal survival concept."

Suddenly, many Americans realized that they'd be on their own in an attack. The government had no plans for sheltering the entire country. As one civil defense official said defensively, "I do not think it is the government's responsibility to take care of you from the minute you're born until you die." The very few homeowners nationwide who had taken the advice to build a shelter found themselves quite popular among friends and neighbors: One Valley Forge, Pennsylvania, shelter owner reported receiving half-joking offers of up to $16,000 from neighbors eager to share his shelter. In the back of everyone's mind, though, was the "Gun Thy Neighbor" debate from the year before. If people were willing to pay money to reserve a spot in a neighbor's shelter, what panic would possess them in a real attack?

As the crisis unfolded, Kennedy wasn't particularly worried about an outright surprise attack by the Soviet Union—he was worried about the two superpowers stumbling into war unintentionally. Americans didn't have to go far to see how nuclear war could start with a stumble; that very month *The Saturday Evening Post* serialized a hot new novel, *Fail-Safe*, by Eugene Burdick and Harvey Wheeler, about how a series of technical failures sent a strike group of SAC bombers toward Russia. But it was another 1962 book—this time a nonfiction one—that obsessed Kennedy through the crisis. Historian Barbara Tuchman's *The Guns of August*, published that spring, traced how the Great Powers, simultaneously headstrong and yet unsure of themselves, slipped, miscalculated, and stumbled into the Great War in the summer of 1914. Kennedy was particularly haunted by a conversation between two German leaders after the war began. One, a former German chancellor, asked the current chancellor, "How did it all happen?" The latter, who had led his nation into war, replied, "Ah, if only one knew." Jack told Bobby on Saturday afternoon, as the crisis looked darkest, that he wanted to avoid someone someday writing a comparable *The Missiles of October*.

As President Kennedy recalled later, "If this planet is ever ravaged by nuclear war, if 300 million Americans, Russians, and Europeans are wiped out by a 60-minute nuclear exchange, if the survivors of that devastation can then endure the fire, poison, chaos, and catastrophe, I do not want one of those survivors to ask another, 'How did it all happen?' and to receive the incredible reply, 'Ah, if only one knew.'"

On Thursday, the Soviet ship *Bucharest* was stopped and searched after passing the quarantine line. After the Navy determined it had no missiles aboard, it was allowed to continue. Twelve other Soviet ships turned around. At the U.N., Ambassador Adlai Stevenson dramatically unveiled photos of the missile sites and asked his Soviet counterpart if they would admit the missiles' presence, saying, "I am prepared to wait for my answer until hell freezes over, if that is your decision." The Soviet forces on Cuba retreated Friday morning to an underground command post outside Havana, stocked with supplies for five or six weeks of fighting if the U.S. attacked. A Cuban foreign ministry officer, Carlos Alzugaray, used U.S. government publications on civil defense and nuclear weapons to summarize for his nation's leaders the results of an American attack. After several hours of research, his report was a single sentence long: "In the event that nuclear weapons are used in or near Havana City, it and we shall be destroyed."

Kennedy's lingering discomfort with Cuba and the Bay of Pigs roiled just beneath the surface of many meetings—he still felt his military advisors had taken advantage of him during the CIA-sponsored invasion. There was little love lost in return, particularly from General Curtis LeMay, the Air Force leader who had done so much to turn SAC into a tightly coiled weapon. As a candidate in 1960, Kennedy cut short LeMay's tour of SAC headquarters after he realized that he was being given a sanitized Potemkin Village brush-off and kept away from the real guts of the Omaha facility. "I don't want that man near me again," Kennedy had spat after another meeting.

Still, as president, he also understood that this was the kind of man he would need in a war—and a crisis like that with the Cuban missiles was precisely why Kennedy had kept LeMay around, even though LeMay's attitude still hadn't warmed toward his new commander. "This blockade and political action, I see leading into war. I don't see any other solution," LeMay said to

Kennedy in one meeting at the start of the crisis. "In other words, you're in a pretty bad fix at the present time."

Dumbfounded by the arrogant hostility, Kennedy assumed he must've misheard: "What did you say?"

"You're in a pretty bad fix," LeMay repeated calmly.

"Well, you're in there with me—personally," Kennedy shot back, hiding his anger behind a laugh.

Luckily for Kennedy, he had a new tool to keep watch over the military. For the first time, the White House staff could monitor the unfolding crisis from the International Situation Room, just one flight below the Oval Office. Kennedy had the alert center built in the weeks after the Bay of Pigs invasion in 1961 as a way to receive direct access to intelligence and news reports. No one, he felt, should have better access to information than the president of the United States. In creating the Situation Room, he hoped to solve a problem that had long dogged the nation's commanders-in-chief. For years, collecting wartime intelligence and having it at their fingertips had been difficult. Sixty years earlier, another Cuban crisis had given rise to the first White House command center. Whereas Abraham Lincoln had often journeyed next door to the War Department in the Old Executive Office Building to read telegraph reports during the Civil War, President William McKinley wanted more direct access during the Spanish-American War. After the explosion of the USS *Maine* in Havana, McKinley converted a sitting room on the residence's second floor into what he had dubbed the "Operating Room," but the press quickly nicknamed the "War Room." From there, he monitored the war using a score of telegraph lines and even the newly invented telephone. A hand-painted map, "probably the best and largest of its kind," filled a wall, where colored pins and flags tracked battles and units. The Army Signal Corps created a Telegraph and Cipher Bureau to run the executive mansion command post, the government's first twenty-four-hour telegraph office, and one of the bureau's expert telegraph operators began accompanying the president when he traveled. "The arrangements were so perfect that President McKinley at Washington was able to communicate with the officers on the firing line in Santiago in less than twenty minutes," news reports of the era bragged.

In the years after McKinley's assassination, Theodore Roosevelt wanted more presidential office space and to separate the White House's residence from its workspace. At the time, both were located on the second floor above the ceremonial rooms. The new West Wing was built in 1902 and expanded upon a second time by William Howard Taft in 1909 to include a new oval-shaped presidential office. FDR in 1933 found the space too small and ordered another expansion that moved the Oval Office to the southeast corner of the West Wing, where it remains today.

For his own command post, Franklin Roosevelt converted a ladies' cloakroom on the ground floor into the White House Map Room, modeled after Winston Churchill's Admiralty Map Room in England's underground Cabinet War Rooms. There, military officers monitored communications around the clock. Oversized wall-mounted National Geographic maps of the Atlantic and Pacific theaters were covered with plastic sheets, and the duty officers used grease pencils to track the movements and positions of Allied and Axis forces. FDR stopped by twice a day, on his way to and from the Oval Office. Truman, after he took over as president, initially used the room to help plan for the postwar era, but his later extensive White House renovation had returned it to its original Georgian appearance.

The Kennedy administration's answer to FDR's Map Room grew to become the Cold War's premier command post—indeed one of the most famous rooms in the world. The need for the command center also marked an important evolution between the commander-in-chief and troops in the field. In the nuclear age, military decisions were as often as not political decisions as well, which—for better or worse—necessitated much closer coordination between the president and generals or admirals in the field.

While popular mythology holds that the Situation Room was created after the Bay of Pigs, the suggestion for the new command post actually arrived at the White House ten days before the CIA-backed invasion of Cuba on April 17, 1961. The Air Force had proposed rethinking "National Cold War Operations," arguing the president needed a large "National Daily Situation Room" to "assist in the continuing review and direction of cold war matters." A week after the botched invasion, Air Force aide Godfrey McHugh passed along a two-page outline to President Kennedy for the "nerve center for the White House" that would be the "war room for the cold war." McHugh underlined the latter phrase for emphasis. After some discussion, the administration settled on a smaller version of the original Air Force proposal, but adopted the original proposed name. The task of building the $35,000 facility fell to Navy aide Tazewell Shepard, who brought in Navy Seabees to rebuild President Truman's old bowling alley in the White House basement—the same group had built the Camp David bomb shelter, as well as the vacation shelters in Nantucket and Palm Beach. The Seabees team spent a week building the four rooms of the newly dubbed International Situation Room, working only at night to avoid disturbing the West Wing staff.

The Situation Room cobbled together a duty staff from the various national security agencies. Tazewell Shepard's office ran operations during workdays; the CIA duty officer was in charge on nights and weekends. The "Sit Room," as it became known, was not part of the White House's underground bunker structure, just a warren of offices in the basement next to the White House Mess. It actually overlooks West Executive Avenue, where the Park Service plants red geraniums in the Sit Room's window boxes. Initially, the space was almost entirely used by the watch staff. Featuring cramped rooms with drop ceilings, piled high with files, it looked nothing like the gleaming war rooms of later Hollywood lore. The first time Kennedy saw the space, he called it a "pigpen," and he preferred meeting with advisors in the Oval Office or the Roosevelt Room. Only with subsequent administrations would presidents begin to use the room as a key meeting facility. The conference room featured low-backed upholstered chairs and extensive wood paneling. Shepard and McGeorge Bundy requisitioned old teletype machines from the East Wing bomb shelter and installed direct links to the State Department, the Pentagon, and the CIA. The White House Army Signal Agency also installed direct telephone lines to the nation's top allies, like Charles de Gaulle in France and Konrad Adenauer in West Germany.* Speaking to the nation's enemies, meanwhile, remained puzzlingly difficult.

Indeed, through the entire Cuban Missile Crisis, communication challenges bedeviled both superpowers—underscoring the era's strange mix of high-tech weaponry and low-tech communication tools. The first

* The line to Great Britain's prime minister, Harold Macmillan, was nicknamed the "Mac-Jack" line by the Situation Room staff.

transatlantic phone line for ordinary citizens had only been laid in 1956 and it had space for just twenty-four simultaneous calls—a very tiny straw through which to connect two continents. Instead, most people—including most of the government—still relied primarily on letters or teletypes.

At 4:42 p.m. on Friday afternoon Moscow Time (9:42 a.m. in Washington), the Soviet government delivered a five-page message for Kennedy from Khrushchev. It took the U.S. embassy in Moscow nearly twelve hours to encode and send it along, meaning the final portion of the letter didn't arrive in Washington until 9 p.m. Friday night. A message from the Soviet embassy back to Moscow relied, in part, on a bicycle messenger from the local Washington Western Union office. "Usually it was the same young black man," recalled Ambassador Anatoly Dobrynin. "But after he pedaled away with my urgent cable, we at the embassy could only pray that he would take it to the Western Union office without delay and not stop to chat on the way with some girl."

As the crisis continued, officials around the capital knew an evacuation order could come at any time. White House staff began to sort through relocation checklists, and most agencies and departments dispatched a handful of staff to Mount Weather and other relocation sites. On paper, it all looked clear. In the early years of the Kennedy administration, the government's Joint Emergency Evacuation Plan (JEEP) provided for emergency helicopter evacuation from Washington to both Mount Weather (HIGH POINT) and Raven Rock (SITE R). When DEFCON 1 was announced, Army and Air Force helicopters would swoop down onto the Pentagon's helipads and into downtown Washington to evacuate a total of 252 government officials, including preplanned teams from the Army, Navy, Air Force, the Joint Chiefs, NATO, and the Office of the Secretary of Defense. Each had special numbered instruction cards that granted the bearers access to the helicopters. While fifty-two staff from the Office of Emergency Planning would be taken to HIGH POINT, hundreds of other officials across the government would be responsible for finding their own transportation to the relocation sites.*

---

* Outside of normal 8 a.m. to 5 p.m. working hours, everyone was responsible for finding their own way to the relocation facilities.

The plans in reality proved messy. As agencies began to study their COG documents, they realized personnel lists were out of date and many staff who were supposed to be involved in the evacuation balked when they discovered that their families wouldn't be saved, too. As Ed McDermott recalled, "When we came so close to implementation of that plan, started tapping on the shoulder and indicating that in connection with your responsibility you are to go here or there, we found that these people were then faced with a choice of responsibility to their government and responsibility to their families. In practically every instance—and I'm not so sure we can be critical of this—the individual felt that his first responsibility was to his family."

"I never took it very seriously," explained Alexis Johnson, who was deputy undersecretary of state at the time. "It was an unrealistic thing, it seemed to me, that we'd all pick up at the ringing of a bell and run for the hills, leaving our families behind."

In many cases, the plans for what would happen after the attack were so secret and so closely held that they were almost useless. According to the Justice Department's secret plans, Maryland U.S. attorney Joseph D. Tydings would become the emergency attorney general for eight mid-Atlantic states. Tydings dispatched two young prosecutors, Stephen H. Sachs and Ben Civiletti—who would later become U.S. attorney general himself during the Carter administration—to Hampstead High School, about thirty miles north of the city, in Carroll County, the office's relocation site. At the school, the two men explained their mission and flashed their Justice Department credentials, but the principal seemed unimpressed. No one had explained to him that his 500-student school was to be requisitioned as an emergency command post. He referred them to the local fire department, where they met with a similarly disinterested response. "No generators, cots, mattresses, fresh water, or food were en route to Hampstead High School," Sachs realized afterward.

At the White House, Press Secretary Pierre Salinger realized the media would need to be included in the emergency plans, and Jacob Rosenthal, a Justice Department public affairs officer, was sent over to the White House to compile the list of reporters who'd survive Armageddon. "I remember painfully going over a list of people and wondering how do you balance a columnist I didn't think very much of as opposed to a reporter who I thought really did work. And that was really hard," he recalled. To accomplish his new task, Rosenthal was given one of the IDs that allowed rare access to Mount Weather. "I was thrilled to get it because it was so James Bond–like," he recalled years later. "All government I.D. at that point was black and white.... Well this was, for God's sake, in color. A color photo of me in a laminated plastic card. And not just color, but woven gold threads across the face of the picture to make it impossible to counterfeit. And it had some numbers on it, but very little writing." Nowhere did it identify its purpose.

Salinger summoned Rosenthal's chosen small group of newsmen and told them about Mount Weather—swearing them to secrecy, but promising that they'd be brought along in an evacuation to report to the world on the president's actions. It wasn't entirely a secret to the press corps that such facilities existed. In the midst of the crisis, one reporter overheard a snippet of conversation as a door to a meeting opened briefly: "The area is beneath several hundred feet of rock. There is plenty of room and a cafeteria."

Reporters telephoned the homes of top government officials asking for family members, just to see if evacuations had taken place. Curtis LeMay didn't make any special provisions for his family, though he talked them through a plan. "The escape plan was to go to Arthur Godfrey's farm in Leesburg, Virginia. They were very close friends. No matter where we were, we were all to meet there. Well, there is no way that you would have ever gotten there because all the highways were civil defense highways," his daughter, Jane, recalled later. The family understood that they wouldn't get any special heads-up from their powerful patriarch just because he was the architect of the nation's offense. "He would always say, 'You read. You become aware of what is going on around you. You pay attention and do what you need to do when the time comes.'"

As the Missile Crisis deepened, President Kennedy's Navy doctor ordered that a briefcase be filled with the president's myriad medications—the steroids for his Addison's disease, painkillers to numb his long-troubled back, antihistamines for his allergies, antispasmodics for his colitis. The brown briefcase was left outside the Oval Office and marked "Personal Effects of the President." It must be ready "to move with the president's party at any time," the doctor wrote. Yet despite such preparations, it remained an open question whether President Kennedy and his senior advisors would agree to evacuate if an attack seemed imminent. Bobby Kennedy's family had taken a vote and decided to stay in town. They wanted to be close to their father. The president's family stayed close, too. Through the week, even as tense discussions unfolded in the West Wing, President Kennedy had taken the time each night to put Caroline and John Jr. to bed upstairs in the residence, reading them good-night stories. Now, as the weekend arrived, Jackie took the family out to Glen Ora, the family's vacation home in northern Virginia, where they'd be out of the immediate fallout zone if Washington was attacked. A small bomb shelter in the basement would serve as their primary protection. "The first problem was going to be to get the President to actually leave or move because of the deep sense of responsibility that he had and his desire to be personally involved up to the very last moment," McDermott recalled later.

Even if the president and his top advisors didn't make it out of Washington before an attack, the military was ready to dig the president and senior staff out of the White House rubble. Just ten days into the Kennedy administration in 1961, the Air Force had established the 2857th Test Squadron at the Olmsted Air Force Base outside Harrisburg, Pennsylvania. A hundred or so miles north of Washington, well outside the capital's blast zone, the innocuously named unit actually consisted of an elite search-and-rescue team, specially equipped to excavate the president from the bunker underneath the White House following a nuclear attack.

As Saturday afternoon turned into evening—the twelfth day of the crisis—a plan to defuse the situation seemed to be coming together. After his lengthy Friday letter, Khrushchev had sent a second transmission—this time publicly, over the airwaves of Radio Moscow, rather than by slow, standard diplomatic channels—demanding that the United States remove its Jupiter missiles from Turkey. Kennedy, for his part, agreed to end the quarantine and guarantee that the U.S. wouldn't invade Cuba if the Soviet missiles were dismantled and shipped back. That left only the Russian demand to withdraw the Jupiter missiles out of Turkey; Kennedy seemed inclined to concede the missiles, which U.S. officials didn't think much of anyway, and suggested that Bobby tell the Soviets privately that the U.S. would withdraw the Jupiters in a few months anyway. That part of the deal, though, had to remain secret to ensure that Turkey didn't feel betrayed.

At 11:08 a.m., Sunday morning, NORAD reported a missile launch from the Gulf of Mexico, heading north toward Tampa. Given how little warning there was, no one could act before the suspected missile should have detonated eighteen miles west of Tampa, so NORAD personnel quickly began to check the Western Union Bomb Alarm System, a government network of blast detectors mounted on telephone poles around the country. Conceived in 1959, the nationwide network had become fully operational earlier in 1962. The one-foot-tall optical sensors, shaped something like a small garbage can and mounted in groups of three to seven around 100 of the nation's largest cities and most vital military installations, ran on Western Union telegraph circuits. Scientists had figured out that a nuclear blast had a unique optical wave pattern that distinguished it from all naturally occurring flashes like lightning: A nuclear flash started with a "fast-rising, short-duration pulse followed by a comparatively slow-rising long-duration pulse" as the fireball grew. Not even nature's most intense thunderstorm could trick the system into mistaking the universe's splitting of an atom.

The system was designed to detect and report the flash of a nuclear blast within two seconds—since light travels so much faster than sound, the alarm would have been sounded long before the blast wave destroyed the detector. To ensure that the sensors were functioning, each detector communicated a "green" message every two minutes to one of six central command centers across the country run by NORAD's 9th Space Division. In the event that two or more Bomb Alarms in a given cluster reported a nuclear explosion, it would trigger a red light on large maps displayed at eleven key government installations—including NORAD, SAC, the Pentagon's NMCC, Raven Rock, and Mount Weather—that would indicate which city had been vaporized. Thus a century after Abraham Lincoln had first relied on telegraph updates from his military field commanders to follow battles in the Civil War, for a few brief moments on a Sunday morning in 1962, the 9th Space Division waited anxiously for a telegraph report about whether Tampa had been obliterated by a nuclear missile. Was this war? That Sunday morning, though, everything stayed green.

An investigation discovered that a radar station in Moorestown, New Jersey, hurriedly reconfigured to look south toward Cuba, had accidentally picked up an object in space coming over the southern horizon and registered it as a missile. A similar mistake would happen later that day at another radar station in Laredo, Texas. Both were false alarms, but they worried officials. There were so many moving parts, so many places for a miscalculation to sneak into the system—and possibly begin a deadly chain of events.

At last, Khrushchev sent a final message on Sunday, announcing his decision to remove the missiles, and again sent it over three routes—including Radio Moscow—to prevent the earlier delays.

Khrushchev had blinked. The crisis was over.

The Cuban Missile Crisis profoundly reshaped the government's thinking about nuclear war. Its legacy included, counterintuitively, both the escalation of the arms race and a general lessening of overall day-to-day tension. Khrushchev had faced America's strong nuclear superiority and been humiliated. In the years ahead, his country embarked on a massive military buildup, boosting ICBM production and achieving a rough parity by the late 1960s.

On the American side, McNamara and Kennedy gave up their earlier ideals about a "counterforce" nuclear strategy in the wake of the crisis. There would be no real way for a nuclear war to be tolerable, they believed. Building any sort of reasonable defensive measures against Soviet missiles would be prohibitively expensive, and it seemed impossible to have a "No cities" doctrine that precisely targeted hundreds of nuclear weapons only on "counterforce," or military, targets. War procedures changed as well. SAC's airborne alert became standard, ensuring that there were always bombers in the sky, ready to respond to a surprise attack.

Another major effect of the Cuban Missile Crisis was that the United States would never again mount a serious, widespread public civil defense effort. The crisis had made everyone recognize how logistically complicated such a massive exercise truly was and how futile. The sole priority, it was decided, would be saving the government—although those plans shifted as well to include new groups. Given that so many officials objected to the evacuation plans that excluded their families, the White House and civil defense officials implemented a new approach: After the officials themselves were evacuated, their dependents and families were to report to the presidential emergency communications tower in Northwest Washington code-named CARTWHEEL, centrally chosen because of the number of White House staff who lived in the surrounding neighborhoods. There, under the watchful eye of the CARTWHEEL security forces, they could await a motorcade to whisk them out of town to another relocation site—not Mount Weather or Raven Rock, but one of the other, smaller, less hardened bunkers. Food and water would be provided to the families during the evacuation, according to a memo, and beyond that the dependents were "urged not to attempt to bring personal belongings."

Press secretary Pierre Salinger also formalized his Doomsday press corps. While the media had participated in exercises like Operation Alert, there had previously not been any accommodation for the working media in actual emergency relocation plans. Salinger created a list of sixteen White House reporters, including the "snoopiest of the lot," and provided them details for evacuation purposes. Certain veteran TV and radio broadcasters—including ABC News's Lewis Shollenberger, NBC's Sander Vanocur, and Steve McCormick of the Mutual Broadcasting Service—were placed on call to ensure that there would be familiar faces broadcasting to the nation during an emergency. Jacob Rosenthal, who had helped select the list during the Missile Crisis, outlined in a series of memos the duties of this press corps—who would report for all of the nation's media, not just their given organizations—and how their efforts would likely be heavily proscribed by the government and the censorship board. The government, for one thing, wasn't at all sure how to limit their access once inside Mount Weather, where in addition to the official news releases they'd have access to casual contacts in the halls, cafeteria, and living quarters, as well as overhear the mountain's closed-circuit public announcements.

In their own exercise, the Emergency Press Pool was helicoptered one night to Mount Weather and taken inside the mountain in trolley shuttles. In one building, they were shown the designated press briefing room, stocked with old wooden desks, telephones, and typewriters complete with extra ribbons. One of the journalists asked during the tour, "What good is it to have a reporter in a very secure place? Whom would he report to?"

In the weeks immediately following the end of the crisis, the Kennedy administration also began an extensive overhaul of what was known as the Defense Resources Act, the standby legislation that would be pulled off the shelf and introduced to Congress during a national emergency. "For the first time, at least in this administration, top leadership in Government has taken a hard look at emergency responsibilities and preparedness deficiencies," McDermott wrote to Bernard Baruch. "We have made considerable progress in this climate of crisis."

Also known as the Standby War Powers Legislation, the Defense Resources Act was a powerful and sweeping rewriting of American government and the U.S. economy, including rationing, price controls, media censorship, property confiscation, the creation of emergency government agencies, the seizure of private industries, and other powers considered too politically toxic ever to be discussed in peacetime. For all intents and purposes, the legislation would allow suspension of the Constitution and Bill of Rights for an unspecified time. It was never introduced—nor disclosed publicly—though its passage by Congress was regularly role-played as part of readiness exercises well into the 1980s. "Only in time of stress will the people or the Congress be ready to consider the creation of a super executive with extraordinary powers," the Office of Emergency Planning's general counsel wrote McDermott in November 1962 after reviewing the draft legislation. "This is not a situation in which the axiom 'half a loaf is better than none' is readily applicable."

After the updates, the draft legislation was returned to the shelf, ready to be unveiled for Armageddon. The legislation included blanks on pages 11, 12, 13, and 19 where a president could fill in the details of the emergency, the name of the enemy, and, of course, the date of the attack.

After devoting so much of 1961 and 1962 to planning for war amid the crises in Berlin and Cuba, Kennedy dedicated himself in 1963 to peace. During his commencement address at American University in June 1963, he passionately called for disarmament and promised the United States "will never start a war." The site was more apropos than anyone realized at the time—the athletic fields where the graduates gathered were a key evacuation point for the government's COG plans. But on June 10, 1963, it was a scene for peace. "I am talking about genuine peace, the kind of peace that makes life on earth worth living, and the kind that enables men and nations to grow, and to hope, and build a better life for their children—not merely peace for Americans but peace for all men and women, not merely peace in our time but peace in all time," Kennedy said.

That summer, representatives of the Soviet Union, the United States, and Great Britain signed the Limited Nuclear Test Ban Treaty, banning testing in the atmosphere, space, and underwater. From that point forward, only underground testing would be allowed.

In the same spirit of cooperation and de-escalation, the two super-powers remedied a simple but critical shortfall underscored during the Missile Crisis: an easy and quick communication link between the leaders of the Soviet Union and the United States. A variety of people—including staff at the State Department Policy Planning Office and the editor of *Parade* magazine, Jess Gorkin—had pushed for it since 1960. The cause had been important to Gorkin since he'd read Peter George's novel, *Red Alert*, which became the basis for Stanley Kubrick's Cold War classic *Dr. Strangelove*. In an open letter, Gorkin highlighted the challenges of Cold War communication, asking, "Must a world be lost for want of a telephone call?"

In June 1963, negotiators in Geneva reached a "Memorandum of Understanding Regarding the Establishment of a Direct Communications Line" that would allow the American president to message the Soviet premier. What came to be known in popular culture as the "red phone" or "hotline" was actually a series of teletype machines installed in the Kremlin and the Pentagon's National Military Command Center. The Americans flew four to Moscow and the Soviets sent four East German–made machines to Washington. Initially, the link was hardly "direct." The main telegraph circuit bounced from Washington to London to Copenhagen to Stockholm to Helsinki before finally reaching Moscow; the backup line transited through Tangier, Morocco.*

There was purposely no voice capability, since—in an era long before crystal-clear telephone communication—both sides agreed speech could be garbled or misunderstood. If the hotline was designed for use in only the gravest situations, it had to convey clearly and accurately what the sender intended.† The teletype machines, referred to as the "Moscow Link" or

---

* The importance of having a backup was underscored when a Finnish farmer plowing his field accidentally severed the primary cable outside Helsinki, forcing the installation of a new line; in another instance, a fire in a Baltimore manhole disabled the line, and on a third occasion a Danish bulldozer cut the line outside Copenhagen.

† This realization has apparently been borne out: Amazingly, despite repeated tech upgrades in the decades ahead—to satellite communications, then fax, then e-mail transmission—the

MOLINK for short, transmitted in both English and Cyrillic to ensure accurate translation, and negotiators settled on using a Norwegian-built ETCRRM II coding machine, which secured the line from eavesdroppers, since the country was seen as impartial. A clock in the receiving room in each capital showed the time in the other city. After a few tests, on August 30, 1963, the U.S. broadcast the first message: THE QUICK BROWN FOX JUMPED OVER THE LAZY DOG'S BACK 1234567890, a pangram that used all of the Latin alphabet. The Russians sent back a similarly nonsensical Cyrillic pangram.

The Pentagon invested $159,849 in the equipment and fielded five two-man teams to staff the MOLINK in eight-hour shifts, each team consisting of one noncommissioned officer who oversaw the equipment and one officer who served as translator. Once an hour each day, the teams transmitted test messages—sometimes poetry, sometimes sports scores, sometimes Shakespeare. One nation tested on even hours; the other on odd. Twice a year, on New Year's and August 30—the link's anniversary—the two communication posts exchange formal congratulatory greetings.*

Even as the tensions of the Cuban Missile Crisis passed and the Cold War appeared to settle into a grim routine, the government's Doomsday apparatus continued out of sight. Across government, hundreds of staff manned bunkers and relocation sites on a daily basis, maintaining communication

---

hotline still has no voice capability as of 2016. The myth that it does, meanwhile, is so powerful that during the Reagan administration, when the State Department raised the possibility of upgrading the hotline for voice calls in 1983, many officials were surprised to discover it didn't already have it.

* The hotline was first used in 1967 during the Arab-Israeli Six-Day War—and quickly proved its improvement over the all-day message process of the Cuban crisis. The first Soviet message was transmitted at 7:47 a.m. Washington time, received at the Pentagon by 7:59, and a quick translation was conveyed to President Johnson by 8:30 a.m. Over the coming days, Johnson and Soviet premier Alexei Kosygin exchanged a total of nineteen messages over the hotline, helping to ensure that neither country's response to the unfolding Middle East crisis was seen as provocative to the other. The first use of the system showed the shortcomings of having the teletypes at the Pentagon, and Robert McNamara had in the years ahead hotline terminals installed directly at the White House and at Raven Rock.

systems and keeping supplies stocked, as well as performing the more mundane office tasks like opening the mail. Such was the lot of the sole duty officer who staffed the Immigration and Naturalization Service's relocation facility in Martinsburg, West Virginia. The INS officer shared the four-story federal building, seventy-five miles outside Washington, with the post office, courthouse, and the one FBI agent assigned to the local office.

On April 17, 1963, the opening of the day's mail unexpectedly became more exciting than usual—the duty officer tore open the envelope and flipped through the papers, puzzling over the contents. At first he was confused, then he realized someone had made a big mistake. He had to make some phone calls. The government needed to get a postal inspector down to North Carolina pronto to find three Cuban emigrants and retrieve from them documents they should have never seen in the first place.

A few days earlier in Banner Elk, North Carolina, the three Cuban emigrants must have been confused themselves when the postmaster handed them the lengthy twenty-one-page questionnaires. Form AE-2, "Application for Certificate of Identity," took forever to fill out, asking all sorts of seemingly invasive questions about their background, family, and other information. When they were done with the questionnaire, the postmaster then took their fingerprints, dutifully completing Form AE-6—the fingerprint card—as they all stood in the lobby of the post office in the tiny town on the edge of the Cherokee National Forest. Then, perhaps most puzzling of all, he handed them certificates proclaiming all three enemy aliens. The carbon copies of Form AE-2 he then mailed to the INS relocation site in Martinsburg, and he mailed the fingerprint cards to the FBI, just as he was supposed to do in the event of war.

Except that the United States wasn't at war. The Banner Elk postmaster had inadvertently given the Cuban emigrants the forms the Justice Department had pre-positioned at every U.S. post office as part of its plans to deal with subversive elements in the event of a national emergency. Indeed, the Post Office—the agency with the widest reach of any arm of the federal government, stretching into every community and with comprehensive lists of where individuals and families lived—had become a key link in post-attack planning during the Cold War. For starters, after an evacuation or attack, individuals and families would be given Form #810,

"Safety Notification Cards," postage-free cards that could be mailed to "any person who might be concerned about your safety." The cards read simply "I am/We are safe and can be reached at this address until further notice," and included space to add names of family members also safe at that location. But the Post Office also had more direct duties, too: In February 1962, with Executive Order 11002, Kennedy had tasked the postmaster general with assembling a national registration program that would help the country understand after an attack who was still alive and where refugees were located; it was to assemble and distribute emergency registration forms to help ensure that families could be reunited and the dead identified. A key part of this program was the registration of foreign aliens, which would help the FBI and other government agencies identify and round up those considered subversive.

That enemy alien roundup was just one part of the Justice Department's own massive emergency plans. Indeed, few U.S. officials during a national emergency would have been more key than the attorney general—and not just because Bobby Kennedy was then the president's brother and most trusted advisor. Like Defense Secretary McNamara, his limousine was equipped with two telephones—one regular phone and a second directly connected with Mount Weather. Everywhere he went, Robert F. Kennedy was accompanied by what was known as the Attorney General's Emergency Briefcase, a portfolio filled with four different sets of documents, each prewritten and ready for presidential signatures.

The documents, known collectively as the Emergency Detention Program, had titles like "Alien Control Program," "Internment of Diplomatic Personnel of Enemy Nations Program," "Handling of Dangerous Nonenemy Aliens Attached to International Organizations," and so forth. Together, they provided the FBI and other federal agencies with sweeping powers to arrest, search, detain, and deport thousands of people who the government decreed might commit "acts inimical to the security of the country in time of emergency."

Part I of the portfolio would allow the president to suspend the "privilege of the writ of habeas corpus," and included what was known as the "Master Arrest Warrant" and "Master Search Warrant," blanket provisions that okayed the arrests and search of "dangerous" persons, both "citizens and aliens alike."

Part II laid out procedures for the control and emergency deportation of "non-dangerous aliens," that is, the college students, tourists, law-abiding immigrants, and so forth who had ties to enemy nations. Again, these powers were sweeping—meant to quickly dispense with anyone who might pose a threat to the United States immediately or in the future as hostilities proceeded. At the very least, all these individuals would be expected to register with the INS at their local post offices and received wartime "Certificates of Identification" for "Alien Enemies." It was these pre-positioned forms that the Banner Elk postmaster had accidentally provided to the Cuban emigrants.

Part III concerned documents, proclamations, and executive orders that could be used in a more nuanced situation—for instance, an unfolding "limited" emergency short of war—that might not necessitate mass arrests, searches, and deportations, but did require immediate targeted actions by the FBI and other federal law enforcement.

Lastly, Part IV of the Attorney General's Emergency Portfolio laid out all the necessary mechanics for declaring civil defense emergencies, activating emergency reserve forces, stockpiles, and so forth.

The Emergency Briefcase and outline of the Emergency Detention Program was never far from the attorney general. A backup briefcase was placed at the Little Rock Field Office in case the original was destroyed or inaccessible in Washington following an attack; beginning in 1959, additional copies were to be stored in a Mount Weather safe accessible only to the Justice Department. There, a full-time Justice Department representative oversaw the department's COG planning and a pre-positioned set of the Presidential Emergency Action Documents, the Master Search Warrant, Master Arrest Warrant, and additional instructions relating to the "Internal Security Programs." Since the U.S. attorneys for Maryland, Northern Illinois, and Colorado were in the chain of succession for the attorney general, other sealed copies of the war plans went to the FBI field offices in Baltimore, Chicago, and Denver.

Theoretically, the Emergency Detention Program could only be activated with presidential authorization and the attorney general's signature. However, under limited circumstances, if the top four officials at DOJ were not reachable, the FBI director or his successor could implement the emergency plans, including the "apprehension and search and seizure provisions of the Emergency Detention Program."*

During each Operation ALERT and readiness exercise, the attorney general and the president ran through activating the detention plans, but they all understood the wartime plans might cause "a real storm of controversy," and so kept them as secret as possible. In 1956, during Operation ALERT, when the president was testing out the procedures for the Emergency Detention Program, the Justice Department had specially dispatched a representative to HIGH POINT's press center to "smother any reference to legal items or decisions" during the exercise.†

The basis for the FBI's Cold War Emergency Detention Program was Congress's controversial 1950 Emergency Detention Act—introduced amid

---

* Of course, such detentions were by no means unprecedented in American history: During the Civil War, President Lincoln suspended the writ of habeas corpus and detained thousands of Confederate sympathizers, and during World War II Franklin Roosevelt ordered the internment of 112,000 Japanese Americans, including 70,000 U.S. citizens. During World War I, a young J. Edgar Hoover had played a key role in the Palmer Raids, an effort by the Justice Department to arrest and deport some 500 suspected radicals, Bolsheviks, and anarchists.

† Eventually, the Enemy Detention Act was repealed by Congress in 1971, with new language that promised "No citizen shall be imprisoned or otherwise detained by the United States except pursuant to an Act of Congress." The Justice Department strongly supported the repeal. As Deputy Attorney General Richard G. Kleindienst wrote to Congress in 1969, "In the judgment of this Department, the repeal of this legislation will allay the fears and suspicions—unfounded as they may be—of many of our citizens." The Justice Department's public push to repeal the law, though, was belied by the fact that in an emergency the government would most likely go ahead and do what it felt it needed to do; in fact, J. Edgar Hoover's original plan for mass preemptive arrests and detention during the Korean War predated by months the technical authority of the Enemy Detention Act. The government clearly felt it didn't need a technical "law" to allow it to make arrests in time of war. Indeed, as crystal clear as the 1971 repeal language might appear, after the 9/11 attacks in 2001, the George W. Bush administration argued that it didn't apply to "the military's wartime detention of enemy combatants," a loophole large enough to allow hundreds to be held without formal charge at Guantánamo Bay and elsewhere.

the fears of McCarthyism and the start of the Korean War, and passed over a presidential veto by Truman. It allowed the government to round up in time of war or national emergency those it suspected might engage in subversive acts. The Enemy Detention Act—which included due process for those detained—was actually seen as a step forward for civil liberties, providing a legal mechanism and framework for what, the legislators admitted, the government would probably do anyway in wartime. West Virginia senator Harley Kilgore later recalled, "Our detention of Japanese in World War II was handled in a manner which did us little credit as a nation, and I felt that it would be well to have orderly detention legislation enacted for use in the event of a national emergency."

In the years that followed, the government renovated World War II prisoner of war camps in Florence, Arizona, and El Reno, Oklahoma, as well as former Army facilities in Wickenburg, Arizona; Tule Lake, California; Avon Park, Florida; and Allenwood, Pennsylvania. Maintained by the Bureau of Prisons, the six facilities were on standby through the early Cold War to receive thousands of people on J. Edgar Hoover's "Security Index," his secret list of suspected Communists and other enemies of the state. During an emergency with the Soviet Union, Hoover had ready a list of 22,663 "hard-core" Communists in the United States. To guard against further saboteurs and subversives, the Border Patrol's force of 1,500 agents would be supplemented in an emergency with a "surge" of between 7,000 and 16,000 additional temporary agents to seal the border.

In mid-November 1963, John F. Kennedy spent the weekend in Florida, relaxing at the family estate in Palm Beach and later, watching the launch of a Polaris missile from the USS *Andrew Jackson*, the first time he'd ever seen that leg of the Nuclear Triad perform. The submarines had allowed a big shift in America's deterrence strategy. "We shall also gain time to think in periods of tension," Admiral Arleigh Burke told a group of retired naval officers. The Navy hoped for a total fleet of forty-five ballistic missile submarines, of which twenty-nine would be deployed at any one time. Those subs, packed with Polaris missiles, would be able to destroy at least 232 targets—more than enough to serve as a counterpunch.

Next up on the president's agenda was a trip to Dallas. When Kennedy left Florida that day, he expected to be back in Palm Beach shortly for Christmas, the second anniversary of the vacation bunker on Peanut Island. It had been used precisely twice for drills when President Kennedy was evacuated from the family estate.

The bunker, as it turned out, would never be used again.

Chapter 9

ANGEL IS AIRBORNE

A surprisingly adoring crowd greeted President Kennedy at Dallas's Love Field on November 22, 1963. The president had looked out the window of the plane that served as Air Force One and turned to George Thomas, his longtime valet from Berryville, Virginia, the small rural community home to Mount Weather, to joke: "I think this is a bigger town than you come from."

An hour later, the president's pilot, Colonel James Swindal, was finishing lunch—a roast beef sandwich—when panicked voices erupted over his radio, making it clear something had gone terribly wrong with the presidential motorcade into the city. With Kennedy dead from an assassin's bullet, Lyndon Johnson's aides and Secret Service pushed the vice president to get back to the plane and escape to Washington. Before leaving Texas, he wanted to take the oath. Passengers were herded toward the main staff area of the plane, though one agent remained with the president's body in the rear. Jackie Kennedy, her skirt still stained with blood, stood next to Johnson as Texas judge Sarah Hughes recited the famous words. The entire process took just twenty-nine seconds, her words and his both barely audible to those even just a few feet away over the whining jet engines. As Hughes reached the end of the oath she added an ad lib: "So help me God." Johnson repeated the phrase, then issued his first order as commander-in-chief: "Now let's get airborne."

Swindal raised the four Pratt & Whitney turbofan engines to maximum throttle. The plane began to move forward, slowly at first, then faster. At

2:47 p.m., the pilot eased his yoke back, tilting the plane upward; Air Force One's wheels left the Texas soil. It banked toward the northeast as news of its takeoff passed through the military radio channels, using the plane's classified code name: "ANGEL is airborne."

The blue-and-white plane that carried Johnson and Kennedy that day represented the physical embodiment of the postwar presidency and American power. It was a relatively new addition, recognizing that the Cold War era required the president to conduct war and diplomacy wherever the commander-in-chief might be.

For the first 117 years of the nation's existence, presidents never ventured far. Unsure of the legality of being "president" outside the country, the first century of presidents carefully remained within the nation's borders. William McKinley agreed in 1901 to meet the Mexican president, but on the border of the two countries. It wasn't until Theodore Roosevelt's trip to Panama in 1906 that a president ever traveled internationally—and he did so as quickly as possible, sprinting aboard a U.S. Navy ship to the Canal Zone and remaining out of territorial waters for only ten hours. A dozen years later, Woodrow Wilson became the first president to journey to Europe, and his trip ignited a firestorm of political criticism. When Wilson left America for the Paris Peace Conference, an absence that would stretch for months, Senator Lawrence Yates Sherman introduced a resolution to declare Wilson "absent" from office and install Vice President Thomas Marshall as the "acting" president until Wilson returned to U.S. shores. "It is a palpable violation of the act of 1790, approved by George Washington, to attempt to exercise the constitutional sovereign powers of the President within the domain of another government," Sherman had thundered, saying, "The President of the United States is not its President in France; he is an alien there, a mere citizen of the Republic, shorn of all his sovereign powers." Yet the country's growing global influence required the president to travel more regularly.

FDR's journey by lumbering Pan Am Flying Boat from Miami to Casablanca made him the first president to travel by air, to fly abroad, and the first to set foot in Africa. Ironically, the president flew because the Secret Service and the military deemed it safer than facing the marauding Nazi U-boats in the North Atlantic. It was a difficult and time-consuming trip: four legs of flying, three stops, and three days' travel each way. All told, FDR spent nearly ninety hours in the air for a trip that today Royal Air Maroc accomplishes in about eight hours. That journey gave rise a few weeks later to the Army Air Corps' decision that the president should have his own airplane. For the long flight to Yalta in February 1945 to meet Winston Churchill and Joseph Stalin as the war wound down, Roosevelt first boarded his four-engine *Sacred Cow*, a DC-4 aircraft painted standard Army olive drab and heavily modified to include a spacious presidential suite and an elevator to lift his wheelchair in and out. The trip, code-named ARGONAUT, represented the far limits of presidential travel; since legislation had to be dealt with within ten days, the five-day journey back and forth to the Crimean Peninsula significantly stretched the presidency to what historian Michael Dobbs called the "logistical limits of the wartime American presidency."*

Truman quickly picked up the air travel habit, boarding *Sacred Cow* just weeks after he took office to fly home to Independence, Missouri—the first domestic flight in presidential history. From that moment forward, presidents seemed to be in near-constant states of travel. Walt Disney offered to design a special insignia for the plane—a smiling cow with a halo over one horn and an Uncle Sam top hat over the other—and it began to be bedecked with the flags of the country it had visited: a total of fifty-one by the time it was retired in July 1947.† When Truman's second plane, a DC-6 named *Independence* after his hometown, was delivered, the designers at Douglas decked it out with an eagle motif, incorporating the cockpit windows as the bird's eyes, and painted a golden beak on the plane's nose.

As the Cold War deepened Allen Dulles pushed Eisenhower to adopt a jet plane—it was critical, he argued, that the U.S. president be seen leading technological advances—and the fact that Khrushchev used jet aircraft meant it was time to retire the presidential propeller planes. In 1959, the first presidential jet had arrived, and in the final months of his presidency, Dwight Eisenhower barnstormed across eleven countries, circling the globe

---

* Shorter, noncritical messages were transmitted via a communications ship docked in Yalta, the USS *Catoctin*.

† Truman even signed the National Security Act of 1947 aboard the *Sacred Cow*, marking it, officially, as the birthplace of the U.S. Air Force.

from Europe to Asia to Africa, over a three-week tour that required massive logistics ranging from delivering special jet fuel to Ankara, clearing cows off the runway in New Delhi, and providing airborne weather reports for the presidential plane over the Afghanistan mountains.

The increasingly advanced and elaborate presidential planes were decked out with survival gear like parachutes—always five extra more than the passengers it carried, in case panicky officials deployed theirs inside the cabin accidentally. When the planes flew over oceans, Navy and Coast Guard ships were stationed in advance every 250 miles on picket duty in case of trouble. Later, as aviation technology advanced, Air Force rescue planes known as "Duck Butts" would accompany the president's plane, stocked with rescue swimmers, life rafts, and medical personnel who could aid survivors if the plane went down at sea.

For the first few decades of presidential flight, each plane had its own nickname. Before the existence of the Air Force as a separate branch of the military, FDR's *Sacred Cow* was known to air traffic controllers as "Army 7451" after the last four digits of its tail number, 42-107451. Later planes were known by the abbreviation for Air Force "Special Air Missions," such as SAM 6505 for Truman's *Independence* plane and Eisenhower's SAM 8610 (which was nicknamed *Columbine II*). While consistent with normal air traffic control call signs, the system proved inadequate for the increasingly crowded skies of the 1950s and the critical status of the president's plane in the nuclear age. The standard call sign didn't distinguish whether the president was on board or if it simply was an empty aircraft; in the nuclear age, knowing the president's whereabouts minute by minute was a necessity. The decades of traditional shorthand came to an end shortly after a 1953 flight to Florida had seen the presidential plane confused with Eastern Air Lines Flight 8610. The military decided that it needed a specific call sign to designate the priority status of the president's aircraft; "Air Force One" was born. The moniker didn't catch on with the public until the press began using it as shorthand to refer to the first jet aircraft delivered to President Kennedy.* That new Boeing 707 (known as a VC-137 in military parlance),

---

* Kennedy, whose private family plane was known as *Caroline*, never nicknamed the presidential aircraft.

tail number SAM 26000, arrived at Andrews Air Force Base for presidential service on October 10, 1962, and became the first presidential plane stationed at the base. It was a model of modern transportation; at 146 feet long, it could carry forty passengers and fly as high as eight miles above the earth. Jackie Kennedy tapped industrial designer Raymond Loewy—best known for designing the logos for Shell and TWA and Coke's remake of its contour bottle—to create a new look for the new plane. He scrapped the traditional U.S. Air Force logo and instead went with a blue-and-white livery, with "United States of America" painted large, oversized presidential seal decals, and the American flag—the familiar design that would be used with few modifications to the present day, instantly conveying American majesty and power.*

Airplane designers had little experience designing VIP jet planes, so they'd put the presidential compartment toward the rear, a carryover from the traditional location for VIP cabins in propeller craft, where it was furthest removed from the noisy engines. Later Air Force planes would relocate the VIP cabins to the front of the plane, where today all first-class cabins in commercial planes also are. Kennedy loved the plane: He put 75,000 miles on it, traveling domestically and internationally. Just a few months earlier, the same plane, SAM 26000, had carried him to Germany, where he'd pledged his allegiance to the people of Berlin with his historic statement: "Ich bin ein Berliner." Boarding it at the end of that day, he'd told Swindal and the other crew, "We'll never have another day like this."

The flight on November 22, 1963, was a remarkable testament to the resilience of the American government. Even as the aides and officials gathered in Dallas, they knew nothing of the assassin who felled their commander-in-chief, knew nothing about the global response, whether it was a lone wacko, the start of a Soviet attack, or a subversive plot on the nation. Yet with just a few words power transferred simply to a new man, and with it the reins of a nation and the codes to all of its nuclear weapons. When he first

---

* The planes used by other government officials, including the usual Air Force Two, had red-painted engines, rather than Air Force One's blue ones, just to make clear the presidential plane.

received word that Kennedy was dead, Sergeant John Trimble, the signal-
man, used the radio call sign "AF 26000" because the plane had no president
aboard. Then, as Johnson had boarded the Boeing jet in Dallas, Trimble assumed a new call sign on the radio with Andrews: "This is Air Force One,"
telegraphing to the nation in its own way the Continuity of Government—
the president is dead, long live the president. Everyone listening on the radio
heard the call sign and knew at once that everything was the same—and yet
everything was also different.

During the flight to Washington, the Secret Service pushed Johnson
to spend the night in the White House, but he made it clear that he didn't
want to seem presumptive. The vice president wouldn't receive an official
residence until the Naval Observatory in 1974, so Johnson had commuted
to the White House compound each day from Spring Valley near the Maryland line.* He would continue to do so now as president—at least until the
Kennedys had some time to arrange their affairs, he said.

As vice president, Johnson's security had evolved. Official Washington
had been so disinterested in Lyndon Johnson that his home telephone number was listed in the phone book. And therein lay the puzzle of the vice
presidency: As John Adams said, there was but one piece of magic in the
otherwise most worthless job in Washington: "I am Vice President. In this
I am nothing, but I may be everything." Secret Service director James Rowley had encouraged Johnson in both 1961 and 1962 to stop traveling on
commercial planes, which didn't allow secure access to the National Command Authorities, and rely instead on U.S. Air Force jets. The Secret Service
argued with Johnson, telling him the world was a more complicated place
and the vagaries of nuclear weapons required more reliable communications.
It wasn't, though, until Kennedy had signed legislation in 1962 that officially
elevated Johnson's security to "the same level of protection as the President"
that the switch was finally made to Air Force Two.

Now that Johnson was president and the situation on the ground was
still unclear, agent Rufus Youngblood urged him, too, "to think of security

---

* His home at 4040 52nd Street NW, known as "The Elms," today serves as the residence
of the Algerian ambassador.

first" and remain at the White House, but Johnson cut off the conversation: "We are going home to The Elms. That's where we live. If you can protect us at the White House, by God you can protect us at home too."

His orders clear, Youngblood scrunched himself into the communications shack aboard the speeding plane to call the White House security chief, Gerald Behn. Though the top-of-the-line radiophone on board the new Boeing 707 supposedly represented a huge upgrade to Air Force One's telecommunications system, each phone call remained a struggle and included a not insignificant transmission lag. While there were nine phone extensions on board, there could be only three simultaneous conversations with people down below. Youngblood's connection was patchy at best—riddled with static, garbled transmissions, and packed with code names.

What are commonly known as "Secret Service code names" are actually code names given by the White House Communications Agency to officials and their families and are grouped around the same letters: All the Kennedy family names began with L; LANCER for JFK, LACE for Jackie, LYRIC for Caroline, and LARK for Jack Jr. The Johnson family had received V names: VOLUNTEER for Lyndon, VICTORIA for Lady Bird, VELVET for Lynda, and VENUS for Luci. White House staff had code names that began with W; altogether, there were more than 200 in use at a given time, including separate code names for major destinations like CROWN for the White House, and VALLEY for the vice president's private residence at The Elms. "Originally the code names were a good idea and did facilitate communications, but like most everything else in government, [they've] gotten out of hand," Sergeant Trimble recalled. It was a lot to keep straight in a conversation—especially in a chaotic one.

"Volunteer will reside at VALLEY for an indefinite time. I repeat: VOLUNTEER will reside at VALLEY for an indefinite time. VICTORIA requests that VENUS will go to VALLEY with agent," Youngblood transmitted.

"Will you say again?" Behn asked from the White House. "Will you say again?"

"VENUS should go out to VALLEY with agent," a White House operator, also on the line, tried to clarify.

"That is a roger," Youngblood said. "That is a roger. VENUS will go to VALLEY with agent. VICTORIA will go to VALLEY after first to CROWN. Do you understand? Over."

"VICTORIA will go to VALLEY after first going to CROWN," the White House operator repeated.

"Okay, that's affirmative," Behn said.

Youngblood signed off: "All right—that is all the traffic I have at present."

A few minutes passed, and then a further thought came from Air Force One: Now that Lyndon Johnson was president, they realized, the public telephone line at his house—the one in the phone book—should be disconnected and new secure phones installed.

Tracking down the various decision makers and top officials in the hours after the assassination proved complicated because most of Kennedy's senior leadership wasn't with the presidential party that day. Six cabinet secretaries—including Secretary of State Dean Rusk and Treasury Secretary C. Douglas Dillon—were on board an Air Force jet, along with officials like White House press secretary Pierre Salinger, en route to Japan for meetings, incommunicado for hours at a time. Thus, aboard Air Force One, in Washington, and aboard the plane to Japan, officials were left to handle the uncertainty as best they could on their own, operating with limited information and limited ability to check with anyone else. In the wake of the assassination, U.S. military commanders around the world had moved their forces to a higher state of readiness, but neither Bundy nor Johnson advocated moving to a higher DEFCON. No sense, they thought, in alarming the Soviets or NATO allies. Similar thoughts preoccupied Johnson's mind as he considered the arrival at Andrews. Even as aides cautioned that Air Force One's landing should be conducted secretly, Johnson wanted a "normal" press arrival. It mustn't, Johnson said, "look like we're panicking."

As Colonel Swindal began the final descent, banking east over Middleburg toward the lights of Washington in the distance, Air Force One glided home. Outside the plane, the seeds of the turbulent 1960s that would confront Lyndon Johnson as president had already been sown. There were already 16,300 U.S. military "advisors" in Vietnam on November 22, 1963, and the social and cultural revolutions that would upend the comparatively quiet and homogeneous 1950s American lifestyle were similarly unfolding; that very day a British rock group named the Beatles had released their second album. After the Cold War had so dominated the day-to-day life of Truman, Eisenhower, and Kennedy, it would fade into the background for Johnson, who saw the morass of the escalation in Vietnam gradually consume his presidency.

After the nationally televised funeral for his slain predecessor, Johnson settled into the Oval Office. He found the Cold War in transition. Defense Secretary McNamara was abandoning the "counterforce" and "no cities" policies that he'd advocated earlier in his tenure and was broadly rethinking many of the tenets of the arms race. In late January 1964, McNamara received the final report of a study group he'd commissioned to examine whether it was worth investing money in the nation's defense. The inquiry, run by Air Force Lieutenant Colonel Glenn Kent, had the relatively obtuse title of *Damage Limitation: A Rationale for the Allocation of Resources by the U.S. and USSR*. It laid out a scenario that could, through a combination of antiballistic missile systems, extensive civil defense planning and operations, and a robust offensive strike capability, enable the United States to protect as much as 60 percent of its population and industry. The catch, though, was obvious: For every three dollars the U.S. invested in "damage limitation" measures, the Soviet Union would only have to spend a dollar on its offensive capabilities to even the score again. In many ways, the Kent Study marked the final stop on McNamara's evolution since he had first tried to bring sanity to an insane military option.

There was, three years of work had concluded, no sane policy to follow. "I cannot imagine any scenario leaders would initiate and hope to gain from it," McNamara said. Instead, as of the beginning of 1964, the United States would threaten Russia with "assured destruction," a policy that called for a strategy sufficient enough to inflict heavy damage on the Soviet Union even after weathering a first-strike attack on the United States. McNamara's team defined that level as killing 30 percent of the Soviet population, destroying 50 percent of its industrial capacity, and leveling a particularly precise "150 of their cities." As the Russian nuclear capability increased, Russia would

also be able to destroy much of the United States even if the U.S. attacked
first. It would become "Mutually Assured Destruction."

Strategists always loved acronyms, so they called the policy simply
"MAD."

And it was.

In August 1964, the Gulf of Tonkin episode, which would drag the na-
tion and the military deeper into Vietnam, caused officials across Washington to reexamine crisis plans that had been largely forgotten since the
Cuban Missile Crisis two years before. As part of those readiness checks,
Ed McDermott, the head of the Office of Emergency Planning, journeyed
to One First Street to talk again with Chief Justice Earl Warren about the
Supreme Court's seemingly dormant evacuation procedures. The Supreme
Court had long worried planners—it seemed quite uninterested in plan-
ning for its own survival—and McDermott's previous attempts to rouse the
Court to action had been politely rejected.

As McDermott again made his pitch, the chief justice explained that
evacuation plans still made no sense to him, and then proceeded to recount
a decade of broken promises by the executive branch. The Court had previously settled on the Grove Park Inn resort in North Carolina as its relocation site, but as the Eisenhower administration's strategy evolved the Court
had been told in 1957 not to finalize its plans for a new relocation facility.
Then more than five years elapsed with no news, and the $97,100 in funds
promised to upgrade the Court's own basement fallout shelter had never
materialized. In 1958, the Court had been told it would get special relocation cards, but again no follow-through. "We do not, in fact, know whether
or not the program of which this was a part has been abandoned," the clerk
had complained in 1963. Nearly all of the Court's plans and fallout shelter stockpiles had fallen into "disuse," all, that is, except for the building's
emergency first-aid kit, which the Court made sure to keep up to date in
the basement.

Finally, during the Kennedy administration, McDermott had visited
Warren to hand him his new gold-threaded color ID granting access to
Mount Weather in the event of an evacuation. The chief justice had warmly
invited McDermott into his office for coffee, but balked when McDermott

tried to hand over his pass. "I don't see the pass for Mrs. Warren," the chief justice had protested.

"You see, sir, you're one of the 2,000 most important people in the United States," McDermott had tried to explain.

"Well, here—you'll have room for one more important official," Warren had replied, handing the ID back.

During the Cuban Missile Crisis, the Kennedy administration had again gone to the Supreme Court to brief them on arrangements for an evacuation, and Robert F. Kennedy dispatched Assistant Attorney General Ramsey Clark, the son of then Supreme Court justice Tom Clark, to tour Mount Weather's facilities and then brief the chief justice. Warren wasn't interested. After Clark's presentation, the chief justice explained, simply, "Ramsey, I'm not going to relocate, I'm going to stay with my family."*

Now, as McDermott went over the 1964 plans during yet another national crisis, Warren found them just as impractical as before. While the chief justice and the other justices would be plucked from the Supreme Court lawn by helicopter and whisked to Mount Weather, there didn't seem to have been a moment's thought put into what would happen after that. There were no plans to move any court records, no room for any additional court personnel or for the justices' families, and the evacuation procedures were only in operation from 9 a.m. to 5 p.m.—an hour *less* than they'd been in operation during the Kennedy years, when at least evacuations would run from 8 a.m. to 5 p.m., exclusive of weekends or holidays. Warren pointed out that he didn't think his staff would be able to rent many trucks in the middle of a nuclear attack to move its papers and records, let alone get its staff onto jam-packed highways to travel to a relocation site or pick up the justices themselves if the attack happened on a night, weekend, or holiday.

Finally, Warren had had enough. He cut off the visiting briefer,

---

* It's a good thing, actually, that Warren didn't try to activate the Court's evacuation plans, which still called for the Supreme Court to relocate to the Grove Park Inn in Asheville, North Carolina. If the Court had shown up at the resort in the Blue Mountains in the midst of the Missile Crisis, it would have found a problem: The resort had actually double-booked for Armageddon, as Cold War historian Bill Geerhart uncovered in 2013. Documents show that in the Kennedy-era shelter frenzy the Grove Park Inn had also agreed to be a fallout shelter for Buncombe County beginning in August 1962.

exasperated: "Then I suppose I should call my wife and say, 'Honey, there is an atomic bomb attack to be made on Washington, and I am flying to safety in Appalachia. Sorry I don't have time to come home and say good-bye, but it is nice to have met you.'"

Warren told the administration liaison that he would not be evacuating—during that crisis or ever. And, he reported, "I heard nothing more about the helicopter or anything else from his office after that."

The Supreme Court would probably not survive Armageddon, if it ever came. But given the host of other preparations by the executive branch, perhaps that was acceptable. The post-disaster government was clearly going to be an executive branch dictatorship—one that drew upon sweeping and likely extralegal emergency powers. During that immediate period, there wouldn't be any need for the traditional constitutional protections overseen by the Court—because there wouldn't be anything resembling the Constitution for months or years afterward.

Even as the McNamara Pentagon plunged deeper into Vietnam, planners worked to address the COG challenges identified during the Kennedy years. In December 1964, the Johnson administration issued the "National Plan for Emergency Preparedness," which would guide U.S. protocol through the Reagan administration. It concluded, "To continue to exist as a sovereign power, the Nation must be able not only to withstand an initial nuclear assault but also to restore its social, political, and economic systems."

To help ensure someone was alive after a nuclear strike, the government explored what it considered the ultimate answer to the problem of survivability: a Kennedy administration plan to build a Deep Underground Command Center (DUCC). The Pentagon had begun in 1962 exploring building one of two designs for the DUCC, one that could hold fifty people and the other that could hold 300. Buried 3,500 feet below the Pentagon, the DUCC would have the twin advantages of being almost instantly accessible to the nation's leaders in an emergency as well as far enough belowground as to be impervious to even the strongest nuclear explosion. McNamara pitched the idea to the White House the following year, just weeks before Kennedy was assassinated. It could survive multiple direct hits of 200 to 300 megatons—a strength four to six times greater than even the largest weapon ever tested, the Soviet Tsar Bomba of 1961. "All other alternatives for assuming survivability of the Presidency—dispersal of Presidential successors, extending the list of Presidential successors, or greater reliance on doctrinal control—appear less desirable than construction of a DUCC," McNamara's office told the White House.

Construction wouldn't be easy or cheap; it would require nearly two years of digging just to arrive at optimal depth for the main facility and would cost about $110 million for the small size and $310 million for the larger one (nearly $1 billion and $3 billion in 2016 dollars, respectively). Plans drawn up by McNamara's office showed the DUCC containing three high-speed entrance elevators—one at the White House, one at the State Department, and one inside the Pentagon, which would open into horizontal reinforced access tunnels buried under the Potomac River. The nation's senior leaders would be able to sneak undetected from their offices in just minutes, with no helicopters, screaming motorcades, or other signs of outward chaos. "It would have the potential of reducing significantly the problems of transition from peace to war," McNamara wrote. "The very existence of a DUCC would also contribute in a very major way to the broad objective of deterrence of enemy attack by making a survivable control posture credible and by creating the impression of a strong will to fight."

The DUCC appeared to be the perfect solution to nuclear age COG—except for one minor problem. There was no clear communication system that would ensure the nation's leaders didn't end up living through a nuclear attack, only to be stuck 3,500 feet below in the world's best-engineered tomb, cut off from the world above as supplies dwindled. That flaw made it unlikely a president would ever utilize the DUCC. Joint Chiefs chairman Maxwell Taylor wrote, "Escape and survivable communications from a DUCC would be problematical in case of a direct attack on Washington with large-yield nuclear weapons." In the end, the DUCC never made it far off the drawing board. While the initial appropriation to begin digging was included in the FY1965 military budget, the House Armed Services Committee didn't approve the full funding. Even as the Pentagon began to study specific sites, the project died a slow death—a casualty of its own shortcomings, of shifting national priorities, and a military budget increasingly focused on ground troops, Huey helicopters, and the other costs of the Vietnam War.

In the years ahead, as McNamara came to endorse the MAD theory of nuclear retaliation, he was increasingly less interested in survivable options like the DUCC anyway. What was the point of building super-fortresses under American cities for the nation's leadership? "If the enemy elects to attack Washington, he is irrevocably committed to full scale destruction and, as long as a doctrine to insure U.S. retaliation is provided, there is no real point in providing a survivable control mechanism at the national level," he argued. If Washington was attacked and the president killed, the COG mechanisms and the National Command Authorities system spread across the globe would ensure the deaths were avenged.

During the fall of 1964, the presidential election—conducted against the backdrop of a nation warily watching the rise of the war in Vietnam and the domestic unrest of the civil rights movement—unexpectedly focused attention on presidential control over the nation's nuclear weapons. GOP nominee Barry Goldwater argued that NATO commanders should have the authority to launch atomic weapons on their own. Goldwater flailed, trying to have what he thought was an important serious and technical discussion about battlefield doctrine that to most of the public came across merely as scary war-mongering. Responding to Goldwater in his Labor Day campaign kickoff speech, President Johnson drew a strong line between his worldview and that of his opponent—saying that the stakes of modern weapons made war too unthinkable to risk. "When it was over, our great cities would be in ashes, and our fields would be barren, and our industry would be destroyed, and our American dreams would have vanished," Johnson said.

That night, his campaign aired what would instantly become one of the most famous political ads of all time, featuring a young girl counting flower petals in a bucolic field, which gave way to an ominous mechanical countdown. As the countdown proceeded, the camera zoomed into the black of the girl's eyes, ending with the flash and footage of a nuclear explosion. Then LBJ's somber voice began: "These are the stakes. To make a world in which all of God's children can live, or to go into the dark. We must either love each other, or we must die." Instantly controversial, the ad never aired again;

Goldwater was "livid" over it and Republicans spent much of the coming weeks vigorously protesting the implied message. Through the fall, the Johnson campaign aired another ad, titled "Telephone Hot Line," which showed a phone labeled "White House" with a flashing light, ringing unanswered. The voice-over intoned, "This particular phone only rings in a serious crisis. Keep it in the hands of a man who's proven himself responsible."* Of course, there was no actual red phone in the White House—or anywhere else—linking Washington and Moscow, but the ad helped cement the MOLINK hotline in the public consciousness.

Johnson's own actions, however, belied his campaign trail critique; he showed little interest in the emergency plans that the Joint Chiefs called the "Gold Book," waiting until August 1964 to participate in a full briefing on SIOP. Just weeks later, the same day that the "Daisy ad" aired, he had flown to his campaign kickoff in Detroit aboard a small twelve-seat JetStar military plane, rather than the traditional Boeing 707, since the Democratic National Committee was paying for the day's travel and Johnson wanted to keep the costs down. While the JetStar found room for five members of Congress, two labor leaders, and a speechwriter, the White House physician and the military aide with the Football were relegated to a second plane for the five-hour round-trip, marking the longest known period that the president had been separated from the Football since the tradition began in the 1950s. The episode was hardly an aberration: His military aide was often as much as fifteen to twenty minutes away during times when Johnson was at his ranch in Texas. Instead, a Huey helicopter was kept on alert at Johnson City Airfield to whisk the Football to him in a crisis.

Out on the campaign trail, Johnson never let on that Goldwater was actually much closer to U.S. military doctrine than the public likely believed. In a Seattle campaign speech, Johnson had said that nuclear weapons were for the commander-in-chief alone: "The responsibility for the control of U.S. nuclear weapons rests solely with the President, who exercises the control of their use in all foreseeable circumstances. This has been the case since

---

* Nearly identical ads would be used by political consultant Roy Spence both in 1988 for Walter Mondale's campaign against Gary Hart, and in 2008 for Hillary Clinton's campaign against Barack Obama.

1945, under four Presidents. It will continue to be the case as long as I am President of the United States."

Except that wasn't really true.

As part of the post–Cuban Missile Crisis reforms, mechanical "Permissive Action Links" had limited access to individual nuclear weapons, but even though McNamara and Dean Rusk had pushed to rescind the "predelegation" orders given to commanders like the head of NATO in Europe, they'd made little progress. In the end, the Johnson administration largely just affirmed the imperfect policy settled upon by the Eisenhower administration. Under the Eisenhower-era program, then code-named FURTHERANCE, U.S. military leaders around the world would have been free to use nuclear weapons on their own discretion in "defense of the free world." In advising Johnson, McGeorge Bundy quoted Eisenhower's old thinking, "When the destructive force of nuclear weapons would hit only military forces, the decision on their use was a very much less serious matter."

Was it?

Chapter 10

THE TYLER PRECEDENT

Lyndon Johnson defeated Barry Goldwater decisively in November 1964, winning a 486-to-52 electoral vote landslide. Johnson's official inauguration on January 20, 1965, also simultaneously installed Hubert Humphrey as the vice president, filling a post that had sat vacant since Kennedy's assassination. Ever since Lee Harvey Oswald's shots in Dallas, House Speaker John McCormack had been first in line for the presidency. While today the presidential line of succession is a subject so widely understood that it's become a regular story line in TV dramas like *The West Wing* or *House of Cards*, it wasn't all that clear until very recently who became president if the elected president died or was incapacitated. Until the late 1960s, in fact, the presidential line of succession was a strange amalgamation of informal secret letters, confusing and shifting congressional legislation, and a seemingly unintended misinterpretation of the Constitution itself. It took the arrival of nuclear weapons—and, specifically, the arrival of nuclear missiles—before the legislative and executive branches would finally clarify the subject.

When the Founders sat down to debate presidential succession, it was more a practical argument than an academic one. In an era where health, daily life, and especially old age were much more uncertain and hazard-filled, colonial governors had a track record of high mortality—nearly a third had died in office. The question was expected: Who should take over in the event of a president's death? Gouverneur Morris of Pennsylvania originally argued for the chief justice of the United States, while others pushed for the president of the Senate; both proposals, however, seemed to the Founders to inappropriately mix the branches of government. The heir to the executive, it was agreed, should come from the executive branch, so a late suggestion came to establish a "Vice-President," who would be elected in the same manner as the president, while also serving as the president of the Senate on a day-to-day basis. After the vice president, only the House speaker and the president pro tem of the Senate stood in the line of succession for most of America's first century—a period during which four presidents and five vice presidents died in office. It was a thin bench for the highest office in the land.

The United States managed to dodge constitutional crises in its first century only through luck and chance. Sixteen different times (a combined thirty-eight years) in the country's first nearly 200 years, the U.S. had been without a vice president. Seven of the first thirty-four presidents—one out of five—suffered some period of incapacitation, during which time there wasn't really anyone technically able to execute the powers of the presidency. James Madison had both vice presidents die in office—George Clinton, who died just months before the outbreak of the War of 1812, and Elbridge Gerry, who died not long after the British burned Washington.*

When William Henry Harrison died in 1841, the first president to die in office, a spirited debate unfurled in Washington over whether Vice President John Tyler actually assumed the presidential office or merely the duties and power therein. John Quincy Adams, himself a former president and in 1841 a member of Congress, believed that Tyler was merely the "Acting President" or "Vice President, Acting as President." Tyler moved into the White House and, despite ongoing attacks from his political opponents who would refer to him as "Your Accidency," was never seriously challenged as president. For years to come, however, he would return unopened any mail that came to the White House addressed to "Acting President" or "Vice President Tyler."[†]

---

* Between an 1813 serious illness that left Madison near death for three weeks and his own risky front-line tours of the British invasion in 1814, Madison could have easily created a scenario that would have thrown the wartime government into chaos.

[†] Tyler himself narrowly escaped death as president when an explosion occurred while he was a passenger on the USS *Princeton* in 1844. Since there was no vice president, his death could have also left the nation leaderless.

The odd thing, constitutional scholars now agree, is that Tyler was almost certainly wrong about becoming president. Little was then known about the debates that went on during the Constitutional Convention— Madison's notes from the debates, for instance, were only published for the first time in 1840 and the first major scholarly review of the convention wasn't published until 1911. Subsequent study has shown that the Founders clearly intended for the vice president to merely "act" as president during a vacancy or inability. At least three other sections of the Constitution actually refer specifically to the vice president only acting as president. The only way the Founders ever intended for someone to become president was to be elected by the nation; anyone else would merely be "acting." Yet Tyler's precedent would guide the nation for the next 120 years.

Over the coming decades, unexpected presidential succession became a semiregular occurrence, with President Lincoln's assassination in 1865, and James A. Garfield's in 1881. Garfield's vice president, Chester A. Arthur, touted the peaceful transitions in each of those crises as he took over after Garfield's death. "No higher or more assuring proof could exist of the strength and permanence of popular government than the fact that, though the chosen of the people be struck down, his constitutional successor is peacefully installed without shock or strain," Arthur said after being sworn in.

Smooth transitions aside, the tenuousness of the office worried officials in Washington. Just four years later, Grover Cleveland's vice president, Thomas Hendricks, died in 1885. Congress was out of session, which meant there was no House speaker or Senate president pro tem—had Grover Cleveland died or become unable to serve, there would have been no clear mechanism for a new president. Aides were concerned enough about the possibility that they recommended Cleveland not even travel to Indiana to attend Hendricks's funeral. That hole in the nation's safety net finally encouraged Congress to act, which passed a new law in 1886 that put cabinet members ahead of congressional leaders in the line both to ensure the continuity of the executive branch and what they hoped would be higher-quality presidents. The president pro tem was chosen, after all, not for executive capability but seniority and parliamentary knowledge. As advocates of the bill argued, more former secretaries of state had been elected to the presidency in the 1800s (six) than House speakers (one) or Senate presidents (one).

Sixty years later, Harry Truman—who lacked a vice president himself after he ascended to the office—pushed Congress to shift the succession process and put the speaker of the House next in line for the presidency; by Truman's argument, the speaker had the closest thing to a national electoral presence and, by virtue of the House's two-year terms, would have had a more recent test at the polls than the Senate's six-year terms. In 1947, Congress took up much of Truman's advice, establishing the modern succession plan, with the speaker second in line, then the Senate president pro tem, and then the cabinet officials in order of their department's founding.*

Yet even though that law cleaned up some of the constitutional questions, it wasn't at all clear the extent to which a president could exercise his duties while injured or sick—Garfield had signed a congressional bill during the weeks he lay wounded following his shooting in a Washington train station, but what if the country had needed a healthy, robust decision maker while Garfield lay dying?

As presidents began to travel further afield from Washington, and as the speed of world events quickened, where various authority lay in their absence from the capital appeared all too amorphous. When Teddy Roosevelt left the capital for long stretches, for vacation or whistle-stop campaign speeches, he designated William Howard Taft, his secretary of state, as the "Acting President." As he famously said upon one departure, "Things will be all right—I have left Taft sitting on the lid." But what could Taft really do? A decade later, President Woodrow Wilson's stroke and incapacitation at the end of World War I left his wife informally running the country for the better part of a year. The "incapacity" question dogged the presidency, especially as nuclear weapons compressed the time frame in which decisions would be required. Garfield could linger on his deathbed for eighty days in the 1880s, Warren Harding could lay dying for four days during the 1920s, but in the era of nuclear weapons, it seemed like someone needed to be clearly in charge.

Eisenhower's presidency in particular gave regular cause for concern.

---

* This is effectively today's system, excepting the postmaster general, who was removed from the line of succession in 1971, and the secretary of homeland security, who was added in 2006.

In 1955, he suffered a heart attack in Denver—an event that left him hos-
pitalized for seven weeks. "It was not until two weeks after the heart attack
that the tension in Washington was eased," Vice President Richard Nixon
recalled years later. "The ever-present possibility of an attack on the United
States was always hanging over us. Would the President be well enough to
make a decision? If not, who had the authority to push the button?" Eisenhower also underwent urgent intestinal surgery from 2:30 a.m. to 4:35 a.m.
on the morning of June 9, 1956, while most of the nation slept. The experience worried Ike long after the fact. "On several occasions afterwards, he
pointed out to me that for the two hours he was under anesthesia, the country was without a Chief Executive, the armed forces without a Commander-
in-Chief," Nixon wrote later. "In the event of a national emergency during
those two hours, who would have had the undisputed authority to act for a
completely disabled President?" Then, just weeks after the launch of Sputnik, on November 25, 1957, Eisenhower suffered a minor stroke that left
him disoriented and his speech slurred.

As the president regained strength, he settled on a new solution. In
February 1958, he summoned Nixon and Attorney General Bill Rogers to
the Oval Office and handed them a four-page letter. It began "Dear Dick"
and outlined an informal agreement about the conditions under which the
vice president could assume the powers of the presidency. He had drafted
it privately and distributed just three copies—one to Nixon, one to Rogers,
and one to the secretary of state. While in the letter Eisenhower promised he would try to inform the vice president if he became unable to fulfill
presidential duties, if he couldn't, Nixon "after such consultations as seems
to him appropriate" could just assume the powers if warning was impossible.
Regardless of duration, however, President Eisenhower could take back the
powers whenever he wanted, the letter explained. The agreement created a
strange and amorphous extra-constitutional system—one that cried out for
a more formal process in the age of nuclear weapons. Eisenhower understandably was nervous that such an agreement only went so far as the president and vice president trusted each other and had a friendly relationship;
otherwise a coup, intentional or unintentional, seemed possible.

Similar letters were handed off from Eisenhower to Kennedy to Johnson. The letter of agreement between Kennedy and Johnson read, in part,

"The Vice President agrees to serve as Acting President 'after such con-
sultation as seems to him appropriate under the circumstances,'" a process
that, while left vague, would likely include gathering support from the
cabinet. Absent any formal process or constitutional clause allowing the
handoff of power, the agreement intended to allow the vice president
to operate "with a free mind that this is what the President intended in
the event of a crisis."

The Kennedy assassination and subsequent Johnson presidency crystal-
lized the swirling fears about presidential succession planning. Kennedy had
died quickly following the shooting in Dallas—but what if he had lingered
for hours, days, or weeks? What if he'd been comatose? When would Lyndon Johnson have become "acting president"? And now that Johnson was
president, and not in great health himself, the two officials in line behind him
were a seventy-two-year-old House speaker and an eighty-six-year-old Senate president pro tem. The nation deserved a vibrant vice president. During
the fourteen months he served as next in line to the presidency after Lyndon
Johnson took over in 1963, Speaker McCormack kept in his office safe a
two-page agreement that the two men had signed on December 23, 1963.
"It is outside the law," McCormack explained, "but it was the only thing
that could be done under the circumstances." The letter notwithstanding, the
vacancy in the vice presidency began to affect negatively U.S. foreign policy.
Without a possible successor to leave behind, President Johnson refused to
travel abroad in 1964 and skipped a meeting with French president Charles
de Gaulle.

The crises of the early 1960s, from the Cuban Missile Crisis to Kennedy's assassination, forced the nation to wrestle with the succession system—
it needed a formal way to determine if the president was unable to serve,
and a new method for ensuring that a vice president could be installed if a
vacancy existed. "Our very survival in this age may rest on the capacity of
the nation's chief executive to make swift and unquestioned decisions in an
emergency," one scholar wrote in the 1960s. The discussion in the nuclear
age added a new wrinkle: Should the line of succession be widened to include officials unlikely to be in Washington, D.C.? Should the line of succession include, if the congressional and cabinet leaders are unable to fulfill
the duties, the state governors, perhaps in descending order of population?

"It is conceivable that, since all of those persons who are presently in the line of succession spend much time in Washington, DC, the whole line could be wiped out in a nuclear attack," one scholar wrote in 1965.

Nelson Rockefeller suggested the creation of a new cabinet post—the first secretary, who would head the National Security Council and be responsible for coordinating domestic and international affairs at the White House, as well as hold the post of second in line for the presidency after the vice president. "He would provide the essential Continuity of Government in our international relations and leadership of the machinery of government," Rockefeller argued.

Ultimately Congress settled on a process that answered many lingering questions about presidential succession, although it did little to address the question of what would happen if everyone in Washington was killed. The Twenty-fifth Amendment of the Constitution, passed by Congress in early 1965, made clear the vice president would officially become president—answering John Tyler's 120-year-old question—and allowed the president to nominate a new vice president in the event of a vacancy, who would then be subject to confirmation by both houses of Congress. The amendment also delineated a clear process to declare a president unable to serve, as well as a clear process for the president to resume power once recovered: The president could either sign over the office to a vice president, if, for instance, he knew he was undergoing an operation with anesthesia, or if the president couldn't or wouldn't sign over the office, the vice president could gather the signatures of a majority of the cabinet, which, when delivered to Congress, would establish the vice president officially as "acting president."

The changes came barely a moment too soon. Soon Richard Nixon, who had weathered Eisenhower's health crises as vice president, would again find himself facing the challenges of presidential succession, but not in a way anyone expected.

By the late 1960s, Mount Weather had settled into a routine. Besides the three-times-a-year ABLE alert exercises, bunker operations were remarkably ordinary from day to day—similar, in most ways, to life in any other corporate office building. Minutes from facilities meetings in the 1960s show discussions of adding a barbershop, regrading the parking lot, the installation of new high-speed printers, and a need to coordinate mail pickup times better.

Mount Weather's parent agency, the Office of Emergency Planning, continued to suffer the same shortcomings that had dogged its predecessors since World War II. In the first three years of Johnson's administration three different former governors passed through the revolving door atop the agency, all friends of the president chosen for political reasons rather than executive vision. In 1968, the agency's name was changed yet again to the Office of Emergency Preparedness, as its mission came to be dominated not by nuclear contingency planning but by the new concern of natural disaster response. OEP leapt into action following the huge Alaska earthquake of 1964—one of the largest ever recorded at the time—and the following year, the devastating Hurricane Betsy swept across Florida and Louisiana, provoking another massive response.

Such incidents, though, little affected Mount Weather—its job wasn't to care about natural disasters, just man-made ones. While it had readied staff and facilities during the Cuban Missile Crisis and in the fear-filled hours following the Kennedy assassination, Mount Weather fully activated only once—when a power blackout at 5:27 p.m. on November 9, 1965, darkened the northeastern United States and left 30 million people without power.

Across the country, the nation's warning systems blinked off—radar systems were knocked out, and twenty-two of the ninety-nine sites of Western Union's Bomb Alarm System, which would have warned of nuclear explosions around major northeastern cities, went offline. Two Bomb Alarms blinked red—seemingly indicating that a nuclear strike had hit Salt Lake City and Charlotte, North Carolina, both far out of the area affected by the power outage. The blackout also silenced the Emergency Broadcast System in the northeastern United States, since it relied on Associated Press and UPI transmission systems idled by the outage. The nation's warning systems were suddenly both blind and dumb.

As the minutes ticked by, the Office of Civil Defense struggled to figure out what was happening and how wide of a region was affected. Since there had been no warning of an air attack before the outages, it seemed likely to be merely a massive mechanical failure, but Mount Weather's director, J. Leo Bourassa, worried that the blackout was the first wave of a Soviet surprise attack. As he said later, "We always suspect the worst. We had probed around for a good half-hour and could not pinpoint the trouble. We couldn't find out if it was sabotage or what, so we got quite concerned." At 6:49 p.m., the facility went to alert. It declared Condition ABLE, ordered staff to report, and dispatched buses to pick up those who lived nearby. ABLE, normally used during an exercise, was one level short of a full Condition ATLAS alert, which would have indicated an impending attack. At 7:45 p.m., all site personnel aboveground retreated to the underground bunker, leaving behind a darkened and concerned East Coast. "It was as if some gigantic creature of night and chaos had swept across the chill Northeast evening, snuffing illumination in Vermont farmhouses and Manhattan skyscrapers, stopping subways in their tunnels and phonograph records on their turntables, halting traffic and emergency surgery, postmen on their rounds and children at their play," *The New York Times* recorded. "The thoughts of the people turned to war and nuclear destruction. Perhaps this was that moment of ultimate dread."

As the evening progressed, it became increasingly clear nothing nefarious was afoot: NORAD found no approaching Soviet bombers or missiles and declared Condition GREEN, normal. Mount Weather stood down at 11:28 p.m., when everyone was satisfied that the emergency was entirely a civil, not a military, problem.

Still, the blackout chastened the nation's emergency planners. As one Mount Weather official said, "The thing that impressed us most was the inability to get information on this particular incident. All we got was negative information. We were unable to isolate the cause. In general, this does not auger well for a real emergency—even with a good communications system." It also caused planners to question how Mount Weather inexplicably lacked insight into key government decisions and intelligence streams. The Pentagon, for instance, had stopped bringing its National Military Command Center watch teams out to Mount Weather for familiarization tours in 1962, so the personnel running two of the nation's key command posts now barely knew each other. In the wake of the blackout, the two command centers began speaking to each other once a shift as a matter of routine. As quiet returned, most days the Pentagon and Mount Weather had little to report.

The daily danger to the nuclear bunker remained mundane: A rabid fox invaded the facility one month, and facility leaders regularly complained about people speeding in their electric carts in the tunnels. Despite its quiet outward appearance, the mysterious facility atop Mount Weather continued to attract curious glances from beyond the barbed wire fence. The Appalachian Trail passed close by and hikers regularly wondered about the facility's heavy-duty security. Very specific ten-foot-tall signs along the perimeter piqued interest but actively discouraged further investigation: "Restricted Area," they read. "Photographing, making notes, drawing maps, or graphic representations of this area or its activities is prohibited." The signs cited as authority the Internal Security Act of 1950, the same law passed by Congress over President Truman's veto that allowed for mass detention of enemy subversives. It wasn't the type of sign that passersby were inclined to disobey.

Then, of course, nearby residents always noticed the snowplows. In snowy weather, the four miles of Route 601 down from Route 7 were always the first and best cleared stretch of road in Clarke County, despite seemingly being a secondary road with little relevance to most of the county's residents. Something on the road required ready access. What was it?

In April 1967, when Lyndon Johnson headed to Uruguay for a Latin American summit, the Navy's USS *Wright* steamed south and secretly waited off the South American coast in case of Armageddon. Little known to the public, the *Wright* represented one of the most unique ships in the Navy, one of just two that served as the National Emergency Command Post Afloat (NECPA), pronounced "NECK-PA" and known colloquially as the "Floating White House."

The NECPA program had begun in March 1962 with the USS *Northampton*, a light cruiser known as CC-1, which served as one of the Navy's first designated command ships. Based in Norfolk, Virginia, the 225-yard-long *Northampton* was always supposed to be a quick helicopter ride away from Washington. More than forty tons of gear, including sixty transmitters and 150 receivers, allowed it to process 3,000 messages a day (considered at the time quite a feat), and the Navy claimed the powerful communications system allowed the ship to set the world record for the fastest around-the-globe message, taking just eight tenths of a second.

A year after the *Northampton* took up station, the Navy completed a lengthy overhaul that added the *Wright*, a Saipan-class light aircraft carrier, to NECPA duty, a vessel that outdid even the *Northampton* as the most sophisticated communications platform ever placed at sea. With its distinctive 156-foot-tall fiberglass aerials installed atop the old flight deck and its former hangar decks turned into operations centers, the ship was "probably as strange and complicated a sea craft as any that man has devised," its publications later bragged.

Over the following decade, either the *Wright* (code-named ZENITH) or the *Northampton* (code-named SEA RULER) was always at sea, alternating every two weeks to ensure that the president and other national leaders could be evacuated in an emergency. From 1962 through much of Richard Nixon's first term, the military considered NECPA the best option for evacuating the president before a nuclear strike. A cramped airborne command post could operate for no more than a couple of days before being forced to land, a hit from a targeted thermonuclear weapon would easily destroy facilities like Raven Rock, and the idea of creating a National Mobile Land Command Post (NMLCP) in the early 1960s had been abandoned. As one 1964 Joint Chiefs memo noted, NECPA alone offered the benefits of "adequate staff support; high volume (not necessarily survivable) communications between the alternate and soft Washington centers; continuous operation for a period of days or weeks; and high survivability of the alternate [command post] itself."*

For most of their life, the NECPA ships cruised aimlessly off the Atlantic coast, almost always alone, normally venturing no further than the Virgin Islands, Nova Scotia, and Bermuda. When the president traveled overseas, however, they'd often shadow him, as the *Wright* did during the Uruguay summit. In 1968, the *Northampton* accompanied Johnson to another summit in El Salvador, slipping through the Panama Canal to wait off the coast near San Salvador, and marking the only time either ship visited the Pacific. Comparatively lightly armed—the *Northampton* had four five-inch deck guns, and the *Wright* had a handful of Bofors 40mm guns—the ships' protection derived from their comparative stealth. Russia's weak

---

* The Navy even considered in the mid-1960s expanding the NECPA fleet to include a nuclear-powered submarine, the USS *Triton*.

navy would have trouble finding them amid the vast stretches of the open ocean.*

The *Wright's* motto, *Vox Imperii*, "Voice of the Leaders," testified to its unique responsibilities: Using massive troposcatter antennae arrays, the ships were designed to communicate with the remnants of the U.S. military through three specially built radio stations onshore, including a large facility at Cape Henlopen on the Delaware shore that repurposed the World War II bunker of an old shore battery. Two other backup facilities were located at Otis Air Force Base in Massachusetts and on Cedar Island, North Carolina. If all shore communications were cut and the continental United States destroyed, the *Wright* had a specially built interlocking-blade QH-43 Kaman helicopter to pull a super very low frequency (SVLF) antenna more than two miles into the air and allow the ship to communicate with submarines around the world. At the time, it was the most powerful VLF antenna in the world.

In addition to the ships' normal complement of about a thousand sailors (200 of which just did communications work), the Joint Chiefs kept a team of 17 officers and 22 enlisted personnel, including a special meteorologist, aboard at all times to serve as the watch staff in case of a national emergency; other agencies like the CIA regularly posted staff as well. Hundreds more staff could join the ship in an emergency. (One young Navy ROTC officer, Bob Woodward, who went on to be a prizewinning investigative journalist behind Watergate, began his naval career aboard the *Wright* as one of the two officers necessary to move or handle the nuclear launch codes.) The president would take charge from an elaborate, carpeted stateroom aboard the ship, equipped with nearly a dozen different color-coded telephones linked to various parts of the nation's military command structure. The ship's emergency operations center, which was decorated with presidential flags and a desk for the commander-in-chief, was kept locked under normal circumstances. Anyone entering had to do so with a security escort—even the captain of the ship. In the event of nuclear fallout, special air filters could have sealed the ship and a saltwater wash-down system would cleanse

---

* Rumors, though, circulated among the ship's crew that a watchful U.S. submarine always trailed protectively behind NECPA when it was out at sea.

the decks. "Everything was spit and polish on the ship," recalled one of the *Northampton*'s sailors decades later. "We had personnel inspections every two weeks, compartment inspections every month. Everything had to be up to snuff."*

During their brief life, the ships were never activated, although the *Northampton* was put on alert status near the Potomac during the Cuban Missile Crisis and the *Wright* was put on alert following the capture of the USS *Pueblo* in January 1968. Twice, though, presidents visited the ship for overnight familiarization tours. The *Northampton* picked up Kennedy on April 13, 1962, in Norfolk, where he greeted a team of Navy SEALs clad in scuba gear. Along with nearly a score of aides, cabinet officials, and congressmen, the president sailed out into the Atlantic while the officials reviewed emergency plans and hosted a ceremonial dinner, complete with a large, three-tiered cake. From the deck the next morning, Kennedy watched naval fleet exercises and then helicoptered away to the USS *Enterprise*, where dozens of members of the diplomatic corps and other members of Congress were also observing the routine. As vice president, Johnson had been kept away from *Northampton* during Kennedy's visit, watching the exercises from a third vessel, the *Forrestal*, to ensure that both leaders weren't aboard at the same time, but Lyndon Johnson and Lady Bird visited after he became president in 1966 as they were on their way to Canada. Sailors later joked that the visit's only purpose, it seemed, was to test if Johnson's large six-foot-four-inch frame would fit comfortably into the presidential berth. The next morning, satisfied it could, Johnson headed on to his meeting with the Canadian prime minister.

Just days after Johnson's summit in Uruguay, as the *Wright* steamed back north on April 17, 1967, SAC achieved one of its longest-held goals: An

---

* Rather than the normal Navy-issue steel-gray dining facilities, the *Wright* featured three different themed dining halls—a rustic Trophy Room, with a fireplace and logs, a Nautical Room, and the Wright Brothers Room, featuring an homage to the ship's namesakes. The fancy accommodations also marked better-than-average food, the crew's favorite NECPA perk. With well-trained chefs ready for VIP visitors, the *Wright* received top honors in the fleet's prestigious Ney Awards for best food for three years running in the late 1960s. As one sailor later recalled, "It carried so many top brass that us peons had it pretty good too."

EC-135 airborne command post flying over Vandenberg Air Force Base in California successfully launched a Minuteman II ICBM from a silo below. With the new technology, the Air Force could remotely launch any Minuteman missile, even if its launch capsule was destroyed or inoperable. The achievement marked a huge step forward in the Doomsday force known as the Post-Attack Command and Control System (PACCS), which piled redundancies atop redundancies, to ensure that somehow, somewhere, on some device, an Emergency Action Message to launch nuclear weapons would go through.

SAC's efforts to diversify its command, control, and launch capabilities had begun in 1959 and 1960 with Project BIG STAR, an audacious plan to mount Minuteman missiles on specially designed rail cars. On paper, it seemed perfect: The missile trains could hide nearly anywhere along the nation's 10,000 miles of railroad track and were virtually impregnable to Soviet attack—requiring, by SAC's estimate, ten Soviet ICBMs to kill each mobile American missile. During the summer of 1960, four different test trains rolled out across the country, each with its own staff, command post, and prototype launch cars. The trains proved difficult to mobilize—they were the heaviest rail cars ever put into operation, were difficult to communicate with, and were actually more expensive than reinforced missile silos. Instead, the Navy's Polaris became the nation's mobile deterrent force.

Launch capabilities, though, were only part of the equation—someone needed to live to actually order the launch. SAC had long worried a decapitation attack might leave the nation's strategic forces leaderless, so it outfitted an EC-135 command aircraft as an airborne command post that could take over headquarters duties if Offutt was destroyed. Since its onboard capabilities mirrored those of SAC's command bunker in Building 501, the missions were code-named LOOKING GLASS. The planes began fifteen-minute ground alert in June 1960 at Offutt; each staffed by a SAC general, a team of weapons controllers, battle staff, and communications experts.

The planes had begun their airborne alert less than a week after the WSEG 50 report gave McNamara the harsh wake-up call about the vulnerability of the nation's leadership. On February 3, 1961, Lieutenant General John P. McConnell took off in his EC-135 from Offutt Air Force Base, becoming the first Airborne Emergency Action Officer in what would ultimately become a continuous string of LOOKING GLASS flights that would stretch, twenty-four hours a day, 365 days a year, in all weather for three decades—some 42,000 continuous shifts right through to the end of the Cold War. The AEAOs, generally one-star or two-star generals, did eight-hour shifts, flying in circles over the prairies, ready to assume command of the nation's nuclear forces.

Originally, the LOOKING GLASS flights were to be backed up by the nation's most secure locations—two 2,000-foot-deep bunkers located in Nebraska and California, and a third facility known as the Deep Underground Support Center. The DUSC, as conceived in the early 1960s, would have been buried two thirds of a mile under the earth, inside an old mine in Cripple Creek, Colorado, where it would have been untouchable even by a 100-megaton nuclear weapon. Packed with computer gear and a 200-person staff to help the airborne command post do data processing and nuclear strike analysis, the DUSC would have been America's ultimate Doomsday bunker. Alas, all three facilities proved too expensive—even for the free-spending period of the early 1960s military budget—and the plan was abandoned. In 1964, with the DUSC idea dead and SAC fully committed to the airborne flights, the Air Force upgraded the authority of the AEAO, making the relatively junior generals a vital link to the National Command Authorities.

Not "breaking the chain" became something of a SAC obsession. GLASS missions began on the ground about forty-five minutes before takeoff when two officers, carrying sidearms, brought aboard the day's war plans and authentication codes. The SAC general AEAO carefully reviewed the papers before locking them away in the plane's red war safe, which sat right next to the general's chair in the battle station. Two padlocks secured the safe; one key was given to each of the plane's two Emergency Action Officers, ensuring that no single person could access the codes. New LOOKING GLASS flights took off each day from Offutt at precisely midnight, 8 a.m., and 4 p.m., for an eight-and-a-half-hour shift, and the preceding GLASS plane would only head home to land once the new flight established communications with NORAD, Offutt, and the Pentagon.* If the next plane in line had a

* While aloft, the planes used randomly assigned call signs to make it harder for eavesdroppers to discern their mission or location.

maintenance problem or crew issue, the airborne plane would remain on station, sometimes for many extra hours. Occasionally, tumultuous Nebraska weather would ground Offutt planes and another EC-135 squadron elsewhere in the country would be scrambled into the air with a general grabbed from some other duty to replace it. "Sometimes we were landing on fumes—it'd come down to just minutes. But we all knew you didn't break the chain," one pilot recalled.*

Following an attack, the plane's staff had a rigorous checklist to determine if they were the last surviving link; if they decided they were, the two Emergency Action Officers would unlock the red safe, known as the "clacker box" because of the plane-wide clacking alarm that went off when it was opened. Then they would begin marching toward war—making contact with SAC's various forces, assessing battle damage, and preparing to execute launch orders. Because of the remarkable autonomy of the airborne launch system, a total of four officers onboard LOOKING GLASS would all have to concur, turning the plane's launch keys within 1.2 seconds of each other to activate a launch.

By the mid-1960s, SAC had two dozen LOOKING GLASS, PACCS command planes, and radio relay planes across the country ensuring that launch orders could be communicated airplane-to-airplane worldwide, never having to touch terrestrial earth. At each unit headquarters, SAC kept other airborne command posts on fifteen-minute ground alert: One team waited at Westover Air Force Base in Massachusetts (call sign GRAYSON), one at Barksdale Air Force Base in Louisiana (call sign ACHIEVE), and another at March Air Force Base in California (call sign STEPMOTHER). The battle staff commanders at the auxiliary posts were generally Navy captains or Air Force colonels, not flag officers, but if the National Command Authorities were destroyed and the LOOKING GLASS command post inoperable, they still had the authority and ability to lead the nation into war and remotely launch any of the nation's thousand Minuteman ICBMs. Twice a week, in GREEN DOT TEN alerts, the entire system was launched and tested.

---

* One of the few perks of the long, mostly boring flights in the air was the ability to tap into the GLASS's "Ground Entry Points" to the nation's telephone network and make easy long-distance telephone calls, which in the 1960s represented a technical feat.

With the arrival of the Airborne Launch Control System in 1967, four more EC-135s were based on ground alert at Ellsworth Air Force Base in South Dakota and Minot Air Force Base in North Dakota. In an OLYMPIC SHOT—the code for an emergency launch—the EC-135s would each fly to a specific Minuteman missile field and, once overhead, contact each launch facility to ensure the missiles were operable; any that the ground-based forces couldn't launch, the ALCS would launch itself using UHF radio commands.

SAC, though, always wanted more redundancies. In case the radio relay planes were knocked out, SAC designed another backup in 1967, the Green Pine network, an arc of radio beacons across the upper reaches of North America, stretching from Greenland to Alaska, to help communicate with Soviet-bound bombers using more resilient UHF signals that wouldn't be disrupted by the electromagnetic pulse of a nuclear weapon. If Green Pine was knocked out, SAC brought online in October 1967 the first of twelve Emergency Rocket Communication Systems (ERCS) at Missouri's White-man Air Force Base. Instead of a warhead, the special ERCS Minuteman missiles contained a powerful UHF transmitter that would broadcast launch orders to U.S. forces along the missile's trajectory, creating, in effect, a high-flying radio broadcasting tower. The launch capsules of the 510th were retro-fitted with large, floor-mounted telephone consoles that the crews quickly dubbed "knee knockers," since they hit their knees on it whenever turning their chairs. With the arrival of ERCS, the very last remnants of the U.S. government in a nuclear war would have likely been the voices of the mis-sileers of Whiteman's 510th Missile Squadron. In an emergency, the crews would use the console to record launch orders onto the ERCS transmitter (the airborne command posts could record an Emergency Action Message remotely). Then either the capsule crew or an airborne command post would have launched the missiles, each set on a different trajectory to blast in a dif-ferent direction. For thirty minutes after launch, ERCS-equipped Minute-mans would broadcast "go codes" to any bomber, submarine, or missile silo along its path, the last communication of a destroyed nation.* For decades,

---

* The high-tech ERCS replaced a much more low-tech 1963 version that relied on three "Blue Scout Junior" rockets scattered across Nebraska at Wisner, West Point, and Tekamah,

ERCS remained so highly classified that even missileers in adjoining squadrons at Whiteman didn't know about it.

Additionally, the Navy built its own separate redundancies to ensure that it could communicate with its own subs starting in 1960 with the most powerful radio transmitter in the world—a sprawling 2,000-acre antenna array near Little Machias Bay in Cutler, Maine, close to the Canadian border. The very low frequency antenna contained two identical star-shaped arrays, with about 2,000 miles of antenna strung back and forth across the arrays, all protected by elaborate deicing features to survive the brutal Maine winters. The Cutler station, which generated a signal about forty times more powerful than a normal commercial mega-station, tied into what would become a global network of outsized radio stations, all focused on providing one-way Emergency Action Messages to missile submarines—including the 5,000-acre Jim Creek Naval Radio Station, an hour north of Seattle, the Lualualei VLF transmitter in Hawaii (the tallest towers in the Western Hemisphere), and the Naval Communications Station Harold E. Holt on Australia's remote northwestern coast (the tallest towers in the Southern Hemisphere).

As massive as the radio facilities were, they faced the obvious threat of being targeted for destruction, so the Navy next built its own fleet of emergency command and relay planes, code-named TACAMO, shorthand for "Take Charge and Move Out," which would be responsible for communicating with the submarines following an attack if the VLF shore stations were destroyed.

Ever-growing knowledge about EMP disruptions led to even more communication redundancies: The Navy's TACAMO planes and LOOKING GLASS planes all had trailing-wire ultra-low frequency antennas that could be unspooled from the tail of the aircraft to transmit "go codes" required for submariners to launch their payloads. The 28,000-foot-long 487L antennas were engineering marvels—their airborne transmitters weighed upward of five tons and their ability to spool out the lengthy antennas in six minutes would, the crews bragged, impress any fisherman who understood the complexity of a long cast. After extending the multi-mile antenna, the planes would orbit

that carried voice recorders with a prerecorded "force execution message" that could be transmitted to all units within line-of-sight.

at 130 knots in a relatively tight circle, creating a spiral in the trailing antenna that allowed it the power necessary to penetrate the water. The long, heavy antennas were finicky, and regularly—despite a flight crew's best effort—would refuse to retract all the way, leaving the plane circling with hundreds and sometimes thousands of yards of cable strung out behind it. For that reason, trailing wire antenna (TWA) tests were always conducted over large bodies of water to ensure the safety of SAC's low-tech solution: Just cut the cable and let it fall harmlessly into the water far below. As one LOOKING GLASS pilot recalled, "It sure reduces the drag when that long wire lets go."

The Navy's first four C-130 TACAMO planes, two each in the Atlantic and the Pacific, came into service in 1965 and eventually grew into two full squadrons—one in Patuxent River, Maryland, and the other in Guam—with the goal of keeping a TACAMO plane airborne over each ocean twenty-four hours a day. "Our props never stop," the TACAMO squadrons bragged. The TACAMO planes each flew more than 135 hours a month—a punishing schedule for an aircraft frame—serving as a tenuous final link between the nation's submarine forces and its commander-in-chief.

Not every nuclear nation invested in such extensive and high-tech Doomsday solutions. Rather than embracing airborne command planes, fancy antennas, and varying radio spectrums, British prime ministers, upon taking office, hand-wrote letters to the commanders of their nuclear missile submarines. Known as "Letters of Last Resort," each individual missive was then locked away in a special safe inside a larger safe in the sub control room. The letters contain personal instructions about what to do if the United Kingdom is destroyed in a nuclear attack. If the government is destroyed, and the submarines left nationless, how should they respond? Should they launch their missiles? Turn themselves over to serve another allied nation? Retreat to another country that's part of the British Commonwealth like Australia or New Zealand? Or maybe leave the ultimate decision up to the sub commander? When the prime minister leaves office, the letters are destroyed unopened—so no one ever knows what the last order of Her Majesty's Government would have actually been.

Johnson had hoped to win a second election, but Vietnam had turned the country against him, and in March 1968 he announced he wouldn't seek another term as president. The month before, the war had already claimed another political casualty when Robert McNamara, the onetime management wonder, was forced from office a broken man. As he left, it seemed that little progress had been made on the core COG and command issues McNamara and Kennedy discovered together seven years earlier. Even with the years of effort McNamara's team had put into remedying the horrifying reality uncovered by the WSEG Report #50—that the nation's leadership could be easily wiped out—a new report in 1968 had reexamined the problem as the Johnson administration wound down and again concluded that the Soviet Union "with a high degree of confidence" could kill the president, vice president, and all fourteen remaining successors within just five to six minutes of the first missile launch. It all really came down to communications: The government could dig deeper holes or send up more planes, but without, as one report explained, "equally survivable communications," it'd all be for naught.

Even as the nation's leadership remained vulnerable, the war machinery itself continued to grow. McNamara's early efforts to curtail the nation's nuclear arsenal were ancient history by the end of his term; the nation's atomic and thermonuclear stockpile reached an overall peak of 32,000 warheads in 1967. Before leaving office, McNamara approved the development of Multiple Independent Reentry Vehicles, a new technology that allowed multiple warheads to be mated to the top of a single ICBM—vastly multiplying the nation's ballistic missile force in one fell swoop. He failed, too, to rein in the worst excesses of SIOP, admitting, "To the day I left, I never did modify the SIOP to reflect realistic operational alternatives." As he left office, he estimated that two out of every three Americans would be killed in a nuclear attack.

One McNamara change, however, did de-escalate the nuclear arms race: SAC trimmed back and ultimately stopped its airborne alert bombers because of solid improvement in "the survival potential" of the nation's strategic forces. While the cost pressures of Vietnam contributed to the decision, two high-profile accidents had underscored the safety concerns of having regular flights of nuclear-armed bombers in the skies overhead—one B-52 crash in 1966 saw one hydrogen bomb disappear into the ocean and three others land in the Spanish countryside, scattering radiation over hundreds of acres.

Another similar crash in Greenland in 1968 sparked a massive icy cleanup effort nicknamed "Dr. Freezelove." Soon after the Greenland accident, the airborne alerts were over forever.

Beyond the two high-profile B-52 crashes, McNamara had gotten all too familiar over seven years with the Pentagon's Pinnacle alerts that brought him news of nuclear accidents. When nuclear incidents occurred, the military unit involved broadcast a Pinnacle alert to the Pentagon's National Military Command Center, the "Operations Event/Incident Report" (OPREP-3) code word indicating "national-level interest" and sending it straight to the nation's top commanders. While OPREP-3's high-priority code words were focused on wartime events—NUCFLASH designated an incident as "a situation that could lead to the outbreak of nuclear war," and FRONTBURNER designated an attack or hostile act against U.S. forces—a series of Native American code words reported less serious nuclear incidents.* OPREP-3 PINNACLE BROKEN ARROW reported an unauthorized launch, jettison, or firing of a nuclear weapon, a release of radioactivity, or an actual unintended nuclear detonation; BENT SPEAR represented a nonserious accident with no radioactivity involved; an EMPTY QUIVER reported the seizure, theft, or loss of a nuclear weapon. Any of the code words would trigger an immediate alert. While there's never been a known EMPTY QUIVER event, one government study found that between 1950 and 1968 there had been 1,200 "significant" BROKEN ARROW and BENT SPEAR incidents. McNamara had weathered many of those, a series that began just three days after Kennedy's inauguration when a B-52 crashed in Goldsboro, North Carolina, carrying two thermonuclear bombs—one of which nearly exploded. As McNamara and Johnson left office and the Cold War began a third decade, it seemed almost a miracle that the nation hadn't experienced an accidental nuclear explosion.

In the broader presidential campaign, the Cold War, the Soviet Union, and nuclear weapons took a backseat to the horror of Vietnam and the festering fears of the American public. The ambitious fallout shelter plans put forth by the Kennedy administration at the beginning of the decade

---

* The code system meant that, in an emergency, the first words that a president was likely to read amid the beginning of nuclear war was OPREP-3 PINNACLE NUCFLASH.

were gone.* Similarly, the gleaming silver bombers of SAC seemed an anachronism of an earlier era—a point underscored when their fearless, cigar-chomping onetime leader humiliated himself on the field of national politics. After retiring from the Air Force in 1965, General LeMay reappeared in public life in the fall of 1968 to take up the vice presidential nomination of the American Independent Party, with the unabashed segregationist George C. Wallace heading the ticket. Together, they represented a perfect antidote in the eyes of angry white voters afraid of progress. It proved a sad coda to a celebrated career. Once a darling of the press, his hawkish policies and bellicosity within the Kennedy administration had rewritten his public persona as a war-monger, parodied in *Dr. Strangelove*, and portrayed as a dangerous fascist in the bestselling novel *Seven Days in May*. Even though he'd long opposed the Vietnam War, he stumbled through the '68 campaign at seemingly every turn, saying awkwardly in defense of using atomic weapons in Southeast Asia, "We seem to have a phobia about nuclear weapons," a comment that reawakened the demons of Goldwater's 1964 campaign, and an embarrassed Wallace spent the rest of the fall trying to backpedal LeMay's remark.

Lyndon Johnson was relieved to hand the White House to its next occupant. As the noon hour passed on January 20, 1969, Johnson relaxed. "When Richard Nixon took the oath," Johnson said later, "the greatest burden lifted from me that I have ever carried in my life." As he explained, "Never a day went by that I wasn't frightened or scared that I might be the man that started World War III."

As the presidential reins passed to Nixon, who had handily defeated Johnson's own vice president, Hubert Humphrey, the nuclear machine continued to chug along. The LOOKING GLASS planes circled endlessly over the prairie; the two "Floating White Houses" alternated standing station off

---

* Steuart Pittman, Kennedy's civil defense chief, was by 1968 penning forlorn op-eds about the lack of civilian protection, but even he hadn't taken his own message to heart. Pittman had long advocated for community shelters, rather than individual ones, to help spare the inequities raised by the "Gun Thy Neighbor" debates of the early 1960s, but when he returned to private life he and his wife started work on a fallout shelter at their Maryland home. "We started it, anyway," his wife said later in an interview. "But after half a day's digging, we gave it up."

the Atlantic coast. Deep underground, men and women watched over the nation day in and day out at Mount Weather, Raven Rock, and Cheyenne Mountain, even as high in the skies overhead a new generation of satellites kept an unceasing surveillance on the Soviet Union's missile fields and bomber bases.

Chapter 11

THE MADMAN THEORY

On his first full day in the West Wing, Henry Kissinger—Richard Nixon's new national security advisor—received an innocuous-looking blue-and-silver binder decorated only with the presidential seal and the single code word FURTHERANCE. As the National Security Council's executive secretary, Bromley Smith, explained, the FURTHERANCE program directed how the military response to an attack by China or the Soviet Union would unfold if the president and the National Command Authorities were unreachable. The Defense Department considered SIOP its crown jewels, creating a unique security clearance designation: "extremely sensitive information" (ESI), a label above top secret, and the binder Smith gave Kissinger was even a level above that, considered so sensitive it was kept in its own White House safe.*

Kissinger, a fixture on the foreign policy stage, had been brought into the Nixon administration to help centralize foreign policy at the White House. "I've always thought this country could run itself domestically without a President," Nixon had said in 1967. "All you need is a competent Cabinet to run the country at home. You need a President for foreign policy." Kissinger had long studied nuclear weapons, dating back to a 1955 stint with

---

* Following a security review in 2013, the precise list of overseas military commands that could have launched nuclear weapons remains classified even nearly fifty years after the fact because of the delicacy of those international arrangements.

the Council on Foreign Relations, where he'd advocated "limited war," saying American leaders should embrace the simpler military goals of the pre-Napoleonic era, that wars on the outskirts of an empire should be focused merely on political leverage, not complete subjugation. Now, though, he was seeing those war plans for the first time, and, as Smith explained, they were anything but limited.*

When Richard Nixon himself sat for his first SIOP briefing, he reacted similarly to the men who preceded him as commander-in-chief: he was "appalled." Nixon's campaign platform was peace, and he had been sworn in as president with his hand resting on the Bible's Isaiah 2:4: "They will hammer their swords into plowshares and their spears into pruning hooks. Nation will not lift up sword against nation, and never again will they learn war." His presidency, though, would prove how difficult that was to achieve.

Earlier that day, January 27, 1969, President Nixon had been questioned at his first press conference about the difference between his goal of military "superiority" over the Soviet Union and Kissinger's standard of "sufficiency." That afternoon in the SIOP briefing, he realized quickly just how minor the differences really were—the decadelong push to transform the all-or-nothing SIOP into a more "flexible response" had increased the options to a grand total of just five. The meeting was a blur of acronyms and charts, minimizing the horror and reducing the death of hundreds of millions to bureaucratic gobbledygook and antiseptic accounting tables. Colonel Don LaMoine, who led the briefing, explained to Nixon that SIOP's "fundamental concept [was] to maximize U.S. power [and] to attain and maintain a strategic superiority which will lead to an early termination of the war on terms favorable to the United States and our allies."

The new plan presented to Nixon, known as SIOP-4, divided targets into three categories: ALPHA, representing China's and Russia's nuclear forces and military command centers; BRAVO, covering conventional military forces;

---

* The Johnson team, as it turned out, had largely kept the Eisenhower nuclear "predelegation" program intact, making just three changes following a 1967 review. First, a commander could launch against only Chinese *or* Soviet targets, not both; second, a commander "cannot make a nuclear response to a non-nuclear attack on his forces unless the U.S. itself is under nuclear attack." The third change allowed for "a less than all-out response in the event the nuclear attack is small scale or accidental."

and CHARLIE, urban and industrial centers. Within those broad categories, SIOP offered just the five options: a preemptive ALPHA strike, requiring 3,200 nuclear weapons against 1,700 targets; a preemptive ALPHA and BRAVO strike (3,500 weapons against 2,200 targets); or a full-out preemptive ALPHA, BRAVO, and CHARLIE strike (4,200 weapons against 6,500 targets). SIOP also included retaliatory strike options against just ALPHA and BRAVO targets or an all-out attack against everything. No option involved fewer than a thousand nuclear weapons. As Nixon said a few days later, "Flexible response is baloney."

Nevertheless Nixon and Kissinger pushed forward their hope of "sufficiency." The desire for limited war options stemmed in part from the fear that by 1969 the superpowers had reached a strategic parity that made the Soviets more likely to take aggressive action in localized conflicts. The Soviets possessed new larger and scarier ballistic missiles—and were building as many as 250 ICBMs and 128 submarine-launched missiles a year—while America's nuclear forces were no longer the sharpened, gleaming spear that they'd been during the Kennedy years. Kissinger's push for limited nuclear war, though, met quickly with stonewalling from the Pentagon and SAC itself.

On May 11, 1969, Nixon flew back to Washington from a Florida trip aboard the EC-135 that served as the National Emergency Airborne Command Post (NEACP), the president's Doomsday plane. In its conference room, the battle staff led the president through a war exercise and the execution of SIOP. "Pretty scary. They went through the whole intelligence operational briefing and a test exercise—with interruptions to make it realistic," wrote chief of staff H. R. Haldeman in his diary that night. "Took P a while to get into the thing (his mind was on the peace plan) but he finally did—and was quite interested. Asked a lot of questions re: our nuclear capability—and kill results. Obviously worries about the lightly tossed-about millions of deaths." After the Pentagon and NEACP briefings, Kissinger knew President Nixon would never execute such insane large-scale attacks. In one meeting, Kissinger bluntly explained, "He has only heard SIOP and if that's all there is, he won't do it."

Nixon's initial efforts to bring peace to Vietnam faltered as the Paris Peace Talks collapsed that summer, with the North Vietnamese declaring that they'd sit silently "until the chairs rot." Unwilling to give up, Nixon and Kissinger sought to restart negotiations by pushing the Soviets to pressure the North Vietnamese along toward peace. "I want the North Vietnamese to believe that I've reached the point that I might do anything to stop the war," Nixon told Haldeman in one meeting. "We'll just slip the word to them that 'for God's sake, you know Nixon is obsessed about Communism. We can't restrain him when he's angry—and he has his hand on the nuclear button.'" The White House set a November 1 deadline to move the peace talks along, and then, to scare the Russians, Nixon embraced what he called the "Madman Theory."

His game-theory-based approach was, in certain respects, merely an extension of Eisenhower's nuclear diplomacy—trying to raise uncertainty in the Soviet mind about whether he'd ever actually resort to a nuclear attack. As Defense Secretary Melvin Laird recalled later, "[Nixon] never [publicly] used the term 'madman,' but he wanted adversaries to have the feeling that you could never put your finger on what he might do next. Nixon got this from Ike, who always felt this way."

Kissinger telephoned the Pentagon to order a "series of increased alert measures designed to convey to the Soviets an increasing readiness by U.S. strategic forces," telling Laird, "Could you exercise the DEFCONs for a day or two in October?" Implementing that "madman" plan fell to Alexander Haig, a West Point graduate whose career mixed politics and the military in a way that few figures in American history ever did. He'd served in Korea with General Douglas MacArthur and done a Pentagon stint under Robert McNamara before returning to combat in Vietnam, where he received the Distinguished Service Cross. (Exploding shrapnel from a grenade left him with a Purple Heart and a permanent scar over his eyebrow.) Then, under Henry Kissinger at the National Security Council in early 1969, his career began to accelerate.

Haig told the Pentagon the readiness tests should be "unusual and significant," but not overtly "threatening," and so beginning on October 13, SAC readied its forces for the staged appearance of a looming nuclear war. SAC put on alert 176 bombers and 189 tankers—nearly the number called for by the nation's nuclear attack plan—and then on the morning of October 26, it launched six armed B-52 bombers, sending them into a lazy circular orbit over Alaska, the first time in twenty months that nuclear bombers had been kept in the air on alert. Coincidentally, the U.S. military's annual nuclear attack exercise, code-named HIGH HEELS '69, kicked off on October 15, bringing teams together at Mount Weather, Raven Rock, and at other facilities like NORAD in Colorado. The OEP director, retired Army General George A. Lincoln, led daily exercise briefings with officials across the government. The combination of alerts and exercises indeed got the Soviets' attention and the Soviet ambassador asked urgently to meet with Nixon and Kissinger. Kissinger, in a background briefing for the president, emphasized, "Your basic purpose will be to keep the Soviets concerned about what we might do around November 1." Then, after scaring the Soviets, the whole exercise just stopped.

Haig was promoted to brigadier general in a festive Oval Office ceremony at the end of October. President Nixon and Kissinger were joined for the promotion ceremony by CIA director Richard Helms and Defense Secretary Laird; all the men were in a good mood, even Nixon was smiling and laughing. They'd just pulled off one of the great nuclear scares of the Cold War—and only the Soviets had noticed, just as intended. Over the months ahead, though, it became clear the feint had done little either to move forward peace talks in Vietnam or alter the U.S. balance with the Soviet Union. The government never received a single inquiry from an allied nation, nor did any reporter ever ask about it; the feints would remain secret until the 1980s.

At precisely 12:59 a.m. on March 1, 1971, five weeks after George White started as the Architect of the Capitol, a caller to the congressional switchboard threatened, "This building will blow up in thirty minutes—evacuate the building." Minutes later, a bomb exploded in the Capitol basement, hidden in a Senate restroom by the domestic terror group Weather Underground. While it didn't kill anyone, it caused extensive cosmetic damage, overturning tables in the neighboring Senate restaurant, leveling most of the barbershop, and destroying a priceless stained glass mosaic. It led to aggressive new security procedures on Capitol Hill—police began searching purses and bags, employees were for the first time issued photo IDs, and the attack generally unsettled the officials who had been preparing for a foreign threat.

Indeed, during most of the nearly quarter century he spent as the head of the Capitol's facilities, White focused himself more on another kind of far more damaging bomb.

A red phone at George White's suburban home might have rung at any hour. The family knew that if or when that phone rang, it'd mean a Capitol evacuation was under way. Daughter Jocelyn White remembers asking her dad who he'd bring with him when that time came—but it wasn't until she was fully grown and the Cold War long over that her family realized the horrible truth: George White would have evacuated alone to a mountain retreat in White Sulphur Springs, West Virginia. "That's one of the most remarkable things about this project, to keep a secret for that long a time," he said years later. "To be put in the middle of something like this was a shock."

In White Sulphur Springs, about 200 miles southwest of the capital, lay one of the most ambitious endeavors of the relocation arc, Project X, where President Eisenhower and congressional leaders had built a secret wartime Capitol—complete with chambers for both the House and the Senate, and support facilities for hundreds of staff—undercover at the Greenbrier, one of the nation's poshest and most storied mountain retreats. First, catering to members of high society who came to "take the waters," it hosted over the years many presidents and officials and, later, as it expanded to include golf courses, skeet shooting, tennis courts, a croquet lawn, and other amenities, it became a key link in the chain of elite East Coast vacation destinations that stretched from Palm Beach, Florida, to Newport, Rhode Island.*

At the outbreak of World War II, the State Department used the Greenbrier to isolate Axis diplomats, ultimately housing some 800 German, Italian, Hungarian, and Bulgarian diplomats under the protection of Border Patrol and FBI agents.† Once the diplomats were all successfully repatriated, the Army requisitioned the Greenbrier as a convalescent facility for wounded soldiers. After the war, it was repurposed back to an upscale resort, redecorated in a flamboyant style known as "Romance and Rhododendrons,"

---

* In 1914, a young well-to-do Boston couple, Joseph P. Kennedy and Rose Fitzgerald, honeymooned at the Greenbrier after they were married by Archbishop William O'Connell.
† In April 1942, the Hungarian and Bulgarian contingents were transferred to the Grove Park Inn in Asheville, North Carolina, and some 400 Japanese diplomats were brought to the Greenbrier from the nearby Homestead resort.

and became a regular vacation spot of Vice President Richard Nixon in the 1950s. Lyndon Johnson, a rising member of Congress, also visited in the years after the war.

In August 1955, President Eisenhower had invited the four congressional leaders—Speaker of the House Sam Rayburn, House Minority Leader Joseph Martin, Senate Majority Leader Lyndon Johnson, and Senate Minority Leader William Knowland—to the White House to argue the necessity of relocation planning. Following the meeting and with the leaders' assent, the Office of Defense Mobilization began to scout locations for a congressional bunker. The entire process would be conducted outside the normal appropriations process—and all but the four leaders of Congress would be kept in the dark. The Greenbrier's sheer scale would make it easier to hide such a large bunker, and it was also right on the rail line from Washington's Union Station. That proximity could speed the evacuation of 1,000 congressional members and staff two blocks away at the Capitol, and they could keep knowledge of the plans contained: The railroad was owned by the same company that owned the Greenbrier, the Chesapeake & Ohio.

While no known record exists of the first entreaty to the Greenbrier, resort historian Robert Conte believes it came during the property's 1956 North American summit, which brought Eisenhower together with the leaders of Canada and Mexico. While historic details are sketchy, Eisenhower appears to have met privately with railway president Walter Tuohy during the three-day summit to discuss the bunker. Then, the day after Eisenhower departed, the congressional leadership wrote him an opaque letter on March 28, 1956: "This is to introduce Mr. J. George Stewart, Architect of the Capitol, who is calling upon you on matters of vital importance to the Congress of the United States. We, the undersigned, representing the leadership of the United States Congress, will appreciate any cooperation you may give us." From there, the plan was in motion.

Government engineers identified the adjacent Copeland Hill as the best bunker location, and test drills were conducted to assess the area's geological profile. The Greenbrier was, coincidentally, in the process of expanding its conference business in the 1950s, as the hotel industry shifted away from relying solely on vacationers, and notices went out to the staff and local residents that the drilling was part of an expanded exhibit hall. Negotiations continued for nearly two years—sorting through the myriad tax, insurance, property, and physical plant questions associated with building a secret government facility as part of a publicly owned company's resort took some time. The C&O officials assigned to the project had to pass special background checks and receive FBI security clearances, and eight members of its board of directors were brought into the loop. In a secret lease, the government agreed to pay Chesapeake & Ohio $27.5 million for the entire property in the event of a national emergency. The hotel would disguise the bunker by building new conference facilities on top of it, leaving part of the emergency congressional meeting rooms open for public use. Since it was logistically complicated for Congress to pay ongoing rent without widening the circle of those who knew about the endeavor, the government agreed to pay for the whole conference expansion outright—covering the cost of the public exhibit hall in lieu of separate payments.

On December 12, 1958, the Greenbrier announced the construction of its new West Virginia Wing, with 22,000 square feet of public meeting space. Another 90,000 square feet were behind the walls for the classified congressional hideout. The hidden facility, surrounded by reinforced concrete walls between three and five feet thick, extended 720 feet into the adjacent mountain—a factor that created the odd sensation that from the resort lobby, one would take an elevator *up* to enter the bunker. It was not designed to withstand a direct attack, but would protect against nearby blasts and be sealed tight from fallout. When the off-the-books ghost project officially got under way in the spring of 1959, it was known by an appropriate code name: CASPER.

Locals raised eyebrows as they saw the massive excavation for the new conference halls begin. The effects were hard to ignore—the nearby St. Charles Catholic Church received a new parking lot as workers filled in a nearby hollow with dirt. Landfill also allowed the Greenbrier's nine-hole golf course to build out to a full eighteen holes. Contractors also questioned why the relatively small exhibit hall needed so many urinals—it seemed like the facility was being built for hundreds more people than the space implied. As construction worker Randy Wickline said years later, "Nobody came out and said it was a bomb shelter, but you could pretty well look and see the way they was setting it up there that they wasn't building it to keep the rain off of them. I mean a fool would have known." Ongoing curiosity resulted in an official denial by the Greenbrier to a local newspaper in February 1959 that it was constructing a presidential hideout—it proved a useful evasion. Time and again over the years ahead, resort officials would offer a version of the quote the Greenbrier's vice president gave the *Gazette*: "I know nothing of a bomb shelter for the president." It was a technically true statement: The facility on the grounds had nothing to do with the executive branch. Mostly, though, rumors didn't go far in the small remote town; the secret was kept.

The Mosler Safe Company, as usual the government's preferred bunker vendor, built massive blast doors, shipping them aboard a specially designed rail car straight from the Ohio plant to the Greenbrier along the Chesapeake & Ohio's railway. The main entrance came through a blast door hidden behind a folding wall in the exhibit hall, while two other Mosler blast doors sealed vehicular entrances on the property's east and west sides.*

During an emergency, the House would meet in the 475-seat Governor's Hall, while the Senate would convene next door in the 125-seat Mountaineer Room. For decades, both rooms hosted thousands of conference attendees who never figured out the location's secret purpose. Each chamber featured scores of microphone outlets, installed in the seat-backs, to ensure that congressional sessions could continue to be recorded as they were under normal circumstances. Just beyond the public areas lay a sprawling multi-floor substructure of 153 classified rooms, including a massive power plant, medical clinic, dentist's office, a 400-seat cafeteria, laundry facilities, three 25,000-gallon water tanks, and three 14,000-gallon fuel tanks, as well as a two-story communication facility for incoming and outgoing messages. Powerful air filters could suck air from the outside and scrub it of radiation before circulating it internally. A secure records room contained the documents and plans necessary for relocating and operating Congress remotely,

---

* The vehicular doors, known as GH1 and GH3 by the Mosler engineers who built them, weighed twenty-eight tons and twenty tons respectively, and had half-ton hinges, but could be opened and closed by a single person.

as well as a small weapons cache and riot control gear for the facility's security force.* An incinerator would have minimized refuse, and also doubled as a crematorium for anyone who died while the bunker was sealed.

Upon arriving at the facility, congressmen and their select few staff would pass through decontamination showers, drop their clothes to be incinerated, and be provided two sets of camouflage army fatigues. A press briefing room would allow Congress to communicate with the outside world using seasonally appropriate photographic backdrops of the Capitol meant to instill a sense of normalcy in a situation that would be anything but. The only people who would have had their own individual beds and conference room were the congressional leadership—everyone else would have been relegated to the eighteen shared dormitories, where double bunk beds were laid out with assigned beds for each congressman; as new members arrived in Washington with each election, the bed nameplates were changed (as with everything on Capitol Hill, they were assigned by seniority). Capitol officials also stocked in the bunker any required prescription drugs or eyeglasses used by each new representative or senator.† In between congressional sessions, the members would have passed time in lounge areas equipped with TVs and exercise equipment, or in the workspaces set up out in the public exhibit hall—which, in an emergency, would be reconstructed as workspace for offices like the Sergeant at Arms, the chaplains, legislative staff, and the Architect of the Capitol.‡

The $14 million construction project wrapped up October 16, 1962, just as the Cuban Missile Crisis loomed. Aware of the escalating situation, officials ordered that supplies be rushed to the facility in case of an emergency evacuation, and the Architect of the Capitol shipped crates full of Congress's vital and historic records to the Greenbrier. No one was the wiser. On the night of October 22, attendees from three different conventions—the

---

* A small store of bourbon and wine was also secreted inside the bunker—staff swore that the stockpile was to be used only to aid a hypothetical alcoholic congressman who might need to be weaned off.

† Even when Congress was primarily male, there was also a stock of birth control pills kept ready at the facility—perhaps recognition that some of the aides and female secretaries might find recreational activities during a prolonged stay?

‡ Rumors that the facility included two boxes of straitjackets have never been confirmed.

Conveyor Equipment Manufacturers Association, the American Coke and Coal Chemicals Institute, and the Folding Paper Box Association—paused at the Greenbrier to watch President Kennedy's address to the nation. None suspected that their exhibit halls, cocktail parties, and banquet dinners were taking place in the very same facilities that would house Congress should the situation in Washington deteriorate.

After that initial flurry of activity, CASPER sat quietly for decades, ready for occupancy with just a few hours' notice. The Army and the Greenbrier funneled funds to run the bunker's payroll and operations through a front company, Forsythe Associates, which purportedly ran the resort's television and communications systems, but actually oversaw the bunker's maintenance. The fifteen or so Forsythe Associates staff tested the telephones daily, the diesel generators weekly, and the elaborate radio communications systems— linked from the resort to surrounding mountaintops—several times annually. Through most of the Cold War, Forsythe maintained a "home office" in suburban Arlington, Virginia, at 927 N. Stuart Street, that was little more than an answering machine.

Forsythe's first Greenbrier manager, John J. Londis, arrived in 1960 to help with the initial installation and construction. Londis was a civilian communications technician for the Army and had just completed a tour of duty at Mount Weather when he was dispatched to White Sulphur Springs. He worked at the Greenbrier until 1976, although in 1963 he was displaced when Congress sent its own representative down to oversee the facility. In 1970, after twenty years in the military, Paul "Fritz" Bugas took over the bunker for Forsythe Associates after Congress's chosen superintendent died unexpectedly. "In doing that job, we spent about 15 or 20 percent of our time doing A/V work for the hotel and about 80 percent of our time doing the necessary work here in the government facility," he recalled. Most Forsythe staff were former military intelligence or communications personnel. Their Greenbrier offices were behind a triple-locked door, and during the winter, when hotel occupancy was at its lowest, Bugas and the Forsythe team would run full-scale drills at the bunker, bringing in as many as 100 personnel and sealing the facility for twelve to sixteen hours at a time.

Inside, bunker tunnels were stocked high with sixty days of military rations, while frozen foods were rotated regularly through the bunker by specially cleared Greenbrier staff and then used by the resort's regular catering kitchens. "Danger: High Voltage" signs near the bunker's hidden entrances and air intakes discouraged nosy explorers. Finding the subterranean working situation both eerie and dreary, Londis and the Forsythe team installed panoramic nature scenes in various locations around the bunker. "We thought we would brighten it up a little bit. It was bad enough being under there—no windows, no nothing—we were trying to brighten it up," Londis said. Later renovations also upgraded the air-conditioning, telephones, and the fire suppression systems.

Originally, the facility wouldn't have allowed anything other than the designated congressional officials to be protected at the Greenbrier, but real doubts were raised as to whether members of Congress would evacuate if they couldn't bring their families—a scenario that could leave Congress paralyzed absent a quorum. House Speaker Tip O'Neill, one of the few briefed on the evacuation procedures, recalled, "I kind of lost interest in it when they told me my wife would not be going with me. I said, 'Jesus, you don't think I'm going to run away and leave my wife? That's the craziest thing I ever heard of.'" Thus, an expansion during George White's tenure as the Capitol Architect created space for another 500 bunk beds and ensured room for at least 1,400 dependents in a pressurized area adjacent to the main bunker. "The facility could have accommodated every congressman, his or her spouse, plus dependent children—generally thought to be one or two children under the age of 18," Bugas recalled later.

Even as elections shifted the political landscape, elevating some leaders and downgrading others, the circle of congressmen and senators who knew about the bunker remained tight. After White became Architect of the Capitol in 1971, one of the first new names added to the list was John Rhodes, who took over Gerald Ford's position as House minority leader when Ford was elevated to the vice presidency the following year. Soon after he ascended to the leadership role, a military officer met with Rhodes to explain the Continuity of Government program and that he was now considered "essential and non-interruptible." It was heady information for the politician. "Yes, I am considered non-interruptible. I am considered essential," he explained shyly later. "There are certain plans made so that I should survive."

Figuring out how to inform rank-and-file members about evacuation procedures proved to be tricky. Moving and coordinating nearly a thousand officials and staff out to the Greenbrier would never be easy. If Congress was in session, the leadership, especially the House speaker and Senate president pro tem, who both served in the presidential line of succession, would be evacuated by helicopter from the National Mall (a scenario that actually came to pass on September 11, 2001). The rest of the representatives and senators—as well as support staff and, eventually, congressional dependents—would board a special train from Washington's Union Station straight to White Sulphur Springs, where evacuees could alight directly across the street from the Greenbrier. That plan, though, was predicated on sufficient time to arrange the special train for the six-hour ride out to West Virginia. As missiles became more of a threat, it was increasingly unclear whether a quorum of Congress would ever make it out of the capital.

There was also a contentious debate within the executive branch about how to handle a congressional evacuation that occurred during weekends or a scheduled recess. Telling all 535 members of Congress the evacuation site's location seemed an unnecessary security risk; the Greenbrier was not built to withstand a direct attack, so if its location became publicly known, its security would be ruined and its safety nullified. Thus, the Office of Defense Mobilization decided Congress simply wouldn't be told in advance where to evacuate in an emergency. ODM suggested instead they be told in an emergency to report to their closest FBI field office, where they'd be given sealed evacuation instructions—ensuring no one would need know the location until the very last moment. With the FBI's national network of field offices, all of which were listed in phone books, it'd be easy for congressmen and senators to find the instructions in an emergency. Senior bureau officials, though, weren't excited by that plan—it could be a manpower drain at a critical moment and involved the FBI in a potential tug-of-war between the executive and legislative branches. What if a powerful senator or congressman showed up at a local field office in peacetime and demanded the location of the bunker? That could negatively affect the bureau's image. Finally, the FBI's two top officials assented, scribbling their approval across the bottom of the proposal. Associate director Clyde Tolson wrote, "If the President wants us to do this, I think it is OK—T," and, later, J. Edgar

Hoover added: "Of course. We must do it if that is the President's desire. H."
The one caveat: The bureau would not seek out nearby members; it would
only be responsible for handing out the information if members of Congress
showed up at a field office themselves.

Thus, sealed envelopes with instructions for senators and representatives were distributed to each FBI field office, designated Appendix 25 and
added to the field offices' war plans. The notification plan—however rudi-
mentary and awkward—remained in place for nearly the entire lifetime of
the Greenbrier bunker. Periodically in the years ahead, the bureau conducted
nationwide security checks to ensure that the sealed envelopes remained
accessible and secure.*

Word of this new evacuation scheme, however, didn't necessarily make
it to all the members of Congress. Hubert Humphrey had been briefed on
the facility by the Office of Emergency Planning when he took office in
1965 as Lyndon Johnson's vice president, helping coordinate the project,
picking up from Johnson himself, who had worked on it as both Senate majority leader and as vice president.[†] Humphrey had even visited the CASPER
facility on multiple occasions under the cover of darkness during vacations
at the Greenbrier. In 1970, after his time as vice president, Humphrey was
reelected to the Senate from Minnesota, where, as a junior senator, he was
no longer privy to the evacuation plans. Even though he knew that the
Greenbrier existed—a fact that put him in an extreme tiny minority inside
Congress—no one ever explained to him what he was supposed to do in an
emergency as a senator. As he said during the Nixon years, "You know, that
has struck me as odd."

Early in the Nixon years, aides worried that emergency procedures had
grown rusty amid the Vietnam War. Military aide James Hughes proposed
increasing OPAL III drills, which practiced evacuating the president by
helicopter from the White House's South Lawn, as well as boosting SILVER

* A 1977 check, for instance, uncovered that one of the Chicago Field Office's sixteen copies had been worn on one end; it was sealed with scotch tape, dated, and initialed.
† In an evacuation, the Greenbrier would have been one of the possible relocation sites for
the vice president, who also serves as the president of the Senate.

DOLLAR drills, which practiced evacuating the National Command Authorities to the presidential "Doomsday" planes, known as NIGHTWATCH. And so at 9 a.m. on January 26, 1972, the president's Coast Guard military aide, Captain Alex Larzelere, waited at the Pentagon helipad in freezing temperatures as the White House ran an unannounced drill.

Larzelere and the other four military aides shared a warren of offices in the East Wing basement of the White House, near the Presidential Emergency Operations Center (PEOC), the "bunker" that dated back to Truman's era. It was the kind of job that ran 24/7; there was even a bedroom in the shelter area for when the aides had overnight duty. Larzelere spent a significant amount of time dealing with the White House Emergency Plans. When Larzelere arrived at the White House six months earlier, he received a pager, the White House Communications Agency installed a special phone at his house for emergencies, and COG planners carefully selected the most convenient place for his own evacuation: He'd be plucked by helicopter from the playground of Pointer Ridge Elementary School, two blocks from his house in Bowie, Maryland. When he wasn't with the president, he scouted and inspected Presidential Emergency Facilities and helped select evacuation sites. For one project, he traveled up and down the Potomac with the Secret Service to identify piers where Nixon could be evacuated from the presidential yacht, *Sequoia*, if an emergency occurred while they were cruising—eventually settling on one at Fort Belvoir and another at the Anacostia Naval Station.

That January morning, Larzelere was standing in for the commander-in-chief during the drill. The helicopter arrived in just five minutes and raced him toward Andrews Air Force Base, even as NEACP readied for takeoff. "I climbed out of the helo and hurried up the steps to the aircraft. The door closed and the plane surged forward," he later wrote in his diary. In the air, the plane's battle staff ran through a war briefing and the current status of Soviet forces. As Larzelere recalled, "I was impressed." Still, how well the plans and planes might have worked in an emergency was questionable. The planes were cramped; Defense Secretary Laird once complained, "Before a person can go to the back of the plane, everyone has to move out of his chair." More seriously, the aging EC-135s struggled to maintain contact with the communications network—problems that became a dark joke among White House staff. One National Security Council aide during a trip to Vietnam sent Al Haig a message, explaining, "You will be happy to know that Hanoi radio is having almost as much trouble communicating as your NEACP aircraft."

NEACP was hardly alone in showing its age. While the Camp David bomb shelter was repainted and renovated by Mrs. Nixon with new beds and bedspreads, furniture, and wall decorations, other problems proved harder than a new paint job. Two decades after Eisenhower's first large-scale COG efforts and a decade after McNamara launched a major expansion, the creaking COG apparatus was being rapidly made obsolete by advancing technology. As satellite surveillance improved, the two "Floating White Houses" were becoming harder to hide from Soviet eyes in space and so the Navy dropped the NECPA program around 1970.* OUTPOST MISSION, the presidential helicopter search-and-rescue team in Pennsylvania, was also disbanded in 1970, as atomic weaponry progressed to the point where there was little chance of digging the president out of the White House rubble after an attack.

On October 28, 1969, Richard Nixon signed Executive Order 11490—updating the government's main COG authority as well as nearly two dozen related orders signed by Truman, Eisenhower, Kennedy, and Johnson. The lengthy, 20,000-word document outlined post-attack responsibilities for twenty-seven critical departments and agencies, everyone from the Pentagon to the Railroad Retirement Board. Those responsibilities ranged from the Justice Department's "emergency plans for the control of alien enemies" to the Treasury Department's need to develop plans for emergency loans "for the expansion of [industrial] capacity" and the "sharing of war losses" to the Post Office's need to provide "emergency mail service" at relocation sites. The Nixon administration also again reshuffled the nation's often orphaned civil defense resources—reorganizing in 1972 the Pentagon's Office of Civil Defense into the Defense Civil Preparedness Agency (DCPA), and, later, abolishing its civilian equivalent, the Office of Emergency Preparedness. COG and stockpile management responsibilities were transferred to

---

* The *Northampton* was sold for scrap in 1977; the *Wright* suffered the same fate three years later.

the General Services Administration, and OEP's responsibility for natural disasters was handed to the Department of Housing and Urban Development's newly established Federal Disaster Assistance Administration. (In 1975, the GSA itself reorganized its civil defense and COG efforts into a new entity, the Federal Preparedness Agency.)

Who—and where—the nation's leaders would be after an attack, to help guide the plans of Executive Order 11490, remained open to question. The nation's creaking command post technology limited just how "flexible" nuclear plans could be. "Command centers do not possess the combination of survivability and capability which is required for the conduct of limited strategic nuclear war," one report concluded early in Nixon's administration. "Those which are survivable have limited capability; those with the required capability are not survivable." While operations like Mount Weather and Cheyenne Mountain had extensive computer systems, NEACP didn't have any computers—meaning the battle staff would have to manually adjust war plans on the fly. LOOKING GLASS and the other airborne command posts also needed major communications upgrades, as did the fleet of TACAMO relay planes. "Our warning assessment, attack assessment, and damage assessment capabilities are so limited that the President may well have to make SIOP execution decisions virtually in the blind, at least so far as real time information is concerned," a Pentagon report cautioned in 1971.

Another report the following year found that with their improved ICBM technology, a Soviet attack by less than one percent of its strategic forces could prevent more than 80 percent of the U.S. nuclear forces from receiving a "go order." The improved Soviet ICBMs meant even hardened command posts like Mount Weather and Cheyenne Mountain would be unlikely to survive a concentrated attack. Though Raven Rock had been reinforced in the 1960s to withstand overpressure of as much as 140 psi, far more than the 50 psi rating of Mount Weather, that probably wouldn't have been enough to survive a direct hit. Mount Weather, engineers had calculated, could be "eliminated with reasonably high probability" by just six to ten weapons in the 10-megaton range.

With Vietnam draining the defense budget and Raven Rock's short-comings becoming increasingly evident, Deputy Defense Secretary David Packard—the co-founder of Hewlett-Packard, who had taken a huge pay cut to work at the Pentagon—wanted in 1969 to put it on standby mode. The Joint Chiefs argued vigorously against it, saying that the underground Pennsylvania command post was still among the best facilities the U.S. had for safely directing a war, but civilian Pentagon leaders limited the upgrades to Raven Rock—after all, what leader would be dumb enough to choose it as a bunker? As Assistant Defense Secretary Eberhardt Rechtin said, "This choice would guarantee suicide."

These problems all pushed the White House and Pentagon toward the conclusion that the airborne command post represented the best evacuation option. Talk in Pentagon circles turned to the idea of building a new "advanced" airborne national command post—one with more space and more capabilities than the EC-135s offered. Then, coincidentally, an opportunity arose to upgrade them. In the early 1970s, Qantas canceled an order with Boeing for two 747s, and the aircraft manufacturer offered the nearly completed airframes to the Air Force, which used the first two to upgrade the aging EC-135 planes and then ordered a third. In his final annual report as Gerald Ford's defense secretary in 1976, Donald Rumsfeld's office had warned that among the National Military Command Center at the Pentagon, Raven Rock, and the Doomsday plane, "Of the three, only the NEACP, if airborne, can be expected to survive a nuclear attack. Moreover, since the NEACP has multiple path, multiple frequency communications to the strategic nuclear forces, its vulnerability to jamming and nuclear weapons effects is low."

It remained entirely unclear, though, whether the NEACP, which always sat under fifteen-minute alert at Andrews Air Force Base, would ever get off the ground. The flying time for a Soviet submarine-launched missile off the Atlantic coast to the runways at Andrews was just thirteen minutes and forty-eight seconds. The ever-shortening time horizons of an attack meant that even evacuating the president from the White House in an OPAL III or SILVER DOLLAR alert would take him out of the decision-making loop at precisely the moment he most needed to be in contact with the military command system. As one report explained, by the 1970s "it became more and more widely agreed that in a real crisis it was highly unlikely that the President would relinquish control of the situation for half-an-hour in order to go to a place targeted by the enemy." The president would be loath to leave a void in the chain at such a critical moment, which would potentially leave "confused and frightened men making decisions under conditions where their authority to do so was questionable and the consequences staggeringly large."

Vulnerabilities and challenges like these began to shift basic tenets of nuclear war. Both superpowers moved away from targeting each other's command posts as officials came to fear there wouldn't be anyone left to turn a nuclear war off. In studying the problems with the readiness exercises in the 1960s, the U.S. government concluded, "Following a heavy nuclear exchange, effective war termination capabilities are marginal." Instead, military strategists suggested treating command posts as "sanctuaries," and focusing initial strikes in a "limited war" on some of the more than 3,000 Soviet targets that would inflict "less than a hundred casualties per target." Leaving each other's command authorities alive would "diminish risks of escalation" and allow those leaders to "negotiate termination of war."

Debates over fine-tuning the nation's nuclear doctrine played out from the headlines. For much of Richard Nixon's second term, the nation was much more concerned about the growing day-to-day leadership void atop government as the White House found itself consumed by the investigations and scandal touched off by the break-in at the Watergate office complex in June 1972.

The scandal rippled through the COG efforts, as well as the nation's emergency and succession plans. As the scandal circled closer to the Oval Office, Nixon knew he had already lost his best protection against impeachment: His unpopular vice president, Spiro Agnew, was forced from office in October 1973 by a federal corruption indictment. Agnew had for so long seemed a wall that would have kept impeachment at bay—no Democratic Congress, however unhappy with Nixon, would have installed him as president instead. But Agnew's absence also created an odd moment for executive succession—suddenly, two Democrats became next in line for the presidency, though neither seemed a strong candidate to lead the nation. The man first in line became Speaker of the House Carl Albert, whose alcoholism was an all but open secret in capital circles, especially after a drunk driving accident in September 1972 where the speaker crashed near one of his favorite bars, the Zebra Room. He spent several weeks after Agnew's resignation in an alcohol treatment facility. Second after Albert was the Senate president pro tem, James Eastland, a wealthy Mississippi plantation owner and unapologetically racist Southern Democrat who had led the fight against desegregation and wasn't of the surest mental faculties. Henry Kissinger, then next in line, was not eligible for the presidency since he was born in Germany. The office, in short order, could have ended up in the hands of the treasury secretary, George Shultz.

It was lucky the Twenty-fifth Amendment arrived when it did. Constitutional scholars have argued that the amendment's clear succession policies allowed Watergate to proceed to resolution; before the amendment's ratification, there would have been no mechanism for Nixon to choose a new vice president and the position would have sat vacant until the 1976 election. Removing Nixon beforehand would have led to Albert's ascension, a politically fraught outcome that might have slowed congressional willingness to pursue an impeachment that could be so obviously dismissed as a political coup and installed such a compromised leader. Such messiness was luckily all avoided, and on October 12, 1973, while he was at Camp David, Nixon chose affable Michigan congressman Gerald Ford as his new vice president.

Succession issues swirled regularly around Watergate, as the scandal continued. Just days later, in attempt to oust Watergate special prosecutor Archibald Cox and avoid a subpoena requiring that Nixon turn over nine tapes of White House conversations, the president fired both his attorney general, Elliot Richardson, and the deputy attorney general, William Ruckelshaus. The "Saturday Night Massacre" stopped only when the Justice Department #3 official, Robert Bork, agreed to fire Cox. Speaking in 2009 to a convention of former U.S. attorneys, Ruckelshaus explained that he and Richardson had "urged Bork to comply if his conscience would permit." At the time, there was no fourth-in-line official at the Justice Department; the chain of successors ended with Bork. "It's not clear what would have happened if Bork had refused," Ruckelshaus said. "We were frankly worried about the stability of the government."*

---

* In the decades ahead, the DOJ line of succession would be built out to more than a dozen officials.

The public revulsion spawned by Watergate also scuttled the government's latest scheme to alert Americans to an impending nuclear attack. During the Kennedy years, the government had tried to supplement the nation's "nearly ineffective" warning sirens with a home-based system called the "National Emergency Alarm Repeater," or NEAR. Small buzzers, available for $5 or $10, could be plugged into any home outlet and triggered by a special high-frequency electrical current transmitted across the national power grid by 500 warning-signal generators.* The multimillion-dollar program was abandoned, though, as its myriad shortcomings became evident. There was no way to provide any more specific detail or information to homeowners about the attack timing, duration, or scale—or instructions on what to do afterward.

To address the problems with NEAR, officials in the Johnson and Nixon administrations developed a new "Decision Information Distribution System," a national radio network to notify citizens of a Soviet strike. DIDS relied on a small $10 device installed in new television sets—or retrofitted onto existing TVs for about $30—that would, following a special government signal, turn the television on at any hour to a special low-frequency warning channel. Within thirty seconds of the warning being issued from Washington, every TV in the country would be alerted, saving precious minutes in the race for shelter. In 1972, DCPA had spent more than $2 million to build the first DIDS transmitter in Chase, Maryland, for WGU-20, "Public Emergency Radio." The program was publicized with a friendly puppy mascot named "PERki" that was emblazoned all over its literature. A poll that year found seven out of ten American households would gladly pay for the warning system. Plans were moving ahead for ten more DIDS stations spread across the country—all controlled from centrally located radio transmitters in Ault, Colorado, and Cambridge, Kansas—when the whole program, estimated to save 27 million lives in an emergency, was quietly scuttled after the Watergate scandal, doomed by public distrust following

* As a test, 1,500 NEAR devices were distributed to the small town of Charlotte, Michigan, near the civil defense agency's headquarters in Battle Creek. On the day of the test, each NEAR-equipped home was given a pink weather balloon to release if its buzzer went off. Spotters on the city's courthouse roof counted the balloons as they rose into the sky to determine how many homes used the warning system successfully.

the dirty tricks and paranoia in the Oval Office. "The technology is there," one federal official explained afterward, "[but] after [Watergate], there was no way we were going to tell John Q. Public that we were going to put something in his home TV that was controlled by the government."

Watergate also caused Congress to take a hard look at the Emergency Government Censorship Board, which came into the spotlight when word leaked that one of the accused Watergate burglars, James W. McCord Jr., was part of the shadow censorship agency's "Special Analysis Division." McCord had participated in monthly meetings with the Office of Emergency Planning to develop censorship plans and helped draft a "National Watchlist" of troublesome Americans who would receive special attention during an emergency.

Wartime media censorship actually had a long history in the United States, dating back nearly to the country's founding, but most of the censorship efforts had been ad hoc operations created in the exigencies of an ongoing war. Only since the Eisenhower administration had the executive branch created a standby censorship structure ready to spring into action. Former Associated Press executive Byron Price had served during World War II as the director of censorship, working with a staff of fifteen to oversee the media's shared "Code of Wartime Practices." While media organizations didn't submit reports before publication to the censors, they relied upon the code and could consult with Price's office anytime a question arose.* That experience had been fresh in officials' minds when ODM created a "Committee on National Censorship Planning" in 1954, naming ODM's deputy, Willard Paul, to lead a nine-agency working group. Over the next four years, it developed a seven-page "Standby National Censorship Agreement," outlining conditions and limitations that news organizations would "voluntarily" accept during a national emergency.†

Johnson and Nixon both expanded the censorship board's powers, and Nixon eventually changed its name from the "Office of Censorship" to the

---

* Thousands more censors actively read public and military mail, telegraph cables, and the like.

† The exact "voluntariness" of the standards would have been debatable, since the draft legislation authorizing the program also prescribed a $10,000 fine and ten years in prison for violations.

friendlier "Wartime Information Security Program." As one historian noted, however, the powers WISP could exercise were "dangerously vague." The agency would have been authorized by either a presidential executive order or under Title XI of the innocuously named Defense Resources Act, the standby legislation that the executive branch had drafted and had waiting on a shelf "for use in a future emergency." The government did not distribute the censorship code in advance, but instead intended to have the wire services—the Associated Press and UPI—distribute it within "forty-five to sixty minutes" of an emergency. Eight standby WISP executives would oversee the system during the Nixon years, an eclectic (and largely retired) group that included a retired CBS TV executive, a head of personnel for the Census, a trade magazine editor, a Hollywood lobbyist, a retired Army officer, an Eastman Kodak executive, a former civil defense leader, and the head of facilities at Western Maryland College. The standby censors all received white ID cards with a thick red border, complete with their identifying information and the Defense Department seal, labeling them as "Federal Emergency Assignee, Office of Emergency Planning." The back side of the card stated: "The person described on this card has been assigned essential emergency duties for the federal government. It is imperative that the bearer be assisted in travel by the fastest means to this emergency assignment."

At the president's command, the eight men would make their way to Western Maryland College—now known as McDaniel College—a small liberal arts school about thirty miles northwest of Baltimore in Westminster.* The government paid the college $100,000 to construct a special sub-basement beneath its science building; faculty wives would periodically set up shop in the facility to test that all the phone lines worked. Upon activation, the WISP headquarters would include a Press Division (to oversee censorship of newspapers, magazines, books, and other publishers), a Broadcast Division (to censor radio and TV), a Telecommunications Division (to censor telephones and telegraph systems), and a Postal and Travelers

---

* Picking the college town as the center of the nation's censorship network added a touch of historic irony: Westminster is famous perhaps for only a single incident in its history— during the Civil War, a mob ransacked the town's newspaper, destroyed the presses, and beat to death the editor after he published an anti-Lincoln editorial. A town jury acquitted the four men charged with the killing, citing "self-defense."

Division (to censor the mail, the communications of people crossing U.S. borders, and all other communications "not within the purview of other elements of the Office of Censorship"), as well as the Special Analysis Division, which would be in charge of collecting and determining what information should be censored in the first place. The staffing for the agency would have been a mix of specially recruited civilians, federal workers transferred from other less essential agencies, and Navy Reserve units with unique training in censorship methods and practices.

After WISP came to public attention, the man who oversaw it, Eugene Quindlen, explained in a moment of candor that any national emergency could allow the president to launch the censorship regime, though he said reassuringly, "It would be unlikely that any element of the Wartime Information Security Program would be implemented in any contingency short of a nuclear attack." The secret draft executive order simply mentioned "the present emergency situation." Promptly after Watergate, Congress defunded WISP entirely in 1974, but the executive orders all still remained drafted—ready for an emergency whenever it arrived.

Gerald Ford was sworn in as vice president on December 6, 1973, taking office even as signs clearly pointed to the unraveling of the Nixon administration. In early August 1974, Senator Barry Goldwater led a delegation of Republican lawmakers to the White House to say that the end had come. The next day, Nixon addressed the nation from the Oval Office at 9 p.m., and three minutes into his speech uttered the fateful words: "I shall resign the Presidency effective at noon tomorrow. Vice President Ford will be sworn in as President at that hour in this office."

The morning after Richard Nixon's unprecedented speech to the nation was foggy. He boarded his helicopter, taking one final look at the crowd assembled on the lawn for his departure and flashing his double-V. On the White House balcony, Defense Secretary James Schlesinger, puffing on a pipe clenched in his teeth, watched alongside a White House chef and an NSC aide named David Michael Ransom as Nixon's helicopter flew away—his presidential nuclear codes, unbeknownst to him, no longer by his side. As Marine One banked southeast by the Washington Monument, Schlesinger took his pipe out and banged it on the metal railing of the balcony to empty it. He had spent the previous days warning the nation's nuclear commanders about taking orders from the despondent Nixon, though given how little time and attention Nixon had spent on SIOP and COG planning, he perhaps need not have worried: As Brent Scowcroft, the deputy national security advisor, said later, "Nixon wouldn't even have known how to give the orders."

The Nixon presidency was growing smaller and receding quickly into the lingering haze over the Potomac. Speaking to no one in particular, Schlesinger announced, "It's an interesting constitutional question, but I think I am still the secretary of defense. So, I am going back to my office."

The Pentagon chief then looked at the chef, dressed in his white uniform, and said, "What are you going to do?"

The chef replied, without a second's pause, "I'm going to prepare lunch for the president." After all, it was noon—and Gerald Ford would be hungry.

Ransom thought, "Of course. The king is dead. Long live the king!" As he explained years later in an oral history, "I've always thought of that as something very important about our country. We may stumble but we don't fall."

Back in his office, Schlesinger sent out two simple communiqués to the military, scattered around the globe from the Pentagon to the barracks in Berlin and the DMZ in Korea to the airspace over Nebraska. The first, a message from Ford himself: "As Commander-in-Chief, I know that I can count on the unswerving loyalty and dedication to duty that have always characterized the men and women of the Department of Defense. The country joins me in appreciation for your steadfast service." The second, from Schlesinger: "Mr. Ford will have, consistent with our best traditions, the full support, dedication, and loyalty of all members of the Department of Defense." The second message, from Schlesinger, annoyed many senior military leaders, who viewed it as unnecessary and redundant. As one general later said, "Civilian supremacy was bred into me."

Eleven days later, thanks again to the new Twenty-fifth Amendment, Gerald Ford, the only man ever to become commander-in-chief without ever having been elected either vice president or president, brought to an end nearly two years of chaos that had tested "Continuity of Government" in ways that no other chief executive ever had—but the system had worked, the Constitution had held, the crisis passed, and, now, Ford could choose among three people to become his own vice president. After considering Republican Party chair George H. W. Bush and the U.S. ambassador to NATO Donald Rumsfeld, Ford nominated Nelson Rockefeller to be vice president. Over the next forty years, ironically, it was Rockefeller who would actually prove to have the smallest impact on the nation of the three.

Chapter 12

MOUNT PONY

A sign at Mount Weather cautioned its occupants and staff, "What you hear here remains here," but as the 1970s progressed, the mountaintop bunker's secrets increasingly spilled out into public view. The facility was under the purview of Bernard T. "Bud" Gallagher—a retired lieutenant colonel, decorated bomber pilot, and former prisoner of war who had taken over as director of the "Western Virginia Office of Controlled Conflict Operations" in 1968 and would hold the post until 1992.

After World War II, Gallagher had spent most of the next two decades engaged in the government's atomic plans; as part of the nuclear tests in the South Pacific and in Nevada, he had flown reconnaissance planes through a dozen mushroom clouds to collect fallout samples. In 1956, during the Suez crisis, he had sat on alert in the cockpit of an F-84 Thunderjet, armed with an atomic bomb, ready to launch an attack if the international tensions escalated. In 1958, he had been transferred to Pennsylvania, where he helped run OUTPOST MISSION, the special helicopter rescue unit based outside the capital's blast zone to rescue the president after an attack. The pilots carried special dark visors and lead-shielded flight suits meant to protect against the flash and effects of a nuclear blast, ready to evacuate Eisenhower, Kennedy, and Johnson from the rubble of the White House. After serving as a U.S. liaison to NATO on nuclear matters, Gallagher had retired from the Air Force in 1965. Three years later, he took over the mountain from Leo Bourassa, who had run it for a decade. Amid the often bland government workforce, Gallagher cut something of a colorful figure with his ever-present white cowboy hat and a pink 1965 Mustang convertible. Despite his long COG service—or perhaps because of it—Gallagher had real doubts about whether the plans would work. "Through the years, we always reacted like we could handle an all-out nuclear attack," he said after his retirement. "I don't think people—even our top people in government—have any idea of what a thousand multimegaton nuclear weapons on the U.S. would do. We'd be back in the Stone Age. It's unthinkable."

Six years into Gallagher's tenure at Mount Weather, on a cloudy December day in 1974 filled with sleet, fog, driving rain, and treacherous winds, TWA Flight 514—a Boeing 727 en route from Columbus, Ohio, to Washington National Airport—was diverted to Dulles because of the weather. Due to confusion between the pilots and the air traffic controllers, the plane descended to 1,800 feet for a landing long before it was safe to do so. It was traveling at about 180 miles per hour when it slammed into the side of Mount Weather at 11:10 a.m., at an altitude of 1,670 feet, some twenty-five miles short of the airport, killing all ninety-two aboard. Rescuers found the treetops shorn off for a hundred yards, and Christmas presents from the plane scattered through the snowy woods. "It looked like a hundred tons of dynamite, like somebody had blown up a building," the local fire chief said. The crash severed the Mount Weather facility's primary telephone line and knocked certain message services offline; still, responding Chesapeake & Potomac technicians restored service within two hours, even as fires from the crash still burned intensely in the rain.

While the crash didn't touch the Mount Weather COG reservation, hundreds of media, officials, and first responders descended on the scene and many had questions about the suspicious activity they spotted nearby. Federal agents sealed the crash site and worked with local police to close the area around the mountain for a five-mile radius. The front-page story in *The New York Times* the next day read, in part, "The plane crashed about one and one-half miles from an underground complex that reportedly is designed to serve as a headquarters for high government officials in the event of nuclear war." A government spokesman would only acknowledge that the facility was operated by the Office of Emergency Preparedness, whose responsibilities included "Continuity of Government in a time of national disaster."

The Washington Post published a story entitled "Hush-Hush Mt. Weather Is a Crisis Facility," calling it "the sort of mountaintop retreat Ian Fleming was always dreaming up for James Bond."

The crash began two years of unwelcome looks into Mount Weather, as Democratic senator John V. Tunney led a series of investigative hearings over the course of 1975 and 1976 into the vast government surveillance network that had grown out of the Vietnam War. Secrecy stymied almost every aspect of his inquiries. "I don't understand what they're trying to hide out there," his subcommittee staff director, Douglas Lea, later complained. "Mount Weather is just closed up to us. I don't believe there's been any effective congressional control over the system."

When the head of OEP, retired General Leslie Bray, testified, he demurred, "I am not at liberty in an open session to describe precisely what is the role and the mission and the capability that we have at Mount Weather, or at any other precise location." The scarce information Congress could gather about Mount Weather's activities did little to ease concerns. Staffers questioned the influence of those in the "Executive Reserves," the businessmen who were predesignated to step into key emergency roles running the country after a nuclear attack, and how they interacted with the regulatory agencies that were supposed to oversee them in peacetime. "In effect, these officials constitute a type of 'shadow government,'" one Senate report warned.

Bray confirmed that Mount Weather maintained a "Survivors List" of names and addresses of people whom the government deemed "vital" to the nation's future and who could provide assistance in maintaining "essential and non-interruptible services" through an emergency. He said it contained 6,500 people nationwide, including a number of private citizens, but refused to release the list.*

"No one seems to be in charge," Tunney complained. "New technologies are developed and seem to be allowed to spread without thought for their future social and political ramifications."

---

* Compiling and maintaining the list, reported one person involved, was "depressing work." It included at one point construction workers who owned earthmoving equipment like bulldozers and diggers, since those would be needed to dig mass graves.

To some degree, Senator Tunney was right: By the early 1970s, Mount Weather, the Office of Emergency Preparedness, NORAD's bunker at Cheyenne Mountain, and the broader COG program had amassed some of the world's most sophisticated computers. A large specially built bubble-shaped pod inside Mount Weather's East Tunnel contained several advanced machines, which were disconnected from the network at 9 p.m. each night so that teams could conduct classified research and computations on them until 8:30 a.m. the next day. Inside the pod, the room-sized UNIVAC 1108 supercomputer, which retailed for about $1.6 million, represented the cutting-edge technology of multiprocessors, allowing for multiple functions at once. "I'm at a loss to describe its maximum capacity," a UNIVAC executive said at the time, awed by the processing power installed at Mount Weather.

The need for Continuity of Government and survivable nuclear command and control facilities had been a key driver in major investments in fledgling technologies during the Cold War. During the late 1950s, at the dawn of the missile era, the military had become obsessed with building resilient and survivable networks to aid in launching a retaliatory second strike. Much of that research fell to the Advanced Research Project Agency (now known as DARPA), a lean and feisty experimental Pentagon research shop established in 1958. "ARPA's existence and sole purpose was to respond to new national security concerns requiring high-level visibility. In this case, it was the command and control of military forces, especially those deriving from the existence of nuclear weapons and deterring their use," explained Stephen J. Lukasik, who served as the deputy director of ARPA from 1967 to 1970, and then spent five years as the overall director. "The goal was to exploit new computer technologies to meet the needs of military command and control against nuclear threats, achieve survivable control of U.S. nuclear forces, and improve military tactical and management decision making."

Under deterrence theory, the harder it was to knock out the American capability to retaliate the less likely an attack would be in the first place. As one scientist involved in the early network development wrote, "The technical solution to avoiding decapitation involved new ways of routing and switching in decentralized and distributed communication systems that could survive damage from an attack." One of the first conceptual breakthroughs was made by Paul Baran, a researcher at RAND, who proposed building a network that relied on "packet-switching." Many iterations later, it was a concept that would form the core of the internet. "The origin of packet-switching is very much Cold War," Baran said later. "The problem was that we didn't have a survivable communications system, and so Soviet missiles aimed at U.S. missiles would take out the entire telephone-communication system."

As the 1960s progressed, ARPA funded a broad array of academics and researchers working on developing these new networks. While there were many disparate teams of academics and scientists working at different institutions, each with different goals and pursuing their own corner of a complicated project, the money that funded their work came from the Pentagon, which had but a single interest in the outcome of their research: the DOD needed a system to help launch missiles, enable COG, and preserve the National Command Authorities. "I can assure you, to the extent that I was signing the checks, which I was from 1967 on, I was signing them because that was the need I was convinced of," Lukasik said. As he said decades later, ARPANet and the birth of the internet was perhaps the best thing to come out of the horrifying possibility of a nuclear holocaust: "[Nuclear weapons] had become a nightmare, but the nightmare had the internet as a consequence."

OEP's needs to handle mass amounts of data in an emergency drove other innovations as well: Under orders from OEP director General George Lincoln to deliver an information-monitoring network in just a week to help address the crisis of President Nixon's August 1971 wage-price freeze—an attempt to wrest the nation's economy out of an inflationary spiral—a young computer scientist named Murray Turoff developed a system in just four days that came to be known as the Emergency Management Information System and Reference Index (EMISARI), which allowed OEP's regional offices to link together in a real-time online chat, known as the "Party Line." EMISARI became the forefather of later electronic chat functions like AOL Instant Messenger and text messaging. "A conferencing capability would be highly useful under [a nuclear attack scenario], particularly during the transattack and immediate post attack period when everybody would have to be holed up and traveling to face-to-face conferences would be impossible," said EMISARI's project manager, Richard Wilcox.

These postwar scenarios that people like Turoff spent their days calculating on the OEP super-powerful computers were becoming important again because the Nixon-era push for "limited war" encouraged the idea that large parts of the nation would survive a nuclear exchange. By January 1974, Nixon had signed a secret new nuclear weapons policy, known as National Security Decision Memorandum 242. It came be known as the "Schlesinger Doctrine," after Defense Secretary James Schlesinger, who explained its goal was to have "more selective" targeting options that did "not necessarily involve mass destruction."*

Throughout the 1970s the Oak Ridge National Laboratory—working with OEP's computer facility in Olney, Maryland—devoted significant resources to calculating which natural resources and infrastructure would likely survive various attacks; it estimated, for example, that 136 of the nation's 224 oil refineries would be destroyed in a widespread nuclear attack— most of the rest, though, would be inoperable due to the loss of electricity. New research in the 1970s also revealed that protein might be harder to come by after a nuclear attack than long thought; the Oak Ridge National Laboratory had been studying pigs that it killed with lethal amounts of radiation and found that earlier predictions that the meat could be safely salvaged weren't true.

The need to ensure a smooth flow of commerce and the exchange of goods following a national attack led the Federal Reserve to open its own Doomsday bunker during the Nixon administration, inaugurating in December 1969 a 140,000-square-foot facility in Culpeper, Virginia, buried in the side of Mount Pony, seventy-five miles outside Washington. Publicly, the Federal Reserve Bank of Richmond, which managed the facility, touted the "Culpeper Switch" as the electronic hub for the nation's 5,700 banks, allowing the instantaneous transfer day to day of funds nationwide. Some $120 billion a day flowed electronically through the Culpeper hub in the 1970s. Yet a closer look at the building revealed that it had some features

---

* Schlesinger at one point tried to convince Congress that, under the more limited options now under way, a Soviet attack on the U.S. missile fields might kill only 25,000 Americans—a number he later raised, under pressure, to 800,000. However, a congressional study showed that the same attack would kill 18 million.

that seemed unnecessary for its day-to-day operations. The building, as it turned out, had some strange features: At the push of a button the windows in the offices that looked out over the facility's parking lot could be covered by a five-inch-thick lead shield. Antitank traps dotted the side of the mountain. The unusual landscaping suddenly made more sense when in 1976 *The Washington Post* outed the facility as the Fed's nuclear war hideaway.

In addition to the computers and the sixty or so staff who handled the electronic transfers that served as the backbone of the nation's financial system, the Mount Pony facility contained room for as many as 500 personnel in an emergency, a thirty-day supply of emergency rations, an exercise room, an incinerator, generators, private water wells, air filtration systems, and cold storage to preserve the bodies of anyone who died while the mountain was sealed up, as well as a weapons range on property for the forty armed guards who patrolled the facility and watched over the grounds from a central security control room. Rows and rows of empty plastic-covered desks filled nearly an entire floor of the facility, each set up with the name of the Fed employee who would occupy that desk in an emergency, and nearby dorm rooms for men and women contained bunks and lockers. The chairman—who would be evacuated by helicopter to the site—had a private office, equipped with two phones to link him to the rest of the nation's leadership.*

Beyond those features, which would be familiar to anyone who had visited one of the government's other ever-multiplying COG bunkers, was a floor unique to the Federal Reserve: a 22,500-square-foot vault, one of the largest in the world, that held nine-foot-tall stacks of cash—more than $4 billion in total. The Mount Pony bunker's 700 million pieces of currency—a substantial chunk of the 1.9 billion pieces the Fed had stockpiled nationwide for Armageddon—would replenish the nation's currency east of the Mississippi River, part of the Federal Reserve Board's emergency mission to regulate and provide for money, credit, and liquidity in the event of a nuclear attack. The Doomsday stockpile was intended to tide the nation

---

* Almost unique among government agencies, the Fed provided room for the families and dependents of its emergency personnel, a perk of the fact that the Federal Reserve Board is self-funding and thus able to spend its money however it wants. "The Board discussed this and it was generally felt that the chance of getting our essential staff to go without their families was pretty slim," the Fed's emergency coordinator, Harry Guinter, said at the time.

over for more than two years, the length of time government analysts expected it would take the Bureau of Engraving and Printing to restart currency printing operations after D.C. was destroyed.*

Each of the nation's twelve regional Federal Reserve branches had its own relocation facility—including an abandoned salt mine in Kansas, a limestone mine in Pennsylvania, a bunker on a military base in Massachusetts, and secure basement facilities on several assorted college campuses across the country. "I can't guarantee our plans will work, but without them—if there is a nuclear war—everyone will take to the hills. We'll be back to tribal warfare and there'll be no hope for national survival and recovery," explained Gordon Grimwood, the Fed's emergency planning officer.

The Treasury Department, meanwhile, would relocate to the Airlie Foundation's 1,200-acre conference center in Warrenton, Virginia, not far from the CIA's relocation facility. Up until the Cuban Missile Crisis, various Treasury components had planned to scatter to cities like Fort Knox, Kentucky; Richmond, Virginia; Greensboro, North Carolina; and Parkersburg, West Virginia, but as part of the reevaluation of plans in the era of ICBMs, the Treasury had consolidated its emergency operations in 1963 into the conference center fifty miles outside Washington. The Treasury Department had done background checks on the conference center's management, given them all security clearances, and installed a secure communications facility in the basement of one building, paying $12,000 a year in rent. In an emergency, it would take over a much larger chunk of the property.

Public scrutiny of COG programs accelerated when journalist Richard Pollock wrote a four-page article in *The Progressive* magazine outlining all that was known publicly about Mount Weather. Readers thought the piece, titled "The Mysterious Mountain," read like science fiction. As Pollock wrote, "interviews with former high-level officials from Mount Weather confirm that the base is much more than a standby administrative complex or storage center for preservation of records; they described the facility as an actual

---

* After 1976, when the Fed reintroduced the $2 bill only to find it unpopular with businesses and the public, many of those bills were redirected into the emergency bunkers. "We had a lot on our hands and we put them into our stockpile," one Fed official said.

government-in-waiting." Mount Weather "more closely resembled a city than an emergency installation," he reported, citing nine federal departments (Agriculture, Commerce, HEW, HUD, Interior, Labor, State, Transportation, and Treasury) and seven agencies (the Postal Service, the FCC, the Federal Reserve, the Selective Service, the Federal Power Commission, the Civil Service Commission, and the Veterans Administration) with contingents based inside the mountain as part of the nation's emergency government.*

By the 1970s, it wasn't at all clear who Mount Weather was hidden from—most U.S. officials involved in COG operations assumed Soviet spies had long figured out both its location and purpose. In the 1960s, the Soviet Union tried to purchase a nearby estate, saying they intended it to be a weekend retreat for their diplomats in Washington, but the State Department blocked the sale. "Everyone around here assumed they wanted to keep an eye on Mount Weather," the editor of the local Leesburg newspaper, Brett Phillips, said in the 1970s.

While the facility itself wasn't necessarily shocking news, the scope of the shadow government's powers certainly troubled a nation worn down by the abuses of Watergate and the revelations of illegal activities by the FBI and the CIA that had come out of investigations like the Church Committee. Pollock asked, "How can a parallel—even if dormant—government be constitutionally acceptable, if Congress has played no significant role in its formation and exercises no control over its day-to-day operations?" The quotes Pollock collected from those running Mount Weather weren't helping, either. "We just act on the orders of the President," one official told him. Another said, "In national emergencies, I imagine we could do whatever needed to be done." "We are not evil men," one COG official said reassuringly, "and no one likes to violate constitutionally guaranteed civil liberties at any time. But if you can save an additional 100,000 lives, some rules might bend under wartime or emergency conditions."

---

* If anything, Pollock surely understated the breadth of organizations represented at the mountain, since the Justice Department, FBI, and the Supreme Court all maintained operations there, too, among other entities.

Senator Frank Church, who had built a reputation of investigating the government's illegal excesses, introduced legislation in August 1974 to codify the ad hoc process for invoking presidential emergency powers. The National Emergencies Act became law in September 1976, signed by Gerald Ford, and ensured a presidentially declared "emergency" could only last two years and gave Congress the option to vote to terminate it.

As the presidential election of 1976 loomed that same fall, pitting Ford against Georgia governor Jimmy Carter, it seemed the nation's COG operations and emergency planning were on the wane. Civil defense spending was still shrinking; the president's emergency powers had been sharply curtailed; and the veil of secrecy had been lifted from some of the Cold War's biggest covert projects. COG, it seemed, might have run its course.

After Ford lost the election, his press secretary, Ron Nessen, indulged in a long-delayed perk of his White House job, touring Mount Weather. He'd meant to do it ever since he'd been informed he was part of the "Presidential Emergency Staff," and now he had just days before he returned to the mass of the American people who would be turned into dust by a Soviet attack. "I felt like I was in a science fiction movie," he recalled, as he was led through the blast doors and down the long tunnels. Staffers walked him past more than twenty barracks built inside the mountain, as well as its hospital, cafeteria, offices, a TV studio for post-attack broadcasts, and "luxury" quarters for the president and the highest officials. "I was taken to the bedroom cubicle assigned to me in case of war. What an eerie feeling it was to stroll around the wartime press office, set up and ready," he recalled. Yet as he passed stacks of emergency rations, he wondered about the unfairness of it all. The last line of his evacuation instructions had been clear: "There are no provisions for families at the relocation or assembly sites." Would he have really abandoned all of his family in the country's hour of need?

In January 1977, as President-elect Jimmy Carter finished the oath of office, Gerald Ford's military aide, Marine Captain Walter Lee Domina, handed Carter's new military aide, Navy Lieutenant Commander J. Paul Reason, the aluminum-sided Football. The plans inside looked largely the same as those Nixon had inherited from Johnson. Despite much effort, neither administration had made much progress on reforming the nation's nuclear plans. The thirty-pound Football's plans were still grouped under three headings—Limited Attack Options (LAOs), Selected Attack Options (SAOs), and Major Attack Options (MAOs). The military aides who carried the Football referred to the options more colloquially: Rare, Medium, and Well-Done. Now that arsenal would be in the hands of a man who would become the unlikeliest hawk of the Cold War.

Chapter 13

THE UNLIKELY HAWK

A week before his inauguration in 1977, Jimmy Carter sat down with the nation's military leaders at Blair House. The generals and admirals spent nearly nine hours walking the president-elect through the nation's defenses, generally making the case that the nation was badly outgunned. At the end of the day, Carter threw out a provocative idea: What if, he asked, the U.S. reduced its nuclear stockpile to just 200 weapons? The idea stunned and horrified the Joint Chiefs, but there was a certain logic to Carter's seemingly crazy idea—after all, the first nuclear war plans, code-named DROP-KICK, had called for targeting 200 targets across 100 cities. Surely that was still sufficient to deter Soviet aggression? As reasonable as it might have been, the Joint Chiefs hadn't confronted such a question in decades. Ever since Truman, incoming presidents had all been experienced in the Cold War's peculiar logic, coming from the ranks of congressional leaders, vice presidents, or military leaders themselves. This Georgia governor, however, was unschooled in it. Joint Chiefs Chairman George Brown was "stunned speechless." Since the beginning of the Cold War, stockpiles had only gone up—the arms race had only sprawled. No one imagined that an incoming president would change that. Yet Carter hoped his administration marked the beginning of a change in direction for the Cold War—one that saw the two superpowers lowering tensions. The dramatic years ahead, though, would change his mind.

Seven days after Carter took office, an emergency order arrived at

Andrews Air Force Base: Evacuate the White House—get the president and the first lady to safety immediately. It was 9 p.m. on a snowy Friday night, the worst possible time for an emergency. Near-gale-force winds buffeted the South Lawn as a green-and-white Marine helicopter loomed out of the darkness, its engines roaring. Two people bundled themselves on board before it took off again. That night, National Security Advisor Zbigniew Brzezinski and his secretary were playing the first couple, helicoptering down the Potomac to the alert NEACP aircraft. A few minutes earlier, Brzezinski had been receiving a briefing on the White House evacuation plans, getting step-by-step descriptions of how COG was supposed to work, when he turned on a stopwatch and ordered the emergency planning officer to launch a simulated evacuation. As Brzezinski recalled, "The poor fellow's eyes practically popped; he looked so surprised."

"Right now?" the officer asked.

"Yes, right now," the White House aide replied.

The alert procedures, so finely tuned during the Eisenhower and Kennedy administrations, had become "rusty, at best" in the intervening years. Brzezinski's stopwatch ticked long past the allotted fifteen minutes—more than double the intended time, in fact. NSC General Robert Rosenberg said the drill was "a nightmare, just a complete disaster."

President Carter had been worried about the plans since before the inauguration, when he discovered that vice presidents had been historically excluded from emergency plan briefings—despite the war plans that assumed the president would be killed in an opening salvo. Carter insisted that his second in command, Walter Mondale, be brought into the fold. Then, at the first White House staff meeting, on January 21, 1977, he tasked Brzezinski with polishing the nuclear procedures, and later in the year ordered a "searching organizational review" of the military command structure, which concluded, "The period of American preeminence following World War II has given way to one of precarious strategic nuclear balance." Indeed, his administration confronted a very different strategic threat than it had a decade before. The war in Vietnam had gutted America's defensive and offensive readiness, leaving little money to modernize and upgrade vital technologies.

Carter devoted significant time in his first year to the problems of the nation's COG operations. On February 11, just three weeks into office, he flew aboard the NEACP plane, taking it for a weekend trip to his family home in Plains, Georgia, spending his time aboard being briefed by staff from the Joint Chiefs. Over the months ahead, he visited bunkers like Raven Rock and Mount Weather and even took a nine-hour trip aboard the nuclear attack submarine USS *Los Angeles* off the coast of Florida.* His self-directed education changed his mind about the nation's military—and about the hopes for peace during the Cold War. All told, the Carter administration would prove to be a remarkable period in COG history, as the onetime Georgia governor, whom history now remembers as an ineffective and disengaged commander-in-chief, actually became the unlikeliest hawk of the Cold War.

On July 9, 1977, Carter's White House ran another OPAL III exercise, dispatching two "Communications Contingency Teams" to hardened facilities outside Washington. The helicopter evacuation drill took fifteen minutes and forty-three seconds to rendezvous with NEACP—a big improvement over the last time. The president himself sat down with COG staff, including his cousin and advisor Hugh, five days later, to review the results, discuss the White House emergency procedures, and the planned response to an imminent nuclear attack. The president wrote in his diary that night, "My intention is to stay here at the White House as long as I live to administer the affairs of government, and to get Fritz Mondale into a safe place, underground or in a command airplane." But just in case Carter survived to coordinate the nation's response, he and Brzezinski scheduled regular telephone calls with military field commanders, in part to familiarize the military leaders with the president's voice and manner of speech—which, they believed, would help build rapport and confidence in a national emergency. As aide General William Odom explained, "He wanted to be able to be awakened at 3 o'clock in the morning and not be confused, and understand what he was going to have to see, or what he was about to hear, what the voice would sound like on the other end of the line, and that sort of thing."

---

* A Naval Academy graduate and former submariner himself, Carter was the only president ever to ride in a submarine while in office; he called it "one of the most interesting days I've ever spent" and "probably the finest military weapon ever devised."

After initial annoyance about the surprise drills, the Pentagon quickly saw value in the president's interest. "It is the first time in years that they have a president who takes his role as Commander-in-Chief seriously," a White House aide bragged. "They're ecstatic." Amid Vietnam, Watergate, and a relatively calm period of the Cold War in general, Johnson, Nixon, and Ford had shown little interest in the emergency procedures, which for the most part had continued to chug along far off the White House's radar. Carter's administration, on the other hand, ran the only full-scale activation of the Greenbrier congressional relocation facility—on cue, the Forsythe Associates team hauled hundreds of desks out of their warehouse on the resort grounds and—while the conference facilities were closed to the public—set up the exhibit hall as if Congress had successfully relocated there. Outside the small Forsythe Associates crew, none of the resort guests or staffers noticed.

One of the few seemingly up-to-date aspects of the nation's Doomsday system were the new Boeing 747 presidential Doomsday planes, known as E-4As, that had arrived in the Air Force fleet in 1974 and 1975. Planners hoped the planes marked the first of what would be seven such aircraft totaling more than a half billion dollars, though the Pentagon only ultimately purchased four. Since the four-engine 747s were rare in the military fleet, the Air Force sent its flight crews to TWA's training facility at New York's JFK Airport to learn how to fly civilian passenger planes before returning to Offutt to join the NIGHTWATCH program. Formally known as the 1st Airborne Command and Control Squadron, the unit's nickname derived from an early commander's love of Rembrandt's famous painting *The Night Watch*, which showed a group of civic guards on the march during the Dutch Golden Age in the mid-seventeenth century.*

One of the first pilots through the NIGHTWATCH training program during the Carter years was Barry Walrath. He had arrived at Offutt in 1979, just as the Air Force received the first E-4B—an upgraded, custom-built 747 variant that included a new hump just behind the cockpit for satellite

* A small copy of the original—one of the largest paintings in the world—still hangs in Offutt Air Force Base in Nebraska today.

communications equipment, and a fine wire mesh that covered the plane's interior and windows to ensure that the plane's electronics wouldn't be fried by a nearby EMP. The mesh, similar to the kind inside a microwave, made the views from inside the plane almost prisonlike. Over the next six years, through 1985, the three first-generation E-4A aircraft were all updated to become E-4Bs.

The white planes, painted with a blue stripe and the words "United States of America" along the fuselage, were little known to the public and much less recognizable than the traditional Air Force One, but in an emergency they were likely the president's best chance to live. The planes were treated specially wherever they went; under a unique FAA directive, FAAO JO 7610.4, NEACP receives "expedited" movement and priority from air traffic controllers, even when the president isn't on board. Dubbed a "White House with Wings" and known to its crew colloquially as "Air Force One When It Counts," the austere NEACP plane had a special suite under the nose of the cockpit for the designated National Command Authorities on board, including a double bunk, a small sitting area, and a half-bathroom—though there were no showers for anyone. Banks of clocks tracked the time in Washington, D.C., local time, Greenwich Mean Time, and the time till the plane was scheduled to land.

The plane's main level featured a nine-seat conference room dominated by a large, wall-sized glowing world map, a larger briefing room that could hold a score of reporters or staff, a main workspace for the thirty-person emergency Joint Chiefs battle staff, and another large workspace for the additional thirty or thirty-five emergency communications staff—about 5,000 square feet of office space in total. Toward the rear, the plane also had a crew rest area and fourteen bunks. All told, NEACP could hold as many as 114 crew and staff—the largest crew of any Air Force plane in the fleet—although under normal operations it only had about twenty communications staff and another twenty battle staff, as well as two pilots, a flight engineer, and a navigator.

The normal NEACP battle staff included a senior commander—either a Navy captain or an Air Force, Marine, or Army colonel—as well as dozens of military personnel (and the occasional CIA officer) with a wide range of specialties. The staff included just about any skill set the designated successor could need to lead a war from tens of thousands of feet above the earth: logistics, conventional weapons experts, intelligence officers, meteorologists, switchboard operators, radio controllers, war planners, and the designated Emergency Action Officers, who oversaw the nuclear codes and launch procedures. An elite, specially trained security team, the forerunner of what would become the Air Force's PHOENIX RAVEN teams in the 1990s, also traveled with the plane, ready to protect and defend it wherever it landed.

In what would be the cargo and luggage area on a normal 747, there were avionics and communications equipment, as well as a cramped workstation for the technician who ran the plane's trailing-wire antenna—the five-mile-long retractable wire VLF antenna that served as the final link in the Pentagon's Minimum Essential Emergency Communications Network (MEECN), its last-ditch one-way communication infrastructure to ensure that, even under heavy enemy jamming or a widespread nuclear attack, the National Command Authorities could communicate with surviving bombers, missiles, and submarines and order a launch. Even if the trailing wire antenna failed to reach anyone on the ground, the LOOKING GLASS and NEACP planes could independently launch the nation's Minuteman missiles, a capability considered so powerful that it had a self-destruct mechanism that would destroy the plane's launch controls if power was lost for just 1.7 seconds, to guard against crashes or sabotage. Overall, the capabilities and technology aboard the NEACP and LOOKING GLASS planes were considered so classified that when Vice President Mondale toured them, his national security staff and military aide weren't allowed to be part of the visit.

Along with LOOKING GLASS, NEACP was an integral part of the World Wide Airborne Command Post system (known in the military by its acronym WWABNCP, pronounced "wah-bin-cop") that circled the entire globe. Until the INMARSAT satellite network negated the need for air-to-air network, special radio-relay planes based in Indiana, South Dakota, and North Dakota helped link LOOKING GLASS and NEACP to the airborne command posts of military forces in Europe, the Pacific, and in the Atlantic.* None

---

* The European plane, based at RAF Midenhall in the United Kingdom, was known as SILK PURSE; the Pacific plane, based at Hickam Air Force Base in Hawaii, was known as BLUE EAGLE; and the Atlantic plane, based in Langley, Virginia, was known as SCOPE

of this extensive network was cheap; in fact, until the B-2 bomber came along, the E-4B laid claim to being the Air Force's most expensive plane, both cost-wise and operations-wise. Through the 1970s, the military spent upward of $200 million annually (about $750 million in 2016 dollars) on technology support for the airborne command posts alone—not counting the flight crews, flight operations, or the planes themselves.

The four NEACP crews alternated one-week alert deployments from Offutt to Andrews, where one NEACP plane always sat "cocked," on alert twenty-four hours a day either at Andrews or within an hour's flight of the president if he was outside the capital. A second plane generally sat alert at Offutt. If an alarm sounded, the goal was to have the engines started just five to eight minutes after the Klaxon. It was an elite assignment—because of the flight experience required to fly the large planes, the NEACP flight crews were older and more senior than other flight wings in the Air Force. Crew wore NEACP baseball hats with an image of the Grim Reaper holding his sickle in one hand, and a button in the other, imposed over a looming mushroom cloud in the background. The hats read: "DOOMSDAY AIR-CREW MEMBER—Don't push me!"

The NEACP planes also regularly traveled with the president overseas, landing at a nearby airport, away from Air Force One, to ensure he'd have access to the nation's nuclear forces even if he was on the other side of the world. During Nixon's historic trip to China, two NEACP planes had been kept ready, in constant flight just off the coast, conducting what the military called "communications training," ready to quickly evacuate the president from the mainland.*

When they weren't on alert, the crews regularly practiced refueling, touch-and-go landings, quick turnarounds on the ground, and rendezvousing with HMX-1, the helicopter of Marine One. To match the requirements for the

---

LIGHT. The NEACP planes were originally known as SILVER DOLLAR, but that code name was later abandoned in favor of more secure daily changing call signs; of course, if the president or his successor was ever on board, it would be referred to as Air Force One.

* Given the E-4s' global mission, their maintenance chief, Air Force Lieutenant Colonel Jim Pike, insisted the planes be outfitted with all FAA-certified parts, which while more expensive than military-issue, meant that they could use standard Boeing spare parts wherever they happened to be in the world.

small runway at D.C.'s National Airport, one of the likely evacuation points for the president, crews trained to land on 7,000-foot runways and to turn around in just 150 feet, both tight challenges for a 747. Through the Cold War, civilian airports like Grand Island, Nebraska, and Indianapolis, Indiana, both of which had runways that closely matched National Airport's specifications, would regularly see NEACP planes practicing touch-and-go landings.

During regular drills, a Pentagon or White House official played the role of the president—once airborne, the battle staff would run the "president" through a scenario and ask for launch orders. Walrath, who sat through many such mock briefings with fake presidents, noticed a clear pattern: "No one would ever press the button—even when it was clearly a drill, even when someone had been told nothing would happen," he recalls. "It just seemed too real. You've suspended disbelief. It was nasty." In every mock training exercise, the "president" would wait until at least one missile had actually hit the United States before ordering retaliation. And often he or she would never order a strike at all, watching as the scenario unfolded and the United States was obliterated. The exercises led Walrath to doubt that in the heat of the moment, faced with the horror of a global thermonuclear war, the U.S. would ever actually launch its nuclear weapons. "I always wondered if the Soviets had had any idea how reluctant we were to launch a missile, they might've felt entirely different," he says. "It wasn't unusual to do nothing at all in response."

While the planes could continue air-to-air refueling indefinitely—and once did a thirty-six-hour flight as part of its initial testing—NEACP only carried enough water and rations for about three days at full capacity, including fifty-seven cases of military MREs (684 MREs total). As prepared as they might be in the air, however, what the plane crews would find when they landed—or even where they'd land—three days after a nuclear attack was anybody's guess.*

The deeper the administration examined the nation's COG and war plans, the less reassured they became. William Odom, a scholarly Army officer and

---

* While rumors circulated that there were designated South American airports meant for the president to evacuate to in case of a nuclear attack on the United States, flight crews from the era say they were unaware of any such plans, either classified or unclassified.

Russia expert who had once been Brzezinski's graduate student at Columbia and was later recruited by Brzezinski to the NSC staff, took over the crisis management portfolio. "I explored the system, tracking the lines of communication and control," he recalled. Despite his reputation as a hawkish hard-liner, Odom found himself horrified by the state of the nation's nuclear structure. "This led to other issues, namely transportation and protection of the president during a nuclear attack, the survivability of the military command and control structure for all U.S. forces, not just nuclear force, and securing the survival and continuity of U.S. government operations." In Omaha, he "could not believe" the "unnerving" plans SAC showed him, and he quickly convinced Brzezinski to visit SAC, where the national security advisor also came away deeply concerned about the state of the nation's preparations.

Determined to find a solution, the foreign policy sage asked Strategic Air Command pointedly about its plans for the days after war erupted—what would happen ten days after the initial attack? Thirty days? "The SAC commander and his staff had no answers," Odom recalled. "Things would just cease in their world about 6 to 10 hours after they received the order to execute the SIOP." That visit to Offutt Air Force Base encouraged President Carter to participate in a large-scale exercise—a seemingly simple act that itself helped reshape the nation's COG infrastructure, when Carter's participation led the military to realize that many of its communications networks were "not secure from foreign intelligence interception." With the president's participation, the Pentagon had hurriedly tried to switch over to secure channels, only to realize more often than not that none existed for the nation's nuclear systems.

The secure networks needed to communicate between the president and the nuclear forces were an early step in what would come to be a significant overhaul of the nation's nuclear telecommunications systems, particularly as Carter's aides discovered the wide-ranging role AT&T played in the nation's military and COG networks and realized how the administration's populist push to break up AT&T's monopoly might impact the nation's ability to respond to a crisis. It was also clear to Carter's team that despite the huge sums and efforts invested in the systems over the preceding two decades, the government had given little thought to the requirements the system should be expected to meet: Was it good enough for the communications networks to operate only through the opening stages of a war, or should the networks be resilient enough to survive a nuclear strike? How long should they be prepared to function in a wartime environment—just long enough to launch SIOP or long enough to keep the National Command Authorities in charge through days, weeks, or months of a prolonged war? Carter was determined to get the nation's defense posture to a point where he had confidence it could execute a nuclear war, no matter how long it lasted.

Improvement was steady; a third OPAL III drill in early October 1977 brought the response time down under fifteen minutes—fourteen minutes and five seconds, to be exact. Later that month, Carter toured SAC on October 22, 1977, inspecting a B-52 bomber, walking through the main war room with Brzezinski and SAC commander Richard Ellis, and sitting at Ellis's red telephone to address the bases around the world. "Very informative," he scrawled in his diary that night. Six weeks later, Vice President Mondale followed, traveling to Omaha for the same set of briefings as part of Carter's insistence that his designated successor know the nuclear war systems as well as he did. The next month, the president spent nearly ninety minutes running through various SIOP drills in the Oval Office with the vice president, the chairman of the Joint Chiefs, the defense secretary, and other officials. "This is the first time any president has done this, which is unbelievable," Carter wrote that night, adding, "We've tried to simplify the process greatly since I've been in office."

Then, just after Christmas, Carter met privately with James Schlesinger, who after his stints as Nixon's and Ford's defense secretary had been appointed as the nation's first energy secretary. The new department, part of the government's efforts to address fuel shortages and the spiraling energy crisis, had also inherited the caretaking of America's nuclear arsenal. Meeting in the Oval Office on a cold morning, the cabinet secretary walked the president through the 25,000 nuclear warheads available to him in a crisis—including 2,251 ICBM warheads, another 6,700 aboard submarines, and more than 6,000 ready to be delivered by SAC's bombers. In the years ahead, Carter would face strong criticism about the nation's relative nuclear strength vis-à-vis the Soviet Union, which had closer to 30,000 warheads at the time, but it would have been hard to sit through Schlesinger's briefing without concluding that the nation did at least possess "sufficient" nuclear weapons to accomplish whatever defensive or offensive efforts it wanted. Carter recorded privately that it was "a sobering experience."

Exactly a year after the first evacuation drill of his administration, President Carter visited the Pentagon's National Military Command Center on January 28, 1978, to participate in a mock readiness exercise and speak with military commands around the world—the day didn't necessarily go as planned. He was never able to establish a secure connection to the NEACP aircraft, a breakdown that led quickly to a $200,000 communications upgrade for all the Doomsday planes. The administration was quick to argue that all of his tests, preparations, and upgrades weren't aimed at actually starting a war. In fact, it just was the opposite. "It is done to help prevent a war from breaking out in the first place," his Defense Civil Preparedness Agency director, Bardyl Tirana, explained. "The existence of the plan itself would diminish or eradicate any possibility of the Soviet Union ever using its capability." If you knew the other side's leadership would survive to launch a counterattack, the deterrence theory of Mutually Assured Destruction held you'd never launch an attack yourself. Left unsaid in Tirana's comments, though, was how such preparations were indeed a fine line: If either superpower got too good at such war planning and continuity operations, it might give false hope that the country could safely weather a retaliatory attack, a conclusion that would threaten to undermine the very heart of MAD.

Along those lines, to help ensure that he never actually had to use any of the apparatus he'd spent the last year perfecting, Carter inaugurated a major upgrade to the Moscow–Washington hotline, moving the primary communications to a U.S. INTELSAT satellite and a Soviet Molniya II satellite, both downlinked to a fifteen-acre site at Fort Detrick, Maryland. Despite the upgrade, an initial nuclear volley would still have blown most MOLINK terminals apart, leaving perhaps Raven Rock as the one surviving hotline terminal. As Defense Secretary Rumsfeld had warned the Carter administration as it took over, "The system is not designed to survive a direct attack." MOLINK could help defuse a crisis before it started, but likely wouldn't have been any use once an attack began.

Carter loved to fish as a way to escape the pressures and the bubble of the White House. And so in August 1978, he took his family to the Salmon River in Idaho for a three-day rafting and fishing trip with his interior secretary, Cecil Andrus, a former Idaho governor. It was, Carter ventured, an "unprecedented vacation" for a modern president, and the pristine wilderness, where they traveled at barely five miles an hour, couldn't have seemed further from the pressures of Washington. But in the nuclear age, the president was always commander-in-chief. While the president and his family, all wearing bright orange life jackets, were together in one rubber raft and the cabinet secretary and his family in another, a third raft of White House staff accompanied them nearby, three other rafts of press and cameramen trailed them out of sight, and dinghies of Secret Service agents scooted up and down and around them on the river. On the raft with the White House staff traveled the president's military aide with the nuclear Football, the briefcase filled with information on launching the nation's nuclear arsenal that had become a constant presence in the president's life. Even on the Salmon River, Jimmy Carter could communicate with the outside world, connected by radio to a network of Air Force planes flying overhead. Helicopters also waited nearby, ready to evacuate the president from the river if necessary.

Only rarely was the Football more than a few steps from the president.* Technically known as the "presidential emergency satchel," the Football got its nickname because the first version of the Single Integrated Operational Plan was code-named DROPKICK. The modern version of the Football is less a satchel than a portable safe—a rugged aluminum briefcase, covered in black

* Being trailed by the aide could be a real source of stress for presidents: Lyndon Johnson commented that one of the things he enjoyed most about his post-presidency was the absence of the Football. As he explained, "It feels good not to have that sergeant with the little black bag a few feet behind me." A November 1975 trip to Paris by President Ford, where the aide had accidentally left the Football locked aboard Air Force One as the motorcade departed, was more the exception than the rule. A speeding staff car quickly caught up with the motorcade and passed the Football to the aide through an open window.

leather and manufactured by a Utah luggage company, Zero Halliburton. Contrary to public mythology, the forty-five-pound Doomsday box is not actually handcuffed to the aide's wrist, but attached through a leather cinch.

By Carter's administration, the documents in the Football were showing their age. As William Odom wrote that fall to Brzezinski, "The emergency decrees which the President carries in the 'Football' for the event of war are badly out of date. Some are even illegal." Updating the Football and the associated Presidential Emergency Action Documents (PEADs) wasn't necessarily a new problem. A few years earlier, Gerald Ford's defense secretary, Donald Rumsfeld, had launched a surprise test of the White House Emergency Plans (WHEP) and discovered that the White House and the Pentagon emergency procedures differed—no one had noticed for years, because there had never been an unannounced and uncoordinated drill. Moreover, Carter felt the Football and its PEADs weren't set up for the quick decisions necessary from a president in an emergency. Over the years, the Pentagon had never really received much guidance from the White House about what to include in the Football, so it erred on including ever more plans and briefings. One effort to pare down the briefcase during the Johnson years, for instance, had elicited a snappy reply from a defense official: "I am sure we can find strong couriers who are capable of carrying an additional pound or two of paper."

The week after the rafting trip and some eighteen months after the PEADs review first began, a frustrated Hugh Carter took the cause directly to James McIntyre, the head of the Office of Management and Budget, which was supposed to be running the process, only to find McIntyre "shocked and unaware" his agency had fallen short. At long last, William Odom wrote to Brzezinski on October 22 that "major progress in a hasty revision has been made, and an adequate set of PEADs should be available soon." The Carter administration stripped the Football down to the essentials. As Bill Gulley, director of Carter's White House Military Office, explained: It was now simply a nine-inch-by-twelve-inch "Black Book" containing about seventy-five loose-leaf pages outlining nuclear retaliatory options, a book that listed classified evacuation locations, a manila folder with a short paper outlining the procedures for the Emergency Broadcast System, and an index card with authentication codes. One military aide,

Colonel Buzz Patterson, would later describe the resulting pared-down set of choices as akin to a "Denny's breakfast menu."

But fixing the Football was just one piece of the puzzle; the months after the rafting trip underscored how much work remained to be done in organizing the nation's war and COG plans. As Brzezinski wrote the president on November 3, "The present state of our Continuity of Government program in FPA is a worry to all those familiar with it." As Odom wrote, similarly exasperated, "Until we work out how the civil side of the federal government would transit from peacetime to wartimes, the PEADs cannot be put in top shape. That issue has not been fundamentally addressed since the 1950s, although serious studies were made in 1962 and 1970."

That fall, the Pentagon and twenty-six federal departments and agencies ran an intense and groundbreaking monthlong command post exercise called NIFTY NUGGET, paired with a civilian exercise known as REX '78, representing the most ambitious readiness exercise the Pentagon had ever conducted. The results were, as one congressman recalled later, "devastating." The nation failed nearly every single test; in the tabletop and computer simulations, tens of thousands of U.S. troops died unnecessarily due to inadequate matériel support. The Pentagon turned out to lack even basic stockpiles of uniforms, weapons, and ammunition. Shortages were evident everywhere: The Air Force didn't have enough forklifts to load its planes, nor enough spare parts to keep them flying. Within the first thirty days of the simulated war, the Army ran out of artillery shells—and planners discovered it would take sixty days to begin manufacturing more. Computer systems meant to handle preplanned logistical movements overloaded when a single Marine unit was switched to deploy to Iceland—causing a ripple effect in the nation's "Aluminum Bridge" airlift capability that crashed the system and forced planners to reroute forces by hand.

More broadly, NIFTY NUGGET exposed a dearth of necessary legal authorities. Differing standards meant Army and Air Force retirees could be recalled to active duty by the president, but that the commander-in-chief had to declare a formal national emergency before recalling those in the Navy. Without anyone noticing, the president had lost the authority to draft physicians into military service in 1973—leaving the nation short thousands of wartime doctors. The Pentagon's readiness command discovered that

Congress had never given it myriad powers necessary for emergency operations. "We couldn't even let a contract or do things like authorize overtime," Lieutenant General Eugene D'Ambrosio, the readiness command's deputy chief, recalled. "We asked the question, 'Has Congress ever given the authority to do this?' The answer was 'No.'"

Other failures were more prosaic—but just as likely to happen in a real emergency. For example, the Department of Health, Education, and Welfare was responsible for handling civilian evacuees from the war zone—but, in real life, the federal worker at HEW who managed that program had retired and hadn't been replaced. In the midst of the exercise, one million Americans "fled" to Europe only to find no plans in place to register, shelter, or feed them.

A follow-up exercise, code-named PROUD SPIRIT, didn't go much better: The computerized World Wide Military Command and Control System collapsed again, going dark for twelve hours in the midst of the exercise. "WWMCCS just fell flat on its ass," one participant reported bluntly. Indeed, thirty years after the nation had first started thinking about nuclear war, it still seemed remarkably unprepared in too many ways, both militarily and on the home front. The years after the NIFTY NUGGET exercise would show, in fact, that the fantastical computers the Pentagon was installing to run its wars were doing more harm than good—bringing the two superpowers closer to an accidental nuclear exchange than they had ever been when humans were in charge alone.

Chapter 14

WAR GAMES

Under normal circumstances, launching a retaliatory strike of the United States nuclear arsenal required a three-step escalation. Suspicious activity discovered by the monitoring systems called first for a "Missile Display Conference," which happened daily—at least 3,703 occurred in 1979 and 1980, according to government records. Run by the NORAD commander, the conferences involved the duty officers at the four major command posts—NORAD, SAC, Raven Rock, and the Pentagon's National Military Command Center—and were often quickly terminated when it was clear no real threat existed.* Nevertheless, the six staff—two officers and four enlisted airmen—inside NORAD's Missile Warning Center were kept busy through their shifts checking various suspicious activities.

Atmospheric abnormalities were easy to identify, since they would register only on one part of the nation's two-pronged early warning system, dependent on both infrared warning satellites and ground-based radar. If, though, the NORAD commander believed a threat might exist because data indicated both the heat signature of a launch and a physical object in motion, he'd order the second escalation, the "Threat Assessment Conference." In would come more senior military personnel, including the chairman of the

* The communications links between the four command posts were kept constantly open and running to ensure that the systems were always working and any outages would be noticed immediately.

Joint Chiefs, and so began the process of activating both a national military response—like scrambling bombers—and also preliminary steps to ensure command survivability. Given the short warning times, it was critical that bombers be airborne and the missile silos warmed up even as the decision to attack was still under way. It took about ninety seconds for the first signs of an attack to be detected and another two minutes for it to be confirmed—a high-pressure moment that felt like it dragged on forever. Unlike Missile Display Conferences, Threat Assessment Conferences were much more rare and might be called only once a month—or even less frequently. If the commanders on the Threat Assessment Conference concurred that an actual launch event and Soviet first strike was under way, they'd trigger the final escalation, convening a "Missile Attack Conference." In United States history, no one has ever called a Missile Attack Conference.

But they've come close.

Guarding North America's 10.5 million square miles of airspace on a daily basis fell primarily to the 500 military personnel working inside NORAD's mountain bunker on the outskirts of Colorado Springs. Predating the Cold War, the North American Aerospace Defense Command had grown out of the darkest hours of World War II, when the Canadian government feared that Great Britain was close to being overrun by Nazi forces and proposed a formal defense alliance to FDR. The resulting alliance, known as the Permanent Joint Board on Defense, would serve as the backbone for a half-century-long partnership during the Cold War. NORAD headquarters was run out of an old 1923 hospital building in downtown Colorado Springs, then a growing city of about 45,000. From there, NORAD watched over an ever-evolving series of warning satellites and football-field-sized ground radars with names like the Distant Early Warning (DEW) Line, the Mid-Canada Line, and the Pinetree Line.

As the job grew more complex, the Pentagon realized it needed a centralized, state-of-the-art facility—one better shielded from an attack than a forty-year-old concrete building on the side of the street. "We must build the best air defense that seems possible, because it might work—not fail to build it because it might not," NORAD advocated. Herman Kahn and the RAND Corporation—who were also busy at the time with a feasibility study encouraging the U.S. to excavate a mass shelter 2,000 feet underground to protect all the residents of Manhattan—advocated to General LeMay that the new NORAD fortress be built underground. After studying five sites, Army engineers picked the 9,000-foot-tall Cheyenne Mountain, off Highway 115 outside Colorado Springs.

To carve NORAD out of its east slope, the Army Corps of Engineers partnered with Utah Construction & Mining—a company that had helped lay the track for the transcontinental Union Pacific railroad, construct the Hoover Dam, and had grown into a massive international mining company.* It seemed a natural contractor for NORAD, arguably the world's most ambitious underground construction project, which would carve out nearly five acres of space from Cheyenne Mountain's rock. To design the facility itself, the government turned to a man experienced in the art of bunker building: Steve Greenfield, an engineer with Parsons Brinckerhoff, had begun his career working on NATO bases in Newfoundland and Iceland and then spent years helping construct the nation's hardened underground facilities, including Raven Rock, or, as his résumé would obliquely refer to it, the "Fort Ritchie Army-Navy-Air Force Communications Center."

In the fall of 1958, a decade after work had started on Raven Rock, Greenfield was brought to Cheyenne Mountain, along with his colleague Thomas Kuesel, who specialized in particularly challenging engineering endeavors. When Greenfield arrived in Colorado Springs to discuss the project, the military pressed him to begin designing that day. "There was this tremendous urgency to get the thing built based on a body of knowledge only a few had," he recalled later. Parsons had built many of the nation's best bunkers, learning through trial and error constructing sites like the civil defense regional headquarters and SAC's underground combat operations center, each, Greenfield said, "an improvement on the last." They were teamed up with Army Corps of Engineers personnel to create America's largest bunker. As Army engineer Robert Selders recalled, "It was an elite group of—what we considered ourselves elite at least—group of people that were the good structural, electrical, mechanical engineers that were given super challenging problems."

---

* In later years, the company would become a major builder of the nation's hardened missile silos.

On May 18, 1961, while workers in the West Virginia mountains were hard at work on the secret Greenbrier congressional bunker, two Air Force generals set off simultaneous dynamite blasts at Cheyenne Mountain for the public groundbreaking of NORAD's new headquarters. Unlike the Greenbrier, the construction of NORAD was public and celebrated—a breathtakingly ambitious project that would keep the nation secure from a new generation of Soviet weapons. Unlike many other command and control facilities like Raven Rock and Mount Weather, NORAD had never been a secret. Its construction was carefully tracked in local newspapers, who called it the "NORAD cave." All told, the three-year-long project to hollow out the entrance tunnels and caverns through the mountain's distinct pink granite excavated nearly 465,000 cubic yards of rock, using nearly two tons of dynamite every day. "That's enough dynamite each month to blow a Cadillac 15 miles high," supervising Army engineer William Curl bragged, choosing a particularly odd analogy.

The massive effort was considered well worth it: No effort or expense appeared too great for the military's new command center. The 1960s, after all, were an era where air defense became a national preoccupation: Just months after construction on NORAD began, the continent's entire airspace was closed for twelve hours—grounding all civilian air traffic—so that SAC's bombers could simulate a Soviet attack on the country and test North America's defense. The SKY SHIELD II exercise, on October 14, 1961, became known in aviation circles as "The Day the Planes Stood Still." Hundreds of NORAD fighters and SAC bombers took to the air to dogfight over American cities, as bombers tried to sneak south from Canada and evade early warning radars. Chaff from dogfights rained down on homes and businesses up and down the East Coast. Even as the generals involved trumpeted the exercises as the "greatest . . . in all our history," the true results, not declassified until the 1990s, were horrifying: No more than a quarter of the "invading" bombers would have been intercepted and much of the country would have been destroyed by the enemy "attack," even with defenders' full knowledge the attack was coming that day.

The NORAD construction project proved more challenging than the engineers ever anticipated. While the mountain's outer granite was solid, the inner core proved brittle, and engineers had to improvise new procedures to ensure that the massive caverns didn't collapse. To prevent the surrounding granite from fracturing, Dr. Clifton W. Livingston, a professor at the Colorado School of Mines, applied a unique blasting method that emphasized small, controlled charges. "He was halfway between a quarry blaster and a sculptor of Mount Rushmore," Kuesel recalled. To strengthen the surrounding walls, 115,000 rock bolts were drilled into the cavern's walls, ensuring the rock could withstand the shockwaves of a nearby nuclear explosion. Then, to help transfer the weight of the brittle rock to more solid stone, the Parsons Brinckerhoff team journeyed to the University of Illinois in Urbana, where they met with Nate Newmark, who, as Kuesel recalled, "literally was writing the book on hardened facilities technology."*

Newmark, known as "Mr. Underground," had spent much of his career working on earthquake engineering, becoming an expert on how energy and shockwaves pass through the earth and turning his civil engineering department at the University of Illinois into one of the nation's leading training centers for aspiring military engineers while building a powerful alumni network. As one officer later recalled, "He was the head of the mafia. . . . They were *it*." In the early 1950s, Newmark had done some of the definitive work on blast-resistant design, developing the "K factor," a mathematical constant that measured how vulnerable a structure would be to the pressure of a nuclear blast, and he later played a role in projects ranging from the Eisenhower-era Gaither Report to the Minuteman missile, as well as civilian endeavors like the trans-Alaska oil pipeline. He was a busy and impatient man; he wore a wristwatch with an alarm that he'd set to fifteen minutes at the start of the meeting. "It went off and your time was up," Parsons Brinckerhoff's Walter Douglas recalled.

Finally, sitting in a run-down café outside the Army Corps building in Omaha, Kuesel and Douglas sketched out on paper an idea for a massive concrete sphere to protect NORAD's combat operations center in the heart of the mountain. Kuesel described it as a "grapefruit with four tin cans attached," which "mutually reinforced and supported each other." His

---

* The books would have the scintillating titles of *Ground Motion Technology Review* and, later, *Approximate Probabilistic Methods for Survivability/Vulnerability Analysis of Strategic Structures*.

description belied its sophistication—the sphere, more than thirty meters in diameter, became the most complex part of the entire project and delayed construction for months as the engineering logistics were hammered out. The protective sphere had to be built outside the tunnel, on land cleared and flattened by the excavation, and then disassembled and transported down the narrow tunnel entrance into the main cavern, where workers then carefully rebuilt it and shored up the core of NORAD.

Though the project's exact specifications stretched to more than 4,000 pages, the general layout of the Combat Operations Center would have been familiar to anyone who knew Raven Rock or Mount Weather, both of which predated Cheyenne Mountain—a curved mile-long access tunnel leading to parallel forty-five-foot-wide chambers that each housed freestanding three-story buildings, carefully balanced on massive man-sized thousand-pound springs and connected by flexible, shielded utility ducts that could sway with a nuclear blast. The interior cavern was shielded by a three-foot-thick, twenty-five-ton blast door similar to those that protected Raven Rock, Mount Weather, and the Greenbrier. Based on suggestions by Newmark, the dozen windowless buildings had an outer layer of thin low-carbon steel plates, like an outer hull, which would shield the facilities from an electromagnetic pulse. "Upside down ships," the site's project manager, Ted Blaschke, called them, "constructed in a cave and floated on a sea of springs."* Planners estimated that the occupants of Cheyenne Mountain had a 70 percent chance of surviving a nearby five-megaton nuclear bomb.

Five separate chambers inside Cheyenne Mountain held reservoirs for water and fuel; the mountain security staff, who used rowboats to patrol the spring-fed water reservoirs, joked it was the nation's only Air Force base with its own navy. By its completion in 1964, the NORAD operations center contained six diesel generators and a total of 170,500 square feet of office space to support the 425 staff who manned the facility twenty-four hours a day. During an emergency, as many as 1,000 personnel could be housed inside for a month of "buttoned-up" operations. Some 72,000 meals were

* Since no model existed for the elaborate spring-mounted, EMP-protected system, the Air Force first built and tested a full-scale replica in Albuquerque.

stockpiled inside, though on a normal day the facility cafeteria served four regular meals, including one at midnight for the overnight shift. Parking for each shift's commuters was easy: The excavated rock had filled in an adjacent canyon and created a 412-space parking lot for the complex's workforce. From there, they journeyed via a converted school bus deep into the mountain.

NORAD's main watch center was built to be the envy of the nation. The cheapest part of the project had actually been the excavation—only about $12 million of the $66 million effort went toward the construction of the bunker itself. Nearly $40 million went into equipping NORAD with the nation's most sophisticated computers and electronics—a process that itself consumed eight months and raised concerns almost from the start. Even before NORAD opened, Pentagon officials expressed concerns about the "complexity" of the computer system and its potential for failure. "There seemed to be an excessive number of computers planned," one report said. There was good reason for their worry: the original NORAD Attack Warning System, installed by AT&T in September 1964, lasted only a month before it was taken out of service due to "numerous malfunctions." The new upgrades were more sophisticated, but also still prone to scary mistakes.

The NORAD facility included three Philco 212 computers and fifteen separate console displays—four for the battle staff and eleven for other personnel, like logistics and damage assessment. For the era, it was a stunning amount of computing power, although each computer required three to four hours of maintenance downtime a day, as was common for the time. A twenty-channel closed-circuit television kept the facility informed as news and events unfolded outside, and the command center was dominated by a 12-foot-by-16-foot, $800,000 projector screen that was able to display a seven-color image of the globe. It was all like magic. It was in this room on November 9, 1979, and on that oversized world map, that the midnight shift at NORAD faced perhaps the most confounding and terrifying moment of the Cold War.

NORAD's warning alarms went off mid-morning. The first report might have been a false alarm—just a month before, the antiquated early warning radar system at Mount Hebo in Oregon had falsely registered some space debris as a possible submarine launch, triggering a Threat Assessment Conference, but false alarms were rare. When Carter had held his first major presidential command exercise at the Pentagon in January 1978, officials reassured him that false alarms were highly unusual—there had been just seven since 1960. Now, though, the computers had detected huge numbers of incoming missiles, making a false alarm appear less likely. Not just a few missiles, but dozens, then hundreds, a full-scale nuclear attack—the long-feared general war appeared to be under way, targeting nuclear forces, cities, command and control facilities, crippling the nation and killing millions. "Here comes our worst-case scenario," Air Force Captain Bob Vouk thought inside SAC's Omaha war room. "Here goes the whole world. Boom!" SAC spun into action—the bunker's blast doors swung shut, sealing inside the watch personnel and leaving their sleeping colleagues aboveground to die.

But, some thought, the attack didn't make much sense. There wasn't any compelling reason in the fall of 1979 for the Soviets to initiate war, and neither U.S. nor European intelligence had reported the increased Soviet activity normally associated with strike preparations. Nevertheless, SAC had just minutes to make critical decisions, and so Colonel Billy Batson, the shift's ranking officer, ordered the system to full alert—aircrews were sent running to their planes at bases across the country; missile silos on the Plains were warned they should be ready to fire. NORAD began launching its interceptor force: Pairs of F-106 fighters in Oregon, Missouri, and at a Canadian base in Ontario roared down the runway into the sky to chase Soviet bombers. Military leaders moved to notify those up the chain of command.

As seconds ticked by, those on watch in the command center still doubted whether an attack was under way. Vouk got on the phone with Fort Ritchie, Maryland, which, according to the radar projections, would be one of the first places the Soviet missiles impacted. Together, the watch officer in Maryland and the SAC officer counted down the seconds to destruction. Nothing happened. Vouk gasped; as he recounted later, he hadn't realized he'd been holding his breath.

The SAC personnel cheered as it became clear they—and the world—weren't going to die that night. Colonel Batson cheered right alongside everyone else, pumping his fist, and then he got back to business: "Now will somebody figure out what the hell is going on around here?" Within minutes, it became clear that someone had screwed up big-time, inserting a training tape into the system's real computers rather than the system used for exercises. News of the false alarm leaked quickly; press reports blamed it on a "mechanical error," and said that the alert had been treated "skeptically." Internally, the Air Force took the incident seriously and NORAD created a new $16 million test facility off-site, to ensure test scenarios never again could be confused with real-world occurrences.

Yet the NORAD computer system continued to provide heart-stopping moments. Officials were coming to understand that as advanced as the computers may appear, the Pentagon networks were prone to glitches. Despite a $10 billion investment to modernize the World Wide Military Command and Control System, known as the WWMCCS—an acronym the military pronounced "Wimex"—the Pentagon's networks were proving deeply inadequate. One whistle-blower, John Bradley, said in 1979 that WWMCCS defects were "enough to keep you awake at night." That much was true: It was, literally, a system bad enough to wake national security officials in the middle of the night.

At 2:26 a.m. on June 3, 1980—barely six months after the training tape incident—Odom woke Brzezinski with stunning news: NORAD had initially notified Odom of two Soviet submarine-launched ballistic missiles, but in the time it had taken him to call his boss, the military was now tracking some 220 Soviet missiles in the air. Unlike the November incident, the surprise attack had a geopolitical basis. The Cold War had chilled gravely. The Soviet Union had invaded Afghanistan, leading to President Carter's announcement that the United States would boycott the 1980 Summer Olympics—set to open in Moscow in just six weeks. The Soviets had retaliated the month before, announcing in May that they would boycott the forthcoming 1984 Los Angeles Olympics.

The chain of command knew it had no more than seven minutes to inform the president and launch a retaliatory strike. A second phone call from Odom to Brzezinski reported a gravely deteriorating scenario: NORAD's screens were reporting a full-scale general nuclear attack—2,200 missiles soaring over the pole toward U.S. targets.

Then, just as suddenly as it started, the whole thing stopped. The attack evaporated. NORAD's checks uncovered no concurring reports from satellites or ground-based radar. The attack existed entirely in the computers—a gremlin somewhere inside NORAD's massive room-sized computers. Brzezinski, sitting at his house in the middle of the night, hadn't bothered to wake his wife. What was the point? Everyone would be dead in half an hour.

Three days later, on June 6, a similar alert went off at 3:38 p.m.; SAC flight crews were alerted and told to spool up their engines, even as NORAD raced to confirm that this was another false alarm. It was—that same gremlin again, somewhere inside Cheyenne Mountain's electronics. NORAD responded by abandoning the computer system, switching to an emergency backup, and set up a round-the-clock conference call between the command posts to rapidly identify false launch warnings.

Finally, technicians isolated the problem: A 46-cent computer chip, deep inside the machine, had failed. Under normal conditions, the NORAD computers broadcast test messages to the other command posts, like SAC in Omaha and Raven Rock in Pennsylvania, to ensure connectivity. In what commanders and technicians realized in hindsight was a bad decision, the test messages were identical to the real alert messages that'd be used in an attack, but simply used zeroes to indicate the number of missiles in the air. The real totals would be filled in during an attack. The faulty computer chip began inserting the numeral 2 in place of zeroes—hence the quickly escalating alert from 2 missiles to 220 to 2,200 Soviet ICBMs. It had been a disaster just waiting to happen. The government's after-action report reported dryly, "Now, that message is in a different format which just indicates the status of the communications system rather than the any indication of numbers of missiles." The Pentagon's classified talking points tried to put lipstick on the pig, celebrating that "The human safeguards which are a central part of our system worked as designed."

Carter found himself under pressure politically from hawks who saw the nation nearing a "window of vulnerability" when the Soviet Union would be more powerful militarily than the United States, but even absent outside pressure, he found his own thinking shifting. His commitment to planning for a prolonged nuclear war only hardened as geopolitical events like the American hostage taking in Iran and the Soviet invasion of Afghanistan unfolded. The Afghanistan invasion, Carter said, "has made a more dramatic change in my opinion of what the Soviets' ultimate goals are than anything they've done in the previous time I've been in office."

His administration's updates to the nation's nuclear weapons policies represented just the third major shift in the Cold War; following Eisenhower's "massive retaliation" and the "assured destruction" of the Kennedy era, Carter was, for the first time, planning for a grinding long-term war. "There would be a 'day after,' and millions of Americans would be around to face the post-strike realities," Odom recalled later. "To pretend that the U.S. Government could simply ignore addressing this responsibility was inconceivable. Yet the command and control system and the SIOP did not include any consideration of post-strike realities."

Over the course of the first seven months of 1980, Carter issued three classified presidential directives that together would prepare the nation for a new style of nuclear war. "We have an NCA [National Command Authorities] 'vulnerability' problem analogous to our ICBM vulnerability," William Odom wrote in one memo to Brzezinski. "A new NCA/Continuity of Government basing mode is critical for maintaining deterrence."

That new strategy began with PD-57, which revived and broadened the nation's mobilization planning; PD-58 pushed the government to dramatically improve its COG operations, investing in new technologies and facilities to ensure that the government would survive; PD-59, meanwhile, sought to address new nuclear strategies incorporating the era of "strategic nuclear equivalence" and the new technologies becoming available to U.S. planners. Odom, who helped oversee the drafting of PD-59, believed that if the world stumbled into a nuclear war, a longer, more drawn-out exchange of weapons might very well occur.* "The confusion and damage created by tactical nuclear exchanges could produce weeks of inaction while both sides try to regain control of their own forces and to locate enemy formations for further nuclear strikes," he said. "The same kind of scenario is not to be discounted for intercontinental nuclear exchanges."

---

* As Odom explained years later, "Under PD-59 the targeting of Soviet forces in East Europe probably would not have prompted an immediate Soviet strike on the United States." Although unknown at the time, historians have since uncovered that the Soviet Union was undergoing its own shift in strategic doctrine, which similarly focused on limiting nuclear attacks to the European combat theater.

The new war plans also, for the first time, brought Soviet "decapitation" into the fore of SIOP planning. The Carter administration knew just how disruptive such an attack could be; one of their exercises had tested a decapitation attack on the U.S., what the military referred to as a Russian attack on "critical C³I nodes." In the exercise, the nation's ICBMs and submarines all survived, but the president and the National Command Authorities were devastated. The president was dead, no one knew which successor had survived—if any—and the military commanders couldn't tell who was alive where to give orders. As one write-up of the exercise explained, "One way of describing the result would have been to say that Russia won the war." With the new SIOP, labeled SIOP-5D, which included thousands of Soviet command and control centers, Carter strategists hoped to inflict similar chaos on the Soviet leadership.

As part of its reform efforts, the administration created the Federal Emergency Management Agency (FEMA) to unite the nation's disaster response with its COG planning. The reorganization stemmed in part from public pressure to improve the nation's response to natural disasters—as the American population had grown and development boomed, hurricanes, tornadoes, and floods had exacted ever-larger tolls on both cities and rural communities. Carter, though, was also concerned about the nation's more secret response to man-made issues. The Federal Preparedness Agency, one report conceded, "has neither the resources required for this priority mission nor an organizational stature sufficient to do the job." As Brzezinski wrote the president in a confidential memo, "The present state of our Continuity of Government program in FPA is a worry to all those familiar with it."

Like the PEADs, many emergency plans turned out to be terribly outdated: nineteen of the twenty agreements for emergency aid between the government and civilian groups like the Red Cross and Salvation Army hadn't been reviewed since the early 1960s. The National Plan for Emergency Preparedness hadn't been updated since 1964, and the classified Federal Emergency Plan D, which would have laid out government functions after a nuclear attack, hadn't been updated since 1970. The board that oversees the National Defense Executive Reserve, which would bring civilian leaders in to help run the response to a wartime situation, hadn't met since early 1973. An April 1978 GAO report found evacuation plans for specific agencies and departments were hardly in better shape: The Department of Health, Education, and Welfare had vacancies of 60 percent on its Team A, 44 percent on Team B, and 23 percent on Team C. HUD had only filled 150 of the 226 emergency relocation slots it was supposed to utilize. Government-wide, only 40 percent of those personnel who were supposed to evacuate in an emergency had ever been to their relocation sites.

The relocation facilities themselves were in rough shape, too. Of the nineteen alternate sites inspected by the GAO, nearly half lacked sufficient fuel to power generators and had inadequate air filtration systems; many also lacked sufficient food or medical supplies. The Department of Labor relocation site had no sleeping facilities at all, and the sites for both the Department of Transportation and the Department of Agriculture had no food at all. "Such major deficiencies would render the facilities nonoperational during an emergency. Officials of all three sites agreed that corrective action was needed but cited lack of funding as a major problem," the GAO reported.

Created in April 1979 under Executive Order 12127, FEMA brought together more than 100 initiatives and offices from across the government— from HUD's Federal Disaster Assistance Administration and the National Weather Service's Community Preparedness Program to the Federal Insurance Administration and the U.S. Fire Administration training programs, as well as programs from the General Services Administration, the White House Office of Science and Technology Policy, and the Pentagon. Publicly, the new agency would be known for coordinating the government's response to natural disasters, but few civilians understood that so much of FEMA's resources went to its primary mission behind the scenes—coordinating the nation's COG efforts—and that much of its funding was actually classified, hidden in the nation's black budget.

Under the new plans, FEMA and the Pentagon shared responsibility for alerting the nation if a real Soviet attack unfolded. Should a Soviet attack trigger a NORAD alert, the military would contact the president and begin the process of activating COG, as the task of notifying the nation fell to two watch officers at FEMA's National Warning Center inside the Cheyenne Mountain bunker—a small civilian corner of the secure military facility. They would activate a special dedicated AT&T party line and announce: "Alternate National Warning Center, I have an emergency message."

"Authenticate," the watch officer at FEMA's alternate facility in Olney, Maryland, would respond. The system's authentication code words—pairs of two- or three-syllable words, one for the activation of a warning, one for the termination of a warning—were distributed in a red envelope quarterly to all the users of the emergency broadcast system, and the caller would have to state the day's correct code word.*

Once the NORAD watch officer authenticated the code, Olney's watch officer would activate the national alert—sounding bells at Mount Weather and all ten regional FEMA headquarters, as well as 400 other federal facilities and more than 2,000 local and state "warning points" like emergency 911 dispatch centers. Each warning point would hear the same message: "Attention all stations. This is the National Warning Center. Emergency. This is an Attack Warning. Repeat. This is an Attack Warning." The FEMA watch officers would also activate a media warning system—breaking into national TV and radio programming. Other alerts would go out from the FAA to all airborne pilots, from NOAA on the national weather radio network, and from the Coast Guard to mariners afloat. Some of the nation's warning systems were more unconventional: Button #13, a Plexiglas-shielded button on the console of the D.C. mayor's emergency command center at 300 Indiana Avenue NW would activate "Emer-zak," seizing control of the capital's entire Muzak network and replacing the piped-in background music of the city's elevators, lobbies, medical offices, and department stores with emergency instructions.

Even with that effort, it wasn't clear how much difference—if any—the warnings would make to the public. Lieutenant Robert Hogan, New York's deputy head of civil defense, explained in 1979, "The people who hear them will run into buildings and be turned to sand in a few seconds anyway." By that point, after all, the government had all but abandoned the pretense of providing civilian aid; across the country, the stockpiles and shelters of the Eisenhower and Kennedy years were mildewing, forgotten and ignored. In 1979, New York City abandoned its efforts to give away the remaining

---

* Generated automatically by an unsophisticated computer, the code words were preprinted the same for every month—meaning that watch officers received code words for days like February 30 and September 31.

supplies socked away inside its 10,800 fallout shelters and began hiring contractors at $38 a ton to transport the stockpiles to landfills.

As it was, two of the people turned to sand in an attack would be none other than President Jimmy Carter and National Security Advisor Zbigniew Brzezinski. A Defense Science Board report in 1978 had concluded that if an attack happened while the president was at the White House, the president would either be able to "command the forces until the attack hit Washington and he was killed or to try to escape and survive, but not both." When it came time to refine the White House emergency plans, since Carter had already decreed that he'd stay to command and refuse to be evacuated in an attack, Brzezinski decided to die with his commander-in-chief. Instead, the OPAL5 III helicopters would try to get Vice President Mondale and the deputy national security advisor to safety aboard NEACP.

The emergency helicopters that did make it out of Washington ahead of an attack would contact BLUEGRASS TOWER, Mount Weather's helipad control station, on frequency 126.20000 as they approached, to provide a list of VIPs aboard. Each arrival would then be checked against the master Survivors List. There was little room for emotion: Bud Gallagher, the facility's director, had imposed a standing order that all arrivals were to be treated equally in terms of medical care, with the exception of the president or his successor, who were to receive extraordinary priority. Those beyond saving—high-ranking government officials with mortal wounds—would be marked with blue triage tags and left to die, so medical personnel could concentrate on the cases where they could make a difference.

Those lucky few inside would find themselves sharing the space with some of the nation's most precious treasures, since, as it turned out, Mount Weather was also intended to protect the cultural legacy of the United States as a nation and an idea. Even as the Carter administration worked to start up FEMA, the General Services Administration ran from 1979 to 1981 a secret project known as the Cultural Heritage Preservation Group to ensure that the capital's major historical institutions and repositories—the National Archives, National Gallery of Art, the Smithsonian Museums, and the Library of Congress—prioritized which artifacts and artworks should survive a nuclear holocaust.

• • •

Planning to protect the nation's history had come a long way since 1814, when Dolley Madison had fled Washington ahead of invading British troops after directing that precious documents and paintings be saved. At that time, many of the nation's most vital documents were hidden inside linen bags at a grist mill upriver from Georgetown. Now, the government had well-organized plans in place to store the nation's history inside one of the most secure facilities ever built, but two items that topped the list during the Cold War hadn't changed: the iconic portrait of George Washington by Gilbert Stuart and the Declaration of Independence that had both been saved by Mrs. Madison 160 years before.

The government had only limited experience protecting cultural treasures. During World War II, the Smithsonian had relocated some of its most important artifacts—including the Star-Spangled Banner, George Washington's uniform, and the desk Thomas Jefferson used to write the Declaration of Independence—for safekeeping in case of a surprise attack on the capital. It also made a careful effort to preserve "type specimens," the original examples of newly discovered plants and animals that natural historians and paleontologists used to describe and compare future discoveries. Altogether, more than sixty tons of American history and science specimens were shipped to a secure warehouse near Luray, Virginia, to ride out the war. Along the National Mall, the museums also removed from display valuables like watches, medals, gems, jewelry, and silverware that might tempt looters following an air raid on the capital.

The National Gallery of Art had opened just months before the U.S. entered World War II and its leaders immediately feared an air attack, so they began to implement the first deliberate plan to protect the priceless collection. They'd seen the damage German air raids had already done to cultural treasures at the British Museum, St. James Palace, and elsewhere in England. Curator David Finley called his friend Edith Vanderbilt, who agreed to hide the nation's most precious artworks—sixty-two paintings and seventeen sculptures—at the Biltmore, her family estate in western North Carolina. There, after a secret 450-mile train trip to Asheville, the artworks were stored in the first-floor music room of the palatial château. Security was crucial to the mission: Workers installed steel doors and bars on the music room's windows, concealing them behind coverings and drapes to avoid arousing the suspicions of visitors and guests, and armed gallery guards stood watch over the room, blending in with the estate's security team. Locked behind the draperies and protected by special fire suppression systems, priceless artwork, including Titian's *Venus with a Mirror*, Raphael's *Portrait of Bindo Altoviti* and *Alba Madonna*—as well as Stuart's portrait of Washington—spent the war resting on steel racks, the public none the wiser. Meanwhile, back in Washington, the gallery supplemented its collection with works from European museums that had been part of traveling exhibits in the United States when the Nazis overran museums in France, Belgium, and the rest of the continent.

The nation's Charters of Freedom were also evacuated from the capital. The attorney general ruled that the Library of Congress had the inherent authority to remove the founding documents without a presidential or congressional order, and so the day after Christmas in 1941 they were smuggled out of Washington. Even as the wreckage of the U.S. Navy still burned in Pearl Harbor, two Secret Service agents hid the U.S. Constitution, the Declaration of Independence, and other important documents aboard a B&O railroad passenger car en route to Kentucky. All were carefully wrapped in manila paper and then padlocked inside a bronze container, which was then sealed with lead and crated inside a larger box; altogether it weighed about 150 pounds. Then, carefully secured in Compartment B of the Pullman sleeper car Eastlake with agents and a Library of Congress staffer occupying the adjoining compartments as guards, the Founders' documents passed without notice all the way to Louisville. The small traveling party was met by troops upon arrival to escort the documents to Fort Knox, where they were kept in a vault with the nation's gold reserves for the war's duration.*

Almost immediately after the war ended and the treasures were returned to Washington, the government began the plan to protect them for the atomic age. Not even two years had passed since the Biltmore works were returned when the National Gallery began to consider its Cold War

---

* Other important papers and artifacts from the Library of Congress and National Archives, like the Gutenberg Bible, were moved outside Washington, too; many vital documents ended up at Washington & Lee University in Virginia.

evacuation plans. This time, though, it wanted its own custom-built wartime repository, a windowless fortress on the grounds of the Randolph-Macon Woman's College in Lynchburg, Virginia, a three-hour drive southwest of Washington. The privately funded $550,000 facility would house sculptures and paintings and included a three-bedroom cottage nearby where the gallery's curator could wait out a war; it was fully stocked through the Cold War, down to napkins and silverware. In Washington, the gallery pre-staged a convoy of trucks in its garage, ready to evacuate the most priceless artworks. Each week, the gallery's security staff would start up the trucks to ensure they were in working order.

In 1952, Harry Truman inaugurated a new display inside the National Archives, housing the Declaration of Independence, the Constitution, and the Bill of Rights inside helium-filled cases that filtered sunlight to minimize further fading. By day, the three Charters were accessible in the Archives' main exhibition hall, but at night and in an emergency, a simple button lowered them mechanically into a custom-built fifty-ton Mosler Safe Company basement vault, sealed by fifteen-inch-thick, five-ton protective doors that would theoretically protect them from an atomic blast.

Later, a special hotline was installed to connect the Archives to the Pentagon, so that it could attempt to evacuate the nation's founding documents should catastrophe strike. The Charters of Freedom, known to the Doomsday planners as "Freedom Documents Group I," would be evacuated by helicopter; truck convoys would follow later with other important documents, if time permitted. The documents in Group II were a more eclectic collection of Americana—according to journalist Ted Gup, they included "the log of the *U.S.S. Monitor*, medical records relating to President Lincoln's assassination, the Japanese surrender documents and an 1804 map of Lewis and Clark's trek across North America." Procedures were also put in place at cultural institutions around the country to protect other valuables: In Philadelphia, a specially trained team of park rangers at the Liberty Bell stood prepared through the Cold War to evacuate the historic one-ton bell from Independence Hall at a moment's notice.*

---

* Doomsday planning went beyond government institutions as well; the atomic age had begun to reshape the museum world within months of Hiroshima. In 1946, wealthy art

Ultimately, it fell to Charles Parkhurst, the National Gallery's longtime chief curator and assistant director, to update the plans during the Carter years. The idea of hiding away from Armageddon in a bucolic farm country cottage had been shelved by the early 1970s as Lynchburg's manufacturing sector grew and the rise of ICBMs meant that the city's industry would likely make it a target for the Soviets.

Parkhurst didn't view preserving such treasures as an entirely abstract idea. A Navy gunner in the Mediterranean during World War II, his prewar art background got him assigned to the units of Monuments Men, who tracked down and repatriated artworks stolen by the Nazis—ultimately recovering more than a million valuable artworks and artifacts hidden in salt mines, castles, and other stashes across Europe. In Washington, Parkhurst's team of curators kept ranked lists of the museum's holdings, ensuring that paintings and sculptures would be saved in an emergency according to their relative cultural history and value. At the National Gallery, curators had settled on a relatively recent addition to its collection to be designated its most valuable painting: a portrait of a fifteenth-century Florentine aristocrat, one of just ten paintings in the world done by Leonardo da Vinci—including the *Mona Lisa* in Paris and *The Last Supper* in Milan—and the only example of those ten in the Americas. The oil painting, just fifteen inches square, was one of his earliest works, done when he was twenty-one years old, depicting Ginevra de' Benci, a Florentine teenage bride, so captivatingly that one contemporary declared, "It seemed to be not a portrait but Ginevra herself." When the National Gallery of Art acquired the work in 1967 from Prince Franz Joseph II of Liechtenstein, it immediately became the museum's most treasured piece.

The first draft of the new evacuation plan called for the rescued

---

collectors Sterling and Francine Clark had been planning to either donate their trove of European art to the Metropolitan Museum of Art or build a small museum near their home in Manhattan, but as the Cold War deepened, Sterling Clark—the heir to the Singer Sewing Machine fortune—became afraid that their extensive art collection could be destroyed by an atomic attack. Rather than keeping their art in New York, the couple settled on building what would come to be known as the Clark Art Institute—now considered one of the nation's top art museums—in the more rural Massachusetts Berkshires near Williams College.

paintings to be transported to Mount Weather and hung on the walls of the COG bunker, not for any special artistic reason nor to inspire the leaders planning the nation's future, but simply because it would be the easiest way to store them. However, fears about the humid conditions inside the hollowed-out cave and tunnels—notoriously damp from the groundwater leaching through the surrounding stone—led the National Gallery to create special climate-controlled crates to house the paintings. The special rolling metal containers, designed by conservator Victor Covey, could be quickly moved through the gallery, with staffers sliding important paintings into designated slots. They'd slip the tiny fifteenth-century painting of St. George slaying the dragon by Rogier van der Weyden into one slot, while the three-foot-wide *Alba Madonna* by Raphael—which had been evacuated to the Biltmore during World War II—would fit into another one. It would take just a few minutes to assemble the score of the gallery's most important works that should be saved, after which the container's lid would be closed and sealed. The paintings would be kept stable by chemicals inside as they were transported to Mount Weather and held safely inside the mountain until civilization was ready to display its greatest treasures again.*

Word leaked to the press about the secret PD-59 in August 1980, just days before the Democratic convention where Carter would face a tough reelection fight; the timing led many to believe that it was a calculated leak to make Carter look tough on the Soviets. The new nuclear weapons strategy created a firestorm of controversy, both inside and outside the government, since the news reports were the first the State Department had heard of the new policy. As the debate over PD-59 spilled into the public, broader concerns emerged, especially when it came to the idea of focusing on "decapitation" attacks. "Who would be there to turn off the war if we nuked Soviet command centers?" asked Jeremy J. Stone, the director of the Federation

---

* The nation would have been puzzled by some of the cultural treasures meant to be preserved during a nuclear attack: When the Pentagon was asked what valuable documents and artifacts should be preserved, it included a list of the oil painting portraits of the Joint Chiefs of Staff.

of American Scientists, the antinuclear group that had evolved out of the original Manhattan Project scientists. The Soviet news agency TASS called the new plans "insanity."

Just days after word of PD-59 leaked, the outlines of PD-58 did as well, sparking more controversy as word spread the government was planning to build additional secret bunkers for its leaders. *The New York Times* editorialized, "What is troubling about the anonymously disclosed information about Directive 58 is how callous it looks to the public. People who know little of the strategic chess games that the Pentagon plays with the Soviets are left to mutter about generals interested in saving themselves." Other critics were more flip. "Dear Mr. President," Russell Baker wrote in his syndicated column, "I have just read about the plan to save certain people in caves, and would very much like to be among them."

Zbigniew Brzezinski feared that the public debate was leaving Carter's "fundamental change" in the strategic doctrine "obscured and confused." In a classified three-page memo, he laid out just how much the president had shifted the nation's COG plans and nuclear weapons policy. It'd be years before the full impact of the changes Carter started would be fully understood—and, indeed, many of the efforts pursued by Carter's successor started in the 1970s. As William Odom lamented later, "The incoming Ronald Reagan administration was both slow to grasp what President Carter had directed and ill-disposed to admitting it." In his final year, Carter had boosted the Pentagon's command and control spending by $1.3 billion, for a total of $11.2 billion; Reagan would boost it another $3 billion for his first year in office. COG and civil defense operations were about to hit overdrive.

Chapter 15

DESIGNATED SURVIVOR

Terrel Bell, Ronald Reagan's new education secretary, was already en route to Capitol Hill on February 18, 1981, when he got the telephone call from White House chief of staff James Baker. It was less than an hour before the cabinet was set to attend Reagan's address to a joint session of Congress about the nation's economic woes. On the car phone, Baker said he had "good news and bad news."

"The bad news is that you don't get to go and hear the speech," Baker told the cabinet secretary. "The good news is that if the Capitol is subjected to a nuclear attack you'll be President of the United States."

For Bell, "starry-eyed" at the idea of attending the joint session, it was a moment of great disappointment. It was also the beginning of a tradition that over the years would become one of the capital's favorite factoids about every major political event: the "designated survivor," a cabinet member chosen in advance and told to skip major events in case of a catastrophe.

In April 1980, President Carter's White House Military Office had instituted new procedures to have FEMA monitor the attendance of all presidential successors "at major, publicly announced functions outside the White House complex," and ensure at least one successor was kept apart. While such gatherings of the U.S. leadership had been commonplace in the past—at inaugurations, States of the Union, state funerals, and the like—the rising tensions of the Cold War made COG planners question their wisdom. "The situation provides an inviting target to enemy attack or terrorist activity, and represents an unnecessary risk to national leadership," the White House Military Office wrote.

These new procedures had been first tested at Reagan's inaugural. There had been little love lost between Jimmy Carter and Ronald Reagan during the 1980 campaign, but Carter had quickly invited the president-elect to the White House, where during a meeting on November 20, 1980, he walked Reagan through major defense initiatives, the nation's COG plans, and what Carter called "the management of our nuclear forces in time of attack on our nation." As Carter later recalled, "I urged him to take plenty of time to learn about these arrangements before Inauguration Day, so that he could be thoroughly instructed on the procedures to be followed in an emergency." The incoming and outgoing administrations agreed that Carter's defense secretary, Harold Brown, would remain in office past the standard noon departure to ensure that there was a national leader in case something catastrophic happened at the inaugural. "Both sides agreed that something should be done," a FEMA official said. Brown resigned later on inauguration day once the Reagan team was firmly in control of the government's levers.

FEMA's Central Locator System, which tracked the whereabouts of everyone in the presidential line of succession and then distributed that info to key outposts like the White House, Mount Weather, Raven Rock, and the Pentagon's National Military Command Center, had figured out that the nation's leadership was all set to attend Reagan's address.* "In peacetime," FEMA's Keith Peterson explained, "we can tell you if a particular successor is in town or out of town on a given day. During a period of increasing tension, we can escalate the reporting requirements so we know when they're in their office, or at home, or in their car, or even when they go down the hall." When such gatherings appeared imminent, FEMA notified the assistant to the president for national security affairs, who would recommend which successor should skip the event.

Now, in advance of Reagan's economic speech, FEMA had notified the

---

* At the Pentagon, for instance, in the NMCC's secure Emergency Actions room, military officials could find anyone in the Constitution's line of succession by checking the screen of a dedicated Zenith Z-150 Central Locator System computer. The CLS computers are protected by a special NSA protocol known as TEMPEST that shields them from electromagnetic snooping.

White House that too many successors were set to attend. The duty officer in the Situation Room tracked down James Baker, who decreed Bell would skip Reagan's speech. "The decision as to who would survive in the line of succession ought to be a conscious decision based upon the national interest," Bud McFarlane wrote in one memo. "Specifically, the 'designated survivor' ought to be someone chosen deliberately for his ability to function as the Commander-in-Chief." Bell, the head of one of the newest cabinet departments and thus normally low on the line of succession, had been chosen to skip Reagan's remarks because he was one of the few cabinet officials who had received FEMA briefings on his succession obligations.

The "designated survivor" program would grow more formal as years passed. Whereas in the Reagan years, officials often just went about their regular lives, by the 1990s the chosen cabinet member would receive a full Secret Service detail, and a White House military aide would arrive with a copy of the Football in case the unthinkable happened and the "designated survivor" needed to be ready to launch the nation's nuclear weapons.

Unfortunately, the "designated survivor" program raised a new problem for planners—the government, it turned out, lacked simple procedures for figuring out who became president after a decapitation event. "One of the things we discovered is that there was no authentication system," Reagan's FEMA director, Louis Giuffrida, said in 1981. "If a successor got on the horn and said, 'I'm the successor,' and somebody said 'Prove it,' they couldn't. So we're working on that, and FEMA will be the authenticating mechanism to say, 'Yeah, this guy's for real. The President's gone and we don't know where the Vice President is . . . and this is the man.'"

One answer to the problem was what came to be known as the Sealed Authenticator System; the SAS cards, carried by officials who were part of the National Command Authorities—like the president, vice president, defense secretary, deputy defense secretary, and the chairman of the Joint Chiefs—each have unique code words that can be used to identify the holder to the military commanders. The cards, known as "SAS cookies," "Gold Cards," or "biscuits" are generated by the National Security Agency, using a specially built machine that randomly generates the authenticator codes, prints them onto the card, and then seals it, all without a human ever seeing the codes.

That question of who was in charge when the president was incapacitated became an issue more immediate—and at a moment of far greater danger—than anyone anticipated that spring. The Reagan administration had been squabbling since the inauguration over its own procedures for handling a crisis. Normally the national security advisor would lead the White House response to a crisis, but Secretary of State Al Haig, who had had a long military career and served in a senior role in the Nixon White House, considered himself the administration's most experienced leader. He had, in his own telling, served almost as deputy president during the dark days of Watergate when Nixon was preoccupied. On March 24, 1981, President Reagan signed a compromise: The vice president, George H. W. Bush, would lead a crisis response, with National Security Advisor Richard Allen and the National Security Council providing staff support to Bush. Just six days after Reagan made his decision, the crisis management system would be put to the test.

The following Monday, March 30, President Reagan addressed an AFL-CIO conference at the Washington Hilton. After the event, he walked out the side entrance of the hotel, past a small cluster of onlookers, where John Hinckley Jr. opened fire with a small revolver. Hinckley squeezed off all six shots in under two seconds. As the shooting started, Lieutenant Colonel Jose Muratti, the president's Army aide with the Football, hit the ground, tightly grasping the black briefcase. Hinckley's first bullet hit White House press secretary James Brady, while the second struck D.C. Metropolitan police officer Thomas Delahanty, who fell forward onto the sidewalk and landed on top of the Football, sprawled on the sidewalk in Muratti's outstretched hand. The third shot missed entirely, but the fourth hit Secret Service agent Tim McCarthy. The fifth and sixth shots both hit the armored limo. The final shot ricocheted off, hitting Reagan as he was shoved into the car by the Secret Service. Reagan was the first president shot in nearly a century—and would turn out to be the first of the five to survive, albeit narrowly. Within four minutes of the incident, Reagan arrived at George Washington University Hospital, collapsing soon after walking through emergency room doors.

Vice President Bush was taking off in Air Force Two from Fort Worth's Carswell Air Force Base, en route to a speech in Austin, when a Secret Service agent on board received word of the shooting. It was a terrible place to be during a moment of crisis—the plane wasn't built to be an effective airborne post and lacked secure voice communications. Al Haig called, patched through by the White House switchboard, and over much static tried to shout, "George, this is Al Haig! Turn around! Turn around!" Meanwhile, FEMA's Central Locator System called House Speaker Tip O'Neill—the next in the line of succession—to ensure he was safe and secure.

At the White House, a string of officials trickled into the Situation Room as news spread—Defense Secretary Caspar Weinberger, Treasury Secretary Don Regan, and Attorney General William French Smith, as well as staffers like David Gergen, White House Counsel Fred Fielding, and the vice president's chief of staff, Admiral Dan Murphy, filled the room, uncertain of what came next. Fielding tried to explain how the president could "pass the baton temporarily," but no one really knew the president's condition. Haig finally asserted, "The helm is right here. And that means right in this chair for now, constitutionally, until the vice president gets here." Except that wasn't correct—the National Command Authorities clearly lay with the defense secretary, not the secretary of state. "At the moment, until the vice president actually arrives here, the command authority is what I have," Weinberger told the group, "and I have to make sure that it is essential that we do everything that seems proper."

"Well, you better read the Constitution," Haig replied.

That afternoon, as Air Force Two returned to the capital, Haig tried to calm the press corps with an impromptu appearance in the briefing room. "Constitutionally, you have the president, the vice president, and the secretary of state in that order," he explained to them. "As of now, I am in control here at the White House pending the return of the vice president."

In the Situation Room one floor below, the other members of the cabinet reacted with horror and surprise.

"What's this all about?" demanded Treasury Secretary Don Regan. "Is he mad?"

"He's wrong! He doesn't have such authority," Weinberger said.*

---

* As upset as Haig's demeanor made the other aides and officials in the Situation Room, the vice president himself wasn't that bothered. As Bush told a *Dallas Morning News* reporter years later, "We understood what [he] was trying to do—namely, send a strong message to our adversaries around the world who might be tempted to take advantage of the chaos of that day."

One reason officials were so eager to understand the chain of command was they worried the Soviet Union might take advantage of the assassination attempt—investigation details were still flooding in and it wasn't clear whether the shooting had foreign ties. As soon as the Pentagon's National Military Command Center learned of the shooting, it issued an OPREP-3 PINNACLE ALERT—the most critical message status. Fears of a Soviet submarine attack sparked debate about launching NEACP or moving bomber crews to higher alert, especially after an intelligence briefer informed Weinberger that a submarine-launched missile was dangerously close to Washington. Normally, there were two Soviet missile submarines lurking off the Atlantic coast, but the subs rotated at the end of every month and given the date—March 30—there were actually four subs off the coast at that moment, the two departing subs and the two relief subs. The Navy knew one was barely a ten-minute missile flight away. "About two minutes closer than normal," Weinberger warned the group. "[SAC] should go on alert or be ready to go on alert," he said. "SAC went on alert with Kennedy's assassination." He ordered 249 SAC crews to "standby alert" status—a process meant to shave three minutes off a launch order by summoning flight crews to their duty stations.

Still, who actually controlled the nuclear machine was a matter of real debate at the White House. The president's own nuclear authentication codes were lost in the chaos at George Washington Hospital; his suit had been cut away and tossed to the floor ("It was literally underfoot," surgeon Drew Scheele recalled later), and with it was the president's wallet, where he carried the Sealed Authenticator System card that would have identified him to military leaders as the commander-in-chief. The FBI had gathered his belongings as part of its criminal investigation into the shooting, and only later did White House officials realize the president's codes were missing. Attorney General William French Smith ordered the bureau to retain the SAS card—but keep it secure. The decision to leave the codes with the FBI was, one official later criticized, an "inconceivable, myopic bureaucratic reaction." Theoretically, the nation's nuclear safety was never in jeopardy, but the disorganization still embarrassed and annoyed both the White House and the Pentagon.

Allen ordered a new copy of the presidential authentication codes, as well as Colonel Muratti and Reagan's Football be brought to the Situation Room—where the briefcase sat for the remainder of the afternoon at Allen's feet under the conference table. The vice president possessed a separate copy of the authentication codes and his own Football aboard Air Force Two.

Luckily, the Reagan shooting wasn't part of an extensive plot—just a lone, deranged gunman who thought he would win fame and actress Jodie Foster's attention by shooting the U.S. president. Around 7 p.m., Vice President Bush returned to Washington. Just as Richard Nixon had during Eisenhower's health episodes, Vice President Bush carefully balanced the need for calm against any sign of usurping the president. Bush vetoed a suggestion that, after returning to Washington, he helicopter directly to the White House: "Only the president," he said, "lands on the South Lawn." By the time Bush arrived at the White House, President Reagan had stabilized—despite having lost more than half of his blood—and the crisis had de-escalated. How, though, the government would have reacted to a more complicated or serious attack that day remained a nervous, nagging thought in the minds of many participants.

In the following days, the White House tried to calm concern about the day's confusion. Spokesman Larry Speakes explained that the vice president had had an "automatic assumption of command authority," but that statement didn't appear to be backed up technically by any specific procedures or legal authorities. One anonymous national security official told *The New York Times* that the military chain of command in the event of presidential incapacitation "is kind of a gray area that never has been looked at as closely as it might," but White House counsel Fred Fielding said he was "confident that the command authority procedures that we have established cover every contingency." Besides, officials explained, normal launch procedure ensured that any attempt to order the use of nuclear weapons could only proceed with the concurrence of multiple officials.*

---

* To avoid some of the confusion from his assassination attempt, Reagan would formally transfer power to Vice President Bush on July 13, 1985, when he underwent surgery, making Bush the first person ever to officially serve as "acting president." He served nearly eight hours, from 11:28 a.m. until 7:22 p.m.

Meanwhile, after being confronted with the limitations of the Situation Room, the White House staff began upgrading their crisis center to better serve officials in an emergency. Admiral John Poindexter was brought in to oversee a $14 million renovation, updating computers and networks and installing a primitive videoconferencing system. The upgrades also introduced to the White House a new tool called "e-mail" that let officials communicate digitally on their own schedule.

President Reagan spent nearly two weeks in the hospital following his shooting and returned to the White House more convinced than ever that he needed to use his presidency to conclude the Cold War once and for all. Reagan had long believed the Soviet Union wasn't merely a traditional geopolitical opponent but, as he said, an "evil enemy" and an "evil empire" that enslaved its own people and its satellite states. Now, since he'd become president, Reagan's tough talk worried the Soviet Union; its leader, Leonid Brezhnev, and the head of the KGB, Yuri Andropov, warned senior officials that they believed the Reagan administration was readying a first strike. Andropov launched Operation RYaN, an acronym for *Raketno-Yadernoye Napadenie*, Russian for "nuclear missile attack." It was a massive intelligence-gathering effort focused on spotting signs that would point to a surprise assault. As Oleg Gordievsky, a senior KGB official who later defected to the West, would later explain, "The origins of RYaN lay in a potentially lethal combination of Reaganite rhetoric and Soviet paranoia."

The world also sensed the renewed tensions. Nuclear war was enough of a possibility when CNN launched in the early 1980s that its founder, Ted Turner, prepared a video to air during the final moments of life on earth. As Turner said, "We'll be on, and we will cover the end of the world, live, and that will be our last event. We'll play the National Anthem only one time, on the first of June [when the network premiered], and when the end of the world comes, we'll play *Nearer My God to Thee* before we sign off." It was the same hymn the band aboard the *Titanic* played during the ship's final moments. The no-frills recording of a joint U.S. military band and honor guard standing at attention sat in the network's archives for years. Slugged as "Turner Doomsday Video," the program's notes read, "HFR till end of the world confirmed," using the network's abbreviation for "hold for release." As Turner explained, "We knew we would only sign off once, and I knew what that would mean."

Even as the Reagan administration pushed ahead with a massive trillion-dollar defense buildup—one that would nearly double the Pentagon's budget in five years and emphasized winning a protracted nuclear war—the first widespread antinuclear movement was building. Globally, scientists had begun to understand the long-term effects of radiation and the possibility of "nuclear winter." The NORAD scares in 1979 and the accident at Three Mile Island, where a Pennsylvania nuclear plant suffered a partial meltdown, encouraged others to speak up against both atomic energy and weaponry. Europeans reacted angrily to a powerful new generation of U.S. missiles, the Pershing II; Easter 1981 saw a massive antinuclear rally in Brussels and subsequent marches of hundreds of thousands of protesters in European capitals like London, Bonn, Rome, Paris, and Amsterdam.

Another major catalyst for the disarmament movement was Jonathan Schell's bestselling book, *The Fate of the Earth*, based on a series of *New Yorker* articles, that confronted the "shrug of indifference that seems to have characterized most people's conscious reaction to the nuclear peril for the last thirty-six years." Writing at the point when the superpowers possessed 1,600,000 times the explosive power of the Hiroshima bomb, Schell's book outlined in 233 pages just how awful a nuclear war would truly be—painting it as not merely a catastrophe for Russians and Americans, but also for the entire human species and the earth's entire biosphere, as fallout contaminated the globe and dust sucked into the atmosphere by nuclear blasts cooled the earth, impacting crops, farmland, and human existence years after the fires had burned themselves out. On the state and local level, the "nuclear freeze" movement rapidly gained strength, and across Europe large protests became a regular occurrence.

On September 14, 1981, presidential counselor Edwin Meese had led the first meeting at the Reagan White House about what came to be its signature military initiative—though the administration later came to call it the "Strategic Defense Initiative," the press quickly chose another moniker: "Star Wars." Reagan had been focused on the idea of a national missile shield since a 1979 visit to the NORAD bunker, when he and an aide, Martin Anderson, had flown out to Colorado for a tour arranged for the presidential

contender by a Hollywood screenwriter friend. They initially didn't think
the compound looked very impressive. "Only a few minutes later, as we
stood in front of a massive steel door several feet thick and watched it swing
open, did we begin to sense the awesome scope of this underground base,"
Anderson later recalled. Through the day, the men were shuttled from one
briefing to another in the sprawling underground city and were taken into
the main command center, where they looked around in wonder—absorbing
the multistory wall-sized map tracking North American airspace and the
dozens of high-tech video screens manned by watch officers, mixed with the
half-filled ashtrays and white Styrofoam coffee cups that marked any other
mundane office space. In the day's final discussion with General James E.
Hill, Reagan had asked what would happen if the Soviets launched a missile
against the United States. "We would pick it up right after it was launched,
but by the time the officials of the city could be alerted that a nuclear bomb
would hit them, there would be only ten or fifteen minutes left," Hill replied.
"That's all we can do."

As president, Reagan intended to alter that dynamic, even though
countless dollars had been poured into antiballistic missile research efforts
since the 1950s—including a billion dollars a year by the Carter administration. The military's brightest minds hadn't found any system cheap or accurate enough that couldn't be overwhelmed by the Soviets simply by building
more inexpensive ICBMs.*

In October 1981 Reagan had signed a secret National Security Decision Directive, known as NSDD 12. Titled "Strategic Forces Modernization
Program," the plan outlined five major initiatives for his administration's nuclear forces. Beyond "improving strategic defenses" and the survivability of
the nation's command and control systems, Reagan hoped to upgrade each
leg of the Triad with new technology—constructing the new B-1 bomber,
upgrading submarine-launched missiles, and deploying a new ICBM. Later
that month, Reagan signed NSDD 13, which replaced Carter's Presidential

---

* The 1974 ABM treaty had reduced ground-based ABM sites to one each in the U.S. and
the Soviet Union. The United States had in 1977 shut down its sole site, which protected a
North Dakota missile field, citing its ineffectiveness. The Soviet Union had kept its sixty-
four ABM missiles focused around Moscow, but the force was so small and ineffective that
Pentagon targeters ignored it in their war planning.

Directive 59, and called for the first time for the United States to "prevail" in a nuclear exchange. As part of the strategic forces update, Reagan proposed committing $18 billion to boosting the nation's command and control systems, expanding COG operations, and ensuring that the country could smoothly weather a limited nuclear war.

A major factor in these missile defense efforts stemmed from fears that the Russians had built a far superior civil defense network. It was, in some respects, the third wave of such concerns—following on the previous "Bomber Gap" and the "Missile Gap," neither of which had been borne out by U.S. surveillance. By the Carter and Reagan years, however, there was no doubt that the Soviets were a powerful nuclear force, at rough "parity" with the United States. In 1975, the journalist wife of a U.S. embassy military attaché in Moscow published in *Air Force Magazine* a lengthy review of Soviet efforts, concluding, "The Soviet leadership has physically and psychologically prepared its people for the possibility of nuclear war. Western leaders have not."

The feeling that the Soviet Union was better prepared to weather a war existed as almost unquestioned gospel among a hawkish foreign policy group known as the Committee on the Present Danger that came to be hugely influential during the Reagan years, as thirty-two of its members entered his administration.* As committee member and NSC aide Richard Pipes explained, the Soviet Union was organizing "a kind of shadow government charged with responsibility for administering the country under the extreme stresses of nuclear war and its immediate aftermath." Of course, the United States had spent decades preparing just that itself—but the worry that the Soviet Union might be creeping ahead, creating—to use the Cold War's parlance—a "COG Gap," was deeply felt by the president. In

---

* The committee traced its origins back to Paul Nitze and the Truman administration's NSC-68; many original members had played key roles in the Eisenhower administration. Nitze helped revive the group in 1976, pushing for a more aggressive stance against the Soviet Union during the Ford-Carter campaign, and Reagan relied heavily on its members to fill out his leadership, including CIA director William Casey, National Security Advisor Richard Allen, Eugene Rostow, the head of the Arms Control and Disarmament Agency, Assistant Defense Secretary Richard Perle, and George Shultz, who became secretary of state after Haig was forced out in 1982.

an October 1981 press conference, a reporter asked, "Is there a winnable nuclear war?" Standing at the podium in the East Room, Reagan answered quickly, "It's very difficult for me to think that there's a winnable nuclear war, but where our great risk falls is that the Soviet Union has made it very plain that among themselves, they believe it is winnable. And believing that makes them constitute a threat."

Reagan's conclusion was actually at odds with the Soviet Union's own public statements. That same month, Brezhnev had been blunt about his own fears: "It is dangerous madness to try to defeat each other in the arms race and to count on victory in nuclear war." As the Soviet leader said, "Only he who has decided to commit suicide can start a nuclear war in the hope of emerging a victor from it."

Reagan himself came face-to-face with the nation's nuclear power during the trip back to Washington from a visit to the Johnson Space Center in Houston, on November 15, 1981, as he flew aboard NEACP as part of the Pentagon's familiarization efforts for incoming presidents. Once aloft, the head of the Joint Chiefs operations division, Lieutenant General Philip Gast, gathered the presidential party—including Reagan, James Baker, and deputy chief of staff Michael Deaver—in the briefing room.* Gast, a decorated Air Force official who had twice received Silver Stars for his role in dogfights over Vietnam, outlined a war scenario and walked the commander-in-chief through the various decision points he would have to make. At the end of the briefing, Barry Walrath, the NEACP squadron commander, and the head of the NEACP team, Colonel George McCoy, gave the president a tour of where he might end up spending the final hours of the world. Reagan visited the flight deck, shook hands all around, and had photos taken with many of the crew and battle staff, before he retired to the small suite reserved for the National Command Authorities.

A few minutes later, Walrath and Deaver were drinking coffee outside the suite's door, at the foot of the spiral staircase up to the cockpit, when Reagan cracked open the door and gestured wildly: "Deaver, Walrath! Either of you have a camera?"

---

* Notably absent from the flight was Richard Allen, the president's national security advisor, who was embroiled in an ethics investigation back in Washington.

The president explained he'd been sitting at the cabin's desk, working on papers, when he heard a snore. He'd pulled back the curtain on one of the suite's twin bunks to discover James Baker, clothed in his full suit and tie, sleeping soundly. Evidently Baker hadn't been too bothered by the thoughts of nuclear doom.

On March 1, 1982, Reagan observed the IVY LEAGUE military exercise—the largest military command post exercise that the United States had run since 1956. It was the first time since Eisenhower that a commander-in-chief personally participated in such an exercise. Like Ike, Reagan wasn't allowed to speak. As an official explained, "No president should ever disclose his hand, even in a war game." Instead, the exercise was led from the White House Situation Room by "President" William Rogers, a former secretary of state, who coordinated with teams at the Pentagon and at Raven Rock.

"War" began on the Korean Peninsula and spread over the unfolding hours and days across the rest of the globe, escalating from conventional weapons to chemical weapons to tactical nuclear weapons (first used to "sink" a U.S. Navy ship in the North Atlantic) to strategic nuclear weapons targeting the superpowers' mainlands. The "vice president," former CIA director Richard Helms, was sent up in NEACP; other officials had been dispersed to Raven Rock, Mount Weather, and FEMA's National Warning Center in Olney, Maryland.* In the first thirty minutes following activation of JEEP, the Joint Emergency Evacuation Plan, helicopters flew forty-four officials out of the capital. Within four hours, fifty-nine personnel were in place at Mount Weather and 194 staffed Raven Rock, joining more than 1,000 personnel worldwide who took part in the exercise. The COG evacuations proved a worthy precaution: "President Rogers" was "killed" in the first Soviet attack on Washington and the Pentagon's National Military Command Center was also "destroyed."

On the third day of the exercise, more officials—and two other presidential successors, Commerce Secretary Malcolm Baldrige and Interior Secretary James Watt—were dispatched with relocation teams to FEMA's

---

* There was even a "White House" set up at a U.S. embassy in Europe, to simulate how to run the nation from overseas, if needed.

regional bunkers in Maynard, Massachusetts, and Denton, Texas, where they, as well as the "surviving" military commanders and national leadership, began the process of rebuilding. "The strategy for reconstitution of the Executive Branch of the Federal Government after a nuclear attack relies on the Federal Regional Offices to be de facto regional governments," one secret FEMA report at the time read. "Because of the uncertainties surrounding a nuclear attack, one of the regional governments may be the national government." Other participating "survivors" included Undersecretary of Defense Fred Iklé, Deputy Secretary of State Walter Stoessel, and Air Force General James Dalton, while Vice President Bush, Secretary of State Al Haig, and National Security Advisor William P. Clark all watched from the exercise's sidelines.

For Reagan, who only participated in the first day of the exercise, even a brief look into nuclear war was troubling. According to one participant, he "looked on with stunned disbelief" as the Soviet nuclear forces escalated attacks on the United States. "After President Reagan watched someone face up to the decision to push the nuclear button," another official recounted, "all of a sudden, there was a sensitivity that wasn't there before."

Most of the staff involved in the exercise emerged from IVY LEAGUE with a different lesson: The COG system had worked—and enough of the leadership had survived, thanks to the bunkers and evacuation plans, that the United States maintained the ability to fight a protracted war. As one official said later, "Protection of key government functions during a crisis is as much of a deterrent to nuclear war as building new strategic nuclear systems." The exercise proved a milestone in the evolution of the nation's nuclear doctrine, and also highlighted the utility of keeping officials moving regularly—effectively creating a shell game. "We probably would not reconstitute in Washington," the head of the National Communications System, Army Lieutenant General William J. Hilsman, explained that same year. "Surviving government would be in Augusta, or in Hartford, or some other place, and decision makers are likely to be moving around."

At the Pentagon, Caspar Weinberger continued the Carter administration's dramatic reshaping of how the United States prepared for war as he drew up the Reagan administration's first comprehensive national security plan. At first glance, the 125-page Pentagon document, entitled

Fiscal Year 1984–1988 Defense Guidance, hardly seemed a watershed moment in American nuclear strategy, but Weinberger's strategy—parts of which became public in May 1982—laid out how the country should be prepared for an extended nuclear war and ensure the ability to "render ineffective the total Soviet (and Soviet-allied) military and political power structure." Because the Carter administration's moves had been little known by the public, the new Reagan doctrine seemed a radical change. While most Americans still believed that a nuclear war would be horrific but brief, Reagan's plan now called for new war-fighting tools, large defense budget increases, and fresh investment in command and control systems that could protect the nation's leadership and manage a long-term war. As the strategy explained, "These systems should support the reconstitution and execution of strategic reserve forces, specifically full communications with our strategic submarines."

By the fall of 1982, Leonid Brezhnev called for a Soviet buildup of its own, warning in an October 27 speech to military and Kremlin leaders that "Washington's aggressive policy . . . is threatening to push the world into the flames of nuclear war." His speech was only about ten minutes long and he slurred so badly that it was mostly incomprehensible to those in the room. The health of the man who had led the Soviet Union for eighteen years—a period that saw the military gain strength even as the general economy stagnated and the population starved—was deteriorating fast. He'd be dead within two weeks, touching off a multiyear turmoil that would be the darkest period of the Cold War since the Cuban Missile Crisis. The Soviet empire was beginning to crack apart; the Polish Solidarity movement was beginning to pressure the empire politically for change.

Propaganda aside, Brezhnev seemed correct that an odd and off-putting cavalierness was permeating many of the Reagan administration's comments about nuclear war. FEMA official William Chipman had optimistically pointed to the experience of Europeans during the Bubonic Plague, which had wiped out a third of the population during the Middle Ages. "It was horrifying at the time, and yet six or eight years later, not only had English society rebounded but, by God, those people went out on an expeditionary force to France," he explained. What he called the "post-attack United States" would, with time, resemble the pre-attack United States and "eventually" even restore traditional institutions and a democratic government: "As I say, ants will eventually build another anthill."

Similarly, the deputy undersecretary of defense for strategic and nuclear forces, T. K. Jones, raised eyebrows around Washington when he appeared to brush off concerns about the threat of war with the Soviet Union. "Everybody's going to make it," he reassured journalist Robert Scheer in one interview, "if there are enough shovels to go around." He proceeded to outline his simple plan: "Dig a hole, cover it with a couple of doors, and then throw three feet of dirt on top. It's the dirt that does it."

Jones firmly believed that nuclear war was not only survivable but that, with adequate preparation, the destruction would be quite limited. "The problem is we've conditioned our people to believe that once the first nuclear bomb goes off, everybody's going to die," he said. "With protection of people only, your recovery time to prewar GNP levels would probably be six or eight years. If we used the Russian methods for protecting both the people and the industrial means of production, recovery time could be two to four years."

After some of Scheer's interview was published in January 1982, the Senate Foreign Relations Committee expressed deep concern, but the "with enough shovels" comment was hardly out of line with other statements. Around the same time, an official in the Office of Civil Defense wrote, "A nuclear war could alleviate some of the factors leading to today's ecological disturbances that are due to current high-population concentrations and heavy industrial populations."

In March 1983, Reagan unveiled his grand plan for missile defense—adding it on his own to a scheduled national security speech so his words weren't watered down by the bureaucracy. His remarks were met with mixed reactions. The idea was not fundamentally new—missile defense efforts had been endorsed in the 1980 GOP platform—but it had never been at the fore of public debate. Critics like Democrats and pundits quickly labeled the fantastical plan "Star Wars," linking it to the blockbuster science fiction franchise sweeping the country's popular culture.* The Soviets strongly

* The reference seemed perfectly timed: The third installment, *Return of the Jedi*, opened just two days after Reagan's Oval Office address, which itself came just two weeks after

objected, with Ambassador Anatoly Dobrynin warning Shultz, "You will be opening a new phase in the arms race." The Soviet Union saw missile defense as a destabilizing force—if the U.S. was able to counter ICBMs successfully, it would put the Soviet Union at a great disadvantage. "SDI was a Soviet nightmare," intelligence official Robert Gates wrote later. "A radical new departure by the United States that would require an expensive Soviet response at a time of deep economic crisis."

Reagan's program, though, was entirely speculative—there was no clear technology on the horizon that could provide the necessary protection—and the years ahead underscored the experience of previous administrations, as SDI became the largest military research program in U.S. history, devouring billions of dollars with little success. The effort, though, did help transform Reagan's image from a hawk to a peacemaker—a transformation that came just as the world turned strongly against the Cold War's militaristic rhetoric.

In early June, Reagan settled in for the night at Camp David to watch a new movie written by his friend Lawrence Lasker. *WarGames* starred Matthew Broderick as a goofy teenage hacker who accesses NORAD's main computer and accidentally begins a countdown sequence for nuclear war. Reagan watched in the president's lodge, just steps from his own bomb shelter, and found himself captivated by the plot, which was based partly on the NORAD scares of the Carter years. The movie clearly underscored the absurdity of Mutually Assured Destruction. The talking computer's final line—and the closing scene of the movie, after a massive computer-launched nuclear strike had been dramatically averted with seconds to spare—focused on the computer realizing how futile thermonuclear war truly would be. "A strange game," it intoned. "The only winning move is not to play." In the days ahead, the movie would become a recurring theme in Reagan's conversations.

Even as *WarGames* opened in the movie theaters, the reality of global thermonuclear war appeared closer than at almost any point since the

---

Reagan had called the Soviet Union an "evil empire," a moment people had already dubbed his "Darth Vader" speech. Only later, after the derisive moniker became widely used shorthand for the project, did the Reagan administration begin to call it the "Strategic Defense Initiative."

Cuban Missile Crisis. On June 16, 1983, Yuri Andropov reported to the Soviet Union's Central Committee that there had been an "unprecedented sharpening of the struggle" between the superpowers. In its efforts to spot U.S. preparations for a first strike, the KGB's Operation RYaN entered a new phase in early 1983: KGB *rezidenturas* (its term for "field offices") were sent detailed instructions to gather information based upon "the growing urgency of the task of discovering promptly any preparations by the adversary for a nuclear missile attack on the USSR." KGB agents were instructed to investigate COG plans, "identify possible routes and methods of evacuation," and "make suggestions about ways of organizing a watch to be kept on preparation and actual evacuation." They were also told to locate major civil defense shelters and "arrange for a periodical check on their state of preparedness."

That same month, Andropov warned U.S. envoy Averell Harriman during a meeting in Moscow that the United States' aggressiveness was pushing both nations toward "the dangerous red line," risking a nuclear war started by "miscalculation." SAC bombers had been regularly circling Russian airspace, making the Soviet military antsy, and in September its fighters shot down the civilian Korean Air Lines Flight 007 over the Sea of Japan when the airliner strayed into Soviet territory. The crash killed all 269 passengers aboard, including a U.S. congressman, Larry McDonald, and underscored for the Soviet Union the poor quality of their own command and control systems. The Korean Air Lines flight had spent hours in Soviet airspace unchallenged and eight of the eleven nearby radar tracking stations had never located it.

Just weeks later, on September 26, 1983, one of the Soviet Union's early warning satellites reported the launch of an American ICBM from Malmstrom Air Force Base in Montana. At the Soviets' control bunker in Serpukhov-15, a small military outpost about fifty miles outside Moscow— its rough equivalent of NORAD—Lieutenant Colonel Stanislav Petrov watched as first one and then four more incoming missiles registered on his tracking computers. The Oko early warning satellite system (named after the Russian word for "eye"), Petrov recounted, was "roaring." As he explained years later, "For 15 seconds, we were in a state of shock. We needed to understand, what's next?" He watched the consoles and made a quick

The USS *Wright*, one of two "floating White Houses," was considered one of the best options for a president during an emergency in the 1960s.

CC-1, the USS *Northampton*, served as the other National Emergency Command Post Afloat.

JFK visited the *Northampton* for an overnight cruise in April 1962 as part of naval exercises, one of two presidents to sleep aboard the NECPAs.

Kennedy witnessed the launch of a submarine's Polaris missile—the final leg of the nation's nuclear triad—during his final visit to Florida, just before his assassination.

The Cuban Missile Crisis led to a brief
revival of interest in civil defense.

The crisis led the White House
to install temporary trailers
to screen visitors through
new security checks.

The Moscow-Washington
"hotline" grew out of the missile
crisis, as the superpowers sought
secure communications.

The construction of Congress's nuclear bunker was disguised
as an expansion of the Greenbrier resort.

The bunker door was hidden behind a wall in
the Greenbrier's conference facility.

Congress's nuclear dormitories would have been tight quarters.

The House of Representatives would have met in a 470-seat auditorium; a similar room next door held space for the Senate.

Congressional leaders could have held and broadcast press conferences from inside the bunker.

The NORAD bunker served as the heart of the
continent's air defenses through the Cold War.

The NORAD command center would have been the
first place to detect a Soviet missile launch.

Cheyenne Mountain holds large reservoirs for NORAD's drinking water, heating, and cooling.

The buildings inside the mountain were mounted on man-sized springs to sway during a nearby blast.

Deep inside the tunnels, massive blast doors could have sealed commanders away from an attack.

Project Elf tried in the 1980s to turn upper Wisconsin and Michigan into a massive radio station to communicate with submarines after a nuclear attack.

During an attack, the Alaskan Railroad Command Post planned to hide military commanders inside tunnels.

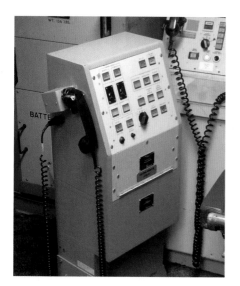

These phone systems inside secret missile silos in Missouri would have recorded a final launch command to broadcast to U.S. forces worldwide using the Emergency Rocket Communications System.

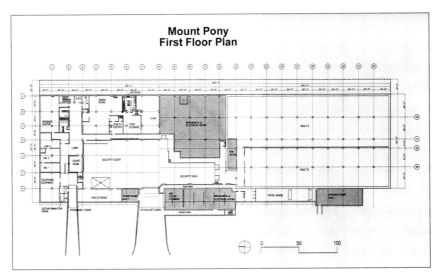

The Federal Reserve's bunker at Mount Pony held
massive vaults filled with U.S. currency.

Drills sought to ensure that not even nuclear
fallout would have interrupted the mail.

The presidential "Doomsday planes" underwent elaborate tests to see
if they could weather an nuclear bomb's electromagnetic pulse.

Once airborne in NEACP, a president would have sat in
this briefing room to order a retaliatory attack.

The NEACP planes held space for scores of military aides and planners.

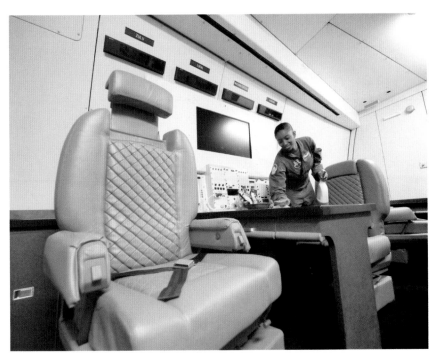

The special cabin reserved for the "National Command Authority"
aboard NEACP, a.k.a., the President or a designated successor.

From the 1960s through 1991, a LOOKING GLASS plane
was always airborne over the Plains to assume control of
the military if the country below was destroyed.

Regular exercises aboard LOOKING GLASS planes ensured the Emergency
Action Officers understood how to launch nuclear missiles.

During the 1990s, many nuclear bunkers were decommissioned. This bungalow hid the entrance to one of Britain's regional command bunkers below.

Canada's own North Bay bunker served as a backup to NORAD.

The massive telephone switchboard inside the UK's central bunker, codenamed BURLINGTON, was never used.

On 9/11, President Bush finally arrived at Offutt Air Force Base midday, deplaning next to the Doomsday planes always kept on station there.

In Curtis LeMay's old underground command post, Bush hosted a videoconference with government leaders on 9/11.

At the end of the day, he met with Vice President Cheney inside the Presidential Emergency Operations Center, the bunker underneath the White House.

To this day, an updated and expanded Mount Weather stands
ready to receive the nation's leaders in a catastrophe.

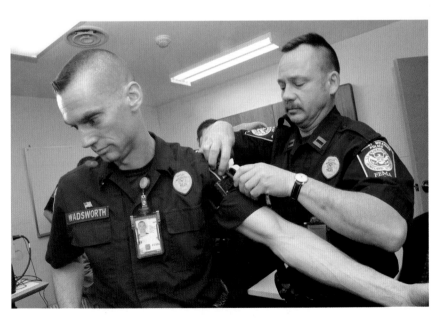

In a rare public photo, Mount Weather's own
police force practice for an emergency.

These Air Force C-20C Gulfstream planes could whisk a president to a special airfield near Mount Weather.

A Doomsday plane is always kept ready on the tarmac in Omaha, Nebraska, its engines turning and powered up.

Today, NORAD is perhaps best known for its annual Santa-tracking operation, but the facility has been reopened and readied for a new Doomsday.

determination; it was probably just a mistake. "I had a funny feeling in my gut," he explained. "When people start a war, they don't start it with only five missiles." He didn't raise an alarm, but it was a close call. The year-old Oko system had extended the Russians' early warning capability to nearly thirty minutes; if Petrov waited until the reported missiles could be validated by the ground-based radar system, that early warning would have squandered half the time, leaving just fifteen minutes to warn the Soviet leadership and activate a nuclear response.

A later investigation found that the satellites had mistakenly registered the sun reflecting off cloud cover as the heat of a missile launch. But given the global tensions, the paranoia of Soviet leader Andropov, and the unfolding Operation RYAN, if Petrov raised the alarm the Kremlin's leadership would have been particularly predisposed to believe Reagan had launched a surprise first strike. The Soviet early warning system was a dangerous mess, leaving the country—and the world—vulnerable to a mistake.

The 1983 tensions culminated with a massive NATO military exercise in November, code-named ABLE ARCHER 83, meant to test the transition from peacetime readiness to general war. Just about every measure tracked by the KGB's Operation RYAN went off the charts as the exercise began— high-level officials relocated, coded communications peaked, military forces moved to alert. On November 5, the KGB alerted its *rezidenturas* that it believed a NATO first strike was possible within seven to ten days. Soviet military bases across Eastern Europe were brought to a heightened alert, and Soviet nuclear bombers went on "strip alert" in East Germany and Poland. By the time the NATO exercise ended normally and on schedule, the allies were none the wiser about the concern they'd caused on the other side.

It was lucky the situation didn't escalate further: Both superpowers would have struggled in executing a war. The Soviet Politburo was wracked by internal tensions and a vacuum of leadership as Yuri Andropov, who had first launched Operation RYAN and who deeply feared an American first strike, lay on his deathbed. In the United States, had Reagan been forced into a nuclear showdown during ABLE ARCHER, he wouldn't have been familiar with the options at his disposal. He had long resisted receiving the traditional presidential SIOP briefing, arguing there wasn't much point in practicing such a terrible event. Finally Weinberger and the chairman of the Joint Chiefs, General John Vessey, provided Reagan with a briefing on SIOP in the Situation Room on November 18, 1983. SIOP-6 had just come into effect on the first of October 1983, the first full update since SIOP-5 took effect during the Ford administration. It focused on "protracted nuclear war" and included nearly 50,000 targets pulled from the National Strategic Target Data Base (NSTDB), among them some 25,000 military targets, 15,000 economic-industrial targets, and some 5,000 focused on the Soviet leadership. "These war games brought home to anybody the fantastically horrible events that would surround such a scenario," Caspar Weinberger explained later. Just as the briefings had been for his Cold War predecessors, Reagan's lesson in the nation's nuclear arsenal "chastened" him, according to Weinberger. The briefing was, Reagan wrote in his diary, "a most sobering experience."

Two days later, on Sunday, November 20, ABC aired a much hyped two-hour $7 million Doomsday movie, *The Day After*, which starred Jason Robards and followed the residents of Lawrence, Kansas, through the awful aftermath of trying to piece society back together after a nuclear attack obliterated America. Graphic and violent in ways that TV had never before depicted, the four-minute attack sequence in *The Day After* as well as the death, maiming, and destruction that followed left viewers unsettled. As one character said, "Hiroshima was peanuts." The movie did little to inspire confidence in the government's ability to respond to such an attack; in one scene, after weeks had passed with little visible help from the government, the American president—who sounded remarkably like Ronald Reagan—delivered a static-filled radio address from a hidden "undisclosed location" that played over a montage of the devastated nation returning to primitive ways of life. The film ended with an on-screen disclaimer: "The catastrophic events you have just witnessed are, in all likelihood, less severe than the destruction that would actually occur in the event of a full nuclear strike against the United States."

The two-hour movie, despite being emotionally draining to watch, turned into a national phenomenon—watched by more than 100 million people, the highest-rated TV movie in history. One viewer, in particular, was impressed. "It is powerfully done," Reagan wrote in his diary. "It's very effective and left me greatly depressed. . . . My own reaction was one of our having to do all we can to have a deterrent & see there is never a nuclear war."* The Soviet head of the armed forces, Marshal Nikolai Ogarkov, had also paid attention. "The danger which is shown in the film really exists," he said. Indeed, to too many people, the impossible suddenly seemed possible: *Time* magazine named Reagan and Andropov its "Men of the Year," writing that the superpowers' two leaders, who would never meet in person, "share the power to decide whether there will be any future at all."

That tense fall of 1983 caused Reagan to reevaluate his own approach to the Soviet Union, a move historian Beth Fischer later dubbed the "Reagan reversal." He was coming to understand just how paranoid the Soviet leadership was and began to take steps to calm the tension. All the education he'd received as president—aboard NEACP, during the Ivy League exercise, and in his SIOP briefing—made him rethink his defense doctrine.† "Nuclear abolition" became a popular applause line for Reagan on the reelection trail during the 1984 campaign, and he started his second term by calling in his inaugural address for the complete rollback of the horror the Manhattan Project had let loose on the world: "We see the total elimination one day of nuclear weapons from the face of the earth."

The Soviet political system was also undergoing a period of immense change and uncertainty. Its elderly leadership had spent the first term of Reagan's presidency consumed by internal challenges—cycling through one aging party leader after another in rapid succession. Brezhnev died in November 1982, to be replaced by Yuri Andropov, who served until his own death in February 1984. Konstantin Chernenko, seventy-two, then took the Communist Party's top position, but was already so ill he could barely read Andropov's eulogy. The *New York Times* obituary of him when he died in March 1985 after just thirteen months in office reported that he left only "a minor imprint on Soviet affairs."

---

* That diary entry is more remarkable than may appear at first glance: Years later, Reagan biographer Edmund Morris reported it was the "first and only admission I have been able to find in his papers" that Reagan was ever "depressed."

† In part to minimize the chance of any misinterpretations, NATO never again conducted exercises akin to ABLE ARCHER.

Reagan said, "How am I supposed to get anyplace with the Russians if they keep dying on me?" Within hours, the Central Committee announced that the comparatively sprightly fifty-four-year-old Mikhail Gorbachev would become the Soviet Union's seventh—and youngest—head of state since Stalin. He understood clearly that the country had to make a change. As he told his wife, Raisa, on the morning of Chernenko's death, "We can't go on living like this."

Chapter 16

NINE NAUGHT EIGHT

Attorney General Ed Meese arrived at Andrews Air Force Base before dawn on June 18, 1986, just one of dozens of government staff from the Pentagon, State Department, White House, and intelligence community streaming onto the base in the Maryland suburbs, ready to practice nuclear war as part of the Reagan administration's covert COG planning. The exercises always started under cover of darkness to help maximize secrecy. Once assembled, the officials would be shuttled to a COG relocation facility—perhaps Raven Rock or Mount Weather or maybe one of the other more mobile locations that the administration was hurriedly preparing to help maximize the chance of avoiding a Soviet decapitation strike. The team knew that morning that the attorney general was stressed, since Chief Justice Warren Burger had announced his resignation the day before. One official at Andrews recalled looking at Meese and joking, "First a Supreme Court resignation, and now America's in a nuclear war. You're having a bad day."

Earlier COG exercises like IVY LEAGUE had concluded that the key to "winning" a nuclear exchange was ensuring that sufficient remnants of the government avoided the opening nuclear salvo and could maintain control over the nation's strategic arsenal, and so large-scale COG exercises became commonplace over the course of the 1980s. Friends of the administration like rising GOP congressman Dick Cheney and former Ford chief of staff Donald Rumsfeld, then head of the pharmaceutical company G.D. Searle in Chicago, had extensive COG knowledge from their own government stints and were among the dozens of people who practiced evacuations, slipping away from their daily lives to participate in covert two-week-long exercises that deployed them to hidden facilities across the country.

During the exercises, they would all be completely incommunicado—reachable only in an emergency by an unlabeled telephone number they left behind with their wives. The relocation teams consisted of forty to sixty staffers, a cabinet member like Meese who would be the designated successor, and a senior team leader like Cheney or Rumsfeld who could step in as White House chief of staff.

Just as in IVY LEAGUE, three different COG teams would take turns leading the country, each working from a different secret relocation facility for three or four days before being "nuked" and then handing off responsibility to the next team. The team leader, designated survivor, and government staff would then pick up the exercise while the "dead" team returned to their normal lives. Throughout the exercise, participants tried to mimic the stress and conditions of an attack as best they could, living at the relocation facilities, eating MREs, and hotly debating the best responses to an unfolding attack. "One of the awkward questions we faced was whether to reconstitute Congress after a nuclear attack," a participant recalled years later. "It was decided that no, it would be easier to operate without them." It was, of course, not a new question: Congress had long represented a sticky situation for COG planners—the body was too large and too slow to participate in the dynamic and fast-unfolding moments of a nuclear attack. During the Reagan era, planners raised more specific objections to its role: If a devastated Congress convened and elected a new speaker of the House or Senate president pro tem, would that congressional leader be seen by the nation as having more legitimacy than the cabinet member who had stepped in to be president?

A COG alert would have begun with a telephone call announcing one of four readiness levels: communications watch, initial alert, advanced alert, or attack warning. At each alert level, phone trees would have gone out through each agency's emergency teams. The first level required no individual action, only that agencies ready their command posts and man their communication systems. An initial alert would require each employee to "be sure your automobile is available with gasoline tank filled." An advanced alert meant that the federal employees should prepare for deployment to relocation fa-cilities and ensure that they had "[made] arrangements for your family's pro-tection and safety."* Under either an advanced alert or an attack warning, the nation's most critical leaders—a total of forty-six government officials who possessed what were known as JEEP-1 IDs—would be evacuated by helicopter, and, separately, teams of retired or former officials—known as the Presidential Successor Support System—would begin to assemble and deploy from their private lives. Another 248 officials, those with JEEP-2 IDs, would be evacuated by air during business hours, but after hours and on weekends would be responsible for reporting to the bunkers themselves. Altogether, the Reagan-era plans called for about 4,000 to 5,000 govern-ment workers to survive and ensure "essential and uninterruptible" services through a nuclear attack and the response.

As that new wave of Reagan administration personnel explored the na-tion's Doomsday bunkers, they were amazed at the scope and sophistication of the government-in-waiting. "It's kind of mind-boggling," said Buford Macklin, HUD's emergency planning coordinator, after visiting Mount Weather. "It's otherwordly—just the size and weight and massiveness of the doors. It's a mini-city—like a space station." Inside the facilities, though, there was plenty of updating to do. Richard Clarke, who worked in the State Department during the Reagan and Bush years, recalled arriving at the de-partment's assigned building inside Mount Weather for an exercise only to find on his desk a phone book labeled "Secretary of State Christian A.

* As had generations of government workers before them, not everyone during the Reagan years agreed in principle with the decision to abandon their families in a crisis. "There's a fifty-fifty chance I'd go," one government official, who had been assigned to relocate to Mount Weather, told a reporter in the early 1980s. "And if I do go, I'll probably take my family with me. What are the guards going to do? I don't think they'll capture me and take me inside. They could turn us all away, but that would miss the whole point of the thing." Others were more pragmatic: Bill Alcorn, the emergency coordinator for the National Labor Relations Board, parked two motorcycles in his garage for his family to use to escape Washington and kept an Airstream trailer at a campsite eighty-five miles outside the city. "I know the roads will be crowded and you won't be able to get out of the city by car, but I think you could get out on a motorcycle," he explained. "My son knows enough to put his mother on the back of the Harley, and along with my daughter they should all head to camp."

Herter." He'd never heard the name before, so when he later returned to his office in Foggy Bottom, he looked it up and discovered that Herter had served more than two decades earlier under Eisenhower. The dusty pencils carefully positioned on Clarke's assigned desk lay untouched, sharpened twenty years before. Improvements only came in fits and starts; while FEMA and the Defense Department paid for overall upgrades to the facility and built aboveground dormitories for staff, each department was responsible for funding its own upgrades to its own buildings and workspaces inside Mount Weather—monies some agencies were more willing to allocate than others.

Under the Reagan-era systems, federal agencies were divided into three tiers for COG purposes—Category A, Category B, and Category C. Those designated "A" had to have extensive relocation plans, Continuity Operations, and the "capability for uninterrupted emergency operations." In general, that required three separate, fully staffed emergency teams—one posted at headquarters, one posted at Mount Weather, and one posted at the department's own relocation site. B-level agencies were required to have plans for "postattack reconstitution as soon as conditions permit." Lastly, Category C agencies would not plan to reconstitute operations until told to do so by the remaining national leadership; federal employees in this third category were told "to make themselves available for other emergency duty."

Most of the A Teams, those who remained at agency headquarters, would die in the opening salvo on Washington—but, just the same, department and agency headquarters outfitted emergency operations facilities, complete with decontamination showers and dormitories in their basements. The Department of Labor's National Office Alerting Plan explained that "Emergency Team Alpha will continue to be in charge of Departmental emergency operations until it is unable to function, at which time Emergency Team Bravo [at Mount Weather] will assume responsibility." The Health and Human Services emergency command post, just a block from the National Mall in Room 313-10 in its headquarters basement, stocked freeze-dried food sufficient to feed three dozen staff for a month, as well radio gear, an infirmary, and, incongruously, an office for the cabinet secretary decorated with photos of the atomic bombings of Hiroshima and Nagasaki, just in case the cabinet official forgot what the world outside would have looked like.

The USDA was allotted sixty-two slots for its emergency team—

including eleven personnel from the secretary of agriculture's office, twenty-four from the Agricultural Stabilization and Conservation Service, whose job would be to direct "use of food resources," three Forest Service personnel who would work on the expected fires in rural areas, three staff from the Food and Nutrition Service to oversee distribution of USDA-donated foods and the "emergency use of food stamps," as well as two staffers from the Soil Conservation Service to work on the radiological contamination of soil and water, among others. Other agencies and departments planned to operate with even fewer staff: The National Mediation Board only had slots for its chair and an alternate; only a dozen staff of the Export-Import Bank were designated to survive Armageddon, as were nine from the Farm Credit Administration, and just seven from NASA were to be sheltered at Mount Weather while another seven were to report to NASA's relocation facility in Olney. As for where all the relocated employees would live, Postal Service security manager David Madden explained, "We make arrangements with local motels for housing," adding, "in the long run, though, it won't matter. There'll be martial law, and we'll just take it."

Among the most important post-attack programs was the Selective Service System, whose plans called for mailgrams to be distributed quickly after a nuclear attack to allow the military to draft new recruits. Backup copies of the national draft registrants' list were stored at the U.S. Naval Training Center in Great Lakes, Illinois, and at the W. R. Church Computer Center at the Naval Postgraduate School in Monterey, California. "We can deliver the first inductees on the thirteenth day," promised one Selective Service "designated survivor." Altogether, the Pentagon's "Master Mobilization Plan" called for 84,600 inductees in the first thirty days.

To keep the government functioning money-wise, the Treasury Department set up fallback payroll offices for each of its major facilities, prepositioning "emergency disbursing kits" and blank checks in places like the post office of Oconomowoc, Wisconsin, in case its Chicago facility was destroyed. As a second fallback, postmasters were to be authorized to run payrolls for local employees using postal money orders. Regardless of whether federal employees were working on the crisis, filling in for other missing staff, or volunteering for civil defense cleanup, their pay rates would remain the same. Regulations were written so standards were clear: "Employees . . .

who are delayed in reporting for work due to disaster conditions . . . should be granted administrative leave for the full period of time it took to reach the relocation site," one personnel manual explained. Those involved in civil defense or unable to report to work "because of disaster conditions" would be similarly eligible for administrative leave, while "Employees reported as dead should be carried on administrative leave until the reported date of death."*

As part of imagining the post-attack world, the Internal Revenue Service ran studies and exercises on how to calculate and levy taxes after a war. After much study from the 1960s to the 1980s, the Treasury Department and IRS concluded that it would be very challenging to levy taxes after a Soviet strike—employers would have lost records needed for W-2s, IRS agents would struggle to verify pre-attack figures during audits, and it seemed unfair to assess homeowners and business owners on the pre-attack tax assessments of their property, since many would likely have seen values reduced drastically by damage. "Consider a firm whose principal assets consist of a professional football team valued, preattack, at $15 million," one study explained. "Any plan to levy . . . a net-worth tax post-attack must face up to the fact that this firm's relative net worth in real terms is certainly not going to be the same as preattack." One of the IRS studies calculated that as much as $2 trillion in property might disappear in a large strike. IRS planners recommended that the government itself assume the underlying mortgages of damaged properties to help ensure that the banking system didn't collapse. Then, instead of relying on income and property taxes to fund the government and the nation's war mobilization, planners suggested that it would likely be necessary to assess a general national sales tax on all goods after an attack—a tax that might range as high as 20 to 24 percent.

---

* Missing employees, though, were more complicated. "There may be some employees whose whereabouts are still unknown by the agency and may therefore be presumed to be missing," the regulations stated. Such employees, if eligible, were to continue to be paid under the federal government's policies for "missing" employees—Subchapter VII, Chapter 55, Title 5 of United States Code—but might have to repay their salaries if they were found to be absent without proper authorization. Later, after an appropriate declaration, missing employees could be presumed dead "for the purpose of adjudicating claims of dependents under the Retirement and Group Life Insurance Acts, or other applicable acts providing benefits in certain circumstances upon the death of an employee."

To assess what was left standing outside the bunkers, FEMA developed a nine-level rating scale, delineating "Basic Operating Situations" to assess a post-attack environment. BOS #1 was known as NEGRAD NEGFIRE, meaning both negligible radiation and fires; BOS #9 was known as HIRAD HIFIRE. (As many as one out of six Americans who weathered a widespread nuclear attack would emerge from the rubble to find BOS #9.) Separately, the nation's satellite network would locate and report nuclear detonations through what was known as IONDS, the Integrated Operational Nuclear Detection System, and the military planned Continental Airborne Reconnaissance for Damage Assessment (CARDA) missions, to allow the Air Force to determine the extent to which major U.S. installations and cities had been damaged. To help evaluate the reports from satellites and CARDA flights, FEMA had carefully collected data, including latitude and longitude, on more than two million structures across the country that warranted monitoring in the event of a nuclear attack—everything from 10,873 grain silos to 8,184 hospitals, not to mention the 316 mines and caves that could be used to house industrial manufacturing and processes in an emergency. Nearly every conceivable statistic had been carefully calculated and stored for later retrieval; a 6,000-megaton attack on the United States, for instance, was estimated to destroy a high proportion of alcohol and tobacco manufacturing relative to the population, meaning that after a war, liquor and cigarettes would require "drastic rationing."

FEMA concluded that while "the death, suffering, misery, and long-term consequences . . . would have few if any parallels in human experience," that was "not the same as saying that recovery would be 'impossible.'" In fact, the agency concluded, hopefully, that "in years of research no insuperable barrier to recovery has been found."

Fears that Russia was far ahead on civil defense spurred efforts inside the Reagan administration to reinvest in similar programs. President Reagan personally intervened to overrule objections by the budget agency about devoting more money to civil defense; there was "no question in his mind that the Soviet Union had a tremendous advantage in civil defense," he explained. During a National Security Council meeting on December 3, 1981, officials walked the president through the sad state of the nation's defensive measures and presented various options for improvement. That night, though, Reagan wrote in his diary, "I approved starting a Civil Defense buildup. Right now in a nuclear war we'd lose 150 mil. people. The Soviets could hold their loss down to less than were killed in WWII."

In the months that followed, FEMA and the government launched one of the most ambitious COG efforts of the Cold War—a secret effort known as Project 908 (or "Nine Naught Eight," as it was called). The National Program Office asked FBI field offices for help finding suitable facilities outside of blast zones. Reports from field offices flooded into Washington over the latter half of the 1980s, detailing large warehouses, automobile facilities, Masonic temples, Elks lodges, casinos, campsites, Coca-Cola bottling plants, Indian bingo halls, country inns, furniture stores, and other potential relocation facilities. In each jurisdiction across the country, agents laid out possible counterintelligence and espionage threats, assessed the local ethnic immigrant populations, ran background checks on business owners to turn up old criminal associations, and investigated political allegiances—all in the name of finding safe havens when war came.

In Arkansas, agents lined up a meeting with Walmart executives to discuss using the company's huge stores for Project 908, explaining as a cover that they wanted to learn crisis management techniques from companies that had large centralized leadership. Denver agents zeroed in on the 31,000-square-foot newly built recreation center in Hanna, Wyoming, an old mining town 200 miles north of Denver, which seemed perfect for a large-scale relocation facility, but after meeting with the rec center's director decided that the town was too small and gossipy to keep such a secret; similarly, they dismissed a closed Coors brewing plant in Colorado because the caretaker was "loose-mouthed." In Geneva, Alabama, agents selected the Fleming Food warehouse as a "priority location"; agents in California settled on the refrigerated Dole Fruit warehouse in Coachella; in Utah they turned to the American Greetings Company to reserve their Payson printing plant; and in Mississippi, Gulf Coast Junior College in Lucedale made the cut. In Redding, California, 160 miles north of the state capital, FBI agents approached the owner of Viking Skate Country ("Redding's fun center for kids!"), known to the government as "Sacramento Site #34," and outlined their proposal. The owner responded enthusiastically, telling agents he was a "fiercely loyal American" and would "cooperate fully." He'd been in Norway during the German occupation in World War II and understood, he explained, all too well the need for secrecy; he promised not even to tell his wife, who ran the rink's operations on a daily basis.

If a building owner proved amenable, the National Program Office then dispatched two "technical consultants" to complete a site survey and collect copies of the building blueprints for the files in Washington. The legal agreements presented to these potential relocation facilities were purposely vague, allowing for occupancy with twenty-four hours' notice when the FBI determined "on a good faith basis" that an emergency situation existed. Lengthy addendums to the contracts outlined required utility and infrastructure upgrades needed to support crisis operations, the costs of which were fully paid by the government, as were separate telephone lines installed at the facility. The government also paid a token annual fee like $1,000 or $2,500 to ease cooperation. During an emergency, the FBI would also pay a daily fee for each day it occupied the facility. Nowhere was any government agency other than the FBI mentioned—there was no sign of FEMA, the National Program Office, the military, or any of the other agencies that would actually be running the facilities in a crisis.

Project 908 became a key part of Crisis Relocation Planning, the 1980s-era program in which the Reagan administration hoped to invest more than $4 billion over five years in civil defense from 1983 to 1989. Under the Crisis Relocation Plan, nearly 150 million Americans—out of the country's total population of 225 million—would be evacuated out of 400 "high-risk" cities into smaller surrounding towns; under FEMA's estimates, some 65 percent of that population could be evacuated in as little as one day and fully 95 percent could be evacuated in three days. Such strategic warning, FEMA estimated, would be achievable under most circumstances, since it was "more likely that [a nuclear attack] would follow a period of intense international tension."

Under FEMA's plans, the agency had a multistage effort for informing civilians about how best to evacuate. First, the agency would air across the country a twenty-five-minute bilingual film, produced in 1978, *Protection in the Nuclear Age*, outlining the threat and putting an optimistic view on a horrible catastrophe, underscoring at every turn that survival was not only possible but—with planning—probable. Copies of the film were distributed in advance to civil defense officials and television stations, and fifteen prewritten newspaper articles distributed by FEMA covered much of the same ground. The low-tech film featured only illustrations and animations of stick figures—no live action—because by the 1970s civil defense planners had grown tired of retaping propaganda films each time fashion or car styles changed. As one FEMA official explained, "Stick figures don't get obsolete."

Next came the evacuation instructions themselves: FEMA would distribute millions of brochures—either door to door or tucked inside a local newspaper. In 1981, as a pilot project, FEMA took out four-page ads in the telephone books of four high-risk target cities that were home to major Air Force bases: Austin, Texas; Limestone, Maine; Marquette, Michigan; and Plattsburgh, New York.* The ads and brochures in Plattsburgh explained, "This area will be evacuated.... All persons living in this risk area must evacuate, when ordered, to lower risk portions of Clinton County called 'host areas.'" The brochures contained seven large letters, A through G, each corresponding to specific neighborhoods that would be evacuated to different, preselected corners of the surrounding county. Residents were to cut out their assigned letter and tape it onto the driver's side windshield before evacuating; along the way, emergency personnel directing traffic would be able to instantly point them in the right direction.†

Nationally, FEMA estimated that the efforts, given three or four days' warning, would save about 80 to 85 percent of the U.S. population—the other 15 to 20 percent, planners estimated, would die simply because they refused to evacuate or because they belonged to groups that couldn't evacuate, including "the sick, the disabled and handicapped, people with mental problems, alcoholics, drug addicts, and some of the elderly lonely."

However impractical in reality, the 152-page plan for evacuating New

---

* FEMA actually had to pay for the ads, since the telephone companies weren't excited about including the public service; even in Washington, D.C., the local C&P Telephone Company refused to include the evacuation information for free.

† According to the phone book ads, for example, Plattsburgh residents south of the Saranac River were to evacuate using Highway 22, Interstate 87, or State Route 374 west to the town of Dannemora and seek out St. Joseph's Grade School, where civil defense officials would be waiting to assign evacuees space in one of the predesignated shelters.

York, drawn up in September 1978, was indeed carefully considered and included a primary plan and eleven alternate plans. Each of the five boroughs would rely on different transit modes to evacuate over the course of precisely 3.3 days to "host areas" within 400 miles of the Big Apple. The per-hour capacity of each road out of New York had been carefully calculated; pre-positioned bulldozers would help ensure travel moved smoothly by quickly removing disabled automobiles. More than 4.8 million "carless" New Yorkers would be evacuated by subway, train, ferry, barge, cruise ships, and civilian and commercial aircraft, as well as by more than 20,000 bus trips. More than 75,000 Manhattan residents would travel up the Hudson to Saratoga using three round-trips of five requisitioned Staten Island ferries, part of the 300,000 evacuated by water. Another 300,000 Manhattan residents would travel by subway to Hoboken and be loaded into boxcars for the trip to upstate New York near Syracuse; 614,000 people in the Bronx would be evacuated up Interstate 87 to Ulster County near Poughkeepsie; and among the 405,360 people evacuated by air, 43,200 residents of Queens would be shuttled by air from LaGuardia to the small town of Bradford in central Pennsylvania.

As complicated as New York's plan was, the evacuation plan for the nation's capital seemed even more unlikely to work. Hal Silvers, the head of civil defense planning for Maryland's Prince George's County, which borders D.C., referred pointedly to CRP by his own name, the "Crisis Relocation Allocation Program," meant to evoke a familiar but less complimentary acronym. Each of D.C.'s eight wards would be sent along a different evacuation route, designated Routes A through H, to its own "host area" and there would be different "host areas" for those evacuating by private transportation or by city-organized buses. Residents with even-numbered license plates were to leave immediately upon an evacuation alarm, while those with an odd-numbered plate were to wait six hours before departure to help ease road congestion.

Under the final CRP developed for D.C., the most affluent residents of the city—who were believed to own the most private vehicles—in Ward 3 would travel the furthest, driving along "Route C" 270 miles out of the city, over seven mountains, to Elkins, West Virginia. Altogether, local planners expected that it would take 10 million gallons of gasoline to run a full evacuation of D.C., so the capital's gas stations would be closed in the early stages of an evacuation and their storage tanks emptied into tanker trucks dispatched to designated refueling points along evacuation routes. Fuel, though, appeared the least of the transportation puzzles: At multiple intersections across northern Virginia, the evacuation routes for various wards crossed each other perpendicularly on two-lane roads, and in Merrifield, Virginia, fifteen miles outside D.C., the evacuation routes for four different D.C. wards overlapped for a thousand feet on U.S. Route 50. How did police expect to smooth the merging and then separation of so many vehicles in a panicked situation?

As the urban evacuations proceeded, construction crews in the "host areas," some of them made up of paroled prisoners, would be hard at work transforming the pre-identified Project 908 buildings into fallout shelters—boarding up windows as dump trucks delivered load after load of dirt and bulldozers and front-end loaders piled the dirt up against the walls and work crews spread dirt over building roofs by hand. Once the evacuees arrived in their new "host areas," they would be "registered" at local collection points like elementary schools. (In theory, evacuees would have used the time traveling en route to the collection point to fill out in duplicate forms listing vital information like name, age, Social Security number, occupation, and other useful data.*) After registering, the evacuees would be directed to their housing in the various government, community, or commercial buildings identified by the FBI in Project 908. Each host area was expected to absorb five times its normal peacetime population and local families would be encouraged to take in relocated strangers. Designated local leaders from each evacuated area, like city councilors or county commissioners, would be dispatched to the new "host areas" to form provisional joint governments.

In an emergency, the U.S. government intended to pay for all the food and supplies necessary to shelter and feed evacuees across the country—all told about $2 billion a day—although the money might not be available immediately, so private businesses would be expected to "maintain complete

---

* Pets were to be left behind—although FEMA optimistically recommended leaving plenty of food and water for them to drink in the hopes that they could be reunited with their owners after an attack.

and accurate records to justify claims submitted after the Crisis Relocation emergency." Stores, medical facilities, laundries, and other vital necessities would be kept open in "host areas" for a minimum of sixteen hours a day to ease access, and most would operate twenty-four hours a day—after all, there wouldn't be any shortage of available labor. Evacuees in the shelters would sleep alternating head-to-toe, "the best position for sleep, in that it decreases the spread of respiratory ailments," explained FEMA's comprehensive 1981 guide, *How to Manage Congregate Lodging Facilities and Fallout Shelters*. Family groups would be placed in the middle of each shelter, with unmarried men and women separated on either side to encourage "high social standards, particularly for sexual behavior."

On paper everything looked neat and tidy: Middlebury College in Vermont, for instance, would be requisitioned to help house some 32,000 residents of Hamden, Connecticut—1,549 would live in the Egbert Starr Library, 343 would move into the Wright Theatre, 1,237 into the Memorial Field House, and 192 into the Mead Memorial Chapel, and so forth. But in reality the rural infrastructure would be deeply strained by the influx of five times the normal population. Across the state line in New Hampshire, locals in Barrington—where a portion of the 8,900 residents of Monroe, Connecticut, would flock in an emergency—looked at the pitched roof of their Congregational church, some forty feet off the ground, and wondered exactly how Washington bureaucrats expected them to bury the church under a foot of dirt. "Damned foolishness," one local said. And, again, what happened if the nuclear attack came during the roughly one third of the year when the ground was frozen solid? You couldn't exactly dig up the dirt then.

That dubiousness, though, came from officials who actually knew and understood the government's plans—many civilians had no idea the role their towns or facilities were meant to play in a crisis. Charles Hoffman, the principal of Fort Defiance High School in Augusta, Virginia, about 150 miles from D.C., had no idea his school was the end of "Route D," the designated reception center for 100,000 residents of D.C.'s Ward 4. "It wouldn't surprise me that we would be, located as close as we are to [Interstate] 81," he said in 1982, when a visitor informed him of his school's nuclear attack plans. Was he aware of any preparations in Augusta for 100,000 evacuees? Nope, he said, "I'm not aware of any."

Beyond the physical infrastructure, a major concern in the national evacuation plans was precisely how smoothly those "host areas" would absorb their new residents. Racial tensions were to be anticipated—particularly in areas that would see large influxes of minority evacuees, like Ulster County, New York, which would see nearly half a million minority Bronx residents descend on its nearly entirely white town. These tense questions around integration were a particular concern of Reagan's first appointee to head FEMA, Louis Giuffrida, who as a colonel in 1970 had written his Army War College thesis on how the government could establish internment camps for "Black Nationalists" in the event that revolutionaries tried to seize control of America's inner cities. The agency Giuffrida inherited in 1981 had spent its recent years studying similar issues about the problems of evacuees upsetting the racial balance of their "host areas." "There could be a lot of opposition because a lot of the white people [in Virginia] don't want a lot of the black people," D.C.'s head of emergency planning, John Colbert, explained. The head of FEMA's predecessor agency, the DCPA, in 1978 had been asked by a reporter: "How are you going to keep those people there from shooting the people coming in?"

"That's tough," Bardyl Tirana said, simply.

"Since you've studied the problem, you no doubt have an answer to this?"

"Don't assume that," Tirana replied.

A FEMA study, done just as the Reagan administration was taking office, laid out myriad problems with evacuating "Blacks, Hispanics, and Orientals" during a national emergency. The fifty-seven-page report, *Special Problems of Blacks and Other Minorities in Large-Scale Population Relocation*, found that emergency management officials thought minority populations would require "more attention (education) to achieve comparable levels of understanding and recognition of the reality and necessity of crisis relocation." Beyond that, they were likely to have a "lower rate of public compliance," less access to both private transportation and private shelters, and have "a greater problem in being accepted in crisis relocation host areas."

As the Pentagon shifted toward thinking about fighting a prolonged nuclear war, it needed a wider set of command tools available. The nation's existing command and control systems were, SAC Commander Richard Ellis concluded in 1981, "essentially soft, fragile peacetime systems, conceived in the late 1950s and put into operation in the 1960s." Most, he said, were "highly vulnerable to attack and destruction." The nation needed much more robust systems, ones that could ensure COG during a much longer war than the "spasm" nuclear exchange of the Eisenhower days. "That was the requirement: six months," recalled Bruce Blair, a SAC officer who worked on the plans during the Reagan administration. "And at the end we had to have a cohesive chain of command, with control over our remaining nuclear forces, that would give us leverage over the Soviets." With the $18 billion the Reagan administration spent boosting command and control systems, the hope was that the U.S. command system could weather a moderate attack of 50 to 150 nuclear warheads and still function.

The Navy's TACAMO planes were upgraded from EC-130s to 707 E-6s, as the presidential NEACP planes were outfitted with new communications that converted them from E-4As to E-4Bs. Across the country, redundancies were piled upon redundancies. On August 25, 1981, NORAD established the Rapid Emergency Relocation Team (RAPIER), to provide continuity and an emergency relocation cadre for its own operations in Colorado. It also established its first airborne command post, an E-3A Sentry AWACS plane based at Tinker Air Force Base in Oklahoma. Nearby Peterson Air Force Base was designated as the primary fallback facility for NORAD should something go wrong at the mountain, and it also had a standby convoy of vehicles known as Mobile Consolidated Command Center (MCCC). If everything in Colorado was destroyed and the Sentry AWACS plane silenced, NORAD's command could be picked up by Canada's bunker at North Bay, Ontario, which served as the final fallback for the North American Aerospace Defense Command.

NEACP also moved in Reagan's first term from Andrews to Grissom Air Force Base in Indiana—still a quick flight from Washington but it wouldn't be able to be caught on the ground by a surprise submarine-launched missile attack on the capital. But that was only a stopgap measure. As Defense Secretary Weinberger said, "We remain concerned, however, about the ability of airborne command posts to operate beyond the first few days of a nuclear war."

SAC created the Headquarters Emergency Relocation Team (HERT),

based at the Cornhusker Army Ammunition Plant about 150 miles west of
Omaha, a convoy of EMP-hardened command posts mounted on tractor-
trailers that would have deployed out into the vast open American West
during an attack. Later renamed the Enduring Battle Management Support Center and staffed by the 55th Mobile Command and Control Squadron, the unit's patch hinted at its Doomsday task: A Grim Reaper sneaking
through the night carrying a lightning bolt. The HERTs, loaded with secure
communications, were part of a massive investment in mobile command centers, including an $85 million project, code-named ISLAND SUN, under which
the Pentagon planned to flood the nation's interstates with convoys of lead-
lined tractor-trailers, staffed by officials like one-star generals, who would be
able to pick up the scattered remains of the U.S. military. The tractor-trailer
plan, though, got off to a bad start when the first two prototypes—built at
exorbitant cost and under a cloak of secrecy—both flunked their road tests
in 1984: The weight of one overweight truck buckled the roadway and the
truck got stuck in rural Virginia; the other truck, too tall for the roadway, got
trapped under an overpass.

  FEMA created its own mobile command center effort, known as Mobile Emergency Response Support (MERS) units—eventually building
some 300 special vehicles and stationing them across the country at regional
command centers. The convoys, the thinking went, would be able to range
across the nation, one step ahead of any Soviet attacks, hiding in the vast
portions of the country that would be unscathed by nuclear attack. The convoys were meant to be entirely self-sufficient for a month, carrying massive
generators and specially equipped fuel tankers that could draw diesel fuel
from abandoned gas stations across the country. Meanwhile, a network of as
many as 500 radio towers known as GWEN, the Ground Wave Emergency
Network, located away from major cities would ensure that the nuclear
forces could still communicate with each other.

  In Alaska, the push for greater command survivability revived one of
SAC's earliest 1960s-era plans for an alternate command post (ALCOP), a
rail-mounted facility. Train-mounted military headquarters were relatively
common in Europe, where the continent has an extensive rail network, and
the Alaska command thought it worth experimenting with. The Alaska
command train included two old passenger cars converted into a command

car and a rolling dormitory, old boxcars retrofitted with water and fuel tanks and mobile generators, as well as a fifth tank car that could be added for extra fuel. To help it blend in while traveling, the ALCOP locomotive was painted with Alaska Railroad's standard yellow-and-blue motif, as were all the passenger cars, but it wouldn't have taken a particularly close observation to realize that the train had a special purpose: All the passenger windows had been covered with metal plates and the cars sprouted forests of various antennae. In a deployment, the train and the sixty-one personnel who made up the alternate command element (ACE) could operate anywhere along the railroad's tracks, although the primary plan was in an emergency to park the train in the midst of one of the track's many tunnels, creating an instant secure underground command post. Understanding their unique environment and the climate's extreme conditions, the train's staff received special training in small arms, woodland survival, and Alaskan geography.

Much of the administration's COG planning fell to a Marine officer on the National Security Council named Oliver North. Early in his White House tenure, North had helped draft in 1982 Reagan's guiding document, National Security Decision Directive 55, titled "Enduring National Leadership," and coordinated with FEMA's National Preparedness Directorate and two new agencies focused on COG planning, known by their innocuous cover names, the National Program Office and the Defense Mobilization Systems Planning Activity, which was based close to the Pentagon at 400 Army-Navy Road in Arlington, Virginia. Together, they represented a vast bureaucracy hidden in plain sight: For every dollar that FEMA spent preparing for natural disasters, the agency's public purpose, it spent $12 preparing for nuclear war and running COG programs. Nearly a third of FEMA's entire workforce existed in the secret black budget, known to only twenty members of Congress and completely unknown to the general public.

The innocuous-sounding National Program Office, run by Vice President George H. W. Bush, gobbled up billions of dollars of its own in classified funds planning for Doomsday. Building off the Eisenhower-era plans to appoint private sector czars to oversee post-disaster response, the National Program Office established a top secret list of former public officials who would be called upon in the event key officeholders were killed.

The COG plan, known as TREETOP, outlined the military aides, war plans, and procedures that would make up the secret program that the National Program Office called the Presidential Successor Support System, or PS3 for short.

The five preselected PS3 teams each consisted of veteran officials who could fill almost every top job in government. Under PS3, which traced its roots to the Carter administration and had no clear constitutional grounding, respected former officials like Howard H. Baker Jr., the onetime Senate Republican leader, former CIA director Richard Helms, former United Nations ambassador Jeane J. Kirkpatrick, and former cabinet secretary James Schlesinger were all readied to return to government following a decapitation attack. In an emergency, the preassigned PS3 teams of retired officials and government managers would each deploy to different bunkers, command posts, and COG facilities to be ready in case a presidential successor needed them. Picked without regard to normal government operations or peacetime organizational charts, the PS3 teams were rooted in the assumption that following a massive attack the presidential successor would likely be a minor cabinet official inexperienced in the complexity of national defense, international affairs, or government recovery operations. Such a figurehead president would need to rely heavily—and quickly—upon more experienced staff to reconstitute a government, defend the nation, and begin to rebuild. Thus, when someone like the commerce secretary or agriculture secretary arrived at an emergency site, he or she would find a White House staff-in-waiting, including an experienced leader like Donald Rumsfeld or Dick Cheney who would serve as a chief of staff designee.

As the classified memo for selecting the five "surrogate" directors of the CIA who would join the PS3 teams explained, "The criteria applicable to ... members of Presidential Successor Support Teams may not be those applied to the selection of peacetime managers of the CIA and the intelligence community. For example, the chain-of-command should probably be ignored in some cases." Instead, it was critical that such successors be chosen for their judgment. "He must be an innovator and improviser," the five-page memo declared. It also explained that given the vagaries of dispersal and evacuation "any of the designated DCI successors could emerge as the intelligence advisor to the President or to a successor President," thus it was critical "his person and personality must be such that he can generate the

NINE NAUGHT EIGHT 315

confidence of the President or any successor." The PS3 teams could call up various government resources to quickly access the necessary COG tools; the Pentagon's general counsel, for instance, ran a special database—the DOD Emergency Authorities Retrieval and Analysis System (DEARAS)—that collected all of its emergency legal authorities.

CNN, which first broke word of the scheme in the 1990s, reported that planners believed "to protect the United States' unique Constitutional form of government from the ultimate threat it was necessary to have this alternate system of succession." As one National Program Office employee told the news channel, "We have to go on the premise that we have enough alternates in enough locations to do the job." William Arkin, a nuclear weapons scholar who had become one of the nation's leading experts on COG programs, concurred that the Constitution simply didn't allow for the flexibility necessary to execute and survive a nuclear war—particularly a surprise attack. "The tension cannot be resolved," he told CNN. "As long as we have nuclear weapons, we're going to have to fudge on the Constitution."

But that left the big question: Given the secrecy around the program, if someone from PS3 emerged from a nuclear disaster as the "president," who among the American public or world leaders overseas would respect that leader? As Duke University law professor William Van Alstyne explained, "If no one knows in advance what the line of succession is meant to be, then almost by hypothesis no one will have any reason to believe that those who claim to be exercising that authority in fact possess it."

Indeed, after realizing that the systems for authenticating a successor were lacking, the Reagan administration began to institute elaborate mechanisms with FEMA and the Pentagon to ensure a successor's legitimacy. The plan called for special coded communications that could prove a successor's identity and establish the highest-ranking official still alive within the government. "There's an elaborate system for the people in this network, first of all, to verify each other's identity," NSC aide Richard Clarke explains. "That person on the other end has a certain password and information that they have to pass for us to believe that they're who they say they are." Then, to establish that the remote PS3 teams were, in fact, controlling the government, the plan called for military demonstrations that proved a new president's authority to foes and allies. "Sometimes, you order U.S.

forces to do something," Clarke says. "You say to the adversary in advance, 'I'm going to order our forces to do X. You will observe that. That's how you know that I'm in charge of U.S. forces.'" One option was to have the new "president" order an American submarine up from the depths to the surface of the ocean as a clear sign that the successor was in full control of U.S. military forces. The Soviet Union or U.S. allies could then independently verify, either by satellite surveillance or firsthand visual confirmation, that such an action followed.*

The supposed secrecy around the nation's COG planning in the 1980s didn't prevent the programs from emerging as public scandals. FEMA chief Louis Giuffrida—who preferred to be called by his National Guard rank, general—resigned in July 1985, just as a congressional report accused him of widespread mismanagement and misappropriation of government resources, including having work done on a government chapel for a friend's wedding. His spending priorities had raised eyebrows almost from the beginning: In 1980, during the final months of the Carter administration, emergency team personnel from each agency had been given "Federal Employee Emergency Identification Cards," which included their name, photo, blood type, and a message asking all authorities to provide "full assistance and unrestricted movement" in a crisis. Just a year after the new ID cards had been distributed, though, Giuffrida decided he wanted a new agency logo, redesigning it to add an eagle and a Latin motto that translated as "Service in Peace and War." At great expense, he distributed new ID cards to all the relevant emergency personnel.†

---

* That same standard—control of the military—is one of the tests the U.S. government uses in deciding whether to deal with a foreign leader after a coup d'état.

† As a precaution against imposters, each department or agency also had a permanent staffer assigned to Mount Weather whose job it was to personally know each of the responding department or agency officials—and would double-check at Mount Weather's gates during an emergency that the person possessing the ID for John Smith was, in fact, John Smith. Whether the passes would get anyone close to Mount Weather was a separate question: Ed Cain, the COG coordinator for the National Communications System, the special network backbone built to keep the National Command Authorities in communication during a nuclear strike, once showed his pass to a Virginia state trooper—who replied that he'd never seen such a pass before. "His reply was not too reassuring," Cain said.

Such waste seemed indicative of a larger problem—the fact that COG operations ran so secretly and without normal oversight allowed the program to squander money. Many aspects of the COG communications systems continued to falter, with seemingly few consequences to those in charge. According to subsequent reports, one major readiness exercise that included House Speaker Tip O'Neill was rigged to ensure the "communications" got through and relied upon a nearby pay phone as an insurance measure. "I do believe Congress was misled by senior-level people in the program," said Tom Golden, a National Program Office staffer during the Reagan administration. Golden argued that the problems with the communications system went deep. "They can get away with things that they would not be able to get away with in any other situation," he recalled years later. "There were contract irregularities. Contracts had been awarded illegally." The communications efforts, much of which were run out of Fort Huachuca in Arizona, were a regular source of problems through the 1980s. Golden eventually went to House Armed Services Committee chair Les Aspin as a whistle-blower, a move that resulted in multiple Army investigations—including one that uncovered a multimillion-dollar contract that had been overseen by an Army general and given to the company that employed his son—and, later, the cancellation of multiple contracts. Golden's voice was hardly the only one: Fred Westerman, another consultant working with the National Program Office to provide security at some of its warehouses scattered around the country, was horrified by the shoddy security at the facilities he was supposed to help protect. When he complained, the Army ended his contract, and he sued the military and FEMA.

Meanwhile, Oliver North's role in the nation's secret COG planning spilled out into the open over 1986 and 1987 as the Iran-contra scandal engulfed the Reagan administration. During the hearings, he was questioned by Congress about REX 84, a secret 1984 exercise that practiced declaring a national emergency, martial law, and detaining thousands of aliens and so-called dissidents. As media reports leaked out about North's work, the planning seemed to indicate that President Reagan was prepared to take drastic action to squash domestic protests in a wide-ranging set of circumstances. Congressman Jack Brooks grilled North, asking, "Colonel

North, in your work at the N.S.C. were you not assigned, at one time, to work on plans for the Continuity of Government in the event of a major disaster?"

North's counsel, Brendan Sullivan, interrupted to stop the line of questioning. Senator Daniel Inouye concurred, saying, "I believe that question touches upon a highly sensitive and classified area so may I request that you not touch upon that?"

Brooks replied, "I was particularly concerned, Mr. Chairman, because I read in Miami papers, and several others, that there had been a plan developed, by that same agency, a contingency plan in the event of emergency, that would suspend the American Constitution. And I was deeply concerned about it and wondered if that was an area in which he had worked? I believe that it was and I wanted to get his confirmation."

Inouye cut it short: "May I most respectfully request that that matter not be touched upon at this stage. If we wish to get into this, I'm certain arrangements can be made for an executive session." That oblique mention was one of the few times that the $8 billion COG program was mentioned publicly during the entire Reagan administration.

In what turned out to be the final years of the Cold War, the military's push for new command tools gave rise to one of the era's most ambitious building projects: Project ELF, a special extremely low frequency radio transmitter that could penetrate the atmospheric disruptions of an EMP and reach the nation's submarines. Whereas commercial radio had wavelengths of a few dozen feet, the ELF end of the spectrum had wavelengths of thousands of miles—strong enough to penetrate deep into the oceans, but which meant it would require a massive transmitter.

The Navy had first begun planning in the 1960s for what it then called Project SANGUINE, a 22,500-square-mile antenna network that would encompass nearly 40 percent of the state of Wisconsin and stretch into Michigan, relying on the unique bedrock the Laurentian Shield to amplify and broadcast one-way launch commands to missile submarines around the world. The original iteration of Project SANGUINE called for 6,000 miles of cables, buried five feet under the ground across Wisconsin and Michigan's Upper Peninsula, connecting 100 hardened transmitters spread across an area the size of Belgium and the Netherlands combined. Together, the system, estimated to cost $1 billion, was sufficiently powerful, large, and scattered that it could not be jammed or destroyed. To prove the concept, the Navy started with a 1962 test in Wisconsin, turning off a forty-three-mile length of high-voltage power lines overnight and converting it into a radio antenna that could broadcast nearly 1,000 miles away to California. Then the Navy built a full test facility, an antenna that stretched over a hundred miles from Lookout Shoals, North Carolina, to Algoma, West Virginia. The ELF transmitter was used in 1963 successfully to broadcast messages to a submerged submarine more than 2,500 miles away.

With billions flooding into the nation's command systems, a scaled-back version of the project, now rechristened Project ELF, finally made it off the ground in the 1980s: Two transmitting sites were built, one at Clam Lake, Wisconsin, with twenty-eight miles of antenna, and another 148 miles away in Republic, Michigan, with its own fifty-six miles of antenna.* When both were operating, their signals could reach a deeply submerged submarine almost anywhere in the world. Thirty-two years after initial work began at the height of Sputnik fears, Project ELF became fully operational in 1989, just as Reagan's vice president, George H. W. Bush, became president, the Berlin Wall fell, and the Cold War ended abruptly.

In quick succession, as the Soviet economy neared collapse, after the Wall's fall, Warsaw Pact forces began withdrawing across Eastern Europe. At the end of May in 1990, Mikhail Gorbachev arrived in Washington for high-level discussions with President Bush. It seemed a new world was at hand; when the two leaders boarded Marine One for the flight to Camp David, Bush looked around the cabin and realized the odd collection of passengers: Both his military aide and Gorbachev's had crowded aboard, as per procedure, meaning that Marine One now held the two leaders and the launch codes for their respective nuclear arsenals targeting each other. Gorbachev, looking down at the Maryland countryside, was fascinated with more quotidian matters: "How do you buy and sell a house?" he asked his

---

* Reagan's deputy assistant for national security, James "Bud" Nance, himself a retired rear admiral, wrote privately at the time, "This [project] has been going on for years and is one of the most political, emotional, stupid, and misunderstood things I have seen."

fellow commander-in-chief. "Who loans the money? Who owns the house?" For all intents and purposes, the Cold War was over.

As the 1980s came to an end, the rapid warming of superpower relations cascaded across the government's COG operations. Dick Cheney, as George H. W. Bush's defense secretary, helped shut down many of the Cold War COG systems and recommended in December 1989, just as the Soviet Union crumbled and the leaders left a summit in Malta, that the round-the-clock LOOKING GLASS flights be ended—a move that would save the Air Force around $20 million annually. A month later in Omaha, an EC-135 code-named CASEY ONE took off from Offutt Air Force Base at exactly 6:59 a.m. on July 24, 1990, the last in a string of LOOKING GLASS flights that stretched in an unbroken chain all the way back to February 3, 1961. On board that day as the Airborne Emergency Action Officer was the SAC commander-in-chief himself, General John T. Chain. When the plane landed at 2:28 p.m., none of the other eight EC-135 planes stood ready to take its place. The chain was broken, the airborne alerts over.

On September 27, President Bush addressed the nation, saying, "The prospect of a Soviet invasion into Western Europe, launched with little or no warning, is no longer a realistic threat." He ordered that SAC's bomber alert stand down and announced that all ICBMs scheduled to be deactivated under the proposed START treaty would immediately go off alert status. He terminated the development of next-generation ICBMs and canceled the replacement program for SAC's air-launched nuclear missiles. The next morning, on September 28, 1991, General George L. Butler assembled the staff at SAC in the facility's underground command and ordered SAC's bombers and refueling tankers to stand down from day-to-day alert status.

On October 21, 1991, President Bush sent a note to Brent Scowcroft: "Does Mil Aide need to carry that black case now every little place I go? Let's discuss." As Bush recalled, "With the Cold War over, I did not think it was necessary for the 'football' to go everywhere with me. However, Brent and others disagreed." (Ultimately, Scowcroft won.) But there was less need for other aspects of the COG system: Raven Rock ceased twenty-four-hour operations on December 1, 1991. At that point, its weekday staffing was about 350, and its weekend staffing only about eighty. On Christmas Day

1991, Gorbachev called President Bush at Camp David to say the nation's leadership transition was going smoothly and he planned to hand over the nuclear codes to the newly elected Boris Yeltsin. "I can assure you that everything is under strict control," Gorbachev said. "There will be no disconnection. You can have a very quiet Christmas evening."

At Raven Rock, the bunker was just completing a long-running renovation begun before the Berlin Wall fell that provided a new tunnel, underground reservoir, and new underground cooling towers, along with updated fire suppression systems. As the project came together, the country lost interest. "You'd feel like you're walking into a dinosaur," an enlisted man stationed at Raven Rock from 1988 to 1992 recalled. "It was a strange feeling. You're there for one purpose—just in case a nuclear war happens. But you get over the weird feeling pretty soon, and then you just feel you're not very needed anymore."

Greenbrier president and CEO Ted Kleisner knew a thing or two about asking too many questions around the resort, and so he was worried the moment journalist Ted Gup arrived at his office in the spring of 1992. Kleisner, a veteran of Hilton Hotels, had started working for the Greenbrier during the Carter administration as the director of operations in 1980, and immediately began assessing the resort's workforce, just as he did whenever he took over a new property. He was surprised to find that the resort carried on its payroll 120 skilled tradesmen—electricians, plumbers, HVAC maintenance staff, and so on—even though the Hilton resort he came from had been three times as large and operated with just a quarter of that staff. In his first weeks, he'd conducted several surprise visits to workshops and pulled workers' time sheets, but even after days of investigation, he couldn't account for nearly sixty of the supposed staff. When Kleisner had pushed several of the shop foremen, they mumbled something vague about "We operate differently here." Another referred him to the resort's president, saying, "Talk to Mr. Pitt about that."

Then an invoice for 10,000 gallons of diesel fuel crossed Kleisner's desk—a surprisingly large amount given that the hotel had only a single vehicle that ran on diesel, a garbage truck. A few days later, he found an invoice for a high-frequency antenna. The resort grouped operating expenses by project numbers, to ensure that each cost center was properly accounted, and both purchases Kleisner noted had been charged to a project known as "CM 232." Now Kleisner knew exactly what was going on: He'd read about this in a textbook years earlier while studying management—someone at the resort was robbing the Greenbrier's parent company, known as the CSX Corporation, by creating a phantom payroll of ghost employees to fund some sort of side business. He took his evidence directly to William Pitt, the resort president, who didn't seem quite as appreciative as he should about the detective work.

"Just be patient, Ted," he said. "There are things you can't be told yet."

Kleisner demanded answers and threatened to go to the company's internal audit department. Finally, Pitt said he needed a couple hours; later that day, Kleisner was told to be at the resort at 7 a.m. the following day, at which time everything would be explained. The next morning, he found Pitt in the lobby of the hotel standing with two other men—Fritz Bugas, whom Kleisner knew as the resort's television repair contractor, and another man who flashed a government ID. Kleisner went to study it more closely, but the mystery man said simply, "Look at it all you want. That's not who I am and that's not who I work for."

Kleisner was led to the warehouse that Forsythe Associates, the television contractor, kept on the grounds—which was filled with TVs and huge stacks of surplus office furniture. The government man, whose real name later turned out to be Jack Sterling and who went by the nickname "Stuff," closed each set of blinds in Bugas's office and Bugas turned on a radio loud. "It's the best we can do without a SCIF," Bugas said, using the term for secure rooms meant for discussing classified materials. Over the following hours, with the radio blaring annoyingly to hinder any eavesdroppers, Kleisner was walked through the history of the Continuity of Government program and the unique facility hidden in plain sight at the Greenbrier, as well as the unrecorded lease of unknown duration that the government could exercise in an emergency. "You may think your main goal is to take care of the resort guests, but we don't care about the customers of the hotel," Bugas said. "Our goal is to have this facility ready 24/7."

Each month, the Greenbrier totaled its CM 232 expenses and passed an invoice along to Forsythe Associates, including an agreed-upon percentage of the resort's executive, maintenance, and security payrolls. The government would reimburse the resort in full monthly, laundering the money through Richmond's SunTrust Bank, whose president, Rick Dean, also served on the CSX board and was cleared into the program. The secrecy created odd information incongruities: While Virginia's governor didn't rate a need-to-know, Virginia's tax commissioners over the years had all been cleared into the secret operation, then known as Project GREEK ISLAND, because Forsythe Associates appeared to be a private Virginia company. The tax commissioner understood, though, that the state tax officials should never look too closely at Forsythe—which suspiciously paid its employees exactly what they'd receive as "real" government workers, provided federal-style benefits, and even provided pensions to those Forsythe workers who retired.

Then Ted Gup showed up, started asking questions—he seemed to know all about the facility—and the jig was up. On Friday, May 29, the president of the Greenbrier summoned staff to his office and announced to their surprise that the West Virginia resort had been host for thirty-five years to a secret facility. A prearranged videotape was played for them, and a narrator explained, "Since the early 1950s the CSX Corporation and its predecessor organizations have been engaged in an extraordinary partnership with the Federal government to assist in the preservation of our constitutional framework. This association has been one of the nation's most closely guarded secrets. Your possession of this video tape means that an event has occurred which has resulted in the public disclosure of this confidential relationship."

That weekend, Ted Gup published a lengthy exposé about the ultimate congressional hideaway. *The Washington Post* wrote that it saw no need to keep the secret any longer: "In the end, we concluded this was a historically significant and interesting story that posed no grave danger to national security or human life."

As the extraordinary news broke in the *Post* and other newspapers, Bugas's Forsythe Associates team took chainsaws to their computer hard drives on the resort's loading dock. A government team arrived quietly and removed the bunker's small arsenal of weapons—the racks of M-16 rifles, M-60 machine guns, and a small contingent of grenade launchers that could have equipped a light infantry platoon. When Kleisner asked Bugas why they were taking away the weapons cache, Bugas explained that FEMA feared congressional officials would descend on the facility to inspect it. "You want to tell Pat Schroeder what we were going to do with these weapons?" Bugas asked, citing the fiery congresswoman.

On June 1, Speaker Tom Foley wrote to Defense Secretary Dick Cheney, "In light of recent press exposure of the emergency relocation facility in White Sulphur Springs, West Virginia, it is my intention to recommend ending support for the facility." That same day, Forsythe Associates dissolved. The Greenbrier bunker for the next three years, as it was wound down, unloaded, and dismantled, was run by the Defense Department. In the fall of 1995, the bunker opened for public tours.

The Greenbrier was hardly the only COG facility discarded in the 1990s. George H. W. Bush's successor, Bill Clinton, closed down many of the National Program Office projects.* On October 1, 1994, the government also shuttered the Defense Mobilization Systems Planning Activity—the cover agency for COG planning, which had burned through $8 billion in the previous eleven years as it prepped for a Doomsday that never came. "They are realizing these requirements are throwbacks to the Cold War," Bruce Blair, who had worked at SAC on war planning in the 1980s, told *The New York Times* that fall. "They are not relevant to today's world." NIGHTWATCH's alert status ended, and the NEACP alert planes returned to Offutt to be rechristened the National Airborne Operations Center (NAOC, pronounced "NI—YOCK") as their mission broadened to include helping FEMA respond to national emergencies.

Other agencies mothballed their COG facilities entirely: NATO abandoned its German bunker, the Kindsbach Cave, returning the property to the family who owned the surrounding land, who opened it for private tours.

---

* Clinton's administration also learned that the plans might not have been as successful in wartime as the government had hoped: The Soviets had actually possessed the blueprints to understand exactly how the U.S. leadership hoped to survive nuclear war. In 1994, the FBI discovered its agent Robert Hanssen—a longtime spy for the Soviet Union—had on August 7, 1989, placed in a dead drop in Eakin Community Park in Fairfax, Virginia, five rolls of film that depicted a highly restricted classified analysis of government COG procedures, perhaps the biggest intelligence coup for the Soviet Union of his lengthy spying career. By the time Hanssen was arrested in 1994, most of those COG secrets were obsolete anyway.

The Interior Department turned its Harpers Ferry bomb shelter into a records warehouse. Amherst College purchased the former SAC bunker in Hadley, Massachusetts, known as "The Notch," and turned it into library storage. The Federal Reserve shelved its plans to relocate to Mount Pony, and by 1998 the billions stashed there had been taken away. The facility was eventually converted into an audiovisual facility for the Library of Congress, which, like Amherst, found that the underground bunker was well suited for the climate control necessary for archival preservation.

Just, though, as the nation forgot the tensions of the Cold War, two unlikely events a month apart refocused the Clinton administration's attention on continuity issues: In March 1995, a Doomsday cult used sarin gas to attack the Tokyo subway, and just a month later the Alfred P. Murrah Federal Building in Oklahoma City was bombed by antigovernment militants, the worst homegrown terror attack in U.S. history. The attack came without warning in an unexpected place, and inside the White House raised new concerns about decapitation of government departments. "That was a serious contingency that we didn't have covered," Richard Clarke says. "It's fine to have a bunker in the mountains, but there's no one there on a daily basis, so in a surprise attack, it's useless."

Continuity planning had long lived at the National Security Council with the official in charge of nuclear war planning—during the Clinton years, a senior director named Robert Bell. Yet, as the 1990s unfolded and the threat from Russia diminished on the global stage, the Clinton administration began to question fundamental tenets of COG planning—it seemed more likely in the post–Cold War era that COG planning should be the responsibility of counterterrorism officials than war strategists. During a tabletop exercise with cabinet secretaries and senior officials during the Clinton administration, COG planners presented a dire scenario: A yacht moored along D.C.'s Maine Avenue waterfront—barely a mile from the White House, the Capitol, and nearly all the cabinet department headquarters—was found to have a smuggled nuclear weapon on board. Among the questions the planners asked the participants: If everyone in the White House and department headquarters was killed right now, who would be left to reassemble the government? "That gripped them," Richard Clarke recalls. "That got them."

The National Security Council decided that it needed to have more routine COG measures that focused on devolving power outside the capital if needed. That changing philosophy was codified in the classified Presidential Decision Directive 67 (PDD 67), signed by President Clinton on October 21, 1998. Among other items, the directive—the full details of which are still classified—called for wider COOP planning within government and transferred responsibility for COG planning from the NSC directorate that oversaw nuclear war planning, run by Bob Bell, to the directorate that oversaw nuclear terrorism, run by Richard Clarke.

President Clinton's administration had also made great progress in one area that had bedeviled generations of his White House predecessors: He turned FEMA—the latest in the ever-shifting set of government acronyms like NSRB, FCDA, OCD, OCDM, OEP, and DCPA that had been responsible over decades for civil defense, homeland defense, and COG programs, and had long been considered a backwater, safe as a dumping ground for political patronage—into a high-functioning agency, capable of smartly and quickly responding to unfolding disasters. By the time George W. Bush took over the White House in 2001, FEMA had the highest public approval ratings it had ever had, and it was known primarily as a natural disaster response agency. Leo Bosner, a former FEMA union president, said, "[FEMA Director James Lee Witt] has focused us on the hazards we face— earthquakes, fires—rather than on what we should do when the bombs start flying."

But for those who knew where to look, FEMA's COG involvement plans continued to chug along, too, out of sight. The agency manual, version 1010.1, laid out the responsibilities for its two most generic and innocuous-sounding divisions—the Special Programs Division ran COG operations and the Program Coordination Division ran COOP operations. And, in tiny corners scattered across the government, aspects of the Cold War planning continued: Twice a day, at 7:35 a.m. Greenwich Mean Time and 7:35 p.m., the National Weather Service still produced fallout wind vectors across the United States, tracing and predicting how a nuclear attack would spread fallout in the upcoming twelve-, eighteen-, and twenty-four-hour windows.*

---

* The program would only wind down in 2010.

And, even as the rest of the nation forgot about it, at Mount Weather in the Blue Ridge Mountains, the FEMA staff kept their watch day in and day out. In June 2001, Ted Gup, the same journalist who had exposed the Greenbrier, wrote about HIGH POINT, calling it "one of the great artifacts of the Cold War." While that issue of *Time* magazine with Gup's article was on the newsstand, on June 28, 2001, CIA director George Tenet wrote a classified assessment for National Security Advisor Condoleezza Rice: "It is highly likely," he wrote, "that a significant al-Qaeda attack is in the near future, within several weeks."

Chapter 17

9/11

The irony of September 11, 2001, was that as dawn swept across the United States, the U.S. government was preparing to fight the Cold War all over again. At Cheyenne Mountain, NORAD's overnight shift had been carefully monitoring Russian bombers and fighters near the Arctic Circle as part of Operation NORTHERN DENIAL. After a long hiatus, Russia had resumed training flights of its Bear bombers, and as summer had turned to fall, the two nations regularly jockeyed in the airspace off Alaska. That September, the U.S. watched as Russian fighters, Tu-160 Blackjack and Tu-95 Bear bombers, practiced missile attacks and air-to-air refueling. Additionally, NORAD units nationwide had been planning to participate that day in VIGILANT GUARDIAN, a large-scale nuclear drill that traced its history back to earlier preparedness exercises like Operations ALERT, HIGH HEELS, and SPADE FORK. The day was scheduled to be busy and high-stakes, as the simulated exercise would escalate, as one officer explained, "from strained diplomacy to the outbreak of conventional warfare that headed inexorably toward nuclear conflict."

The first radio call came in to Northeast Air Defense Sector (NEADS) from the civilian FAA Traffic Management Unit in Boston, which announced at 8:37 a.m. ET, "Hi. Boston Center T.M.U., we have a problem here. We have a hijacked aircraft headed towards New York, and we need you guys to, we need someone to scramble some F-16s or something up there, help us out."

Understandably, there was a good deal of confusion throughout the opening moments of the 9/11 hijackings, as word of the crisis arrived at the headquarters for NEADS, an aluminum Cold War–era bunker at Griffiss Air Force Base in Rome, New York, which had once been a vital hub for the SAGE early warning system. General LeMay himself had christened the sector's SAGE system in 1958, a then state-of-the-art machine to ensure the warning time necessary to launch COG, but by 2001 the Rome base was a shadow of its Cold War self. The air base's half-buried alert facility—where B-52 crews passed the hours waiting for Armageddon playing billiards, poker, or arcade games like ASTEROIDS or BATTLEZONE—lay abandoned.

Air Force Technical Sergeant Jeremy Powell gave the government's first response to the alert: "Is this real-world or exercise?"

"No," the Boston air traffic controller responded, "this is not an exercise, not a test."

It was an exchange that would be repeated across the government as news spread.

At that same moment in Colorado—around 6:40 a.m. local time—NORAD's overnight shift was wrapping up their day and preparing to hand over the watch at 7 a.m. While normally a quiet shift, NORAD had had many of the facility's top staff working overnight to monitor Operation NORTHERN DENIAL, which paired up with the daytime maneuvers in Russia. On the surface, it seemed on that particular September morning NORAD was particularly well suited to coordinate a crisis response—but as the ensuing hours would show, NORAD and the U.S. government weren't prepared very well at all.

Following standard hijacking procedure, NEADS ordered into the air two F-15 alert fighters at Massachusetts's Otis Air Force Base. Within minutes, their afterburners roaring, the planes were airborne en route to New York City, even as reports began to trickle in of a crash at the World Trade Center. The alert fighters' established mission, as one document later explained, was simply to "be there for WWIII," but no one expected World War III anytime soon, so the program, which had once boasted more than sixty ready fighters nationwide, had withered to just fourteen by September 2001. The two F-15s in Massachusetts, along with another pair of alert F-16 fighters at Langley Air Force Base in Virginia, constituted all of the East Coast's air defenses that day.

NORAD's radars faced outward to track incoming threats, so throughout the day the air defense sectors struggled to tap into the FAA's radars. In fact, Cheyenne Mountain struggled to get news of any kind. "All the information we were getting at the time was really off the TV," recalled NORAD official Steven Armstrong. "We were out there in an information void just looking for anything that we could find."*

At 9:24 a.m., two Langley fighters scrambled as NEADS and NORAD chased reports of another hijacked aircraft headed toward Washington. No one told the Langley pilots why they were being scrambled skyward, and so, not realizing they were chasing civilian hijackings, they followed their normal procedures aimed at intercepting incoming threats—heading due east, out over the Atlantic Ocean, toward an airspace known as Whiskey 386 that was reserved for the military. "I reverted to the Russian threat. . . . I'm thinking cruise missile from the sea. You know you look down and see the Pentagon burning and I thought the bastards snuck one by us," one Langley pilot, Craig Borgstrom, told the 9/11 Commission later. "No one told us anything."

As they finally were rerouted toward the capital, one of the Langley pilots heard an urgent request from the Secret Service: "Protect the House." The Secret Service's major concern as the 9 a.m. hour unfolded was securing the White House and the man first in line for succession to the presidency.

When news of the first crash at the World Trade Center spread through the White House complex, Vice President Cheney was in his West Wing office,

---

* The government's stumbling attempts to adapt on the fly to the threat, as others would later put it, represented a failure of imagination—even though this scenario had been on the table before. Richard Clarke, the National Security Council director who helped coordinate COG activities during the Clinton administration, had run senior officials through a 1998 exercise meant to test the response to a terrorist-flown Learjet packed with explosives. And, in an exercise called POSITIVE FORCE in April 2000, the military tested scenarios meant to ensure "Continuity of Operations" if the Pentagon became unusable in the midst of a major war on the Korean Peninsula. As part of that exercise, though, Joint Staff officers rejected a scenario that involved terrorists crashing a plane into the Pentagon. It was "too unrealistic" and disconnected from the purpose of the exercise, officials decided.

dominated by a large mahogany desk and four upright flags that marked his life—the flags of the U.S., Wyoming, the defense secretary, and the vice president. "I was sitting there thinking about it," he recalled two months later. "It was a clear day, there was no weather problem—how in hell could a plane hit the World Trade Center?" Many officials across government shared that same thought as word of the crash trickled out; an attack wasn't the first thing to come to mind. Officials throughout the White House had their TVs on, tuned to the live broadcast of the burning North Tower, when at 9:03 a.m. United Airlines Flight 175 slammed into the South Tower. Smoke and fire billowed out. Even as it became clear that the incident was not an accident, officials weren't yet panicking; it was a New York attack, not a Washington one. Then air traffic controllers noticed a plane rocketing toward the capital and alerted the Secret Service: "We have unidentified, very fast-moving aircraft inbound toward your vicinity, eight miles west."

Around 9:30 a.m., Secret Service agent Jimmy Scott told Cheney he needed to evacuate. Without giving the vice president a moment to consider, Scott and other agents hustled him out. "He put his hand on my shoulder and grabbed me by the back of my belt and propelled me out the door," Cheney recalled. In a moment of reflex, and not wanting to be left without reading material wherever he was going, Cheney grabbed a copy of *The Economist* off his table on the way out. He later recounted that his feet barely touched the ground as the linebacker-like formation rushed through the building, covering the residence in just a minute or two, and delivering the vice president at 9:36 a.m. to the narrow passageway leading into the Presidential Emergency Operations Center.

The successor to the bunker once built for World War II and FDR, then enlarged and improved during Truman's 1948 renovation, the PEOC remained below the East Wing, but bore little resemblance to the spartan quarters where FDR would have hid. Off its main hallway, lined with bunk beds, there was a 600-square-foot operations and communications room, a small executive briefing room, and the main command center, dominated by a conference table that could sit about sixteen officials. On the underside of the table, drawers held white secure telephones. Light beige walls, dark wood moldings, and the thick sound-muffling blue carpeting lent a sense of government-issue majesty to the space, and bright fake skylights over the main conference table helped those inside forget they were hiding in an underground bunker. Under normal circumstances, personnel approaching the PEOC would arrive at its locked vault door, located on the White House's basement "level ZP," and use a telephone to ask the duty officer inside for permission to enter. Today the agents barreled the vice president right inside.

Cheney sat down on a hallway bench and called the president from one of the alcove's phones. The White House, he told Bush, had been targeted. "What I was immediately thinking about was sort of Continuity of Government," Cheney said later. "I urged him not to return until we could find out what the hell was going on."

Second Lady Lynne Cheney had been getting her hair done in northwest Washington when the agents on her detail became concerned. They raced her back to the White House, where she joined her husband around 10 a.m. They proceeded into the PEOC conference room, where the vice president took up a seat under a large presidential seal, facing the wall of TVs used for videoconferencing; a large grade-school-style map of the United States occupied the wall to his left. This would be his command post for the next twelve hours.

A handful of staff had accompanied the vice president to the bunker, and the Secret Service began contacting others Cheney wanted by his side— his counsel, David Addington, had evacuated from the compound and was walking across the bridge over the Potomac toward the Pentagon when his cell phone summoned him back to the PEOC. For many who assembled there, the bunker was an unfamiliar space—while Cheney knew it well from his earlier stints in government, most of the others, including President Bush himself, had never been inside. Aide Mary Matalin was so unfamiliar with the COG operations that she didn't know what the acronym PEOC stood for or where she'd been led within the White House. "All I knew is that I never could have found my way there and couldn't to this day," she said ten years later. Other high-ranking officials, like National Security Advisor Condoleezza Rice and Transportation Secretary Norm Mineta, a holdover from the Clinton administration, were brought down to the PEOC as well. Within minutes of their arrival, the team learned that the Pentagon had been hit. The day was quickly turning from a tragedy to a catastrophe.

Meanwhile, those officials outside the bunker, even high-ranking ones, had little sense of where to go, whom to call, or how to connect back to the government once they had been evacuated—it was the first of many failures of the COG procedures over the course of the day.

Outside, U.S. Park Police captain Sal Lauro pulled from his briefcase a ten-year-old plan for shutting down the area surrounding the White House—a plan originally given to him during the 1991 Persian Gulf War—and worked with the Secret Service and D.C. Metropolitan Police to secure the city blocks around the building. Inside the White House compound, the Secret Service dispatched additional countersnipers, boosted the number of Counter Assault Teams and Emergency Response Teams, and deployed countersurveillance "Prowler" teams around the complex. Worried about further attacks, the Secret Service also alerted the Army Corps of Engineers' structural collapse team in case it needed to dig the vice president out of the PEOC—a task that during the Cold War had belonged to the secret Outpost Mission team in Pennsylvania. The specialized unit, based at Fort Belvoir about twenty miles south of the city, is the military's only advanced urban rescue company, and includes bulldozers, dump trucks, and specially trained personnel. The Secret Service told it to be ready to deploy to the White House within thirty minutes.*

President Bush had been on his way to an education photo op, reading to elementary school students, as the first plane crashed into the World Trade Center. Yet even a simple photo op is never simple for the commander-in-chief—each stop requires sophisticated advance work by the president's staff, the Secret Service, the military, and the White House Communications Agency to ensure that wherever the president might be, he is connected to the White House and the National Command Authorities. One classroom had been converted into a communications suite for the traveling White House, complete with a Motorola SECTEL STU-III—a $2,000

---

* As the scale of the damage to the Pentagon became clear later in the day, the Secret Service released the engineers unit to deploy there instead—but insisted that it remain ready to arrive at the White House on two hours' notice in case a follow-up attack targeted the compound.

handset developed by the National Security Agency in the 1980s that served as the backbone of the nation's secure communications networks through four presidencies, from Ronald Reagan to George W. Bush.

In the classroom, arranged on a child's desk and tested in advance by WHCA staff, the black encyclopedia-sized phone contained a unique plastic KSD-64 Crypto Ignition Key that, when inserted into the phone and connected to other STU-III devices, activated special algorithms—code-named BATON and FIREFLY—to ensure the president could discuss top secret information without fear of eavesdropping. Despite having such sophisticated communications, President Bush learned little more than viewers of CNN as he talked to Condoleezza Rice.

Thinking the incident in New York involved only a small plane, perhaps even an accident, Bush proceeded with his schedule, meeting the principal and students, and was reading to a class when the second plane crashed into the World Trade Center. White House chief of staff Andy Card whispered into the president's ear that the nation was under attack. After Bush finished reading the story—to avoid creating panic, he later said—the presidential party returned to the communications classroom to watch the news and converse. He made a brief statement to the press and then the motorcade hurriedly departed for the airport, arriving at Air Force One after a high-speed race up Florida Route 41 just as the world learned that the Pentagon had been hit.

Air Force One took off at 9:54 a.m., with no specific destination in mind, literally rocketing into the sky at a seemingly impossible steep pitch as it activated for the first and only time in its history a classified system the presidential plane possessed to speed emergency launches. "There are only two 747s in the world that can take off like that—and they're both called Air Force One," a flight steward said, leaning over to one of the passengers. On the ground, the local Sarasota police who had been on escort duty watched in awe. "I've never seen a plane take off like that," Officer Kevin Dowd recalled. "From where we were looking at it, it looked like it was going almost straight up."

"We headed up rapidly, zigzagging in a random pattern towards 45,000 feet," recalled Ari Fleischer, the White House press secretary.

"We were following a Cold War doctrine evasion procedure that was to have been used in the event of a decapitation strike against the country's leadership. Part of the drill for the military is to get the President high into the air if you can't get him into a secure bunker."

Mike Morell, the CIA briefer accompanying the president, recalled the flight crew saying the plane was just going to fly around until they figured things out. "The President kept telling us he wanted to come back in very firm ways all day long and the head of the Secret Service, the Vice President and everyone involved kept telling him, 'No, the system doesn't work that way,'" the NSC's Richard Clarke recalled. On board, presidential aides announced that no one was to use a BlackBerry, cell phone, or other device—a terrorist might be tracking the plane's passengers. Ann Compton, a long-time ABC News reporter who was accompanying the president that day, recalled, "Ari Fleischer said, 'Off the record, President Bush is being evacuated.' And I said, 'Evacuated—you can't say that off the record—that is historic!'"

Meanwhile, the first stumbling COG response was generating even more confusion in an already confused capital. Following standard crisis protocol, an NEACP aircraft launched from Andrews at 9:43 a.m., using the call sign VENUS 77, and after considering flying to Offutt or to Ohio's Wright-Patterson Air Force Base, the pilots decided at 9:47 a.m. to just wait it out over Washington, eventually settling into a holding pattern over Richmond, Virginia. NEACP's unexpected presence in the skies, caught on camera by several news crews, added to the unfolding chaos around Washington. It's possible—perhaps even likely, given a study of the morning's timeline—that reports of the Doomsday plane over the capital are what triggered concerns to evacuate the White House and activate COG procedures. NEACP's takeoff just six minutes after American Airlines Flight 77 hit the Pentagon injected confusion about whether the hijacked plane approaching Washington was still in the air. At 9:52 a.m., CNN's John King, reporting from near the White House, told viewers, "About 10 minutes ago, there was a white jet circling overhead. Now, you generally don't see planes in the area over the White House. That is restricted air space. No reason to believe that this jet was there for any nefarious purposes, but the Secret Service was very concerned, pointing up at the jet in the sky. It is out of sight now, best we can tell."*

Inside the White House Situation Room, an aide asked Richard Clarke, the NSC director who had overseen COG plans since Clinton's PDD 67, whether to institute the protective measures. It was a simple question, but a potentially complicated answer: "How do I activate COG?" Clarke asked.

Clarke seemed like he would have known nearly everything there is to know about COG; he'd been involved in such programs for nearly two decades, since his days at the State Department under Ronald Reagan, and part of numerous elaborate exercises as both a participant and as a leader. During one 1980s exercise, he and a COG team had been evacuated from Andrews Air Force Base, flying for hours across the country before switching to another smaller plane. "And that plane flew off into a desert location, and when the doors opened on the smaller plane, we were in the middle of a desert," he recalled later. "Trucks eventually came and found us and drove us to a tent city. You know, this was in the early days of the program. A tent city in the middle of the desert—I had no idea where we were. I didn't know what state we were in. We spent a week there in tents, pretending that the United States government had been blown up."

Other exercises had tested the participants' stamina and decision making. "It's as though you were living in a play," Clarke explained. "You play-act. Everyone there play-acts that it's really happened. You can't go outside because of the radioactivity. You can't use the phones because they're not connected to anything." Once, during an exercise, the COG team's supply convoy was "intercepted," leaving them without food for a night; on another,

---

* The official silence around the NEACP flight fueled conspiracy theories in the years ahead, especially after the 9/11 Commission left the plane unmentioned in its final report. Commission investigator John Farmer later wrote that the omission of the plane was "regrettable," because it "led some to believe that the plane played a significant role in the events of that morning. It did not." The omission, in fact, Farmer says, was the government's typical knee-jerk secrecy regarding all aspects of COG: "The reason for the omission was that the administration deemed any information regarding the plane or its flight path highly confidential."

participants spent the day corresponding with a Soviet field marshal known as General Vladivostok, only to discover that the man was a rebel leader and not actually in charge of the Soviet Union's military forces. "The exercise is designed for two things—one, to train you with the kinds of questions that might arise but, two, to see if you come up with questions and problems that they haven't thought of," he explained. "These exercises both train the participants and they also train the system."

But now, in the heat of an actual crisis, there was a simple unanswerable question that stumped those in charge of the nation's COG apparatus. During exercises, the person playing the president always activated Continuity of Government. In his absence, though, who had that power? "There was no paperwork that said who could push the button," Clarke recalls. "The directives said that I was explicitly in charge of the procedures, but not explicitly that I could activate it."

His aide, though, thought Clarke possessed the authority, saying, "You tell me to do it."

After a moment's conversation, Clarke agreed: "Tell them I'm instituting COG. Go!"

In the following days, the White House counsel's office investigated the COG confusion and the lack of clarity, but ultimately, Clarke recalls, the matter proved only theoretical and didn't delay activation. No one down the chain of command questioned his order. As he recalls, "The system responded as if I had the authority." But for weeks the question nagged at Clarke: What if someone, somewhere had resisted his decision?

Who exactly activated COG—Cheney or Clarke—remains a matter of some historical dispute: The White House's official "tic-toc" of 9/11 instead has Vice President Cheney ordering at 9:55 a.m. "implementation of Continuity of Government and Continuity of Operations Procedures . . . designed to ensure Constitutional succession and uninterrupted government operations." Whether it was Cheney's order or Clarke's, the decision to trigger COG reverberated across a panicky capital. An Air Force officer with the White House Military Office broke into the crisis videoconference and reported that he had three orders from Deputy National Security Advisor Stephen Hadley: (1) implement Continuity of Government measures; (2) it needed fighter escorts for Air Force One; and (3) a combat air patrol of armed fighters over the capital. Unbeknownst to the White House, all three were already under way.

After Cheney, the two men next in line in presidential succession—Speaker of the House Dennis Hastert and the aging president pro tem of the Senate, West Virginia senator Robert C. Byrd—were both ordered to evacuate. Hastert, who had been watching the attacks unfold from his Capitol suite and already decided to shut down the House of Representatives, was driven to Andrews Air Force Base, about twelve miles outside Washington, which seemed as secure a facility as existed in driving distance of Capitol Hill. Throughout the morning, the speaker tried unsuccessfully to reach the vice president. As Hastert later recalled, "To use the secure phone, you have to push a button and turn a key. On that dreadful day I couldn't make the thing work. No matter what I did, I couldn't connect with the vice president. As the minutes passed, my frustrations grew." Between the communication challenges, unfolding crisis, and Hastert's evacuation, the men who were #2 and #3 in the nation's presidential succession didn't connect until after 11 a.m., two hours after the attacks started.

For his part, the eighty-three-year-old Senator Byrd hadn't been eager to leave the Capitol, either. "Something in me did not want to abandon that grand old structure," Byrd recalled later. He was finally convinced to evacuate by aides, but still didn't go far, standing outside talking to reporters until a large boom from the burning Pentagon encouraged aides to pull him away. Then, unsure of what to do, Byrd—fourth in line to the presidency—just went home.

The rest of Congress improvised its own version of COG. "We had no plan and we certainly had trained with no plan," said House Minority Leader Dick Gephardt. "We had no clue where to go," confirmed Senate Majority Leader Tom Daschle, who added that he couldn't even recall having practiced a fire drill at the Capitol before 9/11. Under normal evacuation procedures from the Capitol, senators were supposed to meet at the Hart Office Building, but now that seemed just as dangerous as the Capitol itself. Instead, members, staff, press, and the public mingled together on the streets and plazas across Capitol Hill; the Senate sergeant at arms, Al Lenhardt, feared that a suicide bomber might attack the crowd.

Finally, Daschle was hustled into an armored Lincoln Navigator and with its wheels spinning in haste, the SUV exited the Capitol grounds—with no destination in sight. "[My security detail] was instructing us to drive around until further orders could be established. We drove with no appreciation for where we were going." Eventually they ended up at the Capitol Police Headquarters, a few blocks from the Capitol, where much of the rest of the congressional leadership was also gathered.

As the morning unfolded, there was, Daschle recalled, "a great difference of opinion" over whether the legislative branch should return to the Capitol, evacuate to Andrews Air Force Base or Mount Weather, or even disperse to multiple locations to avoid concentrating in one location. As an interim solution, Daschle went to a consultant's office nearby and Trent Lott, the Republican Senate leader, went to Andrews Air Force Base.

By mid-morning, confusion over NEACP's presence, as well as one fighter misidentifying another fighter, led air traffic controllers and military commanders to think hijacked aircraft were still on their way toward Washington. While the final hijacked plane, United 93, crashed at 10:03 a.m., in Pennsylvania, the Secret Service continued to update the vice president on an aircraft approaching the capital until at least 10:20 a.m. The vice president's order to shoot down hijacked airliners was transmitted to the Pentagon's National Military Command Center beginning at 10:14 a.m., and it went out from NORAD to NEADS at 10:31 a.m.* By then, NEADS knew United 93 had crashed, so it never broadcast the order to the fighters over Washington. The official account that emerged in the following days—that the Air Force was in position and authorized to shoot down United 93 if it had neared Washington—was simply untrue, though it would take months and years to fully comprehend the morning's timeline.

Vice President Cheney finally connected with Defense Secretary

---

* As she listened to Cheney and Transportation Secretary Norm Mineta authorize the fighters to shoot down civilian airliners, Lynne Cheney thought of the 1962 novel *Fail-Safe*, which had come out in the midst of the Cuban Missile Crisis and featured a U.S. president who ordered the bombing of New York City to appease the Soviet Union after an accidental attack by SAC on Russia—a move that would prevent a wider war. "I remember thinking that with a sort of chill up my spine that this is the kind of thing you only read about in novels," she said later. "It was *Fail-Safe*."

Donald Rumsfeld at 10:39 a.m. "There's been at least three instances here where we've had reports of aircraft approaching Washington," Cheney said. "Pursuant to the president's instructions I gave authorization for them to be taken out."

Cheney heard only silence. "Hello?"

Finally Rumsfeld replied, "Yes, I understand. So we've got a couple aircraft up there that have those instructions at this present time?"

"That is correct," Cheney said, "and it's my understanding they've already taken a couple aircraft out."*

Such conversations were "remarkable, ultimately not as an artifact of history but as an indication of how little-understood the events of the morning remained years later, even—and perhaps especially—to national leaders," argued John Farmer, one of the 9/11 Commission staff. "They honestly believed that their actions in those critical moments made a difference; the records of the day say otherwise."

The ambiguity over the shoot-down order was indicative of the fog of war that engulfed the day's key players. Transportation Secretary Norm Mineta believed he ordered the grounding of the nation's airspace, but that order had originally been given by the FAA's national operations manager and was already under way by the time Mineta made his dramatic statement in the PEOC: "Screw pilot discretion, get the damn planes down." Without waiting for Mineta's order, NORAD and the FAA had activated the war plan known as SCATANA, Security Control of Air Traffic and Air Navigation Aids, which was meant to close the nation's skies, a plan that hadn't been used since the Sky Shield II war game in 1961.

Confusion escalated as threats and attacks seemed to continue even after the four hijacked planes had all crashed: reports came in of an explosion at the Lincoln Memorial; an explosion or fire on Capitol Hill; a plane crashed near the Kentucky-Ohio border. The rumor of a plane heading toward the president's Crawford ranch in Texas led an aide in the Situation Room to call the caretaker—the only occupant at the time—and warn him to "get as far away from there as you can." All four threats, though, turned out to

---

* It wasn't until early afternoon that those in the PEOC found out that the fighter jets hadn't shot down any of the crashed aircraft.

be false. Meanwhile, plans to evacuate personnel and activate COG were confused at points because the plane crash in Shanksville, Pennsylvania, was garbled in various communications as an attack on Camp David. Was it safe to send officials up into the Catoctin Mountains or were terrorists targeting locations there, too? Aides distributed gas masks, while others wrote down the names of those inside to e-mail outside the compound, in case the building was destroyed and rescuers needed to know whom to look for—dead or alive. NSC aide Roger Cressey asked about activating the Emergency Broadcast System to address the nation, but no one knew what they could or would say to calm America.

The videoconference Clarke ran that morning, along with Vice President Cheney, turned into the government's primary source of news—but it was hardly a smooth operation. Incorrect information proliferated, rumors calcified into fact, and agencies came and went from the videoconference intermittently. Some voices were missing entirely: The General Services Administration, which oversees the government's buildings nationwide, never made it onto the call.

When CNN reported that a car bomb exploded at the State Department, Clarke turned to the secure video teleconference to ask Deputy Secretary Richard Armitage: "Rich, has your building just been bombed?"

"Does it fucking look like I've been bombed, Dick?"

"Well, no, but your building covers about four blocks and you're behind a big vault door. And you need to activate your COG site."

"All right, goddamn it, I'll go look for myself," Armitage said, standing to leave and adding to no one in particular as he went off-camera, "Where the hell is our COG site?"

Around 10:45 a.m. ET, amid confusion over a possible incoming aircraft threat, the decision was made to button up Cheyenne Mountain. For the first time outside of an exercise, NORAD's massive twenty-five-ton blast doors swung shut. "Everybody that was in the mountain was going to stay for a while," recalled Canadian Brigadier General Jim Hunter. "Once I realized we had those blast doors closed I think they could have launched airliners at this mountain all day and we never would have felt the effects of it because we have 2,600 feet of granite above us."

Similarly to the COG activation, it wasn't entirely clear to those inside the National Military Command Center who could order the nation's forces to a higher state of alert. As Captain Charles Leidig would recall later, the Pentagon staff had a "historical discussion about how the move to DEFCON 3 went during previous crises, Cuba specifically [the Cuban Missile Crisis in 1962]." Then, after referencing "a book on the shelf," aides showed General Richard Myers, the acting Joint Chiefs chairman, that he had "approval authority to go to DEFCON 3." At 10:52 a.m., an Emergency Action Message went out to the military, taking them to their highest state of alert since the Arab-Israeli war in 1973. Myers told Rumsfeld, "It's a huge move, but it's appropriate."*

Off the National Mall, near the Air & Space Museum, FEMA's headquarters began to spin into action. The Central Locator System, which tracked the presidential successors, began to figure out precisely where each official was. Much like the Kennedy assassination had caught senior cabinet members on their way to Asia and the Reagan shooting had caught Vice President Bush out of town, the senior government was scattered around the globe on September 11, 2001. While President Bush was with the schoolchildren in Florida, Attorney General John Ashcroft was en route to Milwaukee; the chair of the Federal Reserve, Alan Greenspan, was in Europe; Treasury Secretary Paul O'Neill was in Japan; Secretary of State Colin Powell was in Peru; White House deputy chief of staff Joe Hagin was in New York, and the chairman of the Joint Chiefs, General Hugh Shelton, was on a flight to Europe.

Perhaps most inconveniently of all, FEMA director Joe Allbaugh was in Big Sky, Montana, attending the annual conference of the National

---

* Unable to find a master list of what military assets they could use, NORAD personnel opened phone lists and began to call Air Force and Air National Guard bases across the United States one by one, asking if they had any planes they could get airborne. "There were Guard units I'd never heard of calling asking how they could help. And we said, 'Yes, take off,'" recalls one NEADS technician. By the day's end, nearly 400 fighters, tankers, and airborne command posts would be keeping watch from the sky, flying out of sixty-nine different sites around the country. Not even the height of the Cuban Missile Crisis had seen such a huge, rapid military buildup.

Emergency Managers Association, along with the fifty state emergency managers. Allbaugh, who had been appointed to FEMA in February 2001 after helping to manage Bush's presidential campaign, had delivered his keynote address the day before about domestic preparedness and his own efforts to settle in at FEMA. At the time, the agency's role was in flux; unlike President Clinton, Bush had not elevated Allbaugh to cabinet rank and the House had approved cutting $389 million from FEMA's $1.6 billion budget only a few months earlier. At the conference that Tuesday, the emergency managers had been set to hear a session about the risks of animal-borne diseases, but right after breakfast pagers began going off around the conference. Officials trickled into the resort's bar to watch the TVs there; it was clear that they were far from where they needed to be. "I thought it was a movie clip," Allbaugh said later, of watching the second plane hit the Twin Towers. "I did a double-check, double-take like everyone else, blinked, and reality started sinking in."

Hotel staff brought in extra TVs and phones to help run an impromptu command center, as the 350 attendees scrambled to coordinate with their home states, dialing madly to figure out rides home, given that air traffic had been grounded. New York's emergency manager, Ed Jacoby, finally hitched a ride to Albany aboard a two-seat F-16 dispatched from Fargo, North Dakota; from Albany, working out of the underground emergency operations center first built by shelter-fiend Nelson Rockefeller, he then coordinated the work of the thousands of workers flocking to southern Manhattan. An Air Force KC-135 refueling tanker swooped in to pick up Allbaugh—whose six-foot-four-inch frame would, he conceded, have been an "odd fit" for a fighter jet—and his FEMA colleagues for the four-and-a-half-hour flight to D.C., delivering the FEMA director to the White House around 5:30 p.m. Some forty other emergency managers from D.C., Maryland, Virginia, Pennsylvania, and other northeastern states, after an agonizing seven-hour wait at the Bozeman airport, finally caught a ride home aboard an Air Force C-17 transport plane.

Allbaugh wouldn't arrive a moment too soon; FEMA was reeling from the scope of the disaster. Officials at FEMA's Region II office at 26 Federal Plaza in New York could see the second plane hit the World Trade Center from their windows. Unable to communicate with the state's emergency operations center, which was located in World Trade Center 7, staff dispatched Richard Ohlsen to walk down to the site, but initially no one could find a working radio or satellite phone for him to carry. "Communications almost instantly became a problem," Ohlsen later recalled. After the towers fell, Ohlsen headed to the command post at NYPD's One Police Plaza headquarters, but officers initially wouldn't let him in because they "did not recognize his FEMA identification as being official." Only a passing police inspector who recognized him allowed him to join the ongoing crisis response. The ID issue would bedevil countless FEMA officials in the days ahead—the agency's barebones IDs, which lacked many standard government markings like an authorizing signature or specific statute citations, were repeatedly barred by skeptical security personnel.

Once inside the NYPD's command post, Ohlsen's contributions were limited because he did not have with him the special GETS phone card that would have given his calls priority. His attempt to reach FEMA's headquarters fell victim to the same busy signals facing regular Americans that day. Amid the confusion, New York officials resisted FEMA's efforts to deploy pre-positioned supply caches and response teams—and Ohlsen found himself repeatedly unsure of what FEMA could even offer or authorize in the hours after the attack.*

The day almost ended with another tragedy: A specially chartered American Airlines flight, filled with FEMA personnel and government officials dispatched to help from Atlanta, arrived over New York with no clearance from air traffic controllers, and two F-16s from the Vermont Air National Guard came within moments of shooting it down as it approached Kennedy Airport. Even hours after the attacks were over, it was yet one more sign of just how overwhelmed responders were to the day's events.

* Even inside the agency, communication was lacking; many FEMA personnel in New York were confused to find that responsibility for the attack had been transferred to the agency's Region I headquarters in Maynard, Massachusetts, as part of its standard COOP measures. In New York, FEMA created a temporary headquarters at Camp Kilmer, a U.S. Army Reserve base near Edison, New Jersey, where the agency had long maintained space. Three of FEMA's five specialized Multi-Radio Vans were dispatched to New York, while the fourth headed first to the Pentagon. (The agency reserved the fifth as a backup.)

• • •

As the day went on, officials across government grappled with the unprec-edented catastrophe, thousands dead, thousands more missing or injured, four attacks in three states, all aimed at the financial and political heart of the United States; at one point in the PEOC, Condoleezza Rice, who had spent years practicing and running war games and tabletop exercises, said, "You know, it really is like our worst nightmare."

It might have indeed seemed nightmarish in the moment, but the govern-ment had long practiced for worse—even the VIGILANT GUARDIAN exercises scheduled for that day assumed a greater scale of devastation and more dis-ruption to the government's leadership structure. In some ways, 9/11 unfolded as a relatively straightforward test of the nation's COG preparedness—and many of the concerns and tensions that had long dogged COG operations played out just as planners had feared they would. In fact, perhaps the two senior officials in government who knew the most about the secret continu-ity efforts both refused to personally participate on 9/11—ordering subordi-nates and alternates to man the COG bunkers instead.

Perhaps no human being in U.S. history was better prepared to be in command on September 11 than Dick Cheney—he had not only served as White House chief of staff and defense secretary, but also practiced cri-sis management and COG operations during the Reagan administration as part of the Presidential Successor Support System. Cheney understood thoroughly COG's necessity—and also intuitively understood that he was expendable. As soon as he heard that other officials in the line of succes-sion beneath him had been evacuated and secured, he resisted the Secret Service's desire to evacuate him; he knew that the government could go on, legally, at least, without him if necessary. "It's important to emphasize it's not personal," Cheney explained later. "You don't think of it in personal terms. You've got a professional job to do."

Across the Potomac at the Pentagon, Defense Secretary Donald Rumsfeld—both the third cabinet member in the line of succession and a key player in the National Command Authorities—had also been involved in COG operations himself since the 1970s and also participated in the Reagan-era drills. He had been wrapping up a congressional breakfast in the Pentagon when an aide handed him a note warning of the New York attacks;

he then returned to his office on the building's outer E-Ring, where he was when American Airlines Flight 77 hit at 9:37 a.m. "The building shook and the tables jumped," he recalled. Initially, it seemed to many that a bomb had exploded; it would take time before the Pentagon leaders realized that another aircraft had targeted them.

Rather than follow protocols meant to preserve the National Command Authorities, Rumsfeld, accompanied by a few aides and bodyguards, began making his way to the crash site, where he helped carry a stretcher and evacuate injured personnel. Cheney later told a friend that this moment completely transformed Rumsfeld as a leader in the eyes of the military; it also left him out of the chain of command as the White House began frantically trying to figure out what was unfolding across the East Coast. Racing to Air Force One in his motorcade, President Bush grew increasingly frustrated that he couldn't find his secretary of defense in the aftermath of a national attack. Pentagon police officer Aubrey Davis, who was with Rumsfeld at the crash site, heard increasingly worried and confused requests on his radio: "Where's the secretary? Where's the secretary?" Yet the radio frequency was too busy for him to properly respond. "I kept saying, 'We've got him,' but the system was overloaded, everyone on the frequency was talking, everything jumbled, so I couldn't get through." It wasn't until around 10:30 a.m. that Rumsfeld finally arrived at the Pentagon's two-story National Military Command Center. By that point, Cheney and other officials at the White House believed that they had successfully ordered the shoot-down of civilian airliners.

During the Cold War, the September 11th attacks would have been referred to as a BOOB, a Bolt Out of the Blue attack, a surprise assault on an unexpected nation. At its peak, the finely tuned COG systems should have been able to respond to an attack with just fifteen or twenty minutes' warning—but the 9/11 attacks showed just how chaotic those minutes would have really been. The reality was that in the seventy-seven minutes between the first crash impact of American Airlines Flight 11 at the World Trade Center at 8:46 a.m. and the crash of United Airlines Flight 93 at 10:03 a.m. in Pennsylvania, the two key figures in the National Command Authorities were largely absent—President Bush, due to his travel and communication snafus, and Secretary Rumsfeld, first because of confusion and later his own decision to investigate the Pentagon crash site. At the end of those seventy-seven minutes, Rumsfeld remained in harm's way at the Pentagon, and while President Bush had been successfully hidden aboard Air Force One in the vast airspace of the southern United States, it came at the cost to his own ability to communicate with the nation below.

Only about an hour after the Pentagon crash did COG procedures begin to kick into gear at the Department of Defense. Paul D. Wolfowitz, the deputy defense secretary, also ended up at the NMCC after initially evacuating and then returning to the building. "We were in the National Military Command Center and there was this acrid smoke gradually seeping into the place," Wolfowitz recalled later. The smoke, though, "was not killing people," as Rumsfeld explained later, so while he briefly considered relocating to the White House PEOC, the headquarters of the Defense Intelligence Agency across the Potomac River at Fort Bolling, or heading to Raven Rock, he ultimately decided the Pentagon was the best place to fight the unfolding war. "We had things to do and business to conduct and problems to solve," he said later. The hour or so that it would take to evacuate and reestablish command somewhere else just wasn't worth the effort—his decision would have resonated with generations of leaders who had contemplated COG. The precise moment when evacuating would be most important also was precisely when it was most important to remain at the reins of government.* Since there'd be no evacuation at the Pentagon, a special team of Arlington County firefighters battled their way to the NMCC to fight the encroaching smoke and ensure those inside could breathe.

Although it ran contrary to the formal COG procedures that called for him to personally evacuate, Rumsfeld ultimately decided to dispatch Wolfowitz to Raven Rock to ensure continuity. As Wolfowitz recalled, "Rumsfeld simply refused to leave. He finally made me leave, which I was not happy

* Vice President Cheney gave essentially the same explanation for staying at the White House. As he said later, "I didn't want to leave the node that we'd established there, in terms of having all of this capability tied together by communications where we could, in fact, make decisions and act. And if I'd have left, gotten on a helicopter and launched out of the White House, all of that would have been broken down. And we had the presidential succession pretty well guaranteed, so I thought it was appropriate for me to stay in the White House."

about." ("That's life," Rumsfeld said later. "That's what deputies are for.") Wolfowitz was taken to the Pentagon's parade ground, where a helicopter picked him and other officials up for the flight to SITE R; Army Secretary Thomas White, who was second in the line of succession to the defense secretary, also flew to Raven Rock, as did the chief of the Army Reserve, Lieutenant General Thomas Plewes, who ended up being the ranking officer at the alternate command bunker for much of the day. Most officials—especially the highest-ranking ones—insisted on staying at the Pentagon, like Rumsfeld. Even though the plane had destroyed the Navy's Pentagon Command Center, the chief of naval operations, Admiral Vernon Clark, refused evacuation to Raven Rock, instead heading across the Potomac to the Washington Navy Yard to establish a temporary command post at the headquarters of the Naval Criminal Investigative Service (NCIS).

Similarly, across much of government, it wasn't the senior officials who were sent off to Raven Rock and Mount Weather—even though there was the chance to evacuate them—it was the deputies or even the deputies' deputies. FBI deputy director Tom Pickard sent the bureau's #3 official, Ruben Garcia, to Mount Weather instead—packing him into an armored motorcade filled with anxious highly armed agents. Had a large-scale decapitation attack hit Washington on the afternoon of September 11th, it still would have caught many principals in place across the capital—including as many as 250 representatives and senators who had gathered at the Capitol Police Headquarters.

Aside from the attacks themselves, few points in the day threw the government into more confusion than a garbled threat against Air Force One soon after it took off from Sarasota. Even days later, no one really could trace where the threat originated—nor how it was passed, mistranslated, and misunderstood until it took on a life of its own and fundamentally reshaped how the U.S. government responded to the September 11 attacks. Sometime between 9:30 and 10:30 a.m., someone in the White House or military reported a rumored threat to the plane using the specific phrase, "ANGEL is next." The reference to the presidential plane's code name alarmed the Secret Service and the Air Force One crew, though investigation in the days ahead made it appear likely that the original threat had never used the code word.* Then came an even scarier moment: White House communications director Karen Hughes tried to call the plane, but the operator reported, "Ma'am, we can't reach Air Force One." It turned out to be just a momentary communications glitch, not a sign of a further attack, but underscored fear of what lay ahead.

When communications did work, Vice President Cheney alerted the president to the possible threat—and warned him that Air Force One couldn't return to Washington, even though Bush was eager to do so. The Secret Service and aides argued it was better for COG purposes to remain outside the capital—perhaps he could go to Camp David or a NATO bunker in Norfolk, Virginia? "It was very clear that they were going for symbols of power and for the seats of power," Condi Rice recalled. "To bring the president back and to put him in the same building with the vice president would have been foolhardy, frankly, because decapitation then of the U.S. government is quite easy."

Colonel Mark Tillman, the pilot of Air Force One, believed that only a small circle of officials knew the ANGEL code name, and was deeply troubled by the reported threat: "For somebody to call into the White House and say that 'ANGEL was next,' that was just incredible." As he said later, "It was serious before that, but now . . . no longer is it a time to get the president home." No one was really sure what to do, so Air Force One headed for the open sky over the Gulf of Mexico. As Tillman recollected, the military aide's nuclear Football was of little use in managing such an unexpected crisis, so they improvised: "I tell you, this wasn't a nuclear war so as much as you thumb through those secrets, nothing applied. The plan was to move him around, decoy him, until we could figure out exactly what did apply at that point."

Instead, it was decided the president would hide in the air. Tillman asked for an armed guard at the cockpit door, summoning Secret Service and the

---

* What seems likely is that the original threat, if one ever existed, was a more straightforward "Air Force One is next," but that a military or communications aide, in transmitting the threat up the chain of the command translated it to "ANGEL is next" per standard communication protocols.

plane's specially trained Phoenix Raven guards. Agents double-checked the identity of everyone on board, fighter jets scrambled to provide an escort, and the Air Force diverted an AWACS plane to keep an eye on the surrounding airspace. Tillman decided to avoid using the radio entirely, lest he tip the plane's location to an eavesdropping terrorist, and instead called air traffic control on the telephone. The mood on board was tense.

With the threat hanging in the pressurized cabin air, Bush understood he'd have to wait. "I recognized that part of my responsibility was to ensure the Continuity of Government," Bush later wrote in his memoir. "It would be an enormous propaganda victory for the enemy if they took out the president." A few minutes later, the president felt Air Force One bank hard to the west. They were heading for Barksdale Air Force Base in Louisiana to refuel, resupply, and figure out the next stop.

The ensuing criticism that Bush showed cowardice by not returning immediately to the White House rankled Cheney, who thought such critics fundamentally misunderstood the president's responsibilities that day. It wasn't about kowtowing to the press—it was about assuring the office of the presidency. "That's crap," Cheney said in a December 2001 interview. "This is not about appeasing the press or being the macho guy who is going to face down danger. You don't think in those personal terms. . . . This is about preserving and protecting the presidency. His importance lies in the office he holds."

The day's events highlighted the abstract challenges that had always worried COG planners. While the system was trying, with varying degrees of success, to do the right thing to preserve the government's priorities—Continuity of Government, Continuity of the Presidency, Continuity of Operations—the very measures that were best to preserve national leadership were often the very worst for national morale. The public's reaction proved exactly what everyone had imagined it would be: disgust. Throughout the day, news anchors assailed President Bush, who disappeared from public view for hours at a time, even as New York mayor Rudolph Giuliani visited the site of the crashes in Manhattan. As Senator William Fulbright had pointed out, in criticizing the purpose of NEACP in the 1970s, COG undermined the confidence in the nation's leadership at the very moment it was most needed. As Fulbright said, "I am sure that in England during

World War II, when Churchill was standing there trying to encourage his people to resist, it would have been a strange sight if he had taken off in a plane instead." It was a day of tension between the system's executive agents and the optics for politicians—the precise scenario that had troubled presidents leading back to Harry Truman's first air raid scare: Presidents could evacuate or command, but not both.

Air Force One's communication problems were hardly unique. Nearly everywhere officials ended up, they were shocked at how bad the communications were. Paul Wolfowitz's ride to Raven Rock aboard the black-and-gold helicopter from the Army's 12th Aviation Battalion took forty-five minutes, just part of a flood of helicopters, SUVs, and tan military buses trekking to the normally quiet Pennsylvania mountain that day. As he recalled, "I went up to this bizarre location that was prepared to survive nuclear war." Since the end of the Cold War—when, coincidentally, then Defense Secretary Dick Cheney had sent the bunker into a peacetime slumber—SITE R was kept mostly in standby mode and it took hours to assemble the necessary staff, activate communications links, and spin up operations. Wolfowitz reported, "The computer and communications systems there functioned poorly or not at all."

Similarly, PEOC was turning out to be a terrible place from which to run a crisis; at one point a military technician monitoring the bunker's life-support systems reported to the vice president's chief of staff, Scooter Libby, that there were simply too many people inside—specifically, too many people breathing too much oxygen. Carbon monoxide levels were spiking and oxygen was being depleted too quickly. Libby and Cheney's counsel David Addington told all the nonessential staff to leave. As Libby recalled, "Too much CO_2 can affect a person's judgment. This was the wrong time for foggy minds." Beyond its inadequate size, the PEOC lacked a secure line to the Situation Room, forcing aides to shuttle back and forth if they had particularly sensitive information to discuss, and the PEOC couldn't simultaneously play both sound on the TVs and on the videoconference. Mary Matalin recalled, "The vice president obviously wanted to keep talking to the Pentagon, but then he couldn't hear what was on CNN. He just demanded that it get fixed, now. How could it not work? It was as mad as I'd ever seen him up to that point." His complaints that day, though, went unanswered; technicians and aides couldn't fix the problem, leaving officials just guessing at the "breaking news" and "updates" being delivered by anchors and correspondents on the muted television.

According to one official on board NEACP, the flight known as VENUS 77, the nation was "deaf, dumb, and blind" for most of the day—unable to piece together coherent information and unable to communicate effectively among its own leadership.

Air Force One's limitations came into stark relief. President Bush was frustrated to find that the plane initially had just three working secure lines—just as a previous generation of the plane had limited President Johnson on the flight back from Dallas—and couldn't receive satellite TV stations, meaning the president and traveling party were beholden to local affiliates as they flew over the country. "One of my greatest frustrations on September 11 was the woeful communications technology on Air Force One," President Bush recalled. "After a few minutes on a given station, the screen would dissolve into static." He tried several times to reach his wife while she was still at the Capitol, waiting to be evacuated, but the calls kept dropping. Bush couldn't believe that the president of the United States couldn't successfully place a telephone call from his military airplane to the U.S. Capitol building. "What the hell is going on?" he snapped at Andy Card. On the worst day in modern U.S. history, the president of the United States was, unbelievably, often less informed than a normal civilian sitting at home watching cable news.

Colin Powell, who had been in Lima, Peru, later told a committee examining the matter that he was out of touch for nearly the entire flight back to the United States. "They couldn't get a phone line through. I was able to get some radio communications—two radio spots on the way back—but for most of that seven-hour period, I could not tell what was going on here in my capital." The retired Army general and former chairman of the Joint Chiefs, the man who represented the first cabinet leader in the line of succession and was the nation's top diplomat, recalled, "I never felt more useless in my life than on the morning of the 11th of September."

None of the communication limitations that day should've come as a surprise. Earlier in the year, the president had complained to White House deputy chief of staff Joe Hagin after he'd gotten only static when trying to make a telephone call during a routine motorcade around Washington. As Hagin recalled, "He essentially said to me, 'We need to fix this and fix it quickly.' He asked, 'What would we do if something really serious happened and this didn't work?'" Needless to say, Hagin hadn't addressed all the issues in the weeks before 9/11.

Still, even Bush himself had been reluctant to commit the resources to upgrade the COG systems. As part of the Clinton administration's efforts to improve the COG/ECG procedures, the military and the White House had worked out what was supposed to be a large-scale, secret upgrade for the PEOC. In the first months of the Bush administration—when terrorism wasn't on the White House's mind yet—the new PEOC plans were shown to Republican representative Bill Young, the chair of the House Appropriations Committee. The plan was to have Congress unofficially okay the monies outside of the normal appropriations process to preserve the secrecy of the upgrades—similar to how it had approved many of the COG projects over the years. Young, though, hadn't liked the plans—he thought them too expensive for too unlikely a scenario. He called President Bush directly to complain about the construction project and Bush, who hadn't even been briefed that the upgrade plan existed, agreed to nix the project.

Midday on September 11th, as the scope of the attacks became more clear, Richard Clarke went to the PEOC to speak with the vice president; given how tight the security was, Steve Hadley—the deputy national security advisor—had to come to the door of the vault to identify Clarke, who had worked at the White House for more than a decade, before the agents, armed with shotguns and MP5 submachine guns, would let the NSC official into the bunker's narrow entrance hallway. When Clarke talked face-to-face to Cheney, the vice president registered a complaint: "The comms in this place are terrible."

Clarke responded frankly: "Now you know why I wanted the money for a new bunker."

The situation on September 11th would have been much worse except for a little-known government agency that specialized in COG communications. The National Communications System, headquartered in a little-marked but heavily secured Arlington, Virginia, office building, grew out of the Pentagon's realization that it needed ready access to civilian telecom networks in an emergency. The innocuously named National Security Telecommunications Advisory Committee (pronounced "N-stack" in government lingo) held a series of secret meetings from 1982 to 1985 with industry and government officials in Washington, at SAC headquarters in Offutt, and at NORAD to ensure COOP/COG operations in an increasingly splintered telecom environment. As one Pentagon official said during a 1983 meeting at the FCC, "We are looking at trying to make communications endurable for a protracted conflict."

The heartbeat of NCS became its second-floor National Coordinating Center, where close by its 24/7 watch center a corridor known as "logo row" ran along the front of the building. Each of the corridor's offices was staffed by representatives of the nation's major telecom and network companies—the roughly forty companies, each delineated by their logo on their door, included companies like Akamai, AT&T, Comcast, Northrup Grumman, Raytheon, Inmarsat, and HP. In an emergency, these corporate representatives were to work with the Pentagon and FEMA to turn their private networks over to government and military use.

By 9/11, NCS's hundred or so employees managed three special programs meant to help what the government called "emergency communications recovery," coordinating closely with the Defense Information Systems Agency (DISA) and some two dozen participating federal agencies—ranging from the CIA and the cabinet departments to the Federal Reserve, the Postal Service, NSA, NASA, and the Nuclear Regulatory Commission.*

The best-known of NCS's efforts was the Government Emergency Telecommunications System (GETS), a priority phone network with its own dedicated area code (710) and only a single telephone number assigned to it: 710-NCS-GETS (710-627-4387). Officials who dialed that number were prompted for a personalized PIN that not only identified them as

---

* DISA, and its predecessor, the Defense Communications Agency, had grown out of the need in the 1960s to ensure reliable command and control networks. Among other projects, DISA oversees the Moscow–Washington hotline and the MEECN, Minimum Essential Emergency Communications Network, the last-ditch network for the National Command Authorities to ensure its nuclear launch orders could be communicated around the world.

registered users but also allowed the system to prioritize individuals within the calling system, bumping lower-level officials for higher-level ones and so forth. The system was available to select federal, state, and local government officials, as well as to private companies that were "sponsored" by the government that had critical functions for public health, the economy, energy, or other key sectors.*

While GETS, which includes both voice and slow faxlike data speeds, had been in widespread use since the 1990s and was used successfully in the wake of the 1995 bombing of the Murrah Federal Building—when call volume around Oklahoma City nearly tripled and overloaded circuits—the 9/11 attacks represented "the first large-scale emergency event in which the performance of GETS service was tested." Many agencies found that to make any telephone calls, leaders had to rely on the special service; about 20,000 officials—both key government and private sector leaders—had GETS cards on 9/11 and hundreds turned to the system in both Washington and New York to ensure their telephone calls went through even as the public's circuits were overwhelmed. Altogether, nationwide, in the week after 9/11, around 19,000 GETS calls were made—and 18,117 were completed.

NCS also ran the Telecommunications Service Priority (TSP) plan, which focused on restoring disrupted critical communications networks. The highest-priority networks were designated "Emergency services," known as priority E services, considered so critical to the U.S. government that private industry vendors must restore them at the earliest possible time without regard to cost, safety, or resources. (Beyond those E-level services, officials could call upon the networks and carriers for "essential" services that would be dealt with as expeditiously as possible—but the carriers could

---

* In general, five major categories of "essential" government and private services are allowed access to the government's special telecommunications networks: (1) "National Security Leadership," those services essential to national survival of nuclear attack; (2) "National Security Posture and U.S. Population Attack," those services concerning the maintaining of critical defense, diplomatic, or Continuity of Government capability; (3) "Public Health, Safety, and Maintenance of Law and Order," which includes warning systems as well as those needed for maintaining law and order, public health, weather service, and critical transportation; (4) "Public Welfare and Maintenance of National Economic Posture," services to maintain public welfare and economic well-being; and (5) "Disaster Recovery Efforts."

decide for their own safety whether to pursue merely "essential" projects.) In the hours and days following 9/11, forty-six different federal and state agencies tapped into TSP to order 598 different requests for service and repairs—fixes that, among many other uses, delivered extra power generators to MCI, extra phone lines to the FBI's temporary headquarters in New York City, and helped Wall Street firms reconnect before the stock and bond markets could reopen.

It was, though, the third NCS program that put the agency at the center of COG efforts on 9/11. The Special Routing Arrangement Service (SRAS) represented an advanced version of the GETS program, highly restricted only to the government's topmost leaders and focused on preserving Continuity of Government. The classified program rarely is mentioned in public, but in a rare bureaucratic statement the FCC once explained, "SRAS is intended to ensure telecommunications support is provided with the highest likelihood practical during all conditions, particularly during conditions of severe network disruption as may result from acts of war." SRAS operates much like GETS, but with a more exclusive user group—and a more advanced tool set. SRAS provides anonymity of called and calling parties to help ensure that the calls can't give away operations or the location of various officials. As Brenton C. Greene, the retired Navy submarine commander who had taken over the low-profile NCS in April 2001, told the 9/11 Commission, "In a situation where Continuity of Government is put into play, there is a communications system where no one can trace the site of the call on either end."

SRAS relies, in part, on a dedicated communications network between the NCS's National Coordinating Center and the various telecom networks, and by 8:48 a.m. the NCC had been activated. Coincidentally, SRAS itself had been activated as part of the GLOBAL GUARDIAN exercise on September 10 and was already in "exercise" mode that morning, ready for use by government officials as they retreated to their COG locations. Brenton Greene talked throughout the day with telecom leaders, as CEOs called to discuss both their needs and how they could help the government response, and NCS activated military reservists in California, New York, Philadelphia, and Boston to help respond to the crisis.

• • •

By midday, the decision finally came to evacuate the congressional leadership to an "undisclosed location." House and Senate leaders gathered on the Capitol's West Lawn, where helicopters from the Air Force's 1st Helicopter Squadron descended to whisk them away. SWAT teams ringed the landing zone, providing cover as the senators, representatives, and aides hustled toward the blue-and-white Huey helicopters. The Andrews-based squadron, known as Mussel, traced its lineage to that first 1957 helicopter ride by Dwight Eisenhower and had long trained for just this very moment, but it was the first time the pilots and crews had ever landed on the Capitol lawn for a real evacuation. The two helicopters that normally served as the squadron's alert aircraft had been supplemented by as many helicopters as the unit could get into the air that day.

As the loaded helicopters later descended onto Mount Weather, congressional leaders saw gray-uniformed troops carrying M-16s. Senate Minority Leader Trent Lott, Republican Whip Don Nickles, Democratic Whip Harry Reid, and Majority Leader Tom Daschle disembarked to walk inside, where they were joined by Dick Gephardt, Tom Delay, Dick Armey, and David Bonior from the House leadership. Following long-standing protocols, the House and Senate leaders had only been allowed to bring one staffer.

Armed guards brought the evacuees through the double set of blast doors, into the bowels of the bunker. "It was a sense of wonderment," Hastert's aide, John Feehery, recalled. "Oh boy, so this is what we have for the nuclear winter." The aides and members looked around at the spartan facilities and they realized they might be there for quite a while. "It's a very stark place," Daschle said later, recalling his first impressions of Mount Weather. The government bunker was hardly the lap of Apocalypse luxury—nondescript rooms, white walls, basic tables. "The room we were first taken into was more bare bones than I had imagined," he recalled. "It could almost have passed for a police interrogation room." On one bookshelf was a set of law books and the U.S. Code, in case Congress needed to do any legislating from the bunker. The two teams—the skeleton crew manning Mount Weather and the newly arrived congressional leadership—eyed each other warily. As Gephardt's chief of staff, Steve Elmendorf, later recalled, "There was a group of people there who were staffing that location who had been waiting since the Cold War for somebody to show up."

Now, someone had. "They had some sandwiches and potato chips, but they had not really seen any of us before," Elmendorf said. "It was very surreal actually." Lott, who still didn't know where they'd been taken, couldn't get over the structure itself—square, barren rooms stretching back into the bedrock: "There was a granite-like stone on the sides," he said later. "I mean, literally there it was, like a cave."

Congressional leaders eventually moved to a larger room, further into the mountain down a cavelike tunnel, clustering around a U-shaped conference table in one of the bunker's briefing rooms, speaking once an hour or so to the White House via speakerphone. Mostly they just watched TV, awaiting updates. By mid-afternoon, they were tired of being sequestered in the Blue Ridge Mountains and eager to return to Capitol Hill. "It felt like we weren't doing anything," recalls Brian Gunderson, chief of staff to House Majority Leader Dick Armey. "We just spent the day watching TV," Hastert said later.

During one conference call with the White House bunker, Oklahoma Republican senator Don Nickles protested to Cheney that Congress needed to return to Washington. The leadership felt isolated, far removed from its rank-and-file members who had clustered at the Capitol Police Headquarters, waiting for any scraps of information as their leadership communicated by telephone from a secret bunker in who knows where. "That's not where you want to be," Feehery says. As Nickles saw it, Congress needed to come together. The legislature, he argued to the White House, was an independent branch of government and shouldn't require the executive branch's permission to move around. "Don," the vice president replied, pointing out the logistical problem in Nickles's argument, "we control the helicopters."

In Washington that day, Laura Bush had been ready to make history herself, becoming just the fourth first lady to testify before Congress during a Senate hearing on early childhood development. After the plane hit the Pentagon, her Secret Service detail rushed her into a basement room at the Capitol that belonged to New Hampshire senator Judd Gregg, where they hunkered down to wait for reinforcements. She wrote later, "In the intervening years, Judd and I, and many others, were left to contemplate what if Flight 93 had not been forced down by its passengers into an empty field; what if, shortly after 10:00 a.m., it had reached the Capitol Dome?"

Later, the first lady was driven to the Secret Service's headquarters, entering via its underground entrance, and taken up to the director's conference room, where she spent most of the day. An aide returned to the evacuated White House to retrieve the Bushes' dogs.

Midway through the day, an agent approached the first lady to tell her that all of the former presidents and their families were safe. The comment surprised her; she hadn't realized just how far the government's protective embrace would reach that day. Her own children had been secured quickly— Barbara, code-named TURQUOISE, a student at Yale, was taken from campus to the Secret Service's New Haven office at 10:51 ET, while Jenna, code-named TWINKLE, a student at Austin's University of Texas, was awakened by an agent pounding on her dorm door before being taken to the city's Driskill Hotel at 10:57 ET. But the first family represented just the tip of a massive nationwide relocation effort by the Secret Service. After ensuring that Second Lady Lynne Cheney had been secured and delivered to the White House, the Secret Service turned attention to their daughter Liz and grandchildren, ordering agents to locate her children at their private schools and take them to Mount Weather. The agency's reach that day had been long—checking on every first family they'd ever protected: In Dallas, with active duty agents scarce, Heather Vance, the daughter of former first daughter Susan Ford, was pulled from her classes at SMU by a retired Secret Service agent and his wife.*

Around Washington, officials were still struggling to respond to unfolding events. After decades of attention to COG, Crisis Relocation Plans, and so forth, the Office of Personnel Management—the agency charged

---

* Beyond the families of the president and former presidents, such protective efforts were haphazard around the country: Even though Daschle himself couldn't contact his family— the congressional leadership were taking turns using the one working landline phone at Mount Weather—the local police in Aberdeen, South Dakota, took it upon themselves to sweep up his elderly mother and bring her to the police station as a precautionary measure. "She was completely confused," Daschle recalled.

with closing the federal government in the capital—found that on September 11th the only established plan on its books was for a very different scenario: "Basically the only emergency plan that was available that this area had [on September 11th] was the snow emergency plan," OPM's Scott Hatch recalled. Officials across government found themselves left without instructions. One high-ranking Energy Department official, who fled department headquarters with only her purse and a stack of papers grabbed from her desk, said, "I was leaving with senior political people, and we didn't receive any word from anywhere."

The Treasury Department, located adjacent to the White House, evacuated along with the White House complex and, with Secretary O'Neill out of the country, Acting Secretary Kenneth Dam huddled with other officials on the sidewalk before deciding to relocate to the Secret Service's headquarters nearby. At the Commerce Department, no one told Secretary Don Evans what to do, so, after hours waiting in his office, he just had his driver take him back to his house in McLean, Virginia, not far from the CIA's headquarters. The education secretary, Rod Paige, had been left behind in Florida by the departing Air Force One—not purposely, as part of some COG procedure to separate presidential successors, but simply by happenstance. Paige ended up driving home to Washington with aides.

At the Federal Reserve, the nation's central bank tried to sort through a national response, balancing its own evacuation needs with the need to support—and calm—the nation's banks and markets. But it was hardly business as usual. In New York, officers locked the Federal Reserve's vaults just a few blocks from the World Trade Center. In Washington, nearly a hundred staff members remained at the headquarters, just off the National Mall, to help run operations, even as the federal government closed. In Chicago, staffers decided not to evacuate to the bank's relocation site, determining that they didn't have the time to waste.

As they activated the Interior Department's COG plans, National Park Service leaders, unable to find workable phone lines out of their Washington headquarters, e-mailed the agency's Eastern Interagency Coordination Center (EICC) in Shenandoah National Park, and asked it to be the agency's "eyes and ears." "Communications lines within the Washington headquarters broke down or were nonexistent," one report later concluded.

The agency contacted Verizon and Sprint to request a mobile satellite truck, "a so-called cellular on wheels," which came with 150 special mobile phones, and dispatched it to the Interior Department's headquarters in Washington. That truck, which arrived in D.C. about eight hours after the attacks, became the department's key link to the outside world.

In the immediate hours after the attack, the Interior Department's leadership initially tried to relocate to its designated fallback complex in northern Virginia, known as SITE B, but the horrendous, panicked traffic in Washington meant agency leaders spent nearly twenty minutes waiting before they could pull out of the building's garage, so they abandoned the evacuation plan. Later in the day, Cheney ordered Interior Secretary Gale Norton, as well as Agriculture Secretary Ann M. Veneman and Secretary of Health and Human Services Tommy Thompson, to Mount Weather as part of COG, and the Interior Department summoned a Park Police SWAT team to escort them out of the city. As the day wore on, the White House Military Office worked to round up the rest of the far-flung cabinet members and key officials; the Air Force dispatched a C-17 plane to pick up Alan Greenspan in Switzerland, another plane brought former president Clinton home from Australia, where he'd been traveling.

But, even as scattered as the government's response was for key officials, the military wasn't in much better shape with its own personnel. "We don't have a very good feel even for how to account for people," a Pentagon official said. In the hours and days after the attack, the Defense Department resorted to publishing telephone numbers in the media to allow its own key workers to figure out how and where to report to relocation sites. "Not a good way," the official said simply.

If nineteen terrorists, armed with nothing more than box cutters, had managed to wreak this level of havoc on the U.S. government, how, many wondered, would COG hold up during a concerted attack on the leadership itself?

As Air Force One approached Barksdale Air Force Base, the crew and passengers got a stark reminder of the nation's power. The base's workhorse B-52s were all lined up on the tarmac, loaded with nuclear weapons as part of the day's aborted VIGILANT GUARDIAN exercise. It felt, Bush recalled, "like dropping onto a movie set." The press on board were told that they couldn't report where the president was, saying only that he was at an "unidentified location," but the blackout was lifted quickly when it became clear that local press had already reported the presidential arrival—a not-so-friendly reminder of just how complicated it was to evacuate the nation's commander-in-chief during an emergency. "Air Force One is a hard plane to hide," Ari Fleischer recalled.

As President Bush addressed the nation from a base building—the first public statement from the nation's leadership in nearly three hours—the Air Force One crew rushed to resupply the plane, loading on pallets of water and food, not knowing where they would be heading next or how long it might take. Many of the plane's passengers would be left behind at Barksdale, but for the first time, the White House activated the "nuclear pool," choosing a small group of journalists to accompany the president wherever Doomsday might lead. The Secret Service didn't want him back in Washington until they had a better sense of the still-unfolding threat. "There were issues of connectivity and security," Cheney aide Mary Matalin recalled. "It was 'What's the safest place we can get the president to where we can be connected to him to get his orders?'"

The answer to the day's uncertainty ended up being Curtis LeMay's old seat of empire. As Cheney put it, "It's secure as hell, it's a military installation, it's got great communications." As Air Force One took off around 1:30 p.m. for the ninety-minute flight to Nebraska, it marked an important epoch in American history: Offutt had been preparing for this very moment—or, at least, one very like it—since the day General LeMay had arrived there in 1948 to transform SAC into the nation's elite fighting force. Even the president's father agreed: When explaining why his son went to Omaha on 9/11, George H. W. Bush said simply, Offutt "has the most sophisticated command-and-control outside Washington."

Offutt Air Force Base only received confirmation that the president was on his way twenty minutes before the president's plane came into view. As Air Force One pilot Tillman said, "The goal is to get the President underground until everything is secured in Washington, D.C." The large 747 taxied right up next to one of the NEACP E-4B Doomsday planes on the tarmac. "It was a surreal feeling pulling up next to it," aide Dan Bartlett recalled. "It was from a different era for a different purpose, but it was relevant."

The president rode a short distance to the command center's alternate entrance, a concrete blockhouse where stairs and an elevator descended into the ground. Sixty feet underground, the elevator doors opened and President Bush emerged into the war room originally built for Curtis LeMay. He spent nearly twenty minutes in the command center as military briefers brought him up to speed, then entered the adjacent Joint Intelligence Center, where he convened the National Security Council via videoconference around 3:30 p.m. ET. The president opened with the decisive words, "We're at war," and as the call continued the enemy became clear: CIA director George Tenet said he believed the attacks to be the work of al-Qaeda and Osama bin Laden; they'd actually identified the names of al-Qaeda suspects on the hijacked flights.

As the NSC videoconference was wrapping up, confirmation came from NORAD that the last suspect airliner—a flight to the U.S. from Spain—had turned back and landed safely in Madrid. The nation's airspace was fully secure. It was time for the president to go home. "He knew that he had to address the American people, and he wasn't going to do it from here," explained Jay Wentzell, one of Offutt's communications technicians.

Aides had anticipated the president would remain at Offutt for perhaps twelve hours as the government secured Washington, but the stop in Omaha actually lasted just 100 minutes. Bush even beat Tillman back to Air Force One, driving in the base commander's car out to the plane—it was in the air by 4:36 p.m. ET. The escort fighters, who had left their cell phone numbers with the Air Force One crew, didn't know the president was on the move until they heard its engines screaming down the runway. They dashed back to their planes and took off, chasing the president eastward. It was an easy flight, because in the skies over the United States, as Tillman said, "We were the only game in town."

By mid-afternoon, the team at the White House decided to issue another statement—the nation couldn't wait for further reassurance until President Bush's arrival that evening. It seemed wrong for Vice President Cheney to speak, a scenario that hewed too closely to Al Haig's disastrous "I'm in control here" comments during the attempt on Ronald Reagan's life in 1981. Besides, as it turned out, neither PEOC nor the Situation Room had the capability to broadcast to the nation outside their walls. Instead, White House communications director Karen Hughes spoke to reporters down the street at the FBI's headquarters.

Air Force One finally landed at Andrews Air Force Base around 6:30 p.m., with two Langley F-15s tailing it and two F-16s from the D.C. Air National Guard in front of it. The arrival in the capital, nearly nine hours after fleeing Sarasota, was sobering to everyone on board. As Colonel Tillman recalled, "We descended on Washington D.C.; we finally now see what exactly has happened. We can see the Pentagon smoldering. Prior to that, we had seen footage on television, but we hadn't seen anything real at this point."

At 8:30 p.m., President Bush addressed the nation from the Oval Office—finally, many hours later, in control back at his own desk in his own house in his own capital. He told the American people that night, "Terrorist attacks can shake the foundations of our biggest buildings, but they cannot touch the foundation of America. America was targeted for attack because we're the brightest beacon for freedom and opportunity in the world. And no one will keep that light from shining."

Cheney watched the Oval Office address from the bunker, where *The Economist* he'd grabbed that morning remained untouched on the PEOC conference table, surrounded by the chaotic day's detritus: pens, pencils, legal pads filled with the hastily scribbled history of the day, platters of half-eaten sandwiches and trays of cookies, a coffee thermos and Styrofoam cups, Ozarka bottled water from Texas, and Diet Coke—all of which had seemed magically to accumulate over the course of the day courtesy of the White House Mess. "It was surreal," Lynne Cheney recalled two months later. "You know, it was sort of like the polite hostess—there you are in the middle of this amazing crisis, and somebody remembers to put out the cookies."

After his Oval Office address, Bush came to the PEOC himself to lead an NSC meeting. One major COG change began immediately afterward: The president and the vice president would spend much of the subsequent months separated. After the late-night NSC meeting, the Cheneys and two aides—Scooter Libby and David Addington—boarded a helicopter on the South Lawn to fly to Camp David, accompanied by a communications technician, a military aide with a nuclear Football, and the vice president's doctor. It was the Cheneys' first time outside in twelve hours. The Marine Two trip breached protocol, which held that the president was the only person to travel by helicopter to or from the South Lawn.

As the helicopter headed north, the passengers could see the burning Pentagon, lit by giant light towers. "We're flying on our way to hide the vice president," David Addington thought. "My God, we're evacuating the vice president from Washington, D.C., because we've been attacked." He and Libby looked at each other: The Doomsday scenarios they'd trained for throughout their government careers had come to life. At Camp David, Liz Cheney and her family joined them for that first night in an "undisclosed location," a phrase that would become commonplace in the weeks ahead. The vice president slept in Aspen Lodge—the president's cabin, another protocol violation but the cabin had the best access to the camp's bunker.

At the White House, the Secret Service suggested the president and first lady spend the night inside the PEOC—after all, it had been designed to sustain a small group for quite some time. Agents showed the first couple the bed inside the bunker, a foldout that Laura Bush recalled "looked like it had been installed when FDR was president." She and the president both stared at it and finally said no. "We're not going to sleep down here. We're going to go upstairs and you can get us if something happens," the president explained. "I've got to get sleep, in our own bed." That night, he dictated into his own diary, "The Pearl Harbor of the 21st century took place today."

The government had survived the day—but barely. As Major General Angus Watt, the operations director at NORAD, said later, "There is no way NORAD could claim it succeeded on 9/11," he explained, "but we can't say it was a failure either."

Chapter 18

THE DAYS AFTER

Hal Neill had lived next to Raven Rock's entrance for thirty-nine years, mostly ignoring the strange neighborhood institution where his father once worked. In the days since 9/11, he and his wife had noticed the increased guard patrols and regular activity at the few aboveground facilities visible from their backyard. On the eighth day after the attack, his wife called him at work: "Honey, you can't come home," his wife explained. "They've got the road blocked off." The family and others nearby had been evacuated after a truck carrying office furniture, to help alleviate the huge new staffs moving into Raven Rock, had set off an explosives detector at Raven Rock's entrance. For a brief period, rumors and panic flooded the small community—the drivers had tried to crash the gate, then fled—but it all ended up being a false alarm.

As fall arrived in the Appalachian Mountains around Washington, residents of the small communities around Raven Rock and Mount Weather had become used to clattering helicopters arriving and departing—as well as the other disturbances that came with living near the nation's Doomsday headquarters. "Day and night, you hear the airplanes," said Bonnie Wolfe, who owned the hobby shop in nearby Blue Ridge, Pennsylvania. At Mount Weather, black netting went up alongside the perimeter fences bordering the facility to obscure the work and personnel from passersby, and new surface-to-air defenses were loaded into the site.

The lumbering buses, trucks, fighters, and helicopters announced

America's new, permanent "shadow government," a group of 75 to 150 civilian officials spread between Raven Rock and Mount Weather who would support the "presidential successor." The haphazard evacuation on 9/11 had settled in the following weeks into ninety-day rotations of teams working inside the mountains. Most of those pulling "bunker duty" were top civilian managers from the GS-14 and GS-15 ranks of the government workforce, as well as from the Senior Executive Service. "They're on a 'business trip,' that's all," one official told *The Washington Post*. As Richard Clarke explained, "For well over a year after 9/11 the Bush administration had the program on 'warm stand-by.'"

The shadow government's figurehead was the man from the bunker: Vice President Cheney, who explained to Tim Russert on *Meet the Press* the weekend after the attacks that he'd been spending "a good deal of my time up at Camp David since the president returned to the White House just so we weren't both together in the same place so we could ensure the survival of the government."

"My basic role as vice president is to worry about presidential succession," the #2 explained to Russert. "And my job, above all other things, is to be prepared to take over if something happens to the president. But over the years from my time with President Ford, as secretary of defense, on the Intel Committee and so forth, I've been involved in a number of programs that were aimed at ensuring presidential succession. We did a lot of planning during the Cold War, Tim, with respect to the possibility of a nuclear incident. And one of the key requirements always is to protect the presidency. It's not about George Bush or Dick Cheney. It's about the occupant in the office."

The vice president's aides followed a new routine, too: Scooter Libby insisted that Cheney's name not be used by aides on the phone to protect his security, and staff had to keep "go-bags" packed with extra clothes in case of an evacuation. Some high-level aides, like Mary Matalin, relocated to the "undisclosed locations" along with the vice president. The aides and briefers accompanying him became all too familiar with the white tote bags, stenciled with "Office of the Vice President," that denoted their new life on the move. Even years later, spotting one of the bags would bring memories of that high-stress time flooding back. At Camp David, where much of the vice president's time was spent, aides ate breakfast and lunch in the Laurel cabin, and dinner at the Camp David military mess hall, and became fans of the "Frito pie"—chili, Fritos, and cheese—served by the camp's small bar, Shangri-La. "When we were at this location, while I was working, we were kind of in a netherworld," Matalin recalled. "Late one night, I turned on the TV. All this stuff was happening out there in the real world, on this little, teeny screen, and we were so removed from it, and yet so working on it."

Cheney's disappearance from public view and his series of "secure undisclosed locations" became the butt of many jokes, but to many in government he remained a daily presence—a disembodied head on videoconferences where he remained actively involved in planning the unfolding war on terror. "We'd see him on the screen," National Security Advisor Condoleezza Rice recalled. "He was off being the Continuity of Government." White House aides, working with FEMA's Central Locator System, began to carefully track the whereabouts of the president and vice president, color-coding their schedules to show when they'd be in the same place.

Where exactly he was hiding, however, remained a mystery. As Cheney told *The Weekly Standard*'s Matt Labash, "Your undisclosed location could be a secure facility somewhere, or it could be a cornfield in South Dakota where you're hunting, or the South Fork of the Snake [River]." Indeed, as much as the caricature emerged of Cheney hiding in a cave, he actually roamed widely off the radar: pheasant hunting near Pierre, South Dakota; duck hunting near Poughkeepsie, New York, during a two-day trip where he stayed at the local Courtyard Marriott; journeying to Maryland's Eastern Shore to join former treasury secretary Nicholas Brady for another duck hunt; and spending a weekend quail hunting in Georgia with three senators. The hunting trips, which had the added benefit of keeping the vice president far from public eyes, became something of a joke among aides—especially given the high-tension, high-threat environment that enveloped the White House staff. Watching Cheney load his hunting shotguns into a car for one trip, one aide joked that he hoped the latest intelligence wasn't sending the vice president into survivalist mode: "I hope it's not that bad."

Back in Washington, neighbors in D.C.'s Glover Park around the vice president's residence at the Naval Observatory complained in early 2002 about unexplained construction blasts loud enough to rattle windows and shake houses—blasts that continued two or three times a day for more than two months. The Navy refused to explain the noise, telling a neighborhood group, "Due to its sensitive nature in support of national security and homeland defense, project-specific information is classified and cannot be released." Furthermore, the Navy official added, "Please understand we are severely constrained by operation requirements to perform this project on a highly accelerated schedule; therefore, it will not be possible to limit construction activities to the daytime as you request."*

Wherever he was, Cheney was never far from his vice presidential duties. He spent countless hours working on the nation's "decapitation plan," making real the buzzwords "Continuity of Government" and "Enduring Constitutional Government." There was so much work to do. When the GAO studied COOP plans in 2002, it found that twenty-two of the thirty-four plans it examined had never been tested, and that none required any training or orientation for those who were supposed to step into emergency roles. Three agencies it examined had no COOP plans at all. FEMA responded to the shortcomings, in part, by tripling the number of staff it devoted to coordinating COOP planning for other agencies.

The September 11th attacks had made all too clear that it was unrealistic to assume key officials would be able to evacuate to an empty relocation site and get it up and running in a timely manner, so the administration embarked on an ambitious "devolution" plan for its agencies and departments, whereby in the event of an attack they would "devolve" power and authority to existing staff working outside the capital. After all, nearly 90 percent of the nation's nearly two million federal workers lived and worked outside the capital; with planning, there were plenty of high-ranking officials and field offices that could assume power in an emergency. As Richard Clarke explains, "The departments moved to a new plan, that instead of being based on warning, would involve command devolving to an alternate site that was already up and running."

Each department and key agency identified field offices, regional

---

* The likely result of that construction project was inadvertently made public nearly a decade later, when Cheney's successor, Joe Biden, gabbed that he'd found a bunker in his new house—a secure room hidden behind a hallway's heavy steel door.

headquarters, or support facilities that could step into a leadership vacuum during an emergency. If Washington was destroyed or uninhabitable, for instance, the FBI field office in Kansas City might take over the running of the bureau. The Army dusted off its Cold War plans to relocate to the Army War College in Carlisle, Pennsylvania. Collins Hall was set up to handle up to 700 relocated Army personnel. The State Department set up agreements with FEMA to use some of its Olney, Maryland, support facility as a $7 million backup communications and data storage hub that would provide a "highly survivable redundant capability . . . designed to handle any disruption to the Department's communications infrastructure and ensure communications with our overseas posts." Other agencies and departments followed suit.

Just as the Federal Civil Defense Administration had set up its headquarters in Battle Creek, Michigan, during the 1950s, federal agencies and departments began to consider what tasks and offices they could permanently move out of D.C.'s downtown core in the 2000s. The Smithsonian Institution started to move its "wet collections," those specimens preserved in alcohol or other fluid, out of storage inside the buildings along the National Mall and to a new facility in Maryland. New post-9/11 structures, like the Office of the Director of National Intelligence and the National Counterterrorism Center, were built in secure compounds in the Washington suburbs, helping to ensure that an attack on the downtown wouldn't knock them out as well.

Further from public view, command and control upgrades went ahead on Air Force One, so a future president caught in the sky would be better able to communicate with the nation and understand what was transpiring below. By 2004, the presidential planes sported videoconferencing capability and the ability to get live television. Similarly, the once shelved plans to upgrade and expand the White House PEOC finally moved forward. After much work by Joe Hagin and others, the White House Situation Room received millions of dollars in upgrades, its first significant remaking in decades, a project that added three new secure video suites (for a total of five) and a direct feed to Air Force One, if needed. New hardened facilities were built in Colorado and Florida. Relocation facilities like Raven Rock and Mount Weather that had spent much of the 1990s slumbering reopened and resupplied in a hurry. In 2003, the government poured $652 million into supplemental one-time upgrades and construction, on top of the already budgeted amounts, and by 2004 that annual continuity budget topped half a billion dollars. As part of the 2005 budget process, President Bush requested $27 million to help boost FEMA's COG planning, and government-wide COG and command and control expenditures totaled some $2 billion a year. FEMA also poured hundreds of thousands of dollars into a "Next Generation" Central Locator System, to help ensure that it'd be able to find and verify a presidential successor in the event of an attack on the capital.

To address concerns about how the cellular networks were overloaded during the 9/11 attacks, the government quietly launched the Wireless Priority Service in December 2002—a system, similar to the landline-based GETS, that guaranteed critical officials and key private sector industries priority access to cell towers in an emergency. Each user on the system could access the priority calling by dialing *272 from their WPS-enabled cell phone—a privilege for which the government charged agencies and industries $4.50 per device per month—and each user had a unique personal ID code that helped to specify priority levels within the calling system. Over the years, program use skyrocketed: By July 2015, there would be 325,000 GETS calls and 126,000 users. The even more secret network known as the Special Routing Arrangement Service received significant funds in 2005 for upgrades to ensure crisis communications for the nation's key leaders.

The Department of Justice and FEMA also went over the secret, prewritten executive orders and contingency plans for a national crisis. By the time George W. Bush took office in 2001, there were more than twice as many as had originally existed during the Eisenhower era; Eisenhower had had twenty-two of the secret documents, each carefully sealed inside envelopes to be opened in the event of an emergency, and each with its own code name. When the Bush administration's Office of Legal Counsel began its review, there were now forty-eight of the secret plans, all overseen by FEMA's little-known Program Coordination Division, which coordinates "the interagency review, update, and distribution of the Presidential Emergency Action Documents." The PEADs, though, represented just one set of the government's secret standby authorities; an even more classified set of letters go to key personnel, like cabinet leaders or other "Emergency Designees,"

outlining their individual presidential authority in an emergency, while more
general Emergency Action Packages (EAPs) and Major Emergency Actions (MEAs) outline broader authorities for agencies and departments. The
EAPs contain not just the emergency orders, but also the legal justification,
precedents, and documentation necessary to implement the plans.

Rumors abounded of the government's secret new preparations. During
a visit to Des Moines, Iowa, to discuss retirement savings, President Bush
was asked by a reporter, "Is there a shadow government in place since September 11th?"

"A shadowy government or a shadow government?" Bush laughed, then
continued, dodging the underlying question and discussing only the philosophy behind such hypothetical planning: "I have an obligation as the
President . . . to put measures in place that, should somebody be successful
in attacking Washington, D.C., there's an ongoing government. That's one
reason why the vice president was going to undisclosed locations. This is
serious business and we take it seriously."

A terrifying image haunted the post-9/11 discussion of congressional continuity: Had United Flight 93 taken off on schedule, instead of forty-one
minutes late, and the passengers hadn't had time to learn of the other attacks
and storm the cockpit, the plane might very well have successfully continued to Washington and hit the Capitol at about the same time as American Airlines Flight 77 hit the Pentagon. "With hundreds dead and perhaps
hundreds of others in burn units in hospitals, Congress would likely have
been without a quorum, without a building, without the ability to function,"
American Enterprise Institute scholar Norm Ornstein worried.

It wasn't long before another terrifying scenario began to unfold on
Capitol Hill: that fall's anthrax scare, when Senate leaders Patrick Leahy
and Tom Daschle received at their offices envelopes filled with deadly anthrax, forcing the closure of nineteen office buildings. House leaders had
prepared to reconvene the body at D.C.'s Fort McNair, an Army installation
south of the U.S. Capitol building. Absent a custom-built "Capitol" like the
Greenbrier, the best they could do on short notice was to repurpose the fort's
auditorium—importing podiums, a rostrum, and cameras, and setting up

communications, security, record keeping, and voting mechanisms, as well as facilities for the press, as part of an emergency $2 million renovation.

Addressing "Continuity of Congress" proved difficult because, whereas from the outside the legislative branch might appear as a single entity housed in a single domed building, the House and the Senate operate separately, each driven by and respectful of their own traditions and precedents. On succession issues, the Senate, which has a long tradition of appointed members rather than directly elected ones, had relatively clear constitutional policies; the House, meanwhile, had no clear way to reconstitute itself quickly—nor were its leaders inclined to compromise what they saw as their body's unique character in the name of continuity efforts. The House prides itself on the fact that every representative who has ever set foot in the body has been duly elected by the people.

Gathering a quorum of members chosen, sworn, and living—as the Constitution required—was a simple enough standard to meet if members were killed, thereby reducing the House's total number, but it would pose its own post-disaster problems. Would anyone want a subset of just a handful of representatives, perhaps just a dozen, score, or even a hundred, making sweeping decisions about declarations of war, new appropriations, or the massive civil liberties curbs likely to be imposed following a large-scale attack? "Take, for example, an attack that kills all but 9 members of Congress," Ornstein warned. "Five of those nine would constitute a quorum, and that tiny, unrepresentative group could pass legislation out of the House. More troubling was the intersection of the Presidential Succession Act with an attack on Congress. In the case of the death of the president and vice president, a nine-member House could then elect a new Speaker, who would become president of the United States for the remainder of the term."

The procedures for replacing members of Congress and reconstituting the House and Senate would likely leave the legislative branch impotent for weeks or even months after a major attack. State governors could appoint interim senators, but no similar mechanism existed for the House, which filled seats by special elections, a process that took an average of about 117 days under normal circumstances—fine for peacetime, but an eternity in a national crisis. Many states imposed legal waiting periods on those special elections, and some even barred them entirely if it was within 180 days of the scheduled end of the legislative session, meaning that an election year attack could hobble Congress for the better part of a year without a functioning majority.

To suggest solutions, two of the capital's top think tanks, Ornstein's American Enterprise Institute and the Brookings Institution, teamed up to host a new "Continuity of Government Commission" chaired by former White House counsel Lloyd Cutler and former senator Alan Simpson. One idea floated was that each member of Congress should create a political "living will," designating his or her own list of successors in case of death or incapacitation. Several states, including Delaware and Texas, had passed similar bills during the 1950s and 1960s at the height of the Cold War to reconstitute their state legislatures following a nuclear attack. Two former House speakers, Tom Foley and Newt Gingrich, endorsed that "expeditious path" to solving the congressional continuity issue and preserving the House's directly elected "legitimacy." Another suggestion held that it should be up to each governor to decide whether the majority of his or her state's congressional delegation was incapacitated; if a majority of governors declared their members unable to serve, it would trigger the constitutional amendment allowing temporary appointments.

It took years, though, before Speaker Dennis Hastert finally moved forward on "Continuity of Congress" legislation that required states to hold "expedited" special elections within forty-nine days of a declaration by the speaker of the House that more than 100 congressional seats were vacant. Considering the wealth of decisions, executive orders, and precedents that would be set and executed in the first forty-nine days after a devastating attack—decisions that would likely shape the future of the nation in myriad ways big and small—Congress effectively abdicated its responsibility to participate in the nation's governance. Work also began at Fort McNair in 2005 on a massive new $79 million 255,000-square-foot building, Lincoln Hall, that included a cafeteria, meeting rooms, offices, SCIFs for discussing classified information, and a 600-person auditorium. Officially part of the National Defense University, the facility stood ready as an alternate House of Representatives should Capitol Hill again be rendered unusable, as it was during the 2001 anthrax scares.

Maybe there was another reason that the congressional leadership didn't see a need for more robust continuity planning: "Enduring Constitutional Government." ECG plans have never been made public, and the White House will only describe it as "a cooperative effort among the executive, legislative and judicial branches of government, coordinated by the President, to preserve the capability to execute constitutional responsibilities in a catastrophic emergency," but beyond that ambiguous statement, the phrase's true meaning—and the scope of the projects and procedures that it might encompass—remain highly classified.* It's clear ECG policies don't necessarily preserve peacetime constitutional precedents, and instead focus on establishing a streamlined process that could ensure the nation's constitutional traditions could be reestablished over a longer time horizon. In other words, ECG programs are aimed at preserving the spirit of the Constitution, not the letter of it.

One informed theory holds that the secret procedures have a specific, defined role for a small, preselected set of congressional leaders—perhaps as small as the four party leaders of the two houses—who would serve as a "rump" or "skeleton" Congress until a full group could be established months later and would, in the absence of the larger body, serve to approve or disapprove legislation and executive actions. Such a body would mirror the "Gang of Eight" who are kept regularly informed by the president about covert military and intelligence actions conducted around the world. Whereas Congress in general is supposed to be kept informed of U.S. military and intelligence matters, the president could choose in "extraordinary circumstances affecting vital interests" to tell only this smaller group—the four party leaders and the chairs and ranking minority members of the House and Senate intelligence committees—about particularly highly classified, high-risk, or time-sensitive actions. The group, designated as representatives for the larger body and codified in the National Security Act of 1947, have no official say and are sworn to complete secrecy—they can't even, for instance, share concerns about executive actions with other members of

* President Clinton's 1998 PDD 67, entitled "Enduring Constitutional Government and Continuity of Government Operations," remains entirely classified, even though it was replaced by an updated measure in 2007.

Congress—but simply by informing them, the president would be fulfilling his or her responsibility to share. It's easy to see a similar procedure being part of ECG following an attack where it's difficult to share decision making with the full, large, slow, unwieldy Congress.

Such a conclusion is backed up by the one continuity area Congress did tackle successfully after 9/11: starting to appoint its own "designated successor." For decades, a member of the cabinet had skipped major gatherings like the State of the Union to ensure a presidential successor if a disaster struck, and in the weeks following 9/11 Congress did the same. On September 20, 2001, when President Bush spoke to the body, House Majority Leader Dick Armey skipped the event to be the "legislative successor," and for the 2002 State of the Union, House Majority Whip Tom Delay was flown by helicopter an hour outside Washington to ensure legislative continuity. What precisely would the role of a single surviving congressional leader be in the wake of a disaster? That was classified—a procedure, part of Enduring Constitutional Government, hidden away inside the sealed envelopes watched over by FEMA's Program Coordination Division.

In the wake of the attacks, scholars, White House officials, and congressional leaders who began to look at the presidential succession laws foresaw numerous catastrophic scenarios where it would not be clear who could legally claim to be commander-in-chief. As legal scholar Akhil Amar told Congress during one post-9/11 hearing, "The current Presidential Succession Act, 3 U.S.C. Section 19, is in my view a disastrous statute, an accident waiting to happen. It should be repealed and replaced."

Dick Cheney had personally identified one of the holes in the Twenty-fifth Amendment: As the vice president, who had a well-known history of heart trouble, was preparing to take office in 2001, he realized there wasn't any mechanism to replace him should he become incapacitated. His counsel, David Addington, carefully researched the question and discovered an even bigger issue—the procedure for activating the Twenty-fifth Amendment and replacing a president required the vice president to convene the cabinet, so, in theory, a vice president had to exist and be able to step in as acting president. An incapacitated vice president might mean that an incapacitated president couldn't be replaced.

To ensure that his own health problems wouldn't leave the nation without an able vice president, Cheney wrote a secret letter of resignation, dated March 28, 2001, and addressed it to the secretary of state—not unlike the letters that Eisenhower, Kennedy, and Johnson had penned before the existence of the Twenty-fifth Amendment. He handed the letter to Addington with a cautionary speech: "I won't give specific instructions about when this letter should be triggered, but you need to understand something. This is not your decision to make. This is not Lynne's decision to make. The only thing you are to do, if I become incapacitated, is get this letter out and give it to the president. It's his decision, and his alone, whether he delivers it to the secretary of state." Addington slipped the resignation letter inside two manila envelopes, and hid it in a dresser drawer at his home—where it would be safe from even a crisis that destroyed the White House. Cheney told President Bush what he'd done and that Addington had the letter, if the need ever arose. Other than that, their plan remained secret throughout Bush's presidency.

That secret letter only solved one of the many conundrums that scholars began to focus on in the Presidential Succession Act. The nation's existing rules made it particularly vulnerable during presidential inaugurations, when the terms of the president and vice president constitutionally expired at noon on January 20, but their cabinets remained in office until either a resignation was tendered or a successor was confirmed by the Senate, which didn't typically happen for hours or even days after an inauguration. In 2001, as John Fortier (the executive director of the Continuity of Government Commission) explained, a terror attack that targeted George W. Bush's inauguration might have left the nation with a president carried over from the previous administration who would then serve until Congress had a speaker or president pro tem who would "bump" out the president and serve the rest of the four-year term of office. Fortier said, "A country expecting Republican George W. Bush to take office would have found themselves with a Democratic President Larry Summers."*

* As treasury secretary, Summers was the highest-ranking cabinet official eligible for the presidency, since Secretary of State Madeleine Albright had been born in Czechoslovakia. In 1989, at George H. W. Bush's inauguration, the situation would have been even more

The Continuity of Government Commission also raised an issue that had dogged presidential succession since the arrival of the atomic bomb: On a day-to-day basis everyone in the presidential line of succession lives and works in a tiny radius extending a few miles around the White House and the Capitol. "In the nightmare scenario of terrorists detonating a nuclear device, it is possible that everyone in the line of succession might be killed," John Fortier told Congress during one hearing. "Imagine the aftermath: a parade of generals, Governors, and Under Secretaries claiming to be in charge." He proposed creating for the first time a new formal COG structure that included people outside Washington in the succession line, allowing a president to nominate officials like sitting state governors or prominent retired public figures. Once confirmed, these "presidents-of-last-resort" would receive security clearances, regular briefings on national security and economic issues, and perhaps even have a normal role in coordinating regional homeland security efforts or disaster response.*

The commission also confronted one of the strangest and most nettlesome phrases in COG operations—a seemingly unnecessary aside in the language guiding presidential succession known as the "supplantation clause," which held that a prior-entitled presidential successor could supplant a lower-level officer who was serving as "acting president." Harry Truman had felt that "elected" officials should always trump "appointed" officials in presidential succession, and the Presidential Succession Act allowed a newly chosen speaker of the House or Senate president pro tem to take over from a cabinet official who had been serving as "acting president." For instance, in a situation where the president and the congressional leadership

confusing: Michael Armacost, the #3 official at Reagan's State Department, would have been elevated to president of the United States, because the outgoing secretary of state, George Shultz, and deputy secretary of state, John C. Whitehead, had both resigned before the inauguration. Then, with the House in Democratic hands, a newly chosen speaker could have bumped Armacost and given the nation four years of Democratic rule.

* Another proposal, floated during the post-9/11 discussions but dating back to Nelson Rockefeller in the 1960s, would have created a "first secretary," a cabinet official who would have been first in line to the presidency after the vice president and whose sole responsibility would be to remain outside Washington and be the "designated survivor" to head the shadow government if a catastrophic event destroyed the capital.

were killed, but the vice president only incapacitated, the secretary of state would presumably serve as "acting president" until the vice president was able to resume his or her responsibility and become the president. But the "supplantation clause" inserted important ambiguity—could a newly elected speaker of the House or Senate president pro tem insist on replacing the secretary of state even after that person had assumed the office of "acting president"? Could a newly elected speaker supplant a president pro tem? Might the presidency swing widely in a few days, at the height of a crisis, between different officials and different political parties?

Republican senator John Cornyn raised the question of what happened if a speaker of the House or Senate president pro tem ascended to the presidency, but was challenged by the secretary of state, who argued that the legislators didn't count as constitutional officers. "Believe it or not, the secretary actually has a rather strong case, in my view," Cornyn said. No less an authority than James Madison had argued that they were legislators, not constitutional officers, and thus ineligible to succeed to the presidency. It was a question that the Twenty-fifth Amendment had entirely sidestepped, but one that seemed poised to arise at the worst possible moment.

Altogether, without a broad range of fixes—none of which Congress seemed inclined to institute or at least work on—presidential succession remained a recipe for confusion, instability, and perhaps even a silent coup.

As the government reorganized FEMA and other agencies into the Department of Homeland Security—a twenty-two-agency, $36 billion-a-year anti-terrorism behemoth with nearly a quarter million employees—COOP and COG planning remained poorly coordinated and scattershot; in one audit, a cabinet department listed speechwriting for the secretary as an "essential function," but failed to include nine of the ten "high-impact" programs that the White House had charged the department with fulfilling. In fact, the Government Accountability Office found that across the government twenty of the thirty-eight designated "high-impact" programs weren't covered by COOP or COG planning. In December 2003, FEMA put 300 of its staff through a little-publicized exercise known as QUIET STRENGTH, where its emergency group relocated to Mount Weather—the first time FEMA had ever run a full exercise to test its ability to notify, evacuate, and relocate its own emergency workers.

FEMA and DHS also updated "Federal Preparedness Circular 65," a document first issued in 1999 that laid out the specific requirements for government COOP plans. Coupled with other key DHS reports like the National Response Plan (NRP) and the National Infrastructure Protection Plan (NIPP), FPC 65 was meant to lay out the essential functions necessary to keep the nation running smoothly in a crisis. But, even with three years and billions in new spending, Congress wasn't all that sure the nation seemed much better prepared, and it gave FEMA an additional $12 million to boost COOP planning. During a contentious 2004 hearing, Republican representative Tom Davis, whose district covered much of the northern Virginia suburbs packed with federal workers, used puns to chastise Michael Brown's agency. "Chickens are in charge of the COOP," Congressman Davis joked. "We don't want the agencies winging it on their COOP plans, so we will risk ruffling some feathers here today, but I think it's fair to say that the administration's proposals are nothing to crow about."

Brown, for his part, joked about his own desire to escape the grilling, replying, "I'm ready to fly the coop."

Within a year, no one would be laughing about the government's emergency plans.

As planners examined the state of the government's preparations post- 9/11, the judicial branch appeared in poor shape—and, like Congress, its continuity was a minefield of potential problems. In the weeks after 9/11, the judiciary established a new Emergency Preparedness Office, and the government constructed a new judicial relocation facility outside the Beltway, near Dulles Airport, that could serve as a COOP facility if needed. Under normal operations, the Court Operations Support Center in Reston served as the day-to-day back end of the federal courts, working on tasks like payroll processing, but it could be used as a fallback location if the courts were forced from their Capitol Hill offices.

Less easy to solve were the fundamental questions about how to reconstitute the Supreme Court after an emergency. It was an issue that had never received much interest—not even from the Supreme Court chief justices themselves during the Cold War—but real constitutional quandaries might arise from a national disaster that the Court might need to address: Was the language of the Presidential Succession Act constitutional, did the House speaker and Senate president pro tem count as "officers" who could ascend to the presidency? Who would adjudicate competing claims to the presidency? Who could rule on the questions regarding congressional quorums in the case of large numbers of deaths or incapacitations? What would happen if district or appeals courts ruled differently on questions of martial law, the suspension of habeas corpus, press censorship, or the nationalization of various industries? What if a governor or the president tried to suspend regularly scheduled elections that soon followed another attack? On 9/11, New York's governor had suspended the mayoral primary unfolding that day in New York City—but it wasn't entirely clear how he had that power, if he did at all.

Since Supreme Court justices were appointed for life, it made little sense to rush them through, since an emergency transition might give a president—potentially even an acting president who was not elected by the public—the ability to appoint justices who would serve for decades. Presidents had, in limited cases, made recess appointments to the Supreme Court—Ike did with Chief Justice Earl Warren, before submitting him to the Senate for normal confirmation—but if the Court was facing a question about the president's own legitimacy following a disaster, could he or she really handpick the justices who would rule whether the acting president could stay in the Oval Office?

The Continuity of Government Commission suggested that Congress pass legislation creating an interim emergency court made up of the living justices, as well as the living chief judges of the federal circuits. Such a court might end up with as many as eighteen or nineteen justices, but, the commission explained, "The advantage of this arrangement is that it is simple, could be quickly constituted, would allow the surviving members of the court to sit on the emergency court, and would draw on the most senior and experienced leaders of the federal judiciary."*

* As another alternative, the COG Commission also suggested creating a pool of standby justices—nominated by the president from among the sitting federal judges and confirmed

None of the suggestions about the Supreme Court went anywhere. The attention focused on such issues by the Continuity of Government Commission proved brief, quickly lost in the arrival of the Iraq War, the 2004 election, Hurricane Katrina and FEMA's badly bungled response to that disaster, and the many other issues and crises that seemed more pressing in the short term. Just years later, the commission's website was allowed to expire and it has since been taken over by a kinky Japanese sex site. Meanwhile, nearly all of the quandaries it raised would still bedevil the nation in an emergency.

Hurricane Katrina served as a cautionary tale for those who tracked how the nation would respond to an emergency; anyone who argued that the military wouldn't assume massive, near-dictatorial powers had only to look to the streets of New Orleans. Both Mayor Ray Nagin and Governor Kathleen Blanco called publicly for an armed military security force after the storm hit the Gulf Coast. Bush himself, during a speech weeks after Katrina in New Orleans in the city's Jackson Square—a memorial to the man who, ironically enough, first declared martial law in the United States—promised greater military involvement for future catastrophes. As he reassured the nation, "It is now clear that a challenge on this scale requires greater federal authority and a broader role for the armed forces—the institution of our government most capable of massive logistical operations on a moment's notice."

The overarching goal of the nation's emergency plans has always been to preserve the United States—but history has shown that presidents are more than willing to make short-term compromises to America's traditional freedoms if they feel it necessary for the greater good's future survival, decisions that have ranged from Abraham Lincoln's suspension of the writ of

---

each Congress by the Senate—who could step in as interim justices to return the Supreme Court to a quorum. Meanwhile, Randy Moss, a former Clinton-era head of the Justice Department's Office of Legal Counsel, proposed establishing an emergency interim court that could weigh in on settling inter-branch disputes as well as disputes among the nation's judicial circuits. It would serve for a finite time period in an exigency until a quorum could be rebuilt at the Supreme Court level.

habeas corpus in the Civil War to FDR's internment of Japanese Americans during World War II. However repulsive such actions may appear in historical hindsight, the commanders-in-chief viewed them as necessary in the moment. As the U.S. Supreme Court argued, in reviewing the martial law invoked on Hawaii in 1941, such measures could be justified by the goal "to create conditions wherein civil government can be rapidly reconstituted." The precise way that happens, the extent of the compromises, and how "rapid" the return might be to something resembling "normal" governance are matters open to future emergencies.

"Martial law" has no specific constitutional definition; instead, it's an informal set of powers cobbled together through existing law and emergency executive authorities. "Martial law" has been declared in exigent circumstances regularly throughout U.S. history—General Andrew Jackson declared it in New Orleans during the War of 1812, President Lincoln invoked it repeatedly during the Civil War, and Hawaii's territorial governor invoked it after the attack on Pearl Harbor in 1941. Governors have declared more limited martial law in the face of civil insurrections and natural disasters—during labor strikes in the nineteenth century and early twentieth century, in San Francisco after the 1906 earthquake and subsequent fire, and after labor unrest at the North Dakota state capitol in 1933.

If and when a local or national emergency necessitates "martial law," there are, in fact, two vastly different "martial law" scenarios considered: There's one version of "martial law" where, following a fast-moving crisis that affects all three federal branches, the executive branch steps in and runs all of government by fiat, disregarding all of peacetime's constitutional checks and balances, as well as normal state and local prerogatives. Another even more extreme version, though, might see a designated—or self-designated—military commander step in following a devastating crisis and use the might of the armed services to restore order, perhaps with the blessing of a figurehead presidential successor, before returning leadership and full authority to the civilian government, which might or might not entail traditional power sharing and checks and balances with the legislative and judicial branches.

During one post-9/11 interview about COG, Ken Duberstein, a former Reagan chief of staff, was direct when Ted Koppel asked him about the aftermath of a serious attack: "Realistically speaking, if we had that kind of attack again on Washington," Koppel queried, "aren't you left for at least the foreseeable future with some sort of martial law anyway?"

Duberstein's answer was direct: "Yes."

NSC aide Richard Clarke's answer to the same question on the same show was hardly more encouraging. "I think in any war where Washington were destroyed, inevitably there would be a period of, for lack of a better term, something like martial law. The key here is though, that the plans all call for going back to a normal three-branch system as rapidly as possible."

The disaster of Hurricane Katrina helped accelerate a shift in COG planning away from the Department of Homeland Security and more toward the White House; officials realized that any major disaster would require coordination far beyond DHS itself and that it was better to use White House authority to marshal the necessary resources. The government's approach settled into four major umbrellas: Enduring Constitutional Government represented government-wide plans to preserve the nation's core leadership, while COG referred to more specific activities within a single branch to preserve functions and leadership, and COOP referred to the activities of specific departments, agencies, and components to preserve day-to-day responsibilities. Lastly, there was COP—the Continuity of the Presidency— the plans that ensured that there would always be a commander-in-chief, regardless of what transpired.

President George W. Bush privately signed a new order on May 4, 2007, known as National Security Presidential Directive (NSPD) 51, that outlined the nation's continuity policies, established a new "National Continuity Coordinator" who would oversee the efforts from the White House, and introduced a new four-stage COGCON alert system, similar to the military's DEFCON system, to track the government's continuity readiness levels.* It

---

* COGCON 4 signaled normal operations, with the ability to implement continuity plans within twelve hours; COGCON 1 signaled full activation of continuity plans, required all systems operational within two hours' notice, and that each agency must place a headquarters-level successor at its alternate facility.

included eight "National Essential Functions" that should guide continuity planning:

1) Ensuring the continued functioning of government under the Constitution, including the functioning of the three separate branches of government;

2) Providing leadership visible to the Nation and the world and maintaining the trust and confidence of the American people;

3) Defending the Constitution of the United States against all enemies, foreign and domestic, and preventing or interdicting attacks against the United States or its people, property, or interests;

4) Maintaining and fostering effective relationships with foreign nations;

5) Protecting against threats to the homeland and bringing to justice perpetrators of crimes or attacks against the United States or its people, property, or interests;

6) Providing rapid and effective response to and recovery from the domestic consequences of an attack or other incident;

7) Protecting and stabilizing the Nation's economy and ensuring public confidence in its financial systems; and

8) Providing for critical Federal Government services that address the national health, safety, and welfare needs of the United States.

What plans precisely guide those eight "essential functions" remained a tightly held secret. The majority of the document consisted of classified annexes. The only annex released publicly outlined how the government had been partitioned into four categories for COG planning. The top tier, those with the greatest responsibility and necessity to preserve operations and reconstitute themselves in an emergency, included the Departments of State, Treasury, Defense, Justice, Health and Human Services, Transportation, Energy, Homeland Security, the Office of the Director of National Intelligence, and the Central Intelligence Agency. Five components of the cabinet departments were specifically mentioned as playing a key role in ECG: the Army Corps of Engineers, the FBI, FEMA, the Secret Service, and the National Communications System. In NSPD 51, the Defense and Homeland Security Departments were tasked together with providing "secure, in-tegrated Continuity of Government communications to the President, the Vice President, and, at a minimum, Category I executive departments and agencies."*

The ECG program outlines were so highly classified that members of Congress were prohibited from reading the classified documents that out-lined the actual procedures.

---

* The second, less critical tier included the Departments of Interior, Agriculture, Com-merce, Labor, Housing and Urban Development, Education, Veterans Affairs, and nine stand-alone agencies like the FCC, the Federal Reserve, the Postal Service, the General Services Administration, and others. A third tier outlined another thirteen lower-priority agencies, including the FDIC, NASA, the SEC, and the Small Business Administration. All of the rest of the executive branch's agencies, commissions, boards, and bureaus were relegated to Category IV, a group that—if NSPD 51 was consistent with how prior admin-istrations had labeled them—would not have any COG responsibilities at all; they would just sit on the sidelines until (or if) the government returned to normal functioning.

Chapter 19

DOOMSDAY PREPPING

As Barack Obama was sworn in as president on a cold January day in 2009, behind the scenes a disaster government waited anxiously: Defense Secretary Robert Gates skipped the event as the designated presidential survivor and other officials scattered, too—Gates's undersecretary of defense for intelligence, James Clapper, retreated to Raven Rock's caves to serve as the designated survivor for the defense secretary, emerging only when the new commander-in-chief was safely in place.

Upon taking office, the president launched a six-month study of COG that showed real progress in programs that ensured a "survivable core" of officials, but still little planning for what came next. President Obama inherited numerous COG plans, projects, and procedures, all freshly developed and updated by the Bush administration. As his aides were "read into the Special Access Programs," as government speak refers to the process of being told of the existing ECG and COG procedures, they were fascinated to discover the scope of the work done by the Bush and Cheney teams. Redundancies were piled upon redundancies.

In the early days of the administration, new West Wing staffers received briefings on how and where they'd be evacuated. Since senior advisor David Axelrod was designated the main communications evacuee, the alternate, Dan Pfeiffer, joked that he kept a box of snack cakes in his desk to distract Axelrod in an emergency so Pfeiffer could get the coveted spot on the evacuation helicopter instead. Other staffers would be less lucky: They received briefings on nearby rental cars so that, if an attack occurred, they could try to drive themselves to the relocation sites.

Across government, nuclear war plans had been updated to respond to new types of threats: In 2009, President Obama signed Executive Order 13527, decreeing a new post-9/11 role for the Postal Service, which had during the Cold War been responsible for registering the dead in the event of a nuclear holocaust. Now, in the era of terrorism, it would serve as the agency responsible for delivering "medical countermeasures" to biological weapons to the nation since it had "the capacity for rapid residential delivery." Should a wide-scale bioweapon attack like anthrax disrupt a city, state, or region of the country, only the Postal Service would possess the ability to visit every residence in a single day to deliver antibiotics or another antidote from the government's Strategic National Stockpile, DHS explained. In the event that the "Postal Plan" is activated, the Post Office would suspend all mail delivery to the affected region and, escorted by local or state law enforcement, the mail carriers—each of whom would don disposable clothing, protective gloves, and a "NIOSH-approved N-95 disposable particulate respirator"— deliver "a uniform, predetermined quantity of prepackaged medications . . . to each residential mail address along with information sheets."

Much of COG is now a routine part of government life. For instance, there's GSA Form SF 336, the four-page "Alternate Facility Reporting Form," which asks agencies to attest that their facilities have the proper documentation and legal agreements in place to occupy the relocation sites, as well as that the facilities are "NCSD 3-10 compliant," a lengthy and detailed document that lays out the "Minimum Requirements for Continuity Communications Capabilities." The directive requires secure cell and satellite phone capabilities for the senior leadership of all Category I, II, and III organizations, as well as more robust classified systems for the most critical agencies. It also requires agencies to have communication capabilities for leadership in transit to the alternate location—an attempt to limit the problems of 9/11 and to encourage senior leaders to actually travel to the relocation sites if they can.

A day ahead of President Obama's visit to Germany in June 2009, a white unmarked Gulfstream III touched down at Stuttgart Airport. Preparations for the president's visit to Dresden on June 5 had been under way for months, and U.S. matériel had been streaming into Dresden for weeks in advance. Beyond the most visible symbol, the blue-and-white Air Force One 747 that normally transports the president, there are numerous other military aircraft that shuttle staff, communications gear, security teams, helicopters, and armored vehicles ahead of each presidential and vice presidential trip. The Air Force groups those missions into three code-named categories: PHOENIX BANNER, a "special air mission" directly supporting the president; PHOENIX SILVER, a flight supporting the vice president; and PHOENIX COPPER, denoting flights flown in support of the Secret Service for VIPs other than the president and vice president. The basic procedures for such flights fill page after page of a manual, "Air Force Instruction #11-289," and carefully delineate how seats should be configured on transport aircraft (one of the six seats must be reserved for HMX-1 security personnel if a helicopter is on board), how presidential limousines should be loaded (driven forward, not backed in), how weapons can be carried aboard (Secret Service agents are limited to three clips of ammo on their person and three more in their baggage), whether alcohol can be served to passengers (sometimes), and the specific tie-downs necessary for transporting various helicopters.

Aboard those PHOENIX BANNER flights—even though most of the presidential motorcade for that Germany trip would be made up of local black Mercedes sedans—the Secret Service and the Air Force had flown to Dresden multiple heavily armored limousines, Secret Service Suburbans, and communications vans for the president, staff, and security to use, a configuration of vehicles known as the "secure package." Helicopters from HMX-1 had been flown over aboard transport planes to help the president travel around Germany.* While exact costs are nearly impossible to calculate, the Government Accountability Office estimates the Defense Department spends nearly $100 million a year to support presidential and vice presidential trips and the required staff, gear, and vehicles around the world.

Yet despite all these Herculean efforts ahead of the president's trip to Germany, at first glance the $40 million Gulfstream that landed in

---

* The president's use of helicopters is so routine that it's easy to overlook the accompanying logistical feat: The United States is the only nation in the world that supplies its own helicopter "package" to its head of state everywhere in the world.

Stuttgart—an hour's flight from the president's visit to Dresden—appeared to have nothing to do with Obama's trip, blending in among the anonymous business jets that fill most major airports around the world. It had no apparent business in Stuttgart and its crew hung close to the plane. It remained in Germany only a day and took off again around the time the president departed to continue the next leg of his trip in France. As Air Force One went to Caen, France, the Gulfstream flew across the English Channel to the U.K.'s Mildenhall Air Force Base, where it waited in a hangar during President Obama's visit to the Normandy beaches for the anniversary of D-Day on June 6. Then the Gulfstream flew back to the United States. On neither leg of the trip did the plane appear to have any purpose whatsoever. Only someone who looked up its tail number, 60403, would have discovered its secret.

Built in 1985, the Gulfstream was the Air Force's plane 86-0403, one of three special presidential aircraft tasked with the duty of COG evacuations and the preservation of the National Command Authorities. Known as C-20Cs, the planes don't officially exist. They are the president's chameleons, blending in anonymously at airports close to presidential visits—but almost never at the same airport where Air Force One itself is traveling. The Air Force's website doesn't acknowledge the existence of the C-20Cs, neither does the listing of aircraft maintained by the 89th Airlift Wing, the unit at Joint Base Andrews that runs presidential missions. As one Air Force official put it, "Our position is that we do not have any aircraft called a C-20C." One of the only references to the planes is on the government's official master list of aircraft designations, which offers only the vaguest information on the related Gulfstreams known as C-20B, saying the plane "operates on DC power" and offers "upgraded avionics used for the President and other high-ranking officials." The C-20C it describes only as a "modified C-20B with enhanced, secure communications. Used to support senior-level personnel and to provide backup for Air Force One."

For most of its thirty-year existence, the C-20 fleet has consisted of three aircraft, known by their tail numbers as 50049, 50050, and 60403, and delivered to the Air Force as the Reagan administration's massive investment in COG operations upgraded the government's command and control systems. The C-20Cs, like the NEACP planes, had been purposely built with slightly older dial-and-gauge cockpits, rather than the more modern all-glass computer displays, to help protect against an EMP burst following a nearby nuclear explosion. But the gear aboard is top-notch, with satellite communications networks and classified defensive measures that would protect the plane during an attack.

The C-20 planes, while much smaller and able to carry far fewer passengers than a 747, do have distinct advantages from a COG perspective: Their ability to land on a runway just half the length required for a 747 means that they're agile enough to use nearly any airport in the world—which could be very useful if you were suddenly going to be trying to hide a president somewhere in the United States.

Or, specifically, if you're trying to hide a president at Mount Weather.

Mount Weather itself has no airplane runways, just a long grass strip and concrete helipads, but a few miles away, down at the base of the mountain in Upperville, Virginia, the sprawling palatial 2,000-acre estate known as Oak Spring Farms has an odd feature: a paved private airstrip. Paul and Bunny Mellon combined two large fortunes when they married in 1948—he a banking heir, she heir to the Gillette fortune—and devoted themselves to horse breeding, art collecting, and Washington society, where they enjoyed close relationships with the upper echelon of D.C. It was Bunny Mellon, a famed landscape architect, who worked with Jackie Kennedy in the 1960s to make over a stale and worn-out garden dating to the Wilson administration into the modern White House Rose Garden. Mellon in 1969 described her gardening aesthetic as "nothing should be noticed," but the phrase also appeared to help explain the couple's reclusive and publicity-shy lifestyle in Virginia's horse country at Oak Spring Farms. Given their ties to the Washington elite and their aversion to publicity, their estate appeared to be the perfect place to hide an evacuation airfield for Mount Weather.

The estate's private airstrip, which Bunny and Paul Mellon used for their own private plane, originally came into existence in the 1950s, just as government miners began to excavate the bunker at Mount Weather. On charts from the early 1960s, the Mellon runway was just 3,500 feet long—sufficient, for instance, to land a Lockheed JetStar C-140, the plane that served as the day-to-day workhorses of the presidential fleet for staff and VIPs.* By 1962, as the Kennedys became frequent guests—Jackie had her own cottage on the estate—the Mellons' runway had been lengthened to 4,100 feet, and in the early 1970s the paved runway underwent a third expansion to 5,100 feet. By then, it also included lighting to ease night approaches.

In the 1980s, as the Reagan administration began its heavy investment in COG and command and control networks, the Air Force selected the Gulfstream III jet as a replacement for the JetStars.

Its landing requirement? 5,100 feet.

Much of the West's Cold War infrastructure has atrophied or been abandoned in the twenty-first century. Canada's main COG site, the Diefenbunker, is a museum and movie set. In 2016, Northern Ireland put up for sale its sole COG bunker for £575,000, a four-acre site in Ballymena, County Antrim, that once could have housed 235 government leaders. Elsewhere in the U.K., a Scottish nuclear bunker was turned into a museum—a two-story facility complete with a chapel, hidden beneath an ordinary-looking country farmhouse built to conceal the bunker's entrance. Another sold for £200,000 in 2014 to a tech firm that wants to use it for data storage. Britain's main bunker, known as "Site 3," was declassified in 2004, its long double-sided 1960s-style telephone switchboard a relic of a lost age.

Too often, in fact, over the first years of the twenty-first century, the only time when the nation's nuclear systems made headlines was for scandals that seemed to demonstrate just how irrelevant the once-proud Curtis LeMay force had become. In 2003, nearly half the Air Force's nuclear weapons units failed their safety inspections, despite having advance warning. In 2007, in a notable BENT SPEAR incident, the Air Force lost six nuclear weapons for thirty-six hours when a North Dakota ground crew accidentally loaded live nuclear cruise missiles onto a bomber that then flew across the United States to Barksdale Air Force Base, where the plane sat unguarded overnight before anyone noticed that it had real weapons. Twice in 2012, missileers fell asleep in their launch capsule with the blast doors open, a serious

---

* Lyndon Johnson, who used JetStars to ferry back and forth to his Texas ranch, referred to the diminutive planes good-naturedly as "Air Force One-Half."

violation of security protocols. Then, in 2014, a massive cheating scandal hit the Air Force's ICBM crews, leading to the suspension of nearly 100 airmen and the firing of nine top commanders—a scandal that officials blamed in part on the bad morale among the launch crews, who felt they were a Cold War backwater in the armed services. It wasn't hard to feel they might have been right: Even as the Pentagon embraced new high-tech weapons like drones, stealth ships, and fighter planes, the nation's nuclear infrastructure was aging and increasingly downright obsolete. In 2014, a *60 Minutes* story pointed out that Minuteman missile silos still use eight-inch floppy disks as part of their computer launch systems, a technology so ancient that many of the new, young missileers had never seen it before stepping into the launch capsules.*

Even as the nation's nuclear weapons seemed to rust, emotional traits from the Cold War had clearly made the leap to American life post-9/11. The ethos of the disproportionate response—the same mentality that led superpowers to stockpile tens of thousands of nuclear warheads—led to a period of fifteen years in which counterterrorism and homeland security spending dwarfed all other government investments, militarized local police departments, and turned airline travel into a security nightmare. But the most enduring artifact of the Cold War and the nuclear arms race seems to be the era's broad paranoia—the fear that the American way of life could be wiped off the face of the earth in a moment. The September 11th attacks reactivated and worsened that paranoia and created a cultural fascination with Doomsday planning that began to permeate popular culture.

In daily life, the rise of shows like *The Walking Dead* and post-Apocalyptic movies and TV shows seemed to herald a renewed fascination with Doomsday. "Doomsday prepping" itself became a cult phenomenon, as Americans tuned in to cable TV shows to watch their fellow citizens stockpile arms, food, supplies—sometimes even gold or silver coins—to combat the coming End of Days. The survivalists featured on a National Geographic TV show, a modern incarnation of the 1950s and 1960s fallout shelter craze,

---

* Choosing to view the glass as half full, Major General Jack Weinstein told *60 Minutes* that because the technology was so outdated, the ancient IT system actually helped make the missile silos more secure against high-tech cyber-hacking.

explained to viewers their "bug-out bags" and "disaster swag," ready for nuclear war, pandemics, earthquakes, EMPs, or zombies. The "prepper" community was fueled by conferences, expos, and a generalized fear that doom lay just around the corner, and became big business as the internet linked like-minded people around the country on sites like urbansurvivalsite.com. The big-box retailer Costco offers "disaster-preparedness" products on its website, including a $3,199.99 cache of emergency food to feed four people for nine months. Jay Blevins, a former law enforcement officer who lives in Berryville, Virginia, not far from Mount Weather, built a prepper network among his family and friends, whose skills would help complement each other and ensure survival among them in a catastrophe. As he told one reporter in 2012, "his Christian faith drives him to help others prepare, and although he is not certain the end is near, he thinks getting prepared is an act of personal responsibility."

Businessman Robert Vicino founded a company in 2008 named Vivos to turn surplus government bunkers into the ultimate Doomsday shelter. He offered Americans the chance to reserve a spot in an eighty-person shelter in Indiana—which came with pillow-top mattresses, leather couches, flat-screen TVs, and granite countertops and could sustain the group for a year—at a cost of $50,000 per adult and $35,000 per child. His website advertised, though, that "Discounts are available to members with needed skill sets."

While such plans and shows were entertaining mostly because of how far-fetched and out of the mainstream they seemed, it was easy to forget most days that the government's own "Doomsday prepping" was continuing out of sight, and that its entire shadow government is, in many ways, bigger, stronger, and more robust than it ever was during the Cold War. The programs and planning are buried inside innocuous-sounding entities like the Pentagon's Center for National and Nuclear Leadership Command Capability, FEMA's Special Programs Division, the Defense Threat Reduction Agency's Balanced Survivability Assessment branch, or the Joint System Engineering and Integration Office (JSEIO) at the Defense Information Systems Agency (DISA).

To avoid the problems that dogged such programs in the 1970s, when PEADs were regularly out of date and sometimes even illegal, today the special emergency instructions are supposed to be checked and inventoried monthly, on the first Monday of each month, and once a year all the instruc-tions are reviewed and updated. The instructions, tucked inside a sealed and individually numbered envelope marked on the outside only by an obtuse title, laid out all the various ways that the U.S. government, economy, and daily life would be remade in an emergency.

Twice a year, in March and September, the Raven Rock security office collects an updated list from all requisite agencies of the potential relocation personnel—including their Social Security numbers, security clearance levels, and the date of their most recent security check. Every August, the site conducts a complete audit of all its access badges to ensure that each one is accounted for. In the event of a relocation event, or as the site calls it, "Hasty Access," a designated official from each agency would lead its team to Raven Rock and have to provide a specified challenge code word to the military police at the front gate to demonstrate that the lead official is not under duress.* Those who might travel to Raven Rock and the other relocation facilities receive detailed instructions about packing and travel. Coast Guard personnel designated to its West Virginia relocation facility are told, amusingly, to obey carefully the speed limits on Route 9W through Virginia's Loudon County, since "The local police are vigorous enforcers of the law."

Once personnel arrive at Raven Rock ("You will travel 6.8 miles from the Emmitsburg Square and then turn left (south) onto Harbaugh Valley Road. After approximately 0.8 miles on Harbaugh Valley Road, you will turn left up an incline into the SITE R checkpoint. Gladhill Road is directly opposite the SITE R entrance."), drivers are reminded that "there is back-in parking only authorized at SITE R." Moreover, at the site, you might be forced to walk ten to fifteen minutes from your parking spot, so "appropriate weather gear and comfortable walking shoes may be necessary." Many of the seemingly reasonable details in the handbooks and relocation manuals are amusing in context. Relocated staff should plan to bring two sets of clothing and two towels, as well as their own laundry detergent to wash

---

* Officials evacuating to Raven Rock by helicopter, a process governed by the code word programs BLUE LIGHT and IRON GATE, obviously don't show ID before landing, but are cleared in advance. IRON GATE officials are those whom guards are supposed to recognize on sight.

said clothes and towels. They are prohibited from bringing their own radios, knives, or alcohol. Those headed to the bunkers are encouraged to bring combination locks to secure their designated lockers—a strange recommendation to protect against petty theft in the most secure place in the world. Flashlights are also encouraged, since the underground facilities could be dark and the dormitories would be in use twenty-four hours a day for sleeping. According to their "Relocation Procedures and Support Handbook," the triple bunks in the dormitories would be used all day in rotating shifts.

Raven Rock has grown dramatically since 9/11: In 2001, the Defense Department listed the site as consisting of fifty-nine buildings with 450,000 square feet. While there were small additions in the years immediately after the attacks, a building boom hit the complex as the COG machinery grew. For security reasons, the Defense Department for a period stopped listing Raven Rock publicly by name in its annual base reports, but it's still easy to find it if you're looking for it—and by 2012, the facility was composed of sixty-six buildings and 615,000 square feet of space. Just a year later, in 2013, it had grown to sixty-nine buildings and 639,000 square feet. There were huge jumps, too, in its fuel storage, as the underground city added twenty-seven new fuel tanks in 2012, each of which could hold 20,000 gallons.

Most days, life at Raven Rock is like life at any other military base. The normal temperature inside the nation's mountain bunkers is a steady 58 to 60 degrees, but in the confined office spaces there often isn't much supplemental heating since the heat generated by the computers warms the rooms sufficiently. The base proceeds with all the various projects necessary to support a huge, expensive infrastructure, all watched over by the Pentagon Force Protection Agency and the 572nd Military Police Company, known as the "Keepers of the Rock." In 2007, a team of military foresters began a large-scale project to rebuild the forest atop Raven Rock mountain—planting 10,300 new seedlings on the mountain and erecting deer fencing. In 2010, it purchased a new, yellow-and-blue International 7600 pumper truck for the Raven Rock fire department, adding to its six-vehicle firefighting fleet, and the Chickasaw Nation won a contract in 2013 to provide dining services inside Raven Rock at the Granite Cove Dining Facility, the 200-seat cafeteria that serves the base's meals and where lunch costs only $3 to $5. (Granite Cove, by the accounts of workers there, offers a particularly good breakfast.)

Two years later, it was openly advertising on the government's job website for a GS-11 "Supply Management Specialist" (Salary: $63,772 to $82,840) and a "High Voltage Electrician" (Salary: $24.13 to $28.15 an hour), among other jobs.

The veil of secrecy over the alternate Pentagon isn't as all-consuming as it once was, either; its existence and basic mission are not considered classified. Online job postings explain, obliquely, "The Raven Rock Mountain Complex (RRMC) is a unique hardened, survivable, deep underground command center and relocation site with rigorous redundancy, reliability, and security standards charged with a mission to support the Secretary of Defense, the Chairman of the Joint Chiefs of Staff, select DoD components, and as appropriate, non-DoD agencies of the Federal Government to enable the execution of DoD mission-essential functions in support of the National Defense. The Installation includes Site C and encompasses at least 25 distinct tenant activities with varied mission peculiar requirements and representing OSD, JCS, and all branches of the military services with specialized infrastructure and buildings spread out over a 700-acre campus and several distinct and remote sites."

Family members of Raven Rock staff are also now able to attend promotion and retirements in the facility, as well as have Thanksgiving and Christmas dinner with their families in the Granite Cove dining facility if they have to work that day. However, specific capabilities and design details of the facility are classified at the Confidential level, and the complex's plans and COOP operations continue to be classified at the Secret level. Even as those guidelines represent a general loosening of the Cold War secrecy, the military still tries to keep the facility quiet, telling personnel, "Remember: The more the public knows about this facility, the more our adversaries do, and the more vulnerable we become."

At Mount Weather, where FEMA runs regular emergency preparedness seminars and conferences, personnel and authorized visitors can gather in the Balloon Shed Lounge, a little bar in one of the aboveground buildings whose name hints at the facility's origins as a weather station. There, they can drink beer and wine, eat popcorn, and relax with a game on the foosball and pool tables. Upstairs, a larger cafeteria daily serves the facility's masses, both permanent staff and conference attendees alike.

The government now runs so many hardened facilities that their man-agers, engineers, and support personnel gather to share expertise, covering such topics as carbon dioxide management and HVAC, rationing, informa-tion security, bunker security, and the latest in equipment for everything from decontamination to tunnel collapse rescues and pandemic screening. The annual conference rotates around the country—Raven Rock in 2006, Colorado Springs in 2011, Texas's Fort Hood in 2012, and so forth—and brings together personnel from COG sites like Mount Weather as well as military officials in charge of running places like Command Post Tango, the underground bunker complex in South Korea from which a war on the peninsula would be overseen.

The infrastructure and personnel that support these projects is ever-evolving, shifting to meet bureaucratic needs and priorities. The National Communication Services—which ran the government's COG telecom-munications networks like the high-level Special Routing Arrangement Service—was disbanded in 2012 by President Obama, who folded its re-sponsibilities instead into DHS's Office of Emergency Communications. FEMA has continued to build out its own preparedness infrastructure; it now runs eight major logistics centers scattered across the country, as well as fifty additional supply caches belonging to its National Disaster Medi-cal System and 252 pre-positioned containers of disaster supplies scattered across fourteen states. It has nearly 750,000 square feet of warehouses in two locations outside Washington, D.C., alone.

Many of these ever-shifting and evolving projects are visible to the pub-lic only in rare instances, as passersby notice a new antenna here or there, like the new radome that sprouted on SITE D, in Mount Airy, Maryland, in 2013. As part of a hidden-in-plain-sight construction project between the National Mall and the Potomac River in Washington, the U.S. Navy spent more than a decade digging an extensive tunnel and loading in miles upon miles of communications cable as part of a classified COG project done in conjunction with a Maryland construction company and a Nebraska mining company. The Navy took over the four-acre site near East Potomac Park without notice in 2003 and visible work continued well past 2014 behind a ten-foot-tall security fence.

Harder to miss, though, was the massive construction project on the

North Lawn of the White House that began during Obama's first term. Years after 9/11 demonstrated the limitations of the White House bunker and revived the Clinton-era plans to upgrade PEOC, a huge unexplained construction project began on the North Lawn. Officially announced as an upgrade to the White House's utility system, the four-year project involved a deep, multistory pit, shielded by large aboveground walls to hide the work beyond. Officials did everything they could to obscure a project literally being dug under the noses of the White House press corps, even asking construction vehicles to tape over their logos to hide what companies were working on the project. Workers lowered massive concrete blocks and steel beams into the hole for nearly two years, all part of a $376 million project that seemed far too extensive to be merely an air-conditioning upgrade. White House officials begged off knowledge of the project. "It is security-related construction," said one official at the time. "Even we don't know exactly what."

The new White House bunker improvements, though, which theoretically would help ensure that the next crisis is run more smoothly than 9/11, were more the exception than the rule. Much of the COG and COOP system is showing its age; many facilities are now decades old, carved out of mountains during an age in which washing machines were considered cutting-edge technology, and the airborne fleets supposed to protect the nation's leaders date to the Vietnam era. The helicopters that would be the backbone of any evacuation are ancient by today's standards—and there's no clear plan to modernize and replace them. In April 2015, a Mussel helicopter on routine maneuvers made an emergency landing on the athletic fields of a public school in Alexandria, Virginia, and spent the day sitting in the field until a repair crew could get it back in the air. HMX-1, the presidential Marine helicopter squadron, has been warning for years about its aging fleet; while there's never been a serious incident, the helicopters suffered repeated failures and problems during President Bush's administration. "Replacing the current Marine One fleet is urgent," a 2005 congressional report concluded, adding, "The consequences of not providing the President with improved capabilities are potentially dire; such as ineffective crisis response, or even a discontinuity of government." But the first attempt at an upgrade was scuttled by President Obama in 2009 as cost overruns pushed the per-helicopter cost toward $500 million each. Only in 2014 did the program begin to move forward, although replacement helicopters are still years away.

The NEACP planes were originally supposed to be retired in 2010 under a plan proposed by Donald Rumsfeld, who had, coincidentally, also been defense secretary in the 1970s when they were arriving in the Air Force. But, following high-tech upgrades like a switch to fiber-optic broadband, the planes were kept off the chopping block by defense secretary Robert Gates. Their command and control capabilities were too unique to lose, the Pentagon said, and for now the planes—rechristened for a new era with a less scary name, the National Airborne Operations Center (NAOC)—remain a cornerstone of the nation's defense. They're likely now to keep flying well into the 2020s and one of the planes is still rarely far from the president. When President Obama traveled to Hawaii for his Christmas vacation, an E-4B would take up position at Hilo International Airport on the chain's big island, about 200 miles away from the president near Honolulu.

The NORAD bunker, too, once seemed headed for the history books, a victim of the Pentagon austerity instilled by the spiraling costs of Iraq and Afghanistan. NORAD, which cost about $250 million a year just to operate, saw more than $700 million in communications and computer upgrades in the five years after 9/11—one $15 million project in 2004 doubled the main command center's 540 square feet to accommodate more staff—but just a year after NORAD's commander, Navy Admiral Timothy Keating, had hailed the mountain bunker as the "eighth wonder of the world," the Pentagon decided in 2006 to put the facility on "warm standby," moving hundreds of the mountain's 1,100 staff to another base in Colorado Springs. "Cheyenne Mountain is not going away," Keating promised reporters. "There will be a small number of people that will remain at Cheyenne Mountain to maintain the facility in the event we need to stand up for either a real world threat or for exercises."

For many years, the only time the NORAD bunker at Cheyenne Mountain has entered the public consciousness is around Christmas, when its half-century tradition of tracking Santa Claus makes headlines. The practice of carefully monitoring the path of the sleigh and eight tiny reindeer grew out of a child's innocent wrong number on November 30, 1955. By transposing two digits, the boy reached the Combat Operations Center at the forerunner of NORAD. He asked the man who answered the phone if there was a Santa Claus, and a confused Colonel Harry Shoup responded gruffly, "There may be a guy called Santa Claus at the North Pole, but he's not the one I worry about coming from that direction."* That unexpected telephone call, though, gave the air defense team an idea.

By Christmas, the Continental Air Defense Command had put together a "Santa tracking" operation and issued a press release predicting that according to its radars the jolly old elf was on track to arrive in the U.S. on Christmas Eve. In the 1960s, NORAD sent out vinyl records to radio stations that included holiday music from the NORAD house band and prerecorded "reports" about Santa's progress. From year to year, the program grew in ambition as Santa and Christmas became a Cold War bludgeon against the atheistic Communist Soviet Union and offered a friendly sheen over the deadly watch NORAD regularly kept. In the 1970s, NORAD ran three-minute-long TV commercials showing them scrambling jet fighters to intercept an unknown radar track down from the North Pole that turned out to be Santa Claus.

The tradition continued and morphed in the years since, now including a significant online component, with corporate sponsors, fancy graphics, and maps to allow children to follow Santa as he rounds the globe at noradsanta .org. At the command center each Christmas Eve, hundreds of military personnel still answer the phone to update children on Santa's progress, and more than 20 million people visit the website. In recent years, as the program has expanded to include mobile apps and games, First Lady Michelle Obama has even taken a handful of telephone calls, patched through from NORAD to the first family's vacation in Hawaii.

By the end of the Obama administration, new threats brought the bunker back to life. In 2015, the Pentagon announced that it was moving

---

* As the story has become an urban legend, the popularly accepted version has a Sears ad misprinting the telephone number for its Santa hotline and delivering callers to NORAD instead; the myth is persistent—even NORAD's own website tells the wrong version of the story.

personnel back into the facility as the rising threat of an electromagnetic pulse attack against the United States, perhaps even by a new nuclear-armed nation like Iran, meant that the NORAD bunker, which was shielded from the very start of its life in the 1960s from EMP, was a perfect bastion from which to defend the nation. During the Obama administration, NORAD ran its first full-scale continuity drill in decades; for the exercise, the blast doors swung closed, sealing Cheyenne Mountain for a full twenty-four hours for the first time in its history.*

The bunkers, planes, and helicopters remain only one part of the much larger national command and control system designed to sustain Enduring Constitutional Government in an emergency. Much of that activity is now based in and around Fort Meade, the home to the National Security Agency and hub for the military's sophisticated network systems. The area hosts a bevy of corporate headquarters and satellite offices for government IT contractors; as more and more government work is conducted by contractors, these companies have become closely tied into the nation's COG and COOP efforts.

Government contractor SRA International—now combined with an offshoot of the larger firm CSC into the publicly traded firm CSRA—has long maintained a relationship with the White House Military Office working on presidential communications and COG projects, and it employs many retired military personnel who used to work on the president's communication systems. As 9/11 focused many private companies on the need for their own emergency preparedness planning, White House COG operations have turned into a lucrative career development post for staff like Bryan Koon, who spent seven years with the Navy at the White House Military Office working on contingency operations, then transitioned to the private sector, working with SRA as a contractor in the White House Military Office, before leaving to become Walmart's head of emergency management.

---

* Since the military facility had never built sleeping berths, hundreds of cots had been set up in the tunnels outside the bunker's buildings. As Chris Franks, continuity plans and operations chief for NORAD, said, "We've never really slept over in the mountain before as part of an exercise or as a group."

In 2008, the government contractor CACI received a $25 million contract to help upgrade the communications systems for the National Leadership Command Capability Management Office, which helps oversee COG communication systems. Many other contractors provide support as well, including SAIC, which in 2012 received its own $18 million contract to support NLCC; cybersecurity firm Taurean Agile Cyber Defense was brought into the program in June that same year; and IT contractor Koniag Technology Solutions helps to provide systems engineering. KTS, as part of hiring for one of its NLCC jobs, explained vaguely what it's working on: "The Senior NLCC System Engineer will participate on the technical design team for the future presidential senior leadership and COOP/COG architecture development efforts that will describe and integrate all current planning for modification, upgrade, evolution, and modernization of existing nuclear C^3 system components forming the foundation for the NLCC."

Under an obscure line item in the Pentagon budget known as PE 0303131K, SAIC, Raytheon, Booz Allen Hamilton, and an IT contractor named Pragmatics receive about $7.6 million a year for work on the Minimum Essential Emergency Communications Network, the government's nuclear command network of last resort, and provide IT upgrades to planes like Air Force One and NEACP. Verizon, under a separate MEECN project, receives approximately $5.1 million a year, as part of what ultimately will be close to an $85 million contract over more than a decade to work on the project. What are they doing? The budget doesn't say. "All aspects of this project are classified and require special access." Beltway firms with names like Merlin Global Services and Mission Essential have built their businesses around working on COG projects and hiring military and executive branch officials with specific expertise.*

Communication projects held by private government contractors, though—even when uncovered—represent just tiny corners of the massive

---

* The rise of government contractors has created new challenges for COG planners— private sector staff are now used routinely to run so many critical functions inside government, but they aren't legally beholden to government policies in the same way as federal workers. Instead, continuity protocols now call for "appropriate agreements with contractors that are part of a continuity staff that legally bind and specify the contractor's responsibilities and level of participation during a continuity event."

COG architecture, the vast majority of which is hidden inside black budgets and spread across so many different agencies, departments, and line items that it's impossible to construct a full accounting of COG efforts. Internally, and separate from all the other COG programs, the Pentagon, meanwhile, spent nearly $30 million in 2010 just on its own COOP programs—an effort that included nearly seventy-five full-time staff. The Defense Information Systems Agency spent in 2016 upward of $170 million providing communications to the president, the White House Situation Room, COG sites, and other senior government leaders. The Pentagon spends about $60 million a year on maintenance at Raven Rock alone, a number that includes about 140 full-time staff, and about $30 million a year in upgrades and improvements, and more than $1 million a month on security for the complex from the Pentagon Force Protection Agency. Then there are the discrete projects and updates: In 2010, the Pentagon spent $8.4 million upgrading Raven Rock's secondary power to a more powerful generator. In 2014, it upgraded Raven Rock's administrative facility for $32 million and built a new exterior cooling tower for another $4.1 million.* None of that work, though, counts the tens of millions of dollars the Pentagon's Washington Headquarters Service pays to support Raven Rock, nor the personnel costs associated with manning the watch center and battle staffs.

Mount Weather is, as of 2016, in the midst of what FEMA calls "a significant infrastructure upgrade to replace old infrastructure, correct life/safety items, upgrade IT and develop a more resilient facility capable of supporting 21st century technology and current Federal departments and agencies requirements." FEMA's next-generation warning system, known as IPAWS, saw $1.5 million in upgrades in 2016 to the broadcasting facilities at WLS AM-890, Chicago's big talk radio station and one of the designated "Presidential Entry Points" for FEMA's emergency messages, to protect the commercial station against an electromagnetic pulse.

---

* "The renovated facility will include operational spaces, installation of intrusion detection system (IDS), connection to Supervisory Control and Data Acquisition (SCADA), and supporting infrastructure upgrades. Infrastructure upgrades include, but are not limited to HVAC, lighting, voice and data cabling, power, plumbing, intrusion detection, and fire alarm systems," the Pentagon wrote in its budget request, adding, "Additional requirements are classified."

Add in the cost of supporting presidential travel like Air Force One, the C-20 COG aircraft fleet, the Marine One squadron HMX-1, the E-4B Doomsday planes, the COG evacuation helicopters around Washington at Joint Base Andrews and Davison Army Airfield, the other fixed COG sites, FEMA's unclassified continuity programs budget of around $50 million a year, $30 million annual operating costs for Mount Weather, and the government's annual costs for COG easily stretch into the billions of dollars a year. Perhaps, based on some government estimates, it tops $2 billion a year, but the truth is that even the government probably doesn't fully understand how to account for the cost of maintaining its scattered Doomsday infrastructure. It's likely far more than that, especially once one factors in the security details and armored transportation for those in the line of presidential succession and officials who are part of Enduring Constitutional Government.

Sure, some of the money helps the president and White House staff be more efficient and get more done in a given day, but at its core, boiled down to its simplest purpose, all of this money and infrastructure goes into ensuring that at the right moment someone somewhere in the U.S. government is alive and able to order a nuclear missile launch. The plans, though, now have a new name. More than forty years after its creation, the SIOP, renamed in 1991 the National Strategic Response Plans, had finally been replaced with OPLAN 8010, which, the Pentagon promised, offered "a collection of far more differentiated retaliatory choices, tailored to a threat environment of greater nuance and complexity." The new plans will be around for quite some time to come: Despite the hope-filled promises early in President Obama's administration of a nuclear-free world, his presidency would end with 5,000 nuclear warheads in the American arsenal—and a multibillion-dollar effort under way to modernize and build a new generation of nuclear weapons.

Our peaceful normal daily routines remain more fragile than many of us like to consider. Despite years of work on evacuation plans and emergency preparedness, Mother Nature is able to upend life with ease: Washington, D.C., was hammered by brief, unexpected snowstorms in 2011 and 2016—each of which lasted only a few hours but led to more than ten hours of gridlock by hitting on normal workdays during the evening commute. How would a major metro region respond to the chaos of a terrorist attack? The answer, despite however many billions have been spent on such efforts, is almost assuredly: Not well.

In many ways, after many decades, many billions of dollars, and countless advances in technology, the federal government's basic plan to escape a catastrophe in Washington remains the same today as it was during that first Operation ALERT during the Eisenhower administration: Run away and hide in the Appalachian Mountains across Virginia, Maryland, and West Virginia.

The mountaintop redoubt that would in a crisis house many of the nation's spies atop Peters Mountain, near Charlottesville, Virginia, about 120 miles from Washington, D.C., has received a $61 million upgrade since 2007. The long-standing facility, one of AT&T's classified "Project Offices," features massive communications gear and a large corporate logo painted in the parking lot, which doubles as a helicopter landing pad. It would serve in an emergency as a key part of what the Office of the Director of National Intelligence refers to as National Intelligence Emergency Management Activity (NIEMA), a continuity program that "provides for the framework, platforms, and systems to enable the Director of National Intelligence to lead an integrated and resilient IC enterprise capable of sustaining the 'intelligence cycle' under any crisis or consequence management event, both at our headquarters and at our alternate operating locations."

Other new hiding places have taken the place of those that were retired. If you weren't looking for it, you'd be hard pressed to stumble upon the Allegany Ballistics Laboratory, tucked away in the mountainous corner of the Appalachians where West Virginia, Maryland, and Virginia all come together. The mailing address for the massive thousand-acre facility is Rocket Center, West Virginia, a town that technically has no residents and nothing beyond the ABL, a property dating back to World War II that today is split between the Navy and a private contractor named Alliant Techsystems (ATK for short). From State Route 956, which bisects the complex, it looks like just about any other fenced-off anonymous office park, except a closer examination of the surrounding woods will uncover air shafts rising from underground bunkers and a lot more security cameras and patrols than seemingly necessary for such an isolated complex.

Set on the north branch of the Potomac River, 145 miles away from Washington, the Allegany Ballistics Laboratory used to be primarily focused on rocket propulsion—its isolation and scale helped protect the surrounding community and other workers from the volatile experiments and research conducted on rocket fuels. ABL was a critical component of the early Space Race—there researchers worked to perfect the Vanguard rockets that would carry America's first satellite into space after the humiliation of the Soviets' Sputnik launch. It was dangerous work: The ABL's grounds are littered with both new and old storage bunkers, and at least three times from 1961 to 1981 massive accidental fatal explosions leveled parts of the facility. Beginning in 1985, Senator Robert C. Byrd, using his keen eye for appropriations earmarks, sent hundreds of millions of dollars to the hilltop facility—modernizing it, upgrading facilities, and expanding its industrial capacity. As he wrote in his autobiography, "As the Cold War began its final phase, I saw that the continuing evolution of our nation's armed forces into highly technical units presented opportunities to serve the national defense, as well as to expand West Virginia's economic base at ABL."

More recently, ABL's various industrial buildings have built parts for the F-22 Raptor, 30mm shells for the Apache helicopter, and 120mm ammunition for the military, among about eighty different military contracts. The site's primary occupant, Alliant Techsystems, is a publicly traded spin-off of Honeywell's old defense business—another link in the decades-long relationship between the military-industrial complex and the government's secret Doomsday plans.

As the government began to reconsider its need for COG and COOP facilities after 9/11, the Allegany Ballistics Laboratory looked perfect. Its facilities, including the gratefully named Robert C. Byrd Hilltop Office Complex and the Robert C. Byrd Institute for Advanced Flexible Manufacturing, as well as a series of underground bunkers cut into at least two adjoining hillsides, seemed tailor-made for COG and COOP operations. In a short period of time after 9/11, a number of different agencies related to defense and homeland security, including FEMA, set up backup data centers run by IBM on the West Virginia hilltops.

ABL now stands as the primary COOP facility for a group of important agencies, including national security components of the Office of the

Director of National Intelligence and the National Archives. While the National Archives sounds like it'd be an unnecessary appendage during an emergency, it actually runs one of the most vital legal functions of the U.S. government: The *Federal Register* stands as the daily rundown of all the new laws, rules, regulations, and standards that the government announces. To oversimplify the federal paper trail just a bit, nothing is officially enacted or implemented by the government until it appears in the printed *Federal Register*—making it one of the least understood and least known but most critical functions to preserve on a day-to-day basis.

Normally, the *Federal Register* is run out of the Government Printing Office on North Capitol Street in downtown Washington, but in the years since 9/11 the organization has lined up three separate fallback facilities, each further away from its normal headquarters than the last—all dedicated to the goal of continuing the publication of the *Federal Register.* Under the most dire circumstances, "as a result of an attack or threatened attack," the president would through executive order activate the *Emergency Federal Register*—a power laid out by President Reagan in 1988 in Executive Order 12656 and codified in 44 U.S.C. 1505(c). That order, presumably prewritten and never far from the president as part of the packet of draft emergency powers, would short-circuit the normal printing system and launch a website, Emergency-Federal-Register.gov, that could serve as the government's official notice board. "The purpose of the EFR is to preserve the rule of law and a constitutional form of government, as per NSPD-51/HSPD-20," the National Archives says, citing the mysterious 2007 presidential directive that would drive so much of the country's crisis response.

During an emergency that rendered downtown Washington unusable, these (and other) critical functions would end up on this West Virginia mountaintop, moving into anonymous Building 494 of the Robert C. Byrd Hilltop Office Complex. Wherever the president ended up—perhaps hidden inside Mount Weather or Raven Rock or soaring high above the country in an NEACP plane—and whoever the president ended up being, whether it was the chief executive duly selected by the electoral college or a successor in the National Command Authorities like the Senate president pro tem or the secretary of agriculture, the *Emergency Federal Register* would be a vital link in governing the nation, just like the presidential nuclear Football. It's from this hilltop that the string of executive orders, emergency rules, and the implementation of NSPD 51 would unfold, one *EFR* entry at a time.

The rest of the nation—and indeed much of the world—would tune in to the Emergency-Federal-Register.gov website to figure out what our nation would look like after an attack. What would Congress look like—would there be a Congress? How would the Supreme Court participate? What aspects of the long-dormant Cold War plans for martial law, enemy detention orders, and rationing would be pulled off the shelf? Are there today hidden wartime czars waiting among us, as there were during the Eisenhower era? What does "Enduring Constitutional Government" actually mean?

Until an unthinkable catastrophe happens, we won't really know the answers; those of us left alive will be very curious to know.

ACKNOWLEDGMENTS

While this is the first comprehensive attempt to piece together the history of the Cold War's Doomsday plans, many journalists and researchers have tackled parts of this story before me. It's been a long and tiring fight for many to force the government to release documents, figures, and information that seemingly bear little security risk anymore. It's a fight that dates back at least to January 5, 1982—when I was just a few months old—when David Alan Rosenberg's seven-year fight to force the disclosure of the size of the U.S. nuclear arsenal scored its first win: The Department of Energy agreed to release the figures for the 1945 to 1948 years—just three years, numbers that even by 1982 were decades out of date.

Writing this book was racing a clock—declassification on the one hand, but living memories on the other. The contributions of Rosenberg and three journalists who have done extensive research on COG planning were invaluable in this project: The body of work produced by Edward Zuckerman, William Arkin, and Ted Gup allowed me to write this book long after they first broke ground in this field. Three other independent historians and researchers contributed greatly: CONELRAD founder Bill Geerhart, Albert LaFrance, and Tim Tyler, a man whom I've never met but whose pre-9/11 research I found all over. In the early 2000s, CONELRAD's Bill Geerhart, especially, conducted interviews with numerous individuals involved in COG programs who had died by the time I began exploring this subject. I am indebted to his careful research, as are historians to come. Beyond those individuals, three entities have collected invaluable archives of national security–related documents, particularly dealing with the nation's nuclear and military history during the Cold War: Government Attic (governmentattic.org), Federation of American Scientists—a group that was founded in November 1945 originally as the Federation of Atomic Scientists by the founders of the Manhattan Project—and the National Security Archive at George Washington University. All three organizations have done much valiant work to expose and air the history of this era.

I similarly want to give special acknowledgment to a handful of authors and books who unknowingly helped me enormously with background, context, and the conceptual framework for *Raven Rock*. While their works are cited in specific places in the endnotes, I'm also more broadly indebted to them for their historical interpretations, narrative theses, and careful research years or even decades before I began mine. Eric Schlosser's *Command and Control*, David Hoffman's *The Dead Hand*, Daniel Ford's *The Button*, and Fred Kaplan's *The Wizards of Armageddon* all were enormously helpful on the military and strategic side of the nuclear age. Two expansive and well-written memoirs from the Cold War—Robert Gates's excellent *From the Shadows*, and McGeorge Bundy's *Danger and Survival*—helped explain the geopolitics at play, as did *The Cold War: A New History*, by John Lewis Gaddis, whose body of work is critical to anyone researching that era today. I recommend Paul Boyer's *By the Bomb's Early Light*, excellent work to anyone seeking to understand the way atomic weapons changed American culture, and there are also a handful of academics who have done excellent studies of domestic life during the Cold War worth reading: Tom Vanderbilt's *Survival City*, Dee Garrison's *Bracing for Armageddon*, Allan Winkler's *Life Under a Cloud*, Guy Oakes's *The Imaginary War*, Kenneth Rose's *One Nation Underground*, and Tracy Davis's *Stages of Emergency*.

Numerous people shared memories—both major and minor—about their windows into COG. I haven't included all the specific details here, but each conversation helped shape the overall book and its approach. While I've spoken with scores of individuals as part of this research project, I've not cited my own interviews as sources in the footnotes given the sensitivity and classified nature of much of the history included in these pages. Numerous people also contributed a random detail here or there that I never would have found on my own; John Trezise, a faithful POLITICO reader, pointed me to a history of the Interior Department that mentioned the damage to the Lincoln Memorial.

Pieces of the COG puzzle have been hidden in archives all around the country, and I wouldn't have been able to assemble anywhere near as clear a picture as I've done here without the help of dozens of archivists and historians who guided me through their collections. Among them, Arthur Carlson at East Carolina University; Todd Moye and Amy Hedrick at the University of North Texas oral history project; Richard Baker at the Army War College in Carlisle; Yancy Mailes at Global Strike Command in Barksdale, Louisiana; Jayanti Menches at Parsons Brinckerhoff; Alonso Avila at the University of Iowa's Special Collections; and Staff Sergeant Steven Bussey, the keeper of the Oscar-1 missile silo at Missouri's Whiteman Air Force Base. My friend Eric Federing shared his extensive research into Washington's Reagan-era Crisis Relocation Plan, much of which he'd driven personally at the time. Dante Pistone and Darwin Morgan spent a day showing me around the moonscape of the Nevada Test Site. Major Matt Miller, Lieutenant Colonel Martin O'Donnell, and Dr. Jerome Martin helped show me around Curtis Lemay's old haunt at Offutt Air Force Base. Robert Conte and the team at the Greenbrier Resort in West Virginia graciously showed me around and talked extensively with me during two visits there. Mark Tillman, the pilot of Air Force One on September 11, 2001, helped open up that world to me.

This research project took me to the majority of the country's presidential libraries, which together are an underused national treasure. The National Archives writ large and the presidential libraries in particular are a fount of knowledge of the twentieth century. In each of the libraries I visited—from the John F. Kennedy Library in Boston to the Richard Nixon Library a continent away in Yorba Linda, I interacted with talented and knowledgeable staff. The archivists whom I had the chance to work with intimately knew their collections and pointed me to files that I never could have uncovered myself. In Abilene, at the Dwight D. Eisenhower Presidential Library, I'm grateful to Valoise Armstrong and Tim Rives, who also introduced me to some great fried chicken. In Austin, John Wilson navigated me through the archives of the Lyndon B. Johnson Library, and then Lara Hall spent years following up on my declassification requests. In Simi Valley, Ray Wilson helped track down some highly amusing records about Project Elf at the Ronald Reagan Presidential Library. In perusing and quoting the many thousands of documents that made up the research for this book, I should note that I've standardized spellings and cleaned up normal typos and punctuation in official documents or memos where they seemed more a possible distraction than revelatory.

Georgetown journalism dean and my longtime friend Barbara Feinman Todd was a huge help to this endeavor, as were the three very bright researchers who helped me over the course of writing this book—Diana Elbasha, Rebecca Nelson, and Jillian Carter—and I'm deeply indebted to their legwork and careful note-taking. Jillian, especially, helped me through an unexpectedly challenging fall of 2014 and at three vital points helped provide research that kept the book moving. Andy Koenig also aided in gathering various materials. Bob Cooper, Tom Patricia, and Sandy Shenkman believed deeply in this project, and I spent a lovely couple of days traveling COG sites and dodging Mount Weather security patrols with Stephen Scaia and Matt Federman.

I traversed several jobs and several cities in the course of writing this book, and am grateful for the support of my co-workers along the way, especially smart, similarly minded national security writers like Shane Harris and my colleagues at POLITICO Magazine and POLITICO's leadership, John Harris and Robert Allbritton.

Modern publishing is a team enterprise, so I also owe a great deal of thanks to my lawyers—Mark Zaid, Bradley Moss, and Jaime Wolf—and my agents, Will Lippincott, Patricia Burke, Maria Massie, and Rob McQuilkin at LMQ, and Howie Sanders and Katrina Escudero at UTA, who all helped usher this project along. At Simon & Schuster, Jonathan Karp believed in this project from the start, and I was excited to work closely through it all with my talented editor and understanding friend Jofie Ferrari-Adler—thus fulfilling a nearly decade-long desire to collaborate. Julianna Haubner provided a sharp, smart, and careful eye as we beat the manuscript into shape, and helped with a thousand logistical details along the way. Jonathan Evans and the amazing Fred Chase made sure that the text itself was as unembarrassing as they could make it, and I'm grateful to Jay Schweitzer for his yeoman's work helping to hammer this book's many hundreds of footnotes into shape. All remaining typos, of course, are my fault.

There's also a long list of people who have been critical to my being who and where I am today. Among them: Charlotte Stocek, Mary Creeden, Mike Baginski, Rome Aja,

Kerrin McCadden, and Charlie Phillips; John Rosenberg, Richard Mederos, Brian Delay, Peter J. Gomes, Stephen Shoemaker, and Jennifer Axsom; Kit Seeyle, Pat Leahy, Rusty Grieff, Tim Seldes, Jesseca Salky, Paul Elie, Tom Friedman, Jack Limpert, Geoff Shandler, Susan Glasser, and, not least of all, Cousin Connie, to whom I owe a debt that I strive to repay each day. My parents, Chris and Nancy Price Graff, have encouraged me to write since an early age, instilling in me a love of history and research and an intellectual curiosity that benefits me daily, and my sister Lindsay has always been my biggest fan—and I hers. Lastly, I'm deeply grateful to my wife, Katherine, who remained supportive throughout the unexpectedly long process of writing this. Good news! I've finally finished it.

January 2017
Burlington, Vermont

NOTES

xiii   *As Air Force One began to bank:* TerHost and Albertazzie, *Flying White House*, pp. 42–44.

xiv   *"As I am winging my way back . . .":* Woodward and Bernstein, *Final Days*, p. 443.

xiv   *In fact, days before the administration's dramatic denouement:* Robert McFadden, "James R. Schlesinger, Willful Aide to Three Presidents, Is Dead at 85," *New York Times*, March 28, 2014.

xv   *Schlesinger feared that the president:* Werth, *31 Days*, p. 17. The extent to which this contemporaneous story is true remains under debate. No documents or other accounts have emerged to confirm Schlesinger's account of his actions during this period. See Kutler, *Wars of Watergate*, p. 546.

xv   *On its surface, presidential succession:* Kantorowicz, *King's Two Bodies*, p. 333.

xv   *"For me personally, no one ever elected . . .":* Emmett, *Within Arm's Length*, p. 139.

xvi   *In September 1935, Franklin Roosevelt's car:* Hiltzik, *Colossus*, p. 375.

xvi   *In the months after World War II ended:* Alsops' *Saturday Evening Post* article, "Your Flesh Should Creep," from June 13, 1946, quoted in Boyer, *By the Bomb's Early Light*, pp. 148–49.

xvii   *In the event of an emergency, each team:* See, for instance, Armed Forces Staff College, *The Joint Staff Officers Guide*, Pub 1, 1997.

xvii   *Under a truly horrific surprise attack:* "Providing an Order of Succession Within the Department of State," Office of Policy Coordination and International Relations, Executive Order 13252, December 28, 2001, at http://nodis3.gsfc.nasa.gov /displayEO.cfm?id=EO_13251_.

xvii   *Beginning during the Cold War and continuing up to the present day:* While the presidential order of succession is set by the Constitution and has changed just twice in the last forty years, the exact lineup of each cabinet department's succession order is constantly evolving. The Department of Energy's succession lineup has changed nearly six times since 9/11, and the Justice Department's has changed with the political winds: The George W. Bush administration liked the U.S. attorney in South Texas, installing him in the Attorney general succession line, whereas the Obama administration included Minnesota and Arizona—but not Texas.

xviii *While many people are familiar:* The nation has only once gone to DEFCON 2, at the height of the Cuban Missile Crisis, and twice gone to DEFCON 3, during the Yom Kippur War and on September 11, 2001.

xviii *COGCON 4 represents normal peacetime:* Al Cerrone, "DOE O 100.1E Administrative Change 1, Secretarial Succession, Threat Level Notification, and Successor Tracking," U.S. Department of Energy, Office of Management, September 13, 2013, accessed at https://www.directives.doe.gov/directives-documents/100 -series/0100.1-BOrder-E-admchg1/.

xviii *There were some 30,000 nuclear weapons:* Garrison, *Bracing for Armageddon,* p. 5.

xix *Prewritten presidential executive orders sat:* See Folder "Defense Resources Act," Box 29, MsC 241, Edward A. McDermott Papers, 1960, 1965, Special Collections Department, University of Iowa Libraries, at https://www.lib.uiowa.edu /scua/msc/tomsc250/msc241/msc241.htm.

xxi *When Aaron Sorkin was researching:* Author interview with Dee Dee Myers; and Matthew Miller, "The Real White House," *Brill's Content,* March 2000.

xxii *As technology writer Frank Rose:* Rose, *Into the Heart of the Mind,* p. 36.

xxii *The vast secrecy that surrounded the government's atomic weapons:* Brian Fung, "5.1 Million Americans Have Security Clearances. That's More than the Entire Population of Norway," *Washington Post,* March 24, 2014.

xxiii *Modern warfare necessitated quick action:* David Alan Rosenberg, "The Origins of Overkill: Nuclear Weapons and American Strategy, 1945–1960," *International Security,* vol. 7, no. 4 (Spring 1983): 34; L. A. Minnich, "Minutes, Bipartisan Legislative Meeting, January 5, 1954, Staff Notes," January–December 1954 folder, Box 4, Ann C. Whitman File, Dwight D. Eisenhower Papers as President, Dwight D. Eisenhower Library.

xxiii *In 1962, President John F. Kennedy turned:* George Korte, "Special Report: America's Perpetual State of Emergency," *USA Today,* October, 22, 2014.

xxiv *The history of our government's Doomsday planning:* Harry B. Yoshpe, "Our Missing Shield: The U.S. Civil Defense Program in Historical Perspective," Federal Emergency Management Agency, April 1981, p. iv.

xxiv *As Eisenhower said in one meeting:* Nitze, Reardon, and Smith, *Hiroshima to Glasnost,* p. 168.

xxv *And, today, every day, there are still:* "David Alan Rosenberg on: The Bureaucracy of Death," interview transcripts, *American Experience, Race for the Superbomb,* PBS, at http://www.pbs.org/wgbh/amex/bomb/filmmore/reference/interview/rosenberg 03.html.

1 *"I think it is very important that . . .":* McCullough, *Truman,* p. 290.

1 *By the time Woodrow Wilson rallied:* Years later, as political corruption investigations

took down one Missouri colleague after another, Truman wrote privately to his wife, "Looks like everyone in Jackson County got rich but me." Ibid., p. 240.

2   *When Senator Truman called Stimson:* Ibid., pp. 244, 286, 288–89.

3   *So, just a few days later, a detail:* Ibid., p. 334; see also "Oral History Interview with General Harry H. Vaughan," Alexandria, Virginia, January 16, 1963, Harry S. Truman Library, at http://www.trumanlibrary.org/oralhist/vaughan2.htm#78.

4   *"The very fact that no thought was given . . .":* Truman, *Memoirs of Harry S. Truman,* vol. 1, p. 7.

4   *Until the outbreak of World War II:* Brinkley, *Washington Goes to War,* p. 84.

5   *The Secret Service eventually had the Army:* A few real guns were installed, but since none was ever fired, no one knew until years later that the ammunition stacked up beside them was the wrong size. Ibid., pp. 96–97.

5   *A detachment from the Chemical Warfare Service:* Reilly, *Reilly of the White House,* Appendix A: "Air Raid Protection Setup for White House, Shangri-La, Hyde Park, and During Train Travel"; W. D. Nelson, *President Is at Camp David,* p. 10.

6   *Weekly drills began practicing:* Reilly, *Reilly of the White House,* Appendix A: "Air Raid Protection Setup for White House, Shangri-La, Hyde Park, and During Train Travel."

6   *Twelve days after Truman became president:* McCullough, *Truman,* p. 377.

6   *Stimson then introduced General Leslie Groves:* Robert de Vore, "The Man Who Made Manhattan," *Collier's Weekly,* October 13, 1945, pp. 12–13.

7   *Sitting in his special observation seat:* Truman, *Memoirs of Harry S. Truman,* vol. 1, p. 339.

7   *Churchill, who spent part of his time in Potsdam:* McCullough, *Truman,* p. 415.

7   *George Kistiakowsky, who had helped lead:* Ibid., p. 416.

8   *That evening, Stimson carried a coded telegram:* Barton J. Bernstein, "Truman at Potsdam: His Secret Diary," *Foreign Service Journal* (July/August 1980): 29, at http://nsarchive.gwu.edu/NSAEBB/NSAEBB162/38.pdf.

8   *Truman, at the end of a day's negotiations:* Truman, *Memoirs of Harry S. Truman,* vol. 1, p. 416. See also the State Department's Office of the Historian's review of the evidence of this conversation in "Foreign Relations of the United States: Diplomatic Papers, the Conference of Berlin (the Potsdam Conference), 1945, Volume II," p. 379, at https://history.state.gov/historicaldocuments/frus1945Berlinv 02/d710a-97.

9   *Truman shared the news with those around him:* McCullough, *Truman,* p. 455; Truman, *Memoirs of Harry S. Truman,* vol. 1, p. 421. In my research at the Harry S. Truman Library, I found a memo from Stimson to Truman, declassified in 1972, that was worded slightly differently: "Big bomb dropped on Hiroshima 5 August at 7:15 P.M. Washington time. First reports indicate complete success which was even more conspicuous than earlier test. STIMSON" (President's Secretary Files, Box 174).

9   *On NBC radio, Don Goddard:* Boyer, *By the Bomb's Early Light,* pp. 4–5.

9   *Twenty-four hours after the Nagasaki bombing:* McCullough, *Truman,* p. 462.

10   *As the United States emerged from World War II:* Isaacson and Thomas, *Wise Men,* p. 19.

10   *In the weeks following the war's end:* Harry S. Truman, Executive Order 9646, October 25, 1945, at http://en.wikisource.org/wiki/Executive_Order_9646.

10   *Buried in the midst:* Harry S. Truman: "Radio Report to the American People on the Potsdam Conference," 97, August 9, 1945, John T. Woolley and Gerhard Peters, *American Presidency Project,* at http://www.presidency.ucsb.edu/ws/index.php?pid=12165&st=&st1=.

10   *"Everywhere you go, the topic is up . . .":* John J. McCloy, "Personal Impressions of World Conditions," *Proceedings of the Academy of Political Science,* vol. 21, no. 4, European Recovery (January 1946): 98–102.

11   *General Mills offered an "atomic bomb ring":* Boyer, *By the Bomb's Early Light,* p. 11.

11   *Books like* Almighty Atom: The Real Story of Atomic Energy: Ibid., p. 111.

11   *It was an idea many people embraced:* Fleming, *Fixing the Sky,* p. 194.

11   *Hersey's words, vivid details:* Hersey, *Hiroshima,* p. 81.

11   *The magazine's entire print run sold out in hours:* Boyer, *By the Bomb's Early Light,* p. 334.

12   *Hersey's article came out just months after:* Isaacson and Thomas, *Wise Men,* p. 485.

12   *Writer E. B. White captured that new fear:* The remainder of White's meditation holds a specific sadness in the wake of 9/11: "In New York the fact is somewhat more concentrated because of the concentration of the city itself, and because, of all targets, New York has a certain clear priority. In the mind of whatever perverted dreamer might loose the lightning, New York must hold a steady, irresistible charm" (White, *Here Is New York,* p. 51).

12   *The idea was endorsed by such leading lights as Carl Spaatz:* Einstein, *Out of My Later Years,* "Towards a World Government (1946)."

12   *According to social historian Paul Boyer's estimates:* Boyer, *By the Bomb's Early Light,* p. 37.

12   *Military expert Louis Bruchiss explained:* "Underground Civilization Seen as Atomic Defense: Scientist Thinks Nation Should Construct Houses and Railways Beneath Mountains," *Los Angeles Times,* August 21, 1945, p. 5.

13   *Meanwhile, Henry Luce's editors at* Life *magazine:* "The Atomic Age," *Life,* August 20, 1945, p. 32.

13   *"After all, sunlight isn't so wonderful . . .":* Daniel Lang, "Mission to Trout," *New Yorker,* May 17, 1947, p. 76.

13   *They would be built in new design styles:* Boyer, *By the Bomb's Early Light,* p. 326.

13   *Sociologist William Ogburn argued:* William Fielding Ogburn, "Sociology and the Atom," *American Journal of Sociology,* vol. 51, no. 4 (January 1946): 267–75.

14   *Cities like Allentown, Pennsylvania:* Boyer, *By the Bomb's Early Light,* p. 313.

14 *Writing in* The Saturday Evening Post: Alsops' article from June 13, 1946, *Saturday Evening Post*, quoted in Paul Boyer, *By the Bomb's Early Light,* pp. 148–49.

15 *During the Great War, imposing German Zeppelin airships:* British pilot Lieutenant W. Leefe-Robinson became a national hero—and was awarded a Victoria Cross—after becoming the first pilot to shoot down an attacking Zeppelin in September 1916 thanks to a new exploding bullet developed by the military. Londoners across the city had watched the flaming Zeppelin fall from the sky and the following morning, more than ten thousand people visited the crash site.

16 *The government provided resources for the public:* James, *Warrior Race,* p. 625.

16 *The National Gallery moved:* Winston Churchill blocked the gallery's attempt to move some valuable paintings to Canada for the war's duration, writing, "Bury them in caves or in cellars, but not a picture shall leave these islands" (MacGregor, *Whose Muse?,* p. 43).

16 *Tate moved pieces to country estates:* The gallery's keepers safeguarding the underground shelters found themselves having to boil teakettles on portable stoves to keep the rooms' humidity high enough for the priceless art works.

16 *Public Records Office decamped:* Buckingham Palace has never confirmed where the crown jewels were hidden during World War II. Various theories have them spending the war in the U.S. gold depository at Fort Knox, in an insurance company's vault in Montreal, in Cornwall's Carnglaze Caverns, or at Windsor Palace wrapped in brown paper.

16 *By June 1939 the Bank of England had completed:* Hennessy, *Domestic History of the Bank of England,* pp. 173–75.

17 *Winston Churchill toured the facility:* For the history of this amazing facility and Winston Churchill's role, see Holmes, *Churchill's Bunker.*

17 *From September 1939 onward, the operational hub:* Holt, *Deceivers,* p. 172.

17 *"I propose to lead a troglodyte existence . . ."* These details are from J. Moody, *From Churchill's War Rooms.*

17 *The Supreme Allied Commander, Dwight Eisenhower:* Long, *Little Book of the London Underground,* p. 74.

18 *The last time a continental American city:* Lord, *Dawn's Early Light,* p. 153; for details on the career of André Daschkoff, the first Russian diplomat dispatched to the United States, see http://founders.archives.gov/documents/Jefferson/03–01 –02–0265.

18 *As his foreign minister explained later:* N. Thompson, *Hawk and the Dove,* p. 55.

18 *The day after Stalin's speech:* T. R. Kennedy, "Electronic Computer Flashes Answers, May Speed Engineering," *New York Times,* February 15, 1946.

18 *The eight-ton room-sized device:* "Machine Computes Rocket-Fire Data Putting the German V-2 Rocket to Work for a Peaceful Cause," *New York Times,* April 11, 1946.

18 *Then, thirteen days after Stalin's speech, George Kennan:* "X" (George F. Kennan,

writing anonymously), "The Sources of Soviet Conduct," *Foreign Affairs* (July 1947).

19 *On March 5, less than a month:* The Ferdinand Magellan, known as U.S. Car No. 1, is today on display at the Gold Coast Railroad Museum in Miami, Florida, and is the only rail car ever designated a National Historic Landmark. See https://www .nps.gov/NR/TRAVEL/PRESIDENTS/us_car_number_one.html.

20 *Lilienthal immediately understood:* Lilienthal, *Journals of David E. Lilienthal*, vol. 2, p. 641. The David Lilienthal diaries are a delightful and fascinating window into postwar Washington.

20 *His mind was now too valuable:* Ibid., p. 105.

20 *In December 1946, when he was finally told:* Ibid., p. 120.

20 *When the AEC met with President Truman:* "Declassification of Certain Characteristics of the United States Nuclear Weapon Stockpile," Department of Energy Facts, n.d., at http://www.alternatewars.com/BBOW/ABC_Weapons/DOE_Fact _Stockpile_1994.htm.

20 *Truman was shocked:* Lilienthal, *Journals of David E. Lilienthal*, vol. 2, p. 165.

20 *Behind closed doors:* M. Truman, *Harry S. Truman*, p. 359.

21 *Policymakers in the past had always used:* U.S. Congress, Senate, Committee on Military Affairs, Department of the Armed Forces, Department of the Military, Hearings on S. 84 and S. 1482, 79th Congress, 1st Session, October 22, 1945, pp. 98–99, 117. The author found this reference to the hearings in Daniel Yergin's *Shattered Peace* (p. 194).

21 *The resulting Eberstadt Report:* Yergin, *Shattered Peace*, p. 214.

21 *Although he didn't send nuclear weapons:* Quoted in Oakes, *Imaginary War*, p. 12, from the *Rheinische Zeitung*.

22 *Never mind that there weren't ninety:* Ibid., p. 16.

22 *The United States, Truman argued:* Craig, *Destroying the Village*, p. 7.

22 *In LeMay's mind:* Keeney, *15 Minutes*, p. 1.

22 *As LeMay said:* LeMay quoted in DeGroot, *Bomb*, p. 153; Rhodes, *Dark Sun*, p. 228; enhanced transcript, *American Experience, Race for the Superbomb*, PBS, act 1, at http://www.pbs.org/wgbh/amex/bomb/filmmore/transcript/transcript1.html.

23 *When LeMay arrived:* Moody, *Building a Strategic Air Force*, p. 233.

23 *Over the months ahead, LeMay:* Ibid., p. 255.

23 *Pentagon planners meanwhile settled:* Ibid., pp. 148–49.

23 *In 1949, in an unprecedented move:* For more on the "Revolt of the Admirals," see Kaku and Axelrod, *To Win a Nuclear War*, p. 56.

24 *The only man in history:* Lilienthal, *Journals of David E. Lilienthal*, vol. 2, p. 391.

25 *As the Lilienthals drove home:* Ibid., p. 566.

25 *By the light of an oil lamp:* McCullough, *Truman*, p. 748.

26 *The United States couldn't be left behind:* Lilienthal, *Journals of David E. Lilienthal*, vol. 2, p. 577.

26 *The AEC nearly tripled in size:* Rhodes, *Arsenals of Folly*, p. 79.

26 *As Lilienthal's AEC embarked:* McCullough, *Truman,* pp. 756–63.

27 *The document wasn't meant:* Beisner, *Dean Acheson,* p. 238.

27 *Under the 1950 war plan* OFF TACKLE: Moody, *Building a Strategic Air Force,* p. 312.

27 *There was also a subtle but important:* Keeney, *15 Minutes,* p. 59.

27 *"My father made clear . . .":* M. Truman, *Harry S. Truman,* p. 455.

27 *As General LeMay explained years later:* Richard H. Kohn and Joseph P. Harahan, "U.S. Strategic Air Power, 1948–1962: Excerpts from an Interview with Generals Curtis E. LeMay, Leon W. Johnson, David A. Burchinal, and Jack J. Catton," *International Security,* vol. 12, no. 4 (Spring 1988): 78–95.

27 *Between the Korean War and the search:* Lilienthal, *Journals of David E. Lilienthal,* vol. 2, p. 36.

28 *The new budgets and technological improvements:* David Alan Rosenberg, "The Origins of Overkill: Nuclear Weapons and American Strategy, 1945–1960," *International Security,* vol. 7, no. 4 (Spring 1983): 19.

28 *"Boy, we could blow a hole . . ."* Lilienthal, *Journals of David E. Lilienthal,* vol. 2, p. 473.

28 *Meanwhile, the White House was falling:* Truman was very sensitive to the history of the building where he lived. As he said about the White House ghosts: "I sit here in this old house and work on foreign affairs, read reports, and work on speeches—all the while listening to the ghosts walk up and down the hallway. The floors pop and the drapes move back and forth—I can just imagine old Andy and Teddy having an argument over Franklin. Or James Buchanan and Franklin Pierce deciding which was the more useless to the country. And when Millard Fillmore and Chester Arthur join in for place and show the din is almost unbearable" (June 12, 1945, in Ferrell, *Dear Bess,* p. 515).

28 *The subsequent extensive and high-profile:* Klara, *Hidden White House,* pp. 153–54.

29 *As aide David Stowe explained:* "Oral History Interviews with David H. Stowe," Harry S. Truman Library, September 25, 1972, p. 43, at https://www.truman library.org/oralhist/stowe1.htm.

29 *The front page of* The Washington Post*:* "Truman Digs into Special Fund for $881,000 A-Bomb Shelter," *Washington Post,* April 18, 1951, p. 1.

29 *Even as construction progressed:* "Oral History Interviews with Admiral Robert L. Dennison," Harry S. Truman Library, October 6, 1971, p. 97, at https://www.truman library.org/oralhist/dennisn.htm.

30 *"We are living in the atomic age . . .":* "White House Traffic Jams Laid to Threat of Atomic Bomb," *Washington Post,* October 28, 1945.

30 *Then, on the afternoon of November 1, 1950:* Truman received nearly seven thousand letters from the public, concerned about his welfare and glad he was safe. He insisted on personally signing all the responses; for weeks, he was handed a stack of letters daily to sign. McCullough, *Truman,* p. 816.

30 *Two days after the assassination attempt:* Hunter and Bainbridge, *American Gunfight,* p. 317.

30 *"It gives me the willies . . .":* Daniel Lang, "Mission to Trout," *New Yorker,* May 17, 1947, p. 76.

30 *The National Security Act of 1947 had tasked:* "A Recommendation to the President by the National Security Resources Board on Security for the Nation's Capital," NSRB-R-13, White House Confidential Files, Box 27, Harry S. Truman Presidential Library, October 27, 1948.

30 *The Defense Department also began:* Vogel, *Pentagon,* p. 353.

30 *"If we'd known there'd be an A-Bomb . . .":* Memo to the Secretary of Defense, "Report of Ad Hoc Group on Disaster Planning," October 8, 1951, p. 352.

30 *Indeed, when the AEC studied the effects:* "Naked City," *Time,* November 28, 1949, vol. 54, no. 22, p. 68.

31 *Congressman Chet Holifield proposed publicly:* U.S. Congress, Senate, Congressional Record, 81st Congress, 2nd Session, (1950), vol. 96, pt. 2, p. 2030.

31 *As Holifield explained, "The continuity . . .":* Ibid., Appendix p. A1242.

31 The New York Times *covered Holifield's proposal:* Associated Press, "Second Capital Urged in Atom Era; Underground Plan to Be Broached," *New York Times,* February 20, 1950, p. A1.

31 *Other congressmen piled onto the debate:* Associated Press, "Congress Booming Sites for Alternate National Capital, *Wilmington Morning Star,* February 21, 1950, at http://news.google.com/newspapers?nid=1454&dat=19500221&id=hVdgAAA AIBAJ&sjid=xHENAAAAIBAJ&pg=4082,1519349.

31 *Truman asked Congress for $140 million:* United Press, "HST Says No at Alternate War Capital," *Sunday Herald,* July 16, 1950, at http://news.google.com/newspapers?nid=2229&dat=19500716&id=EdUyAAAAIBAJ&sjid=tQAGAAAAIBAJ&pg=6204,1576213.

31 *The Senate Public Works Committee passed a bill:* http://library.cqpress.com/cqalmanac/document.php?id=cqal51–889–29670–1406846.

31 *Dispersal in the hills became:* Quoted in Boyer, *By the Bomb's Early Light,* p. 311.

31 *A D.C. newspaper carried ads:* "Washington Realty Ads Stress Atomic Safety," *New York Times,* July 20, 1950.

31 *"So long as there is any chance at all . . .":* Harry S. Truman, "Address at a Dinner of the Civil Defense Conference," May 7, 1951, John T. Woolley and Gerhard Peters, *American Presidency Project,* at http://www.presidency.ucsb.edu/ws/?pid=14079.

32 *Serious "civil defense" initiatives:* Winkler, *Life Under a Cloud,* p. 110.

32 *Eleanor Roosevelt stepped in:* Garrison, *Bracing for Armageddon,* p. 33.

32 *His leadership quickly established:* Ibid., pp. 35–37.

32 *One newspaper columnist at the time:* Peter Edson, "Washington Notebook," *Southeast Missourian,* April 25, 1955, p. 4, at http://news.google.com/newspapers?nid=1893&dat=19550425&id=yZooAAAAIBAJ&sjid=KNcEAAAAIBAJ&pg=2981,1720354.

32 *Such a conclusion was certainly true:* Harry B. Yoshpe, "Our Missing Shield: The

U.S. Civil Defense Program in Historical Perspective," Federal Emergency Management Agency, April 1981, p. 160.

33 *His "Bible of civil defense" represented:* Joseph E. McLean, "Project East River—Survival in the Atomic Age," *Bulletin of Atomic Scientists,* vol. 9, no. 7 (September 1953): 247.

33 *Whereas Britain closely aligned its military:* "Memorandum for Deputy Secretary Lovett," David H. Stowe Papers, Subject File, 1945–53, Box 5, Harry S. Truman Presidential Library, April 2, 1961. See also the response from Lovett, dated April 19, 1951, in the same file.

34 *the U.S., they noted upon their return:* Ibid., April 2, 1961.

34 *The facility, whose construction was overseen:* FCDA news release, "First Public Exhibition of the Federal Civil Defense Administration's Rescue Street," Document 141, Files of Spencer R. Quick, Papers of Harry S. Truman, Harry S. Truman Library, August 27, 1952.

34 *The public also got a taste of the experience:* "Atomic Fireworks, 1951," Conelrad Adjacent.com, July 4, 2010, at http://conelrad.blogspot.com/2010/07/atomic-fireworks-1951.html.

34 *By the end of 1950, 10,000 of the city's:* "Emergency Taxi Corps," New York Public Radio, January 16, 1951, at http://www.wnyc.org/story/emergency-taxi-corps/.

35 *"No time can be lost," the police:* "Role of the Police Department in Civil Defense," New York Public Radio, March 31, 1951, at http://www.wnyc.org/story/role-of-the-police-department-in-civil-defense/.

35 *Chicago's approach to "helping" kids was even more graphic:* Garrison, *Bracing for Armageddon,* p. 45.

35 *Robert Landry, Truman's Air Force aide:* "Memorandum from Robert Landry to Matthew J. Connelly," White House Central Files, Official File, 1591, Box 1843, Harry S. Truman Presidential Library, February 13, 1948.

35 *The military experimented with creating subterranean:* Lloyd Norman, "Army Works on Underground Plane Plants," *Chicago Tribune,* May 2, 1947, at http://archives.chicagotribune.com/1947/05/02/page/21/article/army-works-on-underground-plane-plants.

35 *To map and identify the nation's:* Walter Winchell, "Helen Hayes Snubs Theater; Operation Spelunk," *Herald-Journal,* June 7, 1948, at http://news.google.com/newspapers?nid=1876&dat=19480607&id=2mEsAAAAIBAJ&sjid=LMsEAAAAIBAJ&pg=3426,4008334.

35 *In 1947, a* New Yorker *writer accompanied:* Daniel Lang, "Mission to Trout," *New Yorker,* May 17, 1947, p. 89.

36 Boys' Life, *the magazine for Boy Scouts:* Clay Perry, "Operation Underground," *Boys' Life,* January 1948, pp. 27, 50, at https://books.google.com/books?id=xvchWC-7f38C&pg=PA27&lpg=PA27&dq=%22Munitions+Board%22+spelunking&source=bl&ots=Z2N4iVOuJ7&sig=_EgSmmvb-EOYIrBSvdKpEk4kOYQ&hl=e

n&sa=X&ei=YL6eVPiTEsiqNoyag8gE&ved=0CCEQ6AEwAQ#v=onepage&q
=%22Munitions%20Board%22%20spelunking&f=true.

36   *Under CONELRAD, as an attack unfolded:* See the press release, Document 151,
     Files of Spencer R. Quick, Papers of Harry S. Truman, Harry S. Truman Library,
     December 2, 1952. CONELRAD, like many parts of these civil defense programs,
     is today a largely forgotten aspect of the Cold War. For more on the program,
     see, for example, the Modesto Radio Museum's online CONELRAD exhibit at
     http://www.modestoradiomuseum.org/conelrad.html.

36   *Even as the Truman administration highlighted:* "Executive Order 10312: Provid-
     ing for Emergency Control Over Certain Government and Non-Government
     Stations Engaged in Radio Communication or Radio Transmission of Energy,"
     December 10, 1951, *Federal Register,* 16 FR 12452, December 12, 1951.

37   *As Truman wrote, "Only an earthquake . . .":* "Longhand Note of President Harry S.
     Truman [includes February 29 and March 2, 1952], February 29, 1952," Truman
     Papers, President's Secretary's Files, Harry S. Truman Library, at http://www.tru
     manlibrary.org/whistlestop/study_collections/trumanpapers/psf/longhand/index
     .php?documentVersion=both&documentid=hst-psf_naid735302–01.

37   *"Every aircraft on the base . . .":* For more on the Carswell tornado, see Abella, *Sol-
     diers of Reason,* p. 84; "Wiley Scores Report on B-36 Tornado Loss," *Washington
     Post,* November 8, 1952, p. 3; "Tornado Left B-36 Wrecked, 106 Damaged," *Wash-
     ington Post,* September 13, 1952, p. 1; "Attack by Tornado," *New York Times,* Sep-
     tember 14, 1952; Kenney, *15 Minutes,* p. 88; and Pate, *Arsenal of Defense,* p. 163.

37   *All told, two thirds of the nation's:* Moody, *Building a Strategic Air Force,* pp. 412–14.

37   *Ten days after the Carswell tornado:* See the Carswell news clippings in Folder 10,
     Papers of National Security Resources Board, White House Central Files, Confi-
     dential Files, Box 28, Harry S. Truman Presidential Library.

38   *In December, as the government still grappled:* "Report to the National Security
     Council by the Acting Executive Secretary of the Council (Gleason)," Report
     No. 958, NSC-139, December 31, 1952, in *Foreign Relations of the United States,
     1952–1954, Western Europe and Canada, vol. 6, pt. 2,* U.S. Government Printing
     Office, 1986.

38   *To supplement the electronic systems:* Michael Hall, "Operation Skywatch," Project
     Blue Book Research Center, National Investigations Committee on Aerial Phe-
     nomena, 1952, at http://www.nicap.org/bluebook/skyw.htm. See also McCray,
     Keep Watching the Skies!, p. 28. Truman's administration struggled to figure out
     how to sell the program to the American public. As aide David Stowe wrote in an
     undated note in his papers at the Harry S. Truman Library (Subject Files, Box 5),
     "Isn't this program at this time as much for training as it is for operational safety?
     If so, should the idea of a 'trained force' be brought in in such a way as to take some
     of the edge off any scare reaction?"

38   *As Truman said, "If an enemy . . .":* "Statement by the President on the Ground
     Observer Corps' 'Operation Skywatch,'" Public Papers of the Presidents, Harry

S. Truman, 1945–1953, Harry S. Truman Library, July 12, 1952, at http://www
.trumanlibrary.org/publicpapers/index.php?pid=2366&st=&st1=.

38 *That same month, on December 12:* "Memo from Charles Johnson to White House
Staff, Air Raid Drill," December 10, 1952, Document 155, Psychological Strategy
Board Files, Papers of Harry S. Truman, Harry S. Truman Library.

38 *"Exercises of this sort are essential . . ."* "Memorandum: Harry S. Truman to Heads
of Executive Departments and Agencies," White House Central Files: Official
File, 1591, Box 1843, Harry S. Truman Presidential Library, November 11, 1952.

38 *While Truman was briefed on each successive set:* "Oral History Interviews with
David H. Stowe," Washington, D.C., September 25, 1972, Harry S. Truman Library, p. 48, at https://www.trumanlibrary.org/oralhist/stowe1.htm.

38 *Only two people had the clearances necessary:* Ibid., May 27, 1969, p. 19.

39 *"All three of us had those powerful little phones . . .":* Ibid., May 27, 1969, p. 16.

39 *Early COG plans consisted of a few:* "Oral History Interviews with Admiral Robert
L. Dennison," October 6, 1971, Harry S. Truman Library, p. 97, at https://www
.trumanlibrary.org/oralhist/dennisn.htm.

39 *"There was also the problem of what files . . .":* "Oral History Interviews with David
H. Stowe," Washington, D.C., September 25, 1972, Harry S. Truman Library,
p. 43, at https://www.trumanlibrary.org/oralhist/stowe1.htm.

40 *In the final year of his presidency, Truman hosted Winston Churchill:* "Oral History
Interview with Brigadier General Cornelius J. Mara," Washington, D.C., June 7
and 9, 1971, Harry S. Truman Library, at http://www.trumanlibrary.org/oralhist
/maracorn.htm#98.

40 *He used it regularly on the Potomac:* McCullough, *Truman,* p. 512; see also "Oral
History Interview with James J. Rowley," Kensington, Maryland, September
20, 1988, Harry S. Truman Library, at http://www.trumanlibrary.org/oralhist
/rowley_j.htm#29.

40 *"The Williamsburg was really a floating command post . . .":* "Oral History Interviews with Admiral Robert L. Dennison," October 6, 1971, Harry S. Truman Library, p. 96, at https://www.trumanlibrary.org/oralhist/dennisn.htm.

41 *The main problem with evacuation:* "Oral History Interviews with David H. Stowe,
Harry Truman Presidential Library, March 18, 1976, p. 17, at https://www.tru
manlibrary.org/oralhist/stowe1.htm.

41 *"The problem in any of these temporary . . ."* "Oral History Interviews with Admiral
Robert L. Dennison," Harry S. Truman Library, October 6, 1971, p. 97, at https://
www.trumanlibrary.org/oralhist/dennisn.htm.

41 *The Secret Service warned Truman:* McCullough, *Truman,* p. 811. McCullough's
source is Roger Tubby's diary, which is now kept at Yale University and not open
to researchers.

42 *Truman's farewell address:* Harry S. Truman, "The President's Farewell Address
to the American People," January 15, 1953, John T. Woolley and Gerhard Peters,
American Presidency Project, at http://www.presidency.ucsb.edu/ws/?pid=14392.

43   *Roy Snapp realized:* Hewlett and Holl, *Atoms for Peace and War,* pp. 1–5.

44   *"Let's not make our mistakes . . .":* Thomas, *Ike's Bluff,* p. 45.

44   *After Eisenhower left the club manager's office:* Hewlett and Holl, *Atoms for Peace and War,* pp. 1–5.

44   *One night they took visiting friends:* Thomas, *Ike's Bluff,* p. 99.

45   *On Memorial Day 1951, with the nation:* Ibid., p. 39.

45   *Eisenhower had campaigned on a "New Look":* Craig, *Destroying the Village,* p. 42; John Dulles, "A Policy of Boldness," *Life,* May, 19, 1952.

45   *The United States, Eisenhower said, needed:* Adams, *Fine Group of Fellows,* p. 64.

45   *To Eisenhower, the point instead:* Ambrose, *Eisenhower,* pp. 227, 275.

45   *Ten days later, Eisenhower was in the Oval Office:* Eisenhower quoted in Hughes diary, March 16, 1953, in Thomas, *Ike's Bluff,* p. 60, and R. Schlesinger, *White House Ghosts,* p. 71.

46   *The resulting speech—delivered under duress:* Thomas, *Ike's Bluff,* p. 65.

46   *That day in April 1953, looking out:* Dwight D. Eisenhower, "Address, 'The Chance for Peace,' Delivered before the American Society of Newspaper Editors," April 16, 1953, John T. Woolley and Gerhard Peters, *American Presidency Project,* at http://www.presidency.ucsb.edu/ws/?pid=9819.

46   *To execute his "New Look," President Eisenhower launched:* Thomas, *Ike's Bluff,* p. 107; see also Pickett, *George F. Kennan and the Origin of Eisenhower's New Look.*

46   *At the conclusion of three hours of presentations:* K. Thompson, *Eisenhower Presidency,* p. 65.

47   *As C. D. Jackson, a White House staffer:* "Submitting Candor-Wheaties Chronology for Lewis Strauss Approval Letter," Nuclear Non-Proliferation Collection, Item Number: NP00173, Digital National Security Archive, George Washington University, September 25, 1954, at http://nsarchive.gwu.edu/nsa/publications/nnp /nuclear.html.

47   *Rather than focusing on the cost of war:* "Chronology—Candor-Wheaties" [Atoms for Peace Proposal], Internal Paper, Nuclear Non-Proliferation Collection, Item Number: NP00175, Digital National Security Archive, George Washington University, September 30, 1954, at http://nsarchive.gwu.edu/nsa/publications/nnp /nuclear.html.

47   *On December 8, 1953, Eisenhower addressed the General Assembly:* "Text of the Address Delivered by the President of the United States before the General Assembly of the United Nations in New York City," December 8, 1953, Dwight D. Eisenhower Presidential Library, at http://www.eisenhower.archives.gov/research/on line_documents/atoms_for_peace/Binder13.pdf.

47   *At the same time, Eisenhower's annual budget message:* "Editorial Note," Foreign Relations of the United States, 1952–1954, National Security Affairs, vol. II, pt. 1, doc. 108, U.S. Department of State, Office of the Historian, n.d., at https://his tory.state.gov/historicaldocuments/frus1952–54v02p1/d108.

47   *More than thirty officials—including a half dozen Cabinet officers:* "The President's

Appointments, Monday February 1, 1954," Dwight D. Eisenhower Daily Appointment Schedule Collection, Miller Center, University of Virginia, at http://web2.millercenter.org/dde/documents/presidential_papers/dde_diary_series/1954/dde_1954_02.pdf.

48 *As MIT President James Killian, the group's leader:* Killian, *Sputnik, Scientists and Eisenhower*, pp. 68–69.

49 *The United States had returned to the Marshall Islands:* Schell, *Fate of the Earth*, p. 53.

49 *Birds spontaneously combusted:* Stephen Salaff, "The Lucky Dragon," *Bulletin of Atomic Scientists* (May 1978): 21–23.

49 *North of Washington, none of the locals:* " 'Beard Lot' Papers Filed," *Gettysburg Times*, March 3, 1951, at http://news.google.com/newspapers?nid=2202&dat=19510303&id=8IElAAAAIBAJ&sjid=3fQFAAAAIBAJ&pg=5333,3073119.

49 *Some sold quickly:* "Countians Give Land Estimates," *Gettysburg Times*, February 4, 1954, at http://news.google.com/newspapers?nid=2202&dat=19540204&id=NTkmAAAAIBAJ&sjid=8v0FAAAAIBAJ&pg=852,929880.

49 *Government lawyers said the land:* "Secret Cold War Bunker No Mystery to Its Neighbors," *Reading Eagle*, November 26, 1997, at http://news.google.com/newspapers?nid=1955&dat=19971126&id=Wi4vAAAAIBAJ&sjid=s6YFAAAAIBAJ&pg=3302,998219.

49 *The most confusing thing was that the government:* "More Land Is Obtained for Army Project," *Gettysburg Compiler*, February 17, 1951, at http://news.google.com/newspapers?nid=2246&dat=19510217&id=EaxcAAAAIBAJ&sjid=hlgNAAAAIBAJ&pg=897,3325706.

50 *Until the government arrived:* W. D. Nelson, *President Is at Camp David*, p. 23.

50 *In fact, the Cold War building boom begun:* Bobrick, *Parsons Brinckerhoff*, p. 124.

50 *"We started design [for Raven Rock] . . .":* "Designing for Defense: NORAD," *Notes* (internal newsletter), Parsons Brinckerhoff, Spring 1988.

51 *Work began in earnest:* "Government Starts Work on 'Beard Lot,' " *Gettysburg Times*, January 27, 1951, at http://news.google.com/newspapers?nid=2246&dat=19510127&id=EKxcAAAAIBAJ&sjid=hlgNAAAAIBAJ&pg=3982,3386736.

51 *Local No. 1167 of the General Laborers' union:* "Say 'Second Pentagon' Being Built in County Hills; Road Is Underway; Tunnel Is Next," *Gettysburg Compiler*, January 27, 1951, at http://news.google.com/newspapers?nid=2246&dat=19510127&id=EKxcAAAAIBAJ&sjid=hlgNAAAAIBAJ&pg=1862,3385645.

51 *Many of the mining team came:* Bill Gifford, "Bunker? What Bunker?" *New York Times Magazine*, December 2000, at http://partners.nytimes.com/library/magazine/home/20001203mag-gifford.html.

51 *Once the $17 million project was running:* "Sunshine Trail Traffic Cut Off," *Gettysburg Compiler*, January 27, 1951, at http://news.google.com/newspapers?nid=2246&dat=19510127&id=EKxcAAAAIBAJ&sjid=hlgNAAAAIBAJ&pg=4361,3384062.

51 *dumping the "spoil":* "Cliff Shelters Peaceful Town, Pentagon in War," *Pittsburgh*

Post-Gazette, August 7, 1985, at http://news.google.com/newspapers?id=6cA 0AAAAIBAJ&sjid=PW4DAAAAIBAJ&dq=site-r%20raven-rock&pg =1842%2C1423160.

51 *In the project's initial days, locals camped out:* "Ban Parking on Highway at Tunnel Digging," *Gettysburg Times,* March 15, 1951, at http://news.google.com/news papers?nid=2202&dat=19510315&id=-oE1AAAAIBAJ&sjid=3fQFAA AAIBAJ&pg=2726,2512815.

51 *On February 2, just weeks after:* "Groundhog Sees More Winter Ahead," *Gettysburg Times,* February 2, 1951, at http://news.google.com/newspapers?nid=2202&dat= 19510202&id=N4dhAAAAIBAJ&sjid=3fQFAAAAIBAJ&pg=1294,4528899.

51 *Locals called the mysterious project:* "Feature Detail Report for: Raven Rock," U.S. Department of the Interior, U.S. Geological Survey, August 30, 1990, at http:// geonames.usgs.gov/apex/f?p=gnispq:3:::NO::P3_FID:1211037.

52 *Raven Rock's presence in the valley:* "Enrollment at Fairfield's School Jumps," *Gettysburg Times,* May 26, 1951, at http://news.google.com/newspapers?nid=2202&d at=19510526&id=gaE1AAAAIBAJ&sjid=nfwFAAAAIBAJ&pg=4079,5079993.

52 *Housing developments were upgraded:* Angelica Roberts, "Fort Ritchie Has Storied History," *Herald-Mail,* June 30, 2008, at http://articles.herald-mail.com/2008 –06–30/news/25163869_1_fort-ritchie-camp-ritchie-training-facility/2.

52 *Both Maryland and Pennsylvania widened:* "Say 'Second Pentagon' Being Built in County Hills; Road Is Underway; Tunnel Is Next," *Gettysburg Times,* January 26, 1951, at http://news.google.com/newspapers?nid=2202&dat=19510126&id=2IE 1AAAAIBAJ&sjid=3fQFAAAAIBAJ&pg=1326,4847600.

52 *The telephone company began:* "Rights of Way Filed by Phone Company," *Star and Sentinel,* April 19, 1952, at http://news.google.com/newspapers?nid=2241&dat=1 9520419&id=uY8lAAAAIBAJ&sjid=yfIFAAAAIBAJ&pg=6082,2118892.

52 *Government officials scouted:* "Magazine Says 'Brass Hats' Go Underground," *Gettysburg Times,* May 26, 1951, at http://news.google.com/newspapers?nid=2202&d at=19510526&id=gaE1AAAAIBAJ&sjid=nfwFAAAAIBAJ&pg=3935,4981845.

52 *The night before, Cutler had told Ike:* Cutler, *No Time for Rest,* p. 304.

52 *Multiple layers of security surrounded:* "Physical Security of the Alternate Joint Communications Center (AJCC)," Army Publications and Printing Command, Army Regulation 190–15, May 6, 1994, at http://web.archive.org/web/2001 0901053654/http://books.usapa.belvoir.army.mil/cgi-bin/bookmgr/BOOKS /R190_15/CONTENTS#GLOSSARY.

53 *At the center of the mountain was the core:* S. K. Johannesen, "Undisclosed Location," *Queens Quarterly,* March 22, 2004, at http://www.thefreelibrary.com /Undisclosed+location.-a0116346788.

54 *It readied what it called the Department:* DACE was uncovered by Cold War researcher Albert LaFrance. For more information, see https://beta.groups.yahoo .com/neo/groups/coldwarcomms/conversations/topics/5382.

54 *In the summer of 1952, the State Department dispatched:* "History of the SCBI

Complex," Smithsonian's National Zoo & Conservation Biology Institute, n.d., at https://nationalzoo.si.edu/conservation/history-scbi-complex.

55 *As Millison recalled, "The vines...":* "Record of Conversation Between Earl G. Millison and Melvin N. Blum," National Archives, Folder "Basic Data in Relocation Site," Box 1, RG 59, Records Relating to the Vital Records Program for Emergency Planning, General Records of the Department of State, National Archives, College Park, Maryland.

55 *Since no one knew how many State Department staff:* "Richard Brown to William Crockett," Folder "Front Royal," Box 1, RG 59, Records Relating to the Vital Records Program for Emergency Planning, General Records of the Department of State, National Archives, College Park, Maryland, December 17, 1962.

55 *The series of barns, converted stables:* "Report of Security Survey, Department of State Relocation Facility," National Archives, Folder "Front Royal," Box 1, RG 59, Records Relating to the Vital Records Program for Emergency Planning, General Records of the Department of State, National Archives, College Park, Maryland, May 18, 1955.

56 *As Senator Henry Cabot Lodge said:* "Memo to Wayne Grover," December 12, 1950; Folder "Front Royal," Box 1, RG 59, Records Relating to the Vital Records Program for Emergency Planning, National Archives; Summary Report on Department's Records Evacuation Program, March 18, 1952; folder "Department of Agriculture Permit Front Royal," Box 1, RG 59, Records Relating to the Vital Records Program for Emergency Planning, National Archives.

56 *The Treasury Department and the Comptroller:* "Preparation of a Mobilization Plan for Records Essential to the National Security," draft, National Security Resources Board, Box 1, RG 59, Records Relating to the Vital Records Program for Emergency Planning, General Records of the Department of State, National Archives, College Park, Maryland, November 18, 1948.

56 *In an era where detailed maps:* "Report by the Joint Intelligence Group, Status of External Security for Cartographic Facilities," JIC 555, Box 1, RG 59, Records Relating to the Vital Records Program for Emergency Planning, General Records of the Department of State, National Archives, College Park, Maryland, January 19, 1951.

57 *During one NSC meeting, he candidly:* "Memorandum of Discussion at the 190th Meeting of the National Security Council," March 25, 1954, doc. 113, in *Foreign Relations of the United States, 1952–1954, National Security Affairs, vol. 2, pt. 1,* U.S. Government Printing Office, 1984.

57 *As Peterson explained:* Davis, *Stages of Emergency,* p. 158.

58 *The $22,500 hospital prototype:* "Federal Civil Defense Administration, Annual Report for 1956," U.S. Government Printing Office, 1957, p. 80, at https://training.fema.gov/hiedu/docs/historicalinterest/fcda%20–%201956%20–%20annual%20report%20for%201956.pdf.

58 *More than 136,000 curious people:* "Federal Civil Defense Administration, Annual

Report for 1955," U.S. Government Printing Office, 1956, p. 80, at https://training.fema.gov/hiedu/docs/historicalinterest/fcda%20–%201955%20–%20annual%20report%20for%201955.pdf.

58 *One of its major campaigns:* Ibid., p. 82.

58 *Sears, Roebuck & Co. erected:* Ibid., p. 79.

58 *Operation* ALERT *1954 became:* Krugler, *This Is Only a Test,* p. 121.

59 *A team of officials gathered:* "Lessons Learned from Operations Alert 1955–57," Publication No. L58–141, Industrial College of the Armed Forces, Washington, D.C., April 30, 1958, at http://www.globalsecurity.org/wmd/library/report/other/l58–141.pdf.

60 *At precisely 6:52 a.m.:* Harrison Salisbury, "Molotov Visits Museum and UN," *New York Times,* June 16, 1955.

60 *As he continued his visit:* Damon Stetson, "Warning Flashed to Control Points," *New York Times,* June 16, 1955.

60 *From* LEMON JUICE, *the yellow:* "Federal Civil Defense Administration, Annual Report for 1955," U.S. Government Printing Office, 1956, p. 97, at https://training.fema.gov/hiedu/docs/historicalinterest/fcda%20–%201955%20–%20annual%20report%20for%201955.pdf.

60 *Air raid sirens sounded:* Peter Kihss, "City Clears Streets Quickly as Big Zone Is 'Wiped Out,'" *New York Times,* June 16, 1955.

61 *When the* APPLE JACK *alert sounded in Washington:* "Dwight D. Eisenhower Daily Appointment Schedule" Collection, Miller Center, University of Virginia, at http://web2.millercenter.org/dde/documents/presidential_papers/dde_diary_series/1955/dde_1955_06.pdf.

61 *For the drill, most of the press corps:* "Lessons Learned from Operations Alert, 1955–57," L58–141, Industrial College of the Armed Forces, Washington, D.C., April 30, 1958, at http://www.globalsecurity.org/wmd/library/report/other/l58–141.pdf.

62 *"The president desires no one . . .":* "Memorandum of Conference with the President," May 25, 1955, Dwight D. Eisenhower's Papers as President, Ann Whitman Diary Series, May 1955, Dwight D. Eisenhower Library, at http://eisenhower.archives.gov/research/online_documents/declassified/fy_2012/1955_05_26.pdf.

62 *As part of that effort, Eisenhower:* "Lessons Learned from Operations Alert 1955–57," Publication No. L58–141, Industrial College of the Armed Forces, Washington, D.C., April 30, 1958, at http://www.globalsecurity.org/wmd/library/report/other/l58–141.pdf, p. 5.

63 *Governors, the administration explained:* "Federal Civil Defense Administration, Annual Report for 1955," U.S. Government Printing Office, 1956, p. 34.

63 *It was clear the FCDA's stockpiles:* Ibid., p. 103.

63 *Confusion continued to swirl throughout:* "Mock Crop Order Arouses Farmers," *New York Times,* June 17, 1955.

63 *Then there were unexpected obstacles:* "Memo from A. H. Belmont to L. V. Boardman, 'Operation Alert 1956,'" Federal Bureau of Investigation (FBI) File Number

66-HQ-18953, War Plans—Emergency Relocation Plans for the Department of Justice (DOJ), 1954–1956, 1966, July 9, 1956, p. 436, at http://www.government attic.org/4docs/FBI-WarPlansEmergRelocatDOJ_1954–1956.pdf.

63 *The State Department, too, had serious concerns:* "Henry Ford to William Crockett," Folder "Front Royal," Box 1, RG 59, Records Relating to the Vital Records Program for Emergency Planning, General Records of the Department of State, National Archives, College Park, Maryland, February 14, 1963.

63 *As syndicated columnist Doris Fleeson:* Sayler, *Doris Fleeson,* p. 231.

64 *Spouses, meanwhile, were left in Washington:* "Official Wives Sit It Out," *Washington Post,* June 16, 1955, p. 35.

64 *Years earlier, he'd participated:* David A. Pfeiffer, "Ike's Interstates at 50," *Prologue,* vol. 38, no. 2 (Summer 2006), at http://www.archives.gov/publications/prologue/2006/summer/interstates.html.

64 *As he argued to Congress in 1955:* Dwight D. Eisenhower: "Special Message to the Congress Regarding a National Highway Program," February 22, 1955, John T. Woolley and Gerhard Peters, *American Presidency Project,* at http://www.presidency.ucsb.edu/ws/?pid=10415.

64 *His effort, known formally:* "Why President Dwight D. Eisenhower Understood We Needed the Interstate System," Highway History, U.S. Department of Transportation, Federal Highway Administration, at https://www.fhwa.dot.gov/interstate/brainiacs/eisenhowerinterstate.htm.

64 *As the network of limited-access highways grew:* "Interstate Frequently Asked Questions," 50th Anniversary, Interstate Highway System, Federal Highway Administration, at https://www.fhwa.dot.gov/interstate/faq.cfm#question37.

65 *The same month as the 1955 Operation ALERT:* "Federal Civil Defense Administration, Annual Report for 1955," U.S. Government Printing Office, 1956, p. 93. See also, for example, "Weather Bureau Makes Public Its Fallout Forecast," *Milwaukee Journal,* September 10, 1956.

65 *As part of the program, fifty-two weather stations:* See also William R. Kennedy Jr., "Fallout Forecasting—1945 Through 1962," Los Alamos National Laboratory, March 1986, at https://fas.org/sgp/othergov/doe/lanl/la-10605-ms.pdf; and "Federal Civil Defense Administration, Annual Report for 1957," U.S. Government Printing Office, 1958, p. 15.

65 *Civil defense planners collected:* "Federal Civil Defense Administration, Annual Report for 1956," U.S. Government Printing Office, 1957, p. 21.

65 *The forecasts would prove helpful:* Ibid., p. 71.

65 *Mobile, Alabama, home to a major Air:* "Federal Civil Defense Administration, Annual Report for 1955," U.S. Government Printing Office, 1956, p. 27.

65 *On September 27th, three months after OPAL '55: The Day Called X,* Cinema History from the Cold War!, CBS Television, Office of Civil and Defense Mobilization, 1957, at http://www.atomictheater.com/adaycalledx.htm.

66 *Still, many ordinary Americans remained:* Garrison, *Bracing for Armageddon,* p. 37.

66　*After an initial fervor, the Air Force struggled:* McCray, *Keep Watching the Skies!*, p. 28.

66　*Recruiting posters showed:* Mark Wolverton, "Oldies and Oddities: When Civvies Scrambled Fighters," *Air & Space* (Smithsonian), July 2011, at http://www .airspacemag.com/history-of-flight/oldies-and-oddities-when-civvies-scrambled -fighters-162566072/#tDMY6bjiKZqAigCl.99.

66　*"The awful truth is that . . .":* See "Aircraft Recognition for the Ground Observer," AF Manual 355–10, US Air Force, Washington D.C., April 1955.

66　*By the mid-1950s, the military began to deploy:* Scott Locklin, "The Largest Computer Ever Built," Locklin on Science, March 28, 2013, at https://scottlocklin .wordpress.com/2013/03/28/the-largest-computer-ever-built/.

67　*Thermonuclear war thoroughly frightened:* See, for example, Gaddis, *Cold War*, p. 66.

68　*Historian Campbell Craig argues that beginning:* Craig, *Destroying the Village*, p. 55.

68　*As Eisenhower told one group of Congressmen:* David Alan Rosenberg, "The Origins of Overkill: Nuclear Weapons and American Strategy, 1945–1960," *International Security*, vol. 7, no. 4 (Spring 1983): 34; L. A. Minnich, "Minutes, Bipartisan Legislative Meeting, January 5, 1954, Staff Notes," January–December 1954 folder, Box 4, DDE Ann C. Whitman File, Dwight D. Eisenhower Papers as President, Dwight D. Eisenhower Library.

68　*He'd tried repeatedly in 1954 and 1955:* Thomas Mallon, "Mr. Smith Goes Underground," *American Heritage*, vol. 51, no. 5 (2000), at http://www.americanheritage .com/content/mr-smith-goes-underground?page=show.

69　*The Court had made some minor efforts:* He later said he "deeply regretted" his role. "Whenever I thought of the innocent little children who were torn from home, school friends, and congenial surroundings, I was conscience-stricken," he wrote in his memoirs. "It was wrong to react so impulsively, without positive evidence of disloyalty" (Warren, *Memoirs of Earl Warren*, p. 149).

69　*As attorney general of California during World War II:* Ibid., pp. 144–47.

69　*As governor of California at the dawn:* Winkler, *Life Under a Cloud*, p. 113.

69　*Court Clerk Harold Willey was dispatched:* "Letter of Harold B. Willey to the Chief Justice," Office of the Clerk, Supreme Court of the United States, Washington, D.C., Manuscript Division, Library of Congress, October 14, 1955, at http://www.scribd.com/fullscreen/137724950?access_key=key-29bn0no34zdw 9pmzyhd2&allow_share=true&escape=false&view_mode=scroll.

70　*Willey also visited the local courthouse:* Ibid. I found these remarkable documents in Krugler, *This Is Only a Test*, p. 168, and at Conelrad Adjacent, "A Resort of Their Own: The Supreme Court's Cold War Relocation Plan," April 24, 2013, at http:// conelrad.blogspot.com/2013/04/a-resort-of-their-own-supreme-courts.html.

70　*With Warren's approval, the court worked:* "Letter of Harold B. Willey to the Chief Justice," Office of the Clerk, Supreme Court of the United States, Washington, D.C., Manuscript Division, Library of Congress, June 6, 1956, at http://www .scribd.com/doc/137724259/Harold-B-Willey-to-Earl-Warren-06-06-1956.

70 *The federal civil defense office, Warren felt:* Warren, *Memoirs of Earl Warren,* p. 230.

71 *In February 1957, the White House announced:* "Copter Trips to Save Time for Eisenhower," *New York Times,* February 20, 1957; see also "2 Helicopters for Ike's Use Undergo Tests," *Chicago Tribune,* April 7, 1957, at http://archives.chicagotribune.com/1957/04/07/page/3/article/2-helicopters-for-ikes-use-undergo-tests.

71 *They were specially modified:* "Bell H-13J," Smithsonian National Air and Space Museum, at http://airandspace.si.edu/collections/artifact.cfm?object=nasm_A19 690013000.

71 *In the months ahead, Draper conducted:* "White House Whirlybird," *Time,* June 10, 1957, vol. 69, no. 23, p. 27.

71 *With a top speed of about 100 miles:* "Dwight D. Eisenhower Daily Appointment Schedule" Collection, July 1, 1957, Miller Center, University of Virginia, at http://web2.millercenter.org/dde/documents/presidential_papers/dde_diary_series/1957/dde_1957_07.pdf.

72 *His aides, meanwhile, had a more pleasant ride:* "Bell H-13J," Smithsonian National Air and Space Museum, at http://airandspace.si.edu/collections/artifact.cfm?object=nasm_A19690013000.

72 *As Virgil Olson, who piloted the Marine transport:* Virgil Olson, "Flying on Foreign Choppers," *Washington Times,* February 1, 2004, p. B5.

73 *No one wanted a repeat:* Williams, *History of Army Aviation,* p. 85.

73 *Their distinctive paint scheme:* Fails, *Marines and Helicopters, 1962–1973,* p. 19.

73 *Jet—faster and more powerful:* "Federal Civil Defense Administration, Annual Report for 1957," U.S. Government Printing Office, 1958, p. 38.

73 *Post-attack planning expanded, too:* Ibid., pp. 14, 18.

73 *Two years later, the Public Heath Service:* Ibid., p. 16.

73 *The Labor Department created handbooks:* Ibid., p. 19.

73 *DELNET, a dedicated teletype system:* "Federal Civil Defense Administration, Annual Report for 1958," U.S. Government Printing Office, 1959, p. 15.

74 *On May 22, 1957, President Eisenhower signed:* James Lay, "Memo: Policy Regarding Use of Atomic Weapons," Executive Office of the President, National Security Council, Washington, D.C., May 16, 1957, at http://www2.gwu.edu/~nsarchiv/news/predelegation2/pre2–1a.htm.

74 *In the field, Eisenhower's "pre-delegation":* Thomas, *Ike's Bluff,* p. 293.

74 *In the event of what RAND strategist:* Albert Wohlstetter, "The Delicate Balance of Terror," RAND Corporation, P-1472, November 6, 1958, revised December 1958, at http://www.rand.org/about/history/wohlstetter/P1472/P1472.html.

74 *The new nuclear "pre-delegation" rules:* Abella, *Soldiers of Reason,* p. 87.

75 *FCDA also launched a major effort:* "Federal Civil Defense Administration, Annual Report for 1958," U.S. Government Printing Office, 1959, p. 4.

75 *Veterans groups adopted the measures:* "Annual Report for Fiscal Year 1959," Office of Civil and Defense Mobilization, U.S. Government Printing Office, 1960, pp. 4 and 9.

75   *During the 1960 election:* "States' Lines of Gubernatorial Powers," National Emergency Management Association, May 2011, at http://www.nlga.us/wp-content/uploads/States-Lines-of-Gubernatorial-Succession-2.pdf; "Annual Report for Fiscal Year 1960," Office of Civil and Defense Mobilization, U.S. Government Printing Office, 1961, p. 8.

75   *The FCDA also released:* "Battleground USA," Ibid., p. 25.

75   *FCDA's stockpiles had soared:* "Federal Civil Defense Administration, Annual Report for 1957," U.S. Government Printing Office, 1958, p. 55.

75   *A dozen FCDA maintenance facilities:* Ibid., pp. 55–57.

76   *More than 900 of the improvised emergency hospitals:* Ibid., p. 58.

76   *The FCDA trained hundreds of police:* "Federal Civil Defense Administration, Annual Report for 1955," U.S. Government Printing Office, 1956, p. 118.

76   *The FCDA even planned:* "Federal Civil Defense Administration, Annual Report for 1958," U.S. Government Printing Office, 1959, p. 10.

76   *In Kansas, officials calculated:* Davis, *Stages of Emergency,* p. 276.

76   *"I don't think we are ever very realistic . . .":* Ibid., p. 277.

77   *Within two months of its reorganization:* "Reorganization Plan No. 1 of 1958," *United States Statutes at Large Containing the Laws and Concurrent Resolutions Enacted During the Second Session of the Eighty-Fifth Congress of the United States of America (1958) and Reorganization Plan and Proclamations,* vol. 72, pt. 1, April 24, 1958, U.S. Government Printing Office, 1959, p. 1799, at https://www.gpo.gov/fdsys/pkg/STATUTE-72/pdf/STATUTE-72-FrontMatter-1-Pgi.pdf.

77   *"The destruction," Eisenhower told his Cabinet:* Nichols, *Eisenhower 1956,* p. 58.

78   *The Defense Department created:* This unit was part of the Pentagon's Office of Civil Defense, the Kennedy-era successor to Eisenhower's Office of Civil and Defense Mobilization.

78   *So in 1950, President Truman authorized:* "Project Nutmeg" fact sheet, DOE/NV 767, National Nuclear Security Administration, U.S. Department of Energy (Las Vegas), August 2013, at http://nnss.gov/docs/fact_sheets/DOENV_767.pdf.

79   *The first of the domestic nuclear tests came:* "Nevada Test Site Guide," DOE/NV-715 REV-1, National Nuclear Security Administration, U.S. Department of Energy (Las Vegas), March 2005, at https://nnsa.energy.gov/sites/default/files/nnsa/inlinefiles/doe%20nv%202001e.pdf.

79   *In 1953 and 1955, the FCDA conducted two major tests:* "Federal Civil Defense Administration, Annual Report for 1955," U.S. Government Printing Office, 1956, p. 44, at https://training.fema.gov/hiedu/docs/historicalinterest/fcda%20–%201955%20–%20annual%20report%20for%201955.pdf.

80   *Clothed mannequins were located in various rooms:* "Interview with Ernest Williams," Nevada Test Site Oral History Project, University of Nevada, Las Vegas, October 27, 2004, at http://digital.library.unlv.edu/objects/nts/1162.

80   *A sign nearby read:* "Nevada Test Site Guide," DOE/NV-715 REV-1, National

Nuclear Security Administration, U.S. Department of Energy (Las Vegas), March 2005, at https://nnsa.energy.gov/sites/default/files/nnsa/inlinefiles/doe%20nv%202001e.pdf.

81 *As physicist I. I. Rabi tried to explain:* James Gleick, "After the Bomb, a Mushroom Cloud of Metaphors," *New York Times,* May 21, 1989.

81 *For the* PRISCILLA *test:* Mary Jo Viscuso et al., "Shot Priscilla: A Test of the Plumbbob Series, 24 June 1957," DNA 6003f, Defense Nuclear Agency, U.S. Department of Defense, 1981, p. 31, at http://www.dtic.mil/dtic/tr/fulltext/u2/a105674.pdf.

81 *Lastly, for the* PRISCILLA *test, the Mosler Safe Company built:* Jim Blount, "Mosler Safe Co., Linked with Banking for Much of Its History, Also Prominent Contributor to U.S. Cold War Defenses," *Employee Reunion,* July 19, 2014, at https://sites.google.com/a/lanepl.org/jbcols/home/2014-articles/mosler-safe-co-linked-with-banking-for-much-of-its-history-also-prominent-contributor-to-u-s-cold-war-defenses. Mosler was also responsible for installing the nation's first drive-through bank teller window, in the First National Bank in Boston in 1939.

81 *"It was our great luck to find . . .":* "Your Products Are Stronger than the Atomic Bomb," Letters of Note, September 16, 2010, at http://www.lettersofnote.com/2010/09/safe.html.

82 *"Your products were admired for being stronger . . .":* "A Tradition of Integrity and Quality," Mosler Safe Co. brochure, Empire Safe Brochure Library, at http://www.empiresafe.com/uploads/0000/0183/A_Tradition_of_Quality_and_Integrity.pdf.

82 *"The damage to the door was only . . .":* Charles D. Price, "Engineering Study of Blast-Resistant Doors, Submitted to U.S. Corps of Engineers, Protective Construction Branch," Mosler Safe Co., p. 10, at http://www.dtic.mil/dtic/tr/fulltext/u2/688173.pdf.

82 *Over the course of the Cold War:* Virginia C. Purdy, "A Temple to Clio: The National Archives Building," in Walch, *Guardian of Heritage,* p. 27.

83 *In* The Washington Post, *journalist Chalmers Roberts explained:* Chalmers Roberts, "Enormous Arms Outlay Is Held Vital to Survival," *Washington Post,* December 20, 1957.

83 *An irritated Eisenhower didn't agree:* Eisenhower, *Waging Peace,* p. 222.

84 *As he told the departing committee:* Nitze, Rearden, and Smith, *From Hiroshima to Glasnost,* p. 168.

84 *Already that morning, he'd sworn in:* "Dwight D. Eisenhower Daily Appointment Schedule" Collection, November 1, 1957, Miller Center, University of Virginia, at http://web2.millercenter.org/dde/documents/presidential_papers/dde_diary_series/1957/dde_1957_07.pdf.

84 *The FBI had accordingly revised its war plans:* "Memo from A. H. Belmont to L. V. Boardman, Buplans—Relocation of Attorney General, October 30, 1957,"

"Sections 5 through 7 (and enclosure 109) of FBI Headquarters file 66–18953: Defense Plans Department of Justice, 1955–1982," p. 50, at http://www.govern mentattic.org/4docs/FBI-file-66-HQ-18953-DefensePlans_1955–1982.pdf.

84   *Eight years before, in November 1949:* "Memorandum, Gordon Dean to James Lay, 'Atomic Energy Commission Memorandum,'" "NSC-Atomic" Folder, Box 202, President's Security Files, Truman Presidential Library, June 24, 1952.

84   *Finally in 1955, Congress allowed the Atomic Energy Commission:* "Why Germantown?" U.S. Department of Energy, Germantown Site History, at http://science .energy.gov/bes/about/organizational-history/germantown-natural-history/ger mantown-site-history/.

85   *This time, however, Eisenhower's dramatic:* Edwin L. Dale Jr., "President, Dedicating A.E.C. Building, Warns of Dangers in the Atom," *New York Times,* November 9, 1957.

85   *As he leaned over to the button, he said:* Dwight D. Eisenhower, "Remarks at the Dedication Ceremonies of the Atomic Energy Commission Headquarters Building," November 8, 1957, John T. Woolley and Gerhard Peters, *American Presidency Project,* at http://www.presidency.ucsb.edu/ws/?pid=10947.

85   *Eisenhower's stubborn resistance:* Brugioni and Taylor, *Eyes in the Sky,* p. 160.

85   *Publicly, the so-called Bomber Gap:* Thomas, *Ike's Bluff,* pp. 181–82.

85   *The junior Massachusetts senator, John F. Kennedy:* Christopher A. Preble, "Who Ever Believed in the 'Missile Gap'?: John F. Kennedy and the Politics of National Security," *Presidential Studies Quarterly,* vol. 33, no. 4 (December 2003): 801–26.

86   *But Ike—and his vice president, Richard Nixon:* "Letter from Mrs. Allan Jones," September 19, 1961, and "Eisenhower to Freeman Dosden," September 25, 1961, quoted in Adams, *Eisenhower's Fine Group of Fellows,* p. 198.

86   *In June 1959, the OCDM's liaison officer:* [Author Redacted], "Memorandum for the Record: Trip to High Point," June 11, 1959, CIA Crest Document CIA-RDP72– 00450R000100350015–7, at https://www.cia.gov/library/readingroom/document /cia-rdp72–00450r000100350015–7.

86   *Dwight Eisenhower's life as commander-in-chief:* Ambrose, *Eisenhower,* pp. 292, 299, 312.

88   *When pressed for details of the raid:* Franklin D. Roosevelt, "Excerpts from the Press Conference," April 21, 1942. John T. Woolley and Gerhard Peters, *American Presidency Project,* at http://www.presidency.ucsb.edu/ws/?pid=16250. This reference actually gave rise to a real U.S. ship: The Navy built an Essex-class aircraft carrier, USS *Shangri-La* (CV-38), that launched in 1944.

88   *When he was in attendance:* Nelson, *President Is at Camp David,* p. 16.

88   *The Secret Service stayed in nearby Thurmont:* Ibid., p. 7.

88   *Truman had inherited the camp:* Ibid., p. 22.

88   *Almost immediately, Mamie set:* Ibid., p. 30.

88   *The presidential cabin:* Memo regarding naming of Aspen Lodge, Box 7, Reading

File Oct. 2, 1958–Nov. 19, 1958, Evan P. Aurand Papers, Dwight D. Eisenhower Presidential Library, November 17, 1958.

89 *A famed New York golf course designer:* Nelson, *President Is at Camp David,* p. 35.

89 *Eisenhower thought Roosevelt's name:* "Letter, President Eisenhower to Friend, Swede Hazlett, Regarding Presidential Retreat Name Change," Folder "Swede Hazlett 1953 (1)," Dwight D. Eisenhower Papers as President, Name Series, Box 18, Dwight D. Eisenhower Presidential Library, July 21, 1953.

89 *In the latter years of Eisenhower's administration:* Eisenhower, *Waging Peace,* p. 433.

89 *Mixing business and pleasure:* "Documents Pertaining to President Eisenhower's Meeting with British Prime Minister Harold Macmillan at Camp David," Folder "Visit by Prime Minister Macmillan, March 19–22, 1959," Dwight D. Eisenhower Papers as President, Beach and Aurand Papers, Box 17, Dwight D. Eisenhower Presidential Library, March 20–22, 1959.

89 *Macmillan recalled in his diary:* Macmillan, *Macmillan Diaries,* p. 212.

90 *Khrushchev had assumed the Soviet:* Taubman, *Khrushchev,* p. 347.

91 *As helicopters across Washington ferried:* Beschloss, *Mayday,* p. 45.

91 *Mount Weather, Kistiakowsky wrote:* Kistiakowsky, *Scientist in the White House,* p. 317.

92 *During a Cabinet meeting:* "Notes on Cabinet Meeting," Cabinet Series, Ann Whitman File, Box 7, Dwight D. Eisenhower Presidential Library, July 25, 1956.

92 *Andrew Goodpaster, the president's national security aide:* "Toledoan Was Asked to Lead U.S. After Attack," *Blade,* March 21, 2004, at http://www.toledoblade.com/frontpage/2004/03/21/Toledoan-was-asked-to-lead-U-S-after-attack.html#BiGKvSG9mifEUHlZ.99.

92 *The president's requests to join:* Hope Yen, "Eisenhower Planned Emergency Government," *USA Today,* March 20, 2004, at http://usatoday30.usatoday.com/news/washington/2004–03–20-eisenhower-secret-government_x.htm.

93 *Nielsen, a mortgage banker by trade:* Tofel, *Restless Genius,* p. 136.

93 *Harold Boeschenstein, the Ohio head:* "The Most Powerful Club in the World? The Links," Valuablebook, October 1, 2012, at http://valuablebook.wordpress.com/2012/10/01/the-most-powerful-club-in-the-world-the-links/.

93 *J. Ed Warren, a longtime oil industry:* "Personalities: Jun. 5, 1964," *Time,* at http://content.time.com/time/magazine/article/0,9171,938633,00.html.

94 *Pace would exercise:* "Frank Pace Jr., Former Secretary of the Army and Executive, Dies," *New York Times,* January 10, 1988, at http://www.nytimes.com/1988/01/10/obituaries/frank-pace-jr-former-secretary-of-the-army-and-executive-dies.html.

94 *All nine men received similar secret:* Knowledge of the existence of the "Eisenhower Ten," as the group of men chosen to assume these emergency positions is known, is predominantly owed to the work of CONELRAD.com founder Bill Geerhart, who has tirelessly shed light upon and compiled many of the historical oddities and quirks that marked U.S. Cold War policy. His invaluable roundup of the

Eisenhower Ten is available at http://www.conelrad.com/atomicsecrets/secrets
.php?secrets=05.

94   *During OPAL '60, Leo Hoegh:* "A Priest, a Rabbi and a Minister Walk into Mount
     Weather . . . ," Conelrad Adjacent, October 23, 2011, at http://conelrad.blogspot
     .com/2011/10/priest-rabbi-and-minister-walk-into.html.

95   *Now Hoegh outlined a plan for the nine men:* Dwight D. Eisenhower, "Executive
     Order 10660—Providing for the Establishment of a National Defense Executive
     Reserve," February 15, 1956, John T. Woolley and Gerhard Peters, *American Presi-
     dency Project,* at http://www.presidency.ucsb.edu/ws/?pid=106365.

95   *"Commercial stocks in the . . .":* "The National Plan for Civil Defense and Defense
     Mobilization," Office of Defense and Civil Mobilization, Washington, D.C., Oc-
     tober 1958, p. 23, in Aksel Nielsen Records, 1956–1959, Box 1, Dwight Eisen-
     hower Presidential Library.

96   *The plans also called for at least two:* "Federal Civil Defense Administration, Annual
     Report for 1955," U.S. Government Printing Office, 1956, p. 108.

97   *As Eisenhower's presidency came to a close:* Pringle and Arkin, *S.I.O.P.,* p. 102.

97   *Fifteen years earlier, in late 1946:* David Alan Rosenberg, "The Origins of Over-
     kill: Nuclear Weapons and American Strategy, 1945–1960," *International Security,*
     vol. 7, no. 4 (Spring 1983): 46.

97   *That first SIOP, which enshrined:* Much of the history of SIOP is pieced together
     through two definitive works: Ibid., pp. 3–71, and Pringle and Arkin, *S.I.O.P.*

97   *The presentation, Eisenhower later told:* David Alan Rosenberg, "The Origins of
     Overkill: Nuclear Weapons and American Strategy, 1945–1960," *International Se-
     curity,* vol. 7, no. 4 (Spring 1983): 8.

98   *When Eisenhower's science advisor:* Pringle and Arkin, *S.I.O.P.,* p. 103.

98   *With the clock running out:* Eisenhower quoted in Thomas, *Ike's Bluff,* p. 389.

98   *"As one who has witnessed . . .":* "Eisenhower's Farewell Address to the Nation,"
     January 17, 1962, at http://mcadams.posc.mu.edu/ike.htm.

98   *A 1959 Consumers Union study:* Winkler, *Life Under a Cloud,* p. 102.

100 *An unfolding nuclear emergency, Eisenhower cautioned:* Details of SIOP are culled
     from Carl Kaysen, "Memorandum for General Maxwell Taylor, Military Repre-
     sentative to the President, Strategic Air Planning and Berlin," National Archives,
     Record Group 218, Records of the Joint Chiefs of Staff, Records of Maxwell
     Taylor, September 5, 1961. This document is a good example of the government's
     crazy classification laws; portions of it have been released to the National Security
     Archive—an invaluable resource at George Washington University—but select
     parts remain classified more than fifty-five years after it was written. The Defense
     Department continues to review releasing the classified portion that pertains to
     it, but the Department of Energy recently upheld the continued classification of a
     portion of the document pertaining to nuclear weapons.

100 *Soon, Ike arrived at the grand finale:* Gibbs and Duffy, *Presidents Club,* pp. 121–23.

101 *An unexpected choice for the job, McNamara:* Sidey, *John F. Kennedy, President,* p. 13.

101 *When McNamara took office in 1961:* See the secret briefing for the Secretary of Defense, "Communications Facilities at National Level," Defense Communications Agency, March 1961, p. 22, at http://coldwar-c4i.net/DCA61/22.html.

101 *"It didn't take me long . . .":* "Robert S. McNamara Oral History," John F. Kennedy Library, April 4, 1964, at http://archive1.jfklibrary.org/JFKOH/McNamara,%20 Robert%20S/JFKOH-RSM-01/JFKOH-RSM-01-TR.pdf.

101 *Even simply hitting the first two:* L. Wainstein et al., "The Evolution of U.S. Strategic Command and Control and Warning, 1945–1972," Study S-467, Institute for Defense Analyses, June 1975, p. 242.

101 *Hitting all the nation's major military commands:* Ibid.

102 *"A judgment [would] be made . . .":* Ibid., p. 243.

102 *McNamara was terrified:* "Letter from Secretary of Defense McNamara to President Kennedy," Foreign Relations of the United States, 1961–1963, National Security Policy, vol. 8, pt. 1, doc. 17, U.S. Department of State, Office of the Historian, at https://history.state.gov/historicaldocuments/frus1961–63v08/d17.

103 *Not even a week later, a CIA-trained:* Sidey, *John F. Kennedy, President,* p. 106.

103 *Over the next two weeks, two U.S. rockets:* Wolfe, *Right Stuff,* p. 239.

103 *Ever since the Truman administration:* "Memo for Admiral Radford, 'Actions and Results Under Conditions of Strategic Surprise,'" November 1, 1956, Department of Defense, FOIA Reading Room, at http://www.dod.mil/pubs/foi/Reading_Room/NCB/999.pdf.

104 *In the early 1950s, the FBI had searched:* Anna Merlan, "In 1951, the FBI Thought the Soviets Might Be Hiding an Atomic Bomb Somewhere in New York City," *Village Voice,* July 22, 2014, at http://blogs.villagevoice.com/runninscared/2014/07 /in_1951_the_fbi_thought_the_soviets_might_be_hiding_an_atomic_bomb _somewhere_in_new_york_city.php.

104 *Several months into his presidency:* Hugh Sidey, "Were the Russians Hiding a Nuke in D.C.?" *Time,* November 12, 2001, at http://content.time.com/time/magazine /article/0,9171,1001206,00.html.

104 *As Hugh Sidey wrote, the first family:* Sidey, *John F. Kennedy, President,* p. 80.

104 *Even before the inauguration:* "White House Army Signal Agency's Equipment at President John F. Kennedy's Estate, Glen Ora (Middleburg, Virginia)," John F. Kennedy Presidential Library, March 2, 1961, at http://www.jfklibrary.org/Asset -Viewer/Archives/JFKWHP-ST-41–4–61.aspx.

105 *It was, Kennedy biographer Richard Reeves:* Reeves, *President Kennedy,* p. 102.

106 *The general recommended tying together:* Pearson, *World Wide Military Command and Control System,* pp. 34–37. Pearson's report, while generally authoritative, misstates the date of Kennedy's NATO remarks as May 1961, significant only because it moves Kennedy's remarks after the Bay of Pigs invasion, establishing a cause and effect. In fact, they predated that debacle by nearly a week.

106 *As one Air Force historian would write:* Ibid., p. 38.

106 *The White House Army Signal Corps maintained:* "Communications Facilities at

National Level," Secret Briefing for the Secretary of Defense, Defense Communications Agency, March 1961, p. 23, at http://coldwar-c4i.net/DCA61/23.html.

106 *According to a partially declassified memo:* "Untitled Binder," Declassified P-95 Records. Accession #66A03, Box 3, Record Group 396, Records of the Office of Emergency Preparedness, National Archives and Records Administration, College Park, Maryland. This document was first discovered by historian Bill Geerhart.

107 *The Pentagon maintained dozens:* "Letter from David M. Shoup, Commandant, USMC, to Edward M. McDermott, Director, Office of Emergency Planning," U.S. Department of the Navy, National Archives, Records Group 396, Declassified P 95 Records, Accession 66A03, Box 6, Folder "Special Facilities Branch," November 2, 1962, at https://www.scribd.com/doc/64015586/1962-Letter-RE-Use -of-Marine-Corps-Schools-Quantico-Virginia-for-Emergency-Services.

107 *Built in 1958 into the side of Bare Mountain:* Wilton Curtis, "Old 8AF PACCS Site," *SAC ACCA Flyer Newsletter,* vol. 16, no. 1 (February 2010): 4, at http:// www.sac-acca.org/newsletter/flyer0210.pdf.

107 *OCDM had also begun burying:* "Annual Report for Fiscal Year 1959," Office of Civil and Defense Mobilization, U.S. Government Printing Office, 1960, p. 5.

107 *Wilson scrambled to contact all three:* B. J. Lewis, "At the Ready for 50 Years," *Denton Record-Chronicle,* February 8, 2014, at http://www.dentonrc.com/local-news /local-news-headlines/20140208-at-the-ready-for-50-years.ece.

107 *When it finally opened, behind schedule:* "Region 6 Federal Regional Center (FRC) 50th Anniversary," fema.gov, at https://web.archive.org/web/20140222054309 /http://www.fema.gov/region-6-federal-regional-center-frc-50th-anniversary.

108 *"We'd be killing each other . . .":* UPI, "In Event of Nuclear War, Federal Government Would Operate from Bothell," *Ellensburg* (Washington) *Daily Record,* August 3, 1978, at https://news.google.com/newspapers?nid=860&dat=19780804&i d=w4RUAAAAIBAJ&sjid=MI8DAAAAIBAJ&pg=6832,2106559&hl=en.

108 *Even local governments began:* "Annual Report for Fiscal Year 1959," Office of Civil and Defense Mobilization, U.S. Government Printing Office, 1960, p.10.

108 *Portland, Oregon, built a $670,000 bunker:* "Kelly Butte Underground Command Center Facts and History," at http://kellybutteunderground.blogspot.com/.

108 *Private corporations got into the mountain:* Zuckerman, *Day After World War III,* pp. 273–74; as well as http://coldwar-ct.com/ATT_Netcong_N.html.

109 *"They had motels there, really . . .":* David Germain, "Abandoned Iron Ore Diggings Became Gold Mine for Savvy Developer: Entrepreneur: Old Hole in the Ground Has Generated Fortunes as Mushroom Farm, Bomb Shelter, Records Vault and Top-Secret Think Tank," *Los Angeles Times,* April 19, 1992, at http://articles.lat imes.com/1992–04–19/news/mn-791_1_iron-mountain-mining.

110 *On a Sunday morning in March:* U.S. Fish and Wildlife Service, Sauta Cave National Wildlife Refuge homepage, at http://www.fws.gov/sautacave/.

110   *At the end of their hike:* Joseph C. Douglas, "Shelter from the Atomic Storm," *Journal of Spelean History,* vol. 30, no. 4 (October–December 1996): 91, at http://caves .org/section/asha/issues/104.pdf.

110   *In an emergency, the Washington sky:* "Memo from Director, FBI, to SAC, Washington Field Office, 'Emergency Relocation of Presidential Successors,'" "Sections five through seven (and enclosure 109) of FBI Headquarters file 66–18953: Defense Plans for the Department of Justice DOJ, 1955–1982," March 18, 1966, p. 151, at http://www.governmentattic.org/4docs/FBI-file-66-HQ-18953-De fensePlans_1955–1982.pdf.

110   *For Vice President Johnson alone:* "Helicopter Pickup Points in the Event of an Emergency Evacuation of the Vice President, November 1, 1962, Vice President Security Files, Box 5, Emergency Evacuation Instructions Folder, Lyndon Johnson Presidential Library.

110   *Beyond the people at the top:* In a memo to the FBI's top agent in Pittsburgh, the office responsible for West Virginia, the bureau noted, "You may be called upon to refer some unusual service for the Attorney General or members of his family during an emergency. You should use every means at your disposal to provide for the safety and security of the Attorney General and his family" (see "Memo from A. H. Belmont to L. V. Boardman, 'Operation Alert 1956,'" Federal Bureau of Investigation (FBI) File Number 66-HQ-18953, War Plans—Emergency Relocation Plans for the Department of Justice (DOJ), 1954–1956, 1966, July 9, 1956, p. 209, at http://www.governmentattic.org/4docs/FBI-WarPlansEmergRelocat DOJ_1954–1956.pdf).

111   *Meanwhile "essential" operations staff:* "Memo from E. D. Mason to Mr. Harbo, 'Relocation Site—Department of Justice,'" May 25, 1954, ibid., p. 26.

111   *Through the 1950s, the FBI had maintained:* Information on the Justice Department's relocation plans are based partly on Rick Steelhammer, "Documents Shed Light on State's Cold War Role," *Charleston Gazette,* January 23, 2011, as well as "Memo from A. H. Belmont to L. V. Boardman, 'Operation Alert 1956,'" Federal Bureau of Investigation (FBI) File Number 66-HQ-18953, War Plans— Emergency Relocation Plans for the Department of Justice (DOJ), 1954–1956, 1966, July 9, 1956, p. 436, at http://www.governmentattic.org/4docs/FBI-War PlansEmergRelocatDOJ_1954–1956.pdf, and "Memo from Director, FBI, to SAC, Washington Field Office, 'Emergency Relocation of Presidential Successors,'" "Sections five through seven (and enclosure 109) of FBI Headquarters file 66–18953: Defense Plans for the Department of Justice DOJ), 1955–1982," March 18, 1966, p. 151, at http://www.governmentattic.org/4docs/FBI-file -66-HQ-18953-DefensePlans_1955–1982.pdf.

112   *"The U.N. being a peace organization . . .":* "Richard Brown to William Crockett," Folder "Front Royal," Box 1, RG 59, Records Relating to the Vital Records Program for Emergency Planning, National Archives, December 17, 1962.

112   *The CIA, meanwhile, settled:* D. Kahn, *Codebreakers*, p. 574; see also David P. Mowry, "Vint Hill Farms Station: 1942–1945," *Cryptologic Almanac*, National Security Agency (Washington, D.C.), at: https://www.nsa.gov/news-features /declassified-documents/crypto-almanac-50th/assets/files/Vint_Hill_Farms _Station.pdf.

113   *For the Bureau of Labor Statistics, set to relocate:* See "A List Dedicated to the Discussion of Various Communications Systems Used by the U.S. Military and Civilian Authorities During the Cold War Era," at https://beta.groups.yahoo.com/neo /groups/coldwarcomms/conversations/messages/7415.

113   *USIA initially set up its relocation facility:* F. Wayne Rhine, "The Voice of America, Greenville, North Carolina," *IEEE Transactions on Broadcasting*, vol. BC-14, no. 2 (June 1968).

113   *During Operation ALERT drills, USIA practiced:* Letter to Dr. Messick, January 25, 1957. Portions of this USIA section are based on fifty-one pages of correspondence between East Carolina University president John Messick and USIA, ODM, and other officials, concerning the relocation facility. The records are stored at the East Carolina University archives. See also "Records of John Decatur Messick's Tenure as President of East Carolina Teachers College and East Carolina College, University Archives UA02–05, East Carolina University Archives, Greenville, N.C., at http://digital.lib.ecu.edu/special/ead/view.aspx?id=UA02–05# catalog.

114   *Greenville became the hub where USIA:* "The International Broadcasting Bureau's Greenville, North Carolina, Transmitting Station," Report Number ISP-IB-05–69, U.S. Department of State and the Broadcasting Board of Governors Office of Inspector General, August 2005, pp. 3–5, at https://oig.state.gov/sys tem/files/124642.pdf.

114   *Staffed with a small contingent:* "Records of John Decatur Messick's Tenure as President of East Carolina Teachers College and East Carolina College, University Archives UA02–05, East Carolina University Archives, Greenville, N.C., at http://digital.lib.ecu.edu/special/ead/view.aspx?id=UA02–05#catalog.

114   *USIA also established a local executive:* Ibid.

114   *One of the only hints of its special function:* Cory O'Kelly, "Opening Up the Diefenbunker," *Midday*, CBC Digital Archive, January 22, 1994, at http://www.cbc.ca /archives/entry/cold-war-opening-up-the-diefenbunker.

116   *Britain, for its part:* One of the best guides to Britain's Cold War BURLINGTON bunker is Steve Fox's history, "Top Secret Acid: The Story of the Central Government War Headquarters," published as a special issue of the British magazine *Subterranea*, no. 22, April 2010. A broader history and guide to Britain's crisis government and Doomsday planning is Peter Hennessy's book, *The Secret State: Whitehall and the Cold War* (Allen Lane, 2002).

116   *As the Berlin Wall rose, the Pentagon and Kennedy:* Carl Kaysen to General Maxwell Taylor, "Strategic Air Planning and Berlin," September 5, 1961, Records of

Maxwell Taylor, RG 218, Records of the Joint Chiefs of Staff, National Archives, College Park, MD, at http://nsarchive.gwu.edu/NSAEBB/NSAEBB56/Berlin C1.pdf.

116 *The attack would likely kill under a million:* Kaysen estimated that given target spacing, the eighty-eight DGZs could be hit by forty-one bombers, and he estimated a 25 percent "attrition" rate, resulting in a total force of fifty-five planes.

116 *Kennedy's war preparations called:* John F. Kennedy, "Executive Order 10952—Assigning Civil Defense Responsibilities to the Secretary of Defense and Others," July 20, 1961, John T. Woolley and Gerhard Peters, *American Presidency Project,* at http://www.presidency.ucsb.edu/ws/?pid=58890.

117 *He nominated Steuart L. Pittman:* Steuart L. Pittman, citation for the Silver Star, at http://valor.militarytimes.com/recipient.php?recipientid=38211.

117 *The veteran-turned-attorney didn't think:* Wigner, *Who Speaks for Civil Defense,* p. 47. Pittman's journey from civil defense booster to disillusioned doubter is readily visible in his afterword to this book of related essays.

117 *The men, working in teams of two:* See "Protection Factor 100 (1963), Conelrad6401240, June 12, 2011, at https://www.youtube.com/watch?v=ONStWz KXb-k.

117 *Buildings that met the standards were then:* "Standard Fallout Shelter Signs," Civil Defense Museum, at http://www.civildefensemuseum.com/signs/.

118 *He proselytized every chance he could:* Garrison, *Bracing for Armageddon,* p. 108.

118 *The result of these two conflicting philosophies:* "Kennedy Favors Shelters for All," *New York Times,* October 7, 1961.

118 *The head of IBM, Thomas Watson Jr.:* Winkler, *Life Under a Cloud,* p. 129.

118 *In the preceding years, the government:* Zuckerman, *Day After World War III,* p. 142.

118 *While some were highly scientific:* "Their Sheltered Honeymoon," *Life,* August 10, 1959, p. 51, at https://books.google.com/books?id=2UkEAAAAMBAJ&pg=PA51&lpg=PA51&dq=Melvin+Mininson+honeymoon&source=bl&ots=IVUPUlEKis&sig=gAZ_RRYb7a4_v5U_w_IVI3JVKm4&hl=en&sa=X&ei=SrcGVfbeF5TdsASswYGIAQ&ved=0CDkQ6AEwBA#v=onepage&q=Melvin%20Mininson%20honeymoon&f=false.

119 *Potential conflicts weren't limited to:* "Gun Thy Neighbor?" *Time,* August 18, 1961, vol. 78, no. 7, p. 60.

119 *Meanwhile, Edward Teller, the scientist:* Kaplan, *Wizards of Armageddon,* p. 314.

119 *The White House also heard from two RAND:* H. Kahn, *On Thermonuclear War,* pp. 10, 19.

120 *Kahn sought to parse:* Ibid., p. 21.

120 *The new plan, SIOP-62:* Pringle and Arkin, *S.I.O.P.,* p. 121.

120 *As the Kennedy family relaxed:* William Anderson, "Kennedy, Frondizi Meet in Palm Beach," *Chicago Tribune,* December 25, 1961, p. 3, at http://archives.chicagotribune.com/1961/12/25/page/3/article/kennedy-frondizi-meet-in-palm-beach; Rabe, *The Most Dangerous Area in the World,* p. 59.

120   *The enthusiasm of Teller and Kahn:* Zuckerman, *Day After World War III,* p. 138.

121   *On December 26, a special team:* Walsh, *From Mount Vernon to Crawford,* p. 142.

122   *As the Seebees worked:* Philip Ward, "Peanut Island: JFK's Last Resort," visitflorida
       .com, at http://www.visitflorida.com/en-us/articles/2011/november/2042-peanut
       -island-off-riviera-beach-was-jfks-last-resort.html.

122   *One successor, the committee concluded:* "Emergency Planning Committee: Committee
       on Assumptions for Non-Military Planning, 1962–1964," Papers of John F. Ken-
       nedy, Presidential Papers, President's Office Files, "Departments and Agencies,"
       p. iv, at http://www.jfklibrary.org/Asset-Viewer/Archives/JFKPOF-094–010.aspx.

123   *The change in plans drastically reduced:* "Letter from William Crockett to Joseph
       Robertson," folder "Department of Agriculture Permit Front Royal," Box 1, RG
       59, Records Relating to the Vital Records Program for Emergency Planning, Na-
       tional Archives, October 11, 1963.

123   *In the mid-1960s, the Alternate:* Thomas A. Sturm, "The Air Force and the World-
       wide Military Command and Control System, 1961–1965," USAF Historical
       Division, Liaison Office, p. 50, at http://www2.gwu.edu/~nsarchiv/nukevault
       /ebb249/doc08.pdf.

123   *The Bureau of the Budget initially tried:* "William Elliott to Acting Secretary,"
       Folder "Front Royal," Box 1, RG 59, Records Relating to the Vital Records Pro-
       gram for Emergency Planning, National Archives, May 19, 1959.

123   *It was important to focus on only:* p. iv. Edward A. McDermott et al., "Report to the
       President: On a Re-examination of Federal Policy with Respect to Emergency
       Plans and Continuity of Government in the Event of Nuclear Attack on the
       United States," Papers of John F. Kennedy, Presidential Papers, President's Office
       Files, Departments and Agencies, Emergency Planning Committee: Committee
       on Assumptions for Non-Military Planning, 1962–1964, John F. Kennedy Presi-
       dential Library, June 11, 1962, p. iv, at http://www.jfklibrary.org/Asset-Viewer
       /Archives/JFKPOF-094–010.aspx.

123   *To do so, Bundy's study group stressed:* Ibid.

123   *A 1960 estimate showed Raven Rock:* "Memo from Joe D. Walstrom, Emergency
       Relocation: The Alternate Joint Communications Center at 'The Rock,'" Folder
       "Front Royal," Box 1, RG 59, Records Relating to the Vital Records Program for
       Emergency Planning, National Archives, July 22, 1960.

125   *Over the next decade, similar hardened communication:* David Rotenstein, "Fort
       Reno's Cold War–Era 'Undisclosed Location,'" Greater Greater Washington,
       December 7, 2010, at http://greatergreaterwashington.org/post/8364/fort-renos
       -cold-war-era-undisclosed-location/.

125   *As more buildings were completed inside:* Edgar B. Stern Jr., "Office Space at AJCC,"
       June 11, 1951, at http://www.globalsecurity.org/wmd/library/report/other/ajcc
       -doc3.jpg.

126   *As one report explained:* Barney Collier, "The Most Embarrassing List in Washing-
       ton," *Harper's,* May 1975.

126 *When the company adopted a new slogan:* This practice extended beyond merely bunkers. The National Reconnaissance Office, the spy agency that runs U.S. satellites and whose very existence was classified until the 1990s, had a sign in front of its Chantilly, Virginia, headquarters saying that the building belonged to defense contractor Rockwell International Corporation. See Tim Weiner, "Ultra-Secret Office Gets First Budget Scrutiny," *New York Times,* August 10, 1994, at http://www.nytimes.com/1994/08/10/us/ultra-secret-office-gets-first-budget -scrutiny.html.

126 *First, it ran in conjunction with:* See the memo from C. F. Usher Jr. to D. E. Felker, November 1, 1971, at http://coldwar-c4i.net/Sequoia/ATTmemo1.html.

127 *The second network, called Autovon:* Abbate, *Inventing the Internet,* p. 15; see also "Historical Summary, January–December 1966," North American Air Defense Command and Continental Air Defense Command, May 1, 1967, p. 36, at http://www.northcom.mil/Portals/28/Documents/Supporting%20documents /(U)%201966%20NORAD-CONAD%20History.pdf.

127 *A fifth emergency level:* "Official Global Autovon Telephone Directory," 1971, at http://www.plexoft.com/SBF/Autovon.html.

127 *Working closely with the military:* "Conus Autovon Switching Centers," at http:// coldwar-c4i.net/AUTOVON/switches.html.

128 *Those five AUTOVON bunkers constructed:* For more, see http://coldwar-c4i.net /ATT_Project/index.html; Albert LaFrance, "Visit to Former AT&T Bucking-ham, VA (Spears Mountain), Project Office," May 21, 2007, at https://groups .yahoo.com/neo/groups/coldwarcomms/conversations/topics/11699.

128 *The only aboveground buildings:* For more, see http://www.drgibson.com/towers/.

128 *Normally staffed by thirty employees:* Jon Elliston, "Big Hole, Deep Secret: Beneath the Chatham County Countryside Lies AT&T's Covert Military Site, the Most Intriguing Local Landmark You're Not Allowed to Visit," *Indy Week,* December 13, 2000, at http://www.indyweek.com/gyrobase/Content?oid=oid:15267.

128 *A local North Carolina construction:* Ibid.

128 *The whole facility was built atop:* Jay Price, "Mysterious Cold War Bunker Closes," *Charlotte Observer,* August 10, 2008, at http://www.charlotteobserver .com/2008/08/10/118719/mysterious-cold-war-bunker-closes.html#.VCWwx itdVOE#storylink=cpy.

128 *"The buildings themselves can shift . . .":* Robert Dietsch, "AT&T Builds Nuclear Safe 'Subway' Line," *Pittsburgh Press,* December 3, 1967, at http://news.google .com/newspapers?nid=1144&dat=19671203&id=za0pAAAAIBAJ&sjid=ok8EA AAAIBAJ&pg=7188,650463.

128 *The sites had their own power:* Albert LaFrance, "Visit to Former AT&T Bucking-ham, VA (Spears Mountain), Project Office," May 21, 2007, at https://groups.yahoo .com/neo/groups/coldwarcomms/conversations/topics/11699; "ATT Cheshire," Coldwar-Ct.com, at http://coldwar-ct.com/Home_Page_S1DO.html.

129 *"An interruption of fifteen . . .":* Charles C. Duncan, "The Role of Commercial

Telecommunications Systems in Preparedness for National Emergencies," address to the Industrial College of the Armed Forces, Washington, D.C., February 19, 1960, at http://coldwar-c4i.net/ICAF_lectures/L60–132.pdf.

129   *AT&T was so tightly integrated:* Merrill Brown, "AT&T System Called Vulnerable to Attack," *Sarasota Herald-Tribune,* May 7, 1981, at http://news.google.com /newspapers?nid=1755&dat=19810507&id=1CMhAAAAIBAJ&sjid=-GcE AAAAIBAJ&pg=6701,3737291; see also Wu, *The Master Switch,* pp. 159–60.

129   *Among other questions it raised:* Dobbs, *One Minute to Midnight,* p. 227.

130   *Mount Weather's name came from:* "Roster of Station Officials and Employees," U.S. Department of Agriculture, Weather Bureau, Washington, D.C., August 1, 1904: http://congressional.proquest.com/congressional/docview/t66.d71.a2928–2?ac countid=11091. To sell Mount Weather reservation, Senate Report No. 44, January 09, 1928: http://congressional.proquest.com/congressional/docview/t47 .d48.8829_s.rp.44?accountid=11091.

130   *The government had spent:* "Record Kite Flight," *Aeronautics,* vol. 7, no. 1 (July 1910): 22; Sean Potter, "Mount Weather: A History," *Climate Station Chronicles,* no. 11 (April 2005): 3, at http://writing.weatherdetectives.com/climatestation chronicles.pdf; "Kite 23,000 Feet in Air; All Records in This Country Broken at Virginia Weather Station," *New York Times,* October 6, 1907.

131   *Finally, Calvin Coolidge proposed:* U.S. Congress, House, "Mount Weather, Va., Communication from the President of the United States Transmitting Supplemental Estimate of Appropriation for the Director of Public Buildings and Public Parks of the National Capital for the Fiscal Years 1929 and 1930 in the Sum of $48,000, Together with Proposed Legislation, to Make Government Property at Mount Weather, Va., Available for the Use of the President," 70th Congress, 2nd Session, February 13, 1929, Document No. 587.

131   *When Coolidge's successor came to office:* "Virginia Site Urged as Summer Capital: Coolidge Asks Congress to Vote $48,000 to Repair Mount Weather; Coolidge Names Site for Vacations," *Washington Post,* February 14, 1929; "Summer White House Chosen in Virginia; Coolidge Asks $48,000 to Convert Property," *New York Times,* February 14, 1929; "Hoover Will Not Use Mount Weather House: He Plans Summer Week-End Trips on the Mayflower and Deep Sea Fishing," *New York Times,* March 17, 1929: p. 29.

131   *In 1936, Mount Weather became a Bureau of Mines:* Drew Pearson and Robert B. Allen, "The Washington Merry Go-Round," *Spokane Daily Chronicle,* November 15, 1934, A1, at http://news.google.com/newspapers?nid=1338&dat=19341115& id=t7szAAAAIBAJ&sjid=_PQDAAAAIBAJ&pg=6331,3557536. See also *Decisions of the Comptroller General of the United States,* vol. 22, July 1, 1942–June 30, 1943, U.S. Government Printing Office, 1943.

131   *As a 1953 Interior Department publication:* U.S. Department of the Interior, *Years of Progress, 1945–1952,* 1953, p. 60, at http://books.google.com/books?id=l3CGA

AAAMAAJ&pg=PA60&lpg=PA60&dq=%22Mount+Weather%22+%22Bureau +of+Mines%22+dynamite&source=bl&ots=mIPRXd3Jjt&sig=e12rl7J4F01JA3h _bRuvg2lH4r4&hl=en&sa=X&ei=rFFxVJSqEemCsQSF1IHAAQ&ved=0CE cQ6AEwCQ#v=onepage&q=%22Mount%20Weather%22%20%22Bureau%20 of%20Mines%22%20dynamite&f=false.

131 *Gilbert Fowler, whose uncle Ernest:* Eugene Scheel, "From the Mysterious to the Mundane, 'The Mountain' Has Weathered It All," *Washington Post,* October 7, 2001.

132 *Fowler, like many of the crew:* Ted Gup, "Civil Defense Doomsday Hideaway," *Time,* June 24, 2001.

132 *The Army Corps of Engineers:* Ibid.

132 *By the Kennedy years, Mount Weather included:* "Jacob 'Jack' Rosenthal Oral History Interview," JFK #1, John F. Kennedy Presidential Library, December 8, 2004, at http://www.jfklibrary.org/Asset-Viewer/Archives/JFKOH-JCR-01.aspx.

132 *Security procedures held that:* Barney Collier, "The Most Embarrassing List in Washington," *Harper's,* May 1975.

133 *On a rainy Washington afternoon soon after:* O'Donnell, Powers, and McCarthy, *Johnny, We Hardly Knew Ye,* p. 285. A slightly different version of this story is told in Reeves, *President Kennedy,* p. 227.

134 *In one July 1962 test:* Charles N. Vittitoe, "Did High-Altitude EMP Cause the Hawaiian Streetlight Incident?" Sandia National Laboratories, System Design and Assessment Note 31, June 1989, at http://www.ece.unm.edu/summa/notes /SDAN/0031.pdf.

135 *National Security Advisor McGeorge Bundy knocked:* Details of the October 16 schedule are pulled from Dobbs, *One Minute to Midnight,* pp. 1–17.

135 *There wasn't a cloud in the sky:* Sorensen, *Kennedy,* pp. 1–3; the weather details are from "Weather History for KDCA—October 1962," Weather Underground, at http://www.wunderground.com/history/airport/KDCA/1962/10/20/Daily History.html.

136 *NORAD raised the nation's readiness level:* "North American Air Defense Command And Continental Air Defense Command Historical Summary," July– December 1962, Directorate of Command History, Office of Information, NORAD/CONAD Headquarters, April 1963, pp. 1–7, at http://www.north com.mil/Portals/28/Documents/Supporting%20documents/(U)%201962%20 NORAD%20CONAD%20History%20Jul-Dec.pdf.

136 *Troop trains packed with soldiers:* "SAC Actions Memo from Air Force Chief of Staff General Curtis E. LeMay to Joint Chiefs of Staff Chairman Maxwell Taylor, 'Additional Decisions,'" Taylor File, box 6, October 22, 1962, at http://www2 .gwu.edu/~nsarchiv/NSAEBB/NSAEBB397/docs/doc%206%2010–22–62%20 LeMay%20memo%20on%20SAC%20readiness.pdf.

136 *One pilot bought fuel for his bomber:* Dobbs, *One Minute to Midnight,* p. 52. For more

details on how Americans across the country responded to the Cuban Missile Crisis, see George's surprisingly bemusing 2003 book, *Awaiting Armageddon.*

136 *In forty-eight hours, AT&T raced:* Angell, *Air Force Response to the Cuban Missile Crisis,* p. 11.

137 *Message traffic was so clogged:* Dobbs, *One Minute to Midnight,* p. 91.

137 *SAC controllers worked feverishly:* "Strategic Air Command Operations in the Cuban Crisis of 1962," *SAC Historical Study,* vol. 1, no. 90 (n.d.): 44.

137 *"This is a joke":* Dobbs, *One Minute to Midnight,* pp. 163–65.

137 *When the Kennedy administration had pushed Power:* Kaplan, *Wizards of Armageddon,* p. 246.

137 *Ground alert only went so far:* "Strategic Air Command Airborne Alert Plan ('Chrome Dome') [includes Memorandum from Robert McNamara to Eugene Zuckert]," U.S. Air Force Directorate of Plans, August 16, 1961.

138 *As part of Project* LIFE INSURANCE*:* Office of the Historian, "Alert Operations and Strategic Air Command, 1957–1991," Strategic Air Command, Offutt Air Force Base, U.S. Government Printing Office, 1991, pp. 4, 13, at http://www.afgsc.af.mil/Portals/51/Docs/SAC%20Alert%20Operations%20Lo-Res.pdf?ver=2016–09–27–114343–960; "History of Headquarters Strategic Air Command 1961," *SAC Historical Study,* no. 89 (January 1962): 12.

138 *SAC's headquarters at Offutt Air Force Base:* "Cold War Infrastructure for Strategic Air Command: The Bomber Mission," Prepared for Headquarters, Air Combat Command, Langley Air Force Base, Virginia, November 1999, pp. 123–24, at http://cryptocomb.org/Cold%20War%20Infrastructure%20for%20Strategic%20Air%20Command-The%20Bomber%20Mission.pdf.

138 *It had replaced SAC's overburdened original:* Karen J. Weitze, "Cold War Infrastructure for Strategic Air Command: The Bomber Mission (Report)," U.S. Army Corps of Engineers, November 1999, p. 3.

139 *Power's daily life revolved around:* Office of the Historian, "Alert Operations and Strategic Air Command, 1957–1991," Strategic Air Command, Offutt Air Force Base, U.S. Government Printing Office, 1991, p. 9, at http://www.afgsc.af.mil/Portals/51/Docs/SAC%20Alert%20Operations%20Lo-Res.pdf?ver=2016–09–27–114343–960.

139 *With the touch of the red ALARM button:* "Post Attack Command Control System," at https://www.scribd.com/doc/115566349/Post-Attack-Command-and-Control-System-overview.

139 *"This is General Power speaking . . .":* "Strategic Air Command Operations in the Cuban Crisis of 1962," *SAC Historical Study,* vol. 1, no. 90 (n.d.): vii.

139 *As one SAC officer listening at a base:* C. Adams, *Deterrence.*

140 *In the days after Kennedy's Oval Office address:* "Major Industries Already Feel Effect of World Crisis," *Los Angeles Times,* October 25, 1962; Victor Gilinsky, "On Tickling the Dragon's Tail," *Bulletin of the Atomic Scientists,* February 26, 2016, at http://thebulletin.org/tickling-dragon%E2%80%99s-tail9192.

140 *Grocers saw runs on sugar:* "Federal CD Officials Speed Drive to Line Up Fallout Shelter Space: No New Program," *Washington Post,* October 25, 1962; "CD Units Placed on Alert; No Shelters Listed Yet: Schools to Hold Drills Today," *Los Angeles Times,* October 25, 1962.

140 *In just two days:* "Stores in Capital Find No Panic: Cuban Crisis Is Top Item of Discussion in Washington," *New York Times,* October 26, 1962.

140 *Not everyone, though, was going to scrimp:* George, *Awaiting Armageddon,* p. 79.

140 *"The nation's flagging interest . . .":* John Goshko, "Civil Defense Queries Rise in D.C. Area," *Washington Post,* October 24, 1962.

140 *The District's civil defense office:* George, *Awaiting Armageddon,* p. 79.

140 *Across the country, schoolchildren:* "Civil Defense Leaders Speed Area Programs," *Washington Post,* October 26, 1962.

140 *Newspapers published descriptions:* George, *Awaiting Armageddon,* p. 75.

141 *Residents of Memphis were told:* Vance Lauderdale, "Helter Shelter," *Memphis Magazine,* March 14, 2011, at http://memphismagazine.com/ask-vance/helter -shelter/.

141 *Chicago school officials mapped:* "188 Civil Defense Workers on Around-the-Clock Alert," *Chicago Tribune,* October 27, 1962.

141 *"This is one of the oldest . . .":* U.S. Congress, House, "Hearings on Civil Defense—1962, Part 1: Testimony of Witnesses," 87th Congress, 2nd Session, February 19, 1962, pp. 136–38.

141 *A fifty-page USDA report:* Allan D. Shepherd et al., "Bulgur Wafer and Adjuncts for Fallout Shelter Rations: A Report of Research Conducted July 1966–June 1967," Agricultural Research Service, U.S. Department of Agriculture, 1967, p. 44.

142 *As one official explained:* Philip Dodd, "In A-Shelter, You'll Dine on Bulgur Wafer," *Chicago Tribune,* December 16, 1961.

142 *As one civil defense official said defensively:* John Murphy, "Area Bomb Shelters Few and Not Marked: CD Head Says Sites Not Ready," *Los Angeles Times,* October 28, 1962.

142 *The very few homeowners nationwide:* George, *Awaiting Armageddon,* p. 77.

142 *Kennedy was particularly haunted:* Kennedy, *Thirteen Days,* p. 127.

143 *As President Kennedy recalled later:* John F. Kennedy, "Address at the University of Maine," October 19, 1963, John T. Woolley and Gerhard Peters, *American Presidency Project,* at http://www.presidency.ucsb.edu/ws/?pid=9483.

143 *At the U.N., Ambassador Adlai Stevenson:* Dobbs, *One Minute to Midnight,* p. 170.

143 *After several hours of research:* Ibid., p. 183; Blight, Allyn, and Welch, *Cuba on the Brink,* p. 248.

143 *"I don't want that man . . .":* Reeves, *President Kennedy,* p. 182.

143 *Still, as president, he also understood:* Tim Weiner, "Word for Word/The Cuban Missile Crisis; When Kennedy Faced Armageddon, and His Own Scornful Generals," *New York Times,* October 5, 1997; the exchange was part of recordings

released years later, available at http://millercenter.org/educationalresources
/youre-in-a-pretty-bad-fix.

144 *After the explosion of the USS* Maine: O'Toole, *Spanish War,* p. 213, for "Operating
     Room"; see "Pres McKinley Now Sent on Forcing Fighting," *Boston Globe,* May 2,
     1898, for "War Room."

144 *A hand-painted map:* Waldon Fawcett, "The War Room at the White House,"
     World's Work, vol. 3, pp. 1841–43, at https://books.google.com/books?id=DFA5A
     QAAMAAJ.

144 *The Army Signal Corps created:* Waldon Fawcett, "Telegraph and Cipher Bureau of
     the White House," *Popular Science News,* September 1902, p. 203, at https://books
     .google.com/books?id=fWLnAAAAMAAJ.

144 *"The arrangements were so perfect . . .":* Waldon Fawcett, "The War Room at the
     White House," *World's Work,* vol. 3, p. 1841, at https://books.google.com/books?
     id=DFA5AQAAMAAJ.

145 *At the time, both were located:* Roosevelt also summarily dismissed the longtime
     director of the Telegraph and Cipher Bureau, Major Benjamin Montgomery, and
     transferred the Army officer to a field command, as part of a decision to consoli-
     date control of the bureau under the president. See "Loses Position at the White
     House," *San Francisco Call,* January 10, 1905, vol. 97, no. 41, at http://cdnc.ucr
     .edu/cgi-bin/cdnc?a=d&d=SFC19050110.2.23.9#.

145 *For his own command post:* Admiral John McCrea, "Setting Up Map Room in White
     House and Other Incidents in Connection with Service There," Oral History In-
     terview by W. W. Moss, March 19, 1973, FDR Presidential Library, at https://
     fdrlibrary.org/documents/356632/390886/mccrea+maproom.pdf/e10e4efe-e
     2cf-4b81-a5b4–06dc2eac74a7.

145 *The Air Force had proposed rethinking:* "Godfrey T. McHugh to the President,
     Memo on 'Nerve Center' for the White House," Papers of John F. Kennedy,
     Presidential Papers, President's Office Files, "Staff Memoranda, McHugh, God-
     frey T.," April 25, 1961, at http://www.jfklibrary.org/Asset-Viewer/Archives/JFK
     POF-064–009.asp.

146 *Tazewell Shepard's office ran operations:* Bohn, *Nerve Center,* p. 35.

146 *The "Sit Room," as it became known:* Ibid., p. 2.

146 *The first time Kennedy saw the space:* McGeorge Bundy, quoted in ibid., p. 32.

146 *The conference room featured:* See, for instance, photos by Robert Knudsen, "The
     West Wing Conference Room," JFKWHP-1962–02–07-E, White House Pho-
     tographs, John F. Kennedy Presidential Library, February 7, 1962.

146 *The White House Army Signal Agency also installed:* Bohn, *Nerve Center,* p. 7.

146 *The first transatlantic phone line:* Johnson, *How We Got to Now,* p. 98.

147 *"Usually it was the same young . . .":* Dobrynin, *In Confidence,* 96.

147 *As the crisis continued, officials:* "Guidance on Actions Which Federal Departments
     and Agencies Should Take in the Event of a Worsening of the Cuban Crisis,"

Executive Office of the President, Office of Emergency Planning, Secret Memorandum, October 25, 1962.

148 *As Ed McDermott recalled, "When we . . .":* "Edward A. McDermott Oral History Interview," by Charles Daly, John F. Kennedy Oral History Collection, John F. Kennedy Presidential Library, June 4, 1964, pp. 41–62, at https://www.jfklibrary .org/Asset-Viewer/Archives/JFKOH-EAM-03.aspx.

148 *"I never took it very seriously . . .":* Ted Gup, "Civil Defense Doomsday Hideaway," *Time,* June 24, 2001.

148 *"I remember painfully going . . .":* "Mount Weather Witness: Jack Rosenthal," Conelrad Adjacent, June 6, 2015, at http://conelrad.blogspot.com/2015/06/mount -weather-witness-jack-rosenthal.html.

149 *"I was thrilled to get it . . .":* Ibid.

149 *In the midst of the crisis:* Sidey, *John F. Kennedy,* p. 285.

149 *Reporters telephoned the homes:* Edward A. McDermott, "Oral History Interview," by Charles Daly, John F. Kennedy Oral History Collection, John F. Kennedy Presidential Library, June 4, 1964, pp. 41–62, at https://www.jfklibrary.org/Asset -Viewer/Archives/JFKOH-EAM-03.aspx. DNSA collection: Cuban Missile Crisis, p. 50.

149 *"The escape plan was to go to . . .":* "Interview with Jane LeMay Lodge, Daughter of Gen. Curtis LeMay," Nebraska State Historical Society, September 10, 1998, p. 10, at http://www.nebraskastudies.org/0900/media/0904_0302jane.pdf.

149 *The family understood that they wouldn't get:* Ibid.

149 *The brown briefcase was left outside:* Dobbs, *One Minute to Midnight,* p. 225.

150 *"The first problem was going . . .":* Edward A. McDermott, "Oral History Interview," by Charles Daly, John F. Kennedy Oral History Collection, John F. Kennedy Presidential Library, June 4, 1964, pp. 41–62, at https://www.jfklibrary.org /Asset-Viewer/Archives/JFKOH-EAM-03.aspx.

151 *The system was designed to detect:* C. R. Deibert and W. D. Buckingham, "Bomb Alarm," *Western Union Technical Review* (January 1963): 32–41, at http://massis .lcs.mit.edu/archives/technical/western-union-tech-review/17–1/p032.htm; see also "(Nuclear Detonation) Bomb Alarm System Study, May 1, 1964," Department of Defense, Office of Security Review, November 4, 2011, at http://www.govern mentattic.org/5docs/BombAlarmSystemStudy_1964.pdf.

151 *In the event that two or more:* C. E. Fritz, "Some Problems of Warning and Communication Revealed by the Northeast U.S. Power Failure of 9–10 November 1965," Weapons Systems Evaluation Group, C.I. Study No. 12, Institute for Defense Analyses Report R-142, April 1968, p. 25, at http://www.dod.gov/pubs/foi /Reading_Room/Science_and_Technology/68.pdf.

151 *An investigation discovered that a radar station:* Sagan, *Limits of Safety,* pp. 130–32. Dobbs, *One Minute to Midnight,* p. 404, fn. 336, corrects Sagan's time from 9:08 ET to 11:08 ET, based on the NORAD logs showing 1608 Zulu Time.

152 *The sole priority, it was decided:* Tazewell Shepard, "Memorandum for Mrs. Lincoln," Presidential Office Files, Box 114, Cuba General, 10/24/62–12/31/62 Folder, John F. Kennedy Presidential Library, October 26, 1962, at https://www .scribd.com/doc/68941196/Relocation-of-White-House-Staff-Dependents -Oct-26–1962.

153 *While the media had participated:* Memo to Pierre Salinger, "White House Emergency Information Program," Memos, Box 3, Folder: "[Memoranda]: 1962–June 1963," Jacob Rosenthal Papers, John F. Kennedy Presidential Library, November 3, 1962.

153 *One of the journalists asked:* Barney Collier, "The Most Embarrassing List in Washington," *Harper's,* May 1975.

154 *"I am talking about genuine peace...":* John F. Kennedy, "Commencement Address at American University in Washington," June 10, 1963, John T. Woolley and Gerhard Peters, *American Presidency Project,* at http://www.presidency.ucsb.edu /ws/?pid=9266.

155 *In an open letter, Gorkin highlighted:* Haraldur þór Egilsson, "The Origins, Use and Development of Hot Line Diplomacy," Discussion Papers in Diplomacy, Netherlands Institute of International Relations "Clingendael," May 2003, at http:// jproc.ca/crypto/hotline_20030500_cli_paper_dip_issue85.pdf.

155 *In June 1963, negotiators in Geneva:* Graham, *Cornerstones of Security,* "The 'Hot Line' Agreements," p. 21.

155 *What came to be known in popular culture:* " 'Hot Line' Opened by U.S. and Soviet to Cut Attack Risk," *New York Times,* August 31, 1963, p. A1.

155 *The main telegraph circuit bounced:* Graham, *Cornerstones of Security,* "The 'Hot Line' Agreements," p. 20; Dobrynin, *In Confidence,* p. 98; Smith, *Doubletalk,* p. 281.

155 *There was purposefully no voice:* Talbott, *Deadly Gambits,* pp. 322–23.

156 *The Pentagon invested $159,849:* Memorandum by Arthur Sylvester for George Reedy, "Proposed DoD Fact Sheet on Washington Moscow Hot Line," Gen Fe 4–1, Box 7, White House Central Files, Papers of Lyndon Baines Johnson, Lyndon Baines Johnson Library, March 16, 1965.

157 *A few days earlier in Banner Elk:* Memo from D. J. Brennan Jr. to W. C. Sullivan, "Enemy Alien Registration, Defense Plans, Immigration and Naturalization Service (INS)," Sections five through seven (and enclosure 109) of FBI Headquarters file 66–18953: Defense Plans for the Department of Justice (DOJ), 1955–1982, April 19, 1963, p. 140, at http://www.governmentattic.org/4docs/FBI-file-66-HQ -18953-DefensePlans_1955–1982.pdf.

158 *Like Defense Secretary McNamara:* Memo from J. Edgar Hoover to Messrs. Tolson, Boardman, Belmont, Nichols, "Relocation Plan for U.S. Department of Justice," Federal Bureau of Investigation (FBI) File Number 66-HQ-18953, War Plans— Emergency Relocation Plans for the Department of Justice (DOJ), 1954–1956, 1966, July 11, 1956, pp. 445–49, at http://www.governmentattic.org/4docs/FBI -WarPlansEmergRelocatDOJ_1954–1956.pdf.

158 *The documents, known collectively:* Memo from L. V. Boardman to the Director, "War Plans," ibid., July 12, 1955, p. 278.

159 *The Emergency Briefcase and outline:* Memo from E. D. Mason to Mr. Harbor, "Emergency Relocation Plan for the Department of Justice," ibid., March 5, 1954, p. 8.

159 *There, a full-time Justice Department:* Memo from R. O. L'Allier to A. H. Belmont, "Defense Plan/Emergency Procedures for Chain of Command of Department of Justice," Sections five through seven (and enclosure 109) of FBI Headquarters file 66–18953: Defense Plans for the Department of Justice (DOJ), 1955–1982, August 4, 1960, p. 104, at http://www.governmentattic.org/4docs/FBI-file-66-HQ -18953-DefensePlans_1955–1982.pdf.

159 *Since the U.S. attorneys for Maryland:* Memo from Director, FBI, to SAC Baltimore, "Instructions for Key Personnel of the Department of Justice in the Event of a Civil Defense Emergency," Federal Bureau of Investigation (FBI) File Number 66-HQ-18953, War Plans—Emergency Relocation Plans for the Department of Justice (DOJ), 1954–1956, 1966, March 11, 1953, p. 129, at http://www .governmentattic.org/4docs/FBI-WarPlansEmergRelocatDOJ_1954–1956.pdf; for more background and context on alien detention efforts, see also Jennifer Elsea, "Detention of U.S. Persons as Enemy Belligerents," Congressional Research Service, July 25, 2013 (R42227); and Louis Fisher, "Detention of U.S. Citizens," Congressional Research Service, April 28, 2005 (RS22130).

160 *In 1956, during Operation ALERT:* Memo from A. H. Belmore to L. V. Boardman, "Operation Alert 1956," Federal Bureau of Investigation (FBI) File Number 66-HQ-18953, War Plans—Emergency Relocation Plans for the Department of Justice (DOJ), 1954–1956, 1966, July 19, 1956, p. 469, at http://www.government attic.org/4docs/FBI-WarPlansEmergRelocatDOJ_1954–1956.pdf.

161 *West Virginia senator Harley Kilgore later:* Cornelius P. Cotter and J. Malcolm Smith, "An American Paradox: The Emergency Detention Act of 1950," *Journal of Politics,* vol. 19, no. 1 (February 1957): 28.

161 *In the years that followed, the government:* Ibid., 20–33.

161 *Maintained by the Bureau of Prisons:* "Declaration of Martial Law in Time of Emergency and Its Effect Upon the Bureau's Operations," Federal Bureau of Investigation (FBI) File Number 66-HQ-18953, War Plans—Emergency Relocation Plans for the Department of Justice (DOJ), 1954–1956, 1966, November 5, 1955, pp. 330–32, at http://www.governmentattic.org/4docs/FBI-WarPlans EmergRelocatDOJ_1954–1956.pdf.

161 *During an emergency with the Soviet Union:* Cornelius P. Cotter and J. Malcolm Smith, "An American Paradox: The Emergency Detention Act of 1950," *Journal of Politics,* vol. 19, no. 1 (February 1957): 20.

161 *In mid-November 1963, John F. Kennedy:* See the video at https://www.youtube .com/watch?v=ZoT3tF6fv3o.

161 *"We shall also gain time . . .":* "GSB [George S. Brown] to Air Force Chief of

Staff Thomas White," March 30, 1959, enclosing "CNO Personal Letter No. 5 to Retired Flag Officers, 'Summary of Major Strategic Considerations for the 1960–70 Era,'" Library of Congress, Thomas White Papers, Box 28, Navy, July 30, 1958, at http://www2.gwu.edu/~nsarchiv/nukevault/ebb275/05.pdf. Also available on Digital National Security Archive, George Washington University, U.S. Nuclear History, 1955–1968, at http://www2.gwu.edu/~nsarchiv/nukevault/ebb275/#doc5.

161 *The Navy hoped for a total fleet:* David Alan Rosenberg, "The Origins of Over-kill: Nuclear Weapons and American Strategy, 1945–1960," *International Security*, vol. 7, no. 4 (Spring 1983): 57.

163 *The president had looked out:* "George E. Thomas Dies, President Kennedy Valet," *Washington Post*, December 15, 1980. A more in-depth account of the flight back from Dallas, Texas, on November 22, 1963, can be found in my story for the fiftieth anniversary of the Kennedy assassination. See Garrett M. Graff, "Angel Is Airborne," *Washingtonian*, November 2013, at https://www.washingtonian.com/projects/JFK-AF1/layout1.html#story.

164 *It wasn't until Theodore Roosevelt's trip:* TerHorst and Albertazzie, *Flying White House*, p. 64.

164 *When Wilson left America for the Paris Peace Conference:* "Senators Clash Over Trip," *New York Times*, December 4, 1918.

164 *FDR's journey by lumbering Pan Am Flying Boat:* The first airplane selected for presidential use, a modified B-24 Liberator bomber named *Guess Where II*, with its bomb bays converted into Pullman compartments that could hold up to twenty passengers, never actually flew Roosevelt—the Secret Service deemed the model too unsafe—though later it did service ably as a VIP transport for numerous U.S. officials.

165 *The trip, code-named ARGONAUT:* Dobbs, *Six Months in 1945*, p. 17.

166 *The military decided that it needed:* The person-specific call signs apply equally to other forms of presidential transport, like Marine One and Army One, when he's aboard helicopters from those branches of the military. The S-3 Viking an-tisubmarine plane that carried President George W. Bush in 2003 to the USS *Abraham Lincoln* for his "mission accomplished" speech declaring the end of the Iraq invasion was the only known use of Navy One. Only once has a president flown aboard a regular commercial airliner: For a vacation trip amid the 1973 energy crisis, President Nixon flew on a United DC-10 from Washington, D.C., to Los Angeles to demonstrate his commitment to conservation. While he was on board, that plane was designated Executive One. An aide carried a portable, secure communications system on board to allow him to reach the military in the event of an emergency during his trip. (The trip, though, didn't really save fuel, since aircraft from the presidential fleet took aides out with Nixon and flew Nixon back from Los Angeles. A *Washington Post* editorial called it "one of those penny-wise, pound-foolish ventures.") Similarly, planes carrying the first family are known as

Executive Foxtrot One and planes with the vice president's family are known as Executive Foxtrot Two. While he was president-elect, Donald Trump's personally branded plane was known as Tyson One.

168   *It wasn't, though, until Kennedy had signed legislation:* Memorandum from James J. Rowley to the Vice President, "The Use of Commercial Aircraft by the Vice President," Vice President Security Files, Box 1, Lyndon Johnson Presidential Library, October 24, 1962.

169   *"Originally the code names . . .":* Trimble recounted his career aboard Air Force One in a short self-published memoir, *Around the World in Twenty-Five Years* (2011).

169   *"Volunteer will reside at* VALLEY *. . .":* Tape transcripts are from the Lyndon B. Johnson Library's special collection, "White House Transcript, Air Force One Recording, 11/22/1963," at http://transition.lbjlibrary.org/items/show/64.

171   *"I cannot imagine any scenario . . .":* Shapley, *Promise and Power,* p. 198.

171   *Instead, as of the beginning of 1964:* "Draft Memorandum from Secretary of Defense McNamara to President Johnson," Foreign Relations of the United States, 1961–1963, Document 151, vol. 8, National Security Policy, Office of the Historian, Washington, D.C., December 6, 1963, at https://history.state.gov/historical documents/frus1961–63v08/d151.

172   *The chief justice had warmly invited McDermott:* "Jacob 'Jack' Rosenthal Oral History Interview," JFK #1, December 8, 2004, John F. Kennedy Presidential Library, at http://archive1.jfklibrary.org/JFKOH/Rosenthal,%20Jacob/JFKOH-JCR-01 /JFKOH-JCR-01-TR.pdf.

173   *During the Cuban Missile Crisis, the Kennedy administration:* "A Resort of Their Own: The Supreme Court's Cold War Relocation Plan," Conelrad Adjacent, April 24, 2013, at http://conelrad.blogspot.com/2013/04/a-resort-of-their-own -supreme-courts.html.

173   *After Clark's presentation, the chief justice explained:* Bill Geerhart, "Grove Park Inn Fallout Shelter License," Historic Memorabilia 1955–1969, Grove Park Inn Archives, Asheville, North Carolina, August 9, 1962, at http://www.scribd.com /doc/137733548/Grove-Park-Inn-Fallout-Shelter-License.

173   *He cut off the visiting briefer, exasperated:* Warren, *Memoirs of Earl Warren,* p. 231.

174   *In December 1964:* "The National Plan for Emergency Preparedness," Office of Emergency Planning, December 1964, p. 3, at http://biotech.law.lsu.edu/climate /FEMA/npep-1964.pdf.

175   *"All other alternatives for assuming . . .":* "National Deep Underground as a Key FY 1965 Budget Consideration," Bureau of the Budget Staff Briefing Paper, National Security File, Box 8, Subject File, Papers of Lyndon Baines Johnson, President, 1963–1969, Lyndon Baines Johnson Library, November 7, 1963.

175   *"It would have the potential . . .":* Robert S. McNamara, "Memorandum for the President, National Deep Underground Command Center as a Key FY 1965 Budget Consideration," Office of the Secretary of Defense, November 7, 1963, at http://www2.gwu.edu/~nsarchiv/nukevault/ebb442/docs/doc%203%20ducc.pdf.

175   *The DUCC appeared to be the perfect solution:* Memorandum from the Joint Chiefs of Staff to Secretary of Defense McNamara, "Deep Underground Command Center (DUCC)," Document 3, *Foreign Relations of the United States, 1964–1968, vol. 10, National Security Policy,* January 10, 1964, U.S. Government Printing Office, 2001.

176   *"If the enemy elects to attack . . .":* Ibid.

176   *GOP nominee Barry Goldwater:* Fendall W. Yerxa, "President Vows to Keep Control Over Atom Arms; Talk Opens Campaign," *New York Times,* September 8, 1964, at http://events.nytimes.com/learning/general/specials/elections/1964/featured_article2.html.

176   *That night, his campaign aired:* For more on the Daisy ad in context, see http://www.conelrad.com/daisy/daisy3.php.

176   *Then LBJ's somber voice began:* See the video at https://www.youtube.com/watch?v=dDTBnsqxZ3k.

177   *Through the fall, the Johnson campaign:* R. Mann, *Daisy Petals and Mushroom Clouds,* p. 72.

177   *The voice-over intoned, "This particular . . .":* Anne E. Kornblut and Shailagh Murray, "Clinton Ad Hints Obama Is Unprepared for Crisis," *Washington Post,* March 1, 2008, at http://www.washingtonpost.com/wp-dyn/content/article/2008/02/29/AR2008022904073.html.

177   *In a Seattle campaign speech:* Lyndon B. Johnson: "Remarks in Seattle on the Control of Nuclear Weapons," September 16, 1964, John T. Woolley and Gerhard Peters, *American Presidency Project,* at http://www.presidency.ucsb.edu/ws/?pid=26506.

178   *Under the Eisenhower-era program:* "Memorandum for the President, Summary of the Existing Plans for Emergency Use of Nuclear Weapons," McGeorge Bundy, White House, September 23, 1964, at http://www2.gwu.edu/~nsarchiv/news/predelegation2/pre3–1.htm.

179   *Gouverneur Morris of Pennsylvania originally:* Feerick, *From Failing Hands,* pp. 32, 44–45.

180   *After the vice president, only the House:* Feerick, *Twenty-fifth Amendment,* p. 39.

180   *James Madison had both vice presidents:* Ibid., pp. 3–5.

181   *Garfield's vice president, Chester A. Arthur:* Feerick, *From Failing Hands,* p. 130.

181   *Aides were concerned enough:* Ibid., p. 141.

181   *That hole in the nation's safety net finally:* Ibid., p. 145.

182   *Sixty years later, Harry Truman:* Ibid., pp. 204–7.

182   *When Teddy Roosevelt left the capital:* Goodwin, *Bully Pulpit,* p. xiii.

183   *"The ever-present possibility . . .":* Nixon, *Six Crises,* pp. 138–39.

183   *"On several occasions afterwards . . .":* Ibid., p. 168.

183   *In February 1958, he summoned Nixon:* Hansen, *Year We Had No President,* pp. 75–77.

183   *The letter of agreement between Kennedy:* "Text of Kennedy-Johnson Accord on Succession," *New York Times,* December 6, 1963.

184   *And now that Johnson was president:* Feerick, *Twenty-fifth Amendment,* p. 59.

184   *During the fourteen months he served:* "Letter, LBJ to McCormack, December 23, 1963," National Security File, Box 7, Files of Walt W. Rostow, Papers of Lyndon Baines Johnson, President, 1963–1969, Lyndon Baines Johnson Library.

184   *"It is outside the law . . .":* Feerick, *Twenty-fifth Amendment,* pp. 55–56, 103–4.

184   *Without a possible successor:* "De Gaulle Meeting Not Expected by U.S.," *New York Times,* March 28, 1964, p. 4.

184   *"Our very survival in this age . . .":* Feerick, *Year We Had No President,* p. 3.

185   *Nelson Rockefeller suggested the creation:* Feerick, *Twenty-fifth Amendment,* p. 72.

185   *Minutes from facilities meetings:* "Federal Agency Representatives Meeting: Special Facilities Branch, January 10, 1964," Lyndon Baines Johnson Presidential Library, Office of Emergency Planning, Box 10, Minutes of Special Facilities Meetings, January 10, 1964–December 16, 1965, at https://www.scribd.com/doc/181386550/Mount-Weather-Meeting-Minutes-1964.

186   *In 1968, the agency's name was changed:* "The Office of Emergency Planning during the Administration of President Lyndon B. Johnson, November 1963–January 1969," Office of Emergency Planning, Box 1, Administrative History Collection, Lyndon B. Johnson Presidential Library, November 1968, p. 98.

186   *Across the country, the nation's warning systems:* Rosenthal and Gelb, eds., *Night the Lights Went Out,* p. 25.

187   *As he said later, "We always . . .":* C. E. Fritz, "Some Problems of Warning and Communication Revealed by the Northeast U.S. Power Failure of 9–10 November 1965," Weapons Systems Evaluation Group, C.I. Study No. 12, Institute for Defense Analyses Report R-142, April 1968, p. 25, at http://www.dod.gov/pubs/foi/Reading_Room/Science_and_Technology/68.pdf.

187   *"It was as if some gigantic . . .":* Rosenthal and Gelb, eds., *Night the Lights Went Out,* p. 17.

187   *Mount Weather stood down at 11:28 p.m.:* "Note for Mr. Phillips, with Log of Emergency Activities, November 10, 1965," Folder "Special Facilities Division—Power Blackouts," Federal Records, Box 10, Records of the Office of Emergency Planning, Lyndon Baines Johnson Presidential Library, at https://www.scribd.com/doc/245954779/Mount-Weather-Northeast-Blackout-Log; "Memorandum to Chief, Special Facilities Division by E. R. McKay, November 18, 1965," Folder "Special Facilities Division—Power Blackouts," Federal Records, Box 10, Records of the Office of Emergency Planning, Lyndon Baines Johnson Presidential Library.

187   *As one Mount Weather official said:* C. E. Fritz, "Some Problems of Warning and Communication Revealed by the Northeast U.S. Power Failure of 9–10 November 1965," Weapons Systems Evaluation Group, C.I. Study No. 12, Institute for Defense Analyses Report R-142, April 1968, p. 110, at http://www.dod.gov/pubs/foi/Reading_Room/Science_and_Technology/68.pdf.

188   *Little known to the public, the* Wright: A third ship, the USS *Saipan,* had been originally meant to be part of the fleet, but it was never converted, instead being

renamed the *Arlington* and reclassified as a Major Communications Relay Ship (AGMR-2).

188 *A year after the* Northampton *took up station:* "CLC-1 Northampton," Global Security.org, at http://www.globalsecurity.org/military/systems/ship/clc-1.htm.

189 *With its distinctive 156-foot-tall fiberglass aerials:* "Sea Lady with a Secret," *New York Sunday News,* November 15, 1964.

189 *"probably as strange and complicated . . .":* "The Command Post," *USS Wright* newsletter, February 1970.

189 *Over the following decade, either the:* Karl C. Priest, "Ghosts of the East Coast: Doomsday Ships," Cold War Museum, at http://www.coldwar.org/museum /doomsday_ships.asp.

189 *As one 1964 Joint Chiefs memo:* "Department of Defense Command and Control Support to the President," Document 86, n.d., and Memorandum from the Joint Chiefs of Staff to Secretary of Defense McNamara, "Deep Underground Command Center (DUCC)," January 10, 1964, Document 3, both in *Foreign Relations of the United States, 1964–1968, vol. 10, National Security Policy,* U.S. Government Printing Office, 2001.

189 *Comparatively lightly armed:* Polmar, *Naval Institute Guide to the Ships and Aircraft of the U.S. Fleet,* p. 170.

190 *The* Wright's *motto,* Vox Imperii: Karl C. Priest, "Ghosts of the East Coast: Doomsday Ships," Cold War Museum, at http://www.coldwar.org/museum /doomsday_ships.asp.

190 *If all shore communications:* See http://politics.slashdot.org/comments.pl?sid=1925 98&threshold=1&commentsort=0&mode=thread&cid=15813107.

190 *In addition to the ships' normal complement:* "Captain Willis Lewis 'Slim' Somervell, Jr.," *Coloradoan,* April 14, 2014, at http://www.coloradoan.com/story /announcements/obituaries/2014/04/14/captcaptain-willis-lewis-slim-somervell -jr/7708347/.

190 *Hundreds more staff:* "Wright at Floating White House," *European Stars and Stripes,* January 27, 1970, p. 10.

190 *Hundreds more staff:* See Bob Woodward's website at http://bobwoodward.com /question-answer.

190 *The president would take charge:* Huey Freeman, "Sailor Recalls Assignment on 'Floating White House,'" *Herald & Review,* February 3, 2009, at http://herald -review.com/lifestyles/sailor-recalls-assignment-on-floating-white-house /article_8026235b-89d8–512a-84ce-e9787bd3fd47.html.

190 *In the event of nuclear fallout:* "Floating White House," *Chicago Tribune Magazine,* August 23, 1964, at http://archives.chicagotribune.com/1964/08/23/page/184 /article/floating-white-house.

191 *"Everything was spit and polish . . .":* See http://politics.slashdot.org/comments.pl? sid=192598&threshold=1&commentsort=0&mode=thread&cid=15813107.

191 *The* Northampton *picked up Kennedy:* For lots of good photos and video of this,

see https://www.youtube.com/watch?v=FjyARoE9_xU#t=53 and https://www
.youtube.com/watch?v=EdgU0HBR-xI.

191 *From the deck the next morning:* "Trips: U.S. Atlantic Fleet, April 1962: 13–14,"
Papers of John F. Kennedy, Presidential Papers, Presidential Office Files, John F.
Kennedy Library, at http://www.jfklibrary.org/Asset-Viewer/Archives/JFKPOF-
107–019.aspx.

191 *Sailors later joked that:* Crawford, *Farm Dies Once a Year,* p. 78.

191 *Just days after Johnson's summit:* "Air Force Plan to Improve U.S. Survivability by
Giving Airborne Command Post a Post-Attack Capability to Launch ICBMs
[Intercontinental Ballistic Missiles] Is Under Study," U.S. Department of De-
fense, August 24, 1965.

192 *During the summer of 1960, four different:* These trains are largely lost to time.
Their history is traced in the unpublished dissertation of Steven Anthony Pome-
roy, "Echoes that Never Were: American Mobile Intercontinental Ballistic Missiles, 1956–1983," Auburn University, August 7, 2006.

192 *The planes had begun their airborne:* The flights originally began with twelve-and-
a-half-hour shifts, with takeoffs at 10 a.m. and 10 p.m.

193 *Originally, the* LOOKING GLASS *flights:* "History of Headquarters Strategic Air Command 1961," *SAC Historical Study,* no. 89 (January 1962): 34.

193 *Packed with computer gear:* L. Wainstein et al., "The Evolution of U.S. Strategic
Command and Control and Warning, 1945–1972," Study S-467, Institute for Defense Analyses, June 1975, p. 324.

193 GLASS *missions began on the ground:* Maj. Greg Olgetree, "History of the 34th Air
Refueling Squadron," *Strategic Air Command Airborne Command Control Association Newsletter,* vol. 3, no. #2 (July 1997), at http://www.sac-acca.org/newsletter
/flyer0797.pdf.

193 *New* LOOKING GLASS *flights:* See the "Looking Glass" episode on the TV show
Lassie. The story, "Peace Is Our Profession," was broadcast on January 28, 1972, in
four back-to-back installments. In Part 2 (season 18, episode 15), Lassie befriends
a diabetic poodle named Sparky who stows away on the LOOKING GLASS to be with
his owner—but Sparky hasn't had his daily insulin shot. The story continues in
Part 3 (season 18, episode 16), when Sparky is discovered aboard the aircraft but,
as the eight-hour tour of duty continues, he begins to show signs of sinking into a
diabetic coma. Just in the nick of time, the aircraft is permitted to land early and
Sparky is saved. The four-part story (Part 1 involved a Minuteman missile and
Part 4 featured a B-52 bomber crew) was later released as a ninety-three-minute
movie with the same title.

194 *Occasionally, tumultuous Nebraska weather:* This happened, for instance, on December 10, 1970, when a blizzard struck Omaha, and the three ACCS squadrons
at Grissom Air Force Base picked a brigadier general from the 47th Air Division. See Major Greg Olgetree, "History of the 3rd Airborne Command and
Control Squadron," *Strategic Air Command Airborne Command Control Association*

Newsletter, vol. 3, no. 3 (December 1997), at http://www.sac-acca.org/newsletter /flyer1297.pdf.

194 *Following an attack:* LOOKING GLASS operational details are pulled from Howard Silber, "SAC Battle Staff in Sky Always Ready," (Omaha) *World-Herald,* c. 1970, at http://www.sac-acca.org/newsletter/flyer0309.pdf.

194 *Because of the remarkable autonomy:* Joseph Albright, "Communications Plane the 'Ultimate Switchboard,'" *Miami News,* September 30, 1980.

194 *By the mid-1960s, SAC had:* Office of the Historian, "Alert Operations and Strategic Air Command, 1957–1991," Strategic Air Command, Offutt Air Force Base, U.S. Government Printing Office, 1991, p. 23.

195 *SAC, though, always wanted more:* "Strategic Air Command's Green Pine Network: The Role of Loring Air Force Base, Maine," all-hazards.com, July 2002, at http://www.all-hazards.com/loring/greenpine/index.html.

195 *If Green Pine was knocked out, SAC brought online:* See the archived "Emergency Rocket Communications System" fact sheet at https://web.archive.org /web/20150302112310/http://www.nationalmuseum.af.mil/factsheets/factsheet .asp?id=8222.

195 *In an emergency, the crews:* "Strategic Air Command Regulation, Emergency Rocket Communications System, Emergency Action Procedures," Department of the Air Force, SAC Regulation 55–45, vol. 10, June 29, 1982, at https://www .scribd.com/doc/95063585/SAC-Reg-55–45-ERCS-Emergency-Action-Proce dures-Redacted.

195 *For thirty minutes after launch:* Office of the Historian, "Alert Operations and Strategic Air Command, 1957–1991," Strategic Air Command, Offutt Air Force Base, U.S. Government Printing Office, 1991, p. 20.

196 *Additionally, the Navy built its own:* See the history of the Cutler transmitter at http://www.navy-radio.com/commsta/cutler.htm.

197 *As one LOOKING GLASS pilot recalled:* Maj. Greg Olgetree, "History of the 3rd Airborne Command and Control Squadron," *Strategic Air Command Airborne Command Control Association Newsletter,* vol. 3, no. 3 (December 1997), at http://www .sac-acca.org/newsletter/flyer1297.pdf.

197 *The Navy's first four C-130 TACAMO planes:* Kent M. Black and Andrew G. Lindstrom, "TACAMO: A Manned Communication Relay Link to the Strategic Forces," *Signal,* September 1978, pp. 6–13, at http://www.navy-radio.com/xmtrs /vlf/tacamo-signal-7809.pdf.

198 *McNamara's early efforts to curtail:* Wigner, *Who Speaks for Civil Defense?,* p. 19.

198 *One McNamara change:* "Rationale for Reduction in Airborne Alert," Secret Memorandum, U.S. Special Assistant to the President for National Security Affairs, June 8, 1966; see also "B-52 Airborne Alert [Includes Memorandum from Alain Enthoven]," Secret Memorandum, U.S. Department of Defense, December 18, 1965.

199 *When nuclear incidents occurred:* Memorandum from Commandant of the Marine

Corps, "Operations Event/Incident Report (OPREP-3) Reporting," MCO 3504.2A, August 7, 2013, p. 1-1, at http://www.marines.mil/Portals/59/MCO% 203504.2A.pdf.

199 *While OPREP-3'S high-priority code words:* L. Wainstein et al., "The Evolution of U.S. Strategic Command and Control and Warning, 1945–1972," Study S-467, Institute for Defense Analyses, June 1975, p. 327.

200 *Once a darling of the press:* See, for instance, Nelson and Matusow, *Scoop*, p. 131.

200 *Stueart Pittman, Kennedy's civil defense chief:* Paul Vitello, "Steuart Pittman, Head of Fallout Shelter Program, Dies at 93," *New York Times*, February 18, 2013.

200 *"When Richard Nixon took . . .":* Anderson and Anderson, *Ronald Reagan*, p. 16.

202 *'I've always thought this . . .":* Memorandum from Smith to Rostow, "Advance Authority to Release Nuclear Weapons," "Furtherance" Folder, National Security File, Box 52, Subject File, Addendum, Papers of Lyndon Baines Johnson, President, 1963–1969, Lyndon Baines Johnson Library, July 10, 1967.

202 *Kissinger had long studied nuclear:* Rostow to LBJ, "Advance Authority to Release Nuclear Weapons," "Furtherance" Folder, National Security File, Box 52, Subject File, Addendum, Papers of Lyndon Baines Johnson, President, 1963–1969, Lyndon Baines Johnson Library, October 1, 1968.

203 *Now, though, he was seeing:* Memo, "President Meets with the Joint Chiefs on FURTHERANCE," "Furtherance" Folder, National Security File, Box 52, Subject File, Addendum, Papers of Lyndon Baines Johnson, President, 1963–1969, Lyndon Baines Johnson Library, October 14, 1968.

203 *When Richard Nixon himself sat:* William Burr, "The Nixon Administration, the 'Horror Strategy,' and the Search for Limited Nuclear Options, 1969–1972: Prelude to the Schlesinger Doctrine," *Journal of Cold War Studies*, vol. 7, no. 3 (Summer 2005): 34; and National Constitution Center, "How Presidents Use Bibles at Inaugurations," January 20, 2017, at http://blog.constitutioncenter.org/2017/01/how-presidents-use-bibles-at-inaugurations/.

203 *Nixon's campaign platform was peace:* Thomas, *Being Nixon*, p. 197.

203 *Earlier that day, January 27, 1969:* Richard Nixon, "The President's News Conference," January 27, 1969, John T. Woolley and Gerhard Peters, *American Presidency Project*, at http://www.presidency.ucsb.edu/ws/?pid=1942.

203 *The new plan presented to Nixon:* William Burr, "To Have the Only Option that of Killing 80 Million People Is the Height of Immorality: The Nixon Administration, the SIOP, and the Search for Limited Nuclear Options, 1969–1974," Electronic Briefing Book no. 173, November 23, 2005, National Security Archive, George Washington University, at http://nsarchive.gwu.edu/NSAEBB/NSAEBB173/.

204 *As Nixon said a few days:* "Notes of National Security Council Meeting," doc. 7, February 14, 1969, *Foreign Relations of the United States 1969–1976, vol. 34, National Security Policy, 1969–1972*, U.S. Government Printing Office, 2011.

204 *The Soviets possessed new larger:* Van Atta, *With Honor*, p. 194.

204   *Kissinger's push for limited:* Burr and Kimball, *Nixon's Nuclear Specter,* p. 51.

204   *In its conference room, the battle:* "Diary entry, May 11, 1969," H. R. Haldeman Handwritten Diaries Special Collection, Richard Nixon Presidential Library, at http://www2.gwu.edu/~nsarchiv/NSAEBB/NSAEBB173/SIOP-5.pdf.

204   *In one meeting, Kissinger bluntly:* "Minutes of Verification Panel Meeting," Foreign Relations of the United States, 1969–1976, doc. 22, vol. 35, National Security Policy, 1973–1976, Office of the Historian, Washington, D.C., August 9, 1973, at http://history.state.gov/historicaldocuments/frus1969–76v35/d22.

205   *"I want the North Vietnamese . . .":* See doc. 59, *Foreign Relations of the United States 1969–1976, vol. 34, National Security Policy, 1969–1972,* U.S. Government Printing Office, 2011, p. 232. Nixon denied this conversation during a 1984 interview.

205   *As Defense Secretary Melvin Laird recalled:* Burr and Kimball, *Nixon's Nuclear Specter,* p. 129.

205   *Kissinger telephoned the Pentagon:* Ibid., p. 128.

206   *Kissinger, in a background briefing:* Ibid., p. 141.

206   *At precisely 12:59 a.m. on March 1, 1971:* Burrough, *Days of Rage,* p. 164.

207   *Indeed, during most of the nearly:* "George M. White, Architect of the Capitol, Dies at 90," *New York Times,* June 23, 2011, at http://www.nytimes.com /2011/06/23/us/23white.html?_r=0. See also https://www.youtube.com/watch?v =jbQCpUhONtk.

207   *"That's one of the most remarkable . . .":* Mark Matthews, "Bunker Spills Secrets to Public," *Orlando Sentinel,* August 21, 2006.

208   *Government engineers identified:* R. R. Roach to A. H. Belmont, "Relocation Site for U.S. Congress," FBI Office Memorandum, June 28, 1957, at https://www .scribd.com/doc/102562220/Greenbrier-FBI-Memos-1957.

209   *As construction worker Randy Wickline said years later:* Ted Gup, "The Ultimate Congressional Hideaway," *Washington Post,* Sunday, May 31, 1992, page W11, at http://www.washingtonpost.com/wp-srv/local/daily/july/25/brier1.htm.

211   *The $14 million construction project wrapped:* Thomas Mallon, "Mr. Smith Goes Underground," *American Heritage,* vol. 51, no. 5 (September 2000): 60.

212   *"In doing that job, we spent . . .":* "Interview with Paul Fritz Bugas," *Race for the Superbomb, American Experience,* PBS, at http://www.pbs.org/wgbh/amex/bomb /sfeature/interview.html.

213   *Finding the subterranean working situation:* CONELRAD founder Bill Geerhart conducted an invaluable interview with John Londis in 2013, just months before he passed away, that today represents the only in-depth interview ever done with the former staff of the Greenbrier bunker. See "The Inside Man: John J. Londis and the Greenbrier Bunker," February 27, 2013, at http://conelrad.blogspot .com/2013/02/the-inside-man-john-j-londis-and.html.

213   *House Speaker Tip O'Neill, one of the:* "Interview with Paul Fritz Bugas," *Race for the Superbomb, American Experience,* PBS, at http://www.pbs.org/wgbh/amex/bomb /sfeature/interview.html.

213 *After White became Architect:* Rhodes retired from Congress in 1982, touching off a fierce GOP primary battle in his district that ended with the election of a former naval aviator, John McCain.

213 *"Yes, I am considered non-interruptible . . .":* Barney Collier, "The Most Embarrassing List in Washington," *Harper's,* May 1975.

214 *Telling all 535 members of Congress:* "Memo from Henry Roemer McPhee to Gordon Gray," November 19, 1957, Harlow, Bryce N. Records, Box 5, File "Civil Defense (1955–60)," Dwight D. Eisenhower Presidential Library.

214 *Senior bureau officials:* "Federal Bureau of Investigation (FBI) War/Emergency Plans and Bureau Assistance for Members of Congress in the Event of War/Emergency, 1955–1977," at http://www.governmentattic.org/4docs/FBI-War PlanCongress_1955–1977.pdf.

215 *In 1970, after his time:* Barney Collier, "The Most Embarrassing List in Washington," *Harper's,* May 1975.

215 *Military aide James Hughes proposed:* Hughes to Erlichmann, October 7, 1969, memo.

216 *When Larzelere arrived at the White House:* Larzelere, *Witness to History,* p. 11.

216 *"I climbed out of the helo . . .":* Mary Meehan, "The Flying Fuhrerbunker," *Washington Monthly,* vol. 6, no. 2 (April 1976): 22.

217 *One National Security Council aide:* "Backchannel Message from Richard T. Kennedy of the National Security Council Staff to the President's Deputy Assistant for National Security Affairs (Haig) in Saigon," Washington, D.C., December 20, 1972, Foreign Relations of the United States, 1969–1976, vol. 9, Vietnam, October 1972–January 1973, doc. 207, Office of the Historian, Washington, D.C., August 9, 1973, at https://history.state.gov/historicaldocuments/frus1969–76v09/d207.

217 *While the Camp David bomb shelter:* W. D. Nelson, *President Is at Camp David,* p. 84.

217 *On October 28, 1969, Richard Nixon signed:* U.S. Congress, House, Committee on Government Operations, Reorganization Plan No. 1 of 1973, House Report No. 93–106, 93rd Congress, 1st Session, U.S. Government Printing Office, 1973.

218 *"Those which are survivable . . .":* Response to NSSM 64.

218 *"Our warning assessment . . .":* L. Wainstein et al., "The Evolution of U.S. Strategic Command and Control and Warning, 1945–1972," Study S-467, Institute for Defense Analyses, June 1975, pp. 432–33.

218 *Though Raven Rock had been reinforced:* Robert S. McNamara, "National Deep Underground Command Center as a Key FY 1965 Budget Consideration," November 7, 1963, U.S. Department of Defense, at http://www2.gwu.edu/~nsarchiv/nukevault/ebb442/docs/doc%203%20ducc.pdf.

219 *As Assistant Defense Secretary Eberhardt:* Quoted in L. Wainstein et al., "The Evolution of U.S. Strategic Command and Control and Warning, 1945–1972," Study S-467, Institute for Defense Analyses, June 1975, p. 420.

219   *In the early 1970s, Qantas:* Donald H. Rumsfeld, "Annual Defense Department Report, FY 1978," January 17, 1977, U.S. Government Printing Office, p. 145, at http://history.defense.gov/Portals/70/Documents/annual_reports/1978_DoD _AR.pdf.

219   *The flying time for a Soviet:* Weapons Systems Evaluation Group Report 179, quoted in L. Wainstein et al., "The Evolution of U.S. Strategic Command and Control and Warning, 1945–1972," Study S-467, Institute for Defense Analyses, June 1975, p. 423.

219   *As one report explained:* Ibid., p. 420.

219   *The president would be loath:* Ernest May, John D. Steinbruner, and Thomas W. Wolf, "History of the Strategic Arms Competition 1945–1972, Part II," Office of the Secretary of Defense, Historical Office, March 1981, p. 607.

220   *Both superpowers moved away:* L. Wainstein et al., "The Evolution of U.S. Strategic Command and Control and Warning, 1945–1972," Study S-467, Institute for Defense Analyses, June 1975, p. 413.

220   *Instead, military strategists suggested:* Burr and Kimball, *Nixon's Nuclear Specter,* p. 57.

220   *Leaving each others' command:* L. Wainstein et al., "The Evolution of U.S. Strategic Command and Control and Warning, 1945–1972," Study S-467, Institute for Defense Analyses, June 1975, p. 431.

220   *The man first in line became:* "Drunk Speaker of the House Crashes into Two Cars," *Washington Post,* September 11, 1972, at http://ghostsofdc.org/2012/12/06 /drunk-speaker-carl-albert/.

221   *Constitutional scholars have argued:* For more on this argument, see Feerick, *Twenty-fifth Amendment,* p. 214.

221   *Such messiness was luckily:* Thomas, *Being Nixon,* p. 469.

221   *"It's not clear what would . . .":* Susan Brenneman, "Watergate's Saturday Night Massacre Gets More Interesting with Age," *Los Angeles Times,* October 18, 2013, at http://articles.latimes.com/2013/oct/18/news/la-ol-saturday-night-massacre -watergate-20131018.

222   *During the Kennedy years, the government:* Peter Braestrup, "Step-Up in Civil Defense Studied by Administration," *New York Times,* October 30, 1961.

222   *Small buzzers, available:* "Annual Report for Fiscal Year 1959," Office of Civil and Defense Mobilization, U.S. Government Printing Office, 1960, p. 19; "Investigations: N.E.A.R Device," transcript, *History Detectives,* PBS, August 2009, at http://www-tc.pbs.org/opb/historydetectives/static/media/transcripts /2011–05–22/709_near.pdf.

222   *There was no way to provide:* "Status of NEACR Program Still Cloudy to Utilities," *Electrical World,* December 18, 1961, at http://coldwar-c4i.net/NEAR/Elec tricalWorld121861–36–37.html.

222   *A poll that year found seven out of ten:* Bennett Z. Kobb, "The Last Radio Network: Long Waves from the Cold War," updated article from *Northern Observer,* no. 22

(November 1990), at http://web.archive.org/web/20080703002044/http://kob
net.net/misc/coldwar/coldwar-c4i.net/PER/WGU20.html.

223   *"The technology is there . . .":* Zuckerman, *Day After World War III,* p. 114.

223   *Watergate also caused Congress:* UPI, "Watergate Suspect 'Drafted Censorship
Plan,'" *Ellensburg Daily Record,* October 23, 1972, p. 3, at http://news.google.com
/newspapers?id=tjkQAAAAIBAJ&sjid=VI8DAAAAIBAJ&dq=censorship%20
nixon%20war%20emergency&pg=5421%2C1133618.

223   *Former Associated Press executive Byron Price:* Wise, *Politics of Lying,* p. 137.

223   *That experience had been fresh:* "News Censorship Mapped for War," *New York
Times,* November 6, 1954, p. 13.

223   *Over the next four years:* See: "Stand-by National Censorship Agreement," at
http://www.foia.cia.gov/sites/default/files/document_conversions/5829/CIA
-RDP80B01676R001100090039–1.pdf; see also DMO X-1, "Establishment of
an Interagency Committee on National Censorship Planning," DMP 1, the Code
of Federal Regulations of the United States of America, Title 32A—National Defense, Appendix, Federal Register, National Archives, December 31, 1956, p. 61.

223   *"Standby National Censorship Agreement":* Wise, *Politics of Lying,* p. 137.

223   *"voluntarily":* Sam Archibald, "Free Press of Future May Dance to Government
Tune," *Prescott-Courier,* October 4, 1970.

224   *As one historian noted, however:* Carpenter, *Captive Press,* p. 113.

224   *The agency would have been authorized:* "U.S. Government Information Policies
and Practices: Security Classification Problems Involving Subsection (b)(1) of
the Freedom of Information Act," pt. 7, Hearing Dates May 1–3, 5, 8, 11, 1972.
Subcommittee on Foreign Operations and Government Information, Committee on Government Operations, U.S. House of Representatives (Sudoc Number:
Y4.G74/7:In3/12/pt.7), p. 2944.

224   *The government did not distribute:* Wise, *Politics of Lying,* p. 139.

224   *Eight standby WISP executives:* Ibid.

224   *The standby censors all received:* Ibid., p. 134.

224   *The government paid the college:* Sarah Hull, "Debunking the Bunker," *McDaniel
Free Press,* March 31, 2014, at http://www.mcdanielfreepress.com/2014/03/31
/debunking-the-bunker/.

225   *After WISP came to public attention:* Wise, *Politics of Lying,* p. 136.

225   *The secret draft executive order:* Ibid.

226   *He had spent the previous days:* Thomas, *Being Nixon,* p. 496.

226   *Speaking to no one in particular:* "Interview with Ambassador David Michael
Ransom," Association for Diplomatic Studies and Training, Foreign Affairs Oral
History Project, November 2, 1999, p. 46, at http://www.adst.org/OH%20TOCs
/Ransom,%20David%20Michael.toc%20ss.pdf.

226   *The first, a message from Ford:* "Message Sent by Commander-in-Chief," *Fort
Hood Sentinel,* August 16, 1974, vol. 33, no. 23, p. 4, at http://texashistory.unt.edu
/ark:/67531/metapth309158/.

226 *The second, from Schlesinger:* Stanley Kutler, "The Imaginings of James R. Schlesinger," *Huffington Post,* April 1, 2014, at http://www.huffingtonpost.com /stanley-kutler/the-imaginings-of-james-r_b_5066130.html.

228 *A sign at Mount Weather cautioned:* Gup, *Nation of Secrets,* p. 65.

228 *The facility was under the purview:* Some of Gallagher's colorful history is recounted in an article entitled "From Denmark," on page 7 of the *Square J Bulletin,* 390th Memorial Museum Foundation, vol. 11, no. 4 (Winter 2006–2007), at http://www.390th.org/wp-content/uploads/Winter2006–2007.pdf.

228 *After World War II, Gallagher had spent:* Details of Gallagher's life are pulled from Ted Gup, "The Doomsday Blueprints," *Time,* August 10, 1992; and "Bernard Gallagher Dies," *Washington Post,* September 8, 2000, at http://www.washingtonpost.com /archive/local/2000/09/08/bernard-gallagher-dies/79d35fbf-693e-470a-b778 –5cb2e933383a/.

229 *"It looked like a hundred tons . . .":* Martin Weil and Tom Zito, "Stormy Weather Forced Diversion from Washington," *Washington Post,* December 2, 1974, A1.

229 *While the crash didn't touch:* Michael Leahy, "25 Years Later, No Place for Their Sorrow: Couple Laments Lack of Memorial in Crash," *Washington Post,* December 1, 1999, p. A01, at http://www.washingtonpost.com/wp-srv/WPcap/1999 –12/01/021r-120199-idx.html.

229 *A government spokesman would only:* Associated Press, "All 92 On Board Killed When Jetliner Crashes in Rain Near Washington," *New York Times,* December 2, 1974.

230 The Washington Post *published:* Ken Ringle, "Hush-Hush Mt. Weather Is a Crisis Facility, *Washington Post,* December 2, 1974, p. A20.

230 *"I don't understand what . . .":* Richard Pollock, "The Mysterious Mountain," *Progressive,* March 1976, p. 13.

230 *"In effect, these officials . . .":* "Staff Report on Emergency Preparedness in the United States," Senate Special Committee on National Emergencies and Delegated Emergency Powers, March 1976, p. 38, at http://fas.org/irp/agency/dhs /fema/srpt94–922.pdf.

230 *Bray confirmed that Mount Weather:* Richard Pollock, "The Mysterious Mountain," *Progressive,* March 1976, p. 15.

230 *"No one seems to be in charge . . .":* Philip Shabecoff, "The President Safety vs. Citizens' Rights," *New York Times,* September 10, 1975, at http://query.nytimes.com /mem/archive/pdf?res=9405EFDD163FE034BC4852DFBF66838E669EDE.

231 *A large specially built:* John Walker, "Typical UNIVAC 1108 Prices: 1968," August 13, 1996, at http://www.fourmilab.ch/documents/univac/config1108.html.

231 *Inside the pod, the room-sized:* Richard Pollock, "The Mysterious Mountain," *Progressive,* March 1976, p. 14.

231 *Much of that research fell to:* Stephen J. Lukasik, "Why the ARPANet Was Built," *IEEE Annals of the History of Computing,* vol. 33, no. 3 (July–September 2011): 4–20.

231 *As one scientist involved:* Ibid.

232 *"I can assure you . . .":* Waldrop, *Dream Machine,* pp. 279–80.

232 *As he said decades later:* Stephen J. Lukasik, "Why the ARPANet Was Built," *IEEE Annals of the History of Computing,* vol. 33, no. 3 (July–September 2011): 4–20.

233 *By January 1974, Nixon had signed:* Terriff, *Nixon Administration and the Making of U.S. Nuclear Strategy,* p. 1.

233 *Throughout the 1970s the Oak Ridge National Laboratory:* Carsten M. Haaland, Conrad V. Chesterp, and Eugene P. Wigner, "Survival of the Relocated Population of the U.S. After a Nuclear Attack," Defense Civil Preparedness Agency, Washington, D.C., June 1976, p. 153, at http://web.ornl.gov/info/reports/1976/3445600218921.pdf.

233 *New research in the 1970s:* "Foresight," Department of Defense, Defense Civil Preparedness Agency, Annual Report, FY 73, February 8, 1974, p. 27, at http://www.hsdl.org/?view&did=34734.

233 *Publicly, the Federal Reserve Bank of Richmond:* "The Culpeper Switch: The Federal Reserve System," Federal Reserve, September 1975, at http://coldwar-c4i.net/Mt_Pony/culpsw04.htm.

234 *The chairman—who would:* Zuckerman, *Day After World War III,* p. 226.

235 *Each of the nation's twelve regional:* Lee Michael Katz, "Mountain of Money," *Washington Post,* January 30, 1983.

235 *"I can't guarantee our plans . . .":* Charles R. Babcock, "Fed Keeps Hillside Vault: Billions in Bills Held in Case of Atomic War," *Washington Post,* February 26, 1976.

235 *The Treasury Department, meanwhile:* Krugler, *This Is Only a Test,* p. 183.

235 *The Treasury Department had done background:* Bill McAllister, "U.S. Pays Airlie a Premium Rental For 'Emergency' Site in the Country," *Washington Post,* April 22, 1978.

235 *As Pollock wrote, "interviews . . .":* Richard Pollock, "The Mysterious Mountain," *Progressive,* March 1976, p. 13.

236 *Mount Weather "more closely . . .":* Ibid.

236 *"Everyone around here assumed . . .":* Ibid.

236 *Pollock asked, "How can a parallel . . .":* Ibid., p. 14.

237 *The last line of his evacuation:* Nessen, *It Sure Looks Different from the Inside,* pp. 321–22.

239 *The generals and admirals spent:* UPI, "Chiefs Brief Carter on Russian Power," *Pittsburgh Press,* January 13, 1977, at https://news.google.com/newspapers?nid=1144&dat=19770113&id=klwqAAAAIBAJ&sjid=AlcEAAAAIBAJ&pg=5911,3970178&hl=en.

239 *At the end of the day, Carter threw:* Carroll, *House of War,* p. 364.

239 *This Georgia governor:* Don Oberdorfer and Edward Walsh, "Carter to Press Liberalizing of Korea, Withdrawal of GIs," *Washington Post,* January 14, 1977, at http://www.washingtonpost.com/archive/politics/1977/01/14/carter-to-press-liberalizing-of-korea-withdrawal-of-gis/cb2f5e6c-dd1c-4743-b5a1-a9910490e7f1/.

240   *As Brzezinski recalled:* Brzezinski, *Power and Principle,* p. 15.

240   *The alert procedures, so finely tuned:* Terence Smith, "White House Springs Surprise Evacuation Alerts," *New York Times,* February 13, 1978.

240   *Brzezinski's stopwatch ticked long:* Thomas Powers, "Choosing a Strategy for World War III," *Atlantic Monthly,* November 1982, p. 95.

240   *Then, at the first White House staff meeting:* Richard Stedman, "Report to the Secretary of Defense on the National Military Command Structure," U.S. Department of Defense, Washington, D.C., July 1978, at http://www.whs.mil/library /Dig/reportjuly1978.pdf.

240   *"The period of American preeminence . . .":* Ibid., p. 3.

240   *The war in Vietnam had gutted:* Karnow, *Vietnam,* p. 24.

240   *On February 11, just three weeks:* "The Daily Diary of President Jimmy Carter," The White House, Washington, D.C., February 11, 1977, Jimmy Carter Presidential Library, at http://www.jimmycarterlibrary.gov/documents/diary/1977/d0 21177t.pdf; see also February 13, 1977, at http://www.jimmycarterlibrary.gov /documents/diary/1977/d021377t.pdf.

241   *Over the months ahead, he visited:* Jimmy Carter, "Port Canaveral, Florida— Question-and-Answer Session with Reporters on Disembarking from the U.S.S. *Los Angeles,*" May 27, 1977, John T. Woolley and Gerhard Peters, *American Presidency Project,* at http://www.presidency.ucsb.edu/ws/?pid=7606. See also Carter, *White House Diary,* p. 58.

241   *The President wrote in his diary:* Carter, *White House Diary,* p. 70.

241   *As aide General William Odom explained:* Thomas Powers, "Choosing a Strategy for World War III," *Atlantic Monthly,* November 1982, p. 95.

242   *"It is the first time in years . . .":* Terence Smith, "White House Springs Surprise Evacuation Alerts," *New York Times,* February 13, 1978.

242   *One of the first pilots:* The Boeing airframe numbers are 73–1676, 73–1677, and 74–0787 for the first-generation E-4As, while the custom-built E-4B was 75– 0125. See Tim Tyler, "Who Are the NIGHTWATCH Stations?" Worldwide UTE News, at http://www.udxf.nl/WUN-str03.pdf.

243   *The planes were treated specially:* Elizabeth L. Ray, "Air Traffic Control," U.S. Department of Transportation, Federal Aviation Administration, no. JO 7110.65W, October 27, 2015, p. 2-1-2, at http://www.faa.gov/documentLibrary/media/Order /ATC.pdf.

243   *The plane's main level featured:* Kenneth Stein, "America's Top-Secret Doomsday Plane," *Popular Mechanics,* May 1994, pp. 38–42.

244   *In what would be the cargo and luggage:* Kenneth Stein, "E-4B Boosts SAC's Communications Net," *Aviation Week & Space Technology,* June 1980, p. 77.

244   *Overall, the capabilities and technology:* Denis Clift to Vice President Mondale, "Unclassified Reporting of US Defense Developments," Remote Archives Capture (RAC) Program Collection, Jimmy Carter Presidential Library, June 19, 1980.

245   *The four NEACP crews alternated:* Staff Sgt. John Dendy IV, "Around the Clock with the E-4B," *Airman Magazine,* May 2000, vol. 44, no. 5, p. 2.

245   *To match the requirements:* Richard Clark, "A 747 Causes Quite a Stir Over Tulsa," News on 6, December 11, 2008, at http://www.newson6.com/global/story .asp?s=9505403.

246   *The deeper the administration examined:* "Interview with Zbigniew Brzezinski," Miller Center, University of Virginia, 2003, at http://millercenter.org/president /carter/oralhistory/zbigniew-brzezinski.

247   *"This led to other issues . . .":* William Odom, "The Origins and Design of Presidential Decision-59: A Memoir," in Sokolski, ed., *Getting MAD,* p. 179.

247   *"The SAC commander and his staff . . .":* Ibid., p. 180.

247   *That visit to Offutt Air Force Base:* Ibid., p. 179.

248   *Later that month, Carter toured:* Bill Neikirk, "Tour of SAC Base Reassuring: Carter," *Chicago Tribune,* October 23, 1977, at http://archives.chicagotribune .com/1977/10/23/page/1/article/tour-of-sac-base-reassuring-carter/index.html; see also "The Daily Diary of President Jimmy Carter," Diehl Residence, Indianola, Iowa, October 22, 1977, Jimmy Carter Presidential Library, at http://www .jimmycarterlibrary.gov/documents/diary/1977/d102277t.pdf.

248   *"Very informative," he scrawled:* Carter, *White House Diary,* p. 122.

248   *Six weeks later, Vice President Mondale:* Jimmy Carter, "Digest of Other White House Announcements Week Ending Friday," December 9, 1977, John T. Woolley and Gerhard Peters, *American Presidency Project,* at http://www.presidency .ucsb.edu/ws/?pid=7001.

248   *The next month, the president:* "The Daily Diary of President Jimmy Carter," The White House, Washington, D.C., November 28, 1977, Jimmy Carter Presidential Library, at http://www.jimmycarterlibrary.gov/documents/diary/1977/d1128 77t.pdf.

248   *"This is the first time . . .":* Carter, *White House Diary,* p. 141.

248   *The new department, part of the government's efforts:* "The Daily Diary of President Jimmy Carter," The White House, Washington, D.C., December 28, 1977, Jimmy Carter Presidential Library, at http://www.jimmycarterlibrary.gov/documents /diary/1977/d122877t.pdf.

248   *Meeting in the Oval Office on a cold morning:* The exact briefing Carter received is not known, but the figures are pulled from historical tables for 1977.

249   *Carter recorded privately:* Carter, *White House Diary,* p. 154.

250   *And so in August 1978:* "Carter Family Awash," *Miami News,* August 22, 1978, p. A1.

251   *As William Odom wrote that fall to Brzezinski:* Memorandum from Odom to Brzezinski, "Weekly Report, October 26, 1978," Remote Archives Capture (RAC) Program Collection, Jimmy Carter Presidential Library.

251   *One effort to pare down:* Michael Dobbs, "The Real Story of the 'Football' that Follows the President Everywhere," *Smithsonian,* October 2014, at http://www

.smithsonianmag.com/history/real-story-football-follows-president-everywhere
-180952779/#ELFRKBD8dcLjGFxX.99.

251 *The week after the rafting trip:* Memorandum from Odom to Brzezinski, "Weekly Report," October 26, 1978, Remote Archives Capture (RAC) Program Collection, Jimmy Carter Presidential Library.

252 *As Brzezinski wrote the president on November 3:* Brzezinski to Carter, "A Director for FEMA," November 3, 1978, Remote Archives Capture (RAC) Program Collection, Jimmy Carter Presidential Library.

252 *As Odom wrote, similarly exasperated:* Memorandum from Odom to Brzezinski, "Weekly Report, October 26, 1978," Remote Archives Capture (RAC) Program Collection, Jimmy Carter Presidential Library.

252 *The results were, as one congressman:* John J. Fialka, "The Lessons of Nifty Nugget," *Daytona Beach Morning Journal,* November 5, 1979, at https://news.google.com /newspapers?nid=1873&dat=19791105&id=UFEfAAAAIBAJ&sjid=H9IEAA AAIBAJ&pg=2672,2169925&hl=en.

252 *Within the first thirty days of the simulated war:* John J. Fialka, "One and One Half Wars Ability in Doubt," *Sarasota Herald-Tribune,* November 12, 1979, at https:// news.google.com/newspapers?nid=1755&dat=19791112&id=hsEqAAAAIBAJ &sjid=qmcEAAAAIBAJ&pg=6840,6310272&hl=en.

253 *In the midst of the exercise:* Pearson, *World Wide Military Command and Control System,* p. 213.

253 *"WWMCCS just fell flat . . .":* John J. Fialka, "The Pentagon's Exercise 'Proud Spirit': Little Cause for Pride," *Parameters,* vol. 11, no. 1 (1981), at http://strate gicstudiesinstitute.army.mil/pubs/parameters/Articles/1981/1981%20fialka.pdf.

253 *The years after the* NIFTY NUGGET: Betts, *Surprise Attack,* p. 186.

254 *Suspicious activity discovered:* Gary Hart and Barry Goldwater, "Recent False Alerts from the Nation's Missile Attack Warning System," October 9, 1980, 96th Congress, 2nd Session, U.S. Government Printing Office, 1980.

255 *"We must build the best . . .": Air Force Magazine,* August 1958, p. 102, as quoted in H. Kahn, *On Thermonuclear War,* p. 101.

255 *Herman Kahn and the RAND Corporation:* "Designing for Defense: NORAD," *Notes* (internal newsletter), Parsons Brinckerhoff, Spring 1988. See also Ghamari-Tabrizi, *Worlds of Herman Kahn,* p. 79.

256 *To carve NORAD out of its east slope:* The history of the Utah Construction & Mining Company is recounted in Hiltzik, *Colossus,* pp. 139, 140, 162–66; as well as in a special collection at Weber State University's Stewart Library, at http:// dc.weber.edu/cdm/ucc.

256 *"There was this tremendous . . .":* "Designing for Defense: NORAD," *Notes* (internal newsletter), Parsons Brinckerhoff, Spring 1988.

256 *As Army engineer Robert Selders recalled:* "NORAD: Cheyenne Mountain," Episode 6, Season 1, *Super Structures of the World,* original air date January 1998.

257 *On May 18, 1961, while workers:* "A Brief History of NORAD," Office of History,

North American Aerospace Defense Command, p. 19, at http://www.norad.mil /Portals/29/Documents/A%20Brief%20History%20of%20NORAD%20(current%20as%20of%20March%202014).pdf.

257　*Unlike many other command and control:* See, for instance, "Miners Walk Off Defense Tunnel Job," *Spokesman-Review,* December 21, 1961.

257　*All told, the three-year-long:* Merwin H. Howes, "Methods and Costs of Constructing the Underground Facility of North American Air Defense Command at Cheyenne Mountain, El Paso County, Colo.," Information Circular 8294, Bureau of Mines, U.S. Department of the Interior, 1966, p. 5.

257　*"That's enough dynamite . . .":* Frank Macomber, "The Detectives," *Lodi News-Sentinel,* November 16, 1961. See also Frank Macomber, "The 'Alarm Clock,'" *Lodi News Sentinel,* November 15, 1961, at http://news.google.com/newspapers?id=3xgzAAAAIBAJ&sjid=vTIHAAAAIBAJ&pg=3176%2C2987805, and Frank Macomber, "The $66 Million Phone Booth," *Lodi News-Sentinel,* November 16, 1961, at http://news.google.com/newspapers?id=4BgzAAAAIBAJ&sjid=vTIHAAAAIBAJ&pg=3098%2C3233569.

257　*Even as the generals involved:* Roger A. Mola, "This Is Only a Test," *Air & Space* (Smithsonian), March 2002, at http://www.airspacemag.com/history-of-flight/this-is-only-a-test-3119878/?all.

258　*To prevent the surrounding granite:* The construction of NORAD, a true engineering marvel, has been the subject of two documentaries worth watching—one by Rocky Mountain PBS, as part of its *Colorado Experience,* and one by National Geographic, as part of its *Megastructures* series.

258　*Newmark, known as "Mr. Underground," had:* William J. Hall, "Nathan M. Newmark, 1910–1981: A Biographical Memoir," National Academy of Sciences, Washington, D.C., 1991, at http://www.nasonline.org/publications/biographical -memoirs/memoir-pdfs/newmark-nathan.pdf.

258　*As one officer later recalled:* Eden, *Whole World on Fire,* p. 133.

258　*Kuesel described it as:* Malcolm, *Parsons Brinckerhoff Through the Years,* p. 185.

259　*Though the project's exact specifications:* "NORAD Combat Operations Center," *Notes* (internal newsletter), Parsons Brinckerhoff, Winter 1963–1964; "Designing for Defense: NORAD," *Notes* (internal newsletter), Parsons Brinckerhoff, Spring 1988.

259　*"Upside down ships . . .":* Bobrick, *Parsons Brinckerhoff,* p. 167.

259　*By its completion in 1964:* Merwin H. Howes, "Methods and Costs of Constructing the Underground Facility of North American Air Defense Command at Cheyenne Mountain, El Paso County, Colo.," Information Circular 8294, Bureau of Mines, U.S. Department of the Interior, 1966, p. 4.

259　*Some 72,000 meals were stockpiled:* "N. America's Defense Tied to City in Mountain," *Lewiston Daily-Sun,* January 4, 1967, at http://news.google.com/newspapers?nid=1928&dat=19670104&id=LmggAAAAIBAJ&sjid=1GYFAAAAIBAJ&pg=2610,463764.

260 *"There seemed to be an excessive . . .":* "Historical Summary, July–December 1964," North American Air Defense Command and Continental Air Defense Command, p. 11, at http://www.northcom.mil/Portals/28/Documents/Supporting%20 documents/(U)%201964%20NORAD%20CONAD%20History%20Jul-Dec.pdf.

260 *There was good reason:* "Historical Summary, January–December 1966," North American Air Defense Command and Continental Air Defense Command, May 1, 1967, p. 45, at http://www.northcom.mil/Portals/28/Documents/Support ing%20documents/(U)%201966%20NORAD-CONAD%20History.pdf.

260 *The first report might have:* Harold Brown to Jimmy Carter, "Questions Brought Up at the Presidential Visit to the National Military Command Center," March 9, 1978, Remote Archives Capture (RAC) Program Collection, Jimmy Carter Presidential Library.

261 *Now, though, the computers:* NORAD computer glitches are based primarily on Comptroller General, "NORAD's Missile Warning System: What Went Wrong?" Report MASAD-81-30, U.S. Government Printing Office, May 1981, as well as supplemental materials gathered by the National Security Archive at George Washington University, Electronic Briefing Book 371, "The 3 a.m. Phone Call," at http://nsarchive.gwu.edu/nukevault/ebb371/.

261 *"Here comes our worst-case . . .":* Matthew Hansen, "Inside Bunker, SAC Crew Feared WWIII Was on Its Way," *Omaha World-Herald,* June 8, 2014, at http:// www.omaha.com/news/metro/hansen-inside-bunker-sac-crew-feared-wwiii -was-on-its/article_77eabaa3-2207-589e-b541-a4fa75163999.html.

261 *Vouk got on the phone:* Ibid.

261 *The SAC personnel cheered:* Busch, *No End in Sight,* p. 59.

262 *Officials were coming to understand:* "HQ/NORAD to Assistant Secretary of Defense C3 and Joint Chiefs of Staff," December 20, 1979, at http://nsarchive.gwu .edu/nukevault/ebb371/docs/doc%2010%2012-20-79.pdf.

262 *Despite a $10 billion investment:* James North, " 'Hello Central, Get Me NATO': The Computer That Can't," *Washington Monthly,* July 1979, pp. 48–51.

262 *One whistle-blower, John Bradley:* Ibid., p. 51.

263 *Brzezinski, sitting at his house:* Gates, *From the Shadows,* p. 114.

263 *Three days later, on June 6:* Department of Defense "Fact Sheet," n.d. [circa June 7/8, 1980], National Security Archive, George Washington University, Electronic Briefing Book 371, "The 3 a.m. Phone Call," at http://nsarchive.gwu.edu/nuke vault/ebb371/.

263 *The government's after-action:* Gary Hart and Barry Goldwater, "Recent False Alerts from the Nation's Missile Attack Warning System," October 9, 1980, 96th Congress, 2nd Session, U.S. Government Printing Office, p. 8.

263 *The Pentagon's classified:* Department of Defense "Fact Sheet," n.d. [circa June 7/8, 1980], National Security Archive, George Washington University, Electronic Briefing Book 371, "The 3 a.m. Phone Call," at http://nsarchive.gwu.edu/nuke vault/ebb371/.

263 *The Afghanistan invasion:* See, for instance, Graham Allison, "A Remarkable Realism on Afghanistan," *Los Angeles Times,* February 17, 1989.

264 *"There would be a . . .":* William Odom, "The Origins and Design of Presidential Decision-59: A Memoir," in Sokolski, ed., *Getting MAD,* p. 182.

264 *"We have an NCA . . .":* Odom to Brzezinski, "Meeting with the Vice President and Hugh Carter on the PEADs and FEMA," Remote Archives Capture (RAC) Program Collection, Jimmy Carter Presidential Library, May 14, 1979.

264 *That new strategy began with PD-57:* William Odom, "The Origins and Design of Presidential Decision-59: A Memoir," in Sokolski, ed., *Getting MAD,* p. 195.

265 *As one write-up of the exercise:* Thomas Powers, "Choosing a Strategy for World War III," *Atlantic Monthly,* November 1982, p. 95.

265 *The Federal Preparedness Agency:* Elmer B. Staats, "Continuity of the Federal Government in a Critical National Emergency—a Neglected Necessity," Comptroller General, Report to the Congress, April 27, 1978, p. i, at http://gao.gov/assets/130/122246.pdf.

265 *Like the PEADs, many emergency:* Ibid., p. 18.

265 *As Brzezinski wrote the president:* Brzezinski to Carter, "A Director for FEMA," Remote Archives Capture (RAC) Program Collection, Jimmy Carter Presidential Library, November 3, 1978.

265 *The board that oversees:* Elmer B. Staats, "Continuity of the Federal Government in a Critical National Emergency—a Neglected Necessity," Comptroller General, Report to the Congress, April 27, 1978, pp. 18–20, at http://gao.gov/assets/130/122246.pdf.

265 *An April 1978 GAO report:* Ibid., pp. 26–29.

266 *"Such major deficiencies . . .":* Ibid., pp. 39–40.

267 *"Authenticate," the watch officer:* See "Emergency Broadcast System, Standard Operating Procedures," Box 9, Folder "Emergency Broadcast System (5)," Ron Nessen Papers, Gerald R. Ford Presidential Library, at https://www.fordlibrarymuseum.gov/library/document/0204/7348021.pdf.

267 *Each warning point would:* Eric K. Federing, "If Washington Had to Be Evacuated—Today," unpublished manuscript, 1982. Materials now in author's personal collection. These details of the Washington, D.C., Crisis Relocation Plans were gathered in the 1980s by journalist Eric Federing, who wrote an extensive paper about the feasibility of the plans at the time. I'm deeply indebted to him for sharing his collected research and draft paper with me.

267 *Lieutenant Robert Hogan, New York's deputy:* Barasch, *Little Black Book of Atomic War,* p. 85.

267 *In 1979, New York City abandoned:* Sewell Chan, "Crackers Are Reminders of New York City's H-Bomb Fears," *New York Times,* March 26, 2006, at http://www.nytimes.com/2006/03/26/nyregion/26shelter.html.

268 *A Defense Science Board report:* "Declassified Pentagon History Provides Hair-Raising Scenarios of U.S. Vulnerabilities to Nuclear Attack through 1970s,"

National Security Archive, George Washington University, Electronic Briefing Book no. 403, November 19, 2012, at http://nsarchive.gwu.edu/nukevault/ebb403/.

268 *Brzezinski decided to die:* Charles Mohr, "Preserving U.S. Command After a Nuclear Attack," *New York Times,* June 29, 1982, at http://www.nytimes.com/1982/06/29/us/preserving-us-command-after-a-nuclear-attack.html?pagewanted=all.

269 *During World War II, the Smithsonian:* Rebecca Maksel, "In the Event of War," *Smithsonian,* April 30, 2007, at http://www.smithsonianmag.com/history/in-the-event-of-war-153775882/#WDUmJ7Grkv5qHkjG.99.

269 *There, after a secret 450-mile train trip to Asheville:* Bryan Mims, "Asheville's Fortress of Art: The Biltmore Estate," *Our State,* September 2014, http://www.ourstate.com/biltmore-estate-art/.

270 *The nation's Charters of Freedom:* Berges, ed., *Charters of Liberty,* p. 61.

270 *Even as the wreckage:* Daniels, *Frontier on the Potomac,* pp. 185–87.

271 *This time, though, it wanted:* While supplemented by my own reporting, many details of the Cultural Heritage Preservation Group were first reported by Ted Gup, "Grab That Leonardo!" *Time,* August 10, 1992, vol. 40, no. 6.

271 *In 1952, Harry Truman inaugurated:* Virginia Purdy, "A Temple to Clio: The National Archives Building," in Walch, ed., *Guardian of Heritage,* p. 27.

271 *By day, the three Charters:* "3 Documents to be Guarded by 50 Ton Safe," *Chicago Tribune,* November 26, 1952, at http://archives.chicagotribune.com/1952/11/26/page/25/article/3-documents-to-be-guarded-by-50-ton-safe#text.

271 *The Charters of Freedom, known to the Doomsday:* Ted Gup, "Grab That Leonardo!" *Time,* August 10, 1992, vol. 40, no. 6.

271 *Procedures were also put:* Alan Littell, "Williamstown Seems Picture Perfect," *Los Angeles Times,* July 2, 1989; Martha Schwendener, "Brotherly Art: The Clarks Who Collected," *New York Times,* May 25, 2007, at http://www.nytimes.com/2007/05/25/arts/design/25clar.html?pagewanted=print.

272 *Ultimately, it fell to Charles Parkhurst:* William Grimes, "Charles Parkhurst, Who Tracked Down Looted Art, Dies at 95," *New York Times,* June 28, 2008, at http://www.nytimes.com/2008/06/28/arts/design/28parkhurst.html.

272 *At the National Gallery, curators had settled:* Leonardo da Vinci, *Ginevra dé Benci,* c. 1474/1478, National Gallery of Art, at http://www.nga.gov/content/ngaweb/Collection/highlights/highlight50724.html.

272 *The first draft of the new evacuation:* Ted Gup, "FEMA," *Mother Jones,* January/February 1994.

274 *Just days after word:* Richard Burt, "Better Protection of Leaders in War Ordered by Carter," *New York Times,* August 12, 1980.

274 The New York Times *editorialized:* "Aiming Missiles, and Dodging Them, Unanswered Worries About Nuclear Targeting, Unanswerable Questions About Whom to Shelter," *New York Times,* August 13, 1980, p. A22.

274 *"Dear Mr. President . . .":* Russell Baker, *Lawrence Journal-World,* September 7,

1980, at https://news.google.com/newspapers?nid=2199&dat=19800907&id=BJ YyAAAAIBAJ&sjid=Q-cFAAAAIBAJ&pg=6581,1247989&hl=en.

274 *As William Odom lamented later:* William Odom, "The Origins and Design of Presidential Decision-59: A Memoir," in Sokolski, ed., *Getting MAD*, p. 175.

274 *In his final year, Carter had boosted:* "Declassified Pentagon History Provides Hair-Raising Scenarios of U.S. Vulnerabilities to Nuclear Attack through 1970s," National Security Archive, George Washington University, Electronic Briefing Book no. 403, November 19, 2012, at http://nsarchive.gwu.edu/nukevault/ebb403/.

275 *On the car phone, Baker said:* Bill Roeder, "Terrel Bell as Stand-by President," *Newsweek,* March 2, 1981.

275 *"The situation provides . . .":* "Memo from William D. Baird," Staff Office Files, Hugh Carter, Subject Files, Folder "Continuity of Gov't Concerns II," Jimmy Carter Presidential Library, July 7, 1989.

276 *There had been little love lost:* Carter, *Keeping Faith,* p. 577.

276 *The incoming and outgoing administrations:* Zuckerman, *Day After World War III,* p. 217.

276 *FEMA's Central Locator System:* "Communications-Electronics (C-E) Manager's Handbook," Department of the Air Force, October 1, 1999, p. 69, at http://nato .radioscanner.ru/files/article63/communications_elect.pdf.

276 *"In peacetime," FEMA's Keith Peterson:* Ed Zuckerman, "Mushroom," Alicia Patterson Foundation, 1981, at http://aliciapatterson.org/stories/mushroom.

277 *"The decision as to who would survive . . .":* "Undated Cover Note from Bud McFarlane to John Poindexter," Folder "Emergency Mobilization Preparedness Board, 1/11/1983–8/8/1983," Box 4, Executive Secretariat, NSC, Agency Files, Ronald Reagan Presidential Library.

277 *"If a successor got on . . .":* Louis Giuffrida, speech to the American Civil Defense Association, 1981, quoted in Zuckerman, *Day After World War III,* p. 65.

279 *White House Counsel Fred Fielding, and the vice president's chief of staff:* Richard V. Allen, "When Reagan Was Shot, Who Was 'in Control' at the White House?" *Washington Post,* March 25, 2011, at http://www.washingtonpost.com/opinions /when-reagan-was-shot-who-was-in-control-at-the-white-house/2011/03/23 /AFJlrfYB_story.html.

279 *That afternoon, as Air Force Two:* Alan Peppard, "Command and Control: Tested Under Fire," *Dallas Morning News,* May 13, 2015, at http://res.dallasnews.com /interactives/reagan-bush/?Src=longreads&utm_content=buffer1d8ef&utm _medium=social&utm_source=twitter.com&utm_campaign=buffer.

279 *As upset as Haig's demeanor made:* Ibid.

280 *"About two minutes closer . . .":* Richard V. Allen, "The Day Reagan Was Shot," *Atlantic,* April 2001, at http://www.theatlantic.com/magazine/archive/2001/04 /the-day-reagan-was-shot/308396/.

281 *One anonymous national security official:* Stewart W. Taylor, "Disabling of Reagan

Provokes a Debate Over Nuclear Authority in Such Cases," *New York Times,* April 4, 1981, at http://www.nytimes.com/1981/04/04/us/disabling-of-reagan -provokes-a-debate-over-nuclear-authority-in-such-cases.html.

282 *President Reagan spent nearly two weeks:* Ronald Reagan, "The President's News Conference," January 29, 1981, John T. Woolley and Gerhard Peters, *American Presidency Project,* at http://www.presidency.ucsb.edu/ws/?pid=44101.

282 *As Oleg Gordievsky, a senior KGB official:* Andrew and Gordievsky, *Comrade Kryuchkov's Instructions,* p. 67.

282 *As Turner said, "We'll be on . . .":* "Signoff," *New Yorker,* September 12, 1988, p. 25; see also Michael Ballaban, "This Is the Video CNN Will Play When the World Ends," *Jalopnik,* January 5, 2015, at http://jalopnik.com/this-is-the-video-cnn -will-play-when-the-world-ends-1677511538.

283 *Another major catalyst for the disarmament:* Schell, *Fate of the Earth,* p. 143.

283 *On the state and local level:* Cannon, *President Reagan,* p. 181.

284 *"Only a few minutes later . . .":* Anderson, *Revolution,* p. 81.

284 *In the day's final discussion:* Ibid., pp. 82–83.

284 *The military's brightest minds:* FitzGerald, *Way Out There in the Blue,* p. 116.

284 *Later that month, Reagan signed NSDD 13:* Ronald Reagan, "Nuclear Weapons Employment Policy," National Security Decision, Directive no. 13, at http://fas .org/irp/offdocs/nsdd/nsdd-13.pdf.

285 *In 1975, the journalist wife:* Zuckerman, *Day After World War III,* p. 250.

285 *As committee member and NSC aide Richard Pipes explained:* Ronald Reagan, "The President's News Conference," October 1, 1981, John T. Woolley and Gerhard Peters, *American Presidency Project,* at http://www.presidency.ucsb.edu /ws/?pid=44327.

286 *Reagan's conclusion was actually:* Andrew Cockburn, "Sure, But What About the Russkies?: Hard Facts About the Soviet Nuclear Threat," *Mother Jones,* September/ October 1982.

286 *Once aloft, the head of the Joint Chiefs:* See http://valor.militarytimes.com/recipient .php?recipientid=24331.

287 *On March 1, 1982, Reagan observed:* "Reagan as Military Commander," *New York Times,* January 15, 1984, at http://www.nytimes.com/1984/01/15/magazine/reagan -as-military-commander.html?pagewanted=all.

288 *"The strategy for reconstitution . . .":* Howard Rosenberg, "Who Gets Saved?" *Washingtonian,* November 1982, p. 117.

288 *Other participating "survivors" included:* "The Doomsday Exercise," *Newsweek,* April 5, 1982.

288 *"After President Reagan watched someone . . .":* "Reagan as Military Commander," *New York Times,* January 15, 1984, at http://www.nytimes.com/1984/01/15/mag azine/reagan-as-military-commander.html?pagewanted=all.

288 *Most of the staff involved:* Pringle and Arkin, *S.I.O.P.,* p. 36.

288 *"We probably would not reconstitute . . .":* Zuckerman, *Day After World War III,* p. 233.

289 *By the fall of 1982, Leonid Brezhnev:* Associated Press, "Brezhnev Cites U.S. 'Threat'; Calls for Soviet Arms Buildup," *Lawrence Journal-World,* October 28, 1982, at https://news.google.com/newspapers?nid=2199&dat=19821028&id=bZky AAAAIBAJ&sjid=VugFAAAAIBAJ&pg=6633,5671202&hl=en.

289 *"It was horrifying at the time . . .":* Robert Scheer, "U.S. Could Survive War in Administration's View," *Los Angeles Times,* January 16, 1982, p. A1.

290 *Around the same time, an official:* Schell, *Fate of the Earth,* p. 7.

290 *In March 1983, Reagan unveiled:* Ronald Reagan, "Address to the Nation on Defense and National Security," White House speech, March 23, 1983, at http://www.reagan.utexas.edu/archives/speeches/1983/32383d.htm.

290 *The Soviets strongly objected:* Shultz, *Turmoil and Triumph,* p. 256.

291 *"SDI was a Soviet nightmare . . .":* Gates, *From the Shadows,* p. 264.

292 *On June 16, 1983, Yuri Andropov reported:* Andrew and Gordievsky, *Comrade Kryuchkov's Instructions,* p. 81.

292 *That same month, Andropov warned:* "Memorandum of Conversation, Meeting with CPSU General Secretary Andropov, CPSU Central Committee Headquarters, Moscow," Collections of the Manuscript Division, Library of Congress, Washington, D.C., June 2, 1983, at http://nsarchive.gwu.edu/NSAEBB/NSAEBB426 /docs/14.%20Memorandum%20of%20Covnersation%20between%20Gen%20 Sec%20Andropov%20and%20Averell%20Harriman-June%202,%201983.pdf.

292 *SAC bombers had been regularly:* Schweizer, *Victory,* p. 8.

292 *The Oko early-warning:* David Hoffman, "I Had a Funny Feeling in My Gut," *Washington Post,* February 10, 1999, p. A19, at http://www.washingtonpost.com /wp-srv/inatl/longterm/coldwar/shatter021099b.htm.

293 *The year-old Oko system:* Geoffrey Forden, Pavel Podvig, and Theodore A. Postol, "False Alarm, Nuclear Danger," *IEEE Spectrum,* vol. 37, no. 3 (March 2000), at http://russianforces.org/podvig/2000/03/false_alarm_nuclear_danger.shtml.

293 *A later investigation found:* "Text of Soviet Statement on Relations with U.S.," *New York Times,* September 29, 1983, at http://www.nytimes.com/1983/09/29/world /text-of-soviet-statement-on-relations-with-us.html.

293 *On November 5th, the KGB alerted:* Nate Jones, "British Documents Confirm UK Alerted US to Danger of Able Archer 83," National Security Archive, George Washington University, at https://nsarchive.wordpress.com/2013/11/04/british -documents-confirm-uk-alerted-us-to-danger-of-able-archer-83/.

294 *"These war games brought . . .":* Fischer, *Reagan Reversal,* p. 121.

294 *Just as the briefings had been:* Gates, *From the Shadows,* p. 264.

294 *The briefing was, Reagan wrote:* The date of Reagan's SIOP briefing is usually stated as having taken place in late October (see, for instance, Fischer, *Reagan Reversal,* p. 120), but according to his own diary and the White House calendar, it happened in late November. This difference is significant.

294 *The two-hour movie:* Reagan, *Reagan Diaries,* p. 186.

294 *"It is powerfully done . . .":* Morris, *Dutch,* p. 498.

295   *"The danger which . . ."*: George Church, "Men of the Year: Ronald Reagan and Yuri Andropov," *Time*, January 2, 1984, vol. 123, no. 1, p. 14.

295   *Indeed, to too many people:* Ibid.

295   *That tense fall of 1983 caused Reagan:* This evolution and the fall of 1983 is covered in depth in Fischer's *Reagan Reversal*.

295   *"Nuclear abolition" became:* Ronald Reagan, "Inaugural Address," January 21, 1985, John T. Woolley and Gerhard Peters, *American Presidency Project*, at http://www .presidency.ucsb.edu/ws/?pid=38688.

295   *The* New York Times *obituary:* Serge Schmemann, "Chernenko Is Dead in Moscow at 73; Gorbachev Succeeds Him and Urges Arms Control and Economic Vigor," *New York Times*, March 11, 1985, at http://www.nytimes.com/learning/general /onthisday/big/0310.html#headlines.

296   *Reagan said:* Gaddis, *Cold War*, pp. 228–29; for more background on Gorbachev's rise, I recommend Kaiser's excellent book *Why Gorbachev Happened*.

297   *Attorney General Ed Meese:* Mann, *Rise of the Vulcans*, p. 140.

298   *The relocation teams consisted:* Ibid.

298   *A COG alert would have begun:* Howard Rosenberg, "Who Gets Saved?" *Washingtonian*, November 1982, pp. 112–13.

299   *"It's kind of mind-boggling . . .":* Zuckerman, *Day After World War III*, p. 223.

300   *The Department of Labor's National Office Alerting Plan:* Ibid., p. 230.

300   *The Health and Human Services emergency:* Ibid., p. 223.

300   *The USDA was allotted sixty-two slots:* Ibid., p. 221.

301   *Other agencies and departments:* Howard Rosenberg, "Who Gets Saved?" *Washingtonian*, November 1982, p. 115.

301   *As for where all the relocated employees:* Zuckerman, *Day After World War III*, p. 225.

301   *"We can deliver the first . . .":* "Master Mobilization Plan," May 1988, Office of the Assistant Secretary of Defense, p. 34, at http://biotech.law.lsu.edu/blaw/dodd /corres/pdf/302036p_0588/p302036p.pdf.

301   *Altogether, the Pentagon's:* Howard Rosenberg, "Who Gets Saved?" *Washingtonian*, November 1982, pp. 107, 116.

301   *To keep the government functioning:* Zuckerman, *Day After World War III*, p. 235.

301   *Regulations were written:* Ibid., p. 234.

302   *One of the IRS studies calculated:* Eugene J. McCarthy, "The IRS' Plan for the Hereafter," *Washington Post*, August 15, 1982, at https://www.washingtonpost.com /archive/opinions/1982/08/15/the-irs-plan-for-the-hereafter/112a3757-d222 –43fd-96ed-6b3d47f3eaa4/?utm_term=.06e1f03703d5.

303   *Separately, the nation's satellite network:* "Plan for the Emergency Security Control of Air Traffic (ESCAT)," Advisory Circular, Federal Aviation Administration, January 18, 2007, at http://www.faa.gov/documentLibrary/media/Advisory_Cir cular/AC_99–1D.pdf.

303   *To help evaluate the reports:* Zuckerman, *Day After World War III*, p. 212.

303   *Nearly every conceivable statistic:* Ibid., p. 213.

303 *FEMA concluded that:* "Recovery from Nuclear Attack," Federal Emergency Management Agency, FEMA 160, October 1988, p. 2, at http://www.defconwarning system.com/documents/recovery_from_nuclear_attack.pdf.

303 *President Reagan personally intervened:* "Monitoring Overseas Direct Employment (MODE) and Civil Defense," Cabinet Room, National Security Council Meeting, December 3, 1981, at http://www.thereaganfiles.com/19811203-nsc-27 .pdf. See also "Editorial Note," Document #110, *Foreign Relations of the United States, 1981–1988, vol. 3, Soviet Union, January 1981–January 1983,* U.S. Government Publishing Office, 2016, at https://history.state.gov/historicaldocuments /frus1981–88v03/d110.

304 *That night, though, Reagan wrote:* Reagan, *Reagan Diaries,* p. 52.

304 *In the months that followed, FEMA and the government:* "Collected Papers Relating to Project 908," released under FOIA, p. 128, at https://archive.org/details /Project908.

304 *In Arkansas, agents lined up:* Ibid., p. 14.

304 *In Geneva, Alabama, agents selected:* Ibid., pp. 59, 80, 134, and 151.

304 *The owner responded enthusiastically:* Ibid.

305 *If a building owner proved amenable:* Ibid., p. 14.

305 *Such strategic warning:* Quoted in Zuckerman, *Day After World War III,* p. 98.

305 *Under FEMA's plans, the agency:* "The Last Movie," Conelrad Adjacent, December 19, 2010, at http://conelrad.blogspot.com/2010/12/last-movie.html.

306 *As one FEMA official explained:* Zuckerman, *Day After World War III,* p. 101.

306 *Next came the evacuation instructions:* Ed Zuckerman, "The Last Picture Show," Alicia Patterson Foundation, APF Fellow 1981, April 4, 2011, at http://aliciapat terson.org/stories/last-picture-show.

306 *The ads and brochures in Plattsburgh:* Ibid.

306 *However impractical in reality:* Details are from Walmer E. Strope and Clark Henderson, "Crisis Relocation of the Population at Risk in the New York Metropolitan Area," *SRI International,* September 1978, at http://www.dtic.mil/get-tr-doc /pdf?AD=ADA061097.

307 *Hal Silvers, the head of civil defense planning:* Margaret Engel, "Civil Defense: Thinking About the Unthinkable," *Washington Post,* November 12, 1981, p. B1.

307 *Under the final CRP:* Federing, "Collected Research and Notes of Eric Federing," Author's Personal Collection, p. 16.

308 *At multiple intersections:* Ibid., p. 72.

308 *As the urban evacuations proceeded:* Wickham and Tiedemann, *Utilization of Equipment Crisis Relocation Program,* pp. 14–15.

308 *In an emergency, the U.S. government:* Zuckerman, *Day After World War III,* p. 109.

309 *On paper everything looked neat:* "What Would Nuclear War Mean for Middlebury College?" *Middlebury College Magazine,* Spring 1982, p. 28.

309 *"Damned foolishness . . .":* "Annual Report of the Town of Barrington, New Hampshire," 1982, p. I-13, at https://archive.org/details/annualreportofto1982barr.

309 *"It wouldn't surprise me . . .":* Federing, "Collected Research and Notes of Eric Federing," Author's Personal Collection, p. 91.

310 *These tense questions around integration:* Ronald Reagan, "Nomination of Louis O. Giuffrida to Be Director of the Federal Emergency Management Agency," February 24, 1981, John T. Woolley and Gerhard Peters, *American Presidency Project,* at http://www.presidency.ucsb.edu/ws/?pid=43453.

310 *"There could be a lot of opposition . . .":* Federing, "Collected Research and Notes of Eric Federing," Author's Personal Collection, p. 9.

310 *A FEMA study, done just:* National Capitol Systems Inc., "Special Problems of Blacks and Other Minorities in Large Scale Population Relocation," Work Unit 4821H, Federal Emergency Management Agency, Washington, D.C., January 1981.

311 *"And at the end we had . . .":* Tim Weiner, "Pentagon Book for Doomsday Is to Be Closed," *New York Times,* April 18, 1994, at http://www.nytimes.com/1994/04/18/us/pentagon-book-for-doomsday-is-to-be-closed.html.

311 *With the $18 billion the Reagan administration:* John D. Steinbruner, "Nuclear Decapitation," *Foreign Policy,* no. 45 (Winter 1981–1982): 25.

311 *On August 25, 1981, NORAD established:* "A Brief History of NORAD," Office of History, North American Aerospace Defense Command, p. 24, at http://www.norad.mil/Portals/29/Documents/A%20Brief%20History%20of%20NORAD%20(current%20as%20of%20March%202014).pdf.

311 *It also established its first airborne:* Maj. Greg Olgetree, "History of the 3rd Airborne Command and Control Squadron," *Strategic Air Command Airborne Command Control Association Newsletter,* vol. 3, no. 3 (December 1997), at http://www.sac-acca.org/newsletter/flyer1297.pdf.

311 *Nearby Peterson Air Force Base:* "21st Space Wing," 21st Space Wing: Heritage of Honor, p. 30, at http://www.chambleyab.com/PDF%20Files/21st%20Wing%20History.pdf.

311 *As Defense Secretary Weinberger said:* Quoted in Zuckerman, *Day After World War III,* p. 65.

311 *SAC created the Headquarters Emergency Relocation Team:* Tim Weiner, "Secret Stash," *Mother Jones,* March/April 1992, p. 26.

312 *The tractor-trailer plan:* Steve Emerson, "America's Doomsday Project," *U.S. News and World Report,* August 7, 1989, p. 28.

312 *FEMA created its own mobile command:* Tim Weiner, "A Growing 'Black Budget' Pays for Secret Weapons, Covert War," *Philadelphia Inquirer,* February 8, 1987, p. A01.

312 *Meanwhile, a network:* Ibid.

312 *In Alaska, the push for greater command:* TSgt William J. Allen, "An Ace in the Hole: A Study of Alaska's Railmobile Command Post," Eleventh Air Control Wing, Elmendorf Consolidated History Office, Elmendorf AFB, Alaska, January 13, 1993.

313 *Early in his White House tenure:* "Secret FEMA Plan Gets Priority," (Fort Lauderdale) *Sun Sentinel,* February 22, 1993, at http://articles.sun-sentinel.com/1993 -02-22/news/9301110256_1_natural-disasters-fema-nuclear-war.

314 *The COG plan, known as* TREETOP: See, for instance, William Odom, Memorandum for the Record, "COG/C3I Working Group Meeting," Remote Archives Capture (RAC) Program Collection, Jimmy Carter Presidential Library, December 7, 1979.

314 *Under PS3, which traced its roots:* Eric Schmitt, "Presidents' Plan to Name Successors Skirted Law," *New York Times,* November 18, 1991, at http://www.ny times.com/1991/11/18/us/presidents-plan-to-name-successors-skirted-law .html; see also "Secret Government Succession Plans," *CNN Special Assignment,* Cable News Network, July 15, 2008, at https://www.youtube.com/watch ?v=ZgpgJPxenFo#t=19.

314 *As the classified memo:* Memo from [Redacted] to William Odom, "Selection and Responsibilities of Potential DCI Successors on Presidential Successor Support Teams," Remote Archives Capture (RAC) Program Collection, Jimmy Carter Presidential Library, December 4, 1979.

315 *The PS3 teams could call up:* "Master Mobilization Plan," May 1988, Office of the Assistant Secretary of Defense, p. 53, at http://biotech.law.lsu.edu/blaw/dodd /corres/pdf/302036p_0588/p302036p.pdf.

315 *CNN, which first broke word:* David Lewis, "Doomsday Government," *CNN Special Assignment,* Cable News Network, November 17, 1991.

315 *The plan called for:* "Secret 'Armageddon Plan' in Motion on 9/11," *Nightline,* ABC News, April 25, 2004, at http://abcnews.go.com/Nightline/story?id=12 8993&page=1.

316 *The supposed secrecy around:* Larry Margasak, "FEMA Chief Denies Mismanagement Charges," Associated Press, March 5, 1985, at http://www.apnewsarchive .com/1985/FEMA-Chief-Denies-Mismanagement-Charges/id-0b773aa04e5a8 cb4af6771d539b37687.

316 *Just a year after the new ID cards:* Zuckerman, *Day After World War III,* p. 225.

316 *At great expense:* Howard Rosenberg, "Who Gets Saved?" *Washingtonian,* November 1982, p. 113.

317 *"I do believe Congress . . .":* David Lewis, "Doomsday Government," *CNN Special Assignment,* Cable News Network, November 17, 1991.

317 *Golden eventually went to:* Steve Emerson, "America's Doomsday Project," *U.S. News and World Report,* August 7, 1989.

317 *Congressman Jack Brooks grilled North:* "Iran-Contra Hearings; North's Testimony: 'Fall Guy' and Foreign Policy," *New York Times,* July 15, 1987, at http://www.ny times.com/1987/07/14/world/iran-contra-hearings-north-s-testimony-fall-guy -and-foreign-policy.html?pagewanted=all.

318 *In what turned out to be:* Walter Sullivan, "How Huge Antenna Can Broadcast into the Silence of the Sea," *New York Times,* October 13, 1981, at http://www.nytimes

.com/1981/10/13/science/how-huge-antenna-can-broadcast-into-the-silence
-of-the-sea.html?pagewanted=all.

318　*The original iteration of Project SANGUINE:* Carlos Altgelt, "The World's Largest 'Radio' Station," at https://www.scribd.com/document/145107136/THE
-WORLD-S-LARGEST-RADIO-STATION-CARLOS-A-ALTGELT.

319　*Together, the system, estimated:* For more SEAFARER history and information,
see the "SEAFARER Extremely Low Frequency (ELF) Submarine Command and
Control Communications System Records," MSS-249, Central Upper Peninsula
and Northern Michigan University Archives, Northern Michigan University, at
http://www.nmu.edu/archives/sites/DrupalArchives/files/UserFiles/MSS-249.html.

319　*To prove the concept:* "Extremely Low Frequency Transmitter Site Clam Lake Wisconsin," Navy Fact File, Department of the Navy, June 28, 2001, at http://fas.org
/nuke/guide/usa/c3i/fs_clam_lake_elf2003.pdf.

319　*With billions flooding into:* Ibid.

319　*It seemed a new world:* Meacham, *Destiny and Power,* p. 404.

320　*Dick Cheney, as George H. W. Bush's defense:* Eric Schmitt, "U.S. Curtails 24-Hour
Duty of Its Flying Command Post," *New York Times,* July 28, 1990, at http://www
.nytimes.com/1990/07/28/us/us-curtails-24-hour-duty-of-its-flying-command
-post.html.

320　*A month later in Omaha:* Robert S. Norris and William Arkin, "Silk Purse Abandoned," *Bulletin of the Atomic Scientists,* vol. 47, no. 7 (September 1991): 48.

320　*On September 27, President Bush:* "Bush's Arms Plan; Remarks by President Bush on
Reducing U.S. and Soviet Nuclear Weapons," *New York Times,* September 28, 1991,
at http://www.nytimes.com/1991/09/28/us/bush-s-arms-plan-remarks-president
-bush-reducing-us-soviet-nuclear-weapons.html.

320　*The next morning, on September 28:* Author Tom Clancy had written earlier that
year that the new facility "had been built because Hollywood's rendition of such
rooms was better than the one SAC had originally built for itself, and the Air
Force had decided to alter its reality to fit a fictional image" (*The Sum of All Fears,*
New York: Putnam, 1991, p. 715).

320　*On October 21, 1991, President Bush:* G. H. W. Bush, *All the Best,* p. 539.

320　*"With the Cold War over . . .":* "Survival Center No Longer Secret," *Tulsa World,*
November 29, 1991, at http://www.tulsaworld.com/archives/survival-center-no
-longer-secret/article_2243fca1-d165–58d2–891d-f3ebcf81fb68.html.

321　*"I can assure you . . .":* Meacham, *Destiny and Power,* p. 495.

321　*At Raven Rock, the bunker:* "Underground Pentagon's Air Conditioning Improved,"
Gettysburg Times, July 18, 1990, at http://news.google.com/newspapers?id=RocyA
AAAIBAJ&sjid=kOYFAAAAIBAJ&pg=6889,1650110&dq=underground-pen
tagon&hl=en.

321　*"You'd feel like you're walking . . .":* David C. Morrison, "And Not a Single Bang for
Their Bucks," *National Journal,* August 13, 1994, p. 1924.

324　*On June 1, Speaker Tom Foley:* Kenneth J. Cooper, "Foley Urges Closing W.Va.

Bomb Shelter," *Washington Post,* June 3, 1992, at https://www.washingtonpost
.com/archive/politics/1992/06/03/foley-urges-closing-wva-bomb-shelter/cb16
0411-e3cb-4bf6–8f8a-de5a82a181ef/.

324 *"They are realizing these requirements . . .":* Tim Weiner, "Pentagon Book for
Doomsday Is to Be Closed," *New York Times,* April 18, 1994, at http://www.ny
times.com/1994/04/18/us/pentagon-book-for-doomsday-is-to-be-closed.html.

324 *Other agencies mothballed:* David C. Morrison, "And Not a Single Bang for Their
Bucks," *National Journal,* August 13, 1994, p. 1924.

326 *By the time George W. Bush:* Scott Higham, "FEMA Chief Brings Order Out of
Chaos," *Baltimore Sun,* July 24, 1995, at http://articles.baltimoresun.com/1995
–07–24/news/1995205004_1_fema-mcmillion-witt/2.

326 *Leo Bosner, a former FEMA union:* Ibid.

326 *The agency manual, version 1010.1:* John W. Magaw, "FEMA Manual 1010.1,"
Office of Policy and Regional Operations, Washington, D.C., February 1, 2001, at
http://www.fema.gov/pdf/library/1010_1.pdf.

326 *Twice a day, at 7:35 a.m. Greenwich Mean Time:* "WSOM Chapter D-42, Fallout
Winds," U.S. Department of Commerce, National Oceanic and Atmospheric Administration, National Weather Service, November 6, 1981, at http://www.nws
.noaa.gov/wsom/manual/archives/ND428119.HTML. See also http://www.nws
.noaa.gov/directives/sym/pd01005018curr.pdf.

328 *That September, the U.S. watched:* "Russian Warplanes Harass U.S. Craft Over Pacific," *Washington Times,* September 11, 2001, at http://m.washingtontimes.com
/news/2001/sep/11/20010911–025331–4897r/.

328 *The day was scheduled to be busy:* Kevin Simpson, "Rearmed Forces: 9/11 Changed
Military Life in Colorado," *Denver Post,* August 27, 2011, at http://www.denver
post.com/news/ci_18768543.

329 *While normally a quiet shift:* Memorandum for Record, "Kevin's NORAD HQ
Notes: Interview with Lt. General Findley," available at: https://www.archives
.gov/declassification/iscap/pdf/2011–048-doc38.pdf; see also "Memorandum for
the Record (MFR) of an Interview with Edward Eberhart of NORAD," Item
261038, Record Group 148, Records of Commissions of the Legislative Branch,
1928–2007, National Archives, College Park, Maryland, at https://catalog.ar
chives.gov/id/2610387.

329 *Following standard hijacking procedure:* Miles Kara, "Memorandum for the
Record (MFR) of a Visit to 119th Fighter Wing of the U.S. Air Force Conducted by Team 8," Record Group 148, Records of Commissions of the Legislative Branch, 1928–2007, October 7, 2003, at https://catalog.archives.gov/id/26
10272?q=2610272.

329 *The two F-15s in Massachusetts:* "Interview of Larry K. Arnold," November 19,
2001, National Guard Bureau, Air Guard History, pp. 4–6, at https://www.ar
chives.gov/declassification/iscap/pdf/2012–042-doc2.pdf.

330 *NORAD's radars faced outward:* NORAD and USNORTHCOM, "In Their Own

Words—NORAD Members Recall September 11: Steve Armstrong,"North American Aerospace Defense Command, NORAD News, September 9, 2011, at http://www.norad.mil/Newsroom/tabid/3170/Article/578477/in-their-own-words-norad-members-recall-september-11-steve-armstrong.aspx.

330   *"All the information we were getting . . .":* Bradley Graham, "Pentagon Crash Scenario Was Rejected for Military Exercise," *Washington Post,* April 14, 2004.

330   *No one told the Langley pilots:* Thomas H. Kean and Lee Hamilton et al., *The 9/11 Commission Report: Final Report of the National Commission on Terrorist Attacks Upon the United States.* Washington, D.C., National Commission on Terrorist Attacks upon the United States, 2004, p. 45, at http://avalon.law.yale.edu/sept11/911Report.pdf.

330   *As they finally were rerouted:* Filson, *Air War Over America,* p. 68.

331   *"I was sitting there thinking . . .":* Evan Thomas, "The Day That Changed America," *Newsweek,* December 30, 2001, at http://www.newsweek.com/day-changed-america-148319.

331   *"He put his hand on my shoulder . . .":* Hayes, *Cheney,* p. 333.

332   *"What I was immediately . . .":* Ibid., p. 335.

332   *Aide Mary Matalin was so unfamiliar:* "Mary Matalin on September 11, 2001," C-SPAN, July 26, 2011, at http://www.c-span.org/video/?300727–1/mary-matalin-september-11–2001&start=2685.

333   *Outside, U.S. Park Police captain Sal Lauro:* McDonnell, *National Park Service,* p. 16.

333   *Worried about further attacks:* Aiden Monaghan, "FOIA, U.S. Secret Service Memos and Timelines,"U.S. Department of Homeland Security, April 23, 2010, at https://www.scribd.com/doc/30764772/Monaghan-FOIA-USSS-Memos-and-Timelines.

334   *In the classroom, arranged:* "History of STU-III," at http://www.cryptomuseum.com/crypto/usa/stu3/#911.

334   *"I've never seen a plane . . .":* "Clear of Skies," episode transcript, *Carte Blanche,* original air date September 8, 2002, at http://web.archive.org/web/20030116190007/http://www.mnet.co.za/carteblanche/display/Display.asp?Id=2063.

335   *"We were following a Cold War . . .":* Philip Sherwell, "9/11: How the Drama Unfolded Aboard Air Force One, Inside the White House Bunker and at the Pentagon," *Telegraph,* September 10, 2011, at http://www.telegraph.co.uk/news/worldnews/september-11-attacks/8754394/911-How-the-drama-unfolded-in-the-skies-and-underground.html.

335   *Mike Morell, the CIA briefer:* For a more in-depth account of being aboard Air Force One on September 11, 2001, see Garrett M. Graff, "We're the Only Plane in the Sky," *Politico,* September 9, 2016, at http://www.politico.com/magazine/story/2016/09/were-the-only-plane-in-the-sky-214230; for a more detailed account of what happened inside the White House PEOC bunker, see Darling, *24 Hours Inside the President's Bunker.*

335   *NEACP's takeoff just six minutes:* Farmer, *Ground Truth,* p. 372, fn. 206.

335 *At 9:52 a.m., CNN's John King:* "The White House Has Been Evacuated," CNN .com Transcripts, September 11, 2001, at http://transcripts.cnn.com/TRAN SCRIPTS/0109/11/bn.06.html.

336 *"And that plane flew off . . .":* "Secret 'Armageddon Plan' in Motion on 9/11," *Nightline,* ABC News, April 25, 2004, at http://abcnews.go.com/Nightline /story?id=128993&page=1.

337 *"The exercise is designed . . .":* Ibid.

337 *Who exactly activated COG:* "September 11, 2001, 'Tic Toc' of Significant Events," The White House, at https://www.scribd.com/doc/12992821/Brief-Timeline-of -Day-of-9–11-Events-drafted-by-White-House.

338 *Throughout the morning, the speaker:* Hastert, *Speaker,* p. 2.

338 *For his part, the eighty-three-year-old Senator:* Byrd, *Losing America,* p. 13.

338 *The rest of Congress improvised:* Dan Balz and Bob Woodward, "America's Chaotic Road to War," *Washington Post,* January 27, 2002, p. A01, at http://www.washing tonpost.com/wp-dyn/content/article/2006/07/18/AR2006071801175_pf.html.

338 *"We had no clue . . .":* "Former Senate Majority Leader Tom Daschle on September 11, 2001," C-SPAN, July 27, 2011, at http://www.c-span.org/video/?300751–1 /former-senate-majority-leader-tom-daschle-september-11–2001.

339 *"[My security detail] was instructing . . .":* Ibid.

339 *The vice president's order:* "Telephone Interview of Mrs. Cheney by Newsweek Magazine," White House, Office of the Vice President, November 9, 2001, at https://www.scribd.com/doc/16942240/NY-B10-Farmer-Misc-WH-3-of-3 -Fdr-11–9–01-Newsweek-Interview-of-Mrs-Cheney-482.

339 *As she listened to Cheney:* Evan Thomas, "The Day That Changed America," *Newsweek,* December 30, 2001, at http://www.newsweek.com/day-changed-america -148319.

339 *Vice President Cheney finally connected:* Farmer, *Ground Truth,* p. 185.

340 *Transportation Secretary Norm Mineta:* Ibid., p. 257.

340 *The rumor of a plane:* Draper, *Dead Certain,* p. 142.

341 *The videoconference Clarke ran that morning:* "Voices of 9–11: 'A Cacophony of Information,'" *National Journal,* August 31, 2002.

341 *When CNN reported that a car bomb:* Clarke, *Against All Enemies,* p. 9.

341 *"Once I realized we had . . .":* "Clear of Skies," episode transcript, *Carte Blanche,* original air date September 8, 2002, at http://web.archive.org/web/20030116190007 /http://www.mnet.co.za/carteblanche/display/Display.asp?Id=2063.

342 *As Captain Charles Leidig would recall later:* "Memorandum for the Record (MFR) of an Interview with Charles Joseph Leidig of the Department of Defense Conducted by Team 8," Record Group 148, Records of Commissions of the Legislative Branch, 1928–2007, April 29, 2004, at https://catalog.archives.gov/id/2610279.

342 *At 10:52 a.m., an Emergency Action Message:* Filson, *Air War Over America,* pp. 74 and 95.

343 *Allbaugh, who had been appointed to FEMA:* Philip Shenon, "White House Battles

Cuts in Spending for Disasters," *New York Times,* June 21, 2001, at http://www
.nytimes.com/2001/06/21/us/white-house-battles-cuts-in-spending-for-disas
ters.html.

343   *"I thought it was a movie . . .":* "America's New War: Healing the Wound in America's Heart," *Larry King Live,* CNN.com Transcripts, October 4, 2001, at http://
www.cnn.com/TRANSCRIPTS/0110/04/lkl.00.html.

343   *Hotel staff brought in extra TVs:* "Edward F. Jacoby Jr., Memorandum to Governor
George E. Pataki," Connecticut State Library, State Archives, Governor John G.
Rowlands Records, Box 48, Folder 6, September 14, 2001, at http://cslib.con
tentdm.oclc.org/cdm/ref/collection/p15019coll5/id/144.

343   *Some 40 other emergency managers:* Emily DeMers, "The Long Way Home," *State
Government News,* October 2001, p. 18, at http://www.csg.org/knowledgecenter
/docs/sgn0110LongWayHome.pdf.

343   *Officials at FEMA's Region II office:* Jim Miller, "Memorandum for the Record
(MFR) of the Interview of Richard Ohlsen of the Federal Emergency Management Agency Conducted by Team 8," Record Group 148, Records of Commissions of the Legislative Branch, 1928–2007, March 16, 2004, at https://catalog
.archives.gov/id/2610505?q=2610505.

344   *Once inside the NYPD's command post:* Ibid.

345   *at one point in the PEOC:* Evan Thomas, "The Day That Changed America," *Newsweek,* December 30, 2001, at http://www.newsweek.com/day-changed-america
-148319.

345   *"It's important to emphasize . . .":* David Kohn, "The President's Story," *60 Minutes,*
CBS News, September 11, 2002, at http://www.cbsnews.com/news/the-presidents
-story-11–09–2002/.

346   *"The building shook . . .":* Goldberg et al., *Pentagon 9/11,* p. 130.

346   *Cheney later told a friend:* David Von Drehle, "Wrestling with History," *Washington Post,* November 13, 2005, at https://www.washingtonpost.com/archive
/lifestyle/magazine/2005/11/13/wrestling-with-history/22e30ed2–4a24–460a
-b6f4–5822b0787563/.

346   *"I kept saying . . .":* Cockburn, *Rumsfeld,* p. 2.

347   *Paul D. Wolfowitz, the deputy defense secretary:* "Deputy Secretary Wolfowitz Interview with Sam Tannenhaus, *Vanity Fair,*" News Transcripts, U.S. Department
of Defense, May 9, 2003, at http://archive.defense.gov/Transcripts/Transcript
.aspx?TranscriptID=2594.

347   *"We had things to do and business to conduct . . .":* "Vice President Dick Cheney
Interview with Tim Russert on NBC *Meet the Press,*" PatriotResource.com,
September 16, 2001, at http://www.patriotresource.com/wtc/federal/0916/VPN
BC2.html.

347   *Since there'd be no evacuation:* Vogel, *Pentagon,* p. 454.

347   *As Wolfowitz recalled:* Goldberg et al., *Pentagon 9/11,* p. 132.

347   *Vice President Cheney gave essentially:* "Vice President Dick Cheney Interview with

Tim Russert on NBC *Meet the Press*," PatriotResource.com, September 16, 2001, at http://www.patriotresource.com/wtc/federal/0916/VPNBC2.html.

348 *Sometime between 9:30 and 10:30 a.m:* David A. Sanger and Don Van Natta Jr., "After the Attacks: The Events; In Four Days, a National Crisis Changes Bush's Presidency," *New York Times,* September 16, 2001, at http://www.nytimes.com/2001/09/16/us/after-attacks-events-four-days-national-crisis-changes-bush-s-presidency.html?pagewanted=all.

349 *"It was very clear that they . . .":* "Post-Attack Tremors," *Moments of Crisis,* ABC News.com, September 15, 2001, at http://web.archive.org/web/20020916203833/http://abcnews.go.com/onair/DailyNews/sept11_moments_4.html.

349 *Tillman asked for an armed guard:* Ibid.

350 *"I recognized that part . . .":* G. W. Bush, *Decision Points,* p. 130.

350 *"That's crap . . .":* Evan Thomas, "The Day That Changed America," *Newsweek,* December 1, 2001, at http://www.newsweek.com/day-changed-america-148319.

350 *As Senator William Fulbright:* Mary Meehan, "The Flying Fuhrerbunker," *Washington Monthly,* vol. 6, no. 2 (April 1976): 22.

351 *As he recalled, "I went up . . .":* "Deputy Secretary Wolfowitz Interview with Sam Tannenhaus, *Vanity Fair,*" News Transcripts, U.S. Department of Defense, May 9, 2003, at http://archive.defense.gov/Transcripts/Transcript.aspx?TranscriptID=2594.

351 *Wolfowitz reported, "The computer . . .":* Goldberg et al., *Pentagon 9/11,* 2049.

351 *Libby and Cheney's counsel David Addington told:* Evan Thomas, "The Day That Changed America," *Newsweek,* December 1, 2001, at http://www.newsweek.com/day-changed-america-148319; see also Hayes, *Cheney,* p. 342.

351 *Beyond its inadequate size:* Draper, *Dead Certain,* p. 143.

351 *Mary Matalin recalled, "The vice president . . .":* "Voices of 9–11: 'A Cacophony of Information,'" *National Journal,* August 31, 2002.

352 *"One of my greatest frustrations . . .":* G. W. Bush, *Decision Points,* p. 130.

352 *"What the hell is going on?":* Ibid., p. 132.

352 *"They couldn't get a phone line . . .":* Verton, *Black Ice,* p. 150.

353 *As Hagin recalled, "He essentially said . . .":* Marc Ambinder, "The Day After," *National Journal,* April 9, 2011.

354 *As one Pentagon official said during:* Donald Goldberg, "The National Guards," *Omni,* May 1987, at http://fas.org/nuke/guide/usa/c3i/870000-ncs.htm.

354 *Each of the corridor's offices:* The National Coordinating Center for Communications publishes a list of participating companies and industries, at http://www.dhs.gov/national-coordinating-center-communications.

354 *The best-known of NCS's efforts:* "Government Emergency Telecommunications Service (GETS) Eligibility," n.d., Office of Emergency Communications, U.S. Department of Homeland Security, at http://www.dhs.gov/sites/default/files/publications/GETS%20eligibility%20final%20041913.pdf.

355 *While GETS, which includes both:* "National Communications System Provides Programs for Priority Calling, but Planning for New Initiatives and Performance

Measurement Could Be Strengthened," August 2009, U.S. Government Accountability Office, pp. 13–14, at http://www.gao.gov/new.items/d09822.pdf.

355 *Many agencies found that:* "Resolution on Recommendations for Use of TSP and GETS in State Emergency and Contingency Planning," National Association of Regulatory Utility Commissioners Board of Directors, February 26, 2003, at http://pubs.naruc.org/pub/539F91D3–2354-D714–5175–5706FBE5D697.

355 *Altogether, nationwide, in the week:* "National Communications System Provides Programs for Priority Calling, but Planning for New Initiatives and Performance Measurement Could Be Strengthened," August 2009, U.S. Government Accountability Office, p. 14, at http://www.gao.gov/new.items/d09822.pdf.

356 *The classified program rarely is mentioned:* "Final Report—Planning for NS/EP Next Generation Network Priority Services During Pandemic Events," Communications Security, Reliability and Interoperability Council, Working Group 7, December 2010, at https://transition.fcc.gov/pshs/docs/csric/CSRIC_WG7 _Final_Report_NGN_Priority_20101216.pdf.

356 *As Brenton C. Greene, the retired Navy submarine commander:* "Memorandum for the Record, Interview of Brenton C. Greene," Record Group 148, Records of Commissions of the Legislative Branch, 1928–2007, March 16, 2004, at https:// catalog.archives.gov/OpaAPI/media/2610184/content/arcmedia/9–11/MFR/t -0148–911MFR-00590.pdf?download=true.

357 *"It was a sense of wonderment . . .":* "Interview with John Feehery, 'Evacuation of House Members and Staff from the Capitol on September 11, 2001,'" U.S. House Historian, at https://www.youtube.com/watch?v=lnSL9vTdBVs.

357 *"It's a very stark place":* Daschle, *Like No Other Time,* p. 115.

358 *As Gephardt's chief of staff:* Interview with Steve Elmendorf, "Learning About the Attacks and Evacuating the Capitol on September 11, 2001," U.S. House Historian, at https://www.youtube.com/watch?v=lMvn4SUvy1o.

358 *"They had some sandwiches . . .":* "Post-Attack Tremors," *Moments of Crisis,* ABC News.com, September 15, 2001, at http://web.archive.org/web/20020916203833 /http://abcnews.go.com/onair/DailyNews/sept11_moments_4.html; see also Lott, *Herding Cats,* p. 221.

358 *"It felt like we weren't doing . . .":* "Interview with Brian Gunderson, 'Congressional Leaders at Secure Location on September 11, 2001,'" U.S. House Historian, at https://www.youtube.com/watch?v=iytb4–3CdkY. See also "Former House Speaker Dennis Hastert on September 11, 2001," C-SPAN, July 12, 2011, at http://www.c-span.org/video/?300449–1/former-house-speaker-dennis-hastert -september-11–2001.

358 *During one conference call:* The story of the Capitol evacuation, subsequent confusion, and the eventual relocation to Mount Weather is told online at "Evacuation," U.S. House of Representatives, at http://history.house.gov/Oral-History/Events /September-11/Evacuation/.

358 *After the plane hit the Pentagon:* Bush, *Spoken from the Heart,* pp. 197–206.

359 *Her own children had been secured quickly:* Ibid.; see also Woodward, *Bush at War,* p. 17.

359 *The agency's reach that day had been long:* "Former Senate Majority Leader Tom Daschle on September 11, 2001," C-SPAN, July 27, 2011, at http://www.c-span .org/video/?300751–1/former-senate-majority-leader-tom-daschle-september -11-2001.

360 *"Basically the only emergency plan . . .":* Jason Peckenpaugh, "Government Creates New Washington Evacuation Plan," *Government Executive,* August 9, 2002, at http://www.govexec.com/defense/2002/08/government-creates-new-washington -evacuation-plan/12252/.

360 *One high-ranking Energy Department official:* Dipka Bhambhani, "Crisis Proves a Need for Disaster Planning," *Government Computer News,* September 23, 2001.

360 *The Treasury Department, located adjacent:* Robert C. Bonner, "Statement," National Commission on Terrorist Attacks Upon the United States, January 26, 2004, at http://www.9–11commission.gov/hearings/hearing7/witness_bonner.htm.

360 *As they activated the Interior Department's COG plans:* McDonnell, *National Park Service,* p. 77.

361 *The agency contacted Verizon and Sprint:* Ibid., p. 3.

361 *"We don't have a very good . . .":* Dipka Bhambhani, "Crisis Proves a Need for Disaster Planning," *Government Computer News,* September 23, 2001.

362 *"Air Force One is a hard . . .":* Fleischer, *Taking Heat,* p. 143.

362 *"There were issues of connectivity . . .":* "Mary Matalin on September 11, 2001," C-SPAN, July 26, 2011, at http://www.c-span.org/video/?300727–1/mary-mata lin-september-11–2001&start=2685.

362 *Even the president's father agreed:* G. H. W. Bush, *All the Best,* p. 647.

362 *The large 747 taxied:* Joe Dejka, "Inside StratCom on September 11: Offutt Exercise Took Real-Life Twist," *Omaha World-Herald,* February 27, 2002.

362 *"It was a surreal . . .":* Evan Thomas, "The Day That Changed America," *Newsweek,* December 30, 2001, at http://www.newsweek.com/day-changed-america-148319.

364 *After his Oval Office address:* Melissa Martin, "Captain from Medford Helps Secure the Sky," *Mail Tribune,* October 25, 2001, at http://www.mailtribune.com /article/20011025/News/310259996.

365 *"We're flying on our way . . .":* Hayes, *Cheney,* p. 346.

365 *Agents showed the first couple:* Bush, *Spoken from the Heart,* pp. 197–206.

365 *That night, he dictated into:* Dan Balz and Bob Woodward, "America's Chaotic Road to War," *Washington Post,* January 27, 2002, p. A01, at http://www.washing tonpost.com/wp-dyn/content/article/2006/07/18/AR2006071801175_pf.html.

365 *As Major General Angus Watt, the operations director:* Ray Dick, "Inside NORAD," *Legion,* November 1, 2004, at https://legionmagazine.com/en/2004/11/inside -norad/#sthash.b6kQd864.dpuf.

366 *On the eighth day after the attack:* Dennis Roddy, "Homefront: Site R Is Secure, but It's Not Undisclosed," (Pittsburgh) *Post-Gazette,* December 16, 2001, at http://old.post-gazette.com/columnists/20011216homefrontp5.asp.

366 *"Day and night, you hear . . .":* Bamford, *Pretext for War,* p. 78.

367 *Most of those pulling "bunker duty":* Barton Gellman and Susan Schmidt, "Shadow Government Is at Work in Secret," *Washington Post,* March 1, 2002; Clarke quote is from "The Armageddon Plan," *Nightline,* ABC News, April 7, 2004.

367 *The shadow government's figurehead:* "Vice President Dick Cheney Interview with Tim Russert on NBC *Meet the Press,*" PatriotResource.com, September 16, 2001, at http://www.patriotresource.com/wtc/federal/0916/VPNBC2.html.

368 *"When we were at this location . . .":* "Voices of 9–11: 'A Cacophony of Information,'" *National Journal,* August 31, 2002.

368 *"We'd see him on the screen . . .":* Hayes, *Cheney,* p. 350.

368 *As Cheney told* The Weekly*:* Labash, *Fly Fishing with Darth Vader,* p. 65.

368 *Indeed, as much as the caricature:* Ellen Gamerman and Chris Guy, "Mostly Hidden, Cheney Hunts on Shore," *Baltimore Sun,* December 21, 2001.

368 *Watching Cheney load:* Evan Thomas, "The Shot Heard Round the World," *Newsweek,* February 26, 2006, at http://www.newsweek.com/shot-heard-round-world-113499?rx=us.

368 *Back in Washington, neighbors:* "Neighbors Complain of Cheney Home Blasts," *USA Today,* December 9, 2002.

369 *Three agencies it examined:* "Continuity of Operations: Improved Planning Needed to Ensure Delivery of Essential Government Services," U.S. General Accounting Office, GAO-04–160, February 27, 2004, p. 17, at www.gao.gov/products/GAO-04-160.

370 *If Washington was destroyed:* U.S. Defense Department, "Barracks Installation Familiarization Briefing," University of North Texas Digital Library, Government Documents Department, September 13, 2005, at http://digital.library.unt.edu/ark:/67531/metadc21913/m1/56/.

370 *The State Department set up:* "Strategic Goal 12: Management and Organizational Excellence," U.S. Department of State, FY 2004 Performance Plan, at http://www.state.gov/s/d/rm/rls/perfplan/2004/20499.htm.

370 *The Smithsonian Institution:* "In the Event of War: How the Smithsonian Protected Its 'Strange Animals, Curious Creatures' and More," Smithsonian.com, April 30 2007, at http://www.smithsonianmag.com/history/in-the-event-of-war-153775882/#WDUmJ7Grkv5qHkjG.99.

371 *In 2003, the government poured:* William Arkin, "How to Pack for the Bunker," *Los Angeles Times,* August 1, 2004.

371 *As part of the 2005 budget process:* See, for instance, DHS Contract Award HS-FEMW06C0052, February 8, 2006, at https://www.usaspending.gov/transparency/Pages/TransactionDetails.aspx?RecordID=B6C0D0F0-E57A-1508-8644-3CD72D138429&AwardID=27379898&AwardType=C.

371   *To address concerns about how:* "National Communications System," December 6, 2007, at http://csrc.nist.gov/groups/SMA/ispab/documents/minutes/2007–12/ISP AB_NCS_SMcDonald.pdf.

371   *By the time George W. Bush took office:* John W. Magaw, "FEMA Manual 1010.1," Office of Policy and Regional Operations, Washington, D.C., February 1, 2001, at http://www.fema.gov/pdf/library/1010_1.pdf.

372   *During a visit to Des Moines, Iowa:* G. W. Bush, "Remarks Following a Round-table Discussion on Retirement Savings and an Exchange with Reporters in Des Moines, Iowa," March 1, 2002, p. 313, John T. Woolley and Gerhard Peters, *American Presidency Project,* at http://www.presidency.ucsb.edu/ws/index .php?pid=12165&st=&st1=.

372   *"With hundreds dead and . . .":* Norman J. Ornstein, "Providing for the Temporary Filling of House Vacancies," House Committee on the Judiciary, February 28, 2002, at https://www.aei.org/publication/providing-for-the-temporary-filling -of-house-vacancies/.

373   *"Take, for example, an attack . . .":* Norman J. Ornstein, "Ensuring the Continuity of the United States Government," Senate Judiciary Committee, September 9, 2003, at https://www.aei.org/publication/ensuring-the-continuity-of-the-united -states-government/; see also Newt Gingrich and Thomas Foley, "If Congress Were Attacked," *Washington Post,* March 17, 2002, at https://www.aei.org/publi cation/if-congress-were-attacked/print/.

374   *To suggest solutions:* Howard M. Wasserman, "Continuity of Congress: A Play in Three Stages," *Catholic University Law Review,* vol. 53, no.4 (2004), at http:// scholarship.law.edu/lawreview/vol53/iss4/4.

374   *Several states, including Delaware and Texas:* "Continuity of Congress in the Wake of a Catastrophic Attack," Hearing Before the Subcommittee on the Constitution, Civil Rights, and Civil Liberties of the Committee on the Judiciary, House of Representatives, 111th Congress, 1st Session (Serial No. 111–17), July 23, 2009, p. 63, at https://www.gpo.gov/fdsys/pkg/CHRG-111hhrg51227/pdf/CHRG-111hhrg5 1227.pdf.

374   *It took years, though, before Speaker Dennis Hastert:* R. Eric Petersen and Jeffrey W. Seifert, "Congressional Continuity of Operations (COOP): An Overview of Concepts and Challenges," CRS Report, Library of Congress, September 9, 2005, at https://fas.org/sgp/crs/secrecy/RL31594.pdf.

375   *ECG plans have never been made public:* See, for example, "National Continuity Policy," National Security Presidential Directive 51, May 9, 2007, at https://www .fema.gov/pdf/about/org/ncp/nspd_51.pdf.

376   *In the wake of the attacks, scholars:* "Presidential Succession Act," Hearing Before the Subcommittee on the Constitution of the Committee on the Judiciary, House of Representatives, 108th Congress, 2nd Session, October 6, 2004 (Serial No. 110).

377   *He handed the letter to Addington:* Cheney, *In My Time,* pp. 320–22.

377   *In 2001, as John Fortier:* "Ensuring the Continuity of the United States Govern-
      ment: The Presidency," Joint Hearing Before the Committee on the Judiciary
      and Committee on Rules and Administration, U.S. Senate, 108th Congress,
      1st Session, September 16, 2003 (Serial No. J-108–40), at https://www.gpo.gov
      /fdsys/pkg/CHRG-108shrg45948/html/CHRG-108shrg45948.htm.

377   *Fortier said, "A country expecting . . .":* John Fortier, "President Michael Armacost?:
      The Continuity of Government after September 11," *Brookings,* September 1,
      2003, at http://www.brookings.edu/research/articles/2003/09/fall-governance-fortier.

379   *Republican Senator John Cornyn raised the question:* "Ensuring the Continuity of the
      United States Government: The Presidency," Joint Hearing Before the Commit-
      tee on the Judiciary and Committee on Rules and Administration, U.S. Senate,
      108th Congress, 1st Session (Serial No. J-108–40), September 16, 2003, at https://
      www.gpo.gov/fdsys/pkg/CHRG-108shrg45948/html/CHRG-108shrg45948.htm.

380   *During a contentious 2004 hearing:* "Can Federal Agencies Function in the Wake
      of a Disaster? A Status Report on Federal Agencies' Continuity of Operations
      Plans," Hearing Before the Committee on Government Reform, House of Rep-
      resentatives, 108th Congress, 2nd Session, April 22, 2004, Serial No. 108-184.

381   *Such a court might end up:* Norman J. Ornstein, Thomas E. Mann, John C. For-
      tier, and Jennifer K. Marsico, "The Continuity of the Supreme Court: The Third
      Report of the Continuity of Government Commission," October 2011, p. 16, at
      https://www.aei.org/wp-content/uploads/2011/10/Supreme-Court-Continuity.pdf.

382   *The attention focused on such issues:* James E. Fleming, "Presidential Succession:
      The Art of the Possible," *Fordham Law Review,* vol. 79, no. 3 (2011), at http://
      ir.lawnet.fordham.edu/flr/vol79/iss3/9.

382   *As he reassured the nation:* "Bush: We Will Do What It Takes," CNN.com, Sep-
      tember 15, 2005, at http://www.cnn.com/2005/POLITICS/09/15/bush.transcript/.

383   *As the U.S. Supreme Court argued:* See, for example, Arkin, *American Coup,* as well
      as Thomas H. Green, "Martial Law in Hawaii, December 7, 1941–April 4, 1943,"
      at https://www.loc.gov/rr/frd/Military_Law/pdf/Martial-Law_Green.pdf.

384   *During one post-9/11 interview about COG:* "The Armageddon Plan," *Nightline,*
      ABC News, April 7, 2004.

388   *Across government, nuclear war plans:* "National Postal Model for the Delivery
      of Medical Countermeasures," Departments of Health and Human Services,
      Homeland Security, Defense, and Justice and the United States Postal Service,
      2010, at http://www.phe.gov/Preparedness/planning/postal/Documents/eo13527
      -section2.pdf.

389   *The Air Force groups those missions:* "Flying Operations: Phoenix, Banner Silver,
      and Copper Operations," U.S. Air Force Instruction 11–289, April 8, 2015, at
      http://static.e-publishing.af.mil/production/1/af_a3_5/publication/afi11–289
      /afi11–289.pdf.

389   *While exact costs are nearly impossible:* "Presidential Travel: DOD Airlift Cost for
      White House Foreign Travel," Report to Congressional Requesters, August

2000, U.S. General Accounting Office, p. 4, at https://books.google.com/books?id=gUXYFRo2o_wC&printsec=frontcover&source=gbs_ge_summary_&cad=0#v=onepage&q&f=false.

390 *As one Air Force official put it:* Dorr, *Air Force One,* p. 16.

390 *The C-20C it describes only:* "Model Designation of Military Aerospace Vehicles," U.S. Department of Defense, Office of the Under Secretary of Defense, 4120.15-L, May 12, 2004, at http://www.dtic.mil/whs/directives/corres/pdf/412015l.pdf.

394 *The big-box retailer Costco:* Erik Lacitis, "Preppers Do Their Best to Be Ready for the Worst," *Seattle Times,* May 14, 2012, at http://www.seattletimes.com/seattle-news/preppers-do-their-best-to-be-ready-for-the-worst/.

394 *Jay Blevins, a former law enforcement officer:* Chuck Raasch, "For 'Preppers,' Every Day Could Be Doomsday," *USA Today,* November 12, 2012, at http://www.usatoday.com/story/news/nation/2012/11/12/for-preppers-every-day-could-be-doomsday/1701151/.

394 *Businessman Robert Vicino founded:* Adam Wren, "Doomsday Profit," *Indianapolis Monthly,* December 2012, at http://www.indianapolismonthly.com/news-opinion/doomsday-profit-get-your-indiana-bunker-now/; see also AP, "Vivos Survival Shelter and Resort a Massive Doomsday Shelter Made from Old Army Facility," CBS News, June 30, 2013, at http://www.cbsnews.com/news/vivos-survival-shelter-and-resort-a-massive-doomsday-shelter-made-from-old-army-facility/.

394 *To avoid the problems that dogged:* Arkin, *American Coup,* p. 18.

395 *Every August, the site conducts:* "Security, Personnel Entry Control Procedures for the Raven Rock Mountain Complex—Site R," USAG Raven Rock Regulation 380–1, U.S. Department of the Army, August, 1, 2003, at http://whitehouse.gov1.info/camp-david/reg%20380–1.pdf.

395 *Those who might travel:* William M. Arkin, "How to Pack for the Bunker," *Los Angeles Times,* August 1, 2004, at http://articles.latimes.com/print/2004/aug/01/opinion/op-arkin1.

395 *Coast Guard personnel designated:* Ibid.

396 *Raven Rock has grown:* "Base Structure Report: Fiscal Year 2001 Baseline," U.S. Department of Defense, n.d., p. Army-11, at http://archive.defense.gov/news/Aug2001/basestructure2001.pdf.

396 *For security reasons:* "Base Structure Report: Fiscal Year 2012 Baseline," U.S. Department of Defense, n.d., p. WHS-1, at http://www.acq.osd.mil/eie/Downloads/BSI/Base%20Structure%20Report%20FY12.pdf.

396 *Just a year later, in 2013:* "Base Structure Report: Fiscal Year 2013 Baseline," U.S. Department of Defense, n.d., p. WHS-1, http://www.globalsecurity.org/military/library/report/2012/120930_fy13_baseline_dod_bsr.pdf.

396 *There were huge jumps, too:* "What the State of Pennsylvania Discloses About Site R," AboutSiteR.com, May 17, 2014, at http://aboutsiter.blogspot.com/2014/05/what-state-of-pennsylvania-discloses.html.

396 *In 2007, a team:* "FY 2011 Secretary of Defense Environmental Awards: Raven

Rock Mountain Complex Natural Resources Conservation, Small Installation," at http://web.archive.org/web/20140301000000*/http://www.denix.osd.mil/awards /upload/Narrative-RRMC-Environmental-Award-2011.pdf.

397 *Online job postings explain:* Postings are viewable on usajobs.gov; postings in 2015 and 2016 included an IT specialist, Powered Support Systems Mechanic Leader, Plans Specialist, Realty Specialist, Maintenance Mechanic, and numerous other positions.

398 *As part of a hidden-in-plain-sight:* Spencer S. Hsu, "Navy Keeps a Secret in Plain Sight: Hush-Hush Project Underway by Potomac," *Washington Post,* November 26, 2004, p. B01, at http://www.washingtonpost.com/wp-dyn/articles/A13265 -2004Nov25_2.html.

399 *"It is security-related . . .":* Will Storey, "Big Hole in White House Lawn Prompts Equally Big Questions," *New York Times,* October 17, 2011, at http://www.nytimes .com/2011/10/18/us/big-hole-on-white-house-lawn-prompts-speculation.html.

399 *HMX-1, the presidential Marine helicopter:* Christopher Bolkcom, "VXX Presidential Helicopter: Background and Issues for Congress," Congressional Research Services, April 1, 2005 (CRS RS22103).

400 *NORAD, which cost about:* Bruce Finley, "Military to Put Cheyenne Mountain on Standby," *Denver Post,* July 27, 2006, at http://www.denverpost.com/nationworld /ci_4103478.

400 *"Cheyenne Mountain . . .":* T. R. Reid, "Military to Idle NORAD Compound," *Washington Post,* July 29, 2006, at http://www.washingtonpost.com/wp-dyn/con tent/article/2006/07/28/AR2006072801617.html; Beverly Allen, "New Command Center Opens at Cheyenne Mountain," NORAD and USNORTHCOM Public Affairs, March 4, 2005, at http://www.norad.mil/Newsroom/tabid/3170 /Article/578094/new-command-center-opens-at-cheyenne-mountain.aspx.

400 *The practice of carefully monitoring:* Matt Novak, "How the US Military Turned Santa Claus into a Cold War Icon," Paleofuture, Gizmodo.com, December 23, 2014, at http://paleofuture.gizmodo.com/how-the-u-s-military-turned-santa -claus-into-a-cold-wa-1664149776.

401 *At the command center:* Yoni Appelbaum, "Yes, Virginia, There Is a NORAD," *Atlantic,* December 24, 2015, at http://www.theatlantic.com/national/archive /2015/12/yes-virginia-there-is-a-norad/421161/.

402 *During the Obama administration:* Tech. Sgt. Thomas J. Doscher, "NORAD, US-NORTHCOM Drills for Continuity of Operations," NORAD and USNORTH-COM Public Affairs, November 19, 2012, at http://www.norad.mil/Newsroom /Article/578546/norad-usnorthcom-drills-for-continuity-of-operations/.

403 *In 2008, the government contractor:* "CACI Awarded $25 Million Contract to Support Office of Assistant Secretary of Defense/Networks and Information Integration," PR Newswire, May 6, 2008, at http://www.prnewswire.com/news-releases /caci-awarded-25-million-contract-to-support-office-of-assistant-secretary-of -defensenetworks-and-information-integration-57144607.html.

403 *Many other contractors provide support:* "SAIC Awarded $18 Million Task Order by Defense Information Systems Agency," PR Newswire, October 17, 2012, at http://phx.corporate-ir.net/phoenix.zhtml?c=193857&p=irol-newsArticle&ID= 1746366.

403 *"All aspects of this project . . .":* "Defense Community Plan Development," U.S. Department of Defense Instruction, no. 3020.42, February 17, 2006, p. 5, at http://fas.org/irp/doddir/dod/i3020_42.pdf.

404 *Internally, and separate from all:* "Fiscal Year 2010 Budget Estimates," Defense Logistics Agency (DLA), May 2009, p. DLA 271, at http://comptroller.defense.gov /Portals/45/Documents/defbudget/fy2010/budget_justification/pdfs/01_Opera tion_and_Maintenance/O_M_VOL_1_PARTS/DLA.pdf.

404 *The Pentagon spends about $60 million:* "Fiscal Year 2015 President's Budget," Department of Defense Revolving Funds, March 2014, p. 7, at http://comptrol ler.defense.gov/Portals/45/Documents/defbudget/fy2015/budget_justification /pdfs/06_Defense_Working_Capital_Fund/DW_Narrative_fy2015_PB.pdf; see also "Fiscal Year (FY) 2013 President's Budget," Department of Defense Revolving Funds, February 2012, at http://www.globalsecurity.org/military/library/bud get/fy2013/dod/dwc-rf.pdf.

404 *Then there are the discrete projects:* "Military Construction, Defense-Wide FY 2010 Budget Estimates," Washington Headquarters Services, May 2009, p. 270, at http:// www.globalsecurity.org/military/library/budget/fy2010/dod/milcon-whs.pdf.

404 *In 2014, it upgraded:* "FY 2014 Military Construction, Defense-Wide," Washington Headquarters Services, March 2013, p. 307, at http://comptroller.defense .gov/Portals/45/Documents/defbudget/fy2014/budget_justification/pdf/07_Mil itary_Construction/14-Washington_Headquarters_Services.pdf.

404 *Mount Weather is, as of 2016:* "Congressional Budget Justification, FY 2016," U.S. Department of Homeland Security, p. 35, at https://www.dhs.gov/sites/default /files/publications/DHS_FY2016_Congressional_Budget_Justification.pdf.

404 *FEMA's next-generation warning system:* Ibid., p. 59.

405 *More than forty years after its creation:* For more information, see Hans M. Kristensen, "US Nuclear War Plan Updated Amidst Nuclear Policy Review," Federation of American Scientists, April 4, 2013, at https://fas.org/blogs/security /2013/04/oplan8010–12/.

406 *The mountaintop redoubt:* William M. Arkin, "The Secret Mountain Our Spies Will Hide in When Washington Is Destroyed," Phase Zero, May 1, 2015, at http://phasezero.gawker.com/the-secret-mountain-our-spies-will-hide-in-when -washing-1701044312.

406 *It would serve in an emergency:* See summary of National Intelligence Emergency Management (NIEMA), at https://www.dni.gov/index.php/about/organization /niema.

407 *Set on the north branch:* See the "Allegany County Economic Development Plan," 2012, at http://www.alleganyworks.org/wp-content/uploads/2013/08/Allegany

CountyEconomicDevelopmentPlan2012DECDAug2013.pdf; see also "Public Health Assessment for Allegany Ballistics Laboratory," U.S. Department of Health and Human Services, Agency for Toxic Substances and Disease Registry, May 21, 2007, at http://www.atsdr.cdc.gov/HAC/pha/AlleganyBallistics/Allegany BallisticsLabPHA052107.pdf.

407 *ABL was a critical component:* Associated Press, "Around the Nation; Two Missing After Blast of Rocket Propellant," *New York Times,* August 12, 1981, at http://www.nytimes.com/1981/08/12/us/around-the-nation-two-missing-after-blast -of-rocket-propellant.html; see also Associated Press, "Ruins Sifted for Cause of Big Blast," *Spokesman-Review,* April 28, 1963, at http://news.google.com/newsp apers?nid=1314&dat=19630428&id=vsxYAAAAIBAJ&sjid=BukDAAAAIBAJ &pg=6383,4632490.

407 *Beginning in 1985, Senator Robert C. Byrd:* Gail Russell Chaddock, "Welcome to Byrd Country," *Christian Science Monitor,* August 15, 2006, at http://www.csmoni tor.com/2006/0815/p01s04-uspo.html.

407 *As he wrote in his autobiography:* Byrd, *Child of the Appalachian Coalfields,* p. 732.

407 *More recently, ABL's various:* See the "Allegany County Economic Development Plan," 2012, p. 2, at http://www.alleganyworks.org/wp-content/uploads/2013/08 /AlleganyCountyEconomicDevelopmentPlan2012DECDAug2013.pdf.

407 *Its facilities, including the gratefully named:* Yevgeniy Sverdlik, "Governors Ask Navy to Consolidate into West Virginia Data Center," DatacenterDynamics, March 8, 2012, at http://www.datacenterdynamics.com/focus/archive/2012/03 /governors-ask-navy-consolidate-west-virginia-data-center.

407 *ABL now stands:* "Annual Audit Work Plan, Fiscal Year 2013," National Archives & Records Administration, Office of Inspector General, pp. 14–15, at http:// www.archives.gov/oig/pdf/2013/audit-plan-2013.pdf.

408 *Under the most dire circumstances:* See U.S. Code, Title 44, Chapter 15, § 1505, "Documents to Be Published in Federal Register," at https://www.law.cornell.edu /uscode/text/44/1505.

SELECTED BIBLIOGRAPHY

Abbate, Janet. *Inventing the Internet*. Inside Technology. Cambridge, MA: MIT Press, 1999.

Abella, Alex. *Soldiers of Reason: The RAND Corporation and the Rise of the American Empire*. Boston, MA: Mariner Books, 2009.

Adams, Chris. *Deterrence: An Enduring Strategy*. iUniverse, 2009.

Adams, Valerie L. *Eisenhower's Fine Group of Fellows: Crafting a National Security Policy to Uphold the Great Equation*. Lanham, MD: Lexington Books, 2006.

Ambrose, Stephen E. *Eisenhower: Soldier and President*. New York: Simon & Schuster Paperbacks, 1990.

Anderson, Martin. *Revolution: The Reagan Legacy*. Stanford, CA: Hoover Institution Press, Stanford University, 1990.

Anderson, Martin, and Annelise Anderson. *Ronald Reagan: Decisions of Greatness*. Stanford, CA: Hoover Institution Press, 2015.

Andrew, Christopher M., and Oleg Gordievsky. *Comrade Kryuchkov's Instructions: Top Secret Files on KGB Foreign Operations, 1975–1985*. Stanford, CA: Stanford University Press, 1994.

Angell, Joseph W., Jr. *The Air Force Response to the Cuban Missile Crisis*. Washington, D.C.: U.S. Air Force Historical Liaison Office, 1963.

Arkin, William M. *American Coup: How a Terrified Government Is Destroying the Constitution*. New York: Little, Brown, 2013.

Bamford, James. *A Pretext for War: 9/11, Iraq, and the Abuse of America's Intelligence Agencies*. New York: Doubleday, 2004.

Barasch, Mark. *The Little Black Book of Atomic War*. New York: Dell, 1984.

Beisner, Robert L. *Dean Acheson: A Life in the Cold War*. New York: Oxford University Press, 2009.

Berges, Steve, ed. *The Charters of Liberty*. American Liberty Press, 2010.

Beschloss, Michael R. *Mayday: Eisenhower, Khrushchev, and the U-2 Affair.* New York: Harper & Row, 1988.

Betts, Richard K. *Surprise Attack: Lessons for Defense Planning.* Washington, D.C.: Brookings Institute Press, 1982.

Blight, James G., Bruce J. Allyn, and David A. Welch. *Cuba on the Brink: Castro, the Missile Crisis, and the Soviet Collapse.* Lanham, MD: Rowman & Littlefield, 2002.

Bobrick, Benson. *Parsons Brinckerhoff: The First Hundred Years.* New York: Van Nostrand Reinhold, 1985.

Bohn, Michael K. *Nerve Center: Inside the White House Situation Room.* Washington, D.C.: Potomac Books, 2003.

Boyer, Paul S. *By the Bomb's Early Light: American Thought and Culture at the Dawn of the Atomic Age.* Chapel Hill: University of North Carolina Press, 1994.

Brinkley, David. *Washington Goes to War.* New York: Ballantine Books, 1996.

Brugioni, Dino A., and Doris G. Taylor. *Eyes in the Sky: Eisenhower, the CIA, and Cold War Aerial Espionage.* Annapolis, MD: Naval Institute Press, 2010.

Brzezinski, Zbigniew. *Power and Principle: Memoirs of the National Security Advisor, 1977–1981.* New York: Farrar, Straus & Giroux, 1983.

Burr, William, and Jeffrey P. Kimball. *Nixon's Nuclear Specter: The Secret Alert of 1969, Madman Diplomacy, and the Vietnam War.* Modern War Studies. Lawrence: University Press of Kansas, 2015.

Burrough, Bryan. *Days of Rage: America's Radical Underground, the FBI, and the Forgotten Age of Revolutionary Violence.* New York: Penguin Press, 2015.

Busch, Nathan E. *No End in Sight: The Continuing Menace of Nuclear Proliferation.* Lexington: University Press of Kentucky, 2004.

Bush, George H. W. *All the Best: My Life in Letters and Other Writings.* New York: Scribner, 2013.

Bush, George W. *Public Papers of the Presidents of the United States, George W. Bush, Book I—January 1 to June 30, 2002.* Washington, D.C.: U.S. Government Printing Office, 2004.

———. *Decision Points.* New York: Crown, 2010.

Bush, Laura. *Spoken from the Heart.* New York: Scribner, 2006.

Byrd, Robert C. *Losing America: Confronting a Reckless and Arrogant Presidency.* New York: W. W. Norton, 2004.

———. *Child of the Appalachian Coalfields.* Morgantown: West Virginia University Press, 2005.

Cannon, Lou. *President Reagan: The Role of a Lifetime.* New York: Simon & Schuster, 1991.

Carpenter, Ted Galen. *The Captive Press: Foreign Policy Crisis and the First Amendment.* Washington, D.C.: Cato Institute Press, 1995.

Carroll, James. *House of War: The Pentagon and the Disastrous Rise of American Power.* New York: Houghton Mifflin Harcourt, 2006.

Carter, Jimmy. *Keeping Faith: Memoirs of a President.* New York: Bantam Books, 1982.

———. *White House Diary.* New York: Farrar, Straus & Giroux, 2010.

Cheney, Dick. *In My Time: A Personal and Political Memoir.* New York: Threshold Editions, 2011.

Clarke, Richard. *Against All Enemies: Inside America's War on Terror.* New York: Free Press, 2004.

Cockburn, Andrew. *Rumsfeld: His Rise, Fall, and Catastrophic Legacy.* New York: Scribner, 2007.

Craig, Campbell. *Destroying the Village: Eisenhower and Thermonuclear War.* Columbia Studies in Contemporary American History. New York: Columbia University Press, 1998.

Crawford, Arlo. *A Farm Dies Once a Year: A Memoir.* New York: Henry Holt, 2014.

Cutler, Robert. *No Time for Rest.* New York: Little, Brown, 1966.

Daniels, Jonathan. *Frontier on the Potomac.* New York: Macmillan, 1946.

Darling, Robert J. *24 Hours Inside the President's Bunker: 9–11–01: The White House.* iUniverse, 2010.

Daschle, Tom. *Like No Other Time: The Two Years That Changed America.* New York: Three Rivers Press, 2004.

Davis, Tracy C. *Stages of Emergency: Cold War Nuclear Civil Defense.* Durham, NC: Duke University Press, 2007.

DeGroot, Gerard J. *The Bomb: A Life.* Cambridge, MA: Harvard University Press, 2005.

Dobbs, Michael. *One Minute to Midnight: Kennedy, Khrushchev, and Castro on the Brink of Nuclear War.* New York: Vintage, 2009.

———. *Six Months in 1945: FDR, Stalin, Churchill, and Truman—from World War to Cold War.* New York: Vintage, 2013.

Dobrynin, Anatoly. *In Confidence: Moscow's Ambassador to America's Six Cold War Presidents.* New York: Crown, 1995.

Dorr, Robert F. *Air Force One.* St. Paul, MN: MBI Publishing, 2002.

Draper, Robert. *Dead Certain: The Presidency of George W. Bush.* New York: Free Press, 2007.

Eden, Lynn. *Whole World on Fire: Organizations, Knowledge, and Nuclear Weapons Devastation.* New Delhi, India: Manas Publications, 2004.

Einstein, Albert. *Out of My Later Years: The Scientist, Philosopher and Man Portrayed Though His Own Words.* New York: Gramercy, 1993.

Eisenhower, Dwight D. *Waging Peace: The White House Years.* New York: Doubleday, 1965.

Emmett, Dan. *Within Arm's Length: A Secret Service Agent's Definitive Inside Account of Protecting the President.* New York: St. Martin's Griffin, 2015.

Fails, William R. *Marines and Helicopters, 1962–1973.* Darby, PA: Diane Publishing, 1978.

Farmer, John. *The Ground Truth: The Untold Story of America Under Attack on 9/11.* New York: Riverhead Books, 2009.

Feerick, John D. *From Failing Hands: The Story of Presidential Succession.* New York: Fordham University Press, 1965.

————. *The Twenty-fifth Amendment: Its Complete History and Application.* New York: Fordham University Press, 1992.

Ferrell, Robert H., ed. *Dear Bess: The Letters of Harry to Bess Truman, 1910–1959.* Columbia, University of Missouri Press, 1983.

Filson, Leslie. *Air War Over America: Sept. 11 Alters Face of Air Defense Mission.* Panama City, FL: Tyndall Air Force Base Public Affairs Office, 2003.

Fischer, Beth A. *The Reagan Reversal: Foreign Policy and the End of the Cold War.* Columbia: University of Missouri Press, 1997.

FitzGerald, Frances. *Way Out There in the Blue: Reagan, Star Wars, and the End of the Cold War.* New York: Simon & Schuster, 2001.

Fleischer, Ari. *Taking Heat: The President, the Press, and My Years in the White House.* New York: William Morrow, 2005.

Fleming, James Rodger. *Fixing the Sky: The Checkered History of Weather and Climate Control.* New York: Columbia University Press, 2012.

Gaddis, John Lewis. *The Cold War: A New History.* New York: Penguin Press, 2005.

Garrison, Dee. *Bracing for Armageddon: Why Civil Defense Never Worked.* New York: Oxford University Press, 2006.

Gates, Robert M. *From the Shadows: The Ultimate Insider's Story of Five Presidents and How They Won the Cold War.* New York: Simon & Schuster, 1996.

George, Alice L. *Awaiting Armageddon: How Americans Faced the Cuban Missile Crisis.* Chapel Hill: University of North Carolina Press, 2003.

Ghamari-Tabrizi, Sharon. *The Worlds of Herman Kahn: The Intuitive Science of Thermonuclear War.* Cambridge, MA: Harvard University Press, 2005.

Gibbs, Nancy, and Michael Duffy. *The Presidents Club: Inside the World's Most Exclusive Fraternity.* New York: Simon & Schuster, 2012.

Goldberg, Alfred, Sarandis Papadopoulos, Diane Putney, Nancy Berlage, and Rebecca Welch. *Pentagon 9/11.* CreateSpace Independent Publishing Platform, 2016.

Goodwin, Doris Kearns. *The Bully Pulpit: Theodore Roosevelt, William Howard Taft, and the Golden Age of Journalism.* New York: Simon & Schuster, 2013.

Graham, Thomas, Jr., and Damien J. Lavera. *Cornerstones of Security: Arms Control Treaties in the Nuclear Era.* Seattle: University of Washington Press, 2003.

Gup, Ted. *Nation of Secrets: The Threat to Democracy and the American Way of Life.* New York: Doubleday, 2007.

Hansen, Richard H. *The Year We Had No President.* Lincoln: University of Nebraska Press, 1962.

Hastert, Dennis. *Speaker: Lessons from Forty Years in Coaching and Politics.* Washington, D.C.: Regnery, 2004.

Hayes, Stephen F. *Cheney: The Untold Story of America's Most Powerful and Controversial Vice President.* New York: HarperCollins, 2007.

Hennessy, Elizabeth. *A Domestic History of the Bank of England, 1930–1960.* Cambridge, U.K.: Cambridge University Press, 2008.

Hersey, John. *Hiroshima.* New York: Vintage Books, 1989.

Hewlett, Richard G., and Jack M. Holl. *Atoms for Peace and War, 1953–1961: Eisenhower and the Atomic Energy Commission.* Vol. 4. California Studies in the History of Science. Berkeley: University of California Press, 1989.

Hiltzik, Michael A. *Colossus: The Turbulent, Thrilling Saga of the Building of Hoover Dam.* New York: Free Press, 2010.

Holland, Max. *The Kennedy Assassination Tapes: The White House Conversations of Lyndon B. Johnson Regarding the Assassination, the Warren Commission, and the Aftermath.* New York: Alfred A. Knopf, 2004.

Holmes, Richard. *Churchill's Bunker: The Cabinet War Rooms and the Culture of Secrecy in Wartime London.* New Haven, CT: Yale University Press, 2010.

Holt, Thaddeus. *The Deceivers: Allied Military Deception in the Second World War.* New York: Skyhorse, 2010.

Hunter, Stephen, and John Bainbridge, Jr. *American Gunfight: The Plot to Kill President Truman—and the Shoot-Out That Stopped It.* New York: Simon & Schuster, 2007.

Isaacson, Walter, and Evan Thomas. *The Wise Men: Six Friends and the World They Made: Acheson, Bohlen, Harriman, Kennan, Lovett, McCloy.* New York: Simon & Schuster, 1986.

James, Lawrence. *Warrior Race: A History of the British at War.* New York: St. Martin's Griffin, 2004.

Johnson, Steven. *How We Got to Now: Six Innovations That Made the Modern World.* New York: Riverhead Books, 2015.

Kahn, David. *The Codebreakers: The Comprehensive History of Secret Communication from Ancient Times to the Internet.* New York: Scribner, 1996.

Kahn, Herman. *On Thermonuclear War.* Princeton, NJ: Princeton University Press, 1960.

Kaiser, Robert G. *Why Gorbachev Happened: His Triumphs and His Failure.* New York: Simon & Schuster, 1991.

Kaku, Michio, and Daniel Axelrod. *To Win a Nuclear War: The Pentagon's Secret War Plans.* Boston, MA: South End Press, 1999.

Kantorowicz, Ernst Hartwig. *The King's Two Bodies: A Study in Mediaeval Political Theology.* Princeton, NJ: Princeton University Press, 1997.

Kaplan, Fred M. *The Wizards of Armageddon.* New York: Simon & Schuster, 1983.

Karnow, Stanley. *Vietnam: A History.* New York: Penguin Books, 1997.

Kean, Thomas H., and Lee H. Hamilton. *The 9/11 Commission Report: Final Report of the National Commission on Terrorist Attacks Upon the United States, including Executive Summary.* Baton Rouge, LA: Claitor's Publishing Division, 2004.

Keeney, L. Douglas. *15 Minutes: General Curtis LeMay and the Countdown to Nuclear Annihilation.* New York: St. Martin's Griffin, 2012.

Kennedy, Robert F. *Thirteen Days: A Memoir of the Cuban Missile Crisis.* New York: W. W. Norton, 1999.

Killian, James. *Sputnik, Scientists and Eisenhower: A Memoir of the First Special Assistant to the President for Space and Technology.* Cambridge, MA: MIT Press, 1977.

Kistiakowsky, George B. *A Scientist at the White House: The Private Diary of President Eisenhower's Special Assistant for Science and Technology.* Cambridge, MA: Harvard University Press, 1976.

Klara, Robert. *The Hidden White House: Harry Truman and the Reconstruction of America's Most Famous Residence.* New York: St. Martin's Griffin, 2014.

Krugler, David F. *This Is Only a Test: How Washington D.C. Prepared for Nuclear War.* New York: Palgrave Macmillan, 2006.

Kutler, Stanley I. *The Wars of Watergate: The Last Crisis of Richard Nixon.* New York: W. W. Norton, 1990.

Labash, Matt. *Fly Fishing with Darth Vader: And Other Adventures with Evangelical Wrestlers, Political Hitmen, and Jewish Cowboys.* New York: Simon & Schuster, 2010.

Larzelere, Alex. *Witness to History: White House Diary of a Military Aide to President Richard Nixon.* Bloomington, IN: AuthorHouse, 2009.

Lilienthal, David E. *The Journals of David E. Lilienthal, Volume 2; The Atomic Energy Years, 1945–1950.* New York: Harper & Row, 1964.

Long, David. *The Little Book of the London Underground.* Stroud, U.K.: The History Press, 2009.

Lord, Walter. *The Dawn's Early Light: The Climactic Shaping of the Land of the Free During the Hazardous Events of 1814 in Washington, Baltimore, and London.* New York: W. W. Norton, 1972.

Lott, Trent. *Herding Cats: A Life in Politics.* New York: William Morrow, 2005.

Macmillan, Harold. *The Macmillan Diaries, Volume II.* New York: Macmillan, 2009.

Malcolm, Tom. *Parsons Brinckerhoff Through the Years: 1885 to 2012.* New York: Parsons Brinckerhoff, 2013.

Mann, James. *Rise of the Vulcans: The History of Bush's War Cabinet.* New York: Penguin Books, 2004.

Mann, Robert. *Daisy Petals and Mushroom Clouds: LBJ, Barry Goldwater, and the Ad that Changed American Politics.* Baton Rouge: Louisiana State University Press, 2011.

MacGregor, Neil. *Whose Muse?: Art Museums and the Public Trust.* Princeton, NJ: Princeton University Press, 2004.

McCray, Patrick. *Keep Watching the Skies!: The Story of Operation Moonwatch and the Dawn of the Space Age.* Princeton, NJ: Princeton University Press, 2008.

McCullough, David G. *Truman.* New York: Simon & Schuster, 1992.

McDonnell, Janet A. *The National Park Service: Responding to the September 11 Terrorist Attacks.* Washington, D.C.: U.S. Department of the Interior, 2004.

Meacham, Jon. *Destiny and Power: The American Odyssey of George Herbert Walker Bush.* New York: Random House, 2015.

Moody, Joanna. *From Churchill's War Rooms: Letters of a Secretary 1943–45.* Stroud, U.K.: Tempus, 2008.

Moody, Walton S. *Building a Strategic Air Force.* Washington, D.C.: U.S. Government Printing Office, 1996.

Morris, Edmund. *Dutch: A Memoir of Ronald Reagan.* Modern Library Paperbacks. New York: Modern Library, 2000.

Nelson, Jack, and Barbara Matusow. *Scoop: The Evolution of a Southern Reporter.* Jackson: University Press of Mississippi, 2013.

Nelson, W. Dale. *The President Is at Camp David.* Syracuse, NY: Syracuse University Press, 2000.

Nessen, Ron. *It Sure Looks Different from the Inside.* New York: Simon & Schuster, 1978.

Nichols, David A. *Eisenhower 1956: The President's Year of Crisis—Suez and the Brink of War.* New York: Simon & Schuster, 2012.

Nitze, Paul H., Steven L. Rearden, and Ann M. Smith. *From Hiroshima to Glasnost: At the Center of Decision: A Memoir.* New York: Grove, 1989.

Nixon, Richard. *Six Crises.* Richard Nixon Library Editions. New York: Touchstone Books, 1990.

Oakes, Guy. *The Imaginary War: Civil Defense and American Cold War Culture.* New York: Oxford University Press, 1995.

O'Donnell, Kenneth P., David F. Powers, and Joe McCarthy. *Johnny, We Hardly Knew Ye: Memories of John Fitzgerald Kennedy.* New York: Little, Brown, 1972.

O'Toole, G. J. A. *The Spanish War: An American Epic, 1898.* New York: W. W. Norton, 1986.

Pate, J'Nell L. *Arsenal of Defense: Fort Worth's Military Legacy.* Austin: Texas State Historical Association, 2011.

Pearson, David E. *The World Wide Military Command and Control System: Evolution and Effectiveness.* Montgomery, AL: Air University Press, 2001.

Pickett, William B., ed. *George F. Kennan and the Origin of Eisenhower's New Look: An Oral History of Project Solarium.* Princeton, NJ: Princeton Institute for International and Regional Studies, 2004.

Polmar, Norman. *The Naval Institute Guide to the Ships and Aircraft of the U.S. Fleet.* 15th ed. Annapolis, MD: Naval Institute Press, 2001.

Pringle, Peter, and William Arkin. *S.I.O.P.: The Secret U.S. Plan for Nuclear War.* New York: W. W. Norton, 1980.

Rabe, Stephen G. *The Most Dangerous Area in the World: John F. Kennedy Confronts Communist Revolution in Latin America.* Mestizo Spaces. Chapel Hill: University of North Carolina Press, 1999.

Reagan, Ronald. *The Reagan Diaries.* New York: Harper, 2007.

Reeves, Richard. *President Kennedy: Profile of Power.* New York: Simon & Schuster, 1994.

Reilly, Michael F. *Reilly of the White House: Behind the Scenes with FDR.* New York: Simon & Schuster, 1947.

Rhodes, Richard. *Dark Sun: The Making of the Hydrogen Bomb.* New York: Simon & Schuster, 1996.

———. *Arsenals of Folly: The Making of the Nuclear Arms Race.* New York: Vintage Books, 2008.

Rose, Frank. *Into the Heart of the Mind: An American Quest for Artificial Intelligence.* New York: Vintage Books, 1985.

Rosenthal, A. M., and Arthur Gelb, eds. *The Night the Lights Went Out.* New York: Signet Books, 1965.

Sagan, Scott D. *The Limits of Safety: Organizations, Accidents, and Nuclear Weapons.* Princeton Studies in International History and Politics. Princeton, NJ: Princeton University Press, 1995.

Sayler, Carolyn. *Doris Fleeson: Incomparably the First Political Journalist of Her Time.* Santa Fe, NM: Sunstone Press, 2010.

Schell, Jonathan. *The Fate of the Earth.* London, U.K.: Jonathan Cape, 1982.

Schlesinger, Robert. *White House Ghosts: Presidents and Their Speechwriters.* New York: Simon & Schuster, 2008.

Schweizer, Peter. *Victory: The Reagan Administration's Secret Strategy that Hastened the Collapse of the Soviet Union.* New York: Atlantic Monthly Press, 1994.

Shapley, Deborah. *Promise and Power: The Life and Times of Robert McNamara.* New York: Little, Brown, 1993.

Shultz, George P. *Turmoil and Triumph: My Years as Secretary of State.* New York: Scribner, 1993.

Sidey, Hugh. *John F. Kennedy, President.* Andesite Press, 2015.

Smith, Gerard. *Doubletalk: The Story of SALT I.* New York: Doubleday, 1980.

Sokolski, Henry D., ed. *Getting MAD: A Nuclear Mutual Assured Destruction, Its Origins and Practice.* Carlisle, PA: Strategic Studies Institute of the U.S. Army War College, 2004.

Sorenson, Theodore C. *Kennedy.* New York: Harper and Row, 1965.

Talbott, Strobe. *Deadly Gambits.* New York: Vintage, 1985.

Taubman, William. *Khrushchev: The Man and His Era.* New York: W. W. Norton, 2003.

TerHorst, Jerald F., and Ralph Albertazzie. *The Flying White House: The Story of Air Force One.* New York: Bantam Books, 1980.

Terriff, Terry. *The Nixon Administration and the Making of U.S. Nuclear Strategy.* Cornell Studies in Security Affairs. Ithaca: Cornell University Press, 1995.

Thomas, Evan. *Ike's Bluff: President Eisenhower's Secret Battle to Save the World.* New York: Back Bay Books, 2013.

———. *Being Nixon: A Man Divided.* New York: Random House, 2015.

Thompson, Kenneth W. *The Eisenhower Presidency: Eleven Intimate Perspectives of Dwight D. Eisenhower.* 4th ed. Vol. 3. Portraits of American Presidents Series. Lanham, MD: University Press of America, 1984.

Thompson, Nicholas. *The Hawk and the Dove: Paul Nitze, George Kennon, and the History of the Cold War.* New York: Picador, 2010.

Tofel, Richard J. *Restless Genius: Barney Kilgore, The Wall Street Journal, and the Invention of Modern Journalism.* New York: St. Martin's Griffin, 2009.

Truman, Harry S. *Memoirs of Harry S. Truman. Volume 1: Year of Decisions.* New York: Doubleday, 1955.

Truman, Margaret. *Harry S. Truman.* New York: Avon Books, 1993.

Van Atta, Dale. *With Honor: Melvin Laird in War, Peace, and Politics.* Madison: University of Wisconsin Press, 2008.

Verton, Dan. *Black Ice: The Invisible Threat of Cyber-Terrorism.* New York: McGraw-Hill Osborne Media, 2003.

Vogel, Steve. *The Pentagon: A History.* New York: Random House Trade Paperbacks, 2008.

Walch, Timothy, ed. *Guardian of Heritage: Essays on the History of the National Archives.* Washington, D.C.: Smithsonian Institution Press, 1985.

Waldrop, M. Mitchell. *The Dream Machine: J. C. R. Licklider and the Revolution that Made Computing Personal.* Sloan Technology. New York: Viking Adult, 2001.

Walsh, Kenneth T. *From Mount Vernon to Crawford: A History of the Presidents and Their Retreats.* New York: Hyperion, 2005.

Warren, Earl. *The Memoirs of Earl Warren.* Garden City, NY: Doubleday, 1977.

Werth, Barry. *31 Days: Gerald Ford, the Nixon Pardon, and a Government in Crisis.* New York: Anchor Books, 2007.

White, E. B. *Here Is New York.* New York: Harper & Brothers, 1949.

Wickham, George E., and Henry R. Tiedmann. *Utilization of Equipment Crisis Relocation Program; Final Report.* Washington, D.C.: Defense Civil Preparedness Agency, 1978.

Wigner, Eugene Paul. *Who Speaks for Civil Defense?* New York: Scribner, 1968.

Williams, James W. *A History of Aviation: From Its Beginnings to the War on Terror.* iUniverse, 2005.

Winkler, Allan M. *Life Under a Cloud: American Anxiety About the Atom.* New York: Oxford University Press, 1993.

Wise, David. *The Politics of Lying: Government Deception, Secrecy, and Power.* New York: Vintage, 1973.

Wolfe, Tom. *The Right Stuff.* New York: Picador, 2008.

Woodward, Bob. *Bush at War.* New York: Simon & Schuster, 2002.

Woodward, Bob, and Carl Bernstein. *The Final Days.* New York: Simon & Schuster Paperbacks, 2005.

Wu, Tim. *The Master Switch: The Rise and Fall of Information Empires.* New York: Vintage, 2011.

Yergin, Daniel. *Shattered Peace: The Origins of the Cold War and the National Security State.* New York: Houghton Mifflin, 1977.

Zuckerman, Edward. *The Day After World War III.* New York: Avon Books, 1987.

INDEX

9/11 attacks and, 352–56

overhaul of, 247–50

radio, *see* radio

"red phone" and "hotline" ideas of, 155, 177

telegraph, 151

telephone, 146–47, 155, 194*n*, 232

teletype, 73–74, 147, 155–56

wireless service improvements, 371

Communism, xxi, 18, 21, 27, 46, 161, 401

Compton, Ann, 335

computers, xxii, 18, 19, 66–67, 138, 231–34, 252–53, 276*n*, 282, 393

internet, xxii, 67, 127, 232

at NORAD, 260–63, 283, 291

Condition Able, 53

Condition Baker, 53

CONELRAD, 36

Congress, xix, xxiii, 62, 64, 68–69, 83, 84, 97, 223

anthrax attacks on, xxiv, 372

continuity of, 373–76

Defense Resources Act and, xix, 153–54

Enemy Detention Act and, 160*n*

Greenbrier bunker for, *see* Greenbrier

House of Representatives, 180–82, 372–76

9/11 attacks and, 338–39

presidential succession and, 181–82, 185

Senate, 2, 31, 290, 373–76

spending and, 27–29, 31, 47, 123, 124, 131

Truman's address to, 20–21

Constitution, xix, 15, 68, 82, 95, 97, 154, 174, 227, 318, 373

Bill of Rights, xix, 154, 271

Enduring Constitutional Government (ECG), xix, 369, 375–76, 384–86, 387, 402, 409

preservation of document, xx, 270, 271

presidential succession and, 179, 181, 182, 279, 315

Third Amendment to, 95

Twenty-Fifth Amendment to, xvi, 185, 221, 226, 376–77, 379

Constitutional Convention, 181

Consumers Union, 98

Conte, Robert, 208

Continuity of Government (COG), xii, xix–xxiv, 4, 29–32, 38–39, 41, 49, 57, 84, 92, 102, 174–76, 185, 198, 216, 217, 226, 231, 232, 236, 273, 274, 276, 285, 320, 350, 359, 369, 379, 384, 387, 388, 399, 402–5, 407

Air Force One and, 168

British facilities for, 15–18

Canadian facilities for, 115

Carter and, 240–41, 246–47, 252, 264–66, 274

Clinton and, 325–26, 330*n*

Congress in, 373–76

construction projects for, 398–99

Continuity of Government Commission, 374, 377–78, 381–82

contractors and, 402–4

decapitation strikes and, 192, 277, 314, 335, 348, 349, 369

Defense Mobilization Systems Planning Activity, 313, 324

designated survivors and, 275–77, 376, 387

devolution plan for, 369–70

discarding of facilities for, 324–25

Enduring Constitutional Government (ECG), xix, 369, 375–76, 384–86, 387, 402, 409

evacuations in, *see* evacuations

Ford and, 226–27

Ivy League exercise, 287–88, 297, 298

National Program Office, *see* National Program Office

9/11 attacks and, 333, 335–38, 341–42, 345–50, 353, 356, 357, 359–65, 367–69, 376

Nixon's updating of, 217–18

people outside of Washington in, 378

presidential succession in, *see* presidential succession

Project 908, 304–10

Reagan and, 287–88, 297–303, 311, 313–18

reevaluation during Kennedy administration, 122

relocation sites, *see* relocation sites

Soviet knowledge of U.S. plans for, 324*n*

spending on, 404–5